Principles of Business: Economics

Principles of Business:
Economics

The Editors at Salem Press

SALEM PRESS

A Division of EBSCO Information Services, Inc.

Ipswich, Massachusetts

GREY HOUSE PUBLISHING

Publisher's Cataloging-In-Publication Data
(Prepared by The Donohue Group, Inc.)

Names: Salem Press, editor.
Title: Principles of business. Economics / the Editors at Salem Press.
Other Titles: Economics
Description: [First edition]. | Ipswich, Massachusetts : Salem Press, a division of EBSCO Information Services, Inc. ; Amenia, NY : Grey House Publishing, [2018] | Includes bibliographical references and index.
Identifiers: ISBN 9781682176726 (hardcover)
Subjects: LCSH: Economics.
Classification: LCC HB171 .P75 2018 | DDC 330--dc23

CONTENTS

PUBLISHER'S NOTE

Principles of Business: Economics is the latest title in Salem's *Principles of Business* series. The first five volumes, *Finance, Marketing, Entrepreneurship, Management* and *Accounting* have been recently published. This series is intended to introduce students and researchers to the fundamentals of important and far-reaching business topics using easy-to-understand language.

The field of economics is vital in the world we live in today, and relevant in any type of business. This work includes topics such as "Behavioral Economics," "E-Commerce," "Financial Globalization" and "Securities Regulations."

The entries in this volume are arranged in an A to Z order, from "Aggregate Demand" to "Transfer Pricing," making it easy to find the topic of interest. Each entry includes the following:
- *Abstract* giving a brief introduction to the topic;
- *Overview* that presents key terms and concepts;
- Clear, concise *presentation of the topic,* including a discussion of applications and issues;
- *Further reading.*

Added features include numerous illustrations and helpful diagrams of relevant topics. The back matter in *Principles of Business: Economics* contains a thorough and valuable glossary of terms as well as an index.

Salem Press thanks the contributors, whose names are listed with each essay. Their diverse backgrounds include graduate degrees in economics, years of business experience, and non-business experience that offers information in language that is often more accessible than that of business specialists, whose explanations may be narrowly focused. A list of contributor's names and affiliations follows the Introduction.

The essays in this volume are written for a varied audience. Our goals include attention to clarity and avoidance of unnecessary jargon. For those readers who desire more specific information on any one topic, each essay includes a list of further reading.

Principles of Business: Economics is, as are all titles in this series, available in print and as an e-book.

INTRODUCTION

Understanding the principles of economics is vital for all businesses and governments entities, as well as for individuals. Economics is a field of study that has a long history dating back several centuries. Many brilliant minds have proposed various theories, tested them, discarded some and found others capable of standing the test of time. Looking back at the evolution of economic thought, one cannot help but marvel at how concepts we consider patently obvious, like supply and demand, weren't always so. It took economic scholars such as Smith, Ricardo, Cournot, Jevons, Menger, Walras, Marshall, and Keynes to explain such theories in a manner easily understood by the masses. Looking to the future, though, the true import of their and other innovative economists' work lies in the synthesis of ideas, new and old, confirmatory or contradictory, into a coherent understanding of economic forces that, when applied, will bring us and future generations good rather than ill fortune.

STAGES OF THOUGHT

Production and trade, investment and profits, poverty and wealth all, of course, predate the rise of capitalism by many, many centuries. Yet the intelligentsia of the ancient world paid scant attention to commercial consideration, instead preferring to debate ethical issues associated with their economies. While profitable commerce benefited the state, making it more powerful in the world, philosophers of the time often condemned those who sought wealth for its own sake. For them, wealth was only a means to an end – the desire to lead a self-reliant and contemplative life.

With the movement away from the land and toward towns, business people gained political influence. The state became increasingly important in protecting their business interests, thus the need for powerful armies and navies developed. Nations began levying taxes and tariffs to pay for their military defenses. However, it was not until later that Adam Smith recognized that the competitive marketplace was the preeminent engine of economic growth. He realized that while self-interest was the predominant force driving human behavior, an economic order must emerge to guide these forces. Smith was the first to recognize that a nation's wealth was based on the goods and services produced by its people.

Smith further believed that the role of government in the economy was a limited one and that the market economy should remain open and free.

Smith forever changed the line of inquiry future economic theorists would take. It would, however, be left to David Ricardo to formalize some of his seminal ideas about income distribution, free trade and economic growth. His ingenious argument in support of free trade between nations, the theory of comparative advantage, is Ricardo's most enduring contribution to economic thought. He considered the cost differential between producing countries far less important than the differential within countries. In purely economic terms, importing goods from a more efficient foreign producer, he reasoned, is preferable to purchasing them from a less efficient domestic one.

While Smith and Ricardo brought new and enduring theories to the field of economics, the most far-reaching theorist in modern economics was John Maynard Keynes. Macroeconomics — the study of how national economies function — effectively began with Keynes. And his central thesis, that aggregate demand in turn is a function of consumer spending and business investment, has figured prominently in debates over both monetary and fiscal policy ever since.

The bottom line is that economics is an observational, not an experimental science. The proof of a theory here thus rests in how well it empirically withstands the counter-arguments hurled at it: That, and the test of time.

ECONOMIC SYSTEMS

There are three basic economic systems in the world today: traditional, free market and command. Each system addresses the fundamental problem of how to allocate scarce resources in a different way. Kinship, custom and religion enter into these decisions in a traditional economy. In a free-market economy, self interest alone matters; buyers and sellers bid freely and openly on goods and services, and the price of purchases directly affects supply and demand. Unlike both traditional and free market systems, orthodox command economies ban all forms of private ownership; the state employs everyone and resources are allocated by central planners.

Economic systems are complex, multidimensional entities where decisions about what is produced, how to produce and for whose benefit have a moral and political context. An economy and the society it serves are inseparable. What differentiates one from the other is the nature of the basic problem being addressed. Social cohesion and regeneration are society's most pressing perennial concerns. Capital formation, productive capacity and full employment are necessary for a healthy economy. Traditional, free-market and command economies approach each of these situations differently. In this work we will examine how successful each system is in today's global economy.

The field of economics has a lengthy history because of its importance in everyone's daily lives on many levels. It is important for members of our society to understand the basic concepts of economics, as well as how these concepts impact our daily lives through our interactions with our government, businesses and with each other. While new situations will require ever-changing methods to deal with these issues, many of the basic premises surrounding economics are here to stay.

BIBLIOGRAPHY

"Chapter 1: Command, market and mixed economies." (2002). In *Understanding the world economy* (pp. 9-31). Oxfordshire, UK: Taylor & Francis Ltd.

Dallago, B. (2002). "The organizational effect of the economic system." *Journal of Economic Issues, 36*, 953-979.

Economy: 4. "The economic process." (2001). In *Discretionary economy: A normative theory of political economy* (pp. 67-87). Piscataway, New Jersey: Transaction Publishers.

Groenewegen, P. (2002). "Part I: Chapter 3: New light on the origins of modern economics." In *Eighteenth century economics* (pp. 76-96). Abingdon: Taylor & Francis Ltd.

Heilbroner, R. (1980). "Modern economics as a chapter in the history of economic thought." *Challenge, 22*(6), 20.

Hopkins, B.E., & Duggan, L.S. (2011). "A feminist comparative economic systems." *Feminist Economics, 17*, 35-69.

Katkov, A. (2013). "Economic goals ranking approach in comparative analysis of economic systems." *Global Conference on Business & Finance Proceedings, 8*, 108-112.

Paun, S. (2009). "The Vestiges of Communism and the Transformation of Party Systems in Post-Communist States." *Economics, Management & Financial Markets, 4*, 231-235.

Petr, J. (1987). "The nature and necessity of the mixed economy." *Journal of Economic Issues, 21*, 1445-1468.

Pressman, S. (1999). Alfred Marshall (1842-1924). In *Fifty major economists* (pp. 64-69). Abingdon: Taylor & Francis Ltd.

— Joan Robinson (1903-83). In *Fifty major economists* (pp. 128-132). Abingdon: Taylor & Francis Ltd.

— Léon Walras (1834-1910) In *Fifty major economists* (pp. 53-57). Abingdon: Taylor & Francis Ltd.

Rosser, M., & Rosser Jr., J. (1999). "The new traditional economy." *International Journal of Social Economics, 26*(5/6), 763-778.

Thoben, H. (1982). "Mechanistic and organistic analogies in economics reconsidered." *Kyklos, 35*(2), 292.

This introduction was based on the essays "Comparative Economic Systems" and "Evolution of Economic Thought" by Francis Duffy, MBA

LIST OF CONTRIBUTORS

Michael P. Auerbach holds a BA from Wittenberg University and a MA from Boston College. Mr. Auerbach has extensive private and public sector experience in a wide range of arenas: business and economic development, tax policy, international development, defense, public administration and tourism.

Seth Azria earned his J.D., magna cum laude, from New York Law School where he was an editor of the *Law Review* and research assistant to a professor of labor and employment law. He has written appellate briefs and other memorandum of law on a variety of legal topics for submission to state and federal courts. He is a practicing attorney in Syracuse, New York.

Sue Ann Connaughton is a freelance writer and researcher. Formerly, she was the Manager of Intellectual Capital & Research at Silver Oak Solutions, a spend management solutions consulting firm that was acquired by CGI in 2005. Ms. Connaughton holds a BA in English from Salem State College, a MEd from Boston University, and a MLIS from Florida State University.

Joseph Dewey holds a Ph.D.

Francis Duffy is a professional writer. He has had 14 major market-research studies published on emerging technology markets as well as numerous articles on Economics, Information Technology, and Business Strategy. A Manhattanite, he holds an MBA from NYU and undergraduate and graduate degrees in English from Columbia.

Dr. Marlanda English is president of ECS Consulting Associates which provides executive coaching and management consulting services. ECS also provides online professional development content. Dr. English was previously employed in various engineering, marketing and management positions with IBM, American Airlines, Borg-Warner Automotive and Johnson & Johnson. Dr. English holds a doctorate in business with a major in organization and management and a specialization in e-business.

Dr. Simone I. Flynn earned her Ph.D in cultural anthropology from Yale University, where she wrote a dissertation on Internet communities. She is a writer, researcher, and teacher in Amherst, Massachusetts.

Marie Gould is an associate professor and the faculty chair of the Business Administration Department at Peirce College in Philadelphia, Pennsylvania. She teaches in the areas of management, entrepreneurship, and international business. Although Ms. Gould has spent her career in both academia and corporate, she enjoys helping people learn new things — whether it's by teaching, developing or mentoring.

Joyce Gubata is a freelance business writer and consultant with more than 20 years experience in business operations, marketing and sales, information technology, and consulting for companies of all sizes in multiple industries.

Dr. Steven Hoagland holds BS and MS degrees in economics, a MS of urban studies, and a Ph.D in urban services management with a cognate in education all from Old Dominion University. His background includes service as senior-level university administrator responsible for planning, assessment, and research. It also includes winning multi-million dollar grants, both as a sponsored programs officer and as a proposal development team member. With expertise in research design and program evaluation, his recent service includes consulting in the health care, information technology, and education sectors and teaching as an adjunct professor of economics. In 2007, he founded a nonprofit organization to addresses failures in the education marketplace by guiding college-bound high school students toward more objective and simplified methods of college selection and by devising risk-sensitive scholarships.

Michele L. Kreidler holds a Ph.D in political science with a specialization in health and aging policy. Her research interest is in states adopting a policy of retiree attraction as a strategy for economic development. In addition she has more than twenty years experience working in health care program development and administration.

Heather Newton earned her J.D., cum laude, from Georgetown University Law Center, where she served as articles editor for *The Georgetown Journal of Legal Ethics*. She worked as an attorney at a large, international law firm in Washington, DC, before moving to Atlanta, where she is currently an editor for a legal publishing company. Prior to law school, she was a high school English teacher and freelance writer, and her works have appeared in numerous print and on-line publications.

Sara Rogers is a lawyer and professor for several major universities. She earned two MS.ED degrees in from City University in Seattle, Washington, and her J.D. from Franklin Pierce Law Center in Concord, New Hampshire. She resides in Phoenix, Arizona, where she teaches, serves as a legal consultant, and writes extensively on current legal issues and policies.

Nancy Sprague holds a BS degree from the University of New Hampshire and a MS in Health Policy from Dartmouth College's Center for the Evaluative and Clinical Sciences. Nancy began her career in health care as a registered nurse for many years. Since earning her BA in Business, Nancy has worked in private medical practice, home health, consulting, and most currently as an administrator for a large Medical Center. Her operational experience as a business manager in private medical practice and for the last decade in a tertiary medical center have allowed her

broad insight into both private and academic business endeavors.

Dr. Richa S. Tiwary holds a Ph.D in Marketing Management with a specialization in Consumer Behavior from Banaras Hindu University, India. She earned her second MS in Library Sciences with dual concentration in Information Science & Technology and Library Information Services from the Department of Information Studies, University at Albany-SUNY.

Michael Jay Tucker was involved for a number of years in trade press journalism during which time he performed many different aspects of editing within the magazine world. In 2002, he went back to academia to attain degrees in history. Currently, he is working on his doctoral studies in U.S. history from Clark University.

Dr. Ruth A. Wienclaw holds a Ph.D in industrial/organizational psychology with a specialization in organization development from the University of Memphis. She is the owner of a small business that works with organizations in both the public and private sectors, consulting on matters of strategic planning, training, and human/systems integration.

Scott Zimmer has a MS in library science, a MS in computer science and a J.D. He is an attorney and a librarian at Alliant International University.

AGGREGATE DEMAND

ABSTRACT

Economic recovery from social conflict, using government intervention to impact aggregate demand, is an attainable goal under certain conditions. This paper reviews the approaches employed by governments of countries that experienced social and/or civil conflict prior to installation of the reformist regime. The author acknowledges that foreign aid can play a role in the redevelopment of war-torn areas—the examples in this paper will be those for whom foreign aid was helpful but not so significant that it directly shaped or established the regime.

OVERVIEW

The World Divided

For most of the twentieth century, the world was apparently divided into two separate camps. To the west

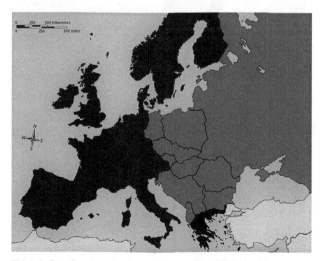

This is the Iron Curtain as described by Winston Churchill during his March 5th, 1946, Sinews of Peace speech in Fulton, Missouri. The Curtain extends down from Szczecin, Poland to Trieste, Italy. The lighter colored countries are behind the Iron Curtain. (Courtesy of BigSteve CC BY-SA 3.0 via Wikimedia Commons)

of what was deemed "the Iron Curtain," governments were formed and operated under democratic principles, whereas eastward, the communist regime held fast. Economically, Western infrastructure hinged on the free market and private industry; in the East, the government was the central figure in virtually any business development undertaking.

Of course, this view of the twentieth century is at best an overgeneralization of the true situation, which was far more complex. After all, the political environment in the United States diverges considerably from that of France, Germany, Spain, and Great Britain (as it does from non-European democracies in Japan, Turkey, and India). The Soviet version of Karl Marx's communist ideal differed sharply from the regimes in China, North Vietnam, and Cuba. Indeed, the concept of a "bipolar" twentieth-century world was largely based on generalizations and politically charged rhetoric: Democracy was democracy and communism was communism.

The truth behind the perceived international economic dichotomy was equally oversimplified. The People's Republic of China, for example, saw enormous economic strides throughout the twentieth century, despite several stumbles back into situations that charged citizens with ethereal, idealistic rhetoric that did little but return that nation to an isolated communist world. Having moved away from the posturing that gave rise to debacles like the Cultural Revolution and the Great Leap Forward, China is now one of the most powerful economies in the world, enjoying unparalleled growth and stature among industrialized nations. The economic architects of China, which was frequently detached from the Western world as "just another communist country" and (at least according to party leaders) proud to be labeled as such, felt comfortable departing from Marxist economics and installing the free and private markets that saw success in the West.

Conversely, the US economy, while ideally free to grow without government intervention, has long featured connections to virtually every level of government. One of the clearest examples of this fact is the American response to the Great Depression of the 1930s. The Smoot-Hawley Tariff Act, which raised tariffs and fortified barriers to economic recovery, is a case in point. In fact, one of the most prominent theories of economic development spawned during that same period in US history: the teachings of economist John Maynard Keynes. Keynes's concepts, which will be given better light in this paper, entail a call for government-introduced financial infusion into a troubled economy (Stegman, 2004) to stimulate aggregate demand. Few adherents to the purist view of a "free market versus communist" world would call Keynes's government bailout representative of the tenets of a Western political economy.

Social upheavals and/or conflicts, such as China's Cultural Revolution (during which thousands died and China spiraled into economic collapse) and the Great Depression give credence to an important point. When a nation is struggling to reemerge economically from social conflict, civil war or regime changes, they may find solace in creating linkages between government and the economy to stimulate aggregate demand.

This article takes a critical look at aggregate demand as a focal point around which economic recovery from political tumult is often built. Employing the ideals of Keynes and the assessments of political economy experts and observers, this paper reviews the examples of three economies that were hit hard by conflict, drastic regime change or civil war, each of which focuses on aggregate demand as a key to fiscal rejuvenation.

APPLICATIONS

Aggregate Demand

One cannot have a thriving economy without consumers. Aggregate demand, the total demand for goods and services within a nation's economy, hinges on the attitudes of the buying public (National Council on Economic Education, 2007). High prices, product reliability and industry confidence all play a role in aggregate demand and, concurrently, supply. In times of recession, low consumer confidence causes people to reduce their spending and,

therefore, aggregate demand flags. Conversely, in times of fiscal health, above-average incomes foster higher demand and consequently, prices. Aggregate demand and supply, therefore, are inversely proportional to each other. The difficulty lies in balancing between the two elements; facilitating economic health without risking inflation or recession. The unenviable task usually falls to lawmakers and regulators.

Enter Keynes

In the 1930s, as the United States suffered the throes of the Great Depression, attitudes abounded as to how to address the situation. For some, signs pointed to the fact that, despite the horrific fiscal state of the union at the time, the United States was in fact continuing to evolve into a prominent world power. In the minds of these economists, the market would correct itself and needed no intervention. Conversely,

Assistant Secretary, U.S. Treasury, Harry Dexter White (left) and John Maynard Keynes, honorary advisor to the U.K. Treasury at the inaugural meeting of the International Monetary Fund's Board of Governors in Savannah, Georgia on March 8, 1946. (Courtesy of the International Monetary Fund via Wikimedia Commons)

British economist John Maynard Keynes, in his treatise, *General Theory of Employment, Interest and Money*, operated from the perspective that the market system was not macro-economically self-sustaining. As one scholar observes, Keynes "thought that the framework of institutions, rules and policies needed to maintain the 'full potentialities of production' was, while not impossible to set up, more elaborate and expensive than that specified by market optimists" (Skidelsky, 2005).

As the polarity among economists seeking an end to market tumult continued, a rather interesting irony emerged: The Soviets remained convinced that the market would correct itself, and held off on instituting corrective economic policies. Keynes, however, felt that the keys lied in reducing unemployment, increasing demand and encouraging investment. A comparison of the two economic regimes demonstrates with great clarity which approach proved successful:

"Keynes's economics provided an important aid to the morale of Western society and its leadership, the Great Depression having badly shaken confidence in the free-enterprise economy. Governmental planning in the Keynesian sense prevented a repetition of high unemployment and dizzying consumption and production plunges, while Soviet economic security became arthritic to the point of paralysis. In the longer competition we know who won" (Felix, 2004, p. 62).

As evidenced by the response to one of the worst economic crises in American history, employing fiscal policy in selective arenas of a free market economy (namely, protecting and/or enhancing the demand side) can be seen as a useful tool for economic revitalization, particularly in times of significant tumult. As the following examples demonstrate, targeted corrective measures designed to bolster consumer confidence and investment can help return an economy to the right track as a nation recovers from large-scale conflict and/or upheaval.

CASE STUDIES
Lebanon
When one looks to the international stage for an example of serious discord, he or she may look no further than the Near East. Lebanon is no exception. In 1975, a civil war erupted in which the capital city of Beirut was shattered into factions, not the least of

The Green Line that separated parts of Beirut in 1982. (Courtesy of James Case from Philadelphia, Mississippi CC BY 2.0 via Wikimedia Commons)

which was a division between east and west. Sunni, Shia and Druze Muslims as well as Palestinians, Christians, Maronites and other factions took hold of the fractured city. In 1982, Israel entered Lebanon in pursuit of the Palestine Liberation Organization (PLO) and, in the process, added to the near chaos of that small nation. In 1982, a multinational force entered Beirut to establish some degree of order, but repeated terrorist attacks killed 300 of their group and drove them out, leaving Lebanon to continue in its own destruction (MIT, 1999).

In the 1990s, however, the conflict drew to an end of sorts. The Lebanese government's first step in the post–civil war years was to reinvigorate the economy. Reconstituting leadership in Beirut, Lebanon's leadership focused its attention on aggregate demand. The banking sector was given the first look, given the ability to redevelop the country's capital domestic market and invite international market access. Still, Lebanon's banking sector is heavily regulated by the central bank. Consumers also have a diversity of private market sectors in which to invest. The result is increased buyer confidence, which will likely continue to improve as long as the government does its part to protect consumers (Embassy of Lebanon, 2002).

Sadly, Lebanon spiraled back into conflict, with terrorist organizations vying for power with the Lebanese government and Israel conducting incursions against those factions. The result is that a reforming market, after adopting a Keynesian approach that seemed to have a positive effect on the economy, returned to a state of stagnancy. Clearly, Lebanon's example, supportive of the notion that government policy making can spur economic growth (particularly when focused on aggregate demand), remains a work in progress.

Lithuania

Whereas Lebanon is a nation attempting to establish order from near chaos, the Baltic state of Lithuania is working to prevent chaos after decades of Soviet-style order. During the era of the USSR, Lithuania's infrastructure was predominantly industrial, comprising about 40 percent of that country's gross domestic product (Economist Intelligence Unit, 2007). This economic sector was reliant on cheap energy prices from and market access to Moscow. Put simply, Lithuania, like other members of the USSR, was kept on a short leash and totally dependent on Mother Russia. There was no policy focusing on consumer demand or investment, since the focus of its economy was service not to investors but the USSR.

Immediately following Lithuania's independence in the early 1990s, matters took a turn for the worse. Lacking Soviet industrial investment (and the inexpensive energy prices available to that industry), Lithuania's nearly homogenous industrial base went into a near free fall. The second-largest industry in that country, agriculture, did not fare much better, again due (in part) to the high cost of fuel and energy.

Lithuanian economic planners, now independent of Soviet control and pursuing free market reformation, found their nation at a crossroads. The sudden transformation to a Western-style economy had an unanticipated consequence: Consumers now had income and the perceived need for services (as well as a scramble for the limited number of jobs available in the post-Soviet era). High demand fostered inflationary conditions. The government acknowledged the situation and initiated anti-inflation policies. Specifically, they sought to cut the national budget deficit, place controls on prices and slow wage growth (Business Monitor International, 2007). By early 2013, Lithuania had experienced stronger than average growth among European countries during the global financial crisis years. Government policy priorities were employment, emigration, energy security and adoption of the euro by 2015. 2012 had seen a rise in household spending and the first drop in unemployment since 2007. Annual average consumer price inflation was just above 3 percent

in 2012, and the current-account deficit narrowed (Country Report, 2013).

Uganda

While Lebanon and Lithuania have struggled to re-emerge from conditions largely created by external factors (interstate intervention and assimilation into the Soviet Union, respectively), the troubles facing most sub-Saharan African nations are largely home-grown. Corruption, sectarian and tribal violence, extreme poverty and even natural disasters have ripped at the fabric of the majority of African nations' infrastructure since their independence from the colonial powers. There are, however, bright spots. South Africa, emerging from international isolation due to the apartheid era, has rapidly seen economic development and growth. Kenya too has grown into a tourism hot spot, and its economy is summarily heading in the right direction. One country, however, is particularly interesting, due in part to its

Idi Amin in 1973. (Courtesy of Archives New Zealand CC BY 2.0 via Wikimedia Commons)

history, its geographical location and its clear desire to reemerge as a "diamond in the rough."

In the 1970s, Uganda became well-known in international circles, but not for a pleasant reason. Tribal infighting that had raged since that country's 1962 independence (save for a brief period of relative peace and economic development under President Milton Obote) gave rise to Idi Amin. Under Amin's watch, not only were hundreds of thousands of Ugandans dying in civil conflict—many more foreigners were being deported or killed. Uganda's economy suffered, with incomes declining 40 percent, previously strong industries declining exponentially and foreign support dwindling. It took Uganda 20 years after Amin's exile to recover to the level of economic progress it saw in 1960 (Siggel, 2004).

President Yoweri Museveni and Ministers of Parliament established frameworks to revitalize the country's strongest industrial assets, combat inflation induced by higher incomes and, most importantly, address poverty. Recently, the International Monetary Fund praised Uganda's macroeconomic policy, using terms like "robust" to describe the country's economy. Citing its cooperative development program with Uganda, the Poverty Reduction and Growth Facility (PRGF), the IMF heralded strong progress in the country's attempts to address its previous economic shortcomings, not the least of which is aggregate demand.

Deputy Managing Director Takatoshi Kato remarked,

> "Under the PRGF arrangement, Uganda has achieved macroeconomic stability and a strong external position, and has implemented a range of key structural reforms. Prudent monetary and fiscal policies, complemented by large external inflows, have contributed to higher growth and broad price stability, setting the stage for increased investments in health, education, and physical infrastructure, and improved living standards for Uganda's fast-growing population" (cited in "IMF Executive Board," 2006, par. 6).

There are concerns, however, that Uganda still has a distance to travel before consumer needs are met. Among them is the nagging issue of poverty: The Organisation for Economic Co-operation and Development recently noted that Uganda's government has been using international aid to eliminate budget deficits, not mitigate poverty. Aid donors, understandably, are becoming increasingly wary of sending funds to Uganda that will simply be used to balance the budget instead of feeding and clothing poor households (Global Consumption, 2006).

Nonetheless, Kiingi (2007) noted that with an overall inflation rate of 2.7 percent and a government that understands addressing consumer demand as the most pressing issue regarding economic development, Uganda at the very least warrants a watchful eye as a model of macroeconomic policymaking after 25 years of internal chaos. In 2013, consumer inflation was 4.9 percent and expected infrastructure development centered on foreign investment in oil production was going slowly owing to political objections and corruption (Country Intelligence Report, 2013).

CONCLUSION

This essay takes a close look at one of the most critical components of an economy: demand. Since the Great Depression, policy makers have looked at consumers as the focal point of recovery from social upheaval, economic collapse (or simply malaise) and even civil/military conflict. Those lawmakers were well-advised to create policy that bolsters this vital sector of the economy. Some nations would rather the economy improve itself through the free market rather than deploy targeted policies to help along redeveloping systems. As the case of the Soviet Union demonstrates, such a lack of intervention can prove detrimental to a return to economic prosperity.

Keynesian Strategies for Economic Strengthening
There are many countries that employed a Keynesian strategy. Some are relative successes, others still a work in progress. The cases offered in this article, however, are rather special. As stated earlier, Lebanon has been situated amid the near chaos of the Middle East, at times absorbing the viciousness of that region within its own borders. Few nearby Near Eastern nations, particularly those that do not produce oil in great quantities, have developed strong economic bases in which aggregate demand is a stable element. The Lebanese government clearly recognizes that demand is an area worthy of consideration in economic recovery. As Keynes suggests, policy makers

who intervene in an attempt to address consumer demand are likely to see long-term economic development in comparison to allowing the free market to correct itself.

In Lithuania, the situation is rather different from that of Lebanon but equally special. Lithuania's plight was worsened by the demise of the only contributor to its economy: the Soviet Union. With few controls, a diversifying economic base and increased worker wages, the Baltic nation is at risk of inflation. Its solution is again reflective of Keynes's thinking: Policy that centers on the needs of the consumer are likely to create effective economic recovery and stabilization.

For more than two decades, Uganda was isolated from the rest of the world largely due to its own actions (or lack thereof). Uganda certainly was not immune to the turmoil of the nations immediately nearby—that country still has a secessionist movement in its north, and the horrific events of Rwanda, Burundi, Sudan and the Democratic Republic of the Congo have spilled within Uganda's borders. Similarly, it was not immune to the corruption, instability and brutal dictatorships that have been a hallmark of central African history. Still, Uganda has prevailed, largely due to its stated commitment to institute free market reforms, repair national infrastructure, combat poverty and restore consumer confidence. Foreign investors and trading partners alike are encouraged by Uganda's example, and despite its erratic performance, most observers believe that nation is not far from prosperity.

There is an element in operation in each of these case studies, as it is in most developing countries. Developing nations of the Near East, the former Soviet Union and Africa all are dependent on international aid. It is, after all, a global economy. While scholars would like to analyze an economic system that is free of external influences (and certainly foreign capital), such systems are not in place any more in the twenty-first century. Regardless of the source of those funds, however, the principle of establishing or reinvigorating aggregate demand elements remains sound—the government in question, at least ideally, seeks to apply available monies to strengthen the consumer base. These funds are ideally used to help less developed (or war-torn) countries rebuild infrastructures. Countless industrialized nations offer similar programs, as does the IMF, the United Nations

(UN) and nonprofit organizations. For example, as stated earlier, the IMF provides such a program to Uganda's government. That program, like others, is designed to empower the consumer with resources not to simply survive but to build or rebuild a thriving economy.

As each of the examples provided in this study demonstrate, Keynesian economics offer viable solutions to countries that are reemerging from economic collapse, social upheaval and even violent intra- and interstate conflicts. The keys, as Keynes suggests, are twofold: First, it is vital for government to play a role in revitalization and redevelopment—under the circumstances of these case studies, markets that are left unassisted are likely to continue free-falling. Second, aggregate demand must be a pivotal focal point of those reforms. Efforts to stave off inflation, safeguard prices, lower taxes, bolster employment and wages, create opportunities for investment and, in general, increase consumer confidence are key to fostering a sustainable macroeconomy.

BIBLIOGRAPHY

Bloomfield, L. & Moulton, A. (1999). Cascon case LBN: Lebanon civil war 1975–90. Retrieved from Massachusetts Institute of Technology Cascon Institute for Analyzing International.

Country intelligence report: Uganda. (2013). *Uganda Country Monitor,* 1–20.

Country Report: Lithuania. (2013). *Country Report. Lithuania,* 1–29.

Embassy of Lebanon. (2002). Profile of Lebanon: The economy. Retrieved from xlink:href="http://www.lebanonembassyus.org/country%5flebanon/economy.html"

Felix, D. (2004). "Keynesian consequences." *Society, 41,* 58–62.

"IMF executive board completes final review of Uganda's arrangement and approves 16-month policy support instrument." (2006, January 24). Press Release. Retrieved September 20, 2007, from International Monetary Fund.

Kiingi, A. (2007, September 3). "Uganda: Inflation crops to 2.7 percent." *The New Vision.* Retrieved from xlink:href="http://allafrica.com/stories/200709040050.html"

Mendita-Munoz, I. (2017). "Wage led aggregate demand in the United Kingdom." *International Review of Applied Economics, 31,* 5, 565–584.

National Council on Economic Education. (2007). "Fiscal and monetary policy process." Retrieved from EconEdLink.

Siggel, E. (2004). "Uganda's policy reforms, industry competitiveness and regional integration: A comparison with Kenya." *Journal of International Trade and Economic Development, 13*, 325–357.

Skidelski, R. (2005). "Keynes, globalisation and the Bretton Woods Institutions in the light of changing ideas about markets." *World Economics, 6*, 15–30.

Stegman, T. (2004, May). "Fiscal policy: Theory and practice." *Ecodate.*

SUGGESTED READING

Chipman, J. S. (2007). "Aggregation and estimation in the theory of demand." *History of Political Economy, 39*, 106–129.

Estes, R. J. (2007). "Development challenges and opportunities confronting economies in transition." *Social Indicators Research, 83*, 375–411.

Hayes, Mark G. (2007). "The point of effective demand." *Review of Political Economy, 19*, 55–80.

Kuodis, R., & Ramanauskas, T. (2009). "From boom to bust: Lessons from Lithuania." *Monetary Studies (Bank Of Lithuania), 13*, 96–104.

Pressman, Steven. (2006). "Economic power, the state and post-Keynesian economics." *International Journal of Political Economy, 35*, 67–86.

—*Michael P. Auerbach*

AGGREGATE SUPPLY

ABSTRACT

The conventional "bipolar" view of supply and demand macroeconomics becomes more complex, particularly on the supply side, when a nation enters into an international trade relationship. Nations may, in an effort to bolster their domestic product or enhance their international standing, employ a number of policies to satisfy the needs of their internal infrastructure—under certain conditions, these efforts may prove fruitful (although controversial to foreign parties).

OVERVIEW

The French economist, statesman and author Frédéric Bastiat (1801–1850) once said, "By virtue of exchange, one man's prosperity is beneficial to all others" (Liberty-Tree.ca, 2007). Indeed, international trade is arguably the most integral component of the now-global economy. However, as difficult as it is to fathom, the present era of global networks and international trade among virtually every nation around the world is relatively young in human historical terms. As recently as the pre–World War II era, the world was a much more disjointed place with factions trading selectively with their allies, and others not trading at all. Even more mind-boggling is the fact that these arrangements were made by choice. Trade relationships, if not long-standing (such as those between the United States and its allies in Europe), were often established not by diplomatic missions, but through wars and post-war negotiations.

Japan, for example, sought to garner many of its most prized resources through military operations in the 1930s. Its strongest trade ally (until its militaristic leanings became apparent) was the United States, through an exclusive, bilateral arrangement made at the end of the Tokugawa era in the late 1860s. After the war and the dismantling of Japan's military machine, the United States largely rebuilt nearly every facet of that country. The United States, whose economy leapt out of the Great Depression, gave new fiscal life to the Japanese people, including a military-based consumer demand (thousands of US soldiers and personnel became part of the Japanese economy after the war). The Korean War exacerbated that dependence, as not just American personnel but troops from 15 other nations descended on Japan as a staging area. Japan did not need to proactively establish trade relationships on the international stage—the world came to Japan.

When the Japanese economic engine restarted in the post-war era, the country looked disproportionately inward at using its aggregate supply to satisfy domestic demand, despite the fact that it has long produced high-quality, exportable goods. Japanese policy has been to focus those products on an intrastate basis and maintain strict import restrictions. Their trade imbalances have also reached significant proportions, as that nation, in 2000, maintained foreign reserves of nearly $300 billion (National Economies Encyclopedia, 2007). Since then, international clamoring over opening Japanese markets to foreign imports has achieved some success, but a clear imbalance remains.

Japan's example above is indicative of the intricacies and delicate nature of international trade and of a sort of "tug-of-war" in economics over aggregate supply. As this paper will demonstrate, international trade tends to pull supply in different and often conflicting directions. To maintain supply for both trading partners and domestic consumers, nations may employ a number of policies to satisfy the needs of their internal infrastructure—under certain conditions, these efforts may prove fruitful (although controversial to foreign parties).

Aggregate Supply & Trade

Plutarch once recalled a fable of Menenius Agrippa about an attempted mutiny by other human organs against the stomach, which they accused of being "the only idle, uncontributing part in the whole body." Only after they ousted the stomach did the organs realize their mistake, as they were left with the arduous task of generating the large supply their appetites demanded (Bartlett, 2005).

As Plutarch's story of Coriolanus suggests, supply plays an absolutely essential role in any macroeconomy. Aggregate supply, the total sum of goods and services produced by an economic system, is a vital counterbalance to consumer demand. There are a variety of elements that influence supply as it relates to demand. Among these factors are the available labor force, employee salaries, corporate and commercial taxes (and, on the positive side, government subsidies), new technologies and consumer investment (Tutor2U.net, 2007).

Without a labor force and the ability to pay them, industries cannot meet the needs of the customer. Likewise, if the government applies a disproportionate tax levy on doing business rather than providing tax incentives or exemptions, business

Oregon gasoline dealers displayed signs explaining the gas crisis flag policy in the winter of 1973–74. (Courtesy of National Archives)

may falter. New technologies also play a role, often making the difference between cost-effectiveness and inefficiency. Furthermore, investment, from either a domestic source or from foreign entrepreneurs, help provide vital resources for manufacturers and service providers to meet the demands of consumers. Still another contributing factor is inflation: If consumer incomes are high and product stock cannot meet customer desire to buy, the imbalance can adversely impact manufacturers and service providers by instigating an increase in prices. Put simply, the supply side of a macroeconomy, as it relates to domestic demand, is already sensitive to a variety of potentially beneficial or harmful influences.

Exacerbating the significant draws on supply resources is international trade. When adding interstate relationships to the mix, the supply side is not only subject to the demands of domestic consumers, but also to the needs of consumers in partner systems. In trade relations, therefore, supply is fluid and dynamic, subject not only to internal forces but also to external elements. If one views macroeconomics as a teeter-totter (with supply and demand in opposing seats), trade acts as a force pulling the supply side in a different direction while it contends with its polar counterpart.

Because of the many directions from which supply is pulled in international trade contexts, it is therefore sensitive and reactive. Nowhere in international economics is this statement truer than it is with oil prices. After all, the price of oil affects transportation, heating, manufacturing and countless other industries. It is no wonder that any spike in oil prices causes a ripple effect in an economy. In a study of the 1973–74 energy crisis (and subsequent inflation), one economist echoes the view that "an increase in oil's relative price will cause an adverse shift in the aggregate supply curve that produces a higher price level and lower output" (Darby, 1982). Judging from the impact of oil price spikes on a wide range of industries (as well as the cost of living in any industrialized country) in the early twenty-first century, this method of thought seems validated.

Are there other factors that can impact aggregate supply in an international trade relationship? Although the oil example provided above, demonstrative of the effectiveness of pricing as a trade mechanism, is a well-established "x-factor" in industry and therefore supply-side economics; it is certainly not alone.

Currency
The trade of goods and services between states necessitates the exchange of currency. The translation of currency plays an integral role in a successful trade relationship. Currency exchange rates (and controls thereof) therefore represent significant influences on aggregate supply.

As stated earlier, an imbalance between large quantities of money and short supply creates inflationary circumstances. If private demand for currency exceeds supply (with domestic central banks making up the difference), that currency is said to be overvalued. This element can wreak havoc on trade relationships for a number of reasons.

- First, as Edna Carew suggests, traders and speculators would be wary of buying currency that is likely to fall (or slough).
- Second, foreign exporters would be unlikely to make payments using their own currency, as that currency would likely be used to offset the differential between the current exchange rate and the actual value of that currency (Carew, 1988).

After the end of World War I, the issue of overvalued currency remained a latent concern for redeveloping countries (including the industrialized European states). Popular belief, which carried into post–World War II reconstruction efforts as well, held that any policy response that entailed devaluation was a recipe for disaster. "Devaluation raises the domestic prices of imports and of exports …" warned one expert, adding, "[it] will tend to raise the prices of import substitutes, of potential exports, and of intermediate goods required for their production" (Sohmen, 1958).

Nevertheless, devaluation (particularly in light of a currency's overvaluation) remains a viable option for those countries seeking to tighten trade relationships and reemerge from economic malaise and/or collapse. In Latvia, this issue had reached a near boiling point in light of an account deficit of over 25 percent of the country's gross domestic product (GDP). With a heavy reliance on the euro as a borrowing currency, fears abounded that any attempt at devaluation of the *lat* would exacerbate inflation and reduce the country's competitiveness. Devaluation at that point might have seemed a bit premature, as the government has just initiated anti-inflation policies that could help mitigate the *lat's* collapse. Although the concern is very real and widespread, Latvia's response is to hang on to its anti-inflation plan before further taking down an already weak currency (Central Europe and Baltic States, 2002). Latavia no longer uses the lat as currency. It replaced the lat with the euro in 2014.

Latvia's fear is based in part on the currency woes of Iceland, which in 2006 downgraded the *krone* about 8 percent in only a few days (Chapman, 2006). Although Iceland is a small country with an equally small economy, such a devaluation created a ripple effect throughout the North Atlantic and Scandinavian region, with investors pulling out of risky ventures in that area. Developing nations like those in the Baltics, unfortunately, fall into this category.

As mentioned earlier, the supply side of international trade is very sensitive. Take, for example, the depreciation of the Thai *baht*, which in the late 1990s fell suddenly and appreciably, sending shockwaves throughout East Asia (Zhao, 2007). Even more painful was the 1998 devaluation of the Russian *ruble*, which in one month fell between 200 and 300 percent—former Soviet satellites who, while politically independent, continued to share 80 to 90 percent of their trade with Russia, were left reeling in fiscal crisis (Perekhodtsev, 1999). Clearly, in a global economy that relies on trade, any currency shock that occurs in one nation affects regional (and even far-reaching) trade partners.

Tariffs

Developing economies simply may not be able to offer a counterbalance to a dynamic potential trade partner or market. Still, they may possess goods or services that are in high demand (and which, therefore, trade partners may be willing and flexible in their price requirements). In these cases, protections applied to those markets, while isolating the fledgling economy from trading on a large scale, may allow infrastructures to grow at a manageable pace and protect demand-side interests such as employment, domestic taxation and pricing.

It goes without saying that such protectionist policies are not advisable for nations or trading blocs

U.S. Secretary of State Rex Tillerson shakes hands with China's General Secretary Xi Jinping before their bilateral meeting in Beijing, China, on March 19, 2017. (Courtesy of the U.S. State Department)

with little clout. However, evidence shows that a viable market, whether in a dominating economy or in a relatively small system, may be able to implement regulations that safeguard domestic systems and industries. These restrictions usually come in the form of tariffs.

In the post-war era, few countries have demonstrated the sort of "economic split personality syndrome" that has been manifest in China. Since 1949's communist revolution, that nation has vacillated between strict adherence to Maoist rhetorical dogma and cultivation of a pro-business, free market regime. However, since Mao Tse-Tung's death in 1976, China has grown to be one of the world's most powerful economies. Despite the sheer immensity of the Chinese markets, however, China has maintained a somewhat unpredictable status in international trade. In one recent example, China, which has a reputation as an area in which products are manufactured inexpensively (and therefore is considered fertile ground for international businesses), has been accused of unfairly blocking foreign-made car parts. The United States (with which China shares "most favored nation" status) and the European Union (EU) take exception to a recently adopted regulation in China that states that "if the value of all imported automobile parts accounts for more than 60% of the value of the whole vehicle, it should be subjected to the import tariff as a 'whole vehicle'" (Lazell, 2006). China has also imposed tariffs designed to encourage domestic high-end steel producers to keep selling in-country rather than going abroad. That tariff amounted to a 17 percent tax on exported steel (Euromoney Institutional Investor PLC, 2005). Indeed, given China's capabilities and resources (both natural and capital), that nation has proven the viability of protectionist practices, especially in light of the continued and extensive trade relationships shared with the economic powerhouses of the West.

Of course, some tariffs are imposed with little international finger-pointing. In Europe, for example, a number of "innovative" tariffs have been imposed on utility prices. Since the products, electricity and natural gas, are the same in the United Kingdom as they are in EU nations, the price for each should be the same. However, the United Kingdom imposes a number of capped tariffs (taxes that remain at a certain rate for a particular period of time) and environmental assessments, some of which are duplicated in other EU partner states in varying numbers, others which are not. Furthermore, some EU countries' utilities combine energy with telecommunications, offering varying services (and associated taxes). Even relatively small nations like Portugal, Denmark and Sweden have been able to implement such tariffs on energy costs and not risk isolation (Market Watch: Energy, 2006). Rather, these trade restrictions and/or additional charges are viewed as simple variances in services whose positives and negatives are gauged as matters of consumer choice.

Exclusive Relationships

Earlier in this paper, this author briefly touched upon the trade relationship between the United States and China. Under "most favored nation" (MFN) status, two of the largest economies in the world, acknowledging their mutual interests and multifarious linkages, established an extensive arrangement in which free trade, in most situations, would occur. In other words, tariffs and similar trade barriers would be largely eschewed.

Such relationships are becoming more commonplace in the global marketplace. Under this sort of arrangement, the two (or more) participating countries create a level playing field under which goods and products are exchanged. The assumption that is made is that the participants are obliged to acknowledge parity in order for exchange to take place. It is in this equitable situation in which the details become murky, at least in a theoretical context. This nebulousness has become a thorn in the side of the World Trade Organization (WTO), as each individual MFN arrangement has different parameters and criteria for the nations to be "like" one another. As one observer writes, "like" has vexing connotations:

["Like"] is one of the most complex issues to define. It does not seem possible to establish a unitary reconstruction valid for the whole WTO system; rather, it is dealt within each of the agreements … case by case, according to the circumstances and context of the situation (Rosembuj, 2007).

MFN and similar trade relationships, in light of the vagueness of the general guidelines (or lack thereof) under which such arrangements are established, can be a great benefit to any nation seeking to advance itself in a global market. The parameters for linking could be based on anything, including strategic and political relationships.

CONCLUSION

In macroeconomics, the casual observer might view the relationship between aggregate supply and demand as two separate arenas that, when balanced form the core of a successful domestic economy. However, the world is not comprised of wholly self-sufficient individual nations—there is another side to aggregate supply, an area affected by the demand of consumers in trade partner nations. International trade, which drives the global economy in a way it never did before the twentieth century, has created interstate networks so intricate and numerous that a simple "supply-demand" portrait is thrown to the wind.

This statement is rooted in the fact that international trade entails one nation building and utilizing its aggregate supply (at least in part) to satisfy not domestic demand but the demand of foreign consumers. Hence, aggregate supply is in fact pulled in two sometimes competing directions. Japan's example at the beginning of this article is demonstrative of this fact. Japan opened its doors to American traders in the late nineteenth century, witnessing economic prosperity and rapid industrialization (predominantly in urban areas) as a result, but that industry was used for foreign trade and the military, not to satisfy domestic demand. Many scholars argue that the fact that Japan was focusing on establishing its international presence instead of the rampant rural poverty that existed at the time was a contributor to the war against the West. When the Depression took hold of the world, Japan (like most countries) looked inward to protect its infrastructure, employing strict tariffs and other restrictions to limit foreign imports. Isolated during the 1930s and 1940s, Japan re-emerged on the world stage. However, for decades afterward, it retained many of the protectionist measures it began before the war; exporting inexpensive products and generating a massive monetary reserve overseas. Clearly, Japan's modern growth over the last century has been remarkable and yet illustrative of the sometimes conflicting pulls on supply caused by international trade.

Establishing trade relationships, particularly for those economies that are either reforming (as is the case in Latvia) or shifting priorities to seize on their potential on the world stage (China), can be vexing when one considers the pull on supply. In order to facilitate trade relationships (or at least level the playing field), nations that are at a competitive disadvantage may employ a number of tactics.

Currency Devaluation

The first of these policies is currency devaluation. Reducing the pressure on an overvalued currency, especially if anti-inflationary policies are in place (thus satisfying domestic demand), may prove viable. There is caution warranted, however, as unilateral devaluation can spark a chain reaction in areas in which interstate trade is heavy but fiscal instability exists. Latvia's potential of lowering the value of the *lat* could have had an impact on the already fragile Baltic region, and this area had already experienced one currency sell off in recent years (Iceland), and the result of that action sent ripples throughout the North Atlantic. However, the lat no longer exists.

Tariffs & Restrictions

The second action is one that any free market enthusiast abhors. Japan's wariness of opening its doors for foreign imports throughout the post-war period left partners crying foul about woefully unbalanced trade relationships. China's propensity for high tariffs and import restrictions has also created consternation in the international community. Still, there are instances, as the example of European utilities illustrates, in which tariffs and restrictions can alleviate supply pressures and appear less like a barrier and more like a matter of consumer choice.

Trading Blocs

Trading blocs or "most favored nation" relationships are a third approach. These arrangements provide an elite trading status between participating nations in which trade restrictions are limited or eliminated. The vagueness of the parameters of such relationships suggests that nations may see symbiotic potentials and even parity despite obvious economic differences between them. It is this parity that can generate strong revenues on either side of the agreement.

There is no "silver bullet" to addressing the sometimes conflicting relationship between aggregate supply, foreign demand and aggregate demand. There are conditions, however, in which certain measures may show success. Devaluation in an otherwise healthy economy (wherein inflation is held in check) may prove useful for Latvia without warding off foreign investment. Tariffs and protections, if applied

in such a way that the foreign consumer is not impacted in an excessive manner, can ensure the long-term health of domestic infrastructure (and supply to meet the demands of that infrastructure). Finally, special relationships can create tight bonds between nations of varying size and resources, fostering economic growth on both sides without isolating domestic demand. Supply, pulled in two directions, may prove more flexible as a result.

BIBLIOGRAPHY

Aggregate supply. (2007). Tutor2U.net. (2007). Retrieved from xlink:href="http://www.tutor2u.net/economics/content/topics/ad%5fas/aggregate%5fsupply.htm"

Carew, E. (1988). "Overvalued currency." In *The language of money*. Retrieved October 2, 2007, from Australia and New Zealand Banking Group, Ltd.

Central Europe and Baltic States. (2002). *Business Eastern Europe, 31*, 7.

Chapman, D. (2006, March). "Rising interest rates, rising geopolitical concerns double jeopardy?" *Union Securities Ltd. Gold-Eagle.* Retrieved from xlink:href="http://www.gold-eagle.com/editorials%5f05/chapmand030306.html"

"China ups tax on steel products." (2005). *Trade Finance, 8*, 12.

Cover, J., Enders, W., & Hueng, C. (2006). "Using the aggregate demand-aggregate supply model to identify structural demand-side and supply-side shocks: Results using a bivariate VAR." *Journal of Money, Credit & Banking (Ohio State University Press), 38*, 777–790.

Darby, M.R. (1982). "The price of oil and world inflation and recession." *American Economic Review, 72*, 738.

Europe's utility tariffs show the value of choice. (2006). MarketWatch: Energy, 5, 21–22.

Fahimnia, B. B., Farahani, R. Z., & Sarkis, J. J. (2013). "Integrated aggregate supply chain planning using memetic algorithm – A performance analysis case study." *International Journal of Production Research, 51*, 5354–5373.

Famous quote from Frederic Bastiat. (2007). Liberty-Tree.ca.: Famous quotations about liberty. Retrieved from xlink:href="http://quotes.liberty-tree.ca/quote/frederic%5fbastiat%5fquote%5f654f"

Hartwig, J. (2011). "Aggregate demand and aggregate supply: Will the real Keynes please stand up?" *Review of Political Economy, 23*, 613–618.

"Japan: Overview of economy." (2007). *National economies encyclopedia.* Retrieved xlink:href="http://www.nationsencyclopedia.com/economies/Asia-and-the-Pacific/Japan-OVERVIEW-OF-ECONOMY.html"

John Bartlett (1820-1905). Familiar quotations (10th ed.). 1919. (2005). *Bartleby.com.* Retrieved from xlink:href="http://www.bartleby.com/100/714.17.html"

Lazell, M. (2006). "China import restrictions anger Europeans." *ICIS Chemical Business, 1,* 13.

Perekhodtsev, D. (1999). "The impact of Russian ruble devaluation on trade and currencies of the CIS countries." *Transforming Government in Economies in Transition (Ford Foundation).*

Rosembuj, T. (2007). "Taxes and the World Trade Organization." *International Tax Review, 35*(6/7), 348–365.

Sohmen, E. (1958). "The effect of devaluation on the price level." *Quarterly Journal of Economics, 72,* 273–283.

Wenfeng, Z. (2007, March 16). "Latvia struggles with currency weakness." *MarketWatch* (online version). Retrieved from xlink:href="http://www.marketwatch.com/news/story/latvian-currency-weakness-raises-emerging/story.aspx?guid=%7B0CE18C17-40E2-4B84-B91B-34FEFF0DE06E%7D"

SUGGESTED READING

Chorev, N. (2007). "A fluid divide: Domestic and international factors in US trade policy formation." *Review of International Political Economy, 14,* 653–689.

Finger, J.M. & John S.W. (2007). "Implementing a trade facilitation agreement in the WTO: What makes sense?" *Pacific Economic Review, 12,* 335–355.

Jensen, J., Rutherford, T. & Tarr, D. (2007). "The Impact of liberalizing barriers to foreign direct investment in services: The case of Russian accession to the World Trade Organization." *Review of Development Economics, 11,* 482–506.

Smith, J. (2007). The death of tariffs. Or not. *World Trade, 20,* 58.

—*Michael P. Auerbach*

AGRICULTURAL ECONOMICS

ABSTRACT

Just as in every other human endeavor, the production and distribution of foodstuffs adheres to certain basic economic principles. Unlike other kinds of competitive markets, though, the dynamics of supply and demand for agricultural goods do not always optimize resource allocation or maximize productive capacity. The most vexing problem here has to do with pricing. Left to its own devices, a commodity market regularly pays out a return that does not even cover the farmer's production costs. Truly efficient farming these days is also far more capital-intensive than it is labor-intensive. Profitability largely depends on successfully leveraging ever larger economies of scale and more cost-effective technology. Yet, most of the world's farmers still till small plots by hand.

OVERVIEW

One word—famine—starkly sums up why, compared to other specialized forms of economic activity, agriculture is "first among equals." Whenever food production falls far short of demand, sooner or later people somewhere starve. Those in the developed world rarely dwell on the sheer precariousness of a sufficient supply of crops and livestock, although this is still a daily fact of life in parts of the developing world. Catastrophic drought, floods and pestilence can and do occur at a moment's notice, wiping out a whole growing season's harvests in the course of months, weeks, or even days. Even industrialized agribusiness is exposed to more risk than most forms of manufacturing.

Natural hazards, moreover, tend to overshadow the seriousness of much more likely economic risks common to highly volatile commodity markets (Clever, 2003). Price-takers by necessity, not choice, farmers always run the attendant risk of supply exceeding demand, which would depress market prices below producer costs. Ironically in such instances, far from earning higher profits, efficient producers actually go deeper in debt. Very real disincentives like this have caused increasing numbers of small-acreage owner-producers to abandon farming as a livelihood when and where circumstances permit. In much of the least developed world and large swaths of the developing one, circumstances do not allow for this. Indeed, the most striking structural feature of the worldwide agricultural sector is the sharp divisions in modes of production, crop yields, types and amounts of capital investments, labor intensiveness, technological inputs and concentration of ownership between developed and developing countries. Agricultural economics looks at the fundamentals in consumption, production, exchange and distribution of foodstuffs in both developed and developing countries (Ise, 1920).

Developing Nations & Farming. In the world's poorest nations, agriculture is practiced today much as it was millennia ago. In small plots tilled mostly by hand, with night soil the only affordable fertilizer

A small scale farmer in the Kasiya area of Livingstone, Zambia practicing conservation farming explains the concept to others on October 4, 2017. She prepared the land herself, applied manure and is now waiting to plant soon as it rains. Despite her age she did all the work. (Courtesy of 13tainonge CC BY-SA 4.0 via Wikimedia Commons)

and rainfall the sole source of water, farm owners or their tenants still eke out a subsistence living. All that is available in the way of technology consists of metal plows, manufactured scythes and hoes and perhaps a beast of burden to help plow or draw water from a deep well. Most of the time, too, any labor-saving device, any soil-enriching agrichemical, any form of genetically modified seed costs money that must be borrowed either from lenders that charge high interest rates or provided as part of a tenancy arrangement. In a tenancy arrangement, farmers are given a plot of land to cultivate in exchange for rentier income such as a sizeable share of the farmer's harvest. The amount of this share is critical, for it must be delivered to the landlord's storehouse no matter how little is left to feed a farmer's typically large family until the next harvest (Bardhan, 1979). There is a point of no return, moreover. Agronomics has established that one out of every three seeds of most cereals must be replanted to sustain future life. A subsistence farmer who consumes more than two-thirds of a grain harvest will not be able to grow enough food to feed his family the following year. Cash-poor, in debt, and subject to the ever present threat of drought or flooding and soil depletion from over-cultivation, farmers in developing nations constantly live at the margins. It is an unenviable position to be in, but it is something nearly one-half of the world's population struggles with daily.

Developed Nations & Farming. Farming in rich nations, by contrast, tends to take place on larger plots of land, using costly fertilizers, herbicides, growth hormones and now genetically modified seeds. Sowing, cultivating and reaping are mostly done mechanically. Elaborately engineered irrigation systems supplement spotty rainfall. This "industrialization of agriculture" has raised the productivity of the individual farm laborer many fold in the last century. The industrialization of agriculture has also improved the farm's crop yield, the metric of agricultural output that measures the amount of a grain (wheat, corn, rice, sorghum, barley, or rye) grown in a standard sized unit of land like the acre or hectare. Indeed, productivity gains alone may well have staved off the dire warnings of nineteenth-century economist Thomas Malthus who rather famously predicted that geometric growth in the world's population would inevitably outstrip arithmetic growth in agricultural

Wheat harvest on the Palouse, Idaho, in 2004. (Courtesy of U.S. Department of Agriculture)

Many farm machines at ARS' Beltsville Agricultural Research Center are running on a mixture of diesel fuel and biodiesel, which is made from soybean oil. – From left to right: John Deere 7800 tractor with Houle slurry trailer, Case IH combine harvester, New Holland FX 25 forage harvester with corn head (Courtesy of Bob Nichols of U.S. Department of Agriculture)

output. It might have been but for the mechanization of farming that occasioned a proportionate geometric growth in output. However, farm machinery, fertilizer and other productivity multipliers are capital goods that depreciate over time and create the need for ongoing investment. Financially, then, the greater the acreage a producer has under cultivation, the more efficiently he can leverage costly technology via economies of scale. Smaller producers cannot compete in the long run because they no longer fall within farming's optimum scale of enterprise, while large producers have every incentive to grow even larger for the very same reason. No wonder, then, that the so-called "family farm" faces extinction; increasing returns to scale favor consolidated operations owned by fewer producers—the modus operandi of agribusiness.

Agribusiness. In the strictest sense of the term, an agribusiness is a corporation dedicated to the high-capacity production of a cash crop. Vertically integrated, an agribusiness is owned and operated using several distinct, interlocking phases that facilitate the process of bringing crops and livestock to the dinner table. Agribusinesses not only cultivate farmland, but can also provide seasonal contract labor; rent out expensive farm equipment; or transport grains, produce or livestock in bulk to food processors through satellite operating companies (Cook & Barry, 2004). In the broadest sense of the term, agribusiness refers to the constellation of industries that produce, process and/or distribute foodstuffs. As long as this process proceeds efficiently, a greater concentration

of ownership is in everyone's vested interest. At a certain point, however, concentration can go too far in the direction of an oligopoly. In such a case, the few remaining firms that supply a given product segment or are instrumental to a necessary stage in the production process will not compete as intensely and allow inefficiencies to creep into production.

FURTHER INSIGHTS

Challenges Faced by Farmers: Agriculture & Competition. "Perfect" competition holds sway in markets in which the exact same product is sold by a large number of suppliers free to enter or exit the market at will; each supplier knows as much about prices as the next. The notion's genesis dates back to the eighteenth-century laissez-faire economic theory of Adam Smith. It endures to this day as a powerful model of free market behavior. Be it of rice, grains, soybeans, produce, poultry or livestock, numerous producers of each certainly supply an identical crop and, to a lesser extent perhaps, share the same pricing information. Given the necessity of land ownership or tenancy and the level of required investments or sunk costs in seed and equipment, however, they all clearly do not have the same freedom to enter or exit the market. Even so, a lot of "same-crop" suppliers also, by dint of their undifferentiated product, make it impossible for any one farmer to charge some buyers more than another, theoretically

15

at least. Of course, transportation costs increase the greater the distance between the buyer and seller. However, Adam Smith and like-minded neoclassical economists of more recent vintage considered location-related matters a burdensome distraction and so simply ignored the problem; a license economic model-builders frequently resort to.

Price Elasticity. The individual producer of any agricultural "staple," then, effectively has one of two choices: sell at the going market price or do not. Storing a staple to be sold at a more favorable price at a later date creates additional costs that must be offset by selling at a price even higher than the one currently sought. Any such decision rests on the anticipation that prices will rise when they may in fact fall; a real possibility that dissuades risk-adverse farmers from this course of action. In either case, the individual producer runs head-on into the price inelasticity of demand for crops. It is a ratio with the percentage change in quantity consumed as the numerator and the percentage change in price as the denominator. When this yields a value greater than one, the item is said to be elastic: a higher or lower price results in a proportionately greater or lesser demand for it. A value of less than one signals the item is inelastic. A price change here has far less effect on consumption levels. Only a comparatively large swing in prices will appreciably increase or decrease demand for it. By its very nature, a staple good like bread tends to be price inelastic; people are going to buy a certain amount except when shortages push the price up exorbitantly. So, only a large increase in price tends to generate higher farm revenue. Conversely, a large decrease tends to depress it. Farming has high fixed costs. Machinery must be repaired and replaced, soil quality chemically refurbished and seasonal labor paid the going rate.

Market Forces & Farming. Making matters worse for the farmer is the economic reality that he is individually powerless to change the going market price because his output accounts for a miniscule fraction of the total quantity available for sale. The question then becomes: Do market forces always efficiently allocate agricultural resources in practice as it does in theory? Not necessarily, for the actual producers rarely receive the full selling price and so are undercompensated for their labor. Transaction and

Farmer's Markets are popular places for farmers to sell their produce in the United States. (Courtesy of U.S. Department of Agriculture via Wikimedia Commons)

transportation costs typically siphon off a farmer's share as does rentier income, the largely unearned share owed by sharecroppers to landlords, and/or interest on outstanding debts (Breiymer, 1974). The producer thus ends up getting a fraction of the selling price as actual income even when prices are high. When prices are low, farmer income can dip below acceptable levels. If a farmer's potential earnings, or opportunity costs as they're called, promise larger earnings than farming does, then this alternate economic activity better meets the farmer's needs. As rational economic agents, we must all look to maximize our utility.

Individual self-interest can conflict with national interests if too many farmers exit the market. If the base of suppliers shrinks past a certain point and automation cannot adequately make up a shortfall in output in the near term, productive capacity will contract. In this situation, imports cannot necessarily come to the rescue due to quotas and tariffs on agricultural goods. Exactly why this is so in the era of "globalization" has as much to do with history and politics as it does with economics. One hundred years ago, farming accounted for a greater share of gross domestic product in developed countries than it does today. Monumental gains in agricultural productivity paled in comparison to much greater gains in manufacturing. Farming employed considerably more of the overall labor force at that time, as well. Protecting rural voters' livelihoods from cheap agricultural imports paid political dividends. With any entrenched power base, there is lobbying and political pressure which, in turn, influences policy and government spending, some of which now regularly goes toward agricultural price supports.

Government Oversight. A larger reliance on imports for staple goods does raise legitimate anxieties about long-term agricultural self-sufficiency. Continuity in the food supply, what is more, can only be assured by maintaining an indigenous agricultural sector capable of feeding an entire country indefinitely. As such, governments have a duty to turn "perfect" competition on its head and intervene in free markets to prop up sagging agricultural prices. The most rudimentary form of intervention is to impose a price on the market above its current equilibrium price. This price floor, as it is called, can be difficult to enforce without regulatory oversight, so governments typically take a more expedient course of action and buy a certain quantity of a commodity in bulk at a set price. In the process, governments literally, as well as figuratively, tinker with market equilibrium by decoupling demand from price to stimulate supply. Of course, they cannot resell what they acquire any time soon for fear of suppliers lowering their output in response. Nor may they ever resell in bulk at a profit when the market once again sets the price. A sudden influx of supply in the absence of a proportionate rise in demand would lower the selling price and demand for staples. It is for this reason that governments finance such purchases with tax payer funds; individuals and firms cannot as readily sustain the loss. Commodities purchased to support a floor price often end up being stockpiled and recycled as foreign aid or humanitarian relief. Finally, as odd as this may sound, agricultural price supports are now so common that governments actually pay farmers directly not to cultivate parcels of land to avoid the costs of additional stockpiling.

ISSUES

Farming & Market Risk. Farming is a seasonal undertaking with comparatively long production cycles. By its very nature, then, it is fairly unresponsive in the short run to changes in market conditions. Expectations of future demand thus play a leading role in deciding how much of which crop to plant at the beginning of a growing season. No matter how

sound these expectations may seem, the reality of events often proves disappointing. Farmers are thus regularly exposed to greater market risk than most manufacturers and service providers. Yet, they are not well rewarded for their risk-taking unlike virtually any other kind of investor. This curious anomaly is one that points to an even more basic contradiction: Namely that for an economic activity so essential to our survival, resources are frequently not as efficiently allocated as one might expect. Nor, for that matter, are the financial returns over time necessarily commensurate with an individual's investment of capital and labor.

The best hope for the world's hungry lies in the spread of "industrialized" farming. But there is a trade-off with which the developing world must reconcile. For all its undeniable advantages—higher crop yields, more nutritious foods, greater availability—there is a price to be paid. In the United States today, farming requires less than 3 percent of the labor force to produce substantial surpluses year in and year out. In the least developed countries, it involves as much as 80 percent of the labor force yet rarely ever produces a surplus. Industrial farming may prove very socially costly for the family farm that still dominates much of the world's landscape. The "problem" of the family farm remains an emotive issue even today in rural America, even almost a century after workers began migrating en masse to the manufacturing and service sectors. A dislocation of far greater proportion over a shorter time span will be required for the developing world to feed its rapidly growing population. Success here may hinge on how well or ill these tradition-bound societies adjust to profound, systemic change as much as on how they amass the capital and expertise required to modernize their agricultural infrastructures.

BIBLIOGRAPHY

Alston, J. M., Anderson, K., & Pardey, P. G. (2016). "Antipodean agricultural and resource economics—introduction." *Australian Journal of Agricultural & Resource Economics, 60*(4), 493–505.

Antle, J. (1999). "The new economics of agriculture." *American Journal of Agricultural Economics, 81,* 993.

Bardhan, P. (1979). "Agricultural development and land tenancy in a peasant economy: A theoretical and empirical analysis." *American Journal of Agricultural Economics, 61,* 48.

Breimyer, H. (1974). "Agricultural economics in a less expansible economy." *American Journal of Agricultural Economics, 56,* 812.

Clever, T. (2002). "Chapter 3: Microeconomics and maroeconomics." In *Understanding the world economy* (pp. 53–67). Oxfordshire, UK: Taylor & Francis, Ltd.

Cook, M., & Barry, P. (2004). "Organizational economics in the food, agribusiness, and agricultural sectors." *American Journal of Agricultural Economics, 86,* 740–743.

Hirvonen, K., Hoddinott, J. (2016). "Agricultural production and children's diets: Evidence from rural Ethiopia." *Agricultural Economics.*

Ise, J. (1920). "What is rural economics." *Quarterly Journal of Economics, 34,* 300–312.

SUGGESTED READING

Barkley, A. P., and Barkley, P. W. (2016). *Principles of agricultural economics.* New York, NY: Routledge.

Colin, J., & Crawford, E. (2000). "Economic perspectives in agricultural systems analysis." *Review of Agricultural Economics, 22,* 192.

Rausser, G. (1982). "Political economic markets: PERTs and PESTs in food and agriculture." *American Journal of Agricultural Economics, 64,* 821.

Roe, T. (1996). "Applications of game theory in agricultural economics: Discussion." *American Journal of Agricultural Economics, 78,* 761.

—Francis Duffy, MBA

AMERICAN BUSINESS HISTORY

ABSTRACT

When examining American business history, it is important to pay special attention to those elements that contributed to the overarching success of the U.S. economy and to look at some of the trends in transaction cost emergence, plummeting transportation costs, and the various coordination mechanisms used by business people throughout U.S. history. It is also important to look at American business history as a viable discipline, reviewing those who contributed to the early days of exploration in the new and rapidly changing field of study. This article will provide an overview of both.

OVERVIEW

The United States experienced its Industrial Revolution in the early part of the nineteenth century, bringing with it less expensive methods of travel and transportation, an increase in factory production, and improved agricultural machinery. These changes allowed for greater production of goods and aided in the expansion of the population across America. Because communities were rural and typically comprised small towns and farms, households previously functioned as small businesses, and due to the rudimentary and close-knit nature of business,

the transactions were often handled in trade and paid down over time (Lamoreaux, Raff, & Temin, 2003).

As the population grew and spread out, the need for goods not readily and locally available increased. Business transactions began to take place over long distances and not just within small towns. To keep the cost of doing business—transportation and communication—down, transactions were often handled through arrangements built and maintained by businessmen in ports or larger cities and with family members or members of familial groups, such as religious communities, where letters of introduction were used (Lamoreaux et al., 2003).

Peddling

As business transactions multiplied, local shop owners were finding it difficult to store expensive and infrequently used durable goods such as clothing and home furnishings; keeping an inventory became a real challenge. This predicament opened towns to the peddling trade—one of the earliest forms of mass marketing in America. Peddlers would travel from town to town, selling their products. However, there were certain setbacks to peddling, as consumers were not accustomed to buying from strangers, and it was difficult for business owners to control how their product was sold, as well as the profits gained. Also, if there were issues with the products such as defects,

Jewish-American fruit peddlers in Saint Paul, Minnesota. Irving Cooper was ten years old when the photo was taken Irving is in the driver's seat. He is working with "Zadie" (Grandfather) Morris. (Courtesy of Jewish Historical Society of the Upper Midwest via Wikimedia Commons)

the peddlers would be long gone and the business owner's distance would make exchange or credit nearly impossible (Lamoreaux et al., 2003).

Wholesaling

When innovations in transport began to occur, (the steamboat, canal, railroad, and telegraph), peddlers started to disappear and the national distribution of goods improved, although that gave rise to other complications, especially as it concerned the distribution and sale of wheat from the Midwest. Farmers who once sacked wheat and paid to have it delivered from their door to the buyers' doors found it easier

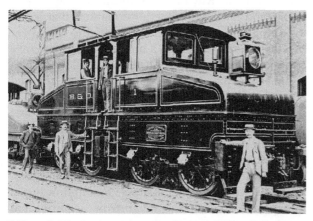

Baltimore & Ohio electric engine in 1895. (Courtesy of Wikimedia Commons)

and less expensive to start pouring the wheat into railroad cars and grain elevators. While convenient, the combining of crops from different farmers allowed for some farmers to mix inferior grain, or even non-grain items, along with their crops to bulk up the weight of the grain and raise their profits. The grain degradation resulted in a lack of consumer trust and the need for a neutral third party. In 1859, the state of Illinois appointed the Chicago Board of Trade to intervene and ensure quality was consistently maintained and that prices were controlled. The Board of Trade implemented a grading process for wheat crops, and while this concept worked well in theory, the board, having power over farmers, allowed for undue influence to occur in wheat grading processes and oversight shifted from the Board of Trade to the Railroad and Warehouse Commission. While this new system worked well with commodities such as wheat, it did not do as well with all goods. This disparity gave rise to wholesalers, who, not tied to personal business relationships, established a network of national, regional, and satellite offices for the sale and distribution of various products (Lamoreaux et al., 2003).

As wholesaling grew and larger cities began developing during the late nineteenth century so, too, did a variety of new business processes, like trade-marking and branding, which added protection and familiarity to new business ideas and products. Wholesaling also gave birth to the five and dime and department stores where a variety of goods were sold and often purchased through wholesalers (although some of the larger stores had no need for wholesalers after establishing their own methods of purchasing goods).

Mail-Order Businesses

As businesses gained more control of their sales, retailers, largely through buyers, were able to collect information on consumer shopping habits that were then used in the development of catalog mail businesses, such as Montgomery Ward and Sears, Roebuck & Company. With information on what consumers were buying, these larger companies were better equipped to tailor the shopping experience to its shoppers. These larger companies were also better able to utilize the railroad to distribute mail-order products and large warehouses to maintain inventory (Lamoreaux et al., 2003).

Sears, Roebuck and Company catalog from 1918. (Courtesy of Wikimedia Commons)

Industrial Districts

Similar to America's present-day technological industry in Silicon Valley, California, and the financial district in Manhattan, industrial districts (business areas containing similar industries with a variety of specialties) emerged. By offering a variety of similar items and services, these districts introduced the beginning of healthy business competition practices. Likewise, joint ventures were commonplace within industries. For instance, in the late 1800s, Philadelphia's textile industry was booming, comprising more than 600 companies, with many concentrating on just one step in the textile manufacturing processes. Companies found that they could each handle one aspect of the process—designing, dying, packaging, etc.—while collaborating on the finished, often unique and specialty, product (Lamoreaux et al., 2003).

Large-Scale Production/Chandlerian Enterprises

While small firms depended on the market for the sale of their product and the purchase of raw materials, larger firms were able to handle all of that internally. Noted business historian Alfred D. Chandler Jr. wrote that this transfer of market power was a vast improvement to American business, in that the larger companies were now easily able to dominate in their business sectors as well as to diversify and dominate in other areas. Large-scale production machinery was introduced and, with it, mass production and distribution. These changes also led to the exploitation of certain worker groups and as a result, during the early part of the twentieth century, the federal government forced large companies to start recognizing and working with unions. At the same time, Chandlerian firms (large, management-heavy companies with tiered structures so named for business historian Chandler) began to emerge. Because of their tiered management structures, these companies were able to operate at lower costs, allowing for lower pricing. But these companies, in order to maintain the lower costs and high output, offered only very standardized products, eliminating any product flexibility. Instead of meeting consumer needs and adapting to consumer habits, firms were then shaping buyers' tastes through their limited inventories (Lamoreaux et al., 2003).

In an attempt to inject some diversity into the mechanized, standardized development and delivery of goods that mass production brought to large businesses, more changes followed. By acquiring or merging with different companies, firms found that they could introduce a wider variety of products and services and a period of mergers and acquisitions began, dominating much of the next century. Much of the activity involved businesses eager to diversify and enter other lucrative markets that led to acquiring other businesses not related to their core products. This resulted in a merger frenzy that grew exponentially during the 1960s and 1970s. It was also at this time that Chandlerian enterprises amassed control over the U.S. economy.

A review of the business environment in the late 1990s indicated that the once strong Chandlerian-style enterprises had deteriorated. Of the 54 U.S. firms ranked in the top 100 globally, less than 20 remained and only 26 had greater capitalizations than at the beginning of that century. In addition to the unexpected chaos that resulted from acquiring too much too soon, international competition spiked during the 1970s. Also, rising incomes caused a shift in consumer habits from the lower priced, standardized products being offered by big business to more unique goods that were of a higher quality. Concurrently, transportation and communication costs dropped and markets became dense; the issues that caused vertical integration were all but eliminated. It now became cost effective for companies to buy rather than produce, making domestic high-production business an outmoded form of business. And while company size increased in the 1990s, growth was apparent not in industry giants, but in moderate-sized firms (Lamoreaux et al., 2003).

Chandlerian firms failed because the executives did not have intimate knowledge of the businesses they acquired and they were unable to properly conduct performance evaluations, interpret financial data, and measure any successes or failures. Managers turned to frequent short-term evaluations, eroding focus on long-term goals and successes. Further, outdated accounting and processing systems were kept in place, eliciting misleading or inappropriate information. The focus appeared to be not on quality—which was what the consumer wanted—but on quantity. All this purchasing of diverse businesses—the expansion of vertical integration—dragged companies down instead of adding to what a company could offer, causing them to lose significant ground in the 1970s. U.S. firms, overwhelmed with the issues presented during the period of mergers and acquisitions, felt little incentive to stay current with emerging, global technologies; technologically advanced rivals dominated. Also, the development and use of large bulk-capacity ships caused transportation costs to fall even further, increasing foreign imports and competition into the United States (Lamoreaux et al., 2003).

Firm Specialization
Capital markets ignored the value of back-office coordination and when they were either unable or unwilling to change, hostile takeovers and leveraged buyouts became the norm, freeing the core firms from its acquired companies. Diversification was all but obsolete, and more than half of those acquisitions made outside of the core firms' interests had been divested. The United States finally began to gain ground back in the 1980s when the huge monolithic enterprises of the 1970s dwindled and allowed the emergence of many smaller, more specialized firms that were able to focus their energies on either one

Amazon allows its customers the luxury of ordering a wide variety of goods from the privacy of their homes via the Internet. Jeff Bezos, one of the world's richest men, is the founder of Amazon. (Courtesy of U.S. Department of Defense photo by Senior Master Sgt. Adrian Cadiz via Wikimedia Commons)

of a small few stages of a process or a small number of offerings. By the 1990s, the hostile methods of conducting business declined and high-level executive compensation began to be tied to a company's performance via its stock performance (Lamoreaux et al., 2003).

Innovations providing consumers with wide selections in a variety of product categories began in earnest at the end of the 20th and beginning of the 21st centuries. The advent of the Internet, coupled with emergent communications technology, brought business back to much of what was offered in the days of early mail-order marketing—seemingly limitless choices in the privacy of one's home. Unlike their predecessors, companies of all sizes use the Internet to brand and advertise. In many cases, books, informational packages, online educational offerings, movies, and music were offered through Internet downloads, totally eliminating any transportation and production needs. The Internet allows companies to amass critical information on consumer preferences, allowing for fewer surpluses and better-directed inventory and marketing of products. All of this is eerily similar to how business was conducted by the craftsmen of the early nineteenth century, but without the physical challenges. Sellers will only produce and offer items for which there is demand, eliminating the stock of underused inventory (Lamoreaux et al., 2003).

APPLICATION

HARVARD SCHOOL OF BUSINESS ADMINISTRATION
Management
Early American business history concentrated on the internal workings of individual American businesses and not on the rise of industries. There was also an obvious focus on management—the heart of American business—that was first explained in the academic as opposed to the business arena. Specifically, Harvard University's Graduate School of Business Administration, which was founded in 1908, focused its teachings on the administrative, decision-making aspects prevalent in business at the time. Teachings were case-study driven and did not necessarily focus on the larger business picture. Lessons were neither meant to be teachings in theory nor vocational instruction. Rather, business education was discussion-driven, based on actual cases and facts, and presented for the purpose of reaching reasonable conclusions on policy and to further the development of business administrators (Supple, 1959).

Linking Economic & Business History
The topic of business saturated academia, allowing for the break of business history from both economic history and business enterprise. Harvard Business School furthered the field of business history with the implementation of the Business Historical Society in 1925 under the direction of Wallace B. Donham, then dean of the school. The society's aim was to further the study of business from a historical perspective. Within two years, the study had grown and a professorship title was endowed in 1927 to N. S. B. Gras—a leading economic historian of that time—who both taught business history at Harvard and

was largely responsible for the evolution of the study until his retirement in 1950. Gras, in collaboration with other economic historians, began to study the links and disparities between economic history and business history, thus allowing for the emergence of a series of growing publications that were very much in league with those developed and presented by Harvard (Supple, 1959).

The studies of society and economics certainly have their impact on the history of business, and Harvard and other business historians continue to review these important relationships; however, through Gras, the development of business policies and results of business management were most closely explored from the standpoint of individual companies and not from general trending information. The overarching feeling was that the administration of business—which it was felt was best explored at the individual business level—was the core of all business and business study (Supple, 1959).

Historical Documentation
A wide array of documentation on American business was being developed, including Harvard's *Bulletin of the Business Historical Society*. This business publication originated in the 1920s and later expanded—in the mid-1950s—to the current *Business History Review*. Although the field of business history was widely accepted as a discipline by the late 1930s, there were still no established links to the other social sciences, resulting in some skepticism. Added to this was the remaining distrust of the business community—especially following the stock market crash. There were also issues with missing records, and there was a decided lack of the combined skills needed to both understand business and document history. Regardless, by the 1950s, documentation had begun to be maintained and the beginnings of business history and scholars who were able to guide the new discipline were emerging (Supple, 1959).

Chandler
Arthur D. Chandler Jr. documented much of his business theories in his three seminal works: *Scale and Scope*, *Strategy and Structure*, and *The Visible Hand* (Pulitzer and Bancroft awards winner). All three books and their related theories added significantly to the documented contributions of Harvard's N. S. B. Gras—considered the founding father of American

business history. Where Gras provided narrative descriptions, Chandler built on Gras's writings by providing analytical theories that he based on reviews and comparisons of business case studies. This allowed for his theories to better resonate with current business practices and economic concerns. Further, rather than theorizing on how one firm handled all business situations, Chandler reviewed and discussed a given business situation through a variety of firms. For example, in his book *Strategy and Structure,* Chandler reviewed four leaders in American business—du Pont, General Motors, Standard Oil of New Jersey, and Sears & Roebuck—and included additional information on at least 80 other companies (Supple, 1991). By the mid-1970s, Chandler had developed his Chandlerian business theory, which says American economic success in the twentieth century was due to the emergence of large firms that dominated important industries with more efficient internal structures in place than the smaller family-owned businesses (Lamoreaux et al., 2003).

Chandler felt that technological advancements allowed some enterprises to reap enormous benefits; however, to maintain economies of scale, firms would also need to ensure operations were maintained at very high outputs, regardless of supply. Chandler felt that the best way to ensure companies did not experience supply shortages was to maintain full control of material production and all activities from inception to sale. No easy task, especially given Chandler's expectation that this type of production output and schedule be maintained for no less than two decades while maintaining profits and ensuring no material overflows. Chandler felt firms able to maintain these activities would experience high productivity and efficiency and would emerge as the competitive leaders in their fields. Further, only firms of equal breadth and depth—other vertically structured, managerially tiered, and capital heavy companies—would be capable of maintaining both healthy competition and economic environments (Lamoreaux et al., 2003).

Emerging Scholars

Although he had built on Gras's information, Chandler's theory was just that, a theory. And, although important, his theory was based on experience. While Chandler's work provided much-needed alternatives to earlier businesses models, it was, in essence, also a narrative theory with little or no way to explain the downfall of those very large firms later in the last century. Other scholars, such as Oliver Williamson, emerged and had tackled some of what was lacking in Chandler's theory and allowed for a more expanded view of the corporation. Williamson began his theory with information gleaned from a 1937 essay written by Ronald Coase. The essay explained that businesspeople could lower their transaction costs by having economic activity occur within the firm rather than in the market. Williamson built on Coase's writing and added that transaction costs rise partly because the principals involved have faulty information. In other words, decision makers are subjective, knowing best their capabilities, not those of the businesses with which they transact. Williamson felt that the larger firms dominated the economic scope because they were able to utilize their vast resources to resolve issues and challenges that would otherwise cripple smaller companies (Lamoreaux et al., 2003).

Learning from History

Historical review of business indicates that the size of a business matters. For instance, face-to-face market—or brick and mortar—transactions, while allowing for potentially lower costs, do not necessarily encourage repeat transactions in the same way in which tiered, large businesses rely. Larger firms can utilize strong branding techniques and rely on long-standing reputations for repeat sales. It is important to note, though, that for those larger, hierarchical entities to be successful, managerial directives must be followed for the larger good of the company. This is not always possible when dealing with employees who disagree with management directives (Lamoreaux et al., 2003).

History proves that long-term business relationships have some advantage over market and hierarchical relationships. Customers may prefer what is tried and true over having to research and seek out a relationship with a different business. Long-term relationships are also beneficial when dealing with situations where the pooling of information—as is common in industry and business districts—is beneficial to all parties, for instance when dealing with emerging technologies, or in changing economic environments where established contracts make renegotiation problematic or prohibitive (Lamoreaux et al., 2003).

Historical review also indicates that regardless of business type—market or long-term relationship—the transactional nature of a business relationship may be improved when all involved parties are members of the same cultural, ethnic, religious, or gender group, hailing back to earlier business practices when letters of credit and introduction were provided in clan and familial groups. Likewise, this familial group dynamic may also affect manager-subordinate relationships within organizations (Lamoreaux et al., 2003).

VIEWPOINTS

There are a variety of ways to write business history that avoid both the narrative nature of reporting history and the practice of viewing one's current environment as the final environment. Attention can be focused on the broader and varied range of business techniques that have evolved historically and in response to a constantly changing economic climate. Given the diverse elements at play—transaction vs. quality, cost vs. location—there remains unpredictability of outcomes, thus business success requires ongoing enhancements to allow for changes in economic conditions, geography, and technology—to name a few—and to withstand uncertainty in future outcomes. Because of the changing nature of business, one method may work well and be the prevailing practice for a period of time—such as the practice of merging and acquiring—to only be replaced by a different method, such as the divesting of unlike businesses that followed the merger and acquisition frenzy. It would be a failure on the part of any business historian to present any one historical viewpoint and theory as a generalization of all possible variables. Alternate theories allow students and researchers of business history to understand that situations at the time of any writing do not remain static; ongoing review and modification are always called for (Lamoreaux et al., 2003). While some historians will focus on the administrative aspect of business, others will separate and report on that which connects business and society, and still others will continue to look at the role of business and economics (Supple, 1959).

BIBLIOGRAPHY

Biswas, M., & Suar, D. (2013). "Which Employees' Values Matter Most in the Creation of Employer Branding?" *Journal Of Marketing Development & Competitiveness*, 7, 93–102.

Jones, C., & Bonevac, D. (2013). "An evolved definition of the term 'brand': Why branding has a branding problem." *Journal Of Brand Strategy*, 2, 112–120.

Lamoreaux, N.R. (2017). "Cultural change and business history." *Business and Economic History On-line: Papers Presented at the BHC Annual Meeting*, 15, 8.

Lamoreaux, N. R., Raff, D. M. G., & Temin, P. (2003). "Beyond markets and hierarchies: Toward a new synthesis of American business history." *American Historical Review*, 108, 404–433.

Robertson, A., & Khatibi, A. (2013). "The Influence of Employer Branding on Productivity-Related Outcomes of an Organization." *IUP Journal Of Brand Management*, 10, 17–32.

Supple, B. E. (1959). "American business history-a survey." *Business History*, 1, 63–76.

Supple, B. (1991). "Scale and scope: Alfred Chandler and the dynamics of industrial capitalism." *Economic History Review*, 44, 500–514.

SUGGESTED READING

Chandler, A. D. Jr., (1990). *Scale and Scope: The Dynamics of Industrial Capitalism.* Cambridge.

Chandler, A. D. Jr., (1977). *The Visible Hand: The Managerial Revolution in American Business.* Cambridge.

Coase, R. (1937). "The nature of the firm," *Economica*, 4, 386–405.

Larson, H. M. (1934). "A China trader turns investor-a biographical chapter in American business history." *Harvard Business Review*, 12, 345-359.

Morton, A. L. (1974). "How to revive the railroads." *Challenge*, 17, 32–37.

McGormick, B. & Folsom B. W. Jr. (2003). "A survey of business historians on America's greatest entrepreneurs." *Business History Review*, 77, 703–716.

Sabel, C. F (1997). "Stories, strategies, structures: Rethinking historical alternatives to mass production." In Charles F. Sabel and Jonathan Zeitlin, (eds.), *World of possibilities: Flexibility and mass production in Western industrialization* (pp. 1–33). Cambridge: Cambridge University Press, 1997.

—*Richa S. Tiwary, PhD, MLS*

APPLIED MACROECONOMICS

ABSTRACT

Macroeconomics is a branch of economics created by John Maynard Keynes, a British economist. Macroeconomics looks at the economy on a large scale either nationally, regionally, or between countries. Keynes's view differed from the classical approach to macroeconomics. The classical view held that there should be no government interference in the economy because it is always in equilibrium or adjusts to put itself in equilibrium. Keynes's view was that certain circumstances, such as a depression, would not improve through self-regulation of the economy and required government intervention. For example, during a depression, unemployment may not automatically improve and often requires government intervention to create jobs. Large-scale macroeconomic indicators can measure the health of the economy and compare the current state of the economy to other periods in time. These measures can also predict what policies and actions will benefit the economy. Applied macroeconomics is applying assumptions about large- scale economic measures to real-world economic problems. Macroeconomic indicators include the unemployment rate, gross domestic product, interest rates, money collected in taxes compared to spending, and the inflation rate.

OVERVIEW

Applied macroeconomics is taking aggregate theories and applying them to real-world scenarios. Aggregate theories are assumptions about aggregate (total or sums) measures in the economy. For example, aggregate supply is the sum of goods and services produced in an economy; it also serves as a measure of how strong the economy is. Applied macroeconomics can be used as a tool to create an accurate picture of current economic events and to suggest approaches for improvement or correcting mistakes. Economists, governments, companies, and individuals have an interest in looking at the economy as a whole because all are affected by changes in the economy. Economists may look at a problem in macroeconomics as an opportunity to predict or design a better future economic state or further the development of the field of economics. Governments may look at macroeconomics to define new policies that address economic issues and support the economy. Companies and individuals may be interested because information about the broad tendencies of the economy can guide decision-making such as looking for a new job or hiring workers and buying equipment.

Some of the big problems and concerns of macroeconomics are based on indicators of the economy. These can include unemployment, inflation, interest rates, and supply and demand. In the United States and other countries including Japan, the economy is based on the free market or capitalist system, in which people may engage in the business of producing and selling goods and services competitively. The government influences business activity by controlling monetary policy and possibly with regulations governing certain aspects of business. Countries take different approaches to creating a healthy and growing economy. These approaches can include how productive resources are used by the producers of goods and the level of government involvement to support and encourage growth. If the economy is healthy, there is the potential to improve the standard of living of the people in that country. A decline in business activity can create a recession and negatively impact spending and incomes. In countries like China, the government exerts additional control over businesses by owning the businesses and deciding how they will be run. Also, in countries where governments control business, they also guarantee full employment by employing all who can work.

A History of Macroeconomics

John Maynard Keynes "was a British economist ... who created macroeconomics, the study of economics on a large scale" (Gilman, 2006, p. 41). Macroeconomics asks a number of questions such as

- What is the unemployment rate?
- How easy or difficult is it to find work?
- What is the strength of the dollar relative to other forms of currency around the world?
- What is the level of prices?
- Are prices rising, falling, staying the same?

- How does this period of pricing compare to prices in another period?
- What revenue is the government collecting in taxes and how does that compare to government spending?
- What is the level of indebtedness to other countries?
- What is the production rate of the country and is the overall income level growing or falling?
- How easy or difficult is it to borrow money based on interest rates?

Schools of Macroeconomic Thought

There are many different versions of macroeconomics beyond what Keynes studied. Some simply disagree with his views, while others build on his ideas. Gottheil (2007, p. 546) lists the following schools of macroeconomic theory and thought

- classical
- Keynesian;
- neo-Keynesian
- rational expectations
- supply-side economics

Gottheil cautions that within each school of thought there can be differences of opinion. Gottheil discusses the schools of thought with respect to unemployment and inflation about which economists desire to uncover the causes and cures. As one example, Gottheil states that classical economists think unemployment is temporary and a condition that will be corrected by the market. Similarly, classical economists believe that prices will eventually move to where they should be. Keynesian economists think that unemployment can go on indefinitely with prices remaining at high levels and that inflation can have many causes. De Rooy (1995, p. 143) describes a phenomenon called demand-pull inflation in which a country's income is growing so fast that it cannot produce goods and services fast enough. The growth comes from an increase in the "supply of money and credit in the economy." Demand-pull inflation can be compared to cost-push inflation, which occurs when there are shortages of certain goods and services. Another scenario is stagflation, when prices are high, inflation is high, and the economy gets progressively worse. Stagflation (stagnation and inflation) was termed in the 1970s and 1980s when unemployment and inflation were simultaneously high. At this time, the economy did not react the way Keynesian economists expected and led to a new movement of neo-Keynesians.

Applied macroeconomics seeks to understand or explain fluctuations in the economy and to determine what actions make sense to respond to the fluctuations (Australian Graduate School of Management, 1997).

Economic Indicators

Moffatt (2009) describes an economic indicator as a statistic about the economy. Examples of economic indicators are unemployment levels and the gross domestic product (GDP). Every economic indicator has three characteristics

- relationship to the business cycle economy
- frequency
- timing

There are three possible relationships to the economy

- procyclic
- countercyclic
- acyclic

Procyclic indicators move with the economy, while countercyclic indicators move against the economy. Acyclic indicators do not have an observable relationship with the movement of the economy.

Frequency

The frequency of an economic indicator refers to how often the indicator is tracked or measured. Some are measured monthly, others quarterly, and still others annually. Economic indicator timing shows the relationship between the appearance of the indicator and the same trend being present in the economy. Economic indicators can be leading, lagging, or coincident. A leading indicator is one that shows up before the economy follows suit. A lagging indicator is "a measurable economic factor that changes after the economy has already begun to follow a particular pattern or trend. Lagging indicators confirm long-term trends, but they do not predict them" ("Lagging indicator," 2009). While leading indicators give an indication of future events, coincident indicators have a direct relationship with the economy and move at the same time as the economy.

Business Cycles

De Rooy discusses business cycles as events that happen in the economy without a single way to measure them all. Indicators could move slowly or quickly in any direction possible. Even in a recession, which is commonly thought of as a downturn, there are parts of the economy that may flourish. People may pay to repair items instead of purchasing new ones. People may take care of some tasks themselves instead of availing themselves of service providers such as beauty or barber professionals. De Rooy (1995, p. 41) lists GDP, business profits, "big-ticket consumer items called durable goods," and short-term interest rates as measures that move with the business cycle. Nondurable goods like food are not as affected by the economy because they are always needed in good times and bad.

The Issues Considered in Macroeconomics

Macroeconomics looks at the economy as whole instead of individual consumer behavior (microeconomics). Macroeconomics studies the decisions that businesses and households make to lead to specific results such as the unemployment rate or inflation. There are two major problems considered in macroeconomics: long-term growth and economic fluctuations. Macroeconomic analysis looks at aggregates or totals of activity in the economy and uses mathematical models to examine the behavior of aggregate information (Drozd, 2008). Economists, governments, individuals, and businesses are directly and indirectly affected by the economy and changes in it. De Rooy (1995, p. xi) noted the importance of economic literacy by stating that skill is only part of one's success and that "your success is significantly influenced by the economic environment."

Economic Growth

Economic growth can mean an improved situation for the citizens of a country. Long-term growth can be determined by examining production in an economy. The economy can grow because of improved means of production and population growth. Both can allow work to be done faster and more efficiently and can help countries benefit from innovation and new knowledge (Burda & Wyplosz, 2004). Since growth may not appear consistently, economists attempt to understand fluctuations in the economy, the causes, and the remedies. Economic growth might be stagnated in third world countries because of high levels of poverty and a limited tax base. In developed countries, fluctuations may be caused by changes in aggregate supply and demand or unemployment. The unemployment rate is the number of workers who are unemployed when compared to all the eligible, employable people. Unemployment affects the entire economy because workers without incomes change their spending habits out of necessity which in turn affects businesses that depend on sales from these now unemployed workers. Unemployment can be devastating to the individual but also to entire communities experiencing high levels of unemployment.

Gross Domestic Product

Countries may look at the gross domestic product because it is the output of the economy and a result of the labor and capital put into the overall economic system. Amadeo (2009) noted that the economy is measured by the gross domestic product and described it as "everything produced by all the people and all the companies in the U.S." Drozd (2008, p. 2) notes that macroeconomics can explain why certain economic conditions exist and allows us to answer questions such as

- What makes a country grow richer or poorer in a given period?
- Why do we have recessions?
- Why did prices tend to rise more rapidly in Russia than in Switzerland?
- Why did [the] inflation rate vary so much in the United States in the 1970s and 1980s?
- What determines the value of the U.S. dollar?

Gottheil (2007, p. 378) suggests similar questions macroeconomists can answer such as

- Why are there periods of recession and inflation?
- What causes prosperity?
- What causes economic growth?

Economists can help present approaches that will lead to better economic results using macroeconomics. The goals of macroeconomics are "long-term growth, high employment, price, employment and output stability" (Drozd, 2008, p. 2). Long-term growth has been sustained in developed countries, but the population growth in these same countries does not match the population growth in underdeveloped countries.

As a result, there have been increases in outsourcing capabilities by which developed countries can benefit from the cheap and easily available labor in other countries. Inflation is "the rate of change of the average level of prices" (Burda & Wyplosz, 2004, p. 7). Massive levels of inflation are called "hyperinflation" when the monthly level of inflation is greater than 50 percent. Intuitively, it is possible to surmise the outcome of incredible increases in the inflation rate. Significant economic instability is likely to result.

Economic Policy

De Rooy (1995, p. 72) defines economic policy as "any government activity designed to improve the condition of the economy." Heijman feels that it is important to understand what the goals of economic policy are in order to easily understand macroeconomics. Heijman (2001, p. 7) lists the commonly agreed upon goals as

- an acceptable level of economic growth;
- full and fulfilling employment;
- a fair distribution of income;
- a stable price level;
- a stable exchange rate;
- equilibrium on the balance of payments or equality in imports and exports; and
- a good environmental quality.

All of these goals are necessary to ensure a sound economy and an environment in which people want to stay and work where they feel they can thrive. Heijman acknowledges the difficulty of getting all of these working at the same time and even acknowledges that these factors may compete with one another. Each government has in place monetary policy experts who will observe the outcomes of the economy and suggest governmental policy or intervention to shape the desired economic outcomes. De Rooy (1995, p. 391) agrees, "A government, through its central bank, will often influence its money's exchange rate to help it improve exports, attract foreign investment, or to reduce inflation." As an example, government policy intervention in the case of high employment might be to

- increase government spending, thus increasing economic activity and hopefully jobs.
- lower wages.

- shorten the work week.
- put more money into circulation to encourage spending and investment (Heijman, 2001, p. 10).

De Rooy notes that there are times when intervention by the government can result in harm to the economy. Harm to the economy does not just come from making the wrong decision about a variable being acted upon. Harm can also come from not understanding what other variables in the economy will be affected. For example, De Rooy (1995, p. 391) says, "When a central bank increases its nation's money supply to devalue it, domestic interest rates are likely to fall." Without considering outcomes from each point of view, a government could increase economic problems instead of improving them.

Supply & Demand Policy

Macroeconomic policy is made up of supply and demand policy. Managing supply and demand can impact the underpinnings of the economy. However, it is often unclear what the long-term benefit of government intervention is. Ulman (2009) notes that the 2008 economic stimulus plan will slow down the increasing unemployment in a particular region but may not have a long-term impact on annual job growth. Demand policy is determining how to bring production to a place where there is full employment and all production capacity is consumed. Demand policy works in the short term and medium long term

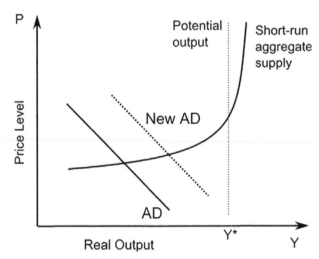

A traditional Aggregate Supply – Aggregate Demand diagram showing a shift in AD and the AS curve becoming inelastic beyond potential output. (Courtesy of Syed CC BY-SA 3. via Wikimedia Commons)

(Heijman, 2001). Supply policy, which emphasizes production capacity, is concerned with the skill and education of workers and is tied to long-term results. McAfee (2006, p. 14) states, "Supply and demand are the most fundamental tools of economic analysis. Most applications of economic reasoning involve supply and demand in one form or another." McAfee (2006, p. 38) also says that supply and demand help economists better understand trade.

Macroeconomic Policy Tools

Heijman (2001, p. 13) lists the tools of macroeconomic policy as

- fiscal policy;
- monetary policy;
- income and price policy; and
- other instruments.

Heijman notes that it is important not only to know what tools are available but also when to use them. Heijman (p. 13) says fiscal policy relates to government taxes and spending while monetary policy is concerned with money circulating in the economy, interest rates, inflation, deflation, and exchange rates. Income and price policies are important because labor is the highest cost in product production, and if the cost is too high, productivity suffers. Similarly, a lack of control of prices can create instability in the economy. The government has tools of legislation "to influence the economic process" (Heijman, 2001, p. 13).

Heijman credits Jan Tinbergen, a Dutch economist, with being the first to devise a process for setting economic policy. Tinbergen suggested four steps policy makers should take that Heijman (2001, p. 15) refers to as the "normative theory of economic policy":

- The policy maker should set specific goals in conjunction with the government's concern for social welfare.
- Targets within the goals should be set.
- The policy maker should determine what instruments or tools are available to affect the policy.
- The policy maker should have an economic model that links the tools to the targets so that the policy maker can play with the variables and maximize the outcomes.

A systematic process implies discipline on behalf of the policy makers. However, it is possible that bureaucracy and politics could affect the policy makers' ability to act systematically.

VIEWPOINT

Macroeconomics & Today's Economic Confusion

The global economic crisis can be frightening and fascinating for economists and individuals. Hanke (2009, para. 1) says, "Shock and confusion describe the state of investors today." Hanke further notes that wealthy people and retirees have lost a large amount of money. "In 2008, the average household net worth dropped by 22.7%" (2009). Hanke feels that the economic experts have led investors astray. "Many investors are walking around like zombies. When they hear economic prognostications, they become even more confused." Shock and confusion mean that the conventional wisdom of what works economically is

Professor Steve H. Hanke in 2017. (Courtesy of Marius Bugge via Wikipedia)

no longer taken at face value. As the economy transitions, it becomes apparent that what worked before may not work again and that even economic experts are not in full agreement on how to solve tough problems (Hanke, 2009, para. 6). Rosen (2009) quotes Hanke as being partially critical of the economic stimulus efforts by the government. Hanke believes that in the late 2000s the United States was in a recession but not a depression. He also believes that the federal stimulus plan would not have an effect of the economic crisis. He was in favor of the "monetary and tax policies" because he felt that they stimulate economic recovery more effectively than government spending (Rosen, 2009, para. 4).

Macroeconomics will likely be updated in light of the new problems the current economic crisis provides. The development of new types of economic problems is not unusual. Drago, Wooden, and Black discuss changing workplace demographics and the need for flexibility in work hours. With the introduction of women into the workforce, the pressure on employers to adapt to the need for flexibility has increased. At different points in everyone's life, the ability to maintain a certain work level changes; not responding to that change affects productivity in the workplace. Given that women are such a large part of the workforce, the effect on the economy could be substantial. There are also men who do not want to be recognized only as "financial" support to their families. Other life-changing events are listed by Drago, Wooden, and Black. Events include marriage, separation, and divorce as well as retirement. The economies of the developed nations will change dramatically as baby boomers begin to age and leave the workforce.

Most importantly, there may not be agreement among economists before, during, or after an economic period on what happened and what would be the best medicine for the economy. Gottheil (p. 546) says there is not very much "consensus among economists on macroeconomic policy" because of imperfect information, different approaches and perspectives and different political stances. While some advocate more government intervention and others less, macroeconomics is filled with economists who spread the ideological spectrum.

BIBLIOGRAPHY

Amadeo, K. (2009, January 14). "What exactly is the U.S. economy?" Retrieved from About.com. xlink:href="http://useconomy.about.com/od/grossdomesticproduct/p/GDP.htm"

Australian Graduate School of Management. (1997, March 27). *What is macroeconomics?* [Lecture]. Retrieved from xlink:href="http://www.agsm.edu.au/bobm/teaching/MM/lect01.pdf"

Baumol, W. J. & Blinder, A. S. (2001). *Economics: Principles and policy,* (8th ed.). Orlando: Harcourt, Inc.

Burda, M. & Wyplosz, C. (2004). "Introduction to macroeconomics." In *Macroeconomics: A European text.* Oxford: Oxford University Press.

Coincident indicator. [Definition]. (2009). Retrieved from Investopedia xlink:href="http://www.investopedia.com/terms/c/coincidentindicator.asp"

De Rooy, J. (1995). *Economic literacy: What everyone needs to know about money and markets.* New York: Three Rivers Press.

Drago, R., Wooden, M. & Black, David. (2009). "Who wants and gets flexibility? Changing work hours, preferences and life events." *Industrial & Labor Relations Review, 62,* 394–414.

Drozd, L. (2008). *What is macroeconomics all about?* [PowerPoint Presentation]. Retrieved from The Social Science Cooperative at the University of Wisconsin-Madison. xlink:href="http://www.ssc.wisc.edu/~ldrozd/my%5ffiles/102files/handout%5f1.pdf"

Gilman, L.A. (2006). *Economics: How economics works.* Minneapolis: Lerner Publications Company.

Gottheil, F. (2007). *Study guide to accompany principles of economics.* Mason, OH: Thomson Custom Solutions.

Hanke, S.H. (2009). "Unconventional wisdom." *Forbes, 183,* 106.

Heijman, W. J. M. (2001). *Applied macroeconomics.* Retrieved from xlink:href="http://library.wur.nl/way/catalogue/documents/macroeconomics.pdf"

Jain, T. R. & Ohri, V.K. (2007). *Introductory microeconomics and macroeconomics.* Retrieved from Google Books. xlink:href="http://books.google.com/books?id=aYPlvkM–FEC&printsec=frontcover"

Kuhry, Y., & Weill, L. (2010). "Financial intermediation and macroeconomic efficiency." *Applied Financial Economics, 20,* 1185–1193.

Lagging indicator. [Definition]. (n.d.). Retrieved from Investopedia. xlink:href="http://www.investopedia.com/ask/answers/177.asp"

Mankiw, N., (1988). "Recent developments in macroeconomics: A very quick refresher course." *Journal* of Money, Credit & Banking (Ohio State University Press), 20, 436–449.

McAfee, R.P. (2006). *Introduction to economic analysis.* Retrieved from xlink:href="http://www.mcafee.cc/Introecon/IEA.pdf"

Miller, M.S., & Epstein, S. (2013). "Teaching applied macro in emergent economies: Lessons from Bahrain." *Journal of Teaching in International Business, 24*, 138–149.

Moffatt, M. (2009). A *beginner's guide to economic indicators.* Retrieved from About.com. xlink:href="http://economics.about.com/cs/businesscycles/a/economic%5find.htm"

Reich, R. B. (1999, March 29). "John Maynard Keynes: His radical idea that governments should spend money they don't have may have saved capitalism." *Time Magazine.* Retrieved xlink:href="http://www.time.com/time/time100/scientist/profile/keynes.html"

Rosen, A. (2009, March 11). "Johns Hopkins University Professor Steve H. Hanke: Things getting worse, but more slowly." *The Daily Record.*

Ulman, D. (2009, February 23). Stimulus package should slow Md. job losses, report says. *The Daily Record.*

"What are leading, lagging and coincident indicators? What are they for?" (2009). Retrieved from Investopedia. xlink:href="http://www.investopedia.com/terms/l/laggingindicator.asp"

"What is economics?" (n.d.). *Undergraduate economics.* Retrieved from Vanderbilt University xlink:href="http://www.vanderbilt.edu/AEA/students/WhatIsEconomics.htm"

What is macroeconomics? (2009). Retrieved from WiseGeek.comxlink:href="http://www.wisegeek.com/what-is-macroeconomics.htm"

SUGGESTED READING

Caetano, J. & Caleiro, A. (2009). "Is there a relationship between transparency in economic and political systems and foreign direct investment flows?" *ICFAI Journal of Applied Economics, 8*, 45–58.

Kumar, S. (2009). "Estimating export equations for developing countries." *ICFAI Journal of Applied Economics, 8*, 17–28.

The economy. (2009). *Country Profile. China,* 22–30.

Vadlamannati, K.C. & Veni, L. K. (2009). "Fiscal synchronization hypothesis in Andhra Pradesh: An empirical testing." *ICFAI Journal of Applied Economics, 8*, 29–44.

—Marlanda English, PhD

B

BEHAVIORAL ECONOMICS

ABSTRACT

Behavioral economics draws upon the fields of economics and psychology to study how people make choices. Behavioral economists believe that the choices individuals make may be neither statistically predictable nor always rational. This article explores concepts of behavioral economics; cites relevant findings; and summarizes some of the contemporary research in the field. The article concludes with a glossary of relevant terms.

OVERVIEW

Behavioral economics draws upon the fields of both economics and psychology to study how people make choices (Lambert, 2006, p. 50). According to Merriam-Webster's Collegiate Dictionary:

Economics is a social science that describes and analyzes the production, distribution, and consumption of goods and services (2000, p. 365) [while] psychology is the study of mind and behavior (2000, p. 940).

Because behavioral economics is concerned with how individuals make their choices rather than how statistical data or calculated notions predict what their choices should be, behavioral economic concepts are differentiated from two well-known economic theories. These theories are: the Bayesian theory, which relies upon statistics to draw conclusions about the future occurrence of a given parameter of a statistical distribution by calculating from prior data on its frequency of occurrence ("Bayesian theory," 2007), and the rational choice theory, which assumes that an individual, using reason, will choose the option that yields maximum advantage or gain and minimizes disadvantage or loss ("Rational choice theory," 2009). In fact, behavioral economists believe that the choices individuals make may be neither statistically predictable nor always rational.

Rather, decisions are heavily influenced by other factors; it is these patterns of irrational choice that form the basis of study for behavioral economists (Fillion, 2008).

Psychology Melds with Economics

In 1982, Daniel Kahneman and Amos Tversky met psychologist Eric Wanner, who wanted to integrate the fields of psychology and economics. Under his presidency of the Russell Sage Foundation, Wanner awarded a grant to economist Richard Thaler to spend the 1984–85 academic year with Kahneman and explore the integration. During that year, psychologists Kahneman and Tversky, and economists Thaler and Jack Knetsch, conducted a series of research experiments that studied the nature and rules of fairness for a variety of transactions (Kahneman, 2002). In 1986, Richard Thaler, Daniel Kahneman, and Jack Knetsch published "Fairness as a Constraint on Profit Seeking: Entitlements in the Market," in the *American Economic Review*. The article described their analysis of a telephone survey that was conducted during the 1984–85 academic year. Among the findings, the survey respondents indicated that they thought it was fair for firms to raise prices or lower wages when profits are suffering, but that it was unfair for firms to raise prices or lower wages for the purpose of exploiting market demand, such as when quantities of an item are temporarily limited, or when unemployment is high (Kahneman, Knetsch, & Thaler, 1986, p. 728). This research on the nature and perception of fairness among individuals provided psychological insight into economic factors in the marketplace: The public applies fairness concepts to their transactions with merchants, landlords, and employers. If the rules of fairness (what individuals have deemed acceptable or unacceptable according to their fairness reference points) are violated, the public will retaliate (Kahneman, 2002). For example, the retaliation may take the form of withholding

Daniel Kahneman shared the 2002 Nobel Memorial Prize in Economic Sciences with Vernon L. Smith for his work on the psychology of judgment and decision-making. (Courtesy of Wikimedia Commons)

business from a merchant who is considered unfair, or by paying more to transact with a merchant because he is deemed to be fair.

In 2002, Daniel Kahneman won half of the Sveriges Riksbank Prize in Economic Sciences—the Nobel Memorial Prize in Economic Sciences—"for having integrated insights from psychological research into economic science, especially concerning human judgment and decision-making under uncertainty" ("The Sveriges Riksbank Prize," 2002). (The "other half" of the prize was won by Vernon L. Smith, an experimental economist.) This prize brought the field of behavioral economics to the forefront as a legitimate and important area of study.

FURTHER INSIGHTS

Concepts & Prospect Theory

Based upon the preliminary research and analysis mentioned above, as well as subsequent research and

study, five prominent concepts within the field of behavioral economics have been identified:

- judgment under uncertainty
- heuristics
- illusion of validity
- intuitive prediction
- prospect theory

Judgment under Uncertainty

Judgment under uncertainty refers to an individual's process for assessing probabilities and predicting values (Tversky & Kahneman, 1974, p. 1124) when choosing an option. As Sleeth-Keppler noted, judgment under uncertainty is not a rigid process, and individuals will often rely upon heuristic strategies to aid their judgment (2007, p. 768).

Heuristics

Heuristics is a method for problem-solving or decision-making that arrives at solutions through exploratory means such as experimentation, trial and error, or evaluation ("Heuristics," 2007).

In 1974, Daniel Kahneman and his long-time collaborator Amos Tversky published an influential paper in *Science*, "Judgment under Uncertainty: Heuristics and Biases." The paper defined three heuristic methods that encompass multiple biases that individuals rely upon to assess the probability of an uncertain event or the value of an uncertain quantity (Tversky & Kahneman, 1974).

These three heuristics include the following:

- judgment by representativeness
- judgment by availability
- judgment by adjustment and anchoring

Judgment by Representativeness

Judgment by representativeness is a determination of the probability that object A belongs to class B, or that event A originates from process B, or that the probability that process B will generate event A (Tversky & Kahneman, 1974, p. 1124).

For example, in the "object A belongs to class B" scenario, an individual is provided with a personality description of a man and then asked to guess the man's occupation from a list of possibilities. The individual, relying upon judgment by representation, will guess the man's occupation to be the one that fits his personality most stereotypically (Tversky & Kahneman, 1974, p. 1124). This practice is referred to as stereotyping. Bodenhausen (1990, p. 319) argues that while stereotyping is convenient and common, it is a less likely strategy when individuals are motivated by personal involvement or are at their peak energy levels.

Judgment by Availability

Judgment by availability is an assessment of the frequency of a class or the probability of an event by the ease with which instances or occurrences can be recalled (Tversky & Kahneman, 1974, p. 1127).

For example, a person may suppose that a new pizza restaurant will fail because three other pizza restaurants in the same neighborhood failed.

Judgment by Adjustment and Anchoring

In judgment by adjustment and anchoring, adjustment involves estimating using a base number that is then altered to garner the final value. Anchoring refers to the phenomenon that different starting points will yield different estimates that are biased toward the initial values (Tversky & Kahneman, 1974, p. 1128). When using adjustment and anchoring to estimate an unknown quantity, an individual uses information he already knows (the anchor) and then makes adjustments from that point to arrive at an acceptable answer (the adjustment) (Epley & Gilovich, 2006, p. 311).

For example, groups of research subjects were asked to estimate the percentage of African countries in the United Nations by adjusting their numbers up or down from a number obtained by spinning a wheel of fortune (the anchor or starting point). Despite the relevance, or lack thereof, the arbitrary anchor numbers represented, subject answers varied according to them (the adjustment) (Tversky & Kahneman, 1974, p. 1128).

Illusion of Validity

Illusion of validity refers to a "complete lack of connection between the statistical information and the compelling experience of insight" (Kahneman, 2002).

Intuitive Prediction

Intuitive prediction refers to a "willingness to make extreme predictions about future performance on the basis of a small sample of behavior" (Kahneman, 2002).

The terms "illusion of validity" and "intuitive prediction" were created by Daniel Kahneman when he first began developing his behavioral viewpoints of individual choice as a psychologist in the Israeli army. After comparing the results of an exercise designed to identify which soldiers showed the best potential to be officers, to the actual success of the same soldiers in officer training, Kahneman deduced that the correlation was minimal. The term he created for this disconnect between statistical information and the experience of insight is the "illusion of validity" (Kahneman, 2002). Kahneman also noted that there was an "intuitive prediction" factor to this method of identifying officers: It resulted in making extreme predictions about future performance based on a small sample of behavior (Kahneman, 2002).

Prospect Theory

Prospect theory "attempts to explain why individuals make decisions that deviate from rational decision-making by examining how the expected outcomes of alternative choices are perceived" ("Prospect theory," 2007).

The term "prospect theory" was created by Daniel Kahneman and Amos Tversky. As they were delving into the intricacies of decision-making, they constructed a theory for risky choice, which they called value theory. They eventually renamed it "prospect theory" when they published their article, "Prospect Theory: An Analysis of Decisions under Risk" in *Econometrica* in 1979. The significance of prospect theory was that it established that "objects of choice are mental representations, not objective states of the world." The publication of the article in *Econometrica*—rather than in a psychology journal—positioned prospect theory to be a strong influence in the field of economics (Kahneman, 2002).

Contemporary Research in Behavioral Economics

Behavioral economists are interested in the benefits of behavioral economics to society. Here are some suggestions from two prominent behavioral economists Richard H. Thaler and Dan Ariely.

Richard H. Thaler

Richard H. Thaler studies the relationships among behavioral economics, finance, and the psychology of decision-making. He discounts the assumption that the economy is totally based on rational and selfish

Richard H. Thaler, 2017 Nobel Memorial Prize Laureate in Economic Sciences, during Nobel Prize press conference in Stockholm, on December 7, 2017. (Courtesy of Bengt Nyman from Vaxholm, Sweden CC BY 2.0 via Wikimedia Commons)

behavior and explores the possibility that human factors are a strong influence. Much of his work focuses on the role of behavioral economics in finance and financial decision-making (University of Chicago Booth School of Business, 2009).

Thaler believes that it is naïve to think that high school students are prepared to be astute consumers. He suggests that financial institutions should be more transparent up-front and teach individuals to be smart consumers by educating them about the costs of their options without limiting them. Thaler calls this approach to teaching financial literacy "libertarian paternalism" (Thaler & Sundstein, 2008).

Thaler's work on retirement savings was influential in the creation of the 2006 Pension Protection Act. In 2008, Thaler described his findings in *Nudge: Improving Decisions about Health, Wealth, and Happiness,* which compared automatic enrollment in retirement plans with opt-in plans and found that people were likely to accept a default decision made on

their behalf. That is, people were unlikely to either opt out of automatic enrollment plans or opt in to freely offered plans (Burstyn, 2011). After moves by the Obama administration to make government data more available to the public, Thaler argued that the response of individuals to such data depended less on actual self-interest than on perceived self-interest, which could be controlled merely by presentation (Thaler & Tucker, 2013).

Dan Ariely

In an article titled, "The Dishonesty of Honest People: A Theory of Self-concept Maintenance," Ariely and two coauthors analyzed the results of six experiments with university students and concluded that they valued honesty and wanted to feel like they were honest. However, they did choose to cheat a little bit if they benefited by it, but did not cheat enough to convince themselves that they were dishonest (Mazar,

Dan Ariely in Camden, Maine, on October 20, 2010. (Courtesy of PopTech CC BY-SA 2.0 via Wikimedia Commons)

Amir, & Ariely, 2008). This has clear implications for behavior theory in general and specifically in determining how people balance their ethical beliefs with their needs.

In 2008, Ariely published his book, *Predictably Irrational*, in which he attempts to describe research findings from behavioral economics and decision-making in non-academic terms so that a broader audience may use the research to improve their lives (Ariely, 2007, p. 5). The book tackles such issues as why a commitment to dieting dissolves when we see a tempting dessert; why we buy items that we don't need; why an expensive aspirin cures a headache better than a cheaper aspirin; and why honor codes reduce dishonesty in the workplace (Ariely, 2007, p. 6).

Homo Economicus vs. Homo Communitatis

H. Joel Jeffrey and Anthony O. Putnam declared in their 2013 article "The Irrationality Illusion: A New Paradigm for Economics and Behavioral Economics" that the old paradigm supported by Kahneman, Ariely, and others of human irrationality in financial decision making—homo economicus—was a mere grafting onto the classical model to explain anomalous decision- making that deviates from utilitarian predictions of human behavior. Jeffrey and Putnam put forward their homo communitatis paradigm, which calls for a framework of principles that asserts that "[b]ehavior choices are made in light of the individual's reasons to engage in one behavior or another" and that "[e]very behavior is an instance of engaging in a social practice of a community" (Jeffrey & Putnam, 2013).

CONCLUSION

Behavioral economics gathers insight from the fields of psychology and economics to try to analyze why people make choices. Behavioral economists do not subscribe to the fact that individual choice always follows rational guidelines or is statistically predictable, but believe that individual choice is heavily influenced by other factors. The importance of behavioral economics as a significant field of study is evidenced by the fact that leading behavioral economist Daniel Kahneman shared the 2002 Nobel Memorial Prize in Economic Sciences "for having integrated insights from psychological research into economic science, especially concerning human judgment and decision-making under uncertainty" ("The Sveriges Riksbank Prize," 2002).

BIBLIOGRAPHY

Amir, O., & Lobel, O. (2008). "Stumble, predict, nudge: How behavioral economics informs law and policy." *Columbia Law Review, 108*, 2098–2138.

Ariely, D. (2008, January 39). *Painful lessons.* Retrieved from xlink:href="http://www.predictably-irrational.com/pdfs/mypain.pdf"

Ariely, D. (2007). Predictably Irrational Web site. Retrieved from xlink:href="http://www.predictably-irrational.com"

Barberis, N. (2018). "Richard Thaler and the rise of behavioral economics." *Yale School of Management*, SSN.

Bayesian Theory. (2007). *Bloomsbury Business Library—Business & Management Dictionary*, 757. London, United Kingdom: A&C Black Publishers Ltd.

Brenner, B.K. (2008). "Create values-based communications to enhance success of employee health plans." *Journal of Financial Service Professionals, 62*, 30–32.

Bruni, L. & Sugden, R. (2007). "The road not taken: How psychology was removed from economics, and how it might be brought back." *Economic Journal, 117*, 146–173.

Bubb, R., & Pildes, R. H. (2014). "How Behavioral Economics Trims Its Sails and Why." *Harvard Law Review*, 127, 1594–1678.

Burstyn, G. (2011). "How a freethinking economist saved your retirement portfolio." (cover story). *Research, 34*, 42–46.

Cosmides, L., & Tooby, J. (1994). "Better than rational: Evolutionary psychology and the invisible hand." *American Economic Review, 84*, 327–332.

Decision making. (2007). *Bloomsbury Business Library—Business & Management Dictionary*, 2285. London, United Kingdom: A&C Black Publishers Ltd.

Decision theory. (2000) *Merriam-Webster's collegiate dictionary* (10th ed.), 298. Springfield, MA: Merriam-Webster.

Economics. (2000) *Merriam-Webster's collegiate dictionary* (10th ed.), 365. Springfield, MA: Merriam-Webster.

Epley, N., & Gilovich, T. (2006). "The anchoring-and-adjustment heuristic." *Psychological Science, 17*, 311-318.

Fillion, K. (Writer). (2008). "Dan Ariely talks with Kate Fillion [Interview]." *Maclean's, 121*, 16–17.

Heuristics. (2007). *Bloomsbury Business Library—Business & Management Dictionary*, 3609. London, United Kingdom: A&C Black Publishers Ltd.

Irrational. (2000) *Merriam-Webster's collegiate dictionary* (10th ed.), 618. Springfield, MA: Merriam-Webster.

Jeffrey, H., & Putman, A.O. (2013). "The irrationality illusion: A new paradigm for economics and behavioral economics." *Journal of Behavioral Finance*, 14, 161–194.

Judgment. (2000) *Merriam-Webster's collegiate dictionary* (10th ed.), 632. Springfield, MA: Merriam-Webster.

Kahneman, D. (2002). *Daniel Kahneman: Autobiography.* Retrieved from Nobelprize.orgxlink:href="http://nobelprize.org/nobel%5fprizes/economics/laureates/2002/kahneman-aut"

Kahneman, D., Knetsch, J.L., & Thaler, R. (1986). "Fairness as a constraint on profit seeking: entitlements in the market." *American Economic Review, 76*, 728–742.

Kahneman, D., & Thaler, R.H. (2006). "Utility maximization and experienced utility." *Journal of Economic Perspectives, 20*, 221–234.

Lambert, C. (2006). "The marketplace of perceptions." *Harvard Magazine*, 108, 50–57, 93–95.

Massachusetts Institute of Technology. Dan Ariel curriculum vitae. Retrieved from xlink:href="http://web.mit.edu/ariely/www/MIT/CV/Ariely%5fCV.pdf"

Mazar, N., Amir, O., & Ariely, D. (2008). "The dishonesty of honest people: A theory of self-concept maintenance." *Journal of Marketing Research, 45*, 633–644.

Ofir, C., & Lynch Jr, J.G. (1984). "Context effects on judgment under uncertainty." *Journal of Consumer Research, 11*, 668–679.

Prelec, D. (2006). "Rebuilding the boat while staying afloat: the modeling challenge for behavioral economics." *Journal of Marketing Research, 43*, 332–336.

Prospect theory. (2007). *Bloomsbury Business Library—Business & Management Dictionary*, 6032. London, United Kingdom: A&C Black Publishers Ltd.

Psychology. (2000) *Merriam-Webster's* collegiate dictionary (10th ed.), 940. Springfield, MA: Merriam-Webster.

Rational choice theory. (2009). Retrieved from *BusinessDictionary.com*xlink:href="http://www.businessdictionary.com/definition/rational-choice-theory-RCT"

"Rational or intuitive? Frameworks for decision-making." (2003). In *Business Strategy* (pp. 66–75). New York: EIU: Economist Intelligence Unit.

Schneider, M. (2007). "Daniel Kahneman." *Yale Economic Review*, 4, 22–27.

"Seeking the Roots of Entrepreneurship: Insights from Behavioral Economics†." (2014). *Journal of Economic Perspectives*, 28, 49–70.

Sleeth-Keppler, D. (2007). "Seeing the world in black and white: The effects of perceptually induced mind-sets on judgment." *Psychological Science, 18*, 768–772.

Stanford University. (1997-98). *Memorial Resolution: Amos Tversky.* (SenD#4782). Retrieved xlink:href="http://facultysenate.stanford.edu/archive/1997%5f1998/reports/105949/1"

Stanford University. (2002, December 6). "Amos Tversky posthumously wins 2003 Grawemeyer Award with Nobel Laureate Daniel Kahneman." Retrieved xlink:href="http://www.stanford.edu/dept/news/pr/02/grawemeyer20031211.html"

"The Sveriges Riksbank Prize in Economic Sciences in Memory of Alfred Nobel 2002. (2002)." Retrieved from Nobelprize.org. xlink:href="http://nobelprize.org/nobel%5fprizes/economics/laureates/2002/index.ht"

Thaler, R. H., & Benartzi, S. (2004). "Save more tomorrow™: using behavioral economics to increase employee saving." *Journal of Political Economy, 112*, S164–S187.

Thaler, R.H., & Sundstein, C. (2008, August 1). "Ignorance lands Americans in debt." *Point for Credit Union Research & Advice*, 18.

Thaler, R.H., & Tucker, W. (2013). "Smarter information, smarter consumers." *Harvard Business Review, 91*, 44–54.

Tucker, B. (2007). "Applying behavioral ecology and behavioral economics to conservation and development planning: an example from the Mikea Forest, Madagascar." *Human Nature, 18*, 190–208.

Tversky, A., & Kahneman, D. (1974). "Judgment under uncertainty: heuristics and biases." *Science, 185*(4157), 1124-1131. Retrieved February 17, 2009.

University of Chicago Booth School of Business. (2009). *Richard H. Thaler.* [Biography]. Retrieved xlink:href="http://www.chicagogsb.edu/faculty/bio.aspx?person%5fid=12825835520"

SUGGESTED READING

Assem, M.J. van den, Dolder D. van, & Thaler, R.H. (2012). "Split or steal? Cooperative behavior when the stakes are large." *Management Science, 58*, 2–20.

Bodenhausen, G.V. (1990). "Stereotypes as judgmental heuristics: Evidence of circadian variations in discrimination." *Psychological Science, 1*, 319–322.

Driscoll, J. C., & Holden, S. (2014). "Behavioral economics and macroeconomic models." *Journal Of Macroeconomics*, 41,133–147.

Gandel, S. (2008). "The campaign to make you behave." *Money, 37*, 126–130.

Goldsmith, M. (2009, January 21). "Human nature: The X factor in economic theory." *Business Week Online*, 13.

"The way the brain buys." (2009). *The Economist, 389*(8611), 105–107.

—*Sue Ann Connaughton, MLS*

BUSINESS IN THE GLOBAL POLITICAL ENVIRONMENT

ABSTRACT

This article will focus on business practices in the global political environment. It discusses globalization and the challenges of political risks for businesses operating in the international economy. This article will provide an analysis of the different types of political risk as well as the strategies most commonly used for identifying, assessing, and managing political risk. Strategies used by companies to mediate political risk, such as political risk insurance and cross-border alliances, will be discussed. In addition, a case study of the political risks facing international e-commerce companies is included as an example of an industry-specific response to political risk.

OVERVIEW

Business practices and operations in the international political environment are influenced by the forces and processes of globalization, including political, social, and policy risks. Political risks refer to the potential effects of a change in government on a business. Social risks refer to pressures put on businesses by environmental or other pressure groups. Policy risks refer to the potential effects resulting from change in policy or rights on a business (Frynas, 2002). The process of globalization refers to the increasingly free flow of ideas, people, goods, services, and capital that is leading to the integration of economies and societies. Businesses have adapted to the changing global political environment by identifying political risks prior to investment in foreign business activities and investments. The following sections provide an overview of the current global political environments and political risks.

Global Political Environment

A political environment is characterized by the regulatory environment, local attitudes toward corporate governance, reaction to international competition, and labor laws. Political environments around the world are changing due to the forces of globalization. Globalization is characterized by the permeability of traditional boundaries of nations, cultures, and economic markets. According to Thruow (1995), the fundamental economic forces and events influencing globalization and political turmoil around the world include the following:

- the end of communism
- the shift from an economy based on natural resources to one based on knowledge industries
- demographic shifts
- the development of a global economy
- increased trade liberalization
- advances in communication technology
- increased threat of global terrorism
- an era without a dominant economic, political, or military power

Globalization creates a turbulent global sociopolitical environment characterized by competing political actors, shifting power relations, and politically driven changes in national economies around the world. Businesses work to find opportunity and profit to be had from these political and economic changes. The political turbulence and upheaval have resulted in a

Back row, left to right: Mexican President Carlos Salinas de Gortari, U.S. President George H. W. Bush, and Canadian Prime Minister Brian Mulroney, at the initialing of the draft North American Free Trade Agreement in October 1992. In front are Mexican Secretary of Commerce and Industrial Development Jaime Serra Puche, United States Trade Representative Carla Hills, and Canadian Minister of International Trade Michael Wilson. (Courtesy of Wikimedia Commons)

move from centralized economies to a decentralized global economy and has created numerous emerging markets. These emerging markets refer to the capital markets of developing countries that have liberalized their financial systems to promote capital flows with nonresidents and have become broadly accessible to foreign investors.

Business opportunities, including international investments and joint ventures, in the global economy are increasingly tied to trade pacts such as the North American Free Trade Agreement (NAFTA) between the United States, Canada, and Mexico; the Mercosur trade pact between Argentina, Uruguay, Brazil, and Paraguay; and the Asia Pacific Economic Cooperation (APEC) trade zone. In addition, business opportunities are resulting from privatization worldwide. Countries are privatizing many state-owned industries and allowing foreign investors to purchase pieces of them through joint ventures or allowing local operations to participate in these projects (Stites, 1995).

Emerging markets, often occurring in countries experiencing political upheaval, will continue to increase in the expanding global market. Businesses, participating in the new global economy, will continue to seek out new manufacturing and sales opportunities in foreign markets and countries. Ultimately, globalization brings businesses new opportunity and

new risks. Political risks are one of the major problems and considerations for businesses in the global political environment. Opportunities and liabilities are growing proportionately in the new global economy. The following section describes and analyzes the influence of political risk on business activities and operations.

Political Risk

Multinational corporations conducting global business in emerging markets experience lucrative investment opportunities as well as challenges and turmoil. Multinational corporations conducting business in today's global political environment are challenged by political risk. Political risk refers to the risk of a strategic, financial, or personnel loss for a firm because of events related to political instability such as riots, terrorism, coups, civil war, and insurrection, as well as non-market factors such as macroeconomic and social policies (fiscal, monetary, trade, investment, industrial, income, labor, and development) (Morales & Kleiner, 1996).

Political risk arises from factors and events such as governmental change, shifts in national ideology or policy, civil war, social unrest, economic instability, nationalization, and corruption. Political, economic, and religious environments influence business operations for exporters, traders, investors, banks, and other organizations involved in international commerce. In addition, national governments may institute forced shutdowns and relocations of foreign business. Companies entering foreign markets for the first time, either as investors or manufacturers, as well as established multinational corporations expanding into new foreign markets or ventures must address certain questions to assess potential political risk (Wade, 2005):

- Is there a tradition of peaceful governmental transition?
- How resilient is the political system?
- How do nongovernmental agencies, such as trade unions, churches, media, and the legal system, influence the society and government?
- Is there demographic stability?
- Are there internal social, ethnic, or religious tensions that could lead to a civil war or unrest?
- What is the country's trade credit history?
- What is the level of unemployment among citizens?

Collage from the Yugoslav wars (1991-1995, excluding the Kosovo war), clockwise from the top: Slovenian police escort captured JNA soldiers back to their unit during the 1991 Slovenian war of independence. A destroyed tank during the battle of Vukovar. Rockets in a Serbian placement overlooking Dubrovnik and the Adriatic coast. New graves for victims of the Srebrenica genocide in 1995. Burial took place on 11 July 2010. UN vehicle driving on the streets of Sarajevo during the siege. (Courtesy of Peter Denton Peter Božič Paul Katzenberger Paalso CC BY-SA 3.0 via Wikimedia Commons)

Political risk, as a general, global category, is characterized by three factors: catastrophic events, business environment, and public policy (Dugan, 1999).

Catastrophic events: Catastrophic events refer to the political developments that can affect operations of all foreign firms in a country. Theoretical examples include racial and ethnic unrest, civil strife, terrorism, civil war, international conflict, and systemic failure. Real-world examples include former Yugoslavia's ethnic unrest, civil war, and international conflict.

Business environments: Business environments face risks either by all foreign businesses in a region or industry specific risks (related to government corruption, labor strife, and the judicial system). Examples include labor and elections. Labor organizations through much of the world are closely tied to political organizations. This connection between labor and politics brings foreign companies into the midst of political struggles and issues. Foreign elections, which seldom influence foreign business operations directly, do influence public policy. Elections may bring in new officials who alter or shift the business environment to match the new regime. For example, new officials may change the tax code or structure.

Public policies: Public policy risks include political initiatives such as changes in the tax system, regulatory structure, and monetary system. For example, when a foreign government is forced to devalue currency due to economic crisis, interest rates rise and alter domestic spending habits. This change in monetary policy could potentially ruin a foreign business's investment.

The new global political environment is often unpredictable or dangerous. Multinational companies may experience work stoppages, hijackings, physical attacks, and more as they manufacture or distribute their products and services in the global business environment. In addition, goods produced by foreign companies may be subject to confiscation by competing political actors and manufacturing facilities may be nationalized (Stites, 1995).

Applications: Assessing and Managing Political Risk
Companies manage political risk through global strategies and organizational planning. These two approaches, global strategy and organizational planning, differ in scale. Global strategy is a macro-level activity that actively tries to connect the proposed project to a firm's overall goals and objectives. Organizational planning is a micro-level activity that actively works to connect the proposed project with project-level goals, objectives, and tools. The following sections describe how global strategy and organizational planning aid companies in the identification, management, and avoidance of political risk.

Global Strategy

Companies develop global strategies, in part, to assess and manage political risk. Global strategy refers to the methods, approaches, and objectives developed by a business to increase competitive advantage in the market by increasing competitive scope worldwide. A global strategy allows a company to determine the real cost of capital for a foreign investment. The majority of global strategies involve a combination of trade and direct investment in foreign countries. Global strategy requires capital investment decisions. The investment decision-making process involves seven steps:

- Determine that the project meets the firm's strategic objectives.
- Compute the costs, revenue, and benefits of the project.
- Assess the risk associated with the project.
- Determine the cost of capital to be used in the evaluation.
- Conduct the evaluation analysis.
- Select or reject the project.
- Perform a follow-up evaluation and tracking on selected project.

Determining the true cost of capital required for a foreign project is crucial to the profit margin of the project. Martinson (2000) argues that the appropriate cost of capital for an investment project is a function of the perceived risk of the investment. Country-specific factors that influence perceived investment risk include political risk, interest rate differential, and tax rate differential. Examples of political risk include frequency of government changes, amount of violence in the country, number of armed insurrection, conflicts with other countries, inflation, balance of payments, deficits, surpluses, and the growth rate of the gross national product (GNP). Country risk surveys and country ratings, produced by independent services, provide the information businesses use to measure political risk. Organizations that rate and quantify political risk of different countries include the following (Martinson, 2000):

Euromoney **magazine:** *Euromoney* magazine produces an annual country-rating risk report based on different countries' access to international credit and payment record.

Economist Intelligent Unit: Economist Intelligent Unit produces an annual country-rating risk report based on external debt, foreign-exchange reserves, and consistency of government policy.

International Country Risk Guide: International Country Risk Guide produces an annual country-rating risk report including composite risk rating as well as individual ratings for political, financial, and economic risk.

Country Forecasts: Country Forecasts produces a semiannual country forecast.

Risk managers are responsible for understanding the potential problems and complex risks of emerging markets. Political risk assessment, including organizational planning, knowledge of the political environment, and diligence, has developed in response to the influence that the political environment has on foreign business operations. A business's foreign or overseas operations will inevitably be influenced by the actions of host governments and competing political actors (Stites, 1995).

Organizational Planning

Political risk to specific foreign investment is managed, in large part, through organizational planning. Organizational planning is conducted prior to final investment decisions. The pre-entry planning or pre-investment stage involves the following steps:

- Describe investment objectives.
- Assess company's knowledge and expertise related to proposed foreign investment.
- Integrate political risk assessment into global strategy.
- Identify opportunities that benefit the company and avoid risk.
- Establish a structure of operations.
- Development of strategy and contingency plans.
- Develop security plans for the protection or evacuation of employees.
- Choose insurance coverage.

Organizational planning occurs both within and outside of organizations. In-house centers gather, process, and disseminate information. Consulting firms also assess country, regional, and global political risk and monitor foreign political environments (Dugan, 1999).

When political risk assessment is completed, the information and knowledge gained through global strategizing and organizational planning allow managers to make informed decisions about the type, degree, and probability of political risk in a business scenario. With this information in mind, political risk managers may choose to mediate political risk through the use of a political risk strategy such as adapting, politick, negotiating, or withdrawing (Morales & Kleiner, 1996).

Issues: Political Risk Insurance and Cross-Border Alliances

In addition to political risk management strategies such as adapting, negotiating, and withdrawing, businesses mitigate political risk by obtaining coverage against possible losses resulting from political actions or inaction by the host government through the purchase of political risk insurance and the formation of cross-border alliances. The following sections describe and analyze political risk insurance and cross-border alliances as they relate to the problem of political risk.

Political Risk Insurance

Worldwide political upheaval has resulted in the demand for political risk insurance (PRI) to protect businesses engaged in international business. Businesses obtain political risk insurance coverage during the initial stages of the project. Businesses pay a small commitment fee to the underwriters and are guaranteed coverage, often for the life of the project.

The market and demand for a political risk marketplace has grown throughout the 1990s. In addition, political risk insurance has expanded and adapted to meet the changing needs of global businesses. Political risk insurance guarantees small business transactions and ever increasing amounts. Increasingly, private sector and public sector political risk insurance underwriters work together to increase insurance capacity (Wagner, 1999). Common political risk insurance options include the U.S. government's Overseas Private Investment Corporation (OPIC) (which pays claims on losses occurring from expropriation, inconvertibility, and political violence) and the World Bank.

The Overseas Private Investment Corporation headquarters plaque in Washington, D.C. (Courtesy of Geraldshields11 CC BY-SA 4.0 via Wikimedia Commons)

The World Bank issues political risk insurance through their Multilateral Investment Guarantee Agency (MIGA). MIGA helps investors mediate political risk by ensuring eligible projects against political losses caused by currency transfer restriction, expropriation, war and civil disturbance, and breach of contract by the host government. MIGA simultaneously works to prevent incidents and claims as well as promises to make prompt payments if a claim is made. MIGA insurance includes services such as the following:

- mediating disputes
- accessing funding
- lowering borrowing costs
- providing extensive country knowledge
- providing environmental and social expertise

The World Bank's political risk insurance, along with political risk insurance in general, creates new investment opportunities for businesses in developing countries by covering risks the private market is unable or unwilling to sustain.

Cross-Border Alliances

In addition to political risk insurance, cross-border alliances offer the opportunity and means to mitigate, reduce, or control political risk. Cross-border alliances are international agreements between two or more independent companies who exploit a tangible or intangible asset. Examples of cross-border alliances include joint ventures, cooperative business arrangements, supplier contracts, and management or technology contracts. Cross-border business alliances involve shared risk, cost, and reward. Cross-border alliances are particularly useful for new market entries and new business start-ups in foreign countries. Cross-border alliances are formed when they promise economic or structural benefits that cannot be achieved by the company alone or through outright acquisition or mergers. Cross-border alliances allow businesses to participate in emerging markets in which involvement of a local partner is desirable or required by the local government.

The main principles for successful cross-border alliance design include the following:

- strategic objective
- mutual dependence
- alliance independence
- shared vision and rewards
- barriers to exit

Challenges to cross-border alliances include management difficulties, costs, inflexibility, coordination difficulties, and risk of competitive conflict (Jagersma, 2005).

Case Study: Political Risk and International Internet Firms

Managing political risk improves global business performance for all types of companies conducting international business. Political risk affects companies with physical and intellectual products alike. For example, Internet companies worldwide are currently struggling to assess and manage political risk caused by government efforts around the world to regulate new technology.

Frynas's study of the political risks faced in international e-commerce reveals that internationally operating Internet firms face serious political and legal challenges in different countries and markets (2002). The country-specific variations between issues such as consumption tax and intellectual property rights demonstrate that Internet firms experience country- or region-specific risks and uncertainties. National governments tax Internet businesses and try to regulate various aspects of Internet activities such as e-commerce. Examples of government efforts

at Internet regulation include the Chinese government's efforts to introduce website censorship and the European Union directives on copyright.

Internet firms face political risks such as non-enforcement of intellectual property rights, uncertainty over the legal validity of electronic contracts, changes in taxation, non-recognition of electronic signatures, and legal liability of Internet service providers for third-party content. Internet businesses are vulnerable to changing national feelings toward technology. Unpredictable changes in political business environments worldwide affect the profits and future of Internet businesses.

Risk managers of international Internet and e-commerce companies minimize risk in the international political environment by following these strategies:

- Research and monitor the legal and political developments in target markets.
- Design the firm's website carefully to ensure strict compliance with the law.
- Carefully choose the jurisdiction when deciding on the home base for the Internet firm.
- Purchase political risk insurance.
- Use legal and political weapons to fight competitors.

In the final analysis, political risk for Internet companies, as for all types of businesses, is a subjective account of how events may affect business activities and operations (Frynas, 2002).

CONCLUSION

Profitable foreign investment strategies in the new global political environment depend on political risk management. Political risk assessment and management is particularly important to foreign direct investment in the economies of developing countries. Companies committed to foreign investment have systems in place for analyzing a country's political risk. The main principles of political risk management include (Morales & Kleiner, 1996) the following:

- staying in touch with a country's daily developments
- analyzing industry, project, and management characteristics
- following a proactive instead of reactive management

Risk assessment and management mediates risks and allows for ever-increasing global expansion of multinational corporations into established and emerging markets.

BIBLIOGRAPHY

Bendell, J., & Kearins, K. (2004). World review. *Journal of Corporate Citizenship, 14,* 6–17.

Dong, M., Li, C., & Tse, D. (2013). "Do Business and Political Ties Differ in Cultivating Marketing Channels for Foreign and Local Firms in China?" *Journal Of International Marketing,* 21, 39-56. doi:10.1509/jim.12.0088

Dugan, W. (1999). "Global dangers." *Risk Management, 46,* 13–16.

Frynas, J. (2002). "The limits of globalization—legal and political issues in e-commerce." *Management Decision, 40,* 871–881.

Jagersma, P. (2005). "Cross-border alliances: advice from the executive suite." *Journal of Business Strategy, 26,* 41–50.

Johnson, A. C., Imam, S. A., & Askar, M. O. (2013). "Managing at the Fringes: The Implications of Politics for Business Strategy." *International Journal Of Business & Public Administration,* 10, 1–13.

Mäkinen, J., & Kourula, A. (2012). "Pluralism in Political Corporate Social Responsibility." *Business Ethics Quarterly,* 22, 649–678.

"Managing political risks with MIGA's guarantees." (2006). The World Bank.

Martinson, O. (2000). "Global investments: discover your real cost of capital—and your real risk." *Journal of Corporate Accounting & Finance, 11,* 23–28.

Moncada, E. (2013). "Business and the Politics of Urban Violence in Colombia." *Studies In Comparative International Development,* 48, 308–330.

Morales, R. & Kleiner, B. (1996). "New development in techniques for analysing diversified companies in today's global environment." *Management Research News, 19,* 41–49.

Ramírez Solís, E., Baños Monroy, V., & Orozco-Gómez, M. (2012). "The Inner Circle: How Politics Affects the Organizational Climate." *Allied Academies International Conference: Proceedings Of The Academy Of Organizational Culture, Communications & Conflict* (AOCCC), 17, 7–8.

Roemer-Mahler, A. (2013). "Business conflict and global politics: The pharmaceutical industry and the global protection of intellectual property rights." *Review of International Political Economy,* 20, 121–152.

Sites, J. (1995). "Going forward with global investments." *Risk Management, 42,* 12–17.

Sovacool. B. (2017). "Political economy, poverty, and polycentrism in the Global Environment Facility's Least Developed Countries Fund (LDCF) for Climate Change Adaptation." *Taylor Francis Online.*

Thurow, L. (1995). "Surviving in a turbulent environment." *Planning Review, 23,* 24.

Wade, J. (2005). "Political risk in Eastern Europe." *Risk Management, 52,* 24–29.

Wagner, D. (1999). "The cluster trend: political risk, Part II." *Risk Management, 46,* 18–22.

"The World Bank." (2006). *World Bank political risk insurance.*

SUGGESTED READING

Althaus, C. (2005). "A disciplinary perspective on the epistemological status of risk." *Risk Analysis: An International Journal,* 25, 567–588.

Bremmer, I. (2005). "Managing risk in an unstable world." *Harvard Business Review,* 83, 51–60.

Noordin, B., Harjito, D., & Hazir, A. (2006). "Political risk assessment of Malaysian based multinational corporations." *Investment Management & Financial Innovations,* 3, 91–99

—Simone I. Flynn, PhD

C

COMPARATIVE ECONOMIC SYSTEMS

ABSTRACT

This article examines the defining features of the world's three major economic systems: traditional, free market, and command. Each system addresses the fundamental problem of how to allocate scarce resources in a different way. In all three cases, the decision revolves around what and how much to produce, for whom to produce, and to whose benefit. Kinship, custom, and religion enter into these decisions in a traditional economy. In a free market economy, self- interest alone matters; buyers and sellers bid freely and openly on goods and services, and the price of purchases directly affects supply and demand. Unlike both traditional and free market systems, orthodox command economies ban all forms of private ownership; the state employs everyone and resources are allocated by central planners.

OVERVIEW

At its most basic level, economics concerns itself with the complex ways we rely upon each other to meet our material needs. Writ large, this pursuit gives rise to hundreds of millions of people engaging in trillions of exchanges (i.e., transactions) on a *daily* basis. Nothing remotely approaching the sheer scale of this activity could ever be sustained purely randomly. It takes structure to coordinate the innumerable elements that go into the production and distribution of goods and services that respond dynamically to changing conditions and needs. A system, in other words, made up of institutions, both formal and informal, following mutually agreed upon rules and practices is required to harness divergent individual interests to serve a common good (Dallago, 2002).

In any economic system, the be-all and end-all is the efficient allocation of resources. This lofty term boils down to the answers of three fundamental questions: What to produce, how to produce it, and for whom? Five thousand years ago, the answers to these questions were moot as early humans were only concerned with food and shelter. But as human populations grew from the small, informal groups where the goal was simple survival, a division of labor along functional lines became necessary. How this division was organized and to what ends was and is the preeminent concern of an economic system. Three major models have since emerged: traditional, free market, and command.

The most long-lived of the major economic systems is the traditional model. It has shaped economic decision-making to one degree or another for more than two thousand years. Rooted in custom and often reenforced by clan, tribal, and sectional ties, supply and demand in traditional economies can be governed as much by sociocultural norms and obligations as by questions of supply and demand. Free market economies employ a more computational signaling mechanism—pricing. Here suppliers are free to charge whatever they want. Those who prosper provide goods and services people find useful, desirable, and affordable enough to buy. The sum of a given item's purchases over time signals that item's relative economic importance. On the other hand, command economies completely disavow the role of tradition or of a self-regulating marketplace. Here the state decides what and how much will be produced and orders state-owned enterprises to meet specific quotas. These quotas are set based partly on statistical forecasts of existing consumption patterns and partly on economic development plans and ideological agendas.

Such are the broad outlines of each major economic system. Ask any practitioner of comparative economics if such and such a system exists in the real world, and he or she will most likely say "no," "not really" or, at best, "not quite." This is so because these "systems" are only conceptual models; clear-cut and idealized versions of much hazier real-world processes. This notwithstanding, they are of value precisely because of the general principles they reveal about the underlying dynamics of supply and demand. Moreover, elements of each system operate to one degree or another somewhere in today's global economy, in many instances cheek by jowl in a mixed economy. Even in the freest of market economies, governments regulate some forms of business. Social, cultural, and even religious mores subtly shape the contours of local and regional commerce in developing and advanced nations alike. Vestiges of the command economies of the last century linger in such emerging world powers as Brazil, Russia, India, and China.

A lot of "isms" quickly surface in any comparison of economic systems: capitalism, socialism, Marxism, colonialism (Economy: 4, 2001). Free market economies can be laissez-faire, corporate, or neo-liberal in disposition. Socialism, in which the state owns and operates major industries and utilities, is a form of command economy that has had several real-world incarnations: the dirigisme of France and the social market system of post-war Germany, and a number of other variations adopted by developing countries at the advent of the post-colonial era. Marxism, of course, is synonymous with communism, a system in which the state literally owns everything and virtually all economic activity is planned. In communism's twentieth-century heyday, Lenin, Stalin and Mao each sought to shape his national economy in his own decidedly ideological mold. Colonialism dominated the global economy in the first half of the twentieth century. Here the major industrial powers occupied and then administered much of the third world for the express purpose of securing access to raw materials and closed markets for their exports.

What matters here is not the distinguishing traits of each offshoot but rather how each major system deals differently with the question of ownership. Private property is a major pillar of the free market economy; it is what people compete to acquire. But, there is always just a fixed amount of land, stocks, savings, and the like. One person adds to his or her wealth (property) at the expense, theoretically speaking, of another. This scarcity of resources inevitably leads to an unequal distribution of wealth. Free market enthusiasts believe this imbalance is not only natural but also morally just. In their view, the rich achieved their wealth by dent of hard work and business acumen. More importantly, they reinvest a

portion of their wealth, thus stimulating economic growth. That investment, in turn, creates jobs and provides additional goods and services and, so, furthers the common good. Proponents of command economies reject these arguments outright. The only cure for a grossly unfair and exploitive economic system, they argue, is collective ownership. The fairest arbiter of the subsequent egalitarian redistribution of income and investment capital is the state.

APPLICATIONS

Economic systems are complex, multidimensional entities in which decisions about what is produced, how to produce, and for whose benefit have a moral and political context. An economy and the society it serves are inseparable. What differentiates one from the other is the nature of the basic problem being addressed. Social cohesion and regeneration are society's most pressing perennial concerns. Capital formation, productive capacity, and full employment are necessary for a healthy economy. Without adequate levels of investment, an efficient manufacturing base, and enough wage earners to buy the goods produced, economies fail. If this happens, the social order itself has the potential to unravel. More often, though, economies simply underperform, and tight credit, high prices, and low wages thwart the average person's aspirations for "the good life." Even when an economy performs well, the prosperity created may be far from universally enjoyed and come with very real social costs. Traditional, free market and command economies approach each of these problems differently.

The Traditional Economy
Over time, methods of production are perfected and kinship or tribal-based patterns of ownership and distribution take root. Material needs are met adequately enough that the community at large grows complacent and/or compliant. Typically, traditional economies are agrarian in nature. They are also relatively static; for example, cultivation techniques changed very little over the centuries, for there was little reason or incentive to innovate. That is because whatever surplus was generated from crop production was usually appropriated by the aristocratic elite. Basic consumer goods like pottery and linen were produced by craftsmen in small-scale, decentralized industries.

Agriculture in China in 2004 performed by landed peasants. (Courtesy of Steve Evans from Bangalore, India CC BY 2.0 via Wikimedia Commons)

Farmer and tradesman alike lived at the subsistence level. Extended family and clan networks fostered the pooling of capital, labor, and technical resources, mitigating the harshness of their predicament.

It would be a mistake, however, to think that this system is now just a fossilized relic of a preindustrial world. In much of the developing world, economies are still agrarian based and land ownership still passes from one generation to the next through inheritance. Extended families are still the primary economic unit and affiliations with clans and tribes are still a ready source of investment capital, labor, technical expertise, employment, and care for the ill and indigent. China and India, two of the world's most dynamic emerging industrial economies, still have in excess of three hundred million landed peasants a piece.

The principle underlying traditional economies are asserting themselves in new ways even as their structural characteristics recede. The sense that an economic actor has concrete obligations to others and must conduct business in accordance with social and religious norms, even at the expense of profits, still resonates in some of the most advanced economies of the Middle East and Asia (Rosser & Rosser, 1999). Islam, for example, forbids the charging of interest and requires the devout to donate a percentage of their annual income to charity. Similarly, family ties proved instrumental to the formation of giant industrial manufacturers in Japan and South Korea. "Crony capitalism," where third world dictators reward friends and family with lucrative contracts and business franchise, is still a fact of economic life in the emerging world.

The Free Market Economy

Unrestrained competition motivated purely by self-gain is the paramount virtue in a free market economy. Purists contend that government intervention of any sort interrupts and detracts from the efficient functioning of the marketplace. Now, despite the almost mystical status assigned it, the marketplace is actually just the sum total of buyers and sellers. Each rational actor decides upon what he or she needs and wants, then looks to the marketplace to find the greatest value at the least cost. The free flow of so-called "perfect" information is vital in this respect. No one likes to buy something only to discover it costs less down the street. Likewise, no one likes to find out that a product does not perform as advertised. Perhaps the single most important piece of information is product price.

While buyers are busy maximizing the utility of their purchases, firms are equally busy trying to maximize their profits by earning as much revenue as they can at the least cost to themselves. The higher this sales revenue on aggregate grows, the greater the number of enterprises supplying the good or service

The Panic - Run on the Fourth National Bank, No. 20 Nassau Street in New York City in 1873. (Courtesy of Library of Congress)

being offered. Conversely, the lower the sales revenues go, the fewer the suppliers. This agile responsiveness to supply and demand is widely considered to be the free market's greatest asset. When supply exactly matches demand, the market is said to be in equilibrium. Any imbalance between the two results in price fluctuations until supply once again matches demand. It is an article of faith among economic theorists that markets are self- regulating and that they will naturally move toward equilibrium.

For an economic system with such anarchistic leanings, free markets operate in a remarkably orderly fashion. This is not to say that they operate smoothly or to everyone's benefit, but simply that, on aggregate, the behavior of buyers and sellers over time exhibits a degree of cyclical predictability. In the short term, though, the behavior of free market economies can be notoriously unpredictable. Herein lies an uncomfortable truth: Risk is ever present in free market economies. Uncertainty and the potential for failure are constants: Some businesses succeed while others go bust, just as some people grow rich and others poor. Limited liability and bankruptcy laws can stem the losses but only to a certain point. Whenever unemployment rises, consumption declines and supply soon exceeds demand. In more severe cases, prices fall so precipitously that some firms go under while others retrench by cutting costs, resulting in longer unemployment lines. Examples of such a situation can be seen in the major American economic depressions of the 1850s, 1870s and 1890s.

The Command Economy

There is, by definition, no unemployment in a communist command economy. In retrospect, this may be its singular virtue. The state owns and runs everything and therefore is in a position to hire everyone. No one, theoretically, ever goes hungry or ends up homeless. Such an outcome is only possible when competition is eliminated from both the supply side and the demand side of an economy. In its place, state planners decide what goods to produce; essentially, which state-run monopolies then manufacture and distribute. In such a system, the consumer plays an indirect role. Central planners factor the needs and wants of consumers into their resource allocations alongside the considerations of industrial development and building public infrastructure. In addition, the ideological appropriateness of any decision is always carefully weighed.

Suits for men are manufactured at the Bolshevichka garment factory as part of the Russian government's command economy. (Courtesy of RIA Novosti archive / Yury Artamonov / CC-BY-SA 3.0 via Wikimedia Commons)

A command economy, simply put, values egalitarianism over efficiency; the collective good over individual freedom. Out of necessity as much as choice, it is highly centralized, a system steeped in top-down decision-making of mind-boggling scope and proportion. No matter how well-intentioned, hardworking and conscientious, critics contend, central planners are all too easily overwhelmed by the sheer complexity of their task. Faced with so much uncertainty, they all too readily fall back on orthodoxy and bureaucratic procedure. Insulated from day-to-day economies, these coddled functionaries arbitrarily decide what people want and then pre-order production runs down to the last item. Not surprisingly, scarcities in the consumer goods people truly desire occur regularly. The quality of the goods actually produced is often inferior, too, for the simple reason that, lacking rivals, state monopolies have little incentive to do better.

Whatever dynamism that may have once marked its economic activity is irretrievably lost, in effect, in a command economy. In its place is an endless series of quotas that workers and managers *must* meet. As deadlines loom, production short-cuts, artificially low projections of productive capacity, laborers working frenzied 20-hour shifts—anything and everything that inches them toward their quota—is resorted to.

If a quota is not met, there are real consequences; one's living stipend, housing allotment, and clothing allowance are, after all, the state's way of recognizing the extent of one's contribution to the "socialist economy." One may be always able to make a living in a command economy, but the "quality" of that life can vary dramatically. The irony here is unmistakable. Even in an egalitarian society where the collective good is the supreme virtue, the economic order still rewards some individuals more than others.

Discourse

The miserable performance and hasty demise of the command economies of the Soviet Union and Eastern Bloc countries is a testament to how unworkable these systems were in practice. In the end, central planning proved far too slow and cumbersome a mechanism of resource allocation. Likewise, developing countries are growing impatient with the glacial pace of progress countenanced in traditional economies. Where is the pool of labor and capital necessary to industrialize going to come from, they ask, if the populace and much of the national wealth are still tied to the land? Free market economies, although clearly in the ascendant, face pressing dilemmas of their own: periodic recessions and bouts of unacceptable levels of unemployment chief among these.

It is probably true that there is always something right and something wrong about a given economic system. Value judgments are a matter of perspective, and people in different circumstances have different perspectives. The whole issue is clouded further by the overly simplistic models of the economic systems themselves. Governments can and do exercise controls over markets capitalists compete undeterred in. Passage of the Sarbanes-Oxley Act tightening financial reporting standards for public companies is just one example. They also fund unprofitable but vital ventures like building roads and bridges, and running schools and public health clinics not only to buttress free market enterprise but also to fulfill obligations considered morally important by the culture at large.

In Cuba, one of the last remaining command economies, people turn to a supply and demand driven "black market" to surreptitiously obtain goods not available in state stores. While in America and the rest of the developed world, consumers looking for a product stare at shelves filled with a plethora of brands. And in Europe, national governments remain major stock holders in the "privatized" reincarnations of formerly state-owned companies. In truth, then, real-world economies are simply too dynamic and too complex to neatly pigeonhole. Look closely enough at any national economy and you are likely to find elements of traditional, free market and command economies at play.

BIBLIOGRAPHY

"Chapter 1: Command, market and mixed economies." (2002). In *Understanding the world economy* (pp. 9–31). Oxfordshire, UK: Taylor & Francis Ltd.

Dallago, B. (2002). "The organizational effect of the economic system." *Journal of Economic Issues, 36,* 953–979.

Economy: 4. "The economic process." (2001). In *Discretionary economy: A normative theory of political economy* (pp. 67–87). Piscataway, New Jersey: Transaction Publishers.

Hopkins, B.E., & Duggan, L.S. (2011). "A feminist comparative economic systems." *Feminist Economics, 17,* 35–69.

Katkov, A. (2013). "Economic goals ranking approach in comparative analysis of economic systems." *Global Conference on Business & Finance Proceedings, 8,* 108–112.

Paun, S. (2009). "The Vestiges of Communism and the Transformation of Party Systems in Post-Communist States." *Economics, Management & Financial Markets, 4,* 231–235.

Petr, J. (1987). "The nature and necessity of the mixed economy." *Journal of Economic Issues, 21,* 1445–1468.

Rosser, M., & Rosser Jr., J. (1999). "The new traditional economy." *International Journal of Social Economics, 26*(5/6), 763–778.

SUGGESTED READING

Aharoni, Y. (1981). "Performance evaluation of state-owned enterprises: A process perspective." *Management Science, 27,* 1340–1347.

Belolipetskii, A. (1992). "Economic agents in a mixed economy." *Problems of Economics, 34,* 82.

Jacobson, D. (1992). "From command economy to market economy with a human face: The potential role of the stakeholder approach." *International Executive, 34,* 237–249.

Raikin, E., & Yousefi, M. (1993). "Some misconceptions about market and non-market economies." *International Journal of Social Economics, 20,* 57.

—Francis Duffy, MBA

COMPUTATIONAL METHODS FOR ECONOMICS

ABSTRACT

Whether employed by theorists, policy makers, or developers, practical applications of the computational models and analytical devices can be used on all levels of economic assessment. The methods themselves are myriad—they range from general algorithms and formulae, to comprehensive state-level modeling, to virtually microscopic sector-based analyses. The results are equally extensive and necessary for truly understanding the systems that build and maintain a macroeconomy.

OVERVIEW

Samuel Johnson once said that "The use of traveling is to regulate imagination by reality, and instead of thinking how things may be, to see them as they are" (Bartlett, 1919). Indeed, it is true that there are

Portrait of Samuel Johnson commissioned for Henry Thrale's Streatham Park gallery. (Courtesy of Joshua Reynolds via Wikimedia Commons)

many concepts that, when applied in different analytical environments, act or appear significantly different from their other incarnations. In the case of the age of exploration, there were those who viewed the world as flat, ending at the edge of the visible horizon. Of course, for those who set out in ships to the New World (and for humanity as a result of their pioneering), the world became a vastly different place.

In the study of any discipline, there are three methods to employ. The first is the theoretical, one in which hypotheses and conceptual themes are given light. In Johnson's metaphor, theoretical adherents use their imagination to view an environment.

The second is the empirical method, which uses data from experiments, interviews, polls, and tests to prove or disprove theories. Empiricists are more rooted in the earth, accepting new ideas only if the evidence of those concepts is truly verifiable.

Bridging the gap between theory and reality is computation. Again using Samuel Johnson's comment, computation is the traveler, inspired by what is theoretically possible and willing to strike out to irrefutably verify or repudiate the idea at hand. Computation rests at the center of the oft-conflicting camps of theory and empiricism. The methods employed using computation result in a new theory, or they may provide evidence that clarifies or discounts previously garnered empirical data. In short, computation's place in an analytical situation is critical and essential for identifying the best possible information.

There are countless forms of methods to employ when assessing trends in economics. Among them are algorithmic formulae, linear modeling, and sector-specific modeling. Economists will utilize any of these methods, tailoring them to better encompass the topic of study much in the same way that a chemist will add or subtract varying volumes of compounds to achieve an experimental result. In this paper, many of the types of computational assessment are, in a general mode, discussed within the broader context of how certain trends and issues are studied.

In economics, the need for both educated theory and empirical data is exceptional. In an ever-changing global economy, many previously established theories and positions have been discounted, and others have yet to be born. This paper takes a close look at some of the aforementioned computational methods used in the study of economics. Using examples from both the theoretical and empirical arenas of macroeconomics, this author highlights the links built between the two in the practice of economic analysis.

Settling the Debate

Since the latter twentieth century and the change into the millennium, academics, policy makers, business forecasters, and observers have taken great pains to grasp the world's economic trends. One of the international economic stage's big stars, globalization, has received a particular amount of attention, as links between national economies are becoming more extensive by the day. In some countries, manufacturing has declined as globalization has become the norm. Experts debated the notion that globalization and this trend of "deindustrialization" were linked—that greater free trade, and enhanced transportation and communications systems caused disinvestment in national manufacturing industries, which were becoming unnecessary in light of inexpensive imports.

Some studies, hinged on theoretical analyses, pointed to economic development and productivity, not globalization, for the decline in manufacturing in certain systems. However, empiricists, seeing holes in such hypotheses, gave a more careful analysis of this decline, focusing attention on the workforces of each manufacturing industry. By employing a curvilinear model as opposed to one of the more traditional "U-shaped" models, one study revealed a connection; one that is more subtle and therefore more revealing. Globalization, the model determined, causes differentiation between manufacturing sectors, which in turn creates a saturated market. This saturation is the culprit in the decline of manufacturing jobs (Brady, 2006).

The example above provides an illustration of the bridge formed between theory and empirical data. The authors, reviewing a theory that purported a lack of linkage between globalization and manufacturing declination and summarily forming an alternative hypothesis, were able to use the data found in "real-world" systems to verify their position.

Helping to Make Effective Policy

In a world in which linkages are being formed not only among long-standing trade partners and industrialized nations but also between so-called "northern" and "southern" states, aid for developing nations has become a tremendous component of international diplomacy and relations. Of course, development monies do not come without strings. In fact, any nation that contributes international aid funds to a developing country or government seeks a return on that investment. Hence, tracking the effectiveness of an international development investment is an important part of government policy making.

On one side of the debate over this issue are those who assert that international development funds do little more than create dependency rather than help generate economic growth. On the opposite end are those who believe that many developing nations do not reach their potential because the funds invested in their growth are insufficient. It is in the analysis of the effectiveness of international aid programs in which an economic method of computation may be useful.

An effective method of analysis in this debate is a sector-specific approach. In other words, economists may focus on the very elements into which international aid is infused: educational institution-building, financial infrastructure development, environmental protection, and other arenas. By studying the growth (or lack thereof) of a sector and the time in which that growth occurs, and factoring in periods of stagnancy (which could be periods in which war, civil unrest, or natural disaster occurred), an accurate picture of each sector can become manifest. One study following this methodology applied American aid, in varying forms (such as conditional grants and unrestricted aid) to this sector analysis. The authors' results paint an extremely interesting illustration of the most effective forms of international aid for nations of varying size, economic status, and geopolitical status (Dovern, 2007).

Addressing Impacts

One of the timeliest of issues facing municipalities in the United States is whether or not to embrace casinos and gaming. In recent years, the number of states to allow casinos and/or casino-style gambling has jumped to 40, with several others presently considering following suit (Cauchon, 2007). The potential economic benefits that states see are sizable— millions of dollars in revenues that could potentially serve as a boon for economically distressed cities and regions. Here too, computational methods may be employed to study not only the monetary potentials

Uptown section of Atlantic City, showing Showboat and The Taj Mahal casino (which closed in 2016). (Courtesy of Bob Jagendorf from Manalapan, NJ, CC BY 2.0 via Wikimedia Commons)

(or losses), but also the social consequences of legalized gambling.

Using a sector analysis approach, one study reviewed several economic factors. One of the most significant elements studied was that of unemployment in the state of Michigan. Popular opinion among advocates maintains that legalized casino gambling will bring jobs to depressed areas. However, a computational study of the empirical data in this arena paints a rather different picture.

In fact, the study suggests, the introduction of casino gambling has been relatively innocuous in mitigating high unemployment rates in certain sections of that state. Unemployment rates remained static in times of economic stagnancy, and moved downward in boom times, in both areas with casinos and without (Koo, 2007).

This analytical work serves as an illustration of the usefulness of a sector analysis. In this case, a popular theory (that legalized gambling generates much-needed jobs in areas experiencing poor fiscal health) that serves as a rallying cry for advocates is proven invalid in the areas under study.

Studying Consumer Behavior

The ever-changing global economy logically creates questions among economists as to how short- and long-term trends affect consumer behavior. In one arena, the increase in liberalized economies has created diversified industrial bases as well as higher incomes. Still, if incomes are higher, how does this change affect demand and consumption? In a similar

vein, with greater wealth across demographic strata, what impact does this trend have on price?

One study, offered by Ray Barrell and Philip Davis, analyzes the impact of economic liberalization on consumption among the United States, Germany, the United Kingdom, France, Japan, Canada and Sweden. Using empirical data models that center on changes to wealth and income, credit restraints and other reductions in liquidity, interest rates and, of course, pricing, the authors find that economic liberalization, and in particular, the removal of fiscal restraints, does have a significant impact on consumption. In fact, the study shows, in a general sense, that removal of those liquidity constraints helps bolster individual wealth and reduces elasticity (Barrell, 2007).

In this case, the methodology used depended not on preestablished theoretical frameworks, as such models disregarded certain elements of an economy that can be a factor in economic development. By focusing on a wide range of components (such as interest rates) and providing individual models of similar but separate economic systems (for example, not combining data from American and Swedish systemic conditions), the authors were able to locate certain truths about the relationships between liberalization and consumer behavior.

Finding Chaos in the Order

The study described above raises another interesting arena in which economic computational methods can prove most useful. In the previous examples, I have demonstrated how computational methods for economics can be used to prove or disprove certain theoretical conclusions. In the following example, however, it becomes clear that theory is slower to appreciate certain trends in economics than is empirical application. Thus, these computational methods can be employed in reverse, bringing empirical data back to the theoretical side of macroeconomics and helping spur the development of new, more updated hypotheses.

In the course of studying the nexus between supply and demand and pricing, there are a number of variables that exist that may play "x-factor" in the establishment of equilibrium in a particular system. In fact, not every market operates exactly the same in a "real-world" setting. At the theoretical level, market behavior is often analyzed under a similar set of "rules," parameters, and formulae. When one takes into account empirical data, however, certain external and previously unanticipated elements can cloud the "clean" model found in a theoretical framework, much in the way atmospheric conditions can impact an experiment once it is removed from the laboratory.

One analysis of monetary policy takes issue with an oversimplified view by theoretical economists that the focal point of fiscal policy should be the relationship between supply and demand and, at the center of that relationship, the establishment of equilibrium. However, there are variables that play a significant role in this general relationship and that may cause unanticipated anomalies within certain models. Among these variables are such factors as floating exchange rates and stock returns. The authors correctly assess that, in light of the inconsistencies that arise when utilizing conventional modeling to analyze certain free markets, a broader and more "outside the box" approach is necessary. Such an action can help foster better modeling at an academic level and, as a result, provide better data-collection methodologies:

[Once] one leaves the narrow preserve of conventional macroeconomics there is mounting evidence that the standard competitive general equilibrium model ... fails to explain [well-documented] and important anomalies in the financial economics area. [Economists] studying the macroeconomy should examine the implications of non-standard preferences ... and staunchly defend [resulting] models if they prove to have empirical content on a par with rival models (Cuthbertson, 2007).

Such approaches may concurrently aid modeling as well as establishing effective monetary policy.

Cost Benefit Analyses

When a development project, such as the construction of a roadway, rehabilitation of an existing building, or even the construction of an industrial site, is being considered, it is critical to conduct another form of computational economic analysis. There are a number of methods that can be utilized, including economic impact assessments, life cycle cost analysis, and a cost-benefit analysis. Each weighs the potential benefits against the risks involved in a major undertaking such as a large-scale project.

The first of these options is the economic impact assessment (EIA), which entails studying the effect

Aerial view of Giants Stadium. (Courtesy of Flickr User Dsearls CC BY-SA 2.0 via Wikimedia Commons)

of the project on surrounding infrastructure, systems, and people. The second, a life cycle cost analysis, examines the expected costs of the project over the entire life of the project. The third, the benefit-cost analysis, examines the costs associated with the investment in direct comparison to the long-term expenses as well as the goal of the project itself (Gabler, 2004).

Any major construction project raises eyebrows. However, the construction of a sports stadium tends to cause even more public scrutiny, as taxpayers are usually wary of using public funds to finance a private development undertaking. In northern New Jersey, a $750 million redevelopment project proposal involving a new football stadium complex to replace the 30- year-old Giants Stadium has been approved. The road to that approval in 2005 was no easy one— an extensive, 35-page project summary was drafted and included a complex EIA. As of 2005 the cost-benefit analysis had yet to be formally conducted, which is much to the consternation of onlookers. One report suggested that, in the long-term, the loss of revenue to sporting events and concerts at the complex far outweigh any tax revenues (Mansnerus, 2005). Absent a thorough benefit-cost analysis and life cycle analysis, both of which had at the time of this study failed to be introduced by an unbiased source, the controversy surrounding this project would have likely continued until all questions were answered satisfactorily.

CONCLUSION

Between the realm of the theoretical study of economics and the "real-world" trends in an economic system are the methods used to study each. Computational methods for economic analysis help provide clarity and even veracity of academic hypotheses. Likewise, such methods can help economists formulate models by which to study empirical data.

In many situations, use of any of the linear, nonlinear, mathematical, or sector-specific models in computational analysis can help settle an issue that rests at the very core of a major economic trend. As is the case with the impact of globalization on demand and, ultimately, price equilibrium, empirical analysis of the individual factors that make up consumer behavior may fill in many of the holes that exist in the ever-evolving study of a global economy.

The computational methods employed to study economic systems can also be used to examine the effectiveness of a national investment program. As shown in this paper, such methodologies can be used to gauge the effectiveness of international aid and development investments. Such data can be critical for establishing long-lasting and mutually beneficial interstate relationships.

Furthermore, economic analysis employing these techniques may help provide evidence of critical trends within an issue area. As shown in the case of the issue of legalized gambling and casinos, the assertion by some that gaming will create jobs is not entirely valid when one takes into account many of the locales in which such gaming already takes place. While this evidence will likely not satisfy either conflicting party, the information it reveals is nonetheless critical and, most importantly, well-founded.

With the global environment establishing interstate linkages in ways and degrees never before seen in human history, the discipline of studying these systems is still quite new. The models that rest between the theoretical and empirical realms are therefore very useful to any researcher. In the case shown in this paper, the Keynesian approach of seeking to understand consumer behavior may benefit from the employment of the very computational methods discussed in this essay.

Computational methodologies for studying economics can also be useful in opening doors for theorists. As this essay has demonstrated, previously unanticipated factors and trends, uncovered with the study of empirical data, can be useful in developing new conceptual models. Hence, the flow of information between the theoretical and empirical arenas goes in both directions with the use of such computational methods. However, the world of analysis is not limited to the traditional approaches, particularly when new and exogenous empirical data (and the methods by which it is tracked) become manifest.

Finally, this paper shows the use of economic computational methods not only for the purposes of national and international policies, but also for the use of local activities. In the case of major construction projects such as the development of the Meadowlands in New Jersey, a series of evaluations of the project's effects on the region and its residents was not only important for the project's progress—it was required by local, state, and federal law.

Whether employed by theorists, policy makers, or developers, practical applications of the computational models and analytical devices can be used on all levels of economic assessment. The methods themselves are myriad—they range from general algorithms and formulae, to comprehensive state-level modeling, to virtually microscopic sector-based analyses. The results are equally extensive and necessary for truly understanding the systems that build and maintain a macroeconomy.

BIBLIOGRAPHY

Aldrich, E., Kung, H. (2017). "Computational methods for production-based asset pricing models with recursive utility." *Economic Research Initiative at Duke.*

Barrell, R. & Davis, P. (2007). "Financial liberalisation, consumption and wealth effects in seven OECD countries." *Scottish Journal of Political Economy, 54,* 254–267.

Bartlett, J. (1919). Familiar quotations. *Bartleby.com.* Retrieved from xlink:href="http://www.bartleby.com/br/100.html"

Brady, D. & Denniston, R. (2006). "Economic globalization, industrialization and deindustrialization in affluent democracies." *Social Forces, 85,* 297–329.

Cauchon, D. (2007, August 13). "Cities gamble on casinos for tax revenue." *USA Today (Online Edition).* Retrieved from xlink:href="http://www.usatoday.com/news/nation/2007-08-13-casinos%5fN.htm"

Chen, S., & Wang, S. G. (2011). "Emergent complexity in agent-based computational economics." *Journal of Economic Surveys, 25,* 527–546.

Cuthbertson, K. & Nietzsche, D. (2007). "Monetary policy and behavioural finance." *Journal of Economic Surveys, 21*, 935–969.

Dovern, J. & Nunnenkamp, P. (2007). "Aid and growth accelerations: An alternative approach to assessing the effectiveness of aid." *Kyklos, 60*, 359–383.

Gabler, E. (2004). "Economics of investment." *Roads and Bridges, 42*, 66.

Koo, J., Rosentraub, M. S., & Horn, A. "Rolling the dice? Casinos, tax revenues, and the social costs of gaming." *Journal of Urban Affairs, 29*, 367–381.

Lewis, S. C., Zamith, R., & Hermida, A. (2013). "Content analysis in an era of big data: A hybrid approach to computational and manual methods." *Journal of Broadcasting & Electronic Media, 57*, 34–52.

Mansnerus, L. (2005, April 23). "New Meadowlands stadium is approved for the Giants." *New York Times (Online Edition)*. Retrieved from xlink:href="http://www.nytimes.com/2005/04/23/nyregion/23giants.html"

Warner, A. G., & Caliskan-Demirag, O. (2011). "An agent-based computational economics approach to technology adoption timing and the emergence of dominant designs." *Journal of Business & Economics Research, 9*, 107–119.

SUGGESTED READING

Camilleri, D., Mollicon, P. & Gray, T.G.F. (2007). "Computational methods and experimental validation of welding distortion models." *Proceedings of the Institution of Mechanical Engineers—Part L—Journal of Materials: Design & Applications, 221*, 235–249.

Dillard, J. & Nissen, M. (2007). "Computational modeling of project organizations under stress." *Project Management Journal, 38*, 5–20.

Missaglia, M. (2006). "Dynamic general equilibrium modeling. Computational methods and applications." *Journal of Economics, 88*, 207–209.

Poe, G.L., Giraud, K.L. & Loomis, J.B. (2005). "Computational methods for measuring the difference of empirical distributions." *American Journal of Agricultural Economics, 87*, 353–365.

—Michael P. Auerbach

D

DEVELOPMENT OF NATIONS IN THE GLOBAL ECONOMY

ABSTRACT

This paper will focus on how people react to the different types of innovations used in developing countries as they attempt to develop in ways that allow them to compete on a global basis. Many have had the perception that the international community should be doing more to close the gap between developed and developing countries since the aid per capita to developing countries has fallen by 6 percent since its peak in 2010 (OECD, 2013). One could argue that developing countries are at a disadvantage and that the scales are tipped against them. To address the different types of inequities that may arise, those in the international business arena must develop policies and procedures that address these issues and create a sense of fairness for everyone involved. Issues such as business ethics, world viewpoint, corporate social responsibility, and trade liberalization will be discussed to develop a framework for how developing countries can be positioned to compete with established countries.

OVERVIEW

According to the 1999 World Development Report, there was a growing gap in gross domestic product (GDP) between the developed and less developed countries (World Bank, 1999); however, more recent data suggests that, overall, this gap is shrinking, especially given the rapid economic development of China, India, South Korea, and other Asian countries (World Bank, 2013). Many had the perception that the international community should be doing more to close the gap since the aid per capita to developing countries was reduced by one-third in the 1990s; aid rose in the early part of the 2000s, but has shrunk since 2010 (OECD, 2013). "As developing countries made strides to open their economies and expand their exports, they were faced with significant trade barriers" and no aid or trade (Stiglitz, 2000).

"To many in the developing world, trade policy in the more advanced countries seems to be more a matter of self-interest than of general principle" (Stiglitz, 2000, p. 438). It appears that good economic analysis is used solely in favor of the advanced countries to support their self-interests. Given the number of opportunities for developing countries to be placed at a disadvantage, supporters of trade liberalization argue that standard economic analysis would benefit a developing country. Common economic theory reasons that losses in one sector will be gained in another sector (i.e., job loss in one sector will be offset by job creation in another sector). However, this relies on the assumption that the markets are functioning properly, which is not always the case. As a result, the anticipated jobs may not be created in another sector, and the process becomes unbalanced. When situations such as this arise, supporters of trade liberalization must be prepared to respond to the resultant challenges.

One could argue that developing countries are at a disadvantage and that the scales are tipped against them. To address the different types of inequities that may arise, those in the international business arena must develop policies and procedures that address these issues and create a sense of fairness for everyone involved. Many believe that there should

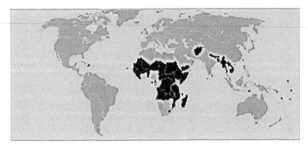

The Least Developed Countries as designated by the United Nations in 2008 are darkened in this chart. (Courtesy of Gabbe & Canuckguy via Wikimedia Commons)

be standards for social responsibility and ethics to make sure that the developing countries are not exploited. Having a formal global approach to these types of challenges can ensure a sense of fairness for everyone involved in the process.

Representational Approaches

Khan (2007) introduced a conceptual framework that identified four representational approaches to understanding how social inequities surface in developing countries as they attempt to venture into international business. When the model was created, it was established that there are many parties involved in the process. Since representation ranged from local workers to international mass media organizations, each party was defined in terms of geography. The two categories introduced are locals and foreigners. Locals were defined as individuals or entities that are primarily located in the developing countries. Locals are very diverse and have different perspectives and interests. Individuals falling into the "foreign" category are those that do not fit into the local category. Significant players in the foreign group would include international businesses that are directly involved in specific situations, and their critics.

Four Approaches to International Business

Both of these groups are considered to be "representers" as they work to resolve issues that arise. Each situation is analyzed and evaluated according to the representers' role in the situation and the worldview of the situation. The approaches attempt to conceptualize the representation of the ethical issues involving international business in the developing world. The four different approaches are:

Approach 1 (No-speak): Foreigners are the representers, and the issue is expressed from a foreign world viewpoint. The local residents have no voice, and they have no input into the worldview. Local worldviews have no place in the development of issues, and the local experience is not considered relevant in social equity issues. Most international business research follows this approach (i.e., Hofstede's *Culture's Consequence*).

Approach 2 (Us-speak): The commonality between this approach and the first approach is that the foreigners are the representers. However, the difference is that the worldview incorporates the local experience. This approach attempts to represent local realities (local view) in a way that the local inhabitants understand the situation. In many instances, the representer places himself in the local's position and attempts to articulate the viewpoint based on the local's perspective.

Approach 3 (Same-speak): The locals are the representers, and the worldview is the same as the foreigner's perception. Locals represent themselves based on one or more worldviews that originate from the West (i.e., modernism, post-structuralism, secular nationalism). Many of the most influential representations of ethical issues that affect international business in developing countries are based on this approach.

Approach 4 (Other-speak): Locals are the representers, and international business issues are explained in the context of local viewpoints. When evaluating this approach, representation is being explained by locals using local concepts.

These approaches provide an explanation as to how foreigners and locals perceive the severity of social issues; an important element to the interactions in the business community. Multinational corporations have to understand the culture and values of the countries in which they do business. Otherwise, the corporation may suffer as a result of conflict on social and business ethics issues. There has to be some sense of social responsibility on the part of the multinational corporation.

APPLICATION

Developing Social Responsibility

According to Griesse (2007), "the introduction of new agricultural biotechnologies has raised a number of concerns regarding the safety of the product for human or animal consumption, the affects the product may have on the environment, the question of patenting living organisms and the power large corporations have over cultivation and food supply" (p. 103). These concerns have created much debate and division in the scientific research field as well as the international business community when it comes to deciding on the best way to feed the growing world

In an effort to reduce corn stem-borer infestations, corporate and public researchers partner to develop local (transgenic) Bt (Bacillus thuringiensis) corn varieties suitable for Kenya. (Courtesy of Dave Hoisington/CIMMYT CC BY 2.5 via Wikimedia Commons)

population. In addition, many believe that these new technologies force the world to reevaluate its views on social responsibility. Some of the key questions that need to be addressed include the following:

- What is the role and responsibility of corporations when laws do not address the issues of the new technologies?
- What are the procedures that governments, scientists, and corporations should follow when developing and approving new technologies?
- What are the new issues that arise as a result of new technologies?
- Is there a difference in how foreigners and locals view and make use of the new technologies?

Historical Stages of International Business Practices
In order to satisfy worldview concerns on socially responsible issues, many organizations have implemented policies that address the concerns. This position was seen as a survival technique. Many corporations have realized that if they did not change their practices, they would be out of business. Sandman (1990) provides an explanation of how corporations have transformed the way they do business. In his opinion, there have been three historical stages.

1. Stonewall Stage — Corporations ignore any responsibility for what happens in a community as a result of their actions.

2. Missionary Period — There is an effort to gain favor in the community by promoting the social and environmental benefits of the product.

3. Dialogue Stage — There is awareness that the local community and worldview may have valid concerns. The corporation opens lines of communication with the public and initiates a process that will repair any damage that has tarnished its image.

Further analysis was conducted by Swift and Zadik (2002) when they defined the three generations of corporate business responsibility. Their work was based on an evaluation of several organizations in Western Europe. Every organization starts at the same base stage where the primary concern is to be in compliance with established laws and regulations. When an organization decides to move to the first generation of corporate social responsibility (CSR), it implements practices and policies that will protect the organization from risks and crises. Actions are reactive as the organization takes a defensive position based on a risk management philosophy.

However, when the organization is ready to move to the second generation of CSR, there is a sense of wanting to be proactively responsible for their actions. The organizations start to see a favorable relationship between social and environmental responsibility and financial gain. By incorporating CSR into their business, there is an opportunity to add value to the product or service, improve the corporate image in the local community, and increase the corporation's ability to attract and retain a qualified workforce (Griesse, 2007). At this stage, there is a systematic approach to integrating CSR throughout all of the business operations.

The third generation is symbolized by the creation of partnership and communication between various stakeholders, especially at the international level. At this stage, corporate social responsibility is no longer an organizational issue. Rather, there is a desire to establish relationships that benefit everyone as the world economy strives for global development. "Social responsibility is seen as part of the very fabric of the economy, in which non-governmental organizations (NGOs), unions, different levels of government, community organizations, industry, and business form a system that strengthens the country's competitive edge" (Griesse, 2007, p. 104).

E.I. DuPont & GMOs in Brazil

The perspectives that have been introduced by the researchers provide a foundation and understanding as to how organizations have evolved over time in their realization of how being socially responsible benefits the corporation and the world. The next section of the application segment will provide an overview of how one organization handled a topic dealing with social responsibility in a host country. The review will detail how E. I. DuPont handled the concern regarding genetically modified organisms (GMOs) in Brazil, one of the largest agricultural countries in the world.

The commercialization of GMOs in Brazil dates back to 1998 when Monsanto received approval for its GM seed, "Roundup Ready." However, the Brazilian Institute for Consumer Defense filed a suit against the release of the product. In addition, the opposition Workers' Party voiced their concern about the use of GM seeds. Many groups joined together to fight the commercialization and cultivation of GM seeds, and they developed arguments to support their position. Some of their concerns included the following:

- Transgenic plants could pose health risks that have not been studied.
- Transnational organizations have not provided sufficient information on their products.
- There are not technical regulations for the secure use of these products.
- GM seeds represent a new form of technology and can have unknown consequences.

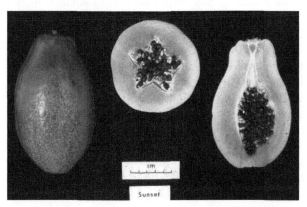

3 views of the Sunset papaya cultivar, which was genetically modified to create the SunUp cultivar, resistant to PRSV. Papayas are exported by Brazil. (Courtesy of Wikimedia Commons)

However, there are two sides to a story and there was a faction that supported the use of GM seeds. Some of the arguments provided by the proponents were the following:

- The exaggeration of risks for transgenic plants was presented by ecologists and activists. Supporters saw these groups as exploiting emotionalism and irrational perspectives in order to validate their position.
- GM seed crops use fewer toxic materials.
- GM crops mean lower costs for farmers because they do not require as many agrochemicals.
- GM crops may offer special dietary benefits.
- GM crops could be used in the production of plastics, which would reduce the need to rely on petroleum.
- Brazil's ability to compete in a global economy would be hindered if the use of advanced technology was minimized.

The Case of DuPont

DuPont is an established corporation and has been around for more than 200 years. The corporation has a history of trying to do the right thing and giving the perception that it is a responsible company. DuPont has invested time, effort, and money in implementing business policies that focus on social and environmental issues. In addition, the organization recognizes that a positive public image in the local community is important.

DuPont has had a presence in the Brazilian community since 1937, and it began work in the GMO field during the mid-1980s. However, Monsanto was the primary corporation fighting the battle for commercialization of GMOs. DuPont recognized the struggles that the organization was encountering and decided to implement policies that would address the concerns of the community. Some of the initiatives included the establishment of a Biotechnology Advisory Panel consisting of independent consultants from universities, nongovernmental organizations (NGOs) and the government sector of various countries, and partnership with major food and seed companies in forming the Conselho de Informacoes de Biotecnologia (CIB), Biotechnology Information Council.

These two strategies were proactive efforts of DuPont that aimed at maintaining its image as a socially responsible multinational corporation that recognizes the sensitivities and viewpoints of the host country. The purpose of the council was to diffuse scientific information on biotechnologies that would promote the advantages of GM technologies and lobby the government for the release of GM seeds (Guerrante, 2004). The purpose of the panel was to assess DuPont's social and environmental commitment as well as to provide guidance during the various phases of product development. DuPont's campaign was successful, and in 2008, Brazil allowed for GMOs to be used. Some of the recommendations that the panel has suggested to DuPont were to:

- make responsible statements when accidents and genetic transfer to wild plants occur;
- share plant genetic resources, especially in developing countries;
- develop biotechnology in developing countries that would benefit the poor;
- increase transparency and seek outside perspectives;
- use its influence to increase transparency and include external perspectives in other industries;
- provide access to scientific knowledge assessment;
- exercise the precautionary principle;
- examine how lessons learned can be applied to emerging issues; and
- continually work to identify new issues (DuPont, 2002).

VIEWPOINT

Innovation Championing Strategies

For economies to grow, there must be change. Unfortunately, all communities do not readily accept innovation (i.e., the biotechnology example). Many of the scenarios discussed in the DuPont case study focused on external groups who either supported or criticized the GM crops. However, multinational corporations should be concerned about internal reaction to change. Some organizations hire from the local community, and these employees may be aligned with the views of their country. Therefore, there may be a need to create innovative championing strategies in order to get buy-in.

Shane, Venkataraman, and MacMillian (1995) have emphasized the necessity of championing strategies. As corporations continue to explore global opportunities, managers will need to "ensure that the process of innovation championing occurs in culturally appropriate ways in each of their national subsidiaries" (p. 948). A champion is a person who promotes the development of new ideas within an organization. There is a need for championing when there is resistance to change. Based on the example provided in the application section, multinational corporations may be required to promote new initiatives to their workforce. "Senior managers will be required to understand if and how national cultural values influence the championing behavior of their subordinates in different countries around the world" (Shane, Venkataraman, and MacMillan, 1995, p. 932).

CONCLUSION

Trade liberalization is an asset to developing countries and the world. However, it must be "balanced in agenda, process, and outcomes, including not only sectors in which developed countries have a comparative advantage, like financial services, but also those in which developing countries have a special interest, like agriculture and construction services" (Stiglitz, 2000, p. 437). One could argue that developing countries are at a disadvantage and that the scales are tipped against them. To combat the different types of inequities that may arise, those in the international business arena must develop policies and procedures that address these issues and create a sense of fairness for everyone involved.

Khan (2007) introduced a conceptual framework that identified four representational approaches to understanding how social inequities surface in developing countries as they attempt to venture into international business. The approaches provide an explanation as to how foreigners and locals perceive the severity of social issues, as this is important to interactions in the business community. To satisfy worldview concerns on socially responsible issues, many organizations have implemented policies that address these concerns. This position was seen as a survival technique. DuPont utilized this approach as it positioned itself to continue work in the GMO field and appease the local Brazilian community.

BIBLIOGRAPHY

DuPont. (2002). "Biotechnology advisory panel report." Retrieved from "http://www.dupont.com/

biotech/images/difference/BiotechPanelReport.pdf"

Griesse, M. (2007). "Developing social responsibility: Biotechnology and the case of DuPont in Brazil." *Journal of Business Ethics, 73*, 103–118.

Khan, F. (2006). "Representational approaches matter." *Journal of Business Ethics, 73*, 77–89.

Organisation for Economic Cooperation and Development. (2013, Mar 4). "Aid to poor countries slips further as governments tighten budgets." *OECD.*

Sandman, P. (1990). "Addressing skepticism regarding responsible care." Retrieved June 7, 2007, from "http://www.psandman.com/articles/cma-care.htm"

Shane, S., Venkataraman, S., & MacMillan, I. (1995). "Cultural differences in innovation championing strategies." *Journal of Management, 21*, 931–952.

Stiglitz, J. (2000). "Two principles for the next round or, how to bring developing countries in from the cold." *World Economy, 23*, 437–455.

Swift, T., & Zadek, S. (2002). "Corporate responsibility and the competitive advantage of nations." Retrieved June 7, 2007, from http://www.ibd-.com.br/default.asp.

Tullo, A. H. (2010). "Global top 50." (cover story). *Chemical & Engineering News 88*, 13–16.

World Bank (1999). "World development report 1999-2000: Entering the 21st century." Washington, D.C.: World Bank.

World Bank. (2013). "World development indicators, 2013." Retrieved from "http://data.worldbank.org/sites/default/files/wdi-2013-ch4.pdf"

SUGGESTED READING

Al-khatib, J., Rawwas, M., & Swaidan, Z. (2005). "The ethical challenges of global business-to-business negotiations: An empirical investigation of developing countries' marketing managers." *Journal of Marketing Theory & Practice, 12*, 46–60.

Barichello, R., McCalla, A., & Valdes, A. (2003). "Developing countries and the world trade organization negotiations." *American Journal of Agricultural Economics, 85*, 674–678.

Beschomer, T., & Muller, M. (2007). "Social standards: Toward an active ethical involvement of business in developing countries." *Journal of Business Ethics, 73*, 11–20.

Devadoss, S. (2006). "Why do developing countries resist global trade agreements?" *Journal of International Trade & Economic Development, 15*, 191–208.

Hertel, T., & Martin, W. (2000). "Liberalizing agriculture and manufactures in a millennium round: Implications for developing countries." *World Economy, 23*, 455–469.

Kessler, F. (2011). "The global financial crisis 2007 fallout: Changing paradigms on trade and development." *Journal of International Business, 3/4(2/1)*, 29–42.

Volkema, R., & Fleury, M. (2002). "Alternative negotiating conditions and the choice of negotiation tactics: A cross-cultural comparison." *Journal of Business Ethics, 36*, 381–398.

—Marie Gould

E

E-Commerce

ABSTRACT

E-commerce is the process of conducting business online through sales transactions and information exchange. There are a number of applications of e-commerce, including online retailing and electronic markets, and online auctions. E-commerce offers many benefits to businesses, including the widening of its marketplace and the reduction of operating costs. E-commerce is often combined with other channels as part of a business's marketing and sales efforts. As with any marketing and sales efforts, careful consideration needs to be given regarding how to best present the business on its website. There are a number of considerations to be taken into account in order to develop a website that will help the organization maximize the effectiveness of its e-commerce efforts.

OVERVIEW

Arguably, the primary goal of information technology and systems is the ability to transmit large amounts of data and information between organizations and individuals quickly and accurately. In addition, information systems often provide the means to automate previously labor-intensive tasks and to add convenience. For example, in many cases, information technology can significantly reduce the time, effort, and expense involved in developing written documents. Similarly, one no longer has to physically go to a store and search aisles for products to purchase. With the advent of information technology, customers frequently have the opportunity to do these tasks electronically by shopping online using e-commerce retailers.

E-commerce is the process of conducting business online through sales transactions and information exchange. Although the term e-commerce is sometimes used interchangeably with e-business, it is actually one of the functions of e-business. In addition to shopping functions, e-business is the process of buying and selling goods or services electronically rather than through conventional means, along with the support activities and transactions necessary to do these tasks.

Online Retailing and Electronic Storefronts. Nearly all businesses have established an online presence. One of the most common applications of e-commerce is online retailing. In this scenario, the organization's home page is the electronic equivalent of a brick-and-mortar storefront, and the various web pages being the electronic equivalent of the aisles of a traditional store. Typically, e-commerce websites allow customers to browse "the aisles" by having links to various categories of products and to search for specific items by various characteristics such as keywords, title, product name, item number, or model number so that they can go directly to a specific product using a search engine.

Online Auctions. E-commerce is not only the electronic equivalent of a physical retail store or mall,

The headquarters of eBay in San Jose, California. (Courtesy of Coolcaesar at English Wikipedia CC-BY-SA-3.0 via Wikimedia Commons)

however. Another popular approach to e-commerce is through online auctions. This approach to e-commerce allows customers to determine the price of products rather than paying a fixed, predetermined amount. There are three online approaches to auctions. In the forward auction, shoppers bid on an item and the seller takes the highest offer. In the reverse auction, bidders list their product or service needs and the maximum they are willing to pay for the product or service. Sellers then bid against each other in an attempt to offer the product or service at the lowest price. The third approach to online auctions is the Dutch auction. In this approach, an item is offered online at a high opening price. At a predetermined interval, if no one has purchased the item, the price is lowered. This continues until someone is willing to purchase the item at the price offered.

Benefits of E-Commerce. E-commerce offers many benefits to businesses. First, e-commerce enables a business to extend its geographic reach to customers around the globe. For example, through e-commerce, customers no longer have to physically go to a brick-and-mortar store to purchase software. Not only can most software be sold over the Internet, but in many cases, it can be downloaded directly from the Internet, thereby eliminating the costs not only of delivery but also of packaging and storing the product. However, even when a product needs to be physically delivered via a transportation carrier, e-commerce can facilitate selling to a larger market. E-commerce also can increase the speed at which transactions can take place. Transaction times are reduced because customers no longer have to wait in line to be served but can complete their own transactions over a secure network simultaneously with other shoppers. Although the transaction speed is irrelevant if the customer still has to wait for delivery of those items that are not available locally, e-commerce can save time because the customer does not physically have to go from store to store to locate an item. Similarly, e-commerce can also increase productivity. Customers can lessen the time needed to find similar products and compare features and prices by doing their research online. This ability means that the customer can make a better-informed decision but also make such decisions in a timelier manner, thereby helping the business's cash flow and saving the customer time.

Incorporating E-Commerce into Business Strategy. As all too many small business owners learned the hard way after the dot-com bubble burst in 2001, e-commerce is not a passive tool that magically brings in business and profits. Those businesses that were able to survive beyond the early 2000s were those that had used the Internet as only one of many marketing channels and were able to fall back on other channels to market and sell their products and services. One of the lessons learned from the bursting of the dot-com bubble is that e-commerce works best when it is only an extension of one's business, not the sole channel. Indeed, in the 2010s, a number of businesses that began as online-only retailers began opening brick-and-mortar stores as well. The use of e-commerce is not an all-or-nothing proposition. Businesses can—and in many cases must—have both traditional capabilities as well as e-commerce capabilities. Nevertheless, in the 2010s, an increasing number of online-only businesses have found success, staying power, and profitability.

There are a number of different ways that businesses can incorporate e-commerce into their strategy. On one end of the spectrum is a primarily off-line strategy with a primary channel that is off-line, and online marketing efforts playing only a supporting role. In this approach, the business may publish a website that provides customers with information about store hours and locations, describes the range of products that are sold, or offers customer-service options. For example, grocery stores may allow customers to go online to read the weekly sales flyer, send comments to the store or corporate manager, or find directions to various store locations. However, to do e-commerce, the business must also allow customers to purchase items online. To do this, the off-line-focused strategy is often used when a sophisticated distribution system is needed to provide goods, personal consultation services can only be done in person, or there are contractual restrictions among the channel partners that prohibit more online involvement. Other organizations can primarily use the online channel for their marketing efforts, and some businesses only do business online and use traditional marketing methods (television and print advertisements; infomercials; sales calls) to point the customer to their website. This strategy can allow both the business and the customer to bypass the "middleman" or to take advantage of the lower costs associated with the online channel, which obviates the need for the overhead associated with leasing and maintaining a physical retail store.

Physical Resources and E-Commerce. Another lesson to be learned from the dot-com bubble was that it is sometimes best to devote as few physical resources to e-commerce as possible. The fact that the purchasing transaction is being conducted electronically does not obviate the need for the rest of the supply chain. Products still need to be produced, stored, transported, and delivered to the customer. When the organization already has a brick-and-mortar support infrastructure in place, the potential failure of its e-commerce activities to meet the anticipated volume of business or profits will not affect its overall ability to conduct business. Similarly, it has been found that it is beneficial to work with other organizations already successfully working in e-commerce so that one does not have to invest in duplicate e-commerce infrastructure, although if e-commerce becomes a major revenue source for a

Target Corporation headquarters in Minneapolis, Minnesota. (Courtesy of 2008-0712-MPLS-panorama.JPG: Bobak Ha'Eri derivative work: Xnatedawgx CC-BY-SA-3.0 via Wikimedia Commons)

business, it may no longer be worthwhile to allow a partner to take a cut of the profits. For example, when Target first ventured into the e-commerce marketplace in 2001, it partnered with online retail giant Amazon, but as Target's online sales grew, it began developing an e-commerce platform of its own, finally parting ways with Amazon in 2011.

Website Design. To be an effective tool for conducting e-commerce, a website must be well designed. This means that it is attractive and otherwise memorable so that customers will think of that site and the organization when they again need a similar product or service. In addition, the website must be user friendly, that is, easy and intuitive for the customer to use. Most consumers who use the Internet for e-commerce have experienced websites that are difficult to navigate, do not provide all the necessary information needed to make a transaction, or that attempt to force the consumer to provide personal information that is not necessary to the transaction. When such qualities become egregious, consumers are unlikely to complete a transaction or return to the site in the future. Without the loyalty of repeat customers, the e-commerce venture is unlikely to be a success. There are a number of considerations to be taken into account when developing a website for e-commerce purposes.

Development of a Strategic Plan. First, one must consider the place of e-commerce within the greater strategic plan for the business and the strategy of the electronic channel specifically. Success in business—whether it is through conventional or electronic means—must be based on a well-developed strategy. This strategy is a plan of action to help the organization reach its goals and objectives. Strategic planning is the process that helps the organization determine what goals to set and how they are to reach them. Through strategic planning, the organization determines and articulates its long-term goals and develops a plan to use its resources—including materials, equipment and technology, and personnel—in reaching these goals. The resultant business plan summarizes the operational and financial objectives of the organization and is supported by detailed plans and budgets to show how these objectives will be achieved over time. The business plan also analyzes the risk involved in reaching these goals. In business terms, risk can be defined as the quantifiable probability that a financial investment's actual return will be lower than expected. Higher risks mean both a greater probability of loss as well as the possibility of a concomitant greater return on investment.

In addition to the objectives or end goals that the organization is trying to reach, strategic planning should also consider what resources are necessary to accomplish these. This should include the financial resources of the organization such as capital structure, new issues of common stock, cash flow, working capital needed, dividend payments, and collection periods. In addition, the strategic planning process also needs to give consideration to the resources necessary to accomplish the other objectives, including costs of maintaining a web presence, physical infrastructure, employees needed, and so forth.

Website Content and Design. Once a strategic plan has been developed, the next step is for the organization to flesh out its concept and design a website. Part of this process is the choice of a domain name. This is a unique, easily understood identifier for a set of addresses on a network. Having a domain name that is easily remembered and associated with the company's name can help customers find the company's website in the future for additional transactions. Domain names that are not closely associated with the organization and its products, however, are less likely to be remembered and revisited.

The design of the website must also take into consideration the image that the business wishes to project.

Toys "R" Us Express store at the Oaks Mall, Gainesville, Alachua County, Florida. Toys "R" Us is one of many businesses that has a successful Web Site presence. (Courtesy of Michael Rivera CC BY-SA 4.0 via Wikimedia Commons)

Branding is just as important for e-commerce as it is for conventional marketing efforts. For example, the design of a website for a high-end consulting firm would undoubtedly be different from the design of a website for a firm that is selling toys, not only in content but also in terms of layout and other design features. The consulting firm, for example, might want to include a video message from its president, use a subdued color palette that conveys the serious nature of the services offered, and include a significant amount of white space or quotes from satisfied customers. The website for the toy company, however, might include animation, bright colors that appeal to children and convey the notion of fun, and use a lot of color pictures of toys. An organization needs to work closely with its web designer to develop a concept that will help convey what kind of organization it is. No matter the type of product or service offered by the website, consideration needs to be given to the inclusion of appropriate customer service features. Websites can collect data for use in customer relationship management, including organizing, tracking, and analyzing customer data and buying patterns. As mentioned above, e-commerce websites also need to be user-friendly, allowing customers to easily navigate the site and find the information that they need. Although this often means the inclusion of search engine capabilities, it also means providing a way for customers or prospective customers to contact the business to get the information that they need. This can be done by providing contact information for phone and mail, having a pop-up email message form or an online form to fill out to submit questions, or online chat feature with customer service representatives.

BIBLIOGRAPHY

Abingdon, D. (2006). "Winning with E-commerce." In D. Abingdon (ed.), *Out of the box marketing* (pp. 110–130). London: Thorogood Publishing.

Chuan-Lin Kang. (2013). "Product virtuality and firms' performance in e-commerce: a transaction cost approach." *Journal of International Management Studies, 8,* 68–76.

Einav, L., Levin, J., Popov, I., & Sundaresan, N. (2014). "Growth, adoption, and use of mobile e-commerce." *American Economic Review, 104,* 489–494.

Hogan, S. M., & Ivey, J. S. (2014). "What every entrepreneur should know about taxation of internet commerce." *Journal of Internet Law, 18,* 13–19.

Hortaçsu, A., & Syverson, C. (2015). "The ongoing evolution of US retail: A format tug-of-war." *Journal of Economic Perspectives, 29*(4), 89–112.

Lucas, H. C. Jr. (2005). *Information technology: Strategic decision making for managers.* New York: John Wiley and Sons.

Martinez, M. J. (2002). "A cautious look at e-commerce." In M. J. Martinez (ed.), *Practical tech for your business: Using today's technology to make your business more efficient, creative and flexible* (pp. 111–138). Washington, DC: Kiplinger Books.

Mikitani, H. (2013). "Rakuten's CEO on humanizing e-commerce." *Harvard Business Review, 91,* 47–50.

Pascaly, A. (2016). Changes on the horizon: Sales and use tax in the e-commerce era. *Computer & Internet Lawyer, 33*(12), 5–8.

Perrigot, R., & Penard, T. (2013). "Determinants of e-commerce strategy in franchising: a resource-based view." *International Journal of Electronic Commerce, 17,* 109–130.

Senn, J. A. (2004). *Information technology: Principles, practices, opportunities* (3rd ed.). Upper Saddle River, NJ: Pearson/Prentice Hall.

Sherman, A. J. (2002). "Growth through E-commerce and internet-driven strategies." In A. J. Sherman (ed.), *Fast-track business growth: Smart strategies to grow without getting derailed* (pp. 301–337). Washington, DC: Kiplinger Books.

Turban, E., Outland, J., King, D., Lee, J., Liang, T., Turban, D. (2017). "Intelligent (Smart) E-Commerce." *Electronic Commerce 2018,* 249–283.

SUGGESTED READING

Black, G. S. (2007). "Consumer demographics and geographics: Determinants of retail success for on-line auctions." *Journal of Targeting, Measurement & Analysis for Marketing, 15,* 93–102.

Dou, W. & Krishnamurthy, S. (2007). "Using brand websites to build brands online: A product versus service brand comparison." *Journal of Advertising Research, 47,* 193–206

Fang, Y., Qureshi, I., Sun, H., McCole, P., Ramsey, E., & Lim, K. H. (2014). "Trust, satisfaction, and on-line repurchase intention: The moderating role of perceived effectiveness of e-commerce institutional mechanisms." *MIS Quarterly, 38,* 407–427.

Gaile-Sarkane, E. (2007). "Impact of e-commerce on marketing development." *Economics & Management,* 356–362.

Reingold, J., & Wahba, P. (2014). "Where have all the shoppers gone?" *Fortune, 170*(4), 80–84.

Roman, S. (2007). "The ethics of online retailing: A scale development and validation from the consumers' perspective." *Journal of Business Ethics, 72,* 131–148.

Selko, A. (2016). "E-commerce drives the demand for logistics real estate." *Material Handling & Logistics, 71*(3), 27–28.

Yang, J. G. S. (2013). "Emerging issues in e-commerce taxation." *Journal of State Taxation, 31,* 15–44.

—*Ruth A. Wienclaw, PhD*

ECONOMETRICS

ABSTRACT

Econometrics can be defined as the application of mathematical statistics tools, and related techniques, to economic problems such as the analysis of economic data and the testing of economic theories and models. Although economists are not often able to collect primary experimental data, econometric tools are available that can readily be applied to secondary data, whether they are cross-sectional or time series in nature. In some ways, the analysis of this type of secondary data gives economists a better understanding of real-world phenomena and processes than would more controlled—but smaller in scope—experimental studies that allow for the manipulation of variables. The combination of secondary data and econometric data allow economists to develop and test empirical models to better understand economies and make forecasts.

Economics is a social science focusing on the creation, allocation, and utilization of goods and services; the distribution of wealth; and the allocation of resources as well as the theory and management of economic systems. One of the primary goals of economics is to understand and explain how economies work and how economic decisions are made. To advance understanding in these areas, economics is concerned with the theories, principles, and models of economic systems. As a result, many economists are engaged in the development, testing, and application of economic theories with the ultimate goal of being better able to understand and predict real-world behavior. To help in such endeavors, economists apply the scientific method to better parse the large quantities of data available and understand the processes that underlie their action.

Testable Theories

To help them better understand the nature and actions of economies, economists are concerned with the development of testable theories and concomitant models that are based on empirical evidence. As shown in Figure 1, the theory-building process begins with inductive reasoning in which inferences and general principles are drawn from specific observations or cases. This type of reasoning is a foundation of the scientific method and enables the development of testable hypotheses from particular facts and observations. For example, one might observe that employees with greater levels of training and education are more likely to have successful careers. However, unless one is able to operationally define these terms and articulate the exact theorized nature or the relationship between the variables of training/education and career success, this preliminary theory is nothing more than an opinion. Although it may be a considered opinion based on empirical evidence, untestable theories are of little use to science on their own. The theory-building process, therefore, goes on and builds on the work of the inductive reasoning process by applying deductive reasoning. This is a type of logical reasoning in which it is demonstrated that a conclusion must necessarily follow from a sequence

Inductive Process

Deductive Process

of premises, the first of which is a self-evident truth or agreed-upon data point or condition. Deductive reasoning is the foundation upon which predictions are drawn from general laws or theories.

Inductive & Deductive Reasoning

As shown in Figure 1, both inductive and deductive reasoning are essential to the theory-building process. Without careful observation of real-world phenomena and the development of these observations into testable theories and models, economics—or any science—cannot advance. Although one may be convinced, for example, that training and education are positively linked with eventual career success and salary, unless one can articulate a testable hypothesis and subject this preliminary theory to the rigors of the scientific method, this theory cannot be confirmed. For example, even in this simple example, there are many other variables that may influence career success such as job experience, intellectual capacity, native skills and abilities, and interest. Depending on their importance in determining career success, they, too, need to be included in the model.

Econometrics

To determine whether a model actually adequately and accurately reflects the phenomena and processes of the real world, it needs to be tested. Econometrics is a subfield of economics that is concerned with the application of quantitative tools to analyze economic data, validate theories, and test models of economic behavior. Econometrics is more than the mere measurement and capture of economic data as the word implies. Econometrics can be defined as the application of the tools of mathematical statistics and related techniques to economic problems, including the analysis of data and the testing of theories and models. Econometric tools are used to estimate economic relationships, test economic theories, evaluate economic policies, and forecast important macroeconomic variables (e.g., interest rates, inflation rates, gross domestic product). Econometric testing is an important component of economics because it helps economists determine the adequacy and accuracy of their theories. Without econometrics and the objective checks that it provides for the reasonableness of models, it would be difficult (if not impossible) to test the validity of economic models and their strength in forecasting real-world situations. The application of econometrics to test economic theories and models is an important part of the theory-building process for economics.

Secondary Analysis

In the physical sciences, one can often experimentally manipulate variables to establish the relationship between the independent variable and the dependent variable. For example, in metallurgy, one might be interested in the strength of a given metal after being subjected to various temperature ranges. In the social sciences—including economics—however, the direct manipulation of variables is often not possible not only for logistical reasons (e.g., difficulty collecting data, inability to manipulate variables), but for ethical ones as well. For example, not only would it be logistically impossible to deprive the people in a given country or economy from the education they need to succeed in a career, but such an action would also be considered morally and ethically reprehensible. Therefore, economists and other social scientists are often forced to rely on secondary analysis to collect data and test their theories. Secondary analysis is a further analysis of existing data that have typically been collected by a different researcher. The intent of secondary analysis is to use existing data to develop conclusions or knowledge in addition to or different from those resulting from the original analysis of the data. Secondary analysis may be qualitative or quantitative in nature and may be used by itself or combined with other research data to reach conclusions.

Types of Data

To develop and test practical models to be used in forecasting, most economists rely on two types of data: cross-sectional and time series. Cross-sectional data are quantifiable observations or measurements on a wide variety of variables during one time period rather than across time periods. For example, one might be interested in the training and education level of individuals from a representative cross-section of the general population in order to determine the relationship of training and education to career success. Therefore, one would look not only at assembly line workers in the garment industry, for example, but also across industries and along all career levels. Otherwise, the theory—even if validated—would only be applicable to assembly line workers in

the garment industry. The second type of data commonly used by economists is time series data. These are data gathered on one or more specific characteristics of interest over a period of time at intervals of regular length. These data series are used in business forecasting to examine patterns, trends, and cycles from the past in order to predict patterns, trends, and cycles in the future. Time series analysis typically involves observing and analyzing the patterns in historical data. These patterns are then extrapolated to forecast future behavior.

Random Sampling

Whether the economist uses cross-sectional or time series data, it is important that the data be randomly sampled. Rather than collecting data from a group from which it is easy to collect data but that has a low likelihood of representing the population that one wishes to test, one instead should take a sample of individuals from the larger group that reflects the characteristics of the larger population. A random sample is a sample that is chosen at random from the larger population with the assumption that such samples tend to reflect the characteristics of the larger population. The sample that is selected in this way can then be used in econometric analysis to represent a cross-section of the population as a whole. It is very important that sample selection allows one to draw a sample that is representative of the population and the characteristics in which one is interested. Otherwise, the sample may be biased and the results of the model will not represent the results that would have been obtained from the population in general.

APPLICATIONS

Data Patterns

One of the major uses of econometric methods is in the development and testing of models that can be used to forecast how behavior patterns will continue into the future. In this meaning of the term, models are a concise mathematical description of past events. To develop such models, time series are analyzed through several techniques including naïve methods, averaging, smoothing, regression analysis, and decomposition. These econometric techniques assume that the sequence of observations is a set of jointly distributed random variables. Through the analysis of time series data, one can study the structure of the correlation (i.e., the degree to which two events or variables are consistently related) over time to determine the appropriateness and usefulness of the model in predicting future behavior.

Stationarity, Trends, and Business Cycles

Time series data can take several distinctive forms. As shown in Figure 2a, sometimes data remain fairly constant over time and are said to be constant about the mean (an arithmetically derived measure of central tendency in which the sum of the values of all the data points is divided by the number of data points). This characteristic of the data is referred to as stationarity. If a process is assumed to be stationary, the probability of a given fluctuation in the process is assumed to be the same at any given point in time. If time series data do not demonstrate stationarity (see Figure 2b), however, in some cases they may be transformed to approximate stationarity so that they can be econometrically analyzed. Such approximations allow the development of models to help the economist better understand the underlying mechanisms in the data series. Time series data can also be influenced by variables for which there are specific causes or determiners (see Figure 2c). These deterministic variables include trends, business cycles, and seasonal fluctuations. Trends are persistent, underlying directions in which a factor or characteristic is moving in either the short, intermediate, or long term. Business cycles are continually recurring variations in total economic activity. Business cycles tend to occur across most sectors of the economy at the same time. Seasonal fluctuations are changes in activity that occur in a fairly regular annual pattern and which are related to the seasons of the year, the calendar, or holidays.

Modeling

Econometrics offers several approaches to modeling time series data. One of the primary tools for analyzing time series data and developing a mathematical model of real-world situations is regression analysis. This is a family of statistical techniques that allows the economist to develop a mathematical model for use in predicting one variable from the knowledge of another variable. Modeling of time series data can also be done through autoregression, a multiple regression technique in which future dependent variable values are estimated based on previous values of the variable. Autoregression takes advantage of the relationship of values to the values of previous time periods. Another family of techniques used in building models from time series data is smoothing techniques. One approach to smoothing time series data is the use of naïve forecasting models that assume that future outcomes are best predicted by the more recent data in the time series. Smoothing of time series data can also be done using averaging models. These techniques take into account data from several time periods, thereby neutralizing the problem of naïve models in which the forecast is overly sensitive to irregular fluctuations.

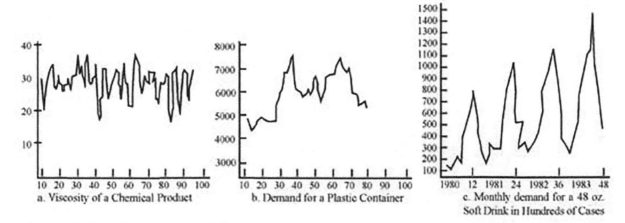

a. Viscosity of a Chemical Product

b. Demand for a Plastic Container

c. Monthly demand for a 48 oz. Soft Drink in Hundreds of Cases

(from Mastrangelo, Simpson, & Montgomery, p. 828)

Case Study: Analysis of Oil Supply

An example of the analysis of time series data is given in a study of the seasonality of non-OPEC oil supply by Jazayeri and Yahyai (2004). The cost of oil has far-reaching effects not only on the individual's pocketbook but also on the ability of businesses to support the travel of personnel and the transportation of goods. For this reason, it is vital to be able to accurately predict oil supply trends and changes. Although decisions about supply are coordinated between the member countries of OPEC (which provides approximately two-thirds of the world's oil supply), this is not true for non-OPEC countries. Therefore, analysis of this industry segment is particularly important for forecasting the supply of oil.

Time series data of oil supply in non-OPEC countries show the effects of seasonality, an important factor in understanding and predicting the availability of oil from these countries as well as for planning within these countries. Some of the factors affecting the seasonality include demand for oil, price of oil, stock levels, annual maintenance schedule at production facilities, the psychology and manipulation of the market, timely completion of development projects, as well as irregular and random factors including severe weather, floods, earthquakes, and strikes. Seasonal weather fluctuations and the concomitant changes in demands for heating oil, cooling systems, and vacation travel also affect the demand for oil.

Jazayeri and Yahyai performed an analysis of seasonality of non-OPEC supply in order to help improve the accuracy of short-term supply forecasts. In their analysis, the authors assumed that observed seasonality cycles are independent of other factors and that they will continue into the future. The authors then decomposed the data into the four components of

These workers are "fracking" in the Bakken Formation in North Dakota. Shale "fracking" in the U.S: is an important new challenge to OPEC market share. (Courtesy of Joshua Doubek CC BY-SA 3.0 via Wikimedia Commons)

trends, business cycles, seasonal fluctuations, and irregular or random variables to better understand the phenomena related to oil demand. Using the decomposition technique of Fourier spectral analysis, they found that non-OPEC supply follows a seasonal pattern that repeats annually irrespective of other trends. These results can be very useful for analysts forecasting oil supply across the various seasons of the year.

CONCLUSION

Econometrics is the application of the tools of mathematical statistics and related techniques to economic problems, including the analysis of data and the testing of theories and models. The use of such quantitative methods allows economics to be a science in which theories are empirically tested rather than an armchair philosophy whose theories cannot be empirically tested. Although it is rare that an economist can manipulate variables and collect primary data as is possible in many of the physical sciences, econometric tools are available that can readily be applied to secondary data whether they be cross-sectional or time series in nature. In some ways, the analysis of this type of secondary data gives economists a better understanding of real-world phenomena and processes than would more controlled—but smaller in scope—primary studies that allow for the manipulation of variables. The combination of secondary data and econometric data allow economists to

OPEC Conference delegates at Swissotel, Quito, Ecuador in December 2010. (Courtesy of Cancillería Ecuador CC BY-SA 2.0 via Wikimedia Commons)

develop and test empirical models to better understand economies and make forecasts.

BIBLIOGRAPHY

Bendic, V. (2013). "Econometric model of multiple equation of different shape." *Internal Auditing & Risk Management*, 8 (2), 211–218.

Black, K. (2006). *Business statistics for contemporary decision making* (4th ed.). New York: John Wiley and Sons.

Coleman, R. D. (2006). "What is econometrics?" Retrieved xlink:href="http://www.numeraire.com/download/WhatIsEconometrics.pdf"

Dosescu, T., & Raischi, C. (2011). "Another category of the stochastic dependence for econometric modeling of time series data." *Economic Computation & Economic Cybernetics Studies & Research*, 45 (4), 1–15.

Jazayeri, S. M. T. & Yahyai, A. (2004). "An analysis of seasonality of non-OPEC supply." *Maritime Policy & Management*, 30(3), 213–224.

Koop, G. (2009). *Analysis of economic data* (2nd ed.). New York: John Wiley and Sons.

Mastrangelo, C. M., Simpson, J. R., & Montgomery, D. C. (2001). "Time series analysis." In Saul I. Gass, S. I. & Harris, C. M. (eds.), *Encyclopedia of operations research and management science* (pp. 828-833). New York: Wiley.

McMillen, D. P. (2012). "Perspectives on spatial econometrics: Linear smoothing with structured models." *Journal of Regional Science*, 52 (2), 192–209.

Pindyck, R. S. & Rubinfeld, D. L. (1998). *Econometric models and economic forecasts*. Boston: Irwin/McGraw-Hill

Nazem, S. M. (1988). *Applied time series analysis for business and economic forecasting*. New York: Marcel Dekker.

Stock, J., Watson, M. (2017). "Twenty years of time series econometrics in ten pictures." *Journal of Economic Perspectives*, *31*, 2, 59–86.

Wooldridge, J. (2008). *Introductory econometrics: A modern approach*. Florence, KY: South-Western College Publishing.

SUGGESTED READING

Barelli, P. & De Abreu Pessôa, S. (2009). "On the general equilibrium costs of perfectly anticipated inflation." *Annals of Finance*, 5(2), 243–262.

Foroni, C., & Marcellino, M. (2013). *A survey of econometric methods for mixed-frequency data*. Norges Bank: Working Papers, (6), 1–42.

James, R. N. III. (2009). "An econometric analysis of household political giving in the USA." *Applied Economics Letters*, 16(5), 539–543.

Partridge, M. D., Boarnet, M., Brakman, S., & Ottaviano, G. (2012). "Introduction: Whither spatial econometrics?" *Journal of Regional Science*, 52 (2), 167–171.

Tabak, B. M. & Lima, E. J. A. (2009). "Market efficiency of Brazilian exchange rate: Evidence from variance ratio statistics and technical trading rules." *European Journal of Operational Research*, 194(3), 814–820.

—*Ruth A. Wienclaw*

ECONOMIC ANALYSIS OF LAW

ABSTRACT

This article will provide an overview of the economic analysis of law. The article will explain the basic concepts that are foundational to an economic analysis of legal theories, including efficiencies, positive law, normative law, and the Coase theorem. In addition, this article also explains how economic analyses have been integrated into the basic areas of the common law, including torts, contracts, and property law. Economic analysis of law is also critically important in government regulations that have been created and enforced to regulate financial markets. This article explains how government regulations affect antitrust enforcement, intellectual property protections, and oversight of the various financial markets. Finally, examples are provided that illustrate how an economic analysis of the law continues to shape our modern legal framework. These examples include discussions of distributive justice, taxation, and law enforcement within the criminal justice system.

OVERVIEW

Economic analysis of law is a method of incorporating ideas taken from the discipline of economics and melding them into considerations of legal theories and principles. Economic analysis of law generally involves both the study of human behavior in response to legal rules and the economic implications of that behavior and an evaluation of the economic and social effects of legal principles across the spectrum of socioeconomic and sociological classifications. While economic analysis of the law has become an increasingly influential field, it is not a modern school of thought. In the eighteenth century, economist and philosopher Adam Smith wrote about the economic effect of legislation on merchants and commerce. However, the study of economics in relation to laws that regulate non-market activities, such as due process or law enforcement, is a relatively new phenomenon.

Engraving of Adam Smith in 1805. (Courtesy of Library of Congress)

The inception of the modern school of law and economics is often considered to be the publication of two articles in the early 1960s by economists Ronald Coase and Guido Calabresi that revolutionized legal theory and laid the groundwork for many of the ideas that were developed in the following years. Coase and Calabresi, working independently from each other, published "The Problem of Social Cost" and "Some Thoughts on Risk Distribution and the Law of Torts," respectively. The movement gained even more traction with the publication of Richard A. Posner's "Economic Analysis of Law," which he wrote while a professor at the University of Chicago. Posner's work, which was followed by other academics and legal theorists associated with the University of Chicago, led to an era of economic principles being applied to all aspects of the law, which became dubbed the "Chicago School" of thought. This period of legal theory in particular examines the impact on the law when courts adopt economic efficiency as their guiding standard. More recently, the study of law and economics has essentially been divided into two classes—one that seeks to oppose the efficiency view of the Chicago School by maintaining that there is an ideological bias inherent in the application of economics to law, and the other that seeks to incorporate law and economics into a broader spectrum of interdisciplinary theories about law.

Economic analysis of law is usually divided into two subfields: positive and normative. Positive law and economics uses economic analysis to predict the effects of various legal rules. The positive school restricts itself to the study of the incentives produced by the legal system, largely because its adherents believe that efficient legal rules evolve naturally. On the other hand, the normative school, historically associated with the early contributions of the Yale school, sees the law as a tool for remedying "failures" that arise in the market. Thus, a positive economic analysis of liability as it relates to tort law would predict the effects of a strict liability rule as opposed to the effects of a negligence rule. Normative law and economics would make policy recommendations based on the economic consequences of various liability theories.

As these schools of thought have developed, the theories stemming from the economic analysis of law have become increasingly influential. Today, courts, legal professors, and even attorneys frequently apply economic principles to a range of potential legal outcomes to aid in the process of arriving at a more equitable outcome in a legal dispute or a greater understanding of the social costs of legal precedents. The following sections will provide a more detailed discussion of the basic concepts of the economic analysis of law.

Basic Concepts on the Economic Analysis of Law

The application of economics to law can help explain the consequences of laws and legal outcomes in terms of their social and economic impact. The economic analysis of law therefore uses economic methods and principles to evaluate how well laws and legal outcomes advance legal and moral objectives and the degree to which they also serve such social objectives as efficiency or fairness. Efficiency, as a social objective, is based upon the concept of allocative efficiency, or the allocation or distribution of resources according to their most valuable uses to the members of a society. In addition, economic analysis of law is usually divided into two subfields, positive and normative. Positive law and economics uses economic analysis to predict the effects of various legal rules, while the normative approach suggests ways to reform legal doctrines and institutions in light of a society's core beliefs. The following sections will further explain these concepts.

Efficiency

Efficiency in business or economic terms is often associated with the concept of accomplishing an outcome at the lowest possible cost. However, there are other concepts of efficiency that are also important in an economic analysis of the law. For instance, allocative efficiency is the study of whether an industry is producing the appropriate amount of a particular good or service. For instance, it is economically sensible for a company to produce an item as long as the value attributed to it by buyers exceeds the social cost of its production. This is because the demand for the item will likely ensure that the supply of items produced will be consumed, and thus the resources allocated to the production of the good will have been used efficiently. Companies will likely continue to produce the good as long as it is allocatively efficient, or economically advantageous, to do so, which is generally until the demand and supply for a good

Italian economist Vilfredo Pareto.

intersect. Any continued production of the good after that may meet with diminishing demand, and thus continued allocation of resources for the production of that good is no longer efficient.

Another concept of efficiency is Pareto optimality and Pareto superiority. Vilfredo Pareto, an Italian economist, studied the distributions of wealth in different countries. Pareto noted that, consistently, only a minority, or about 20 percent of the population, controlled the remaining majority, or approximately 80 percent, of a society's wealth and resources. This same distribution has been observed in other areas and has been termed the Pareto effect. For instance, the Pareto effect has been noted in the context of quality improvement, in that 80 percent of problems usually stem from 20 percent of the causes. This concept led to the development of two further theories of efficiency, which are that an allocation is Pareto superior if achieving it means at least one person is better off and no one is made worse off, and an allocation is

Pareto optimal if any movement from that allocation would make at least one person worse off.

Finally, a more recent version of efficiency is the Kaldor-Hicks, or wealth maximization, theory. In the context of legal analysis, the Kaldor-Hicks efficiency theory holds that in order for a law to be efficient, those individuals made better off by the law would have to be made sufficiently better off that they could compensate those who are made worse off. In other words, the Kaldor-Hicks criterion requires not that no one be made worse off by a change in allocation of resources, but only that the increase in value be sufficiently large that the losers can be fully compensated.

Positive Law

The positive approach to the economic analysis of law seeks to understand how the behavior of people is affected by incentives created by the law. This approach uses the analogy of the law as a type of pricing machine. The law "prices" various forms of human behavior through the use of fines, penalties, and other measures. These alter the balance of costs and benefits individuals face in deciding whether or not to engage in certain behavior.

For example, this approach might predict that implementing mandatory automobile safety legislation, such as requiring the use of seat belts, penetration resistant windshields, and other safety equipment, would be unlikely to reduce the number of driver

A sign reminding motorists in the state of California about the national "Click It or Ticket" seat belt education campaign. This sign was photographed on State Route 4 near Discovery Bay. (Courtesy of Coolcaesar CC-BY-SA-3.0 via Wikimedia Commons)

deaths. An economic analysis of such legislation might argue that such equipment—by reducing the probability of death following an accident and thus reducing the implicit "price" of speeding—would increase the incidence of speeding, or the amount of speeding drivers are willing to implicitly "purchase," and thus increase the number of accidents. In actuality, one study of accident statistics showed that the increase in the number of accidents just balanced out the decrease in driver deaths, resulting in no net decrease in driver deaths but a net increase in the number of pedestrian deaths from car accidents.

Normative Law

The normative approach to the economic analysis of law proposes an efficiency criterion for shaping the legal system based on wealth maximization. Wealth maximization is based upon the maximization of the sum of the "willingness to pay" exuded by a society's members. In an economic context, willingness to pay is a measurement of the value in dollars that people are willing to pay for something or the dollar amount that they demand to give it up. In the legal context, this approach asks how much each individual would be willing to pay to either get rid of or keep certain laws or rules.

For example, economists could determine how much a safe workplace means to people by examining employees who work in unsafe environments and figuring out how much higher their wages must be to compensate for the unsafe workplace. This concept is also used by insurance companies that seek to determine the point at which a rise in premiums would result in behavioral changes of the insured.

The Coase Theorem

A final concept that has been extremely influential in the economic analysis of law is the Coase theorem, attributed to Ronald Coase, whose work earned him the Nobel Memorial Prize in Economic Sciences in 1991. The Coase theorem holds that in the absence of transaction costs, or costs associated with buying and selling investments, resources will ultimately be allocated to their most valuable uses, regardless of how the resources are initially allocated, because interested parties will bargain privately to correct any inefficiency in the allocation. However, many critics have argued that the Coase theorem can only exist on paper because transaction costs are almost always present and are frequently set too high to facilitate the most efficient bargaining.

Ronald Coase working in 2003 at the University of Chicago Law School. (Courtesy of University of Chicago Law School via Wikimedia Commons)

Economics and the Common Law

The common law is the body of law that has developed in the United States, based on principles and precedents developed in England and Great Britain, that includes customs, general principles, and precedents set by court decisions that are applied to situations not covered by statute. The common law forms the basis for many significant areas of law, such as torts, contracts, evidence, criminal law, and even wills and trusts. Economic analysis has been applied to all areas within the body of law. The following sections explain the intersection of economic analysis of law and the basic subjects of common law, including torts, contracts, and property.

Torts

A tort is a civil wrong that subjects the wrongdoer to a suit for damages by the victim. Torts may be intentional or unintentional, and the economic implications of each is different. In unintentional torts, the injury occurs from an accidental harm that one person causes to another. An economic approach to unintentional torts seeks to minimize the costs of accidents by allocating the costs of accidents resulting in injury to the persons or parties who are in the best position to avoid or minimize the losses. This is because, in theory, that person or party is able to make a decision about whether the benefits of the activity outweigh the costs to which the activity gives rise, including the risk of injury.

The most significant scholarly work to examine this theory is Guido Calabresi's "The Costs of Accidents." In his work, Calabresi identifies three types of costs

Judge Learned Hand. (Courtesy of Library of Congress)

that result from accidents. Primary costs are those associated with the harm to the injured party, such as the cost of medical care and lost earning capacity. Secondary costs are the societal costs resulting from accidents. The third type of costs is associated with administering the tort system. Calabresi noted that eliminating or minimizing one cost may not be consistent with minimizing another cost. For example, a system that always assigns the primary costs of accidents to the party that causes the accident may be very expensive to administer, and this raises the question of whether that is the most efficient allocation of costs associated with accidents.

Further, while categorizing the types of costs is a useful way to enumerate the harms and costs associated with accidents, an economic analysis of tort law would not necessarily seek the minimization of these costs. For instance, at some point the cost of avoiding accidents inevitably becomes greater than the harm that would be caused by those accidents, and thus a more appropriate economic analysis would be to both search for a way to minimize the sum of the costs of accidents and the costs of prevention efforts to avoid accidents.

In intentional torts, the economic analysis shifts from accident avoidance and prevention to compensation of the victim and retribution or punishment for the wrongdoer. Tort law has adopted a number of economic theories to develop the principles of negligence, liability, and damages. For instance, in the landmark case *United States v. Carroll Towing Co.*, 159 F.2d 169 (2d Cir. 1947), Judge Learned Hand saw the issue of liability as being the function of three variables: the probability of the harm (P), the amount of harm should an accident occur (L), and the cost of prevention (B). Judge Hand noted that P multiplied by L is the "expected harm." Thus, under the Hand formula, when PL exceeds B, or when the expected harm is greater than the cost of prevention, a party is regarded as negligent. Conversely, if the expected harm is less than the cost of prevention, the party is not negligent.

If a party is not negligent, the party may still be required to bear the costs of the injured based upon a finding of strict liability. Strict liability means that a party is liable for damage caused by her activity even if there is no showing of negligence. This theory is justified in terms of economic efficiency in that, presumably, those parties who are more likely to be in control of the activity and could have taken measures to prevent the injury will be the ones held strictly liable. Furthermore, streamlining the fault-finding process can reduce the administrative costs of the legal process, and this cost savings can also be allocated toward compensating the victim.

If a party is found negligent or strictly liable, the victim is entitled to collect damages from the wrongdoer. Compensatory damages compensate the victim for actual damages suffered by the injury, while punitive damages are awarded to the victim to punish the wrongdoer and to attempt to deter the defendant and other persons from pursuing a course of action such as that which damaged the plaintiff. Generally, negligence victims are only entitled to compensatory damages, while victims of an intentional tort may sometimes obtain punitive damages as well as compensatory damages.

Contracts

The economic function of modern contract law is to facilitate the voluntary transaction of property rights so that goods and services move into the hands of those who value them the most. While the actual exchange of goods or services for money may also

be regulated by other areas of the law, contract law governs the process of the exchange, once the terms of the exchange are agreed upon. Because contracts are frequently created in situations in which the performance of both parties does not occur at the same time, the lapse in time between when the contract is formed and when the parties perform as agreed introduces the possibility that unforeseen events will disrupt performance and that one of the parties will be tempted to exploit any strategic opportunities that may arise during this interval. Contract law includes remedial measures that courts may implement to deter people from exploiting unforeseen events to the detriment of the counterparty, and to make costly self-protective measures unnecessary.

Another important function of contract law is to protect the parties' expectations in the event of an occurrence that is not covered by the contract's provisions. The longer the interval between contract formation and performance, the harder it becomes for the parties to foresee every contingency that may affect the performance of one or both parties. Moreover, while parties may be able to conceive of some contingencies, these events are so unlikely to occur that the costs of dealing with them might exceed the benefits associated with providing for the event in the contract. When this occurs, a contract may be silent on a matter before the court, and in certain circumstances, the court may fill in the contractual term necessary to deal with the contingency if and when it occurs.

If a court is asked to apply a contract to a contingency that the parties did not foresee, the court will generally imagine how the parties would have provided for the contingency if it had occurred to them to do so. In doing so, courts have to think in economic terms to determine the most efficient way of dealing with the contingency. Courts can use fundamental economic principles to guide the process. For instance, parties have an obvious interest in their own profit maximization, but they also frequently have an interest in joint profit maximization as well; the larger the joint profit, the bigger the "take" of each party is likely to be. A corollary of this is that parties likely also have a mutual interest in minimizing the cost of performance. Economic principles such as these help courts fill in gaps in a contract in a way that is likely keeping with what the parties would have approved at the time of making the contract.

Property

The law of property is concerned with creating and defining property rights, which are rights to the exclusive use of valuable resources. Thus, a property right, in both law and economics, is a right to exclude everyone else from the use of some scarce resource. This right is absolute in the sense that someone who wants a resource that belongs to another person cannot justify simply taking or using the resource by arguing that he will put the resource to better use. For example, if A's land includes a sunny field while B's land is dry and rocky, B cannot plow A's land and plant crops, even if B plans to use the produce to give to needy neighbors. B must negotiate with A for use of the land, and refrain from entering the land if A refuses to accept an offer for B to use the land.

Because the law of property is so broad and includes a wide range of rights, there is no singular economic analysis of property rights. Instead, the interplay between economics and property rights turns on the type of property right at issue. For instance, property rights include trespass and eminent domain. In trespass cases, although a trespasser may claim a superior use of certain land, the owner of the land may still eject the trespasser without altering his use of the land. Or, the landowner may negotiate a deal with the trespasser in which the trespasser is able to pay for a right to use or access the land upon payment of a fee. However, if the government wants to use the land, it can seize the land under the eminent domain power without negotiating with the landowner at all, although it must compensate the landowner by paying just compensation for the property. The eminent domain power enables government to pursue the highest use of property that best enhances a community's use of its land and resources, while the requirement that the government pay just compensation serves as a check to ensure that the government does not abuse this right.

Other property laws, such as nuisance prohibitions, easements, zoning requirements, and even intellectual property rights, also create different analyses of the benefits and costs associated with protecting these rights against violations. In each circumstance, however, any economic analysis includes such factors as transaction costs, transference rights, and competing uses in reaching a determination of settling property disputes.

Law and Economics: Government Regulation of Financial Markets

While financial markets are regulated in one sense by competition in the marketplace, the U.S. government has also implemented regulations that affect almost every area of industry and the financial markets. The purpose of these regulations is to correct imperfections and inefficiencies in the market that, left unaddressed, may cause valuable resources to be misused or even abused. For instance, in markets that are not sufficiently competitive, consumers may be faced with higher prices or artificially limited supplies. Government regulations can help control price fluctuations or preserve competition in the market by preventing companies from merging or acquiring competitors. In addition, in an unregulated market, businesses may not have incentives to provide consumers with accurate or sufficient information regarding products and services. Regulations can help minimize these dangers by requiring that companies disclose information about the ingredients or possible side effects of products, or the energy efficiency of an appliance or gas mileage of an automobile. The following sections provide explanations of some of the areas in which the government has created regulations that balance the competing economic interests of property owners, businesses, consumers, and the society at large.

Antitrust Laws

Antitrust laws protect competition. Free and open competition benefits consumers by ensuring lower prices and new and better products. In a freely competitive market, each competing business generally will try to attract consumers by cutting its prices and increasing the quality of its product or services. Consumers benefit from competition through lower prices and better products and services. Inefficient firms or companies that fail to understand or react to consumer needs may soon find themselves losing customers or even facing bankruptcy.

When competitors agree to fix prices or act in collusion, consumers lose the benefits of competition. The prices that result typically begin to spiral upward, until they no longer accurately reflect the cost of the item. When this occurs, the resources of consumers are no longer allocated efficiently and the inefficiencies begin to clog the flow of money and resources.

Standard Oil (Refinery No. 1 in Cleveland, Ohio, pictured) was a major company broken up under United States antitrust laws. (Courtesy of Wikimedia Commons)

Antitrust regulations aim to prevent actions that would eliminate competition from the marketplace. Both the Federal Trade Commission and the Department of Justice have implemented regulations that these public enforcement agencies enforce through legal actions against companies that violate antitrust laws. Economists help government regulators determine how to best shape and apply antitrust laws. Economists study such factors as the defining of the relevant market in any industry and the impact of any potential antitrust violation by considering alternative definitions of the market. Economists also help define the market structure for many industries and consider the effects of mergers, acquisitions, or the disappearance of competitors from the market on factors such as price increases and pricing issues, including predatory pricing, price discrimination, price fixing, brand pricing, bundling, and tie-ins.

Intellectual Property Laws

Economists have long known that economic innovations are a more powerful force in determining how fast an economy's productivity and output rises than either increases in capital investment or improvements in the skills of workers. Thus, the economic advantage in inventing and creating new technologies and new ways of doing business depends heavily upon protections for the intellectual property embodied in every innovation. However, the innovations that most enhance economic activity originate primarily in advanced economies in which commitments to research and development are strong, the political and economic environments are stable, barriers to starting new businesses are relatively low, and intellectual property rights are respected.

Developing countries face different concerns with regard to intellectual property and globalization. These countries have less economically valuable intellectual property and hence are often significant importers of innovative technologies and expertise. This prospect may tempt developing countries to simply ignore foreign intellectual property rights. This is especially true because during the period in which a patent applies, intellectual property rights guarantee that its owner can charge prices substantially greater than its marginal costs to produce the good. Hence, recourse to piracy or counterfeiting can significantly reduce the costs of a given patented product in a developing country. In many parts of the developing world today, however, lack of respect for intellectual property rights or lax enforcement of those rights remains the rule rather than the exception.

Because of these marked differences in economically valuable intellectual property and respect for intellectual property rights in countries around the world, the economic analysis of intellectual properties law occurs at the global level. Today, it has become readily accepted that analysis and evaluation of intellectual property law is conducted within a framework of economic efficiency. In forming appropriate intellectual property laws and regulations, courts and legislators grapple with questions such as how to enable the creator of intellectual property to enjoy the fruits of his labor when his creation is heavily influenced by the cumulative process of his education and adaptation of other intellectual properties that influenced his creative process.

In addition, the modern world of seamless technologies and the broadening range of the public domain are causing economists to reconsider how best to craft copyright protections that protect the creative effort while allowing for inputs and adaptations of intellectual property. In terms of trademark protections, economists consider how to optimize the value of a trademark and reduce consumer search costs in the face of unfamiliar or confusing trademarks. Finally, economists continue to study the costs and benefits of the limits of durational protections provided by copyrights and trademarks.

Regulation of Financial Markets

The confidence that investors have in the fairness of the financial markets has a significant impact on the amount of capital available for businesses to use. If the general public believes that investing is for a privileged few who can profit from insider connections, there is limited investment and limited economic growth as well. In contrast, capital flows into financial markets that the public perceives as basically fair. Overall, the United States has enjoyed solid growth in its financial markets. Some of this can undoubtedly be attributed to the federal, state, and industry regulatory systems that regulate and protect U.S. financial markets. Regulation of financial markets helps to minimize systemic risks in the market and enhance an efficient allocation of funds. Also, regulations can protect consumers from unethical practices so that the markets are fair, efficient, and transparent.

In the United States, the financial markets are protected with layers of regulation. At the federal level, the Securities and Exchange Commission consists of four departments—Corporate Finance, Market Regulation, Investment Management, and Enforcement—that regulate specific areas of the business and financial services industries. In addition to other federal statutes and administrative agencies that play a role in regulating the financial markets, states have also enacted legislation to protect consumers and enhance market efficiencies. Finally, the financial services industry has developed self-regulatory organizations, known as SROs, that provide a mechanism for the expertise and practical experience of the industry to contribute to the development of regulatory policy.

While critics have argued that the corporate fraud, accounting debacles, and mutual fund trading scandals that have occurred in recent years illustrate the ineffectiveness of these layers of regulations, still others have pointed out that those misdeeds were ultimately uncovered and that the ensuing investigations and prosecutions have led to significant adaptations to the financial industry and its regulatory framework that have further enhanced the security and efficiency of these markets. Thus, while regulation of financial markets is not fail-proof, it can assist in balancing investor protections, competition in the market, and the growth objectives of business and individual portfolios.

APPLICATIONS

Law and Economics in the Modern World

The basic function of law in a wealth-maximization environment is to alter incentives and thus regulate behavior to facilitate the most advantageous and efficient allocation of resources. Yet the law must also protect the social and economic interests of individuals who have neither the education nor the resources to maximize their own wealth or to protect themselves from the unethical behavior of others. Without a legal framework to regulate wealth-maximization, the disenfranchised and impoverished classes of people are left to the mercies of the most resourceful. Thus, economists must consider the social implications of the allocation of goods and the costs of social services within the context of taxation and redistribution of income. Finally, economists must weigh the extent to which economic policies impact criminal activity and law enforcement. These issues will be discussed in more detail below.

Distributive Justice

Distributive justice concerns what is just or right with respect to the allocation of goods in a society. In essence, distributive justice is concerned with the fair allocation of resources among diverse members of a community. Fair allocation typically takes into account the total amount of goods to be distributed, the distributing procedure, and the pattern of distribution that evolves from the allocation process. Often contrasted with procedural justice, which is concerned with just processes, such as in the administration of law, distributive justice concentrates on just outcomes and consequences. The most prominent contemporary theorist of distributive justice is the philosopher John Rawls.

Because societies have a limited amount of wealth and resources, a question arises as to how those benefits ought to be distributed. One answer is that public assets should be distributed in a reasonable manner so that each individual receives a "fair share." But this leaves open the question of what constitutes a "fair share." Various principles might determine how goods are distributed. For instance, equality, equity, need, and social utility are all common criteria for the appropriate distribution of goods. If equality is regarded as the ultimate criterion in determining who gets what, goods will be distributed equally among all persons so that every person receives the same amount. However, due to differences in levels of need, this will not result in an equal outcome.

Another possibility is to proceed according to a principle of equity, and distribute benefits in proportion to the individuals' contribution to the society. Thus, those individuals who make the greatest productive contribution to the group deserve to receive more benefits. This sort of distribution is typically associated with an economic system in which there is equal opportunity to compete. In addition, goods can be distributed according to need. Finally, resources can even be distributed according to social utility, or what is in the best interests of society as a whole. Regardless of the distribution method, economists must still grapple with the reality that no allocation process is perfect and thus whatever system is used, there will likely be inefficiencies and failures in the process that must be addressed.

Taxation

Taxation can be used to alter the allocation of resources or the distribution of wealth and as a means for funding the provision of public services. The origin of taxation in the United States can be traced to its earliest days, when the colonists were heavily taxed by Great Britain. The colonists had no voice in the establishment of the taxes, and their disdain for this taxation without representation fueled a series of revolts, such as the Boston Tea Party. After many years of debate and compromise, the Sixteenth Amendment to the Constitution was ratified in 1913, and provides Congress with the power to lay and collect taxes on income. The objectives of the income tax were the equitable distribution of the tax burden and the ability of the federal government to raise sufficient revenues to function. Since 1913, the U.S. income tax system has become very complex, and taxes are imposed on more than just personal and business incomes.

Today, the Internal Revenue Service (IRS) is the agency of the U.S. Department of the Treasury that is responsible for collecting income taxes from individuals and businesses. In addition to income tax, the IRS collects several other kinds of taxes for the government, including Social Security, estate, excise,

and gift taxes. The agency's other responsibilities include enforcement of U.S. tax laws, distribution of forms, and instructions necessary for the filing of tax returns and providing counseling to businesses and individuals with uncertainties about the tax regulations.

Income tax, in particular, has been the subject of a great deal of debate among economists and legal theorists. Income tax is a levy imposed by public authority on the incomes of persons or corporations within its jurisdiction. The fairness of personal income taxation is based on the premise that one's income is the best single index of one's ability to contribute to the support of the government. In addition, personal income taxation assumes that as people's financial circumstances differ, their tax liabilities should also differ. The income tax structure in the United States is based on a system of progressive taxes, in which taxes fall more heavily on those who earn more money, and individual income tax deductions are allowed for items such as interest paid on home mortgage debt, certain medical expenses, philanthropic contributions, and state and local income and property taxes.

Critics of income tax systems have argued that they can be extremely complex, requiring detailed record-keeping, lengthy instructions, and complicated schedules, worksheets, and forms. In addition, critics have also claimed that income tax systems can penalize workers, discourage saving and investment, and hinder the competitiveness of businesses.

Law Enforcement

Economic analysis of crime and punishment is based upon the premise that punishment is a method of imposing costs on criminal activity and thereby altering the incentives to engage in it. The economist is interested in how the criminal justice system, which constitutes a form of government coercion, is used and how it could be used more effectively to prevent wasteful private activities, such as theft and murder. In addition, economists consider such issues as how to prevent the criminal justice system from being misused, and how to ensure that the distribution of wealth and justice is allocated efficiently within the governing legal framework.

Various studies have examined the benefits and costs of criminal activity. The benefits or gains obtained from a criminal act vary. For instance, some gains from crime are monetary, such as goods acquired through theft, robbery, or fraud. Others gains are social or psychological, such as the thrill of danger, peer approval, a sense of retribution as in a bank robbery, or a sense of accomplishment. The costs of crime could include material costs, such as acquiring equipment, guns, or vehicles and psychic costs, such as guilt, anxiety, or fear. In addition, punishment costs include all formal sanctions, including fines and various forms of incarceration, as well as pecuniary costs arising from lawsuits, and informal sanctions, including any personal losses connected with arrest, prosecution, and conviction. The more severe these sanctions are, the higher the costs.

Finally, any economic analysis of criminal activity and law enforcement must consider the socioeconomic statistics that link decreased income and educational levels with the potential for increased criminal activity. The lower a person's income, for instance, the lower the opportunity cost of crime, in that the yields from criminal activity may be greater than the costs associated with giving up earning a legal income. In addition, ineffective law enforcement activities may waste valuable resources without minimizing criminal activity, or even worse, may result in increased forms of retributive criminal behavior aimed at striking back at perceived injustices in the legal system. Thus, economists and legal theorists, along with courts and legislatures, must consider many socioeconomic, racial, psychological, and sociological factors in weighing how best to shape a society's economic, legal, and criminal justice framework to provide incentives to effect the desired behavior while fairly imposing penalties on those who violate laws without the penalties becoming too onerous that they tax the society's resources.

CONCLUSION

The economic analysis of law is a broad, dynamic field that examines the intersection of law, economics, morality, and even sociology and psychology. Every individual and corporate action has economic implications. Economists and legal theorists study the incentives that motivate people to make behavioral changes that follow the society's moral and legal framework and the economic consequences of developing areas of law and past legal precedents. Basic theories, such as efficiencies, positive law, normative

law, and the Coase theorem provide economists with the basic building blocks for shaping an economic analysis of the law. In some areas of the law, such as torts, contracts, and property, the economic implications of legal principles in those fields have been well established. In other areas, such as antitrust, intellectual property, and the financial markets, economists are still studying the interplay between economics and the law, and how both of these fields inform and shape the development of the other. Finally, an economic analysis of the law does not stop with the study of resource allocation or assignment of liability. Instead, economists must consider how economic policies and the legal process affect the administration of justice and resources to the poor and uneducated and the role that the criminal justice system and law enforcement activities play in shaping the behavior of members of a society.

BIBLIOGRAPHY

al-Nowaihi, A.M., & Dhami, S. (2013). "The hyperbolic punishment function." *Review of Law & Economics, 8,* 759–787.

Baird, D. (1997). "The future of law and economics: Looking forward." *University of Chicago Law Review, 64,* 1129.

David, B. (2012). "Contemporary readings in the economic analysis of law." *Economics, Management & Financial Markets, 7,* 209–214.

Edlin, A. (2006). Review essay: "Surveying two waves of economic analysis of law." *American Law & Economics Review, 2,* 407.

"Foundations of economic analysis of law." (2005). Harvard Law Review, *118,* 2485.

Hornik, J., Villa Illera, C. (2017). "An economic analysis of liability of hosting services: Uncertainty and incentives online." *Bruges European Economic Research Papers.*

Lombardo, S. (2011). "The comparative, law and economics analysis of company law. Reflections on the second edition of The Anatomy of Corporate Law. A Comparative and Functional Approach." *European Company & Financial Law Review, 8,* 47–64.

Rosenberg, G. (1997). "The implementation of constitutional rights: Insights from law and economics." *University of Chicago Law Review, 64,* 1215.

Siegel, N. (1999). "Sen and the hart of jurisprudence: A critique of the economic analysis of judicial behavior." *California Law Review, 87,* 1581.

Shavell, S. (1999, Spring). "Economic analysis of law." *NBER Reporter,* 12–15.

Soon, J. (2000). "The economic analysis of law." *Policy, 16,* 58.

Sunstein, C. (1997). "The autonomy of law in law and economics." *Harvard Journal of Law & Public Policy, 21,* 89.

SUGGESTED READING

Jacobsen, J. (2007). "Law and economics: Alternative economic approaches to legal and regulatory issues." *Feminist Economics, 13,* 224–226.

Ostas, D. (1998). "Postmodern economic analysis of law: Extending the pragmatic visions of Richard A. Posner." *American Business Law Journal, 36,* 193.

Posner, R. (1998). "Social norms, social meaning, and economic analysis of law: A comment." *Journal of Legal Studies, 27,* 553.

—Heather Newton

ECONOMIC APPLICATIONS OF GAME THEORY

ABSTRACT

This article focuses on the economic applications of game theory. The foundation for the basis of game theory is introduced followed by examples of some simple games. The concept of two-person zero-sum games is evaluated. There is also a discussion on how social norms influence behaviors when playing games. One particular game, the exclusion game, is highlighted.

OVERVIEW

Economically speaking, people have choices, wants, and needs. The ultimate goal of economic action is to satisfy one's desires. While it is expected that individuals will act in a rational way in order to be in compliance with social norms, the process is complicated due to external factors such as prices, production, gains, and expenses. Additionally, individual behavior is dictated by choice, or free will. The act of making a rational decision regarding choices involves what is referred to as social exchange economy.

Social Exchange Economy Models
A social exchange economy can be described in terms of three models:

■ Robinson Crusoe Economy
This type of economy focuses on how the economic well-being of a single person is influenced by a single will. The person in this model must decide how to satisfy a need to obtain commodities that will provide maximum satisfaction. For example, Crusoe is given information that describes his desires and commodities. His goal is to select a combination of choices that will give him maximum satisfaction. The key to this model is that Crusoe controls all of the variables that influence the decision.

Once Crusoe enters into a social exchange economy, he loses some of his autonomy. He no longer has control over all of the variables as he seeks to enter into an exchange relationship with another person.

■ Free Competition
In contrast to the Robinson Crusoe model, free competition is a theory that emphasizes the notion that there are many people involved in a social exchange economy. In addition, these individuals are aware that their choices have an effect on the decision-making process of others. The participants in this process believe that as more people enter into the equation, the influence of each person becomes a moot point. Free competition encourages diversity and variety while discouraging seller involvement in monopolies, duopolies, and oligopolies.

■ Lausanne Theory
This theory values individual planning as well as an interrelated network of individual plans. One can assume that this theory takes the best of the Crusoe model as well as the free competition philosophy. In essence, each individual develops an individual plan

and utilizes it to interact with the masses and obtain maximum satisfaction.

As one looks at the individual and collective behaviors of a group, the focus centers on how one obtains maximum satisfaction, which could be referred to as the game.

Individuals play the game, which is governed by a set of rules. Each player has the choice of making a move, which ultimately has consequences. In many cases, the players participate in two types of procedures: direct and inverted signaling.

Game Theory

Game theory came to prominence in 1944 when von Neumann and Morgenstern published a book entitled "Theory of Games and Economic Behavior." The second edition was published in 1947. One of the reasons for the book's popularity was its focus on decision-making involving more than one decision maker. World War II activities led many scholars to seek opportunities to model decision situations. At the time, the military was a large proponent of game theory.

Game theory can be viewed as a mechanism for resolving conflicts of interest (Thomas, 1984). Conflicts of interest evolve as a result of disagreement between people. According to Thomas (1984), game theory:

- is a way to resolve these types of conflicts;
- describes types of results that may occur;
- suggests the best solution to the game and how the players should respond; and
- suggests which players will work together to resolve problems (p. 15).

Some of the key assumptions for a game include the following:

- There are at least two participants who are referred to as players.
- Players make moves, which are decisions made by the players.
- Players receive a payoff at the end of the game.
- Players develop strategies in order to win the game.

Players are constantly developing strategies throughout the game. The goal is to anticipate moves to make, which will lead to ultimate victory. Players seek to gain the greatest payoff in order to win. Payoff

can be explained in terms of two concepts—zero-sum and non-zero-sum games. Zero sum occurs when the payoff for all players is zero regardless of the strategy. In this scenario, there is always a winner and a loser. Poker is an example of this strategy. On the other hand, games that do not have a clear distribution of wins and losses are considered non-zero-sum games.

Game Theory and Economics

How is game theory applied to economic decision-making and forecasting? Firstly, forecasting involves the ability to predict future behavior based on historical evidence. For example, forecasting models are applied to problems that need to be resolved on a number of levels (i.e., managerial strategic plan, operational decisions). A manager may want to review sales from previous years to predict what the sales will be for a certain product line in the future. There is a review of consumer trends to predict future spending habits. Game theory allows the manager to speculate what the different alternatives will be as he seeks to make the decision that will yield the greatest sales.

Shefrin (2002) has argued that "traditional game theory assumes that players are fully rational in respect to preferences (expected utility), judgments, and strategic choices" (p. 375). Scholars have supported the concept of rational choice theory to support this notion. The concept of rational choice theory is significant in microeconomics. In the model, the assumption is that individuals will make choices based on favorable conditions, preferences, and constraints.

When making a choice, one can assume that all parties will make decisions based on amount of return. Each player studies all of the possible choices and determines the return for each. The alternative with the optimum "win" should be selected for this process to yield great economic outcome.

To take advantage of all economic tools, one may elect to create a simulation by role-playing. Role-playing can be argued as a more plausible way of forecasting given its outcomes. "Role-playing outcomes emerge from the actual interaction of real human beings, whereas, game theoretic outcomes emerge from the theoretical interaction of idealized human beings" (p. 382). There may be times when a player cannot theoretically conceive what the possible outcomes could be given the limitations of the environment. However, if the players engage in a role-playing scenario, each can use external factors and the environment to visualize what potential outcomes could be.

APPLICATION

Two-Person Zero-Sum Games

A two-person zero-sum game involves two players; one player wins and one player loses. According to Rapoport (1966), the following occurs in this type of scenario:

- The game begins by one or more of the players making a choice among a number of specified alternatives. For example, in the game of Tic-Tac-Toe, the first player has a choice of eight boxes to make a mark of "X" or "O."
- After the choice associated with the first move is made, a certain situation occurs. This situation determines who is to make the next choice and what alternatives are open to the player. Once the player places an "X" or "O" in a box, the next player will make a mark.

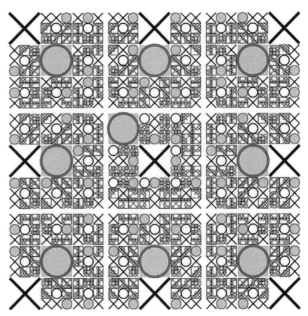

Optimal strategy for player O in Tic-Tac-Toe based on "A Fractal Guide to Tic Tac Toe" by Ian Stewart on August 1, 2000, in Scientific American. Player O can always force a win or draw by taking center. If it is taken by X, then O must take a corner. (Courtesy of Nneonneo CC BY-SA 3 via Wikimedia Commons)

- The choices made by the players may or may not become known. In the game of Tic-Tac-Toe, the choices are known.
- If a game is described in terms of successive moves, there is a termination rule. Each choice made by a player determines a certain situation. When such a situation occurs, the game is ended. The game ends when one player has placed three of his marks in a row. A win can occur as soon as the fifth move takes place.
- Every play of a game ends in a certain situation. Each of these situations determines a payoff to each bona fide player (pp. 18–21).

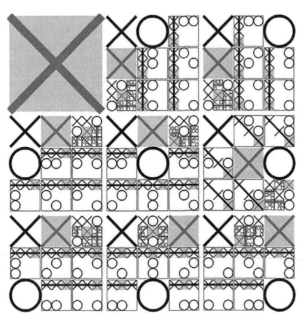

Optimal decision tree for player X in Tic-Tac-Toe based on "A Fractal Guide to Tic Tac Toe" by Ian Stewart on August 1, 2000, in Scientific American. In each grid, the shaded X denotes the optimal move, and the location of O's next move gives the next sub-grid to examine. Note that only two sequences of moves by O (both starting with center, top-right, left-mid) lead to a draw, with the remaining sequences leading to wins from X. (Courtesy of Nneonneo CC BY-SA 3 via Wikimedia Commons)

Another way to describe a two-person zero-sum game is in terms of the process of the game. One can list all of the possible sequences of moves that a player can make and what the payoff is at the end of the sequence. A tree graph is a way that this information can be documented. When creating the graph, one can list multiple move points, which represent at what point a move must be made. A move is considered a decision made by one of the players or a chance event. All possible moves that can be made are represented by lines that are drawn to the designated point on the tree graph (Thomas, 1984).

VIEWPOINT

Role of Norms in Game Theory

Some may consider norms to be the basis for human behavior. For example, it has been said that a norm can dictate an individual's behavior. Theft is considered to be an illegal act. Therefore, the norm is that one does not steal if he/she does not want to go to jail. A person who steals understands that it is an illegal act against the rules of society. Researchers in this area have determined that:

- an individual's behavior is a reflection of society's norms;
- aocial order is a result of norms encouraging cooperation and pro-social behavior (Arrow, 1974; Elster, 1989).

There are social researchers, who believe that norms affect behavior as a result of their influence on a person's motivation (Elster, 1989; Gintis, 2003; Becker, 1996). For example, if an individual's motivation is to win at all costs, this particular individual may consider cheating (a behavior) even if it is against society's norm of appropriate behavior. The individual has insulated himself against feeling any type of remorse for acting in a deviant manner because the motivation to win at all costs has superseded the need to be in compliance with society.

Given this scenario, it is not surprising that "self-interest and opportunism have recently become the target of criticism by behavioral economics theorists, who urge the introduction of a more complex account of the motivations of economic agents" (Sacconi & Faillo, 2005, p. 57). Sacconi and Faillo (2005) conducted a study to determine at what point players who have contributed to the choice of a norm actually comply with the norm, especially when the norm does not align with the motivation of the players. In essence, under what conditions will a player desert the characteristics of a person adhering to the self-interest-based model?

The study was based on an experiment called the Exclusion Game. The participants were asked to choose how to play the game once they had agreed to play according to specific rules. The experiment was conducted at the Computable and Experimental Economics Laboratory of the University of Trento. There was a total of 150 participants. Fifteen participants were active in each session, and there was a total of 10 sessions.

The participants were divided into groups of three individuals. Two of the participants were active players and one player did not have an active role. This one player, the "dummy player," had to rely on the decisions of the active players and his/her rewards were determined by the decisions made by the active players. The three choices were to ask for half of the money, ask for one-third of the money, or ask for one-fourth of the money. The agreement was that if both of the players asked for half of the money, the dummy player would not receive anything. However, if both active players asked for one-third of the money, the pot would be split equally among the three players.

Saconi and Faillo (2005) found that:

- about 85 percent of the players chose the second principle at least once in the first phase.
- considering the players in phase one who chose the second principle at least once, and in phase two chose the first principle (approximately 60 percent of the players), those who expected that the other active players would select the first principle agreed to support this decision.
- choosing a principle induced a change in the behavior of a significant number of the players (p. 103).

CONCLUSION

As one looks at the individual and collective behaviors of a group, the focus centers on how one obtains maximum satisfaction; or, how one plays the game. Within such games, each player has the choice of making a move, which ultimately has consequences.

Game theory came to prominence in 1944 when von Neumann and Morgenstern published a book entitled "Theory of Games and Economic Behavior." The second edition was published in 1947. One of the reasons for the book's popularity was its focus on decision-making involving more than one decision maker. World War II activities led many scholars to seek opportunities to model decision situations. At the time, the military was a large proponent of game theory.

This is John von Newumann's Los Alamos Laboratory wartime badge photo. He was a respected mathematician, physicist and computer scientist who made contributions in a number of fields, including his work on the Manhattan Project during the period of WW II. (Courtesy of U.S. Department of Energy via Wikimedia Commons)

Game theory can be viewed as a mechanism for resolving conflicts of interest (Thomas, 1984). Conflicts of interest evolve as a result of disagreement between people. According to Thomas (1984), game theory:

- is a way to resolve these types of conflicts;
- describes types of results that may occur;
- suggests the best solution to the game and how the players should respond; and
- suggests which players will work together to resolve problems (p. 15).

Some of the key assumptions for a game include the following:

- There are at least two participants who are referred to players.
- Players make moves, which are decisions made by the players.
- Players receive a payoff at the end of the game.
- Players develop strategies in order to win the game.

Researchers in this area have determined that an individual's behavior is a reflection of society's norms;

and, social order is a result of norms encouraging cooperation and pro-social behavior (Arrow, 1974; Elster, 1989). However, there are social researchers who believe that norms affect behavior as a result of their influence on a person's motivation (Elster, 1989; Gintis, 2003; Becker, 1996). For example, if an individual's motivation is to win at all costs, this particular individual may consider cheating (a behavior) even if it is against society's norm of proper behavior. The individual has insulated himself against feeling any type of remorse for acting in a deviant manner because the motivation to win at all costs has superseded the need to be in compliance with society.

BIBLIOGRAPHY

Arrom, K. (1974). *The limits of organization.* New York: Norton & Company.

Becker, G. (1996). *Accounting for tastes.* Cambridge, MA: Harvard University Press.

Brink, R., Katsev, I., & Laan, G. (2011). "A polynomial time algorithm for computing the nucleolus for a class of disjunctive games with a permission structure." *International Journal of Game Theory, 40,* 591–616.

Elster, J. (1989). "Social norms and economic theory." *Journal of Economic Perspectives, 3,* 99–117.

Gintis, H. (2003). "The hitchhiker's guide to altruism: Gene-culture coevolution, and the internalization of norms." *Journal of Theoretical Biology, 220,* 407–418.

Owen, G. (2013). "Applications of game theory to economics." *International Game Theory Review, 15,* 1.

Qin, C. (2013). "Contests, managerial incentives, stock price manipulation, and advance selling strategies: introduction." *Pacific Economic Review, 18,* 162–163.

Rapoport, A. (1966). *Two-person game theory: The essential ideas.* Ann Arbor, MI: The University of Michigan Press.

Richardson, B. (2006). "Game theory: History and applications." Retrieved March 1, 2009, from education.uncc.edu/cmste/summer/2006%20History%20of%20Mathematics/ Ben.doc

Sacconi, L., & Faillo, M. (2007). "Norm compliance: The contribution of behavioral economics theories, Discussion Paper." Department of Economics, University of Trento.

Sacconi, L., & Faillo, M. (2005). "Conformity and reciprocity in the Exclusion Game: An experimental investigation, Discussion Paper." Department of Economics, University of Trento.

Shefrin, H. (2002). "Behavioral decision making, forecasting, game theory, and role playing." *International Journal of Forecasting, 18*, 375–382.

Thomas, L.(1984). *Game theory and applications.* New York: Ellis Horwood Limited.

SUGGESTED READING

Dogan, G. & Assen, M.V. (2009). "Testing models of pure exchange." *Journal of Mathematical Sociology, 33*, 97–128.

Ferreira, N., Kar, J. & Trigeorgis, L. (2009). "Option games." *Harvard Business Review, 87*, 101–107.

Finkelstein, N., Facey, B.A. & Finkelstein, J. (2009). "Game theory and the Competition Act: Winners and losers in Canadian merger review." *World Competition: Law & Economics Review, 32*, 113–133.

Guastello, S.J. (2009). "Evolutionary game theory and leadership." *American Psychologist, 64*, 53–54.

—*Marie Gould*

ECONOMIC GROWTH

ABSTRACT

This article focuses on economic growth. It provides an analysis of the main theories of economic growth, including neoclassical growth theory, new growth theory, and modern political growth theory. Economic growth trends in the U.S. economy and the global economy are discussed. The differences between economic growth and economic development are addressed.

OVERVIEW

Economic growth, according to the World Bank, refers to the quantitative change or expansion in a country's economy. The economic growth of a nation is measured as the percentage increase in its gross domestic product during one year. Economic growth occurs in two distinct ways. Economic growth of a nation occurs when a nation grows extensively by using more physical, natural, or human resources or intensively by using resources more efficiently or productively. Economic growth is generally considered to be either extensive or intensive in nature. Extensive economic growth refers to growth scenarios in which an increase in the gross domestic product is absorbed by a population increase without any increase in per capita income. Intensive economic growth refers to growth scenarios in which gross domestic product growth exceeds population growth creating a sustained rise in living standards as measured by real income per capita (Snowdon, 2006). According to the

World Bank's approach to promoting and facilitating the economic growth of nations, intensive economic growth of nations requires economic development.

Economic Growth and Labor Productivity

Economic growth is a focus of study and concern for economists, governments, and private sector development organizations. Economists are concerned with forecasting and measuring economic growth. Governments and private sector development organizations focus on forecasting and promoting economic growth of regions and nations. Economic growth is generally promoted through efforts to increase labor

The World Bank Group Headquarters building in Washington, D.C. (Courtesy of Shiny Things CC BY 2.0 via Wikimedia Commons)

productivity. Labor productivity growth is crucial to the strength and growth of economies. Labor productivity is promoted in four main ways (Vanhoudt & Onorante, 2001):

- Expand the physical capital of workers through the purchase of better machines, tools, and infrastructure.
- Improve the knowledge capital of the workforce through education and training.
- Foster a new economy by introducing new technologies to improve the productivity of all workers.
- Strengthen relations between public and private sectors to facilitate the working of the labor market and limit economic distortions caused by taxes and passive labor market policies.

Tracking and Measuring Economic Growth

Economic growth is generally tracked and measured by national governments and nongovernmental economic research organizations. For example, in the United States, the National Bureau of Economic Research (NBER), the United States' leading nonprofit economic research organization, determines and records dates for economic growth cycles and business cycles in the United States. The NBER published its first business cycle dates in 1929. The NBERhas, since its establishment in 1920, worked in its capacity as a private, nonprofit, nonpartisan research organization to promote a better general understanding of the way the economy works. NBE R associates, including 600 professors of economics and business, develop new statistical measurements, estimate quantitative models of economic behavior, assess the effects of public policies on the U.S. economy, and project the effects of alternative policy proposals. The NBER established itself as the predominant research organization on the topic of U.S. business cycles and economic growth tracking through the bureau's early research on the aggregate economy, business cycles, and long-term economic growth in the United States.

The following section provides an overview of the main theories of economic growth: neoclassical growth theory, new growth theory, and modern political growth theory. This section provides the foundation for later discussion of economic growth trends in the U.S. economy and the global economy, and the relationship between economic growth and economic development.

Theories of Economic Growth

Economic growth has been a focus of study by economists since the eighteenth century when Adam Smith published The *Wealth of Nations*. Scholarly interest in economic growth reached its peak in the mid-twentieth century following World War II. Following World War II, economists and national governments worked to find the factors and variables that controlled post-war economic growth (Snowdon, 2006). Economic growth is considered by economists to be a natural result of market activity. Economists have long been interested in the relationship between income inequality and economic growth. Growth theories refer to the theories that explain the factors and relationships that promote the economic growth of nations. Economic growth theories incorporate variables representing the effects of production factors, public expenditure, and income distribution. The following factors influence the effect that income distribution has on growth: investment indivisibilities, incentives, credit market imperfections, macroeconomic imperfections, macroeconomic volatility, political economy aspects, and social effects (Alfranca, 2003). In the history of economic growth theories, there are three main waves or theories of economic growth: neoclassical growth theory, new growth theory, and modern political growth theory.

Neoclassical Growth Theory

The neoclassical growth theory, also referred to as the exogenous growth model, focuses on productivity growth. The neoclassical growth theory, promoted by economists Robert Solow and Trevor Swan, was the predominant economic growth theory from the nineteenth to mid-twentieth centuries. Exogenous growth refers to a change or variable that comes from outside the system. Technological progress and enhancement of a nation's human capital are the main factors influencing economic growth. Technology, increased human capital, savings, and capital accumulation are believed to promote technological development, more effective means of production, and economic growth. The neoclassical growth theory prioritizes the same factors and variables as neoclassical economics. The field of neoclassical economics emphasizes the belief that the market system will ensure a fair allocation of resources and income distribution. In addition, the market is believed to regulate demand and supply, allocation of production, and the optimization of social organization. Neoclassical economics, along with the neoclassical growth model, began in the nineteenth century in response to perceived weaknesses in classical economics (Brinkman, 2001).

There are numerous criticisms of neoclassical growth theory. Criticism of the neoclassical growth theory focuses on the long-run productivity limitation created from the theory's exclusive focus on the addition of capital to a national economy. In addition, the neoclassical model predicts that different countries will have different levels of per capita income, depending on the variable factors that determine income levels. The range of income levels between countries shows the magnitude of international differences is actually vast and variable. The neoclassical model also predicts that an economy will reach its steady state, which is then determined by savings and population growth rates. Comparisons of the growth rates of rich and poor countries suggest that the neoclassical model does not successfully predict the rate of convergence of all countries, as poor economies tend to grow more rapidly than rich economies (Mankiw, 1995).

New Growth Theory

The new growth theory, also referred to as the endogenous growth theory, began in the 1980s as a response to criticism of the neoclassical growth theory. Endogenous growth refers to a change or variable that comes from inside and is based on the idea that economic growth is created and sustained from within a country rather than through trade or other contact from outside the system. The new growth theory identifies the main endogenous factors leading to sustained growth of output per capita including research and design, education, and human capital (Park, 2006). There are three main criticisms of new growth theories: First, the new growth theory is criticized for lack of conceptual clarity in its underlying assumptions. Second, the new growth theory is criticized for lack of empirical relevancy. Third, the new growth theory is criticized for claiming to be a wholly new theory when it is closely tied to growth theories that came before. Economists debate the significance of this last criticism. The new growth theory claims to represent a total break from neoclassical theory, but the continued focus on technology (whether exogenous or endogenous

technology) and its relationship to economic growth connects the two main growth theories in significant ways (Brinkman, 2001).

Modern Political Growth Theory

The modern political growth theory focuses on the fundamental determinants of economic growth such as the quality of governance, legal origin, ethnic diversity, democracy, trust, corruption, institutions in general, geographical constraints, natural resources, and the connection between international economic integration and growth. The modern political economic growth theory asserts that poor countries, although they have the potential for economic growth, will never achieve economic growth so long as the countries lack supporting institutions.

These three theories vary in their argument about what causes economic growth and what role technology plays in the economic growth of nations. Neoclassical growth theory and new growth theory emphasize the conditions associated with growth while the modern political growth theory focuses on fundamental causes or determinants of economic growth (Snowdon, 2006).

Elements Necessary for Sustained Economic Growth

Ultimately, sustained economic growth, as represented by enhanced productivity and growth, may require structural transformation within the nation. Economic growth, while encouraged and facilitated by factors such as a large labor supply,

The World Trade Organization Ministerial Conference of 1998 in the Palace of Nations, Geneva, Switzerland. (Courtesy of World Trade Organization from Switzerland CC BY-SA 2.0 via Wikimedia Commons)

national infrastructure, and a resource-rich environment, is hindered by economic problems and cultural obstacles inherent in the business climate and troughs in the business cycle. Economic problems refer to factors that hinder the functioning and growth of an economy. Economic problems of all kinds, including structural, fiscal, and cultural, impact economic development efforts by national governments, corporations, and international development organizations. Economic development encompasses a wide range of programs and strategies aimed at promoting growth in a part or whole of an economy. Developing countries with limited economies or economies in transition are particularly sensitive to economic problems of child labor, creditworthiness, corruption, and poverty and its related conditions. Economic growth may require creative destruction of an old system of institutions, modes of production, and relationships. Limin, Chaobo, and Junliang (2013) looked at China's growth between 1987 (a period of rapid inflation, budgetary instability, and relatively low per capita income levels) and 2010 and found that exports were a powerful driver of economic growth during the period, especially in the more developed eastern region. Toward the end of the period, however, exports became less important, imports increased, and foreign direct investment (FDI) accelerated. China's entry to the World Trade Organization in 2001 undoubtedly affected the dynamics of growth in China, driving up labor costs on the one hand and facilitating FDI on the other. China, with rising income, an expanding infrastructure, and technological advances, was a natural draw for investors exploring new markets.

APPLICATIONS

ECONOMIC GROWTH OF THE U.S. AND GLOBAL ECONOMIES
Monetary and Fiscal Policy
The U.S. government controls economic activity and economic growth through the creation and implementation of monetary policy and fiscal policy. Monetary policy is a tool used by the federal government to control the supply and availability of money in the economy. Fiscal policy controls the expenditures by federal, state, and local governments, and the taxes levied to finance government expenditures.

The federal government promotes economic growth by adjusting government spending, interest rates, setting the tax rates, and monitoring the nation's money supply.

Economic Competitiveness
In addition to the active economic growth efforts of the United States, nations around the world are working to increase their competitiveness in the global economy and marketplace. Economic competitiveness of nations is measured and tracked with tools such as the Growth Competitiveness Index and the Business Competitiveness Index. As global competition increases and influences economic growth, these indexes are being eclipsed by the Global Competitiveness Index, which tracks and measures both macroeconomic and microeconomic factors of a country's performance in the global marketplace. Competitiveness refers to the set of institutions, policies, and factors that determine the level of productivity. Increased productivity creates growth (Snowdon, 2006). The growth of nations varies between regions and historical eras. Economic and political changes promote or depress the growth of nations depending on variables such as national leadership, political and economic stability, natural resources, international relations, and infrastructure. The current era of the global economy, a product of economic globalization, is creating strong, though variable, national economic growth and development worldwide (Jones, 2005).

The Global Growth Economy
The global growth economy is characterized by the growth of nations, both in populations and in output and consumption per capita, interdependence of nations, and international management efforts. Indicators of global growth and interdependence include the huge increases in communication links, world output, international trade, and international investment since the 1970s. The global economy is built on global interdependence of economic flows linking the economies of the world. The global economy is characterized by economic sensitivity. National economic events in one region often have profound results for other regions and national economies. National economies exist not in isolation but in relationships and tension with other

economies worldwide. The global economy includes numerous economic phenomena and financial tools shared between all countries. Examples include the price of gold, the price of oil, and the related worldwide movement of interest rates. Ultimately, national governments participate in the global economy in an effort to increase economic growth of their own nation.

ISSUES

THE RELATIONSHIP BETWEEN ECONOMIC GROWTH AND ECONOMIC DEVELOPMENT
Foreign Aid and Economic Growth

The relationship between foreign aid and economic growth is strongly debated. Economists question the efficacy of foreign aid as a tool for economic growth and poverty alleviation. Private sector development organizations promote economic growth and development in developing countries in an effort to combat widespread poverty. Poverty, which encompasses a lack of basic necessities as well as a denial of basic opportunities and choices that permit human development, is a persistent, widespread, and intractable economic problem in developing regions. According to the World Bank, extreme poverty, and its related conditions such as hunger, affects more than one billion people in the world. The measure of extreme poverty is based on individual income or consumption levels of below $1 a day. Economic development efforts in developing countries are based on the argument that poverty reduction is tied to economic growth. Economic development, as it is practiced today, involves numerous public sector and private sector stakeholders, such as development agencies, national governments, corporations from industrialized countries, businesses from developing countries, community agencies, and populations in need, committed to ending poverty, and related conditions, in developing countries.

Combating Global Poverty

Combating global poverty is an economic development goal that unites international development organizations, national governments, and corporations around the world. For example, in 2000, the United Nations Millennium Summit was held to create time-bound and measurable goals for combating poverty and related conditions. The millennium

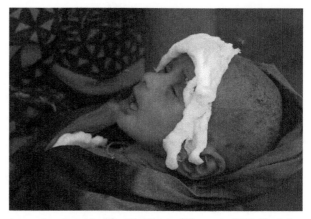

A severely malnourished Somali refugee at Hilaweyn health facility, being held by his mother.
(Courtesy of Peter Heinlein via Wikimedia Commons)

development goals (MDGs) have become a blueprint of sorts for national governments, development agencies, and corporations committed to aiding the world's poorest people. The United Nations concluded the MDGs in 2015, and as of 2016, initiated the UN Sustainable Development Goals. The millennium development goals included the following objectives:

- eradicate extreme poverty and hunger;
- achieve universal primary education;
- promote gender equality and empower women;
- reduce child mortality;
- improve maternal health;
- combat HIV/AIDS, malaria, and other diseases; and
- ensure environmental sustainability.

An HIV/AIDS educational outreach session in Angola. (Courtesy of USAID Africa Bureau via Wikimedia Commons)

Develop a global partnership for development (Millennium Development Goals, 2000). While contemporary forms of economic development are focused primarily on eradicating extreme poverty and related conditions, economic development has been in existence, in some form, since the end of World War II. The modern era of aid to developing countries began in the 1940s as World War II ended. After the war, world leaders and governing bodies put structures into place, such as the World Bank, the United Nations, the World Trade Organization, and the International Monetary Fund, to prevent the economic depressions and instability that characterized the years following World War I. The modern trend of globalization, and resulting shifts from centralized to market economies in much of the world, has created both a need and opportunity for economic development in developing countries and regions of the world. International development organizations, national governments, and corporations are coming together to focus on building frameworks for economic development as the basis for achieving sustainable economic growth.

International Governance Organizations and New Growth Theory

International governance organizations, such as the Organisation for Economic Co-operation and Development and the United Nations, base their development and economic growth efforts on the principles of the new growth theory (also referred to as endogenous growth theory). International governance organizations, a product of the global economy, promote development and growth in nations through the adoption of principles, tools, technologies, and aid from outside the nation rather than from within the nation. More than $1 trillion was spent on foreign aid in developing countries in the last 50 years. The sum has not effectively eradicated extreme poverty. In fact, foreign aid alone has been shown to be ineffective in reducing poverty. The majority of countries report low per capita income even after receiving large amounts of foreign aid. Due to speculation that foreign aid alone cannot eradicate poverty, the World Bank reported that total foreign aid disbursements, in particular to sub-Saharan Africa, the Middle East, and North African countries, went down from 0.33 percent of donor countries' gross national product in 1990 to 0.24 percent of their gross national product in 1999. Alvi and Senbeta (2012) disaggregated foreign aid to determine whether types of aid produce different impacts on poverty and found that multilateral source aid was more effective than aid from bilateral sources and that loans were ineffective, although grants had good results. Importantly, poverty reduction seemed to correlate with the development of financial systems. The relationship between foreign aid and economic growth suggests that greater amounts of foreign aid can, in some instances, inhibit economic growth. The conclusion that greater foreign aid may lead to lower economic growth will likely influence the direction and scope of foreign aid and foreign policy (Ali & Isse, 2005).

Economic Growth vs. Economic Development

Ultimately, economic growth and economic development are not the same process. When nonprofit development organizations provide foreign aid alone to developing countries, the organizations are not promoting the structural changes necessary for economic development. There is a clear distinction between economic growth and development. The substantive nature of the economic growth and economic development processes vary. The economic growth process includes a complete transformation of a country's economic and social framework. The economic development process includes the upward movement of the entire social system. Social systems include non-economic factors such as education and health infrastructure, class stratification, the distribution of power, and general institutions and cultural attitudes. In addition, the structure and form of economic growth and economic development processes vary. Economic growth alone is the replication of a given structure. Continued economic growth does not lead to structural transformation and economic development. Ultimately, economic growth cannot occur before the infrastructure and institutional structures for economic development are in place (Brinkman, 1995).

CONCLUSION

In the final analysis, economic growth theories, including neoclassical growth theory, new growth theory, and modern political growth theory, explain economic growth trends in the U.S. economy and the global economy. Economic growth occurs when a nation grows extensively by using more physical, natural, or human resources, or intensively by using resources more efficiently or productively. Economic growth, which is generally considered to be either extensive or intensive in nature, requires infrastructure, human resources, and organizational support (Snowdon, 2006).

BIBLIOGRAPHY

Alfranca, O., & Galindo, M. (2003). "Public expenditure, income distribution, and growth in OECD countries." *International Advances in Economic Research, 9,* 133–139.

Ali, A. & Isse, H. (2005). "An empirical analysis of the effect of aid on growth." *International Advances in Economic Research, 11,* 1–12.

Alvi, E., & Senbeta, A. (2012). "Does foreign aid reduce poverty?" *Journal of International Development,* 24, 955–976.

Brinkman, R. (2001). "The new growth theories: a cultural and social addendum." *The International Journal of Social Economics, 28,* 506–526.

Brinkman, R. (1995). "Economic growth versus economic development: Toward a conceptual clarification." *Journal of Economic Issues, 29,* 1171–1188.

Cavusoglu, N., & Tebaldi, E. (2006). "Evaluating growth theories and their empirical support: An assessment of the convergence hypothesis." *Journal of Economic Methodology, 13,* 49–75.

Delink, R., Chateau, J., Lanzi, E., Magne, B. (2017). "Long-term economic growth projections in the shared socioeconomic pathways." *Global Environmental Change, 42,* 200–214.

De Long, J. (1996). "A short review of economic growth: theories and policies." *University of California at Berkeley and National the Bureau of Economic Research.*

Dougherty, C., & Jorgenson, D. (1996). International comparisons of the sources of economic growth. *American Economic Review, 86,* 25–29.

Gwartney, J., Lawson, R., & Holcombe, R. (1998). "The size and functions of government and economic growth." Joint Economic Committee Study.

Herbst, A. F., Wu, J. K., & Ho, C. (2012). "Relationship between risk attitude and economic recovery in optimal growth theory." *Global Finance Journal, 23,* 141–150.

Jones, B., & Olken, B. (2005). "Do leaders matter? National leadership and growth since World War II." *Quarterly Journal of Economics, 120,* 835–864.

Limin, Y., Chaobo, B., & Junliang, Y. (2013). "Research on economic development stage and marginal effects of trade and fdi on economic growth in China." *International Journal of Economics & Finance, 5,* 37–45.

Mankiw, N. (1995). "The growth of nations." *Brookings Papers on Economic Activity, 6,* 25–29.

"Millennium Development Goals." (2000) United Nations Development Programme. Retrieved from UNDP.com

Mitchell, D. (2005). "The impact of government spending on economic growth". The Heritage Foundation. Retrieved from"http://www.heritage.org/Research/Budget/bg1831.cfm"

Park, C. (2006). "The theory of economic growth: a "classical" perspective." *Science and Society, 70,* 558–562.

Snowdon, B. (2006). "The enduring elixir of economic growth." *World Economics, 7,* 73–130.

Vanhoudt, P. & Onorante, L. (2001). "Measuring economic growth and the new economy." EIB Papers. Retrieved from "http://eib.eu.int/Attachments/efs/eibpapers/y01n1v6/y01n1a03.pdf"

SUGGESTED READING

Alexander, W. (1997). "Inflation and economic growth: Evidence from a growth equation." *Applied Economics, 29,* 233–238.

Eicher, T., & Turnovsky, S. (1999). "Non-scale models of economic growth." *Economic Journal, 109,* 394–415.

Skonhoft, A. (1997). "Technological diffusion and growth among nations: The two stages of catching up." *Metroeconomica, 48,* 177–187.

—Simone I. Flynn, PhD

ECONOMIC PROBLEMS OF DEVELOPING AREAS

ABSTRACT

This article will focus on the economic problems of developing areas. It will provide an overview of the United Nations' criteria for developing country classification as well as an analysis of different types of economic problems that affect developing areas. The economic problems of infrastructure, creditworthiness, corruption, and poverty will be described and analyzed. Economic problems will be discussed within their respective related cultural, social, political, and historical contexts. In addition, the issue of colonization's lasting influence on business climates in developing countries will be introduced.

OVERVIEW

Developing areas, including developing countries and regions, have a unique set of economic problems and challenges to economic development. Developing countries, taken as a whole, refer to countries characterized by an underdeveloped industrial base, low per capita income, and widespread poverty. Developing countries are often referred to as least developed countries (LDCs) by international development organizations such as the United Nations (UN) and the World Bank. Least developed countries have, by definition, small- to medium-sized economies and structural handicaps that hinder economic development. In 2003, the U N Economic and Social Council, along with the U N Committee for Development Policy (CDP), formalized the use of

The United Nations headquarters is located in New York City. This is a view of the building from Roosevelt Island. (Courtesy of Neptuul CC BY-SA 3.0 via Wikimedia Commons)

the following three criteria for the identification of least developed countries:

- **Low-income:** A three-year average estimate of the gross national income (GNI) per capita under $750.
- **Human resource weakness:** A low composite Human Assets Index (HAI) score based on indicators of nutrition, health, education, and adult literacy.
- **Economic vulnerability:** A composite Economic Vulnerability Index (EVI) based on the instability of agricultural production, the instability of exports of goods and services, the economic importance of nontraditional activities, the handicap of economic smallness, and the percentage of population displaced by natural disasters (Ghaus-Pasha, 2007).

According to the UN framework, least developed countries may "graduate" from the least developed countries list when they meet or exceed the thresholds for two of the three criteria in two consecutive reviews by the Committee for Development Policy. The least developed countries list is fluid and dynamic. For example, in the early 2000s, Senegal was added to the least developed countries list and Cabo Verde and Maldives qualified for graduation from the least developed countries category.

The United Nations, as of 2017, classifies the following countries as the least developed countries:

- Least developed countries: Forty-eight countries including Afghanistan, Angola, Bangladesh, Benin, Bhutan, Burkina Faso, Burundi, Cambodia, Central African Republic, Chad, Comoros, Democratic Republic of the Congo, Djibouti, Eritrea, Ethiopia, Gambia, Guinea, Guinea-Bissau, Haiti, Kiribati, Lao People's Democratic Republic, Lesotho, Liber ia, Madagascar, Malawi, Mali, Mauritania, Mozambique, Myanmar, Nepal, Niger, Rwanda, Samoa, Sao Tome and Principe, Senegal, Sierra Leone, Solomon Islands, Somalia, Sudan, Timor-Leste, Togo, Tuvalu, Uganda, United Republic of Tanzania, Vanuatu, Yemen, and Zambia.
- The least developed regions and countries of the world experience economic problems caused and

exacerbated by shared characteristics, structures, histories, climates, and practices. For example, developing countries tend to have high levels of income inequality, low life expectancies, small or limited industrial sectors, outward migration from rural to urban areas, market imperfections (or market absence), and a history of colonial rule. This list of shared characteristics, while not present in all developing countries, illustrates the complexity of economic problems in developing countries. Economic problems do not occur in isolation. Economic problems, which are products of particular historical events, patterns, and structures, are related to social, political, and cultural problems and practices.

The following sections describe economic problems in their respective cultural, social, political, and historical contexts. The economic problems of child labor, creditworthiness, corruption, and poverty will be described and analyzed. In addition, the issue of colonization's continued influence on business climates in developing countries will be introduced.

APPLICATIONS

Economic Problems of Child Labor, Creditworthiness, Corruption, and Poverty

Economic problems refer to factors that hinder the functioning and growth of an economy. Economic problems of all kinds, including structural, fiscal, and cultural, affect economic development efforts by national governments, corporations, and international development organizations. Economic development must address a wide range of programs and strategies aimed at promoting growth in a part or whole of an economy. Developing countries with limited economies or economies in transition are particularly sensitive to economic problems of child labor, creditworthiness, corruption, and poverty and its related conditions.

Child Labor

Exploitative child labor, which refers to any economic activity performed by a person under the age of fifteen, is a major economic and social problem in developing countries. The International Labour Organization (ILO) estimates that there are about 250 million children between the ages of five and

Child labor is common in informal mining industry of Africa. Above, children engaged in diamond mining in Sierra Leone. (Courtesy of USAID via Wikimedia Commons

fourteen involved in at least part-time labor. The ILO estimates that there are 120 million involved in hazardous and exploitative full-time work. Child labor by region suggests that it is a global problem: There are an estimated 152.5 million child laborers in Asia, 80 million in Africa, and 17.5 million in Latin America (Palley, 2002). The ILO reports that child labor is used in multiple industries and sectors, including agriculture, fishing, forestry, hunting, manufacturing, retail, trade, community and personal services, transport, storage, communications, construction, mining, and quarrying (Tierney, 2000).

Child labor is deeply connected to the economic life and prosperity of many developing countries. Child labor in developing countries cannot be eradicated without solving the problems that afflict developing country labor markets. Labor market dysfunction and underdevelopment are believed to be

Home-based carpet weaving enterprise in Egypt deploying child labor. (Courtesy of Endlisnis CC BY 2.0 via Wikimedia Commons)

the fundamental causes of exploitative child labor practices in developing regions of the world. The eradication of exploitative child labor practices requires the development and implementation of economic development programs that strengthen the economies of developing countries.

International development organizations, national governments, and corporations debate whether voluntary practices or required labor rules should be used to solve the problem of child labor in developing countries. Corporations are increasingly adopting voluntary practices, such as private labeling schemes, as part of corporate social responsibility (CSR) efforts, which certify to global consumers that a product has been produced without child labor. While voluntary efforts by corporations to use adult labor rather than child labor is a positive step, voluntary practices alone are not believed to be sufficient to eradicate child labor in developing countries. International labor standards, which address the root

causes of child labor such as labor market dysfunction and underdevelopment, have a better chance for success than voluntary practices alone.

The ILO, as described in the 1998 Declaration of Fundamental Principles and Rights at Work, promotes five main international labor standards which, if adopted by developed and developing countries alike, would likely significantly affect the problem of child labor (Palley, 2002):

Freedom of Association: The ILO Freedom of Association and Protection of the Right to Organize Convention (No. 87) establishes the right of workers to form and join organizations, including unions, of their own choosing.

Effective Recognition of the Right to Collective Bargaining: The Right to Organize and Collective Bargaining Convention (No. 98) protects unions from outside interference.

The Elimination of All Forms of Forced or Compulsory Labor: The Forced Labor Convention (No. 29) and the Abolition of Forced Labor Convention (No. 105) require governments to suppress all forms of forced and compulsory labor in their territories.

The Effective Abolition of Child Labor: The Minimum Age Convention (No. 138) sets a baseline minimum working age of fifteen.

The Elimination of Discrimination in Respect of Employment and Occupation: The Discrimination Convention (No. 111) requires governments to establish national policies that eliminate discrimination on the basis of race, color, sex, religion, political opinion, and national origin (Palley, 2002, p. 605).

Creditworthiness
Many developing countries depend on international loans and grants from both the public sector and private sector to fund economic development programs and initiatives. International institutions use creditworthiness scores to determine a developing country's loan eligibility. Numerous national governments, international aid and development organizations, and for-profit reporting agencies compile and distribute sets of economic indicators, in part,

to meet the demand for quantifiable data about economic development and activity. International organizations that depend on and produce economic indicators include the United Nations and World Bank. Common economic indicators include national income per capita, age-dependency rates, fertility rates, migration, unemployment rates, the number of mothers in paid employment, childcare costs, tax on labor, unemployment benefits, students' performance, material deprivation, earnings inequality, gender wage gaps, intergenerational mobility, public social spending, poverty persistence, housing costs, and pension replacement rates.

Development agencies, which refer to either public or private organizations, that lead the economic development and regeneration efforts in developing countries or regions of the world use multiple economic tools and products to promote economic growth and its related social, cultural, and political gains. One of the most important economic tools that development agencies use to promote economic growth in developing countries are loans for small- and large-scale businesses and initiatives. Development agencies use the criteria of creditworthiness to determine the type and amount of development loan that a developing country business or local government may receive. Ultimately, creditworthiness is directly tied to increasingly important and competitive development funds.

The World Bank produces a set of statistics on developing countries based solely on income. These income-based country classifications are used to determine creditworthiness and development loan eligibility. The World Bank's main criterion for classifying developing country economies is gross national income (GNI) per capita. Gross national income per capita classifies economies and countries as low income, lower middle income, upper middle income, or high income. The gross national income categories correspond to the following income levels:

- Low income: $875 or less
- Lower middle income: $876–$3,465
- Upper middle income: $3,466–$10,725
- High income: $10,726 or more

While classification by income does not always correctly represent development status, low-income and middle-income economies are usually categorized as developing economies. Developing countries are eligible for different types of loans based on their gross national income per capita and perceived creditworthiness. The most common economic development loans made to developing countries are made by the International Development Association (IDA) and the International Bank of Reconstruction and Development (IBRD).

The International Development Association lends money to low-income countries that have difficulty borrowing on international markets. IDA loans and grants, which carry a zero interest rate, are intended to promote economic growth and improve living conditions. IDA loans are concessional loans offering interest rates below those available on the market and long grace periods. Sixty-six countries, with a per capita income in 2005 of less than $1,025, qualified for IDA loans and grants. For the fiscal year ending in June 2013, IDA commitments surpassed $16 billion, with about 50 percent of those loans going to African countries. The International Bank of Reconstruction and Development provides loans to sixty-four developing countries. IBRD loans are nonconcessional, meaning they do not offer exceptionally low interest rates or long grace periods. IBRD loans are only offered to developing countries considered, based on economic indicators, to be financially creditworthy.

In addition to private sector development use, as described above, developing country creditworthiness indicators, also called risk indicators, are developed and used by commercial lending institutions. Commercial creditworthiness ratings (country-specific risks) refer to the likelihood that a certain country will fail to repay its debt. Default risk is evaluated using specific information about a country's political and economic development levels thought to affect its ability and willingness to repay its loan. Commercial creditworthiness indicators determine both the volume and the rates of commercial bank loans to developing countries. Commercial creditworthiness indicators are influenced by variables such as economic fundamentals, regional location, and structure and content of its exports. Economic fundamentals refer to the ratio of non-gold foreign exchange reserves to imports, the ratio of the current account balance gross domestic product (GDP), growth, and inflation. Three main rating agencies, including Institutional Investor, Euromoney, and

Economist Intelligence Unit, produce and publish commercial creditworthiness indicators for developing countries for use by commercial lending institutions (Haque, 1996).

Corruption

Corruption is a social pathology that affects both developing and developed countries. Corruption refers to abuse of the agent-client relationship, misuse of public office, legal violations, opposition with public opinion, and not acting in ways that promote the public interest, trust, or duty. Three main factors influence the economic impact of corruption in developing countries. These factors include the following:

- The amount of resources wasted through each corrupt action.
- The periodicity of corrupt activities.
- The amount of people involved in the corrupt action.

Corruption can be separated into two categories including small scale and large scale. Small-scale corruption extracts public resources to supplement the income of one or a few individuals. Large-scale corruption is systemic and supported by power networks. Corruption hinders growth and development. Scholars cite the following variables as the root causes of large-scale corruption: protection of self-interest,

A Somali pirate with weapons aboard a vessel. (Courtesy of Jan van Rijn, Dutch mariner, via Wikimedia Commons)

unfair laws, pathology of the market structure, ineffective control systems, bureaucracy, lack of knowledge, economic need, job dissatisfaction, and lack of power.

Ultimately, large-scale corruption results from power networks (social networks that function through horizontal and vertical exchanges) that profit through the exploitation of opportunity and the diversion of economic gains from the public into the pockets of a small number of corrupt individuals. Power networks depend on economic, political, technical, historical, and ideological support. Large-scale corruption affects programs, law, and organizations and has a major negative impact on economic development. Corrupt networks grow quickly. Police and legal systems are major targets and places for large-scale corruption as these arenas offer the elements that corruption needs to grow. Large-scale corruption is an obstacle to economic development. Corruption reduces the resources available for development and limits the development of new institutions and ways of operating (Carvajal, 1999). Corruption and political instability threaten trade in developing countries. For example, bread-bulk shippers, which refer to shippers handling cargo that cannot be stored in liquid containers or steel container boxes, transporting goods to developing countries face corruption problems and related conditions. Corruption is often part of a wide range of economic-related problems, including piracy, regime change, thieves, difficult terrain, lack of transportation infrastructure and ports, political instability, and unstable or disputed succession (Leach, 2006).

Poverty

Poverty, which encompasses a lack of basic necessities as well as a denial of opportunities and choices that permit economic and personal development, is a persistent, widespread, and intractable economic problem in developing regions. The United Nations provides two separate metrics for measuring poverty: the Human Development Index (HDI) and the Human Poverty Index (HPI) (Norton, 1998).

The Human Development Index measures human capabilities through health, education, and a high standard of living based upon gross national income per capita.

A poor boy sitting in the streets of Mumbai, India. (Courtesy of Joshua Doubek CC BY-SA 3.0 via Wikimedia Commons)

The Human Poverty Index provides a metric to compare the well-being of the most deprived people in a community for the purposes of economic planning and advocacy.

According to the World Bank, extreme poverty, and its related conditions such as hunger, currently affect more than one billion people in the world. The measure of extreme poverty is based on individual income or consumption levels of below $1.25 a day. Economic development efforts in developing countries are based on the argument that poverty reduction is tied to economic growth. Economic development, as it is practiced today, involves numerous public sector and private sector stakeholders (such as development agencies, national governments, corporations from industrialized countries, businesses from developing countries, community agencies, and communities in need) committed to ending poverty, and related conditions, in developing countries.

Combating global poverty is an economic development goal that unites international development organizations, national governments, and corporations around the world. For example, in 2000, the United Nations Millennium Summit was held to create time-bound and measurable goals for combating poverty and related conditions. The millennium development goals (MDGs) have become a blueprint of sorts for national governments, development agencies, and corporations committed to aiding the world's poorest people. The millennium development goals include the following objectives: eradicate extreme poverty and hunger; achieve universal primary education; promote gender equality and the empowerment of women; reduce child mortality; improve maternal health; combat HIV/AIDS, malaria, and other diseases; ensure environmental sustainability; and develop a global partnership for development by 2015 (Millennium Development Goals, 2005). The UN concluded the MDGs in 2015, and as of 2016, initiated the UN Sustainable Development Goals.

While contemporary forms of economic development are focused primarily on eradicating extreme poverty and related conditions, economic development efforts have been in existence, in some form, since the end of World War II. The modern era of international aid to developing countries began in the 1940s as World War II ended. After the war, world leaders and governing bodies put structures into place, such as the World Bank, the United Nations, the World Trade Organization, and the International Monetary Fund, to prevent the economic depressions and instability that characterized the years following World War I. The modern trend of globalization and the resulting shifts from centralized to market economies in much of the world has created both a need and opportunity for economic development in developing countries and regions of the world. International development organizations, national governments, and corporations are coming together to focus on building frameworks for economic development as the basis for achieving sustainable economic growth.

CONCLUSION

Colonial Legacy and Business Climates
Economic problems of developing areas, while not intractable, are often caused by the persistence of

colonial-era influences on business climates. In many developing regions, the forces of economic globalization promise to challenge and change the colonial legacy of fixed class and power relations, limited production bases, and outdated economic institutions. In developing regions, business climates or environments (which refer to combined factors such as tax structure, public services, government regulations, labor force, and infrastructure that affect the profitability and experience of conducting business in a particular country or region of the world) are often shaped by a colonial legacy or history. Factors such as power relations (including class and race), institutional structures (including banking or tax systems), cultural biases (including gender and work-day perceptions), resource use, and planning are, to varying degrees, shaped by local histories. For example, urban land use patterns in Nigeria, a developing country, are considered to be an outdated colonial legacy. The "traditional urban planning framework, its administration, and the associated master planning which still dominates planning in Nigeria, does not adequately respond to evolving changes in cultural, economic and social developments" (Ogu, 1999, p. 347).

In the final analysis, economic problems of developing areas, while not uniform or fixed, may be classified into broad categories (such as child labor, creditworthiness, corruption, and poverty as described in this article) as part of the process of problem identification and long-term problem solving.

BIBLIOGRAPHY

Bahmani, S. (2013). "Exchange rate volatility and demand for money in less developed countries." *Journal of Economics and Finance, 37*, 442–452.

Carvajal, R. (1999). "Large-Scale corruption: definition, causes, and cures." *Systematic Practice and Action Research, 12*, 335.

Chakraborty, S., & Lahiri, A. (2007). "Costly intermediation and the poverty of nations." *International Economic Review, 48*, 155–183.

Criteria for the identification of the LDCs. (2007). The United Nations.

Data and statistics. (2006). The World Bank. Retrieved May 09, 2007.

Dedrick, J., Kraemer, K. L., Shih, E. (2013). "Information technology and productivity in developed and developing countries." *Journal of Management Information Systems, 30*, 97–122.

Definition of major areas and regions. (2006). The UN's 2006 Revision Population Database.

Ghaus-Pasha, A. (2007). *Governance for the millennium development goals: core issues and good practices.* Department of Economic and Social Affairs of the United Nations.

Haque, N., Kumar, M., & Mathieson, D. (1996). "The economic content of indicators of developing country creditworthiness." *International Monetary Fund Staff Papers, 43*, 688–725.

Kennedy, T. F., Bardy, R., & Rubens, A. (2012). "Economic growth and welfare: how foreign direct investment contributes to improving social order in less developed countries." *Journal of Organisational Transformation and Social Change, 9*, 185–205.

Leach, P. (2006). "Political instability threatens trade with third world countries." *Shipping Digest, 83*(4368), 12.

Ogu, V. (1999). "Evolutionary dynamics of urban land use planning and environmental sustainability in Nigeria." *Planning Perspectives, 14*, 347–368.

Norton, S. (1998). "Poverty, property rights, and human well-being: a cross-national study." *CATO Journal, 18*, 233.

Palley, T. (2002). "The child labor problem and the need for international labor standards." *Journal of Economic Issues, 36*, 601–615.

Roggero, P., Mangiaterra, V., Bustreo, F., & Rosati, F. (2007). "The health impact of child labor in developing countries: evidence from cross-country data." *American Journal of Public Health, 97*, 271–275.

Seers, D. (2017). "Back to the ivory tower? The professionalism of development studies and their extension to Europe." *IDS Bulletin, 48*, 1A.

Tierney, J. (2000). "The world of child labor." *The World & I, 15*, 54.

United Nations Millennium Development Goals. (2005). The United Nations.

SUGGESTED READING

Bird, G. (1996). "The International Monetary Fund and developing countries: A review of the evidence and policy options." *International Organization, 50*, 477–511.

Prasad, B. (1998). "The woes of economic reform: poverty and income inequality in Fiji." *International Journal of Social Economics, 25*, 1073.

Shourie, A. (1973). "Growth, poverty, and inequalities." *Foreign Affairs, 51,* 340–352.

Silva, E. G., & Teixeira, A. A. C. (2011). "Does structure influence growth? A panel data econometric assessment of 'relatively less developed' countries, 1979–2003." *Industrial and Corporate Change, 20,* 457–510.

—Simone I. Flynn, PhD

ECONOMIC UNIONS

ABSTRACT

Economic unions are a natural response to the realities of globalization and represent one stage in the process of economic integration. In theory, nations move from free-trade agreements to form customs unions and then common markets before forming economic unions. In practice, however, the path is not always that clear. Economic unions often are characterized by a common currency and centralized bank, in which case they are sometimes referred to as economic and monetary unions. The best example of a contemporary economic and monetary union is the European Union (EU). In many ways, the EU is a living laboratory for observing the effects of macroeconomic policy cooperation on regional growth and cross-border economic, trade, and investment ties.

OVERVIEW

Globalization brings with it many changes. From a business point of view, globalization increases the marketplace in which a business can sell its goods and services. On the other hand, globalization often makes doing business more difficult, requiring, for example, the management of an international supply chain, dealing with the intricacies of managing an international workforce, or marketing to different cultures. In addition, globalization affects not only businesses but also the countries within which a business operates. Before globalization, most countries were able to be economically self-sufficient and did not rely on international trade or imported goods to survive. However, with increasing globalization comes an increasing reliance on the goods and services of other countries. Thus, while an international company can market its goods and services in other countries, those other countries can market their own goods and services locally to the new company. To help facilitate the economic realities of globalization, a number of nations are forming economic unions.

An economic union is a type of common market that permits the free movement of capital, labor, goods, and services. Economic unions harmonize or unify their social, fiscal, and monetary policies (often including having a united currency). Examples of economic unions include

- the African Union;
- Andean Community (Comunidad Andina);
- Arab Maghreb Union (Union du Maghreb Arabe);
- Association of Caribbean States;
- Association of South East Asian Nations;
- Caribbean Community;
- Commonwealth of Independent States;
- East African Community;
- European Union; and
- Pacific Community.

African Union Conference Center and office complex (AUCC) in Addis Ababa, Ethiopia. AU's new headquarters was inaugurated at the 18th AU summit during the week of January 23 – 30, 2012. (Courtesy of Maria Dyveke Styve CC BY-SA 3.0 via Wikimedia Commons)

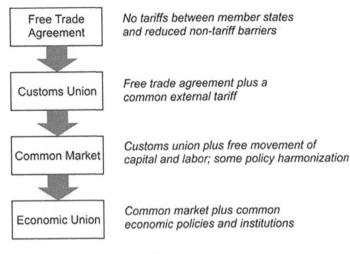

Free Trade Agreement	*No tariffs between member states and reduced non-tariff barriers*
Customs Union	*Free trade agreement plus a common external tariff*
Common Market	*Customs union plus free movement of capital and labor; some policy harmonization*
Economic Union	*Common market plus common economic policies and institutions*

(adapted from Holden, 2003).

Although in practice, the path from national economic self-sufficiency to economic integration varies from situation to situation; in general, there are four stages to this transformation:

- free-trade agreements;
- customs unions;
- common markets; and
- economic unions (Holden, 2003).

These stages are summarized in Figure 1.

Free-Trade Agreements. The first stage toward economic integration is represented by the free-trade agreement. Free trade is the exchange of goods and services between countries or sovereign states without high tariffs, nontariff barriers (e.g., quotas), or other inhibiting requirements or processes. Free trade does not apply to capital or labor. Free-trade agreements (also referred to as preferential trade agreements) eliminate import tariffs and quotas between the signatories to the agreement. They may apply to all aspects of international trade between the signatories or may be limited to a few sectors. Often, free-trade agreements include formal mechanisms that are to be used to resolve disputes. The primary advantage of the free-trade agreement is that it liberalizes trade among the member nations. However, free-trade agreements otherwise place few limitations on the member nations. In order for a free-trade agreement to properly function, it must

also include rules of origin that apply to all third-party goods imported from outside the free-trade area.

Customs Unions. The next stage in economic integration comprises the development of customs unions. Customs are duties or taxes that are imposed by a country, sovereign state, or common union on imported goods. In some situations, duties or taxes may also be imposed on exported goods. Customs unions remove internal trade barriers and require participating states to harmonize external trade policies. Part of this harmonization includes the development of a common external tariff. These are shared customs duties, import quotas, preferences, or other nontariff barriers imposed by a customs union or common market on imports to any or all countries in the union or market. Common external tariffs are actually a simple form of economic union. Customs unions may prohibit the use of trade remedies with the union and may also negotiate multilateral trade initiatives. Because all goods imported into a customs union are subject to the same tariff no matter their point of origin, customs unions have no need for rules of origin as required in free-trade agreements. However, in order to gain the benefits of a customs union, participating nations must by necessity relinquish their right to establish an independent trade policy. As a result, member nations also experience some restriction of foreign policy.

Common Markets. The third stage in economic integration is the development of a common market. This is a group of countries or sovereign states within a geographical area with a mutual agreement to permit the free movement of capital, labor, goods, and services among its members. Although common markets promote duty-free trade for the member nations, they impose common external tariffs on imports from countries that are not members. Common markets have unified or harmonized social, fiscal, and monetary policies. This feature of common markets severely limits the ability of member nations to implement independent economic policies. However, common markets offer gains in economic efficiency that could not otherwise be realized. Because of the nature of common markets, both labor and capital can move within the area of the common market, leading to a more efficient allocation of resources than could otherwise be achieved.

The Economic Union. The fourth stage in economic integration comprises the economic union. This is a type of common market that permits the free movement of capital, labor, goods, and services. Economic unions harmonize or unify their social, fiscal, and monetary policies. When economic unions also have a common currency with a concomitant central bank for all member states, they may be referred to as economic and monetary unions. Economic unions include significant harmonization of policy among the member states, particularly the formal coordination of monetary and fiscal policies, and labor market, regional development, transportation, and industrial policies.

APPLICATIONS

The European Union. Arguably, the best-known economic union is the European Union (EU) comprising twenty-eight different sovereign states in

Europe by 2013. According to the Delegation of the European Union to the United States, the roots of the EU trace back more than fifty years ("Economic & Monetary," 2007). The EU started as a "customs union that allowed trade to move freely among its member states" (p. 1). The EU facilitates the flow of labor, capital, goods, and services by providing a single market among the member states. The EU went a step further and became an economic and monetary policy with "coordinated fiscal policies and a common currency, the euro" (p. 1). In many ways, the EU is a living laboratory for observing the effect of macroeconomic policy cooperation on regional growth and cross-border economic, trade, and investment ties.

The roots of the modern EU began in 1970 with the publication of the first feasibility report for a European monetary union. At this time, much of Europe was suffering from stagnant and unstable economies. In 1973, the gold standard was broken up, and in 1979, the European Monetary Standard was established. These steps paved the way for

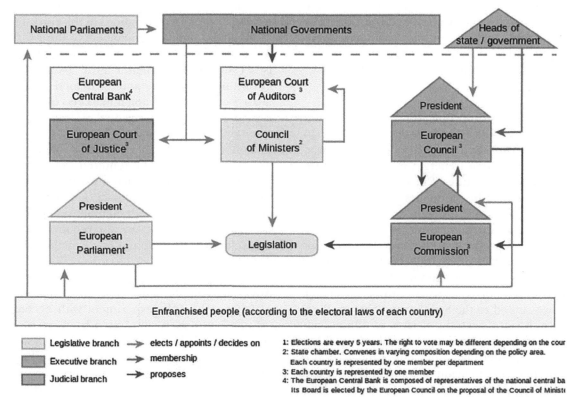

Political System of the European Union. (Courtesy of 111Alleskönner CC BY-SA 3.0 via Wikimedia Commons)

economic and monetary union in Europe. In 1989 and 1992, the Delors Report and the Maastricht Treaty respectively set out a single currency for the EU. In 1999, member states of the EU entered the first stage of becoming an economic and monetary union by more closely coordinating economic policies and beginning to dismantle the barriers to the free movement of capital within the EU ("Economic & Monetary," 2007).

In 1994, the second stage toward becoming an economic and monetary union was entered. At this time, the EU liberalized the movement of capital and payments to non-EU countries. Member states of the EU also adopted a budget and debt ceilings and instituted a monitoring system. In 1998, Austria, Belgium, Germany, Finland, France, Ireland, Italy, Luxembourg, the Netherlands, Portugal, and Spain qualified to join the European economic and monetary union and adopt its currency parities. In 1999, the third stage was entered, and the euro was introduced. At this time, monetary authority in the euro zone was transferred to the European System of Central Banks. Also in 1999, eleven of the euro area member states fixed their exchange rates and adopted the euro. In 2001, Greece became a member of the euro area. In 2002, euro notes and coins were introduced within the euro area. In 2013, Croatia also joined the euro area ("Economic & Monetary," 2007).

Monetary Policy. Most people associate the creation of the euro with the transformation of the EU to being an economic and monetary union. However, this is only the tip of the iceberg. Underlying the euro is an entire infrastructure of economic policies intended to integrate the economies of member states, maintain low and stable inflation and interest rates, foster sustained economic growth, and improve competitiveness and productivity. Because the success of the EU is dependent on the efforts of the member states, they have agreed by treaty to address economic policies as a common concern. Accordingly, member states have agreed to the Stability and Growth Pact, which requires the central government within each member state to maintain an annual budget with a deficit of no greater than 3 percent of the gross domestic product and to maintain a public debt of less than 60 percent of the gross domestic product. The European Central Bank (ECB), an independent

Euro Banknotes as of 4/4/2017. (Courtesy of 636Buster via Wikimedia Commons)

bank with a governing board that represents all euro area member states, determines and implements the monetary policy for all nations in the euro area.

Monetary policy for members of the EU that are not members of the euro area, on the other hand, is set by their national central banks. Similarly, government budgets and structural policies for labor, pensions, and capital markets continue under the jurisdiction of individual EU member states whether or not the state belongs to the euro area ("Economic & Monetary," 2007). Member states within the euro area are required to pay a financial penalty or face other sanctions if they do not meet these requirements of the pact (barring exceptional circumstances). Although member states that do not belong to the euro area are also required to avoid excessive deficits, they do not face sanctions if they do not or cannot comply.

Advantages of the Euro. Despite prognostications of failure, the EU's experiment with becoming an economic and monetary union has been successful. Before the EU became an economic and monetary union, inflation in Europe was as high as 10 percent in some European countries. By 1998, however, inflation had dropped to 1.5 percent and has remained under 2 percent across the euro area. In addition, the introduction of a common currency has resulted in benefits not only for businesses, consumers, and travelers but also for Europe in general and for the world economy. Since the implementation of the euro as a common currency, doing business in member states has become easier for businesses, consumers, and travelers. Because of lower inflation rates and more sound public finances, both businesses and consumers are faced with less economic uncertainty than before. In addition, businesses are no longer faced with exchange rate risks when doing business within the euro area. The use of the common euro also reduces requirements for paperwork and transaction costs resulting from the use of multiple currencies. Having a common currency also reduces corporate accounting requirements because there are fewer transactions involving multiple currencies.

The new economic environment within the European economic and monetary union also makes investment more attractive to foreign entities due to the lower costs of doing business and obviates the necessity for travelers of exchanging currency. As a result, member states have become more attractive tourist destinations. Similarly, lower interest rates also make it easier for euro area companies and consumers to borrow money ("Economic & Monetary," 2007). Banks, insurance agencies, and pension funds also have greater flexibility in the types of financial services they can offer because they are no longer affected by fluctuating exchange rates. The use of the euro also allows consumers, wholesalers, and traders to compare prices more easily. This leads to greater competition and a resultant lowering of prices.

The movement of the EU to become an economic and monetary union has also resulted in benefits for Europe in general. By banding together in the common euro area, member states are better protected from crises in the international economy. For example, member states can adjust more easily to fluctuations in external exchange rates with other currencies including the U.S. dollar and the Japanese yen. The transition to becoming an economic and monetary union has also given the EU a more prominent place in international institutions such as the G-8, the World Bank, and the International Monetary Fund ("Economic & Monetary," 2007). In addition, the establishment of the euro area has led to greater trade within the area. This has resulted in higher employment in the manufacturing and service industries

and has also stimulated economic growth and expanded the tax base. In addition, the establishment of the euro area has impacted the world economy. This move has resulted in a stronger, more competitive economy in Europe with greater price and exchange rate stability and lower interest rates.

Opting Out. Not all member states of the EU are part of the euro area. For example, Denmark negotiated an opt-out clause in the treaty allowing it to retain its own national currency. Member states of the EU, however, have committed to adopt the euro once they meet certain criteria. First, member states desiring to join the euro area must have an inflation rate no more than 1.5 percent greater than the three best-performing EU member states for the previous year. In addition, the national budget deficit for the applying member needs to be less than 3 percent of the nation's gross domestic product, and the ratio of its debt to its gross domestic product cannot exceed 60 percent. The national exchange rate for the applying member also needs to have been within predefined margins for the past two years. Interest rates within the applying state can be no higher than two percentage points above those of the three best performing EU member states during the previous year ("Economic & Monetary," 2007).

In early 2010, eurozone member Greece began imposing measures to rein in its expanding public debt. Greece was only one of a number of EU countries with substantially unbalanced budgets. The global financial crisis was creating massive demand for public services, and very high levels of unemployment limited those countries' ability to raise revenues. The European Central Bank, following the lead of German chancellor Angela Merkel, demanded deep austerity measures in Greece, Ireland, Portugal, Italy, and Spain in return for bailouts to prevent national insolvency. Resistance by recession-battered populaces pitted economically strong Germany and to some extent France against the eurozone's weaker but still important members. As the political situation in Greece became increasingly unstable and stock markets globally began to sink, the U.K. urged a solution be found more rapidly. Ratings agencies downgraded not only Greece, Portugal, and Spain (all reduced to junk bond status) but also Italy, Belgium, France, and Austria. By 2013, stock markets had bounced back, though the weaker EU members remained fragile, and Cyprus joined the list of troubled eurozone countries.

In the aftermath of the crisis, El-Erian (2013) warned that the euro was fragmented, freely circulating in some areas of the eurozone and trapped by capital controls in others. The euro was also subject to flight, especially to Switzerland and the United States. Neo-Keynesian Hetzel (2013) concluded that the ECB should purchase as many government securities as necessary to drive growth in aggregate nominal demand and commit to structural reform, allowing the inflation rate of affected countries to exceed 2 percent. The UK, though financially regulated chiefly from Brussels, retained its own currency, and fears arose that resentments might negatively impact the financial services sector there (Dale, 2013). The role of Germany, though critical to sustaining its poorer sister countries in the eurozone, was not free from criticism. German wealth was undoubtedly the product of a culture of financial prudence, with an emphasis on savings, and repeated demands for bailouts from what it deemed profligate nations was met with resentment. As Greeley (2013) pointed out, however, German euros were invested aggressively—and profitably—in the very countries it later accused of reckless borrowing. In other words, the euro flowed from weaker countries to stronger countries, and EU policy did not adequately foster a return trip of euros to weaker countries in the form of growth.

CONCLUSION

Economic unions are a natural response to the realities of globalization. As nations develop and begin to interact more with their neighbors, free-trade agreements are often developed to eliminate tariffs between parties and to reduce other nontariff barriers to trade. As interaction and interdependency increase, customs unions form to impose a common external tariff in addition to the benefits of a free-trade agreement. When the benefits of a customs union become insufficient to promote trade at the level desired by the participating parties, common markets may be developed. These provide the benefits of a customs union along with free movement of capital and labor as well as some policy harmonization. The next step in responding to increasing globalization is the development of an economic union. This not only provides the benefits of a common market but also establishes common economic policies and institutions for the member states. A further refinement on the economic union is the economic and monetary union that also gives the member states the benefit of a common currency and centralized bank. The best example of an economic and monetary union is the EU.

BIBLIOGRAPHY

Beck, G. W. & Weber, A. A. (2005). "Inflation rate dispersion and convergence in monetary and economic unions: Lessons for the ECB." *CFS Working Paper Series, 2005/*31.

Borsi, M., & Metiu, N. (2015). "The evolution of economic convergence in the European Union." *Empirical Economics, 48*(2), 657–681.

Dale, S. (2013). "MEPs warning of EU's resentment towards UK." *Money Marketing,* 5.

"Economic and monetary union in the EU: A force for European and global economic stability." (2007, January). *Eufocus.*

El-Erian, M. A. (2013). "Europe's hard choices." *Fortune International (Asia), 167*(6), 12.

Fichtner, F., & König, P. (2015). "A stronger Union through crisis? 25 years of monetary integration in Europe." *DIW Economic Bulletin, 5*(27), 376–384.

Greeley, B. (2013). "Can the Germans admit their role in the crisis?" *Bloomberg Businessweek,* (4346), 49–50.

Hetzel, R. L. (2013). "ECB monetary policy in the recession: A new Keynesian (old monetarist) critique." *Working Papers Series (Federal Reserve Bank of Richmond), 13*(7), 2–43.

Holden, M. (2003, Feb). "Stages of economic integration: From autarky to economic union." Retrieved from Government of Canada Web xlink:href="http://dsp-psd.tpsgc.gc.ca/Collection-R/LoPBdP/inbrief/prb0249-e.htm"

Howarth, D., & Quaglia, L. (2013). "Banking union as Holy Grail: Rebuilding the single market in financial services, stabilizing Europe's banks and 'completing' economic and monetary union." *Journal of Common Market Studies, 51,* 103–123.

Kostenko, N. (2014). "Geo-economic strategy of the European Union: Experience for Ukraine." *Economics and Business, 25,* 54–60.

Nau, H. R. (1979). "From integration to interdependence: Gains, losses and continuing gaps." *International Organization, 33*(1), 127–155.

Rittberger, B. (2014). "Integration without representation? The European Parliament and the reform of economic governance in the EU." *Journal of Common Market Studies, 52*(6), 1174–1183.

Semmler, W. (2013). "The macroeconomics of austerity in the European Union." *Social Research, 80*(3), 883–914.

SUGGESTED READING

Afontsev, S. A. (2014). "From the customs union to the common economic space." *Problems of Economic Transition, 56*(12), 3–18.

Archer, C. (2014). *The European Union* (2nd ed.). London, England: Routledge.

Avery, W. P. & Cochrane, J. D. (1973). "Innovation in Latin American regionalism: The Andean Common Market." *International Organization, 27*(2), 181–222.

Bainev, V., & Vinnik, V. (2015). "Approaches to harmonizing the industrial policy of countries in the customs union and common economic space." *Problems of Economic Transition, 57*(10), 66–79.

Etro, F. (n.d.). "International policy coordination with economic unions." Retrieved from Intertic Website xlink:href="http://www.intertic.org/Unions"

Lorz, O. & Willmann, G. (2007, Nov.). *Enlargement vs. deepening: The trade-off facing economic unions.*

McLure, C. E. Jr. (2008). "Harmonizing corporate income taxes in the European Community: Rationale and implications." *NBER/Tax Policy and the Economy, 22*, 151–195.

Srivastava, R. K. & Green, R. T. (1986). "Determinants of bilateral trade flows." *Journal of Business, 59*(4), 623–640.

—*Ruth A. Wienclaw*

ECONOMICS OF BUSINESS REGULATIONS

ABSTRACT

This article focuses on the economics of business regulation in the United States as well as the impact of national business regulations on the global economy. The economics of federal business regulations and compliance are described and analyzed. The regulatory burden of different-sized businesses is summarized. The economic issues associated with differences in international business regulations are also addressed. The regulatory impact of international trade agreements, such as the North American Free Trade Agreement, and environmental pacts, such as the Kyoto Protocol, are discussed.

OVERVIEW

In the United States and around the world, governments actively regulate business and industry. Business regulations refer to the use of laws or rules by a government regulatory agency to protect consumers and investors as well as to provide orderly and predictable business procedures. Government regulations, in general, refer to statutes established by federal departments or agencies that are enforceable by law. The U.S. government, as represented by approximately 160 different federal agencies, issues more than 8,000 rules and regulations each year. Due to the impact of business operations on the lives of citizens, health of the environment, and the strength of the national economy, business regulations comprise a significant portion of regulatory activities. In the United States, local, state, and federal governments regulate business structures, intellectual property, reporting, hiring, retirement, fair and equitable treatment of employees, working conditions, wages, waste disposal, product advertising and distribution, trade, environmental impact, taxes, employee savings plans, benefits, business safety, and business accounting. Governments develop business regulations to protect the general public from business abuses, preserve the natural environment and ecosystems, and, in some cases, control anticompetitive practices between businesses.

Business regulations impact both the economics of businesses themselves and national economies as a whole. First, compliance with business regulations is a massive expense for most businesses. Second, the specifics of national business regulations make nations more or less competitive in the global marketplace. For example, business regulations affect a business's ability to legally hire foreign workers, import and export goods, manufacture products in foreign countries, sell business interests to foreign investors, use foreign-made products in manufacturing, and advertise foreign and domestic products.

Business regulations are highly responsive to events and trends in the private sector as well as to demands expressed by the electorate. The U.S. government created the following laws and accompanying business regulations in response to perceived public problems:

Clean Water Act. In 1972, the Environmental Protection Agency developed and passed the Clean Water Act in response to increasing public awareness and concern over water pollution. The Clean Water Act established the regulations concerning the

discharge of pollutants, by individuals and business, into the waters of the United States.

Emergency Planning and Community Right-to-Know Act. In 1986, the Environmental Protection Agency developed and passed the Emergency Planning and Community Right-to-Know Act (EPCRA) as concerns about the environmental and safety hazards created by the storage and handling of toxic chemicals increased. The EPCRA establishes regulations for businesses, as well as the federal, state, and local governments and Indian tribes, regarding emergency planning and "Community Right-to-Know" reporting on hazardous and toxic chemicals.

USA PATRIOT Act. In 2001, the federal government passed the USA PATRIOT Act, which includes a host of new business regulations, in response to the September 11, 2001 attack on the World Trade Center. The USA PATRIOT Act, which stands for Uniting and Strengthening America by Providing Appropriate Tools Required to Intercept and Obstruct Terrorism Act and includes the International Money Laundering Abatement and Financial Anti-Terrorism Act, empowers federal regulators to obtain information from a wide range of businesses (Van Cleef, 2003).

The Sarbanes-Oxley Act. In 2002, The Sarbanes-Oxley Act, which includes numerous new business accounting and reporting regulations, was passed in response to the Enron Corporation's accounting scandal. The Sarbanes-Oxley Act was actualized to

President Richard M. Nixon signed the Clean Water Act into law in 1972. (Courtesy of Library of Congress)

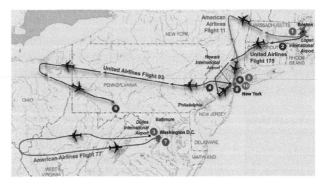

Flight paths of the four hijacked planes used in the terrorist attacks on September 11, 2001. The U.S. Patriot Act was enacted as a response to this act of terrorism in 2001. (Courtesy of the U.S. Federal Bureau of Investigation via Wikimedia Commons)

help investors defend against corporate accounting fraud. The Sarbanes-Oxley Act requires that corporations engage in risk assessment and risk auditing to monitor their financial reporting and auditing processes. Section 404 of the Sarbanes-Oxley Act, which focuses on management's assessment of internal control over financial reporting, instructs corporations to conduct a top-down market risk assessment to evaluate the corporation's internal controls systems.

Securities & Exchange Commission Regulations. In 2005, the Securities and Exchange Commission (SEC) issued new corporate risk reporting and disclosure regulations. The SEC requires business reporting on risk factors in three main categories of market behavior, including industry risks, company risks, and investment risks. The SEC's new corporate risk reporting requirements, as represented by changes to annual report requirements on Form 10-K and quarterly reports on Form 10-Q, further the SEC's commitment to integrating corporate disclosure and processes first described in the Securities Act of 1933 and the Securities Exchange Act of 1934. Corporations must now disclose risk factors in their annual reports and describe changes in previously disclosed risk factors in their quarterly reports. Risk factors are believed to present a summary of the risks facing the company and identify factors that investors should consider when making an investment. The SEC's new corporate risk disclosure requirement, as described in Item 503(c) of Regulation S-K, instructs that, when appropriate, a company has to engage in a discussion identifying the major factors that may negatively affect the issuer's business, operations, industry, financial position, or its future financial performance. The SEC argues that the new reporting requirements and regulations should not be burdensome as the SEC noted that companies should already be in a position to recognize new or changing material risks affecting their businesses. The SEC argues that disclosure of risk factors will alert investors to risks specific to the company or its industry that make an offering speculative or high risk (Banham, 2004).

Business regulations, while usually supported by society at large, are often opposed by business interests on grounds that complying with a business regulation is unduly burdensome to the business or that the business regulation is unwarranted or based on inaccurate assumptions. The business sector is generally in favor of deregulation. For example, Ronald Reagan was elected president in part owing to his promises to provide regulatory relief to businesses (Levine, 1989). In the twenty-first century, businesses wishing to change or challenge business regulations have two options. First, businesses may lobby and petition Congress for a change. Second, businesses may bring a lawsuit against government. As business regulations continue to grow in number and scope rather than shrink, lawsuits against regulators are increasingly common. For example, in 1998, the National Mining Association had over 40 pending court cases challenging federal regulations for air and water quality standards. Ultimately, national governments weigh the economic impact of business regulations with the well-being of citizens, environmental goals, and the sociopolitical climate when making business regulations. In many instances, businesses chafe at the expense of compliance and the limitations that business regulations impose (Andelman, 1998).

This article will describe the economics of business regulation in the United States as well as the impact of national business regulations on the global economy. The following sections provide an overview of the economics of federal business regulations. This section serves as the foundation for later discussion of the economic issues associated with differences in international business regulations.

APPLICATIONS

Economics of Federal Business Regulations

The U.S. federal government develops business regulations in a highly transparent and participatory process. The federal government publicizes proposed business regulations, and government regulations in general, in the *Federal Register*. The *Federal Register* is the government's official daily publication, which delineates all the current rules, proposed rules, notices from federal agencies, executive orders, and other presidential documents. Proposed business regulations that become law are added to the *Code of Federal Regulations* (CFR). The *Code of Federal Regulations* is the organizational system for the rules published in the *Federal Register*.

The federal government's regulation-making process is generally referred to as rulemaking. Rulemaking refers to the process followed by federal agencies to formulate, amend, or repeal a regulation. The rulemaking process includes two main stages: the proposed rule stage and a final rule stage. In the proposed rule stage, the regulatory agency provides notice of a proposed regulation. During a 30-, 60-, or 90-day period, any person or organization may review this document and submit comments on it in writing to the regulatory agency. The regulatory agency is legally bound to consider the public comments received on the proposed regulation. In the final rule stage, the regulatory agency incorporates a response to the significant issues raised by those who submitted comments, discusses any changes made to the regulation, and publishes the complete text of the final regulation in the *Federal Register* (How to Solve, 2005).

The federal government, as part of the eRulemaking Initiative, is committed to providing public access to regulatory information for individuals and businesses. The eRulemaking Initiative is intended to "allow citizens to easily access and participate in the rulemaking process; improves the access to, and quality of, the rulemaking process for individuals, businesses, and other government entities while streamlining and increasing the efficiency of internal agency processes" (Federal Register, 2004). To further the federal government's eRulemaking Initiative, the federal government maintains two informational websites about federal regulations and compliance procedures. RegInfo.gov is a central website for federal regulatory information. Regulations. gov, established in 2003, is considered by the federal government to be the federal regulatory clearinghouse. The website provides the public with access to rules open to discussion. Citizens can read full texts of any associated documents and submit comments to the appropriate federal agency. The website includes compliance information for business regulations governing advertising and marketing, emergency and disaster planning, environmental compliance, finance, franchises, government contracting, human resources, information security, intellectual property, international trade, licenses and permits, taxes, and workplace health and safety.

The federal government categorizes all proposed business regulations into two categories: economically significant and not economically significant. Executive Order 12866, "Regulatory Planning and Review," requires that economic analysis be undertaken for all proposed federal regulations considered to be economically significant. In 1996, an interagency group developed best practices procedure for preparing the economic analysis of a significant regulatory action. Regulators are required to undertake the following steps in their economic analysis of all proposed regulations:

- Develop a statement of need for the proposed action and appropriateness of alternatives to federal regulation.
- Undertake an examination of alternative approaches.
- Perform an analysis of benefits and costs.

Congress and all relevant government agencies review the economic analysis of all proposed business regulations prior to final decision-making.

Compliance with federal, state, and local business regulations is one of the major expenses of business operations in the United States. Regulatory compliance, which is generally overseen in a business by compliance officers or in-house lawyers, costs U.S. businesses billions of dollars and hours per year. The cost of compliance with business regulations, often referred to as the regulatory burden, has grown over the past twenty years. In 1988, according to the United States Office of Management and Budget, the private sector spent 5 billion hours and approximately $100 billion complying with government business regulations and paperwork requirements (Kurland, 1993). By 2000, the cost of compliance with business regulations, and federal regulations in general, grew to approximately $843 billion, or 8 percent of the U.S. gross domestic product (GDP). The United States Small Business Administration argues that small businesses bear the largest burden from the costs associated with regulatory compliance. For example, in 2000, regulatory compliance cost small firms with fewer than 20 employees approximately $7,000 per employee per year and medium-size firms with 20–499 employees approximately $4,300 and large firms with 500 or more employees approximately $4,500 per year per employee. Ultimately, the cost of regulatory compliance in 2000 was 55 to 60 percent higher for small businesses than medium or large businesses (Crain & Hopkins, 2000).

The expense for compliance with business regulations is raised by compliance problems that require additional resources to address. There are, according to federal regulators, six common categories of regulatory mistakes made by across businesses and industries:

- Failure to comply with the books and records regulations
- Inaccurate documents
- Weak or nonexistent internal controls
- Insider trading compliance
- Personal securities transaction compliance
- Antiterrorism compliance

Businesses with compliance issues, such as those described above, may face federal fines and penalties. Compliance problems may be resolved through the formation and oversight of an in-house compliance committee. Compliance committees work to ensure that business operations occur within the parameters established by federal regulations. Compliance committees work to mitigate compliance risk. In addition to the costly compliance problems common across businesses and industries, there are compliance problems specific to industries or areas of business. For example, 401(k) administrators and plans, as a group, have been found to commit compliance mistakes specific to their business specialty. Examples of 401(k) administrator and plan compliance mistakes include the following: plan administrators fail to remit contributions and loan repayments to the plan; plan sponsors fails to monitor the plan's mutual funds; and plan administrators fail to fully and accurately apply a plan's definition of compensation. These compliance mistakes may result in substantial federal fines and business audits (Kelvin, 2003).

ISSUES

International Differences in Business Regulation

Business regulations vary significantly between nations. Business regulations and national financial systems are generally shaped by the cultural, social, and political climate of a country. The international differences in business regulations are creating economic problems in the global economy. The global economy is characterized by growth of nations, both in populations and in output and consumption per capita, interdependence of nations, and international management efforts. Indicators of global growth and interdependence include the huge

President Lyndon B. Johnson signing the 1967 Clean Air Act in the East Room of the White House. (Courtesy of Mike Geissinger via Wikimedia Commons)

increases in communication links, world output, international trade, and international investment since the 1970s. The global economy is built on global interdependence of economic flows that link the economies of the world. The global economy is characterized by economic sensitivity. National economic events in one region often have profound results for other regions and national economies. National economies exist not in isolation but in relationship and tension with other economies worldwide. The global economy includes numerous economic phenomena and financial tools shared between all countries. Examples of the interrelationship of the global economy include the international price of gold, the price of oil, and the related worldwide movement of interest rates.

In some instances, the differences and variations in international business regulations create economic tensions and trade incompatibility between countries. For example, national differences in business regulations and financial systems have posed serious economic challenges to member nations of the European Union. Significant national differences in business regulations have challenged trade relationships and the goal of achieving a single and unified European Union market (Cole, 2006). The World Bank compiles and publishes international comparisons of business regulations. The statistics and descriptions are compiled to aid businesses involved in international commerce and trade to understand foreign business practices and regulations (Matthes, 2005).

In some instances, nations come together to create complimentary business regulations. Examples include trade pacts such as the North American Free Trade Agreement (NAFTA) and global environmental pacts. The North American Free Trade Agreement, which was implemented in 1994, is an agreement between the United States, Canada, and Mexico intended to remove most barriers to trade and investment among member nations. Business regulations, as negotiated and specified in international trade agreements such as the North American Free Trade Agreement, tend to be complex and fixed. Businesses involved in trade among the United States, Canada, and Mexico need to understand and follow the business regulations concerning import licensing, certificates of origin, health codes, and labeling.

One of the largest global environmental pacts, the Kyoto global warming pact created in 1997, imposes limits on emissions of carbon dioxide and other gases scientists believed to be associated with rising world temperatures and melting glaciers. The Kyoto Protocol has been ratified/approved by 191 countries. The United States, as of 2013, supports but has not ratified the Kyoto Protocol. Canada withdrew in 2012. Environmental regulation began in the United States with the passage of the Clean Water Act and the Clean Air Act. Regulation to address the problems of future and past hazardous waste disposal include the Resource Conservation and Recovery Act (RCRA) and the Comprehensive Environmental Response, Compensation, and Liability Act (CERCLA) or the Superfund program. Environmental regulation began in Europe with a common environmental protection policy built into the Treaty of Rome (1987) and was extended and expanded by the Treaty on European Union (1992). Environmental regulation has been criticized by businesses for ignoring production processes and being expensive and excessive. Critics argue that environmental regulation has traditionally focused on "end-of-the pipe" solutions (such as emissions or waste control) rather than addressing the basic processes that created the problem initially (Anderson, 1999).

NAFTA and international environmental alliances are designed to promote economic growth in all member nations. Internationally coordinated and complimentary business regulations have the potential to create the economic growth of nations. The growth of nations varies among regions, nations, and historical eras. Economic and political changes promote or depress the growth of nations depending on variables such as national leadership, political and economic stability, natural resources, international relations, and infrastructure. The current era of the global economy, a product of economic globalization, is creating strong, though variable, national economic growth and development worldwide (Jones, 2005). The process of globalization, a process of economic and cultural integration around the world caused by changes in technology, commerce, and politics, requires complementary national financial systems. The future strength of the global economy depends on the international coordination of business regulations.

CONCLUSION

In the final analysis, business regulations create rules and regulations for all aspects of business operations and industries. Business regulations are shaped by public problems. For example, the environmental and civil rights movements in the United States during the 1960s resulted in the creation of significant business regulations. The growth of environmentalism, along with increased civil rights laws and international immigration, significantly influenced business activities in the United States and around the world. Federal business regulations shape how businesses hire and treat employees, manufacture products, advertise products, transport products to markets, and dispose of waste. In the twenty-first century, the private sector is exploring global connections of people, politics, products, and culture. The public sector is responding by creating business regulations that strengthen global trade relationships and the global economy.

BIBLIOGRAPHY

Andelman, D. (1998). "Taking regulators to court." *Management Review, 87,* 30.

Anderson, D. (1999). "Incorporating risk management into environmental management systems." *CPCU Journal, 52,* 115.

Angulo, M., Perez-Monero, S., & Abad-Guerrero, I. (2017). "How economic freedom affects opportunity and necessity entrepreneurship in the OECD countries." *Journal of Business Research, 73,* 30–37.

Banham, R. (2004). "Enterprising views of risk management." *Journal of Accountancy, 197,* 65–71.

Chen, N., & Wang, W. (2012). "Kyoto Protocol and capital structure: a comparative study of developed and developing countries." *Applied Financial Economics, 22,* 1771–1786.

Chrisman, J., & Fry, F. (1983). "How government regulation affects small business." *Business Forum, 8,* 25.

Cole, G. (2006). "Becoming similar while remaining different: company law in the EU." *Managerial Law, 48,* 533.

"Compliance corner: Solutions to common compliance mistakes." (2003). *Community Banker, 12,* 21.

Compliance guides. (2007). Business.gov. Retrieved from xlink:href="http://www.business.gov/"

Crain, M. & Hopkins, T. (2000). "The impact of regulatory costs on small firms. The Office of Advocacy, U. S. Small Business Administration." Retrieved from xlink:href="http://www.sba.gov/advo/research/rs207tot.pdf"

Dermine, J. (2013). "Bank regulations after the global financial crisis: good intentions and unintended evil." *European Financial Management, 19,* 658–674.

Economic analysis of federal regulations under Executive Order 12866. (1996). Office of Management and Budget. Retrieved xlink:href="http://www.whitehouse.gov/omb/inforeg/riaguide.html"

Federal Register, 69, 25155. (2004). Retrieved from xlink:href="http://www.pubklaw.com/regs/69fr25147.pdf"

"How to solve the top nine 401(k) plan compliance mistakes." (2005). *Managing 401(k) Plans, 2005,* 1–13.

Kelvin, J. (2003). "Common compliance mistakes." *Journal of Financial Service Professionals, 57,* 26–29.

Jones, B. & Olken, B. (2005). "Do leaders matter? National leadership and growth since World War II." *Quarterly Journal of Economics, 120,* 835–864.

Kohl, J. & Mayfield, M. (2004). "Human resource regulation and legal issues: Web sites for instructional and training development." *Journal of Education for Business, 79,* 339–343.

Kurland, O. (1993). The mounting burden of processing paper. *Risk Management, 40,* 16–18.

Levine, R. (1989). "Unfinished business: Reagan's regulatory relief." *Management Review, 78,* 18.

Lovely, M., & Popp, D. (2011). "Trade, technology, and the environment: Does access to technology promote environmental regulation?" *Journal of Environmental Economics & Management, 61,* 16–35.

Matthes, J. & Schroder, C. (2005). "Business regulation in international comparison: Aggregating World Bank data." *CESifo Forum, 6,* 42–50.

Regulations. (2007). Regulations.gov. Retrieved xlink:href="http://www.regulations.gov/fdmspublic/component/main"

Van Cleef, C. (2003). "USA Patriot Act: Statutory analysis and regulatory implementation." *Journal of Financial Crime, 11,* 73.

Yan, W., & Carr, D. A. (2013). "Federal environmental regulation impacts on local economic growth and stability." *Economic Development Quarterly, 27,* 179–192

SUGGESTED READING

Fri, R. (1976). "How to live with the new regulators." *Management Review, 65,* 42

Martin, J., & Leeder, S. (1994). "Deregulation by delegation: The regulatory review process in Queensland." *Australian Journal of Public Administration, 53,* 95.

Stender, N. (2002). "The risks of technology deregulation." *China Business Review, 29,* 24.

—*Simone I. Flynn, PhD*

ECONOMICS OF CLIMATE CHANGE

ABSTRACT

Climate change is moving to the top of humankind's priorities list as the debate over whether it exists or not gives way to the debate over how best to forestall and counteract its more onerous effects. In this regard, the possible economic impacts of action or inaction have been discussed far less than the science, for the fact of the matter is that no one really knows for sure what changes lie in store for producers, markets, and consumers. That there will be profound structural changes is less in doubt than whether we collectively are up to the task of successfully dealing with global warming. Here, fortunately, we have a large body of research to fall back on, most notably the welfare economics of Pigou and Hicks and sustainable-development theory, to guide our decision-making.

OVERVIEW

Although skeptics still contest that climate change exists and is a result of human action, the scientific evidence overwhelmingly supports these conclusions. As the perils of "irreversible" climate change loom ever larger and more imminent in the public's imagination, the calls for action grow ever louder, with good reason. As little as a two-degree centigrade increase in Earth's average temperature by 2100 might well make fertile land arid, submerge densely populated coastal regions, and magnify the destructiveness of extreme weather. And therein lies a dilemma of the first order, because ours is a carbon economy. Humankind has prospered far more since the late eighteenth century from industrialization, powered first by coal and then by oil, than it ever did over the preceding millennia. To halt global warming, atmospheric emissions of carbon dioxide (CO_2) must be severely curtailed. But how can this happen without sacrificing the very productive capacity responsible for the high standard of living many enjoy and others aspire to? It is a daunting question.

Economics examines how resources are allocated in conditions of scarcity, so the ideas of constraints and

President George W. Bush meets with the American 2007 Nobel Award recipients in the Oval Office on Nov. 26, 2007. They are, from left: Harlan Watson, Oliver Smithies, Mario Capecchi, former Vice President Al Gore, Eric Maskin, Susan Solomon, Roger Myerson and Sharon Hays. Gore won the 2007 Nobel Peach Prize with the Intergovernmental Panel on Climate Change for their work on manmade climate change issues. (Courtesy of Eric Draper via Wikimedia Commons)

trade-offs are hardly new. Nor, for that matter, are concerns about the potentially disastrous consequences of unrestrained economic growth. Early nineteenth-century economic theorists like Malthus and Ricardo feared such growth would bring a precipitous rise in population that would quickly deplete available food stocks. Pessimists like Malthus held that only war and famine could right the balance again; optimists like Ricardo believed agricultural imports and farm machinery might postpone but ultimately would not prevent widespread calamity. Convinced that future events can never be predicted with any real certainty, John Stewart Mill was more circumspect. He thought one of three outcomes possible (Pressman, 1999b):

- Increasingly expensive cultivation would continue to keep pace, with prices paid by workers and profits earned by landowners both rising;
- The division of labor and new technologies would more than keep pace, and workers' wages would increase; or
- Capital-intensive farming would keep pace, though just barely, with wages remaining constant, profits declining, and overall economic growth slowly grinding to a halt.

Economists pondering the likely economic impact of climate change face a far more complex problem set. To begin with, though there is growing agreement about why climate change is occurring, beyond sweeping generalities, the when, the where, and the how are still far from clear. What is clear is the sheer scale of the structural change the global economy faces, be it in heavy industry, energy, transport, or agribusiness. And with it will come new opportunities as well as threats. Though the impetus for change may in the end be political, the mechanism will always be economic. New green industries will supplant existing smokestack ones, renewable energy will replace fossil fuels, and so on—provided, that is, that the necessary changes are undertaken before the damage is irreversible and the social, political, economic, environmental, and humanitarian distress it brings becomes too great. But before this can happen, the very real question of who pays for the enormous upfront investments required must first be settled, and as yet no clear-cut consensus has emerged about the how to go about this. Fortunately or not, climate change is just a rather dissonant variation on a recurring theme in twentieth-century economics; the problem of externalities and a workable solution may well lie there.

APPLICATIONS

Externalities
The term *externalities* was coined in 1920 by the English economist Arthur Pigou, welfare economics' first major theorist. This term stems from the fact that manufacturing any good creates not one but two outputs, a physical commodity and a waste by-product, for matter can never be destroyed, only transformed. As long as the effect of these waste by-products on the larger community is benign, the material and economic benefits of production outweigh its social costs. Customers pay for the former but rarely for the latter. Nor do producers whose prices cover only the private costs of production—the raw materials, plant, equipment, labor, and capital required to make a profit. What happens when the social costs, measured as the investment necessary to counter the harmful side effects of a given production process, outstrip manufacturers' private costs (Pressman, 1999a)?

Strictly speaking, externalities arise whenever consumers not party to a transaction either benefit or lose as a result of it. A lighthouse is a much-discussed example of a positive externality: shipping firms and their passengers benefit directly from something paid for from the public purse. Air pollution is an example of a negative externality: emitters profit at the expense of the public at large. The emitters' behavior is countenanced in the first place because the utility of the goods they produce exceeds or equals the utility of cleaner air. However, this seemingly straightforward trade-off is often much more one-sided. The benefit to the producer and the producer's customers is immediate; the cost to the community in worsening air quality is cumulative.

Negative Externalities & Free-Market Economies
Early proponents of welfare economics, such as Pigou and Hicks, saw negative externalities as market failures of the first order, ones that only government regulations, taxes, subsidies, or court action could correct. Laissez-faire marketplaces, they argued, have no built-in mechanism to effectively counter the so-called free-rider problem. This problem arises whenever too many economic agents ask, Why foot part of the bill for some public resource when others are sure to pay it off? Given the option, in other words, why not get something for nothing? Unscrupulous, perhaps, but it is a tempting proposition in any milieu where narrowly defined self-interest trumps all other considerations. Of course, if too many of us think this way, the bill is not paid, the benefit never materializes, and everyone is worse off. In the absence of government regulation, the temptation to leverage free or grossly underpriced environmental assets to lower production costs is always there—especially since, as public goods, their consumption by one party does not lessen the supply available to other parties, and once these goods are available, no party can be denied access to them. In addition, these non-rival, non-excludable characteristics make them unattractive private investments (Reinhardt, 1999). Without the outside stimulus of government funding or regulatory enforcement, essentially, a market for their development and upkeep would not materialize on its own.

Revisiting the issue decades later, economist Ronald Coase questioned the universality of this premise. Perhaps, he suggested, given certain circumstances, private solutions could remediate a negative externality more efficiently. When property rights are clearly established and transaction costs are low, the better option lies in contesting parties agreeing amongst themselves about what course of action to take, for the party that stands to gain the most economically has a vested interest in resolving a dispute quickly and cost-effectively. And the aggrieved parties have every reason to expect either relief through remedial action or reparations in keeping with the Kaldor-Hicks compensation principle, a major tenet of orthodox welfare economics, which maintains that overall utility is served even if some suffer from a change in the economy—provided, that is, that the injured parties are remunerated for their loss.

A market-based alternative to government-mandated solutions, the Coase theorem does not preclude the possibility of victims paying perpetrators to change their production processes, nor of perpetrators compensating victims for the ill effects that their ongoing operations cause. Of course, polluters may decide that in the long run it might be cheaper to invest in more environmentally friendly equipment, and victims believe that their health is more valuable. In either case, the parties choose to return to the bargaining table instead of the courts. A quick resolution where all parties benefit to one degree or another is preferable to a lengthy and costly legal impasse. Bargaining increases the chances of maximizing the utility of the ensuing outcome, which matters more in the Coasian hierarchy of values than who is to blame.

A very different notion of utility lies at the heart of conventional welfare economics. Here, the true test of the worthiness of any remedial course of action, whether government mandated or market inspired, lies in whether or not it achieves Pareto optimality. A marked contrast to the win-lose dynamic of zero-sum game theory, Pareto optimality is reached where there are winners but no losers. Its cardinal principle rejects any reallocation of resources that enriches some at the expense of others. In the best-case scenario, everyone benefits, perhaps a few more than most; in the worst-case scenario, only a few prosper, but nobody is poorer for it.

The very same premise lies at the root of sustainable-development theory, an alternative to the conventional growth paradigm of neoclassical economics and its emphasis on yearly net increases in productive output as an end in itself. In this conventional paradigm, utility is considered nigh on synonymous with consumption, a linkage that sustainable-growth advocates reject. They too call for steady rises in per capita income, but only insofar as near-term increases do not deplete the physical, environmental, human, and social capital bequeathed to future generations. These assets must be left intact; otherwise, their Pareto optimality will be sacrificed before they are even born. In effect, the world's populations must rely solely on the interest of their accumulated wealth, what welfare economists call their Hicksian income, to bankroll future consumption and investment. If they do not, someday their offspring will confront head-on a much starker, Malthusian limits-to-growth model (Davidson, 2000).

Remediation Mechanisms

The time when pure theory sufficed has ended. With the constraints, both real and imagined, of climate change more pressing with each passing day, attention has turned to finding efficient transition paths out of negative externalities for markets otherwise in equilibrium. Two diametrically opposed types of mechanisms are being contemplated, though the use of one in some markets does not exclude the use

Solar panels are one option being used to reduce the use of fossil fuels for energy. This Solar Settlement is located in Freiburg, Germany. (Courtesy of Andrewglaser at English Wikipedia CC BY-SA 3.0 via Wikimedia Commons)

of the other elsewhere. Of the two, government-imposed command-and-control measures are the most direct. Uniform standards for emissions and for types of inputs and technologies used by manufacturers can be enforced, or quotas on outputs can be set (Mulder & Van Den Bergh, 2001). But critics charge that the fiats of regulators smack of central planning that, according to experience, only warps the overall efficiency of free markets. And though these measures may or may not deal effectively with a problematic externality, they almost certainly will dampen economic activity, slowing or reversing its growth.

Yet, the externality arose from these very same markets and, so the counterargument goes, will only worsen if said markets are left to their own devices. A better approach, consequently, might be for governments to provide incentives for change rather than mandates: subsidies, tradable permits, and tax breaks to encourage compliance, with punitive taxes or levy cleanup costs as a last resort to sway the recalcitrant. However, for such market-based instruments to work, everyone affected has to have a very accurate idea of the pluses and minuses involved. Indeed, major environmental policy initiatives have been the subject of formal cost-benefit analysis since Eckstein's "Water Resource Development" and Krutilla and Eckstein's "Multipurpose River Development" of 1958 (Pearce, 2002). Standard accounting practices make the valuation of any tangible asset a straightforward exercise: a machine costs X and produces goods that earn sales

Harnessing wind is another viable option to fossil fuels for energy. In India wind farms are used in numerous areas. This one is located in the midst of paddy fields. (Courtesy of Yahoo! Blog from Sunnyvale, California, USA CC BY 2.0 via Wikimedia Commons)

According to the UN's Intergovernmental Panel on Climate Change (IPCC), climate change of 2.5 degrees Celsius could cost the world 2 percent of global GDP (cited in Morales, 2014). For comparison, in 2013, output in industrial countries grew at around 3.5 percent over the preceding year (Central Intelligence Agency, n.d.); in the long run, then, unimpeded climate change will slow their future expansion, perhaps significantly. At first glance, it would thus seem that economically speaking, remediation is the less favorable option, since it would on the whole cost more. But these costs are largely derived from forecasts of the likely negative impact of the Kyoto Protocol on the U.S. economy, by far the world's largest emitter of greenhouse gases, and some of these forecasts were grist for the mill in a contentious political debate. Forecasting is an imprecise science to begin with, in part because basic assumptions must always be made. When these assumptions are ideologically tinged, biases can be and are introduced, often unintentionally, making an already imprecise science only more so. Forecasts supporting pro or con positions on climate-change abatement, therefore, should not necessarily be taken at face value.

It is not yet clear just how much of a mitigating factor new technologies will be in slowing or reversing climate change. Much indeed hinges on the kind and degree of "substitutability" of human for natural capital. Is our ingenuity and technological prowess up to the challenge of marshalling non-carbon-based sources of energy, of remaking our material world with non-petrochemical-based substances, of supplying enough fresh water to counter the salination of arable land and slake human thirst? And can all this and more be done in conditions of Pareto optimality? Or will efforts be too little and too late? Must a great and terrible price be paid by Earth's people generations hence? Alarmists raise that possibility to galvanize action, of course, but that does not mean their dire predictions will not come true. Even believers in sustainable development's viability are divided on the question of substitutability. Advocates of strong sustainability think no amount of human or economic capital can make up for the likely loss in natural capital, and present efforts must focus on their preservation. Conversely, advocates of weak sustainability think that technology and green investment can make a difference, and present efforts must focus on creating the required incentives. Only time will tell who is right.

of Y. Lacking a marketplace to set prices, the valuation of intangible assets such as air quality is much more difficult. At best, their monetization can only be approximated indirectly via observable changes in the prices of tradable commodities affected. A newly contaminated watershed, for example, will dramatically lower the resale value of a house. Environmental economists call this alternate approach revealed-preference valuation. When no such proxy exists, stated-preference valuation is relied on instead. In stated-preference valuation, individuals are queried about how much they are prepared to pay to improve a particular environmental problem.

No matter how rigorous, no cost-benefit analysis can predict with any real certainty what the long-term economic effects of climate change will be.

VIEWPOINTS

While little can be said with absolute confidence about the future economic effects of climate change, one such certainty is that it will occasion structural change of the first order. How exactly this restructuring will unfold is open to interpretation. Carbon-emitting industries are still the cornerstone of much of the world's economic output, and sudden and drastic change would throw markets into a disequilibrium that may take decades to reverse. By contrast, measured, incremental change might not reach critical mass in time to stave off catastrophic irreversibility. What is clear is that new government policies and market mechanisms will be needed, and soon, to deal with what is an already enormous and still-growing negative externality.

BIBLIOGRAPHY

Arndt, C., Chinowsky, P., Robinson, S., Strzepek, K., Tarp, F., & Thurlow, J. (2012)." Economic development under climate change." *Review of Development Economics, 16*(3), 369–377.

Central Intelligence Agency. (n.d.). World. Retrieved November 5, 2014, from *The world factbook.*

Davidson, C. (2000). "Economic growth and the environment: Alternatives to the limits paradigm." *Bioscience, 50*(5), 433.

Dawson, G. (2006). *Economic impact of climate change.* Retrieved from xlink:href="http://www.open.edu/openlearn/society/international-development/international-studies/economic-impact-climate-change"

Drajem, M. (2013). "The cost of climate change is up 60 percent." *Bloomberg Businessweek,* (4335), 30–31.

Harvey, F. (2012, September 25). "Climate change is already damaging global economy, report finds." *Guardian.* Retrieved xlink:href="http://www.theguardian.com/environment/2012/sep/26/climate-change-damaging-global-economy"

Hassler, J., & Krusell, P. (2012). "Economics and climate change: Integrated assessment in a multiregion world." *Journal of the European Economic Association, 10*(5), 974–1000.

Morales, Alex. (2014, August 27). "Irreversible damage seen from climate change in UN leak." Retrieved from *Bloomberg*xlink:href="http://www.bloomberg.com/news/2014-08-26/irreversible-damage-seen-from-climate-change-in-un-leak.html"

Mulder, P., & Van Den Bergh, J. (2001). "Evolutionary economic theories of sustainable development." *Growth & Change, 32*(1), 110.

Pearce, D. (2002). "An intellectual history of environmental economics." *Annual Review of Energy & the Environment, 27*(1), 57.

Pressman, S. (1999a). "Arthur Cecil Pigou (1877-1959)." In *Fifty major economists.* Abingdon: Taylor & Francis Ltd.

Pressman, S. (1999b). "John Stewart Mill (1806-1873)." In *Fifty major economists.* Abingdon: Taylor & Francis Ltd.

Reed. B., Mendelsohn, R., & Abidoye, B. (2017). "The economics of crop adaptation to climate change in south-east Asia." *Climate Change Economics, 8*, 3.

Reinhardt, F. (1999). "Market failure and the environmental policies of firms: Economic rationales for beyond compliance behavior." *Journal of Industrial Ecology, 3*(1), 9–21.

Staten, M., & Umbeck, J. (1989). "Economic inefficiency: A failure of economists." *Journal of Economic Education, 20*(1), 57–72.

Yamaguchi, R. (2013). "Discounting, distribution and disaggregation: Discount rates for the rich and the poor with climate as a source of utility." *Scottish Journal of Political Economy, 60*(4), 440–459.

SUGGESTED READING

Nordhaus, W. (2001). "Global warming economics." *Science, 294*(5545), 1283.

Parry, I. (2002). "Are all market-based environmental regulations equal?" *Issues in Science & Technology, 19*(1), 38.

Ratnatunga, J. (2014). "Costing life: Air, water and food." *Journal of Applied Management Accounting Research, 12*(1), 1–12.

Scrieciu, S., Barker, T., & Ackerman, F. (2013). "Pushing the boundaries of climate economics: Critical issues to consider in climate policy analysis." *Ecological Economics, 85*, 155–165

"The climbing cost of climate change." (2001). *Earth Island Journal, 16*(2), 19.

Thorning, M. (2003). "Heroes and villains?" *Power Economics, 7*(4), 26.

—*Francis Duffy, MBA*

ECONOMICS OF MEDICAL CARE

ABSTRACT

This essay examines the application of economic norms and theories to the study of medical care and medical care costs. Using a landmark article published in 1963 by Nobel Prize–winning economist Kenneth J. Arrow as a launching point, the analysis of medical economics is presented from the perspective of medical care in a competitive market. A series of retrospective articles presented in the *Journal of Health Politics, Policy and Law* provides further perspectives on Arrow's article. The essay concludes with a brief look at work in the area of market forces in the medical care market and a consideration of the role of the Internet in providing information on quality and price to medical providers and consumers.

OVERVIEW

Is the medical care market a "competitive" market as defined by the discipline of economics? Can the general norms and theories of economics be applied to medical care? These are the questions that are discussed in this article. First, it is important to note that the language used here is "medical" economics and not "health" economics. "Medical economics" refers to the study of the medical industry as represented by goods and services produced and provided by physicians, ancillary providers, clinics, and hospitals. Health economics implies a state of being that includes factors such as diet, exercise, and individual risk behaviors such as smoking, drinking, non–seat belt use, etc. The exploration of health economics is not considered in the scope of this article and best left for a separate discussion.

The Birth of Medical Care Economics

In December 1963, the *American Economic Review* published an article by noted economist Kenneth J. Arrow, "Uncertainty and the Welfare Economics of Medical Care." This article marks the beginning of the study of medical economics (Hammer, Haas-Wilson & Sage, 2001). The importance of Arrow's article was observed some forty years later as the October 2001 issue of the *Journal of Health Politics, Policy and Law* provided a series of retrospective articles examining the thesis set forth in Arrow's article in light of the tremendous changes in medical care delivery and finance in subsequent decades.

First, to put his article in context, Arrow was writing before the era of health maintenance organizations (HMOs), managed care, and many of the major technological advances in medicine that have since become commonplace. These would include advanced imaging such as magnetic resonance imaging (MRI), as well as major new classes of drugs used in infection control, cancer treatment, mental health, and other conditions. Thus, the retrospective analysis published in October 2001 sheds additional information on Arrow's original thesis in the context of contemporary understanding of medical economics.

Arrow's thesis in his 1963 article was that "the role of moral hazard in medical insurance arises from inequalities of information between the insurer on the one hand and the physician and patient on the other" (as restated in Arrow, 2001). The concept of moral

Kenneth Arrow, winner of the Nobel Prize in Economics in 1972. (Courtesy of Linda A. Cicero / Stanford News Service CC BY 3.0 via Wikimedia Commons)

hazard is defined as the effect of insurance on the behavior of the insured (Nicholson, 1990). In general, the availability of insurance creates the potential for increased demand. This is clearly seen in the medical care market where the spread of insurance, in particular Medicaid and Medicare, has created an increased demand for medical services (Millenson, 2001; Arrow, 1963). Arrow and others argue that medical care markets fail to address increased demand through increased prices because medical care is a noncompetitive market. Arrow's contention that medical care is a special market distinct "from the norms of welfare economics" is explored in the following sections (Reinhardt, 2001).

Pareto Optimality & the Health Care Market

The concept of Pareto optimality, as first described by Vilfredo Pareto in 1897, states that competitive equilibrium exists in a market when an allocation of resources is such that giving one additional allocation to one person results in making another person worse off. Stated another way, a condition of Pareto optimality resource allocation is such that all participants in a market are in equilibrium and a change to make one better off makes another one worse off. Pareto optimality can be further understood by examining the first and second theorems of optimality.

First Theorem of Optimality

The first theorem of optimality states: "If a competitive equilibrium exists at all, and if all commodities relevant to costs and utilities are in fact priced in the market, then equilibrium is necessarily optimal: There is no other allocation of resources to services which will make all participants in the market better off" (Arrow, 1963, p. 942). Reinhardt (2001) further states that the assumptions underlying the first theorem are as follows:

- Both buyers and sellers understand fully the good and services available in the market.
- Both buyers and sellers are price takers because neither has influence over prices in the market.
- All relevant prices are known to all participants before a purchase transaction takes place.

Second Theorem of Optimality

The second theorem of optimality states: "If there are no increasing returns in production, and if certain other minor conditions are satisfied, then every optimal state is a competitive equilibrium corresponding to some initial distribution of purchasing power" (Arrow, 1963, p. 943). To apply this theorem to the reality of the medical care market, one assumes that an equal distribution of purchasing power exists to insure a state of equilibrium. In its most practical sense, an equal distribution of purchasing powers is achieved through taxes and subsidies. Thus, the question of how the purchasing power gets redistributed becomes a question of politics and social justice and not necessarily economics.

If one argues that the medical market operates in such a manner as to efficiently meet the needs of both patients and providers, e.g., buyers and sellers, one must also argue that the medical market meets the criteria of a market in a state of competitive equilibrium, e.g., fulfills the assumptions of the first and second theorems of optimality.

The significance of the Arrow article is that he was the first to systematically apply the standard norms and assumptions of economics to the medical market, especially with respect to competitive equilibrium and Pareto optimality. His work opened the door for subsequent important research and theoretical discourse that continues in the literature to this day.

Asymmetrical Information

Arrow and subsequent researchers theorize that it is the asymmetry of information between patients and providers, mainly physicians, that causes the medical market to be characterized as a noncompetitive equilibrium. Researchers, economic and noneconomic alike, contend that medical economics are "different" because of the role of information (Robinson, 2001). Asymmetrical information means that the distribution of information between buyers or sellers is skewed, i.e., not equal. In the case of the medical market, the distribution of information is not equal. Buyers, e.g., patients, do not have access to all or the same information as sellers, e.g., physicians. The health care delivery system is built on the assumption that doctors are more knowledgeable about medical diagnosis and treatments than their patients. Because of that knowledge, as a society we give doctors the medical, legal, and political authority to not only provide medical care but also to set policy and determine the pricing structure of medical care.

Uncertainty in Medical Care

This imbalance, or asymmetry, of information is manifest along several dimensions. First is the role of uncertainty in medical care. According to Arrow, uncertainty occurs in two ways. When a patient sees a doctor, he or she is uncertain about the consequences of his or her decision to purchase treatment in the first place and uncertain about the effectiveness of that treatment in the second place. At the time that Arrow was writing, there was almost no way for a patient to obtain information about his or her own condition prior to seeing the doctor, no way to determine which doctor was best suited to treating the condition, and no way to evaluate treatment options or outcomes of the treatment (Haas-Wilson, 2001). The Internet has provided an avenue for patients to gain a great deal more information about diagnosis and treatment options, but by and large, physicians still hold a monopoly on medical information.

This information monopoly on the part of physicians is an outcome of the growth and development of medicine as a profession. As scientific treatments evolved and medical education became more sophisticated, physicians sought to withhold this specialized knowledge from anyone other than a trained physician. This was accomplished by strict licensure requirements and by increasing levels of specialization within the profession (Starr, 1982). In addition, mistakes made by doctors with regard to diagnosis or treatment outcome are kept within the community of physicians. Unethical behavior is also withheld from the public by the bonds of the professions (Starr, 1982).

Value of Treatment

Second, related to uncertainty in diagnosis and treatment is the observation that patients lack an understanding of the value of what they purchase. Certainly if the disease is cured and he or she feels better, the patient values the treatment. But what the patient probably does not know is what alternative treatments exist and what the cost of those alternative treatments may have been. This raises the question, did the patient get the best treatment for the dollar amount expended? An impediment to this knowledge is the fact that the treatment was most likely paid by a health insurance plan. The patient may have no knowledge of what the total cost of the treatment was and little incentive to find out since his

or her co-payment would likely vary little no matter which treatment alternative his or her doctor may have selected.

Physician Knowledge & Practice

Lack of information about outcomes is not restricted to patients. Surprisingly, physicians often lack knowledge about specific outcomes from the treatments they prescribe. In 1989, the federal government established the Agency for Healthcare Research and Quality (AHRQ) for the purpose of evaluating clinical treatments and their outcomes. An initial round of research looked at four treatments: smoking cessation, chlamydia screening of adolescents, diabetes care in underserved areas, and treatment of respiratory distress syndrome in preterm infants. Among the findings of the initial round of research was that there was wide geographic variation in what treatments were prescribed and what the outcomes of those treatments were. In addition to the government, health plans have also been collecting data from within their provider and enrollee panels to determine which treatments appear to have the greatest effectiveness and at what cost.

There is growing acceptance in both medical practice and medical education for the application of evidence-based medical treatments (EBM). EBM refers to the application of medical treatment based on evidence of clinical effectiveness as determined and validated by extensive scientific study. Although treatments have historically been evaluated for effectiveness by conducting clinical trials, these trials are

The Department of Health and Human Services headquarters are located by the National Mall in Washington, D.C. The Agency for Healthcare Research and Quality is one of 12 agencies within the U.S. Department of Health and Human Services. (Courtesy of Matthew G. Bisanz CC BY-SA 3.0 via Wikimedia Commons)

frequently conducted on a smaller scale, from a few dozen to a few thousand subjects. EBM goes a step further by formulating standardized treatment recommendations that emerge from meta-analysis of the scientific literature and rigorous statistical analysis of data sets compiled from insurance claims, hospital records, and medical expenditure data.

FURTHER INSIGHTS

While many medical economics researchers have focused on the role of asymmetrical information and competitive equilibrium in medical care markets, additional research is ongoing with regard to other important issues in medical economics.

Moral Hazard & Adverse Selection

The first of these are the issues of moral hazard and adverse selection. Moral hazard, as defined earlier, is the effect of insurance on the behavior of the uninsured. Medical insurance does not have the same effect in the market as other types of insurance. Insurance is generally purchased to protect the insured against financial risk in the event of a catastrophic incident, for example, the repair or replacement of a car in the event of a collision. Medical insurance does not provide a straightforward transfer of money to the insured but rather is used to reduce the cost of medical care on a more or less continuous basis, such as for the costs of preventive care and ongoing treatment. Because the true cost of care is typically unknown to the patient, there is overconsumption of services. Despite the emergence of insurance products, medical savings accounts, for example, where there is a tax benefit for consumers and increased awareness of true costs, enabling consumers to make more informed treatment purchase decisions, there has been reluctance for consumers to fully embrace this type of insurance product (Nichols, 2004). Part of this reluctance may be that despite the tax and savings benefit, consumers also assume more risk with this type of insurance product.

"Adverse selection" refers to the behavior of insurance companies to insure only the consumers with the lowest risk. With respect to medical care, this means that insurers generally refused coverage to all but the very healthy. One possible explanation for this was the transaction costs involved with writing policies for high-risk patients (Glied & Remier, 2002).

Price Elasticity of Demand

A third consideration is price elasticity of demand in medical care. Price elasticity of demand is defined as the percent change in quantity of goods or services demanded in response to a corresponding percent change in its price (Nicholson, 1990). Price elasticity is expressed as the change in quantity demanded by each 1 percent change in price. Studies have suggested that spending on medical care is highly inelastic. In other words, the quantity of medical care demanded does not change in to an appreciable degree regardless of price change (Phelps, n.d.; Nicholson, 1990; Arrow, 1963; Aron-Dine, Einav & Finkelstein, 2013).

Price Competition

A fourth consideration in regard to the study of medical economics is the issue of price, namely price competition and physician pricing behavior. There is little price competition among physicians, nor do they make their fees known to the public. The consumer typically does not know in advance what the price of a treatment will be and typically does not ask. Their particular medical insurance plan obscures the true cost of medical care. Physician fees may be predetermined on a contractual basis. Physicians may also adjust their fees based on the financial circumstances of their patients. This practice was especially prevalent prior to the enactment of Medicaid

On July 30, 1965, President Johnson signed the bill, the Social Security Amendments of 1965 that established Medicare and Medicaid, making it Public Law 89-97. The signing took place in Independence, Missouri and was attended by former President Harry S. Truman. The following are in the background (from left to right): Senator Edward V. Long, an unidentified man, Lady Bird Johnson, Senator Mike Mansfield, Vice President Hubert Humphrey, and Bess Truman. (Courtesy of National Archives)

and Medicare in 1965. Fee adjustment, or a sliding fee scale, masks the true price of medical care in a medical market.

Government intervention in the market also violates the assumptions of a true competitive market. Federal and state governments are major figures in the medical market. Medicare and Medicaid are the major health programs, but others include the Veterans Administration, social security, and public health programs at state and federal levels. It has been well documented that medical expenditures increased dramatically with the enactment of Medicare and Medicaid. Initially, providers (physicians and hospitals) were reimbursed on a 'usual and customary' basis. There was little question about the claims that were submitted for payment. As costs continued to escalate, Medicare implemented a prospective payment system based on diagnosis-related groups (DRGs). DRGs created approximately 500 groups of related diagnoses based on comparative hospital resource use. This prospective payment system was implemented in 1983 and became a model future development of managed care plans. While initially prospective payment systems appeared to have some effect on cost containment, that effect leveled off and health care costs continued to escalate.

In the 2010s patients and internists, who make patient referrals, began pushing for greater transparency in medical costs. As a result, some insurers launched online databases to communicate the price of common medical procedures at various hospitals and clinics in their coverage areas. Consumer advocates have warned that such pricing data may be unhelpful if it is not given in the context of other information, such as the frequency with which the test or procedure is ordered and the quality of care, as defined by patient outcomes (Herman, 2015). There is some hope that increased transparency in both price and quality will increase competition in this historically noncompetitive market.

Patient Protection and Affordable Care Act

In 2010 U.S. president Barack Obama signed the Patient Protection and Affordable Care Act (PPACA; also known as the Affordable Care Act or Obamacare) into law. The act faced considerable resistance in Congress and from conservative bodies due to some of its elements, including its individual mandate. The act officially went into effect on January 1, 2014. The

President Barack Obama signing the Patient Protection and Affordable Care Act on March 23, 2010, at the White House. (Courtesy of Pete Souza via Wikimedia Commons)

act requires that Americans be insured (or else face a penalty), changes the qualifications for Medicare, has affected premiums, and prevents insurers from denying coverage for preexisting conditions, among many other provisions. The goal of the Affordable Care Act is to lower the number of uninsured by reducing costs and expanding coverage—it is expected to reduce health care inflation and lower government spending for Medicare and Medicaid. Notably, the act also includes insurance exchanges and mandates.

Other Directions

Economists continue to grapple with the issue of competitive markets in the context of "market forces," addressing many of the same issues originally presented by Arrow in his 1963 article (Hammer, Hass-Wilson, & Sage 2001). One researcher, Alain Enthoven, has espoused the development of managed competition to use market forces to create quality and efficiency in the medical market. The features of the managed competition model are the provision of a standard set of benefits covering routine doctor visits, hospitalization, and surgery; acceptance of all applicants regardless of preexisting conditions; and price competition with complete cost information available to both providers and patients. The approach is a means of building on the model of market-based private health insurance and operated within certain government restraints. Managed competition was first put forth in the early 1990s and was a key component of proposed health care reform under President Clinton.

Nichols et al. conducted a series of longitudinal surveys tracking changes in health care markets in sixty communities. In their 2004 paper "Are market forces strong enough to deliver efficient health care systems? Confidence is waning," they focus their analysis on 12 health care markets and conclude that even with changes in the market since the early 1990s, there is still a need for stronger government intervention. Their findings show that there is still limited choice offered by employer-based health plans with most consumers choosing a preferred provider organization (PPO) that is little different from traditional fee-for-service plans. Employers have had a disincentive to offer fixed-benefit plans due to the tax benefit of offering company-paid insurance. And finally, there is still a lack of information available for employers and consumers to make meaningful decisions about the price and quality of medical care.

The issue of information and its role in the medical market appears as persistent and pervasive as it was at the time of Arrow's landmark article. Despite changes such as the introduction of prospective payment, rise of managed care and health maintenance organizations, and early attempts at strengthening market forces, access to solid data on medical care quality and price remain at the heart of medical economics. Data from research such as that promoted by the Agency for Healthcare Research and Quality are promising. The exponential growth of information available from the Internet also provides a degree of optimism for the availability of information for use by insurers, employers, providers, and consumers. By 2013 the field of health informatics had grown to integrate medicine and information science for things like medical records, patient and doctor communication, and clinical guidelines.

BIBLIOGRAPHY

Andel, C., Davidow, S. L., Hollander, M., & Moreno, D. A. (2012). "The economics of health care quality and medical errors." *Journal of Health Care Finance, 39,* 39–50.

Aron-Dine, A., Einav, L., & Finkelstein, A. (2013). "The RAND health insurance experiment, three decades later." *Journal of Economic Perspectives, 27*(1), 197–222.

Arrow, K. J. (2001). "Reflections on the reflections." *Journal of Health Politics, Policy & Law, 26,* 1197–1204.

Arrow, K. J. (2001). "Uncertainty and the welfare economics of medical care." *Journal of Health Politics, Policy and Law, 26,* 851–884.

Custer, W. S. (2014). "Experiments in health care cost management." *Journal of Financial Service Professionals, 68,* 31–32.

Enthoven, A. C. (2004). "Market forces and efficient health care systems." *Health Affairs, 23,* 25–27.

Fevurly, K. R. (2012). "Alternatives to long-term care insurance." *Journal of Financial Service Professionals, 66,* 61–68.

Foy, A., Sciamanna, C., Kozak, M., & Filippone, E. J. (2014). "The medical care cost ratchet." *CATO Journal, 34,* 83–98.

Glied, S. A. (2001). "Health insurance and market failure since Arrow." *Journal of Health Politics, Policy & Law, 26,* 957–966.

Glied, S. A., & Remier, D. K. (2002). "What every public finance economist needs to know about health economics: Recent advances and unresolved questions." *National Tax Journal, 55,* 771–788.

Haas-Wilson, D. (2001). "Arrow and the information market failure in health care: The changing content." *Journal of Health Politics, Policy & Law, 26,* 1031–1045.

Hammer, P. J., Haas-Wilson, D. & Sage, W. M. (2001). "Kenneth Arrow and the changing economics of health care: 'Why Arrow? Why now?'" *Journal of Health Politics, Policy & Law, 26,* 835–850.

Herman, B. (2015). "Insurer tells public how much it pays providers." *Modern Healthcare, 45*(35), 0030.

Millenson, M. L. (2001). "Moral hazards vs. real hazard: Quality of care post-Arrow." *Journal of Health Politics, Policy and Law, 26,* 1069–1080.

Nichols, L. M., Ginsburg, P. B., Berenson, R. A., Christianson, J. & Hurley, R. E. (2004). "Are market forces strong enough to deliver efficient health care systems? Confidence is waning." *Health Affairs, 23,* 8–21

Nicholson, W. (1990). *Intermediate microeconomics and its application.* Orlando, FL: Dryden Press.

Reinhardt, U. E. (2001). "Can efficiency in health care be left to the market?" *Journal of Health Politics, Policy & Law, 26,* 967–991.

Robinson, J. C. (2001). "The end of asymmetric information." *Journal of Health Politics, Policy & Law, 26,* 1045–1054. Retrieved from Academic Search Premier.

Saini, V., et al. (2017). "Drivers of poor medical care." *The Lancet, 10090,* 8–14, 178–190.

Skinner, J. (2013). "The costly paradox of health-care technology." *Technology Review, 116*, 69–70.

Starr, P. (1982). *The social transformation of American medicine.* New York, NY: Basic Books, Inc.

SUGGESTED READING

AHRQ profile: Advancing excellence in healthcare. (2001, March). Agency for Healthcare Research and Quality, Rockville, MD. U.S. Department of Health and Human Services.

Bhattacharya, J., & Packalen, M. (2012). "The other ex ante moral hazard in health." *Journal of Health Economics, 31*, 135–146.

"Communicating costs to patients." (2015). *Health Care Registration: The Newsletter for Health Care Registration Professionals, 24*(7), 1–12.

Fuchs, V. R. (1986). *The health economy.* Cambridge, MA: Harvard University Press.

Kapoor, R., & Lee, J. M. (2013). "Coordinating and competing in ecosystems: How organizational forms shape new technology investments." *Strategic Management Journal, 34*

McCue, M. (2012). "Financial performance of health plans in Medicaid managed care." *Medicare & Medicaid Research Review, 2*, E1–E9.

Phelps, C. E. (1992). *Health economics.* New York, NY: Harpers Collins Publishers Inc.

—*Michele L. Kreidler, PhD*

ECONOMICS OF PUBLIC PROBLEM-SOLVING

ABSTRACT

This article will focus on the economics of public problem-solving. It will provide an overview of the economic history of public problem-solving in the United States. This overview will serve as the foundation for discussions on the relationship between democratic values and public problem-solving as well as tools of economic analysis and public problem-solving. In addition, the relationship between public policy, funding structures, and public problem-solving will be described and analyzed. Numerous real-world examples of public problem-solving will be discussed.

OVERVIEW

Public problems such as poverty, child abuse, smoking, crime, aging, and terrorism are characterized as undesirable conditions that impinge on a society. All undesirable conditions within society do not become classified as public problems. Citizens and their elected officials establish their public problem agendas based on their levels of tolerance for specific adverse conditions. Theoreticians use decision or choice theory, which studies how real or ideal decision makers make decisions and how optimal decisions can be reached, to explain how public problems are solved in ideal circumstances. In reality, historical, social, and economic variables make many public problems difficult to solve if not intractable.

The U.S. government addresses and solves public problems through multiple means and strategies. In government, public administrators and politicians are responsible for solving many types of public problems. A common, generally applied problem-solving

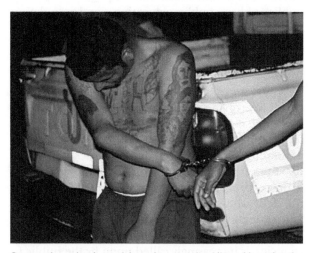

Gangs and associated gun violence has created public problems that the federal government is attempting to solve. Here an MS-13 suspect bearing gang tattoos is handcuffed. (Courtesy of U.S. Federal Bureau of Investigation via Wikimedia Commons)

or decision-making model includes the following steps:

- Determine whether a problem exists.
- State decisional objectives, alleviations, or solutions.
- Identify the decision apparatus and possible action options.
- Specify alternatives.
- State recommendations.
- Ascertain ways to implement recommendations.

Public problems may be routine, out-of-the-ordinary, small-scale, or large-scale. Systematic decision-making processes may or may not be used in their entirety to solve or alleviate the public problem. Factors influencing the formal adoption and use of a problem-solving process or model include agency or department regulations, personal preference of the public administrator, and the variables of the public problem at hand (Hy & Mathews, 1978).

Problem-solving strategies are often situation- or condition-specific, requiring carefully selected problem-solving strategies and techniques such as the multiple criteria decision-making model (MCDM), consensus or group decision-making, ethical decision-making, and finance-based or budget-maximizing decision-making. The federal government's problem-solving process involves activities such as intergovernmental collaboration, public budgeting, public policy, public education, and regulation (Andranovich, 1995). Important trends in public problem-solving include increased community participation in government decision-making and collaborative public decision-making (Irvin, 2004).

While the federal government as a whole uses multiple problem-solving models and approaches to solve and alleviate the public problems arising from, for example, overuse of the urban infrastructure, pollution, unemployment, public education, childhood poverty, aging Americans, sanitation problems, drunk driving, gangs and gun violence, nearly all of the federal government's problem-solving efforts and processes are significantly influenced by economics. The federal government, and its numerous agencies, is increasingly called upon by the public to improve financial and operating performance. The current government-society relationship is characterized by demands for government accountability

in spending and programs. For example, current public budgeting is characterized by variables such as governmental accountability, performance requirements, and program justification.

The political economy of public problems, and closely related public policy, is a long-established area of study and interest. The economics of public problem-solving involve at least three different elements:

- The federal government prioritizes the value of economics, and a strong economy, when solving public problems.
- The federal government uses economic tools for analysis, such as strategic accounting, serial cost-sharing, cost-based systems, activity-based costing system, and total unit cost-output model, when solving public problems.
- The federal government has budget formats and funding structures in place that influence the scope and parameters of problem-solving public policy.

This following section will provide an overview of the economic history of public problem-solving. This section will serve as the foundation for later sections describing and analyzing the three ways, described above, that the federal government uses economic approaches and justifications to solve and alleviate public problems. In addition, a case study describing the economics of managed beach erosion will be included at the end of the article as an opportunity to examine the ways in which economics influence the definition and solution of a real-world public problem.

Economic History of Public Problem-Solving
In the United States, the economic history of public problem-solving, including the development and implementation of a wide range of fiscal and public policy as well as regulatory agencies, began in the late eighteenth century. Following the American Revolution, the individual economies of the states were faltering, paper money had little value, and there was conflict between borrowers and lenders. The original thirteen states came together to draft the U.S. Constitution, in part, to stabilize and strengthen the U.S. economy. The U.S. Constitution and its amendments were drafted to solve and alleviate social and economic problems.

Destitute pea pickers during the Great Depression in California. Florence Thompson is shown with several of her children in a photograph known as "Migrant Mother." (Courtesy of Library of Congress)

From the Civil War through the beginning of the Industrial Revolution, the U.S. economy was characterized by cycles of growth and contraction. By 1920, the U.S. had begun mass production of standardized goods in factories and the practice of commercial advertising on the radio. The development of commercial radio meant that companies could promote their products and services to a larger audience of potential consumers than ever before. The federal government founded the Federal Communications Commission (FCC), an independent United States government agency that regulates interstate and international communications by radio, television, wire, satellite, and cable, in 1934 to monitor, solve, and alleviate the public problems caused or exacerbated by telecommunications activity in society.

The Great Depression, the severe economic recession in America that lasted from 1929–1939 was caused by instability of the American economy created, in part, by new mass manufacturing processes,

uneven distribution of wealth and profits, and the government's investment in new industries rather than agriculture. The depression ended after President Franklin D. Roosevelt took office in 1933 and initiated a recovery plan. Roosevelt's New Deal Campaign, an example of a successful public problem-solving campaign, outlawed gold coins, set farm quotas, and established government work programs to generate confidence and money within the U.S. economy.

In the 1930s, following the Great Depression, the United States government began a program and approach of economic problem-solving that created mixed fiscal and monetary policies in an effort to produce sustained economic growth and stable prices (for goods, services, and natural resources). The government, with a strong record in the latter half of the twentieth century for controlling cycles of expansion and contraction, remains challenged by inflation and related problems of unemployment. The government, including budgets, policies, and regulatory agencies, has been growing steadily since the 1930s. In 1930, the federal government accounted for 3.3 percent of the nation's gross domestic product (GDP) while in 1999, the federal government accounted for 21 percent of the nation's gross domestic product (Conte, 2001). The scale and scope of the federal government has grown in the twentieth century in proportion to the demand from society for increased public problem-solving by government agencies and leaders.

APPLICATIONS

Economic Approaches to Public Problem-Solving

Economics influences what public conditions citizens and their representatives consider to be public problems as well as the strategies that the federal government uses to alleviate or solve the public problem. The following three sections, including values and public problem-solving, tools of economic analysis and public problem-solving, and funding structures and public problem-solving, combine to illustrate the ways in which economics influences the federal government's public problem-solving efforts.

Values & Public Problem-Solving

Public problems are categorically different than private problems. Examples of public problems include

The juxtaposition of the homeless and well-to-do on Broadway is common in New York City. (Courtesy of Sonyblockbuster CC BY-SA 3.0 via Wikimedia Commons)

gun violence, beach erosion, domestic violence, drunk driving, teen pregnancy, low voter turnout, childhood poverty, gang colors worn in school, and homelessness. Examples of private problems include marital trouble, deciding between colleges, flat tires, deciding how to dress, or lack of childcare. Some issues, such as access to childcare, straddle the line between public and private problems. For many families, the cost of childcare may outweigh the financial benefit of a low-wage job, and for low-income families, the conflict between employment and childcare can be an economic trap. Some researchers argue that government-provided or subsidized childcare allows low-income earners to escape poverty (Huston, A.C., et al., 2011) and is therefore economically positive; whereas, others caution that policies requiring employment as a condition of public assistance come at a social cost (Albelda, R., 2011).

How do individual or general conditions become public problems? Public problems, such as poverty,

child abuse, smoking, crime, aging, and terrorism, are characterized as undesirable conditions that impinge on a society. A society defines its public problems, its public agenda, through a process in which indicators, preexisting perceptions, and focusing events combine to create the push needed for policy change. The public problem definition process is often described as an issue of tolerance. The threshold model of collective behavior, as applied to public problem definition, argues that individuals have tolerance costs and thresholds that must be met before they will take a public stand and declare a condition, issue, or event to be a public problem. Individual tolerance thresholds vary based on their tolerance costs and values attached to siding with the majority (Wood & Doan, 2003).

Public and private problems often overlap but are usually solved through different means and approaches. Solving public problems is the combined responsibility of voters and their elected officials. The solutions to public problems always reflect the shared or majority public values of society. The relationship between public values and public problems illustrates why people and their government choose the public problem solutions that they do. Public problems have at least four main features:

- Public problems involve facts and values.
- Public problems are solved through value-based decisions and approaches.
- Public problems affect people as public citizens rather than as private individuals.
- Public problems occur in public settings rather than in private settings (Boyle, 2001).

Public problems are related to at least four main public values, guaranteed in the U.S. Constitution, including liberty, equality, community, and prosperity. Liberty refers to a person's freedom, choice, and individuality. Equality refers to equity, fairness, and justice for all. Community refers to safety, security, social order, and protected quality of life. Prosperity refers to efficiency, economy, and productivity for all people. These public values are the cornerstones of American civil rights and civil liberties as guaranteed in the U.S. Constitution. Americans often disagree about which values to prioritize and under what circumstances. The federal government often prioritizes the value of economic prosperity as shown, in part, by the government's expansive and enduring support for the private business sector.

Public problems involve choices for individuals and elected officials based on values and facts. Public choice refers to the situation in which the public and their elected representatives must decide which values and facts to prioritize and use when solving a problem. Public problems result when there is disagreement among the public and politicians about which value to prioritize when solving a problem in society. Public problems result when people disagree about which values are more important for promoting the common good. Public problems also occur when an issue or an event affects people as public rather than private citizens or when an issue or an event occurs in a public setting. For example, drinking alcohol to the point of impaired judgment is legal at home as a private citizen but illegal on shared city streets or roads where people must act as public citizens (Boyle, 2001).

Public problems are, for the most part, not directly solved by individuals in society. Instead, individual voters elect representatives who share their values to solve public problems on their behalf. Elected officials work together in government to solve public problems. People often disagree about the proper role and responsibility that government should undertake to solve public problems. Common areas of debate about the proper role of government in solving public problems, and legislating society in general, include scope, power, and finances. For example, some people want expanded social programs and spending and increased national security while others want an end to "big government" and a much smaller tax system (Boyle, 2001).

Tools of Economic Analysis & Public Problem-Solving

Current economic models that inform and structure federal public problem-solving include the practices of institutional and managerial economics. These two economic approaches advocate the use of specific tools of economic analysis to solve and alleviate public problems and make organizational decisions. Institutional economics focuses on understanding the role of human-made institutions in shaping economic behavior. Institutional economics considers efficiency to be a means of problem-solving through the application of instrumental reasoning that facilities effective social functioning. Institutional

economics works to help institutions reduce transaction costs (Klein & Miller, 1996).

Managerial economics, or business economics, applies microeconomic analysis to specific organizational decisions. Managerial economics offers tools of economic analyses that work to optimize an institution's decisions based on economic objectives and goals. Common techniques of managerial economics include risk analysis, production analysis, pricing analysis, capital budgeting, and serial cost-sharing. Risk analysis refers to the quantification techniques utilized to assess the associated risks of a specific decision. Production analysis refers to the economic techniques used to evaluate production efficiency, optimal factor allocation, costs, and economies of scale. Pricing analysis refers to economic techniques used to assess pricing decisions including transfer pricing, product pricing, price discrimination, price elasticity estimates, and optimal pricing method. Capital budgeting is an investment theory used to examine an agency's capital purchasing decisions. Serial cost-sharing is a mechanism used to apportion shared resources among its users as well as split the corresponding cost.

In addition to these tools, federal budget reform during the 1990s produced the zero-based budgeting model that works to justify and rank programs based on performance and economic efficiency. In this budget format, social programs, which are created to solve and alleviate a wide range of public problems, are ranked in importance and successfulness based on the relationship between economic efficiency and performance. Zero-based budgeting creates budgets that subject all programs, activities, and expenditures to a justification process that may or may not recognize and continue to fund socially important programs (Morgan, 2002). The federal government uses tools of economic analysis that reflect the needs and standards of society at the time in which the tools were developed.

Funding Structures & Public Problem-Solving

Public problems are addressed, alleviated, and solved by government through the development and implementation of public policy. Public policy refers to the basic policies that provide the foundation for public laws. Public policy is often defined as a social goal, enabling objective, or social solution. The public policy process is a problem-solving activity that solves or alleviates a problem or conflict in society. For example, urban public policy regulates, oversees, and alleviates contemporary urban public problems such as health care, education, economic development, employment and training, nonprofit sector, immigration, housing and land development, welfare, drug control, environmental policy, transportation, local government, leadership, social policy, information access, poverty, historical preservation, and community development. Public policy, requested by society and enacted by government, bridges the gap between society and government. Public policy develops within a specific historical context, sociocultural context, and political system.

The economic goals of the United States government include maintaining high levels of employment, establishing stable prices for goods and services, and controlling the pace of economic activity. The United States government uses the tools of fiscal policy and monetary policy to achieve those goals. Fiscal policy refers to expenditures by federal, state, and local governments and to the taxes levied to finance these expenditures. Fiscal policy supports and funds the federal budget, aids the federal government's social policies, and promotes overall economic growth and stability. Federal spending includes contracts, grants, loans, and direct payments such as social security.

In the early twentieth-first century, large concerns developed over the increasingly unaffordable cost of health care and the scientific community's consensus that carbon emissions were causing global climate change. After numerous attempts to pass reforms in the way health care is funded in the United States, the Patient Protection and Affordable Care Act was signed into law on March 23, 2010 (Sonfield, A., & Pollack, H.A., 2013). The mechanisms for funding the massive universal care program were complex and involved unprecedented private/public interrelationships and mandates that remained controversial throughout the lengthy rollout. Administration projections were optimistic; however, challenges to its feasibility were vociferous. Researchers, such as Macinko & Silver (2012), proposed methods for measurement and analysis to determine over time whether the extraordinary new entitlement program is successful in achieving its policy goals while remaining economically positive. Climate change mitigation, like health care reform, was criticized as a problem for the free market to solve by economists

who charged that government regulations are by nature inefficient and "job killers." The consequences of climate change were variously viewed as socially and economically catastrophic and overly pessimistic, but the challenge for policy makers was to measure the considerable social and economic costs of either acting or doing nothing (Jones, Clark & Tripidaki, 2012).

Once public and fiscal policies have been developed at either the federal or state level, policies require funds for administration and implementation. Congress established the modern system of grants-in-aid to support state and local governments in the early twentieth century. Grants-in-aid refer to the federal funds appropriated by Congress for distribution to state and local governments to implement and support public policy initiatives. Congress awards four kinds of fiscal grants: categorical grants, block grants, project grants, and formula grants.

The funds for state and local public programs and policy implementation come from federal grants, as described above, as well as indirect taxes and personal income taxes. Trends in government grants to state and local governments have followed social and public policy interests over the past few decades. For example, state and local spending during the latter half of the twentieth century was characterized by the need to finance and support public education and Medicaid (Penner, 1998). Social, fiscal, and public policy, shaped by the parameters of federal funding structures described above, address and alleviate a wide range of public problems.

The following section provides an in-depth example of a public problem to illustrate the influence of economics in defining and solving a real-world public problem.

ISSUES

The Economics of Beach Erosion Control

Beaches (defined as natural forms composed of sand and other loose sediments moved and deposited by waves, currents, and storm over-wash) and the natural environment in general would seemingly be outside any discussion of the economics of public problem-solving. In actuality, beaches, which are legally and socially considered to be a public good, are an increasingly common public problem. Public goods refer to items, locations, or events that

Damaged homes along the coast of Mantoloking, New Jersey, left by Hurricane Sandy five months after the storm. This photo was taken from a miniature Quadcopter along the coast of Mantoloking, New Jersey. (Courtesy of Wendell A. Davis Jr./FEMA)

are indivisible, jointly consumable, and nonexclusive in nature. Laws governing the use of a public good serve two main purposes:

- Common good rules and laws protect the common property from damage that would adversely affect the flow of services demanded.
- Common good rules and laws order uses in such a way as to reduce the elements of adversity among users.

Sandy beach zones, a common good with high land values, often suffer chronic erosion as well as storm erosion. Sandy beach zones experiencing erosion are considered by many citizens and politicians to be important public problems; the loss of developed sandy beaches is a major economic and social problem. Beach erosion is officially defined as a public problem in order to receive the following economic protections, often in the form of public use policy or fiscal subsidy, from society and government:

- Protection of valuable beach residences
- Protection of tourist-related businesses
- Protection of sandy beach space for recreation
- Protection against storm damage inland
- Protection of public infrastructure servicing beach users (Fischer, 1990)

Beach erosion is considered to be a public problem due to economic property losses caused by storms

and hurricanes. The condition of beach erosion, an environmental condition exacerbated by over-development, is defined as a public problem by citizens and their elected representatives when, and only when, beach erosion causes financial loss and damage to a sufficient number of citizens and communities (Fischer, 1990).

CONCLUSION

In the final analysis, citizens and their elected representatives work together to define public problems. Democratic government guarantees public choice in defining public problem agendas. The federal government works to address and solve public problems primarily through education, participation, and representation:

- The government solves public problems by educating citizens about problems and choices beyond their immediate self-interests.
- The government solves public problems by helping citizens understand the choices between these values by promoting opportunities for citizens to participate in public problem-solving and decision-making.
- The government solves public problems by helping citizens prioritize democratic values in framing public problems (Boyle, 2001).

The federal government, as empowered by founding documents such as the Declaration of Independence and the U.S. Constitution, is responsible for safeguarding the four democratic values of liberty, equality, prosperity, and security in the public problem-solving process (Boyle, 2001). While the government does indeed develop and implement public policy solutions that protect all four of these basic democratic values, the role of economics in public problem-solving, as described in this article, is pervasive and enduring.

BIBLIOGRAPHY

Albelda, R. (2011). "Time binds: US antipoverty policies, poverty, and the well-being of single mothers." *Feminist Economics, 17,* 189–214.

Andranovich, G. (1995). "Achieving consensus in public decision making: Applying interest-based problem solving to the challenges of intergovernmental collaboration." *The Journal of Applied Behavioral Science, 31*, 429–446.

Boyle, P. (2001). "Public problems, values, and choices." *Popular Government*, 18–23.

Conte, C. & Karr, A. (February 2001). *An outline of the U.S. economy.*

Fischer, D. (1990). "Public policy aspects of beach erosion control: the public interest requires that all relevant interests have access to decision-making." *American Journal of Economics & Sociology, 49*, 185–197.

Huston, A.C., Gupta, A.E., Walker, J., Dowsett, C.J., Epps, S.R., Imes, A.E., & McLoyd, V.C. (2011). "The long-term effects on children and adolescents of a policy providing work supports for low-income parents." *Journal of Policy Analysis & Management, 30*, 729–754.

Hy, R., & Mathews, W. (1978). "Decision making practices of public service administrators." *Public Personnel Management, 7*, 148.

Irvin, R., & Stansbury, J. (2004). "Citizen participation in decision making: is it worth the effort?" *Public Administration Review, 64*, 55–65.

Jones, N., Clark, J., & Tripidaki, G. (2012). "Social risk assessment and social capital: A significant parameter for the formation of climate change policies." *Social Science Journal, 49*, 33–41.

Klein, P., & Miller, E. (1996). "Concepts of value, efficiency, and democracy in institutional economics." *Journal of Economic Issues, 30*, 267–277.

Macinko, J., & Silver, D. (2012). "Improving state health policy assessment: An agenda for measurement and analysis." *American Journal of Public Health, 102*, 1697–1705.

Morgan, D. (2002). *Handbook of public budgeting.* [Electronic Version]. Portland, OR: Hatfield School of Government, Portland State University.

Penner, R. (1998). *A brief history of state and local fiscal policy.* The Urban Institute.

Sonfield, A., & Pollack, H.A. (2013). "The affordable care act and reproducting health: potential gains and serious challenges." *Journal of Health Politics, Policy & Law, 38*, 373–391.

Wood, B., & Doan, A. (2003). "The politics of problem definition: applying and testing threshold models." *American Journal of Political Science, 47*, 640–653.

SUGGESTED READING

Gerrits, L., & Moody, R. (2011). "Envisaging futures: An analysis of the use of computational models in complex public decision making processes." *Emergence: Complexity & Organization, 13*(1/2), 96–114.

Jun, J., & Storm, W. (1990). "Social design in public problem solving." *Public Administration Quarterly, 14*, 19–30.

Nelson, B., & Leone, R. (1999). "Diversity and public problem solving: ideas and practice in policy education." *Journal of Policy Analysis & Management, 18*, 134–155.

Romney, G. (1969). "Public problem solving." *Vital Speeches of the Day, 35*, 329.

—*Simone I. Flynn, PhD*

ECONOMICS OF REGIONAL DEVELOPMENT

ABSTRACT

This article focuses on the economics of regional development. It provides an overview of regional development theory and approaches. Regional development strategies, which have different effects on economic growth, inflation, welfare, income distribution, and interregional economic inequality, are assessed. The connections between regional development, planning theory, and neoclassical development theory are described. The funding issues of public-sector and private-sector regional development organizations are included. Issues associated with measuring the economic effectiveness of regional development networks are also addressed.

OVERVIEW

Regional development efforts and programs occur worldwide. The modern trend of globalization, and the resulting shifts from centralized to market economies in much of the world, has created both a need and an opportunity for economic development in depressed regions worldwide. International development organizations, national governments, and corporations are coming together to focus on building frameworks for development in order to achieve sustainable economic growth and solve economic problems. Regional development strategies address the inequalities that form between municipalities and between urban cores and suburban peripheries. Examples of regional development goals include reduced poverty, improved infrastructure, and the provision of job training. Different regional development strategies have different effects on economic growth, inflation, welfare, income distribution, and interregional economic inequality (Kim & Kim, 2002).

Issues in regional development include the following:

- Divergence and convergence
- Resource-dependent regional growth
- The spatial centralization of the economy
- Spatial divisions
- The social construction of regional identity
- Differentiation between the capital cities and rural areas
- Indigenous issues
- The suburbanization-versus-centralization debate
- The regional effects of economic reform
- Regional policy debates
- Industry clusters (Maude, 2004)

Traditional principles of regional development have led countries to group development initiatives by geography to maximize growth potential of the country as a whole. This approach tends to result in significant economic growth for the economy in general but also serious interregional income disparity.

Modern regional development efforts work to distribute development efforts in a manner that strengthens the economies of core and periphery zones alike. Nations encourage decentralization of industries and industrialization in regions without industry to promote growth in small and medium-sized cities. Regional development programs are expected to create growth on the regional and national levels simultaneously.

Regional development is affected by agglomeration, deglomeration, production factors, infrastructure, and access to markets and information.

The connections between investment in regional infrastructure and regional development are very strong. Strong infrastructure lays the foundation for regional growth and development. Nations have different goals for regional development, including equitable interregional income distribution, productivity growth, increased gross domestic product and gross national product, and international competition (Kim & Kim, 2002).

The following section provides an overview of regional development theory. This section serves as the foundation for later discussion of the funding options of regional development organizations. The issues associated with measuring the economic effectiveness and success of regional development networks are addressed.

Regional Development Theory & Its Influences

Development efforts, whether local, regional, or national, have historically been influenced and guided by the predominant theories of economic development and growth. Development theory, closely related to economic growth theory, examines productivity, growth, income distribution, and economic equality. Development efforts and theory incorporate aspects of the following theories:

- Regional science theory
- Planning theory
- Neoclassical development theory
- New growth theory
- Modern political growth theory

Regional Science Theory

Regional development is informed by regional science theory. Regional science theory includes a collection of social science tools used to address regional problems. Regional science, which combines environmental analysis, transportation analysis, policy analysis, resource analysis, and special analysis, studies the connection between regional geography and regional economies.

Planning Theory

Regional development efforts and theory also incorporate aspects of planning theory. Planning theory, which began in the 1940s, combines civic design, corporate management, and systems analysis. Planning involves an understanding of the

Transportation is a regional problem. New York City is known for its subway system. Picture is a map of the New York City Subway as of January 2017. (Courtesy of CountZ at English Wikipedia CC BY-SA 3.0 via Wikimedia Commons)

President Clinton is awarding Robert Solow the National Medal of Science. (Courtesy of Wikimedia Commons)

development process, a long-term outlook, and planning processes or strategies. Planning theory has distinct aspects, including planning practice, political economy, and metatheory. Planning practice encompasses planning processes and outcomes. The political economy approach studies the connection between planning and capitalism. Planning metatheory encompasses theories on epistemological and methodological questions, planning procedures, actions, and behavior. Ultimately, the planning field does not have a defining paradigm. Instead, planning is shared perspectives, interests, and concerns (Brooks, 1993).

Neoclassical Growth Theory
Regional development efforts and theory were guided throughout the twentieth century by neoclassical growth theory. The neoclassical growth theory, also referred to as the exogenous growth model, focuses on productivity growth. The neoclassical growth theory, promoted by economists Robert Solow and Trevor Swan, was the predominant theory of economic growth and development from the

nineteenth to the mid-twentieth century. Exogenous growth refers to a change or variable that comes from outside the system. Technological progress and enhancement of a nation's human capital are the main factors influencing economic growth. Technology, increased human capital, savings, and capital accumulation are believed to promote technological development, more effective means of production, and economic growth. The neoclassical growth theory prioritizes the same factors and variables as neoclassical economics, which emphasizes the belief that the market system will ensure a fair allocation of resources and income distribution. In addition, the market is believed to regulate demand and supply, allocation of production, and the optimization of social organization. Neoclassical economics, along with the neoclassical growth model, began in the nineteenth century in response to perceived weaknesses in classical economics (Brinkman, 2001). Criticism of the neoclassical growth theory focuses on the long-run productivity limitation created from the theory's exclusive focus on the addition of capital to a national economy.

New Growth Theory

Over the last three decades, regional development has been strongly influenced by new growth theory. New growth theory, also referred to as the endogenous growth theory, began in the 1980s as a response to criticism of the neoclassical growth theory. Endogenous growth refers to a change or variable that comes from inside and is based on the idea that economic growth is created and sustained from within a country rather than through trade or other contact from outside the system. The new growth theory identifies the main endogenous factors leading to sustained growth of output per capita, including research and design, education, and human capital (Park, 2006). There are three main criticisms of new growth theory:

- It lacks conceptual clarity in its underlying assumptions.
- It lacks empirical relevancy.
- It claims to be a wholly new theory when it is closely tied to growth theories that came before.

Economists debate the significance of this last criticism. The new growth theory claims to represent a total break from neoclassical theory, but the continued focus on technology and its relationship to economic growth connects the two main growth theories in significant ways (Brinkman, 2001).

Political Growth Theory

Regional development efforts are, in some instances, highly politicized events. The modern political growth theory argues that development, both regional and national, is heavily influenced by political and power relationships. It focuses on the fundamental determinants of economic growth, such as the quality of governance, legal origin, ethnic diversity, democracy, trust, corruption, institutions in general, geographical constraints, natural resources, and connection between international economic integration and growth. The modern political growth theory of economics asserts that although developing and poor regions have potential for economic growth, they will never achieve this growth so long as the countries lack supporting institutions and infrastructures (Snowdon, 2006). Ultimately, the theories described in this section—planning theory, regional science theory, neoclassical development theory, new

growth theory, and modern political growth theory—have influenced regional development efforts and theory since the end of the nineteenth century.

APPLICATIONS

Regional Development Organizations

Regional development programs are undertaken at the local, regional, and national levels by both private- and public-sector stakeholders. Public- and private-sector stakeholders direct development activities differently. Regional development organizations from the private sector, the public sector, and public-private partnerships all tend to have similar structures, consisting of a governing board (which makes policy decisions, goals, and objectives) and an administrative workforce (which carries out the board's instructions). What varies between regional development organizations is the level of participation and funding from either the private or public sector (Whitehead & Ady, 1989). The economics and funding sources of regional development organizations are described below.

Private-Sector Regional Development

Private-sector regional development is a strategy for promoting economic development by private industries that benefits the poor in developing regions of the world. The private sector comprises all the micro, small, medium, and large enterprises that are outside of government ownership and control. Modern private-sector regional development involves numerous private-sector stakeholders—such as development agencies, corporations from industrialized countries, businesses from developing countries, community agencies, or populations in need—who are all committed to ending poverty and related conditions in developing regions. Private-sector regional development is funded by contributions from business, industry, and private individuals. Economic development functions include a range of activities such as creating, attracting, and retaining jobs and capital investments. Board members may come from a wide range of nongovernmental organizations, such as bankers or small-business owners. Operational advantages of private-sector regional development organizations may include freedom from political boundaries or restrictions, freedom to maintain confidentiality about important issues, and knowledge of the business sector's interests and needs. Organizational disadvantages include lack of control over development issues requiring government involvement, such as investment incentives and infrastructure planning. Private-sector regional development organizations may choose the legal form of a nonprofit organization.

Public-Sector Regional Development

Local and national governments fund public-sector regional development organizations. The public-sector model is often referred to as the government-agency model. While the governing body of private-sector regional organizations is usually a board of directors, the governing body of the public-sector regional organization is most often an elected or appointed government official, such as a mayor or city council member. Public-sector regional development functions, similar to those of the private-sector regional development organizations, include creating, attracting, and retaining jobs and capital investment. Operational advantages may include control and direct access to investment incentives, such as tax abatements, and control over infrastructure planning, such as roads and utilities. In addition, the public-sector model invites, and sometimes requires, input and participation from all sectors of the community. Public-sector regional development organizations are legally defined as government agencies for tax-reporting purposes.

Public-Private Regional Development

The private and public sectors both fund public-private regional development organizations. Policy direction, objectives, and goals are determined through collaboration between public and private interests. Governing boards include members from business and government posts. The public-private regional partnership model is the most prevalent among economic development organizations today. Public-private partnership organizations are often called balanced organizations. Reasons for the growing number of public-private partnership organizations include the burdensome and escalating costs of regional development activities. In many instances, those involved in regional development combine public- and private-sector resources in order to acquire sufficient funds and staff to accomplish development projects and goals. Public and private sectors combine their respective operational advantages to benefit their regional communities and service areas.

Choosing an Economic-Development Model

Regional development organizations consider two important organizational issues when choosing a model of economic development. First, there are numerous benefits gained from combining a new regional development organization with an existing agency, either nonprofit or government. This practice is called piggybacking. The public-private regional partnership often allows the new organization to use the legal status of the established organization, thus saving time and money resources. Second, regional development organizations must choose the legal form and tax status most suited and advantageous to their organization. For example, the legal designation of a nonprofit organization allows for tax-exempt status, which means that organizational revenues are not taxed and donations are tax deductible for the donor. Regional development organizations usually apply and are approved for tax-exempt status. The organizational structure of a regional development enterprise has the potential to influence the performance and success of regional development organizations and projects.

ISSUES

Measuring the Effectiveness of Regional Development Networks

Trends in development practices, including economic and environmental or sustainable development, are moving away from local and national development and toward regional development. The predominant regional development model at the beginning of the twenty-first century was the regional development network. These networks include regional networked environments and regional trade partnerships. New networked development environments in regions worldwide form in response to the forces of the new information society and globalization. There are three main types, or archetypes, of regional development networks:

- Large and loose
- Heterogeneous, multi-actor, and innovative
- Closed, homogeneous, and public actor

Economists increasingly consider subnational regions to be the real players in international competition. Regional economies interact and trade in the global marketplace (Harmaakorpi, 2007).

Economic Integration

At the beginning of the twenty-first century, regional trade partnerships were found in every region of the world, and economic integration efforts between nations characterized international relations. Economic integration refers to the integration of commercial and financial activities between countries through the abolishment of nation-based economic institutions and activities. Economic integration between nations includes the following four stages:

- Free-trade agreements (FTA)
- Customs unions (CU)
- Common markets
- Economic unions (Holden, 2003)

Nations choose different levels of economic integration and trade partnerships based on variables such as the strength of their national economy and trade relationships and forecasted trade prospects. Nations may have multiple trade relationships and levels of economic integration with other countries, or they may have none at all. Nations that reject or do not pursue economic integration, as described above, are characterized as autarkic. An autarkic nation is a self-sufficient country that does not participate in international trade. Autarky, which derives from a Greek word meaning "self-sufficient," confers independence from other states, resulting in both benefits and costs (Anderson & Marcouiller, 2005). The stages of economic integration and partnership are rarely fixed or permanent; rather, they are generally fluid and overlapping.

Economic Indicators

Different models and incarnations of trade partnerships produce a wide range of economic outcomes. Nations and economic development organizations track trends in economic development at the regional and national levels. Economic indicators, which are statistical data reflecting general trends in the economy, reveal discrepancies between economic development in regional and national economies. Examples of economic indicators include monthly sales of goods and services, gross domestic product, productivity levels, manufacturing shipments and inventories, wholesale trade, new construction, personal-income figures, and balance of trade. The model of regional development driven by and based on innovation and trade argues that regional trade and information networks create growth. Regional trade and information networks produce different outcomes and levels of economic growth (Werker & Athreye, 2004).

Index-Based Regional Analysis

Different regional development strategies generally create different levels of economic growth, inflation, welfare, income distribution, and interregional economic inequality than national-development planning. Nations and regional development organizations measure regional development efforts to assess the effectiveness of strategies and programs. The main tool for measuring regional development results and levels is index-based regional analysis, which is used throughout the world to compare development efforts in different regions. For example, the Republic of Korea, which has numerous regional development organizations that produce different economic outcomes, uses index-based regional analysis. The West Coast regional development program in Korea created substantial gains in gross domestic product and a reduction in regional income disparity (Kim & Kim, 2002). The three Korean coastal-area development strategies—East Coast, South Coast, and West Coast—and the Seoul-Pusan development corridor strategy have created different levels of efficiency and equity distribution.

Index-based regional analysis is also used throughout eastern Europe. Giannias et al. (2000)

The automotive line Hyundai is a key sector in South Korea's industry. This is a 2010 Hyundai Genesis Coupe photographed in Middleburg, Virginia. (Courtesy of IFCAR via Wikimedia Commons)

ranked the members of the former Soviet Union and the regions of Russia on a regional development index that includes per capita income and various socioeconomic measures and components. According to the index, of the former Soviet Union states, Lithuania ranked the highest and Tajikistan ranked the lowest. An analysis of Russia's various regions shows that the central-southern region and the Sackha Republic in the west ranked the highest, while parts of western and central Russia ranked the lowest (Giannias et al., 2000).

Regional Networks

Ultimately, regional economic integration and development between developing and developed countries is common and believed to lead to economic stability and development. Developing countries and international development organizations, such as the World Bank and the Organisation for Economic Co-operation and Development, promote regional economic networks and regional trade agreements as a means of facilitating stability, development, information sharing, and trade creation. Examples of regional trade agreements include the European Free Trade Association (EFTA), the Southern African Customs Union (SACU), the Gulf Cooperation Council (GCC), the Monetary and Economic Community of Central Africa (CEMAC), the Southern Common Market (Mercosur), and the West African Economic and Monetary Union (UEMOA). Tracking the effectiveness of these regional networks has become the responsibility and challenge of all stakeholders. Index-based regional analysis is one method by which the economic effectiveness of regional development programs, networks, and partnerships is evaluated.

CONCLUSION

The economics of regional development changes as a result of new global forces of economic integration and globalization. Nations, which once centralized their economic development efforts in single or multiple cores, are suffering from the problems associated with unequal development and income distribution. Nations attempting to strengthen regional economies are allocating resources to create infrastructure, jobs, and industry. Regional development efforts may be funded by the public sector, the private sector, or public-private partnerships. Economic analysis of regional development efforts suggests that sustained regional development, as represented by enhanced productivity and growth, may require structural transformation within the nation. Economic development and growth, while encouraged and facilitated by factors such as a large labor supply, national infrastructure, and a resource-rich environment, is hindered by economic problems and cultural obstacles inherent in the business climate and by troughs in the business cycle. Economic problems of all kinds, including structural, fiscal, and cultural, impact regional development efforts by national governments, corporations, and international development organizations. Regional development encompasses a wide range of programs and strategies aimed at promoting growth in a part or whole of an economy. Successful regional development may require a nation to undertake creative changes to its old economic institutions, modes of production, and power relationships.

BIBLIOGRAPHY

A gender agenda: "New directions for planning theory." (1992). *Journal of the American Planning Association, 58,* 49–60.

Anderson, J., & Marcouiller, D. (2005). "Anarchy and autarky: Endogenous predation as a barrier to trade." *International Economic Review, 46,* 189–213.

Brinkman, R. (1995). "Economic growth versus economic development: Toward a conceptual clarification." *Journal of Economic Issues, 29,* 1171–1188

Brooks, M. (1993). "A plethora of paradigms." *Journal of the American Planning Association, 59,* 142.

Giannias, D., Belokrilova, O., Shevchenko, I., & Chepurko, Y. (2000). "Index based regional analysis: The case of the former Soviet Union and Russia." *Economics of Planning, 33,* 71.

Harmaakorpi, V. & Niukkanen, H. (2007). "Leadership in different kinds of regional development networks." *Baltic Journal of Management, 2,* 80.

Holden, M. (2003). "Stages of economic integration: From autarky to economic union." Government of Canada Depository Services Program. Retrieved from xlink:href="http://dsp-psd.pwgsc.gc.ca/Collection-R/LoPBdP/inbrief/prb0249-e.htm"

Jain, A. (2012). "An integrated model of subnational regional and urban economic development: Framework of analysis applied to the city of Casey,

Victoria, Australia." *Australasian Journal of Regional Studies, 18,* 206–231.

Kim, E., & Kim, K. (2002). "Impacts of regional development strategies on growth and equity of Korea: A multiregional CGE model." *Annals of Regional Science, 36,* 165.

Maude, A. (2004). "Regional development processes and policies in Australia: A review of research 1990-2002." *European Planning Studies, 12,* 3–26.

Melnikas, B. (2013). "Transformations and regional economic development in central and eastern Europe: Typicalities and new perspectives." *Region Formation & Development Studies, 9,* 102–113.

Oort, F., & Bosma, N. (2013). "Agglomeration economies, inventors and entrepreneurs as engines of European regional economic development." *Annals of Regional Science, 51,* 213–244.

Park, C. (2006). "The theory of economic growth: A "classical" perspective. "*Science and Society, 70,* 558–562.

Snowdon, B. (2006). "The enduring elixir of economic growth." *World Economics, 7,* 73–130.

Werker, C., & Athreye, S. (2004). "Marshall's disciples: Knowledge and innovation driving regional economic development and growth." *Journal of Evolutionary Economics, 14,* 505–523.

Whitehead, W., & Ady, R. (1989). "Organizational models for economic development." *Economic Development Review, 7,* 8.

SUGGESTED READING

Estrada, M. (2013). "The Global Dimension of the Regional Integration Model (GDRI-Model)." *Modern Economy, 4,* 346–369.

Matuschewski, A. (2006). "Regional clusters of the information economy in Germany." *Regional Studies, 40,* 409–422.

Mcmaster, I. (2006). "Czech regional development agencies in a shifting institutional landscape." *Europe-Asia Studies, 58,* 347–370.

Ward, N., Lowe, P., & Bridges, T. (2003). "Rural and regional development: The role of the regional development agencies in England." *Regional Studies, 37,* 201.

—*Simone I. Flynn, PhD*

ECONOMICS OF URBAN DEVELOPMENT

ABSTRACT

This article focuses on the economics of urban development. It provides an overview of the connection between urban decline and urban development. This article examines how economic policy solutions address and remedy the problems of economic disinvestment, economic underdevelopment, and urban decline in urban neighborhoods and communities. The main urban development strategies, public policies, and programs, including impact fees, congestion pricing, tax-base sharing, special taxing districts, concurrency planning, reverse commuting, affordable housing strategies, regional government, and growth management are described. A case study of urban development in the United States is included as an opportunity to explore how the federal government structures its efforts to halt urban decline and promote urban development in American cities.

OVERVIEW

Cites are considered to be the engines of national economies worldwide. In the United States, the majority of Americans live in metropolitan regions or areas. The U.S. Census Bureau recognizes 381 metropolitan areas in the United States. Despite the prominence of American cities, urban communities in the United States, and around the world, have struggled with urban flight, poverty, housing discrimination, isolation, budget deficits, declining tax bases, and rising public sector costs (Stegman, 1996). Factors that shaped U.S. metropolitan cities in the twentieth century include generational shifts, demographic shifts, sociopolitical orientations, real estate economics, income inequality, technology, social divisions, housing, zoning, and transportation (McDonogh, 2004). American cities, such as Washington, DC, and Detroit, are suffering from the negative externalities created by urbanization such

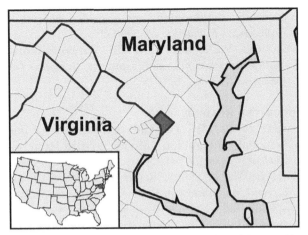

Location of Washington, D.C., in the contiguous United States and in relation to Maryland and Virginia. (Courtesy of USA_Counties.svg: U.S. Census Bureau Blank_USA,_w_territories.svg: Lokal_Profil via Wikimedia Commons)

as unemployment or underemployment, economic and social inequalities, challenges to social cohesion, urban sprawl and congestion, environmental problems, and housing shortages. Numerous American cities are suffering from urban decline and do not have the local or federal fiscal support to fix the situation. Urban decline is characterized by problems such as unemployment, underinvestment in physical infrastructure, homelessness, decrease in local population, and decrease in private sector presence and investment (Freudenberg, 2006).

Policy makers address the problem of urban decline through urban fiscal policy and urban development.

- Urban fiscal policy, negotiated and carried out at the federal, state, and local levels, affects the ability of cities to meet the economic and social needs of diverse resident and business populations. Urban fiscal policy refers to a wide range of tax, budget, and economic and other related public policy issues that affect the quality of life and the economic well-being of people in cities. Areas of concern and influence for urban fiscal policy makers include the causes and future consequences of the urban fiscal crisis, the optimal tax and spending rate for local governments, and public infrastructure funding. The goal of urban fiscal policy is a strong urban economy and a thriving populous. Urban fiscal policy promotes, supports, and facilitates urban development efforts.

- Urban development refers to largely government initiated and sponsored enterprises focused on redeveloping derelict urban land and communities. Urban development includes multiple efforts such as job programs, housing initiatives, reverse-commuting efforts, tax-sharing, regional governance, and congestion fees. The economics of urban development is complex. Stakeholders debate the following issues and questions: Who should fund economic development? How should economic development resources be allocated? Who is responsible for urban decline? In most cities, funding for urban development comes from both public and private sources.

This article explores the economics of urban development. The article examines how economic and fiscal policy solutions address and remedy the problems of economic disinvestment, economic underdevelopment, and urban decline in urban neighborhoods and communities. The following section provides an overview of the connection between urban decline and urban development. This section serves as a foundation for later discussion of many prominent urban development strategies and programs. A case study of urban development in the United States is included at the end of the article as an opportunity to explore how the federal government structures its efforts to halt urban decline and promote urban development in American cities.

URBAN DECLINE & URBAN DEVELOPMENT
America's Urban Crisis

Many economists, urban studies experts, and policy makers consider America's urban metropolises to be in crisis. Throughout the twentieth century, centers of industry moved from highly industrialized cities to urban-suburban hubs. As a result of industry transformations, population switches from urban to suburban living, and globalization, American cities experience uneven development and, in many instances, urban decline. Different parts of metropolitan regions experience disparities in standards of living, housing options, employment opportunities, and quality of public services. The economic health of American cities influences the physical infrastructures and services provided in a city. The fiscal issues facing local governments in the United States are complex. Local governments that serve urban areas in the United States receive funds from the federal government (in the form of grants) and the local populations (in the form of taxes). Local governments must use funds as specified by the grants given by the federal government and must meet the needs of the local population.

Budget Imbalance

Urban decline affects industry, quality of life, availability of services, and infrastructure. Numerous urban regions in the United States face large structural budget imbalances in which there exists a persistent gap between the regional government's ability to raise revenues and the cost of providing basic services. Large budget expenditures include the high cost of living, public safety, and social service needs. One result for this fiscal imbalance is a long-term underinvestment in city physical infrastructures. In the interest of a balanced budget, local governments are often forced to defer infrastructure maintenance, improvement, and expansion. Federal contributions are necessary to address structural budget imbalances that cannot be addressed or remedied at the local level (Lazere, 2005). Urban revenue sources are, in many instances, shrinking. Revenue sources, including income tax and corporate profit tax, are not growing in proportion with the needs of urban areas. Direct federal aid to local governments is also decreasing or leveling off. For example, the Community Development Block Grant (CDBG), a federal program that serves over 1,000 communities

Aerial view of downtown Detroit, Michigan, with the Riverfront looking up Grand River Avenue. (Courtesy of Robert Thompson CC BY-SA 4.0 via Wikimedia Commons)

and provides fiscal flexibility to local officials, was cut from $4.45 billion in 2010 to $3.5 billion in 2013; the budget was due to be cut even more in fiscal year 2014 (Cohen, 2013).

The problem of budget deficits in state and local governments affects the economic health of the whole country. The nonprofit Center on Budget and Policy Priorities (CBPP) makes recommendations for how state policy makers can make substantial improvements to their state fiscal systems in upcoming legislative sessions. Proposed strategies for fixing state and local revenue problems, addressing budget gaps, and financing new initiatives include the following (Johnson, 2007):

- Expand the corporate income tax flaws.
- Modernize state sales taxes.
- Separate state tax codes from the federal tax code.
- Raise state cigarette taxes.

Ultimately, American urban areas may be understood as economic organizations similar to public corporations. While a corporation has shareholders, a board of directors, and a chief executive officer, a city has landowners, a city council, and a mayor. The main economic purpose of a city is to offer resources and services such as infrastructure, safety, and schools. Cities must provide the services that its residents need or the residents will leave, creating falling real estate prices and unemployment. Efficient cities attract investment and development. Inefficient cities go bankrupt. In fact, Detroit, once the center of the American auto industry, filed for bankruptcy in 2013. American cities in fiscal crisis will need to rely on urban fiscal policy, drafted at the federal, state, and local levels, and private-sector urban investment to provide resources for urban change and growth.

Suburban Growth

In the United States, the postindustrial urbanization and restructuring processes have been affected by significant economic and sociocultural change. Since the 1950s, low-density suburban environments have grown around most American cities. The residential structure of American cities has changed (Wyly, 1999). Contemporary urban change has resulted in uneven development and disparities between metropolitan regions. The urban and suburban regions of New York, Chicago, Philadelphia, Detroit, Boston,

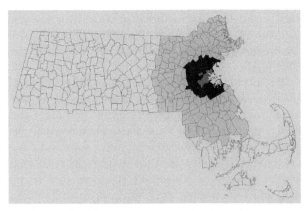

Light gray represents the area in Massachusetts known as Greater Boston, while dark gray represents the Metro-Boston area and the smallest gray area represents the City of Boston.

Washington, DC, Cleveland, and St. Louis expanded faster than their populations. Policies are now being developed and implemented to accomplish the following pro-development goals (Wiewel, 1999):

- Reduce urban decline, suburban sprawl, and resulting costs and inequalities.
- Make the city more attractive to investors.
- Allocate costs more effectively so those who create them are responsible for them.
- Redistribute the benefits of growth more equitably.

Urban development efforts include multiple stakeholders: government, business, city residents, and suburban residents. The fields of urban economics and land use, as well as urban studies, urban geography, economic geography, social geography, and central planning, combine to help understand and guide the economics of urban growth and urban restructuring.

APPLICATIONS

Urban Development Programs
Policy makers use public policy to address the imbalance in distribution of costs and benefits between the public and private sectors and different parts of the population. Public policies address inequities and correct growth patterns; slow deconcentration in the future; and redistribute the benefits of growth (Wiewel, 1999). Examples of public policies that attempt to address and halt urban decline include

impact fees, congestion pricing, tax-base sharing, special taxing districts, concurrency planning, reverse commuting, affordable housing strategies, regional government, and growth management. These policies, described below, are classified as economic urban development policies.

- Congestion Pricing: Congestion pricing is a mechanism that accounts for traffic-related costs and imposes them on local businesses and commuters. One of the main examples of congestion pricing is peak-hour road pricing, during which drivers have to pay higher toll amounts if driving on congested highways during peak hours.
- Impact Fees: Impact fees refer to charges that localities levy on developers to produce revenue rather than make existing residents pay for capital projects necessitated by development. Examples of impact fees include schools, roads, or other public infrastructure.
- Concurrency Planning: Concurrency planning refers to situations in which public services and infrastructure must be provided at the same rate as new development is being built.
- Reverse Commuting: Reverse commuting programs promote, and in some cases provide, inner-city residents with transportation to and from suburban jobs.
- Affordable Suburban Housing: Affordable housing programs aid city residents in moving to the outer suburbs without losing access or proximity to job growth centers. These programs may include loans, information, zoning changes, grants, and subsidized suburban housing.
- Tax-Base Sharing: Tax-base sharing programs refer to a tax system in which urban and suburban municipalities share revenue with each other rather than keeping it for the exclusive use of their area. Tax-sharing programs address the problem of unequal taxable property and businesses.
- Growth Management: Growth management refers to a specific plan with future goals that involves shaping and controlling growth through certain procedures and policies. Examples of growth management programs include limits on development density allowed through zoning or restrictions on subdivisions; architectural design and human capacity standards for buildings; requirements to provide adequate public facilities or imposition of

impact fees; urban growth boundaries; greenbelts; and regional review.

- Regional Governance: Regional governance refers to a governance model that includes greater geographic scope. Under this model, cities and their suburbs share governance and resources. The regional governance model reduces public resources inequalities and disparities between the central city and its outer suburbs. Local governments that have previously tried many of the strategies described above to address the problems of urban decline and the need for urban development are increasingly turning to new forms of urban governance. New forms of urban governance are being tried in urban regions worldwide (Keil, 2006).

Cities around the world have incorporated these development strategies to address the economic problems of urban decline and promote urban development. These strategies and programs vary in revenue sources and wide-scale applicability.

Case Study: Urban Development in the United States

Urban problems, including poverty, isolation, declining tax base, and crime, are public problems that require policy solutions. The U.S. government addresses urban problems with urban development initiatives. Urban development initiatives, often a form of public policy, are closely connected to economic policy. Important urban development policies of the twentieth century included the following:

- The U.S. Housing Act of 1937 established the United States Housing Administration.
- The Housing and Urban Development Act of 1965 established the Department of Housing and Urban Development (HUD).
- The Housing Act of 1968 established Government National Mortgage Association.
- The Housing and Urban Development Act of 1970 established the Federal Experimental Housing Allowance Program and Community Development Corporation.
- The Housing and Community Development Act of 1974 consolidated numerous urban development programs into the Community Development Block Grant program.

- The Housing and Urban-Rural Recovery Act of 1983 established the Housing Development Action Grant and Rental Rehabilitation program.
- The Indian Housing Act of 1988 established the connection between HUD and Native Americans and Alaskan Indians.
- The Federal Housing Enterprises Financial Safety and Soundness Act of 1992 created HUD Office of Federal Housing Enterprise Oversight.

All of the policies described above include economic and social components. In the twenty-first century, the federal government actively promotes urban development through two large-scale economic programs:

- The Department of Housing and Urban Development (HUD)
- Community reinvestment policy

The Department of Housing and Urban Development Act

The Department of Housing and Urban Development Act, established in 1965, is the part of the government most responsible for national urban development. The Department of Housing and Urban Development's stated mission is "to increase homeownership, support community development, and increase access to affordable housing free from discrimination" (Pennisi, 2010, ¶1). The efforts of the Department of Housing and Urban Development to strengthen communities are led by economic development efforts. The Department of Housing and Urban Development's economic development focus is on creating and retaining jobs in our urban communities. The Department of Housing and Urban Development promotes urban development through the designation of Renewal Communities and Urban Empowerment Zones.

The Department of Housing and Urban Development's Renewal Communities and Urban Empowerment Zones are designed to redress urban decline. The Renewal Communities program includes a tax incentive program for all businesses of all sizes in the Renewal Communities area. Examples of tax incentives include employment credits, a 0% tax on capital gains, and accelerated depreciation through commercial revitalization deductions. The tax incentives are intended to encourage businesses to open, expand, and hire local residents. The Empowerment Zone program also includes a tax incentive program for small and large businesses in Empowerment Zones. These incentives, which include employment credits, low-interest loans through EZ facility bonds, and reduced taxation on capital gains, give businesses incentives to expand and hire local residents. As of 2013, there were 30 communities designated Urban Empowerment Zones.

The Department of Housing and Urban Development's Renewal Communities and Urban Empowerment Zones programs are part of the federal government's larger urban development efforts. The federal government requires active community reinvestment nationwide. Community reinvestment refers to the practice in which depository institutions, such as federally insured banks and thrifts, help to meet the credit needs of the communities in which they operate with safe and sound business practices and operations. Community reinvestment, as a form of urban development, combines and addresses the fiscal and social needs of urban dwellers.

Community Reinvestment Act

Minority communities in the United States have experienced unequal and lagging economic growth and development throughout the twentieth century. The existing economic inequality experienced by minority communities was exacerbated by the reluctance of banks to fully service minority communities. The federal government responded to the reported bias and neglect by banks in low- and moderate-income neighborhoods by passing the Community Reinvestment Act. The Community Reinvestment Act, enacted by Congress in 1977, encourages economic development in low- and moderate-income neighborhoods. The Community Reinvestment Act requires depository institutions, such as federally insured banks and thrifts, to help meet the credit needs of the communities in which they operate by providing safe and sound business practices and operations. The federal government passed the Community Reinvestment Act to ensure that banks and thrifts were meeting the lending and credit needs of all people and groups within their communities regardless of income, age, or race.

The Community Reinvestment Act was enacted to eliminate the practice of redlining and the resulting disinvestment that occurs when banks export deposits from one community in order to increase available credit in another community. The practice of redlining creates a flow of funds from low- to moderate-income neighborhoods to middle- to high-income communities. Redlining refers to the act of refusing to offer services or increasing the cost of services, such as banking and insurance, to residents in low-income areas. Mortgage discrimination is one of the forms of redlining most responsible for lagging economic development. The Community Reinvestment Act, along with the Fair Housing Act of 1968, which prohibited housing discrimination based on race, religion, gender, familial status, disability, or ethnic origin, effectively stopped the practices of redlining and mortgage discrimination in many minority neighborhoods. The Community Reinvestment Act has facilitated and promoted urban development in the United States for decades.

The Community Reinvestment Act has affected private-sector urban development practices in numerous ways. For example, the Community Reinvestment Act has affected lending institutions and the communities in which they operate in equal measure. Lending institutions and their practices, procedures, goals, and objectives are altered by increased Community Reinvestment Act regulatory oversight, the public release of Community Reinvestment Act performance ratings, and the relationship between Community Reinvestment Act performance and possible denial or delay of an institution's application for a merger or acquisition (Bostic & Robinson, 2003). The Community Reinvestment Act has changed banking practices and communities throughout America. The Community Reinvestment Act has resulted in significant economic growth and opportunity for underserved and underdeveloped communities as well as strengthened relationships between banks and the communities they serve. The Community Reinvestment Act has encouraged banks to open new branches, provide expanded services, adopt more flexible credit underwriting standards, and increase lending to underserved segments of local economies and populations. The Community Reinvestment Act has begun to remedy the problems of economic disinvestment and economic underdevelopment in urban neighborhoods and communities (Matasar & Pavelka, 2004).

CONCLUSION

In the final analysis, urban decline requires creative economic and social solutions. Urban development, initiated and funded by both the public sector and private sector, combines economic and social programs to address negative externalities created by urbanization such as unemployment or underemployment, economic and social inequalities, challenges to social cohesion, urban sprawl, congestion, environmental problems, and housing shortages.

BIBLIOGRAPHY

Bin Y. (2017). "Analysis on sustainable urban development levels and trends in China's cities." *Journal of Cleaner Production, 141*, 10.

Bostic, R., & Robinson, B. (2003). "Do CRA agreements influence lending patterns?" *Real Estate Economics, 31*, 23–51.

Cohen, R. (2013 June 21). "GOP demands CDBG cuts to the tune of $1.19 billion." *Nonprofit Quarterly.*

Freudenberg, N., Fahs, M., Galea, S., & Greenberg, A. (2006). "The impact of New York City's 1975 fiscal crisis on the tuberculosis, HIV, and homicide syndemic." *American Journal of Public Health, 96,* 424–434

Johnson, N. (2007). "Improving state fiscal policies in the 2007 legislative sessions."

Junnila, S., & Ristimäki, M. (2012). "Public demand for eco-efficient concepts in urban development." *International Journal of Strategic Property Management, 16*, 21–36.

Keil, A. (2006). "New urban governance processes on the level of neighborhoods." *European Planning Studies, 14*, 335–364.

Lazere, E. & Garrison, D. (2005, November). "A new federal contribution to the District of Columbia? The need, likely impact, and some options. Retrieved from the D.C. Fiscal Policy Institute Web site."

Matasar A. & Pavelka, D. (2004). "Minority banks and minority communities: Are minority banks good neighbors?" *International Advances in Economic Research, 10*, 43–58.

McDonogh, G. (2004). "Urban economics and land use in America: The transformation of cities in the twentieth century." *Choice, 42*, 742–744.

Mission and history. (2007). U.S. Department of Housing and Urban Development. Retrieved from "http://www.hud.gov"

Paulsen, K. (2013). "The effects of growth management on the spatial extent of urban development, revisited." *Land Economics, 89*, 193–210.

Pennisi, M. (2010). "US department of housing and urban development." Coldwell Banker Residential Brokerage - Summit Office. Retrieved from "http://michaelpennisi.com/hud-.asp"

Sawicky, M. (2002, June). "U.S. cities face fiscal crunch: federal and state policies exacerbate local governments' budget shortfalls." *Economic Policy Institute Issue Brief*, 181.

Stegman, M., & Turner, M. (1996). "The future of urban America in the global economy." *Journal of the American Planning Association, 62*, 157.

Wiwel, W. (1999). "Private benefits and public costs: Policies to address suburban sprawl." *Policy Studies Journal, 27*, 96–115.

Wyly, E. (1999). "Continuity and change in the restless urban landscape." *Economic Geography, 75*, 309–339.

SUGGESTED READING

Bovaird, T., Gregory, D., & Martin, S. (1988). "Performance measurement in urban economic development." *Public Money & Management, 8*, 17–22.

Ohls, J., & Pines, D. (1975). "Discontinuous urban development and economic efficiency." *Land Economics, 51*, 224.

Stokes, C., Mintz, P., & VanGelder, H. (1965). "Economic criteria for urban redevelopment." *American Journal of Economics & Sociology, 24*, 249–255.

Vitkien?, E. (2011). "Relationship between urban and regional development in global context." *Human Resources: The Main Factor of Regional Development,* 311–320.

—*Simone I. Flynn, PhD*

ELASTICITY

ABSTRACT

Presenting some applications and insights to undergraduate students on the topic of elasticity, this essay contains discourse that aims to facilitate their understanding of the concept. The essay addresses several variants of elasticity along with definitions, calculations, and examples. A large portion of this essay covers price, cross, and income elasticities of demand. The author devotes an ample amount of attention to those demand elasticities striving to alleviate learning difficulties. Frequently, students encounter problems associated with line graph characteristics, expenditure and revenue changes, and elasticity determinants. The article also presents price elasticity of supply and its comparative relevance to those who incur the tax burden on some items.

OVERVIEW

Elasticity is a concept of central importance to business, marketing, and economics. Studies in economics begin by expressing the importance of the *ceteris paribus* ("all else is held constant") assumption and by focusing on relationships between the possible prices of an item and the quantities consumers are willing and able to purchase at each price; likewise, the quantities suppliers are willing and able to produce. On the consumer or demand side, students learn very early in their coursework that an inverse relationship exists between price and quantity in accordance with the law of demand. Relatively speaking, smaller amounts are in demand at higher prices, and vice versa. On the producer or supply side, they learn that a positive relationship exists according to the law of supply. Whether one chooses to focus on demand or on supply, elasticity is a concept that helps us understand in precise terms exactly how much quantity changes in response to a price change.

Many students who complete and evaluate introductory courses in economics for non-business majors find the elasticity topic easy to comprehend. In addition, they report that the topic makes perfect sense to them and is highly relevant to their everyday exchanges. However, they report having difficulties mastering the varied types (price, income, and cross)

of elasticity. To overcome those obstacles, they encourage other students to elicit examples from their professors and to practice calculating, interpreting, and applying elasticity.

Some commonly used textbooks in economics (Arnold, 2005; Guell, 2007; McConnell & Brue, 2008; Parkin, 2000) provide basic topical coverage, but unfortunately very few articles present economic elasticity in a straightforward manner, without references and narrow application to a specific context. Furthermore, those contexts usually require readers to have an advanced understanding of economics and other business disciplines. In a demonstration of how the elasticity concept is relevant to marketing, Dickinson (2002) makes the case that textbook presentations of elasticity provide a weak foundation for studying price-quantity interactions and for simulating behavioral complexities of consumers in the marketplace. From an economics education perspective, this article represents one effort to facilitate an undergraduate student's understanding of the elasticity concept.

APPLICATIONS

Price Elasticity of Demand

Cigarette smokers, beer drinkers, and motor vehicle drivers are consumers who are likely to identify most readily with the elasticity concept. Examples pertaining to alcohol and tobacco will follow later, but gasoline prices serve as an excellent example for starters. Motor vehicle drivers probably retain their awareness of the daily price for gasoline and its fluctuations during any given period. Furthermore, it is likely that these consumers will purchase greater quantities when the price of gasoline falls and fewer quantities when the price rises. Calculations of the price elasticity of demand for gasoline allow us to determine precisely in percentage terms how sensitive drivers' purchases of fuel are in response to changes in its price. Though most dislike rising gasoline prices and generate some noise about it, the evidence strongly suggests that consumer demand is relatively unresponsive, or inelastic, as they tend to purchase the same amounts over time irrespective of price. To explore this observation further, students need to

Sign showing gas prices in front of Sheetz in Mt. Jackson, Virginia, on August 31, 2005, just as Hurricane Katrina began to make its mark on the price of gasoline. Prices had risen thirty cents since the previous day, and would rise an additional twenty cents before the day was over. (Courtesy of Ben Schumin via Wikimedia Commons)

understand demand elasticity coefficients, calculate them, and determine whether demand for gasoline is truly inelastic.

Guell (2007, p. 41) summarizes a few studies on the price elasticity of demand for gasoline, stating that any given 10 percent increase in its price will result in a decrease of less than 3 percent in quantities purchased; coincidentally, the gasoline prices can fluctuate by 10 percent or more during any given week. The latter percentage varies depending on how long consumers have to adjust their driving and spending habits; for example, the amount of gasoline in their car's tank and the remoteness of their geographic location jointly influence whether they can afford to shop for cheaper gasoline. In 2014, the U.S.

Energy Information Administration (EIA) reported the estimated price elasticity of demand for gasoline at about 0.02 to 0.04 in the "short run." The EIA noted that factors beyond price, such as changing employment status, urbanization, and increasing vehicle fuel efficiency, can play a role in changing the price elasticity of demand for gasoline over time.

Calculating & Presenting Demand Elasticity Coefficients
Note the simplifying omission of the negative sign from the aforementioned coefficients because of the explicit inverse relationship that exists between price and quantity demanded. Calculations of the elasticity coefficient involve division of the percentage change in quantity demanded by the percentage change in price. The coefficient is unit-free, and its basic formula is

Percent change in quantity demanded/Percent change in price
Percent change is the observed difference between two points—namely, the starting point and the endpoint—divided by the value at the starting point. Readers of textbooks will find variants in the formula that are merely designed to accommodate calculations whether one holds an interest in observing the elasticity at the starting point, the endpoint, or somewhere near the middle of those two points and when facing different shapes of the line that represents all the price-quantity combinations.

Another justification for omitting the negative sign is to simplify interpretations of a price elasticity of demand coefficient by examining it as an absolute term. In the broadest sense, we can think about and talk about elasticity of a specific item at its extremes along a demand spectrum. The demand for an item is either elastic, inelastic, or unitary elastic when the respective coefficient as an absolute term is greater than one, less than one, or equal to one. The coefficient in the gasoline example is less than one, which informs us that the demand for gasoline is inelastic; in other words, consumers are unresponsive to changes in the price of gasoline. We generally dislike the price hike, but collectively gasoline consumers maintain their purchase levels.

Think of the larger array of items that you purchase on a regular basis. My guess is that readers of this article, like other consumers, are more responsive to changes in price for some items and not so for other items. In absolute terms, price elasticity of demand coefficients range between zero and infinity extending outwardly from unitary elasticity, which is where the coefficient is equal to one. Those extremes carry specific names. At one extreme, your purchases of an item will cease or go to zero quantity when a price increase occurs. Demand is perfectly elastic in this instance. At another extreme, your purchases of an item will remain the same regardless of price. Demand is perfectly inelastic in this instance.

Demand Line Graphs & Elasticities

The coefficient of elasticity is different than, but has some relation to, the slope of a straight line. The slope formula calls for dividing the rise by the run or, in other words, the change in the vertical direction by the associated change in the horizontal direction. In general, rearrangement of the elasticity coefficient formula will reveal that coefficient is the product from multiplying a point on the line by the inverse of the line's slope. This rearrangement allows for the calculation of elasticity at a specific point on the line using the slope of the line. In addition, it allows for applications to straight lines or curved lines.

Another important distinction between elasticity and slope is that the slope is the same along a straight line at any given point on the line, but its elasticity varies. Conversely, the slope varies along a curved line at any point on the line, but its elasticity is the same. At this point, let us put these technical considerations aside and return some additional characteristics of graphs that display demand as taking the form of a straight line.

Three regions of elasticity exist along the demand line. The upper segment of the line is where demand is elastic. The lower segment is where it is inelastic. The segment in the middle is where demand is unitary elastic. Recall that the "price elasticity of demand" is a term that describes how sensitive consumer purchases are in relation to changes in price. In a relative sense, these regions inform us that consumers are more sensitive to changes in price for items having high prices than they are for items having low prices.

At two extremes, the demand line can be horizontal or it can be vertical. These extremes carry the term "perfect" with respect to elasticity. On the one hand, demand is perfectly elastic when the line is horizontal. This means item purchases will cease for any change in price. On the other hand, demand is perfectly inelastic when the line is vertical. This means item purchases will persist regardless of any change in price.

Consumer Expenditures & Producer Revenues

Suppliers would love to sell only those items for which demand is perfectly inelastic. However, such a fantasy is often a far cry from reality with few exceptions. In actuality, their revenues increase in concert with price rises but only to a point. As market prices move higher along the demand curve and begin to enter its upper region, consumers exhibit greater sensitivity to price changes and they begin to curtail their purchases. Consequently, purchase quantities fall faster than prices rise resulting in decreases in consumers' total expenditures and suppliers' total revenues.

Unabated price increases or decreases eventually move past the point at which demand is unitary elastic (for instance, where the price elasticity of demand coefficient in absolute terms is exactly equal to 1.00). The total revenue test and, conversely, the total expenditure test, as they are commonly known, direct attention to danger of constant increases in an item's price and to the appeal of constant decreases in an item's price. In summary, upward movements in price through the middle region of the demand line tend to decrease sellers' total revenues and consumers' total expenditures whereas downward movements tend to increase them.

Determinants of Elasticity

Elasticity depends on a set of factors known as the determinants of elasticity. The set includes the number and relative availability of items considered to be viable alternatives or substitutes for any given item. Are there items considered as close substitutes? In addition, the set includes whether an item is something that a consumer needs and wants (a necessity like food, clothing, or shelter) or something that a consumer wants but perhaps doesn't need (a luxury like jewelry, cruises, or newest electronic gadgets). Is the item a necessity or is it something else? A third factor is the portion of the consumer's budget spent on the item. The last factor within the set of determinants is the amount time available to a consumer in making a purchase decision. Is a delay in the item's purchase a wise decision? Recall the gasoline example in

A Rolls-Royce Phantom is a luxury vehicle. Pictured is one parked on the streets of London in 2008. (Courtesy of Damors CC BY-SA 2.0 via Wikimedia Commons)

which the long run or the short run depend largely according to your geographic location when the gas tank gauge indicates it is near the empty mark.

Cross & Price Elasticities of Demand

Other types of elasticity need some discourse as we move toward closure in this essay. Attention up to this point was on the price elasticity of demand. Before we move to a discussion of a supply-side related elasticity, this article describes two additional types of demand-side related elasticities: cross elasticity and income elasticity. All these remaining elasticities serve a purpose in economics and use percent changes to portray how quantities change in relation to a change in income or price. A brief description of each comprises the sections that follow.

Some instructors spend a considerable amount of time with their students comparing apples to oranges. Those comparisons are highly appropriate when examining the cross elasticity of demand concept. One might begin by asking the following question: What happens to the purchases of oranges when there is an increase in the price of apples? In more precise terms, the economics instructor may inquire by adding the word "percentage" with respect to the changes in price and quantity.

Calculating cross elasticity of demand and its examination will reveal whether consumers switch between apples and oranges and/or whether they eat them in some combination. They are likely to be substitutes, but it is possible that they group goods

in combinations of complements; an example of the latter would be hot dogs and hot dog buns. If the coefficient for the cross elasticity of demand is a positive number, we can conclude with some certainty that apples and oranges are indeed substitutes; for instance, the percentage increases in price and in quantity move the same direction. On the other hand, if the coefficient is a negative number, we can be certain that they are complements; for instance, the percentage increases move in opposite directions.

Leaving cross elasticity behind and moving to another type of elasticity, we can determine whether an apple, an orange, or some other item is a normal good or an inferior good. Accordingly, we look at the percentage change in the item purchase quantities in relation to the percentage change in consumer income, and then we seek to determine whether the income elasticity of demand coefficient is positive or negative. If the coefficient is positive, then we can conclude that the item is a normal good; for example, an increase in income may generate an increase in apple consumption. In other words, the normal case is that higher incomes generate additional purchases and larger quantities. If it is negative, then we can conclude that the apple is an inferior good. Next, we introduce the price elasticity of supply concept, which is the last concept, and its relevance to economic decision-making.

PRICE ELASTICITY OF SUPPLY
Tax Burdens & Price Elasticities Comparison

Calculation of coefficients for the price elasticity of supply is slightly different than those for demand, the differences being the use of percentage change in quantities of an item supplied or sold as opposed to quantities demanded or consumed and the positive or direct relationship between price and quantity supplied. A major benefit of knowing the price elasticity of supply accrues by analyzing the potential impact that a tax will exert on an item's exchange. We can think of the imposition of a tax as being quite similar to a price increase, except that it has implications for demand and/or supply quantities.

Taxes on tobacco and alcohol are government agency revenue generators. The evidence suggests the demand for these items is inelastic, probably a result of their habit-forming or addictive natures. The World Health Organization reported the price elasticity of demand among adults for cigarettes in 2012 was –0.40

Some states in the United States operate their own retail stores for the sale of certain types of alcohol, such as this state-run liquor store in Cottonwood Heights, Utah. (Courtesy of FancyPants via Wikimedia Commons)

in high-income countries and –0.2 to –0.8 in low- to middle-income countries. A 2013 meta-analysis by economist Jon P. Nelson of studies on alcohol price and income elasticity from a number of countries found that for beer, the price elasticity is –0.3, while for all alcohol it is –0.6. Thus, price increases would produce a negligible change in consumption patterns.

The supply of these items could be inelastic as well, or it could be elastic. Comparisons between the price elasticity of supply and the price elasticity of demand will reveal whether the consumer or the producer will pay any tax imposed on an item. If the evidence indicates that suppliers are more sensitive than consumers to price changes, then the latter will likely bear the tax burden. Empirical data on price elasticity of supply are available elsewhere including the articles of the suggested reading list, but it stands to reason that sellers would be more sensitive than consumers to tax-induced price increases and therefore ready to pass the tax burden along to their customers. In closing, this essay seeks to provide information in a clear and concise manner in order to promote elasticity concept mastery among undergraduate students.

BIBLIOGRAPHY

Arnold, Roger A. (2005). *Economics* (7th ed). Mason, OH: Thomson South-Western.

Cuddington, J. T., & Dagher, L. (2015). "Estimating short and long-run demand elasticities: A primer with energy-sector applications." *Energy Journal, 36*(1), 185–209.

Dickinson, J. (2002). "A need to revamp textbook presentations of price elasticity." *Journal of Marketing Education, 24,* 143–149.

Guell, R. C. (2007). *Issues in economics today* (3rd ed.). Boston, MA: McGraw-Hill Irwin.

Gordon, B.R., Goldfarb, A., & Yang, L. (2013). "Does price elasticity vary with economic growth? A cross-category analysis." *Journal of Marketing Research (JMR) 50,* 4–23.

Hamilton, R., Thompson, D., Arens, Z., Blanchard, S., Häubl, G., Kannan, P., & … Thomas, M. (2014). "Consumer substitution decisions: An integrative framework." *Marketing Letters, 25*(3), 305–317.

Auboin, M., & Borino, F. (2017). "The falling elasticity of global trade to economic activity: testing the demand channel." *WTO Staff Working Paper.*

McConnell, C. R. & Brue, S. L. (2008). *Economics* (17th ed.). Boston, MA: McGraw-Hill Irwin.

Oner, E. (2013). "Simultaneous effects of supply and demand elasticity with market types on tax incidence (graphical analysis of perfect competition, monopoly and oligopoly markets)." *International Journal of Economics & Finance, 5,* 46–55.

Parkin, M. (2000). *Economics* (5th ed.). Reading, MA: Addison Wesley Longman.

Sethuraman, R., Tellis, G., & Briesch, R. (2011). "How well does advertising work? generalizations from meta-analysis of brand advertising elasticities." *Journal of Marketing Research (JMR), 48,* 457–471.

SUGGESTED READING

Baltagi, B., & Goel, R. (2004). "State tax changes and quasi-experimental price elasticities of US cigarette demand: An update." *Journal of Economics & Finance, 28,* 422–429.

Friedel, E. (2014). *Price elasticity: Research on magnitude and determinants.* Frankfurt am Main: Peter Lang AG.

Goel, R., & Nelson, M. (2006). "The effectiveness of anti-smoking legislation: A review." *Journal of Economic Surveys, 20,* 325–355.

Grossman, M., Sindelar, J., Mullahy, J., & Anderson, R. (1993). "Policy watch: Alcohol and cigarette taxes." *Journal of Economic Perspectives, 7,* 211–222.

Pearce, D. W. (Ed.). (1992). *The MIT dictionary of modern economics.* Cambridge, MA: MIT Press.

—*Steven R. Hoagland, PhD*

ELECTIONS AND ECONOMIC GROWTH

ABSTRACT

What is the connection between electoral politics and economic growth? This paper provides an in-depth analysis of the impact government has on the American economy and, as a result, the role elections play in proposing and implementing policies designed to foster economic development, address fiscal shortcomings, and meet the financial needs of current and future constituencies.

OVERVIEW

Author and columnist Barbara Ehrenreich once observed that a free enterprise economy depends solely on markets. In turn, those markets, according to the most advanced mathematical macroeconomic theory, depend on the moods of the people she called "the Boys on the Street." She went on to explain, "When the Boys are in a good mood, the market thrives; when they get scared or sullen, it is time for each one of us to look into the retail apple business" (Columbia World of Quotations, 1996).

While Ehrenreich's statement may be interpreted as a somewhat glib and a bit overly simplistic assessment of the way the modern economy operates, one cannot deny the impact on the economy that the human element delivers. After all, prices are set based on the willingness of investors to purchase or sell as they are by the costs involved with manufacturing the product or providing the service. If one investor sees another individual sell his or her stock in apparent panic over information he or she receives, the former investor may act similarly. Markets, after all, thrive when consumer confidence is high and wane when investors' fears are manifest.

In macroeconomics, the relationship between supply and demand is an integral theme. There is little doubt that government has long played a central role in the U.S. economy throughout the nation's history. However, America's implementation of a free-market economy has been accented by a tacit understanding that government should adopt a Hippocratic Oath of its own with regard to the country's business institutions: "First, do no harm." Government's role has long been to facilitate economic growth and create the underpinnings that will give the economy long-term stability. For the first century of American history, the legislative and executive branches adhered to that policy.

Then again, when the nation was faced with one of the worst fiscal disasters in its history, the Great Depression, which was compounded by the horrific events of World War II, government's active presence in rebuilding devastated economies in North America as well as Europe and Asia was not reluctantly requested by the citizenry—it was overwhelmingly expected.

Since the Great Depression, politicians have maintained an active role in seeking economic growth. Their interest is clear—if the voters are concerned with the state of the economy, then the issues facing the fiscal system must be a priority. The colloquial statement uttered by Democratic strategist James Carville in the 1992 presidential campaign, "It's the economy, stupid," remains true to the present, evoked by political candidates from both sides of the American political aisle.

What is the connection between electoral politics and economic growth? This paper provides an in-depth analysis of the impact government has on the American economy and, as a result, the role elections play in proposing and implementing policies designed to foster economic development, address fiscal shortcomings and meet the financial needs of constituencies.

Leadership & Economic Growth

As far back as the Reconstruction, economics and electoral politics have experienced linkages. After the Civil War, attentions rightly turned to two fronts: cultural reparations between whites and former slaves and economic development. The success of America's elected leaders, it is believed, was increasingly becoming based on how the American economy fared, especially in the decades that followed one of the country's darkest eras. One study, however, indicates that while these linkages existed prior to the turn of the twentieth century, they were amplified by the Depression and Second World War. This upturn is attributed to the fact that government was called upon to stabilize the markets, stimulate

The Southern economy had been ruined by the Civil War. Pictured is Broad Street in Charleston, South Carolina in 1865. (Courtesy of Library of Congress)

business development, and get Americans back to work (Lynch, 1999).

INDICATORS OF ECONOMIC STATUS
GDP

In order to understand these linkages, it is prudent to study the tenets of economic growth itself. There are a variety of factors that can be used to measure economic growth. The Federal Reserve, for example, employs several indicators as measuring sticks when establishing economic policy. The first of these is also the most prominent: gross domestic product (GDP). This indicator can be defined as the total value of goods and services produced within the borders of the United States, regardless of who owns the assets or whether or not the product or service was created by a U.S. or foreign-born worker (Federal Reserve Bank of New York, 2006).

Consumer Confidence

A second indicator is that of consumer confidence. A useful mechanism for monitoring the behavior of shoppers is the Consumer Confidence Index (CCI), which measures the attitudes of consumers regarding the economic environment. In late 2013, this important survey revealed a decline in citizens' belief in

The Federal Reserve Bank of New York Building at 33 Liberty Street as seen from the west. (Courtesy of Beyond My Ken CC BY-SA 4.0-3.0-2.5-2.0-1.0 via Wikimedia Commons)

the short- and long-term strength of the economy. In November of that year, the index declined to 70.4, while the Expectations Index declined from 72.2 to 69.3 from October to November. However, there was some optimism on the job front, as 11.8 percent of those polled indicated that jobs were "plentiful," representing a 0.2 percent improvement from the previous month (The Confidence Board, 2013).

While U.S. stocks are up more than 150 percent from their 2009 lows, during the midst of the economic recession, investment authorities advised caution entering 2014; the likelihood that stock prices will continue to rise at such a rate are unlikely, and economic prognosticators are mixed on the direction of the U.S. economy (T. Rowe Price, 2013). Because the U.S. economy remained volatile, despite signs of continued economic recovery (including a reduction in unemployment), it affected both the 2014 midterm elections and the 2016 presidential elections.

Quality of Life

A third indicator of economic growth is manifest through an analysis of the population's quality of life. While assessments of manufacturing productivity, unemployment rates and consumer confidence are critical, a nation's standard of living is also an invaluable measuring stick by which the country's true economic health is revealed. In fact, an individual's ability to pay higher interest rates, purchase a home, commute to work, pay for medications and health care, shop for groceries, and other activities is a vital bellwether for determining the country's actual state of fiscal health.

Standard of living is a central issue in the aftermath of the recession. Although the unemployment rate in October 2013 (7.3 percent) had declined significantly from its recession height of 10 percent in 2010, it was still much higher than its prerecession rate of 4.4 percent in May 2007 (BLS, 2013). These facts are certain to be taken into consideration in the 2014 election cycle. Inflation-adjusted wages and benefits have changed very little since the beginning of the twenty-first century; in fact, wages dropped for the bottom 70 percent of earners from 2007 to 2012 (Economic Policy Institute, 2013). Furthermore, the rising cost of health care, skyrocketing oil prices, and increases in the price tags on other necessities are eating away at individual paychecks (Colvin, 2006).

A stagnate U.S. economy does not sit well with the voting electorate. However, as details about the status of the GDP and CCI are likely to be appreciated only by those familiar with such issues, these indicators may not create a tidal wave of voter sentiment. Then again, standard-of-living issues hit a larger number of households more directly and with greater clarity. Their responses to such situations can impact an election, as they did in 2008, 2010, and, to a certain extent, 2012.

POLITICS & THE ECONOMY
The U.S. Government & Iraq Policy

In 1992, President George H. W. Bush was coming off a wave of popularity from the success of military operations designed to oust Iraqi forces from Kuwait. However, his popularity, stemming from his unquestioned leadership and poise in that campaign, would be short-lived. The economy was showing signs of wear, and neither the Bush administration nor the private sector seemed to be able to counter what would ultimately become a painful economic recession. One writer, invoking the school of thought known as "polimetrics" (which calculates how economic conditions affect voter behavior), posited that Bush's post-Iraq popularity would not be a factor in his reelection. Rather, Bush's bid for a second term would be determined by the state of the economy, which by the time of the election would be anemic (Koretz, 1991).

The following decade, the United States again dealt with a situation in Iraq, but that time, the Bush

President George W. Bush makes a statement to reporters about the war in Iraq after his meeting with senior national defense leaders at the Pentagon May 10, 2007. From left, Army Chief of Staff Gen. George Casey, Air Force Chief of Staff Gen. T. Michael Moseley, Vice Chairman of the Joint Chiefs of Staff Navy Adm. Edmund P. Giambastiani, Secretary of Defense Robert Gates, President George W. Bush, Chairman of the Joint Chiefs of Staff marine Gen. Peter Pace, Chief of Naval Operations Adm. Michael G. Mullen and Commandant of the Marine Corps Gen. James T. Conway. (Courtesy of DoD Staff Sgt. D. Myles Cullen, U.S. Air Force via Wikimedia Commons)

A nice home is an indication of a satisfactory quality of life. Pictured is the "Gingerbread House" in Essex, Connecticut. (Courtesy of Gregoryj77 via Wikimedia Commons)

who occupied the White House was not running for reelection. Additionally, the campaign in that Middle Eastern country was anything but popular, and the fact that it cost the lives of American soldiers (as well as many civilian Iraqis) gave President George W. Bush's opponents an opportunity to propel Democrats into majority leadership in Congress in 2006 and to retake the White House in 2008. Every Democratic candidate for president in 2008 (even those who voted to send troops to Iraq in 2002) called for the troops to come home, and even a few Republican presidential candidates echoed such demands.

Interestingly, however, the "troop surge" deployed by President Bush, while unpopular among Democratic candidates, initially showed improvements in terms of reductions in violence and greater stability. Fewer and fewer reports of bombs and chaos were seen on television. Voters, previously vehemently opposed to the war and keeping troops in Iraq, seemed increasingly less focused on the conflict. Some even called the Democratic demands for immediate troop withdrawal unrealistic and, although still opposed to the war, turned their attentions to domestic issues. Chief among these concerns was the economy (Halloran, 2007).

Ironically, the issue that solidified the Republican Party leading up to the 2008 presidential election was the "war on terrorism," of which the Iraqi front is part. Republican candidate and former prisoner of war John McCain highlighted the good news of increased Iraqi stability. However, McCain's candidacy was done in by his refusal to address the economy as it spiraled downward as the 2008 election approached.

An Economic Downturn
In 2008, with the increased number of housing foreclosures (and related credit issues) and a consistently upward trend in oil prices, the U.S. economy entered a prolonged recession, which affected the 2008 election and nearly cost President Barack Obama his reelection bid in 2012.

The voting population picked up on the economic warnings in 2008, and, coupled with a general distrust of the Republican Party mostly based on the Bush administration's agenda, overwhelmingly elected Obama in 2008. The United States has a staggering trade deficit, with the United States paying more in overseas interest than it is receiving from foreign investments. Millions lost their homes to foreclosures,

Notices accumulate on the door and window of a foreclosed, unoccupied house. (Courtesy of Daniel Case CC BY-SA 3.0 via Wikimedia Commons)

and millions more were unable to sell their properties in a dead market. In addition to increasing oil prices were the high costs of health care and college tuition, but cost-of-living adjustments are hardly keeping up with such upward trends (Borosage & Vanden Heuvel, 2007). Though the recession seemed to solidify Obama's election in 2008, it continued to be an issue during the midterm elections of 2010; so much so, that a contingent of far-right Republicans known as the Tea Party was able to make significant headway in electing officials that took strong anti–big government stances, blaming Democratic spending for the continuation of the recession.

More than any other issue, the economic climate has strongly affected the American voters' decisions since 2008. In a 2013 Gallup poll, Americans indicated that dysfunctional government and the economy were the biggest problems facing the country (Newport, 2013).

The Economy's Effect on Political Candidacy
Since 2008, candidates have taken notice of voter sentiments regarding the plight of the U.S. economy. While the economy is without a doubt a bipartisan issue, the response by presidential candidates has largely been divided. They have chosen advisors from a variety of schools of thought, including those from previous administrations and Congress.

Unsurprisingly, the positions of the Democratic and Republican candidates, at least rhetorically speaking, have been typical for the party lines. Democratic candidates tend to lean toward demand-side economics, seeking infusions of cash to help

President Barack Obama signs into law the American Recovery and Reinvestment Act of 2009 on February 17, 2009, as Vice President Joe Biden looks on. (Courtesy of Pete Souza via Wikimedia Commons)

bolster the workforce as well as to serve those who are out of work. This philosophy is best exemplified by the American Recovery and Reinvestment Act of 2009, a massive program implemented by the Obama administration to stimulate the American economy through investment in multiple economic sectors. The Democrats are more likely to embrace tax increases in the hopes that the wealthy will pay more into public coffers, which can be used to serve the middle class and those below the poverty line.

Republicans, on the other hand, have tended to lean toward the supply side, favoring business-friendly tax cuts and incentives in order to foster and support corporate growth. They appear warm to across-the-board tax cuts and espouse cuts in capital gains taxes, hoping that the latter will encourage more citizens to invest in the stock market.

CONCLUSION

An economy is not unlike an ecosystem. It relies on the establishment and maintenance of a delicate balance between the varying components that comprise it. In a macro-economy, this accord rests between the countervailing supply and demand elements. On the supply side, production must be consistent, while the system must remain conducive to continued business. On the side of demand, consumers must feel confident and remain capable of making purchases and investments.

At the same time that balance is maintained, the system must continue to grow. Without some form of growth, the equilibrium between supply and demand destabilizes. This unfortunate situation weighs heavily on the minds of political leaders as well as economic observers and the business community. Even the layman ultimately finds reason for concern at the notion of a faltering economy, particularly when the shortcomings of the system place his or her way of life in danger.

For this reason, vigilant observation of economic growth indicators remains essential for safeguarding against fiscal malaise. Candidates for elected office in particular keep a careful eye on the electorate's attitudes concerning the economy, and they also seek vigilance on changes in these indicators. If production sloughs, consumer confidence wanes, or any sort of unanticipated fiscal event occurs, they will undoubtedly be called upon to address such issues.

In fact, government has, since the early twentieth century, been expected to right the problems of a supposedly free-market economy (and, by its definition, a system that is free of government interference). Since the Depression and the rise of Keynesian economics, political institutions have had a strong presence in the U.S. economy—setting interest rates, creating tax incentives for business development, and even providing subsidies, among other activities. It comes as no surprise, therefore, that candidates for political office may be asked for solutions to a weakening economy.

A point made clear in this paper, however, is that in an election year, candidates (particularly challengers) have very full dockets and very little air time in which to propose truly comprehensive solutions. In speaking to the uninitiated, would-be leaders must introduce positions that are direct responses to the voters: If unemployment is up, a candidate may advance a job training program. If the housing market is up, he or she might propose more funds to aid less-affluent potential homebuyers. He or she may understand that a program designed to retrain laid-off workers is but a drop in the bucket, but without the time (or voter attention), he or she must remain myopic.

Polimetric studies do show a linkage between economic growth and voter participation. As the recession damaged every layer of the American economy, voters became less concerned with global politics and issues such as the War on Terror, and shifted their focus to issues such as the cost of living, jobs, and their ability to buy, maintain, and sell a house. In turn, political candidates have shifted their attention away from foreign military campaigns and onto the domestic economy.

Nonetheless, candidates must speak to their bases, and their policy responses, whether as proposals or actual legislation, remain essentially the same. Tax cuts for businesses, increases in minimum wages, housing grants, sector investment, and economic stimulus packages may all see modest success, but they also can cause other problems (tax cuts, for example, cost budgets losses in revenues and make sector investment and development grants less available).

In an election year, economic growth is an absolutely critical issue. President George H.W. Bush learned this lesson the hard way, falling victim to a faltering economy in the 1992 election only two years after his extremely successful campaign in the Persian Gulf. And McCain seemingly paid at the polls for the younger Bush's mistakes. Obama nearly lost his 2012 reelection bid because of the economy, and the 2016 candidates for president also had to contend with economic issues facing the country in the wake of eight years of Democratic policy.

BIBLIOGRAPHY

Asher, A. (2017). "Politics and local economic growth: evidence from India." *American Economic Journal: Applied Economics, 9*, 1, 229–273.

Bartiromo, M. (2007). "The unvarnished McCain. "*Business Week, 4037*, 114–115.

Borosage, Robert L. & Vanden Heuvel, K. (2007). "The economy debates." *Nation, 285*(7), 6–8.

Bureau of Labor Statistics. (2013, Dec 3). "Labor force statistics from the current population survey." Retrieved from data.bls.gov/timeseries/LNS14000000.

Columbia World of Quotations. (1996). Retrieved from xlink:href="http://www.bartleby.com/66/33/18533.html"

Colvin, G. (2006, July 10). "The imagination economy." *Fortune, 154(1)*.

The Conference Board. (2007, December 27). "The Conference Board Consumer Confidence Index improves moderately in December." Retrieved from xlink:href="http://www.conference-board.org/economics/ConsumerConfidence.cfm"

Conference Board. (2013, Nov 26). "Consumer confidence declines again in November." Retrieved from xlink:href="http://www.conference-board.org/data/consumerconfidence.cfm"

Cook, C. (2007). "It's the economy, maybe." *National Journal, 39*(48).

Englund, M. (2007, November 15). "GDP estimate: Trimming the sales." *Business Week Online.*

Federal Reserve Bank of New York. (2006, April). Retrieved from xlink:href="http://www.newyorkfed.org/education/bythe.html"

Halloran, L. (2007). "With casualties down, the war retreats as a political issue." *US News and World Report, 142*(22), 40.

Koretz, G. (1991, December 9). "The economic tea leaves say Bush could lose in '92." *Business Week,* (3243), 24.

"Consumer confidence continues to free fall amid holidays." (2007). *Las Vegas Business Press, 24*(49).

Lynch, G. P.. (1999). "Presidential elections and the economy, 1872-1996." *Political Research Quarterly, 52(4)*, 825–844.

Mishel, L., & Shierholz, H. (2013, Aug 21). "A decade of flat wages: The key barrier to shared prosperity and a rising middle class." *Economic Policy Institute.*

Newport F. (2013, Oct 9). "Dysfunctional gov't surpasses economy as top US problem." *Gallup.* Retrieved from xlink:href="http://www.gallup.com/poll/165302/dysfunctional-gov-surpasses-economy-top-problem.aspx"

Novak, R. (2007). "Advising the candidates." *International Economy, 21*(4), 24–29.

Schneider, W. (2007). "A 'bad times' election?" *National Journal, 39*(46/47), 75.

SUGGESTED READING

Benjamin, M. (2004). "The war for your wallet." *US News and World Report, 137*(13).

Investor's Business, D. (2013, June 27). "Backward priorities kill Obama economy." *Investor's Business Daily* A01.

Schneider, W. (2007). "A 'bad times' election?" *National Journal, 39*(46/47), 75.

Zuckerman, Mortimer B. (2007). "Let's put it to a vote." *US News and World Report, 142*(23), 72.

—*Michael P. Auerbach*

ENVIRONMENT AND THE GLOBAL ECONOMY

ABSTRACT

This article will focus on the relationship between the environment and the global economy. This article will provide an overview of the global economy and the global environment. This overview will serve as a foundation for discussions about the three main ways that the global environment is managed and protected in the global economy: voluntary corporate environmental protection, national environmental regulation, and international governance by global policy regimes. Examples of global environmental governance, including the United Nations Earth Summit, the Kyoto Protocol, and Organisation for Economic Co-operation and Development's environmental efforts, will be described and analyzed. The environmental concepts of ecology, biodiversity, and sustainable development will be introduced.

OVERVIEW

Economic globalization complicates the relationship between the global economy and the global environment. Economic processes, such as the production of goods, and waste disposal, strip-mining, over-farming, and the transportation of goods to and from markets, impact Earth's ecosystem and result in polluted landfills, ozone depletion, global warming, and loss of biodiversity. The global environment, including resources such as air, freshwater, oil, timber, coal,

Coal strip mine in Wyoming. (Courtesy of Bureau of Land Management via Wikimedia Commons)

natural gases, gold, salt, and arable land, is used in the global economy. The use of these environmental resources for economic purposes, such as manufacturing of goods, farming, and energy production, creates new environmental problems and scenarios. The global economy-environment relationship is often referred to as entropic in nature (Preston, 1996). *Entropic*, or *entropy*, refers to the steady deterioration of a system. Economic globalization processes, such as the internationalization of trade, ubiquity of gas-powered modes of transportation, migration, and the transnational development and production cycle of goods, challenge the traditional nation-based environmental protection strategy of sustainable development. Neither the global environment nor the global economy respects national boundaries.

In the twenty-first century, global environmental affairs are characterized by an inextricable link between the world economy and the global environment. Global environmental politics are coordinated and managed by non-state actors such as nongovernmental organizations (NGOs). The connections between the global environment and the global economy are demonstrated in global environmental policies such as those that govern hazardous waste collection. For example, international trade, production, and financial relationships determined the direction and extent of the toxic waste trade between industrialized and developing countries until the practice of toxic waste trade was ended in 1992 through the Basel Convention on the Control of Transboundary Movements of Hazardous Wastes and Their Disposal (Clapp, 1994).

Economic globalization has shifted economic, political, and environmental power from local, national, and regional bodies to international governing institutions. The goals and objectives of global environmental governance are complicated by the agenda and motives of economic governance. Global environmental governance has the challenge of simultaneously protecting global *and* local environments. The need to protect local and global environments as well as promote the economic growth demanded by the global market is challenging. Consumers, producers, and cities need to think globally and locally to protect Earth's environment. For example, cities must address urban air pollution problems to benefit local residents and, in part, to solve global warming problems. Ultimately environmental governance in the global economy will likely require reducing demand and using financial instruments, such as corrective taxes on fuel, to curb consumption (Eskeland, 1998).

The following sections provide an overview of the global economy and the global environment. These sections will serve as a foundation for later discussions about the three main ways that the global environment is managed and protected in the global economy: voluntary environmental protection, national environmental regulation, and international governance by global policy regimes. Examples of global environmental management including the United Nation's Earth Summit, the Kyoto Protocol, and Organisation for Economic Co-operation and Development's environmental efforts will be described and analyzed.

The Global Economy

The global economy is characterized by growth in populations and in output and consumption per capita, in interdependence of nations, and in international management efforts. Indicators of global growth and interdependence include the huge increases in communications links, world output, international trade, and international investment since the 1970s. The global economy is built on global interdependence of economic flows that link the economies of the world. The global economy is characterized by economic sensitivity. National economic events in one region often have profound results for other regions and national economies. National economies exist not in isolation but in relationship and tension with other economies worldwide. The global economy includes numerous economic phenomena and financial tools shared among all countries. Examples include the price of gold, the price of oil, and the related worldwide movement of interest rates. The new global economy is characterized and controlled through global management or governance efforts. International organizations, both public and private, work to establish norms, standards, and requirements for international financial governance. These international organizations, including the G-20, Financial Stability Forum, International Organization of Securities Commissions, Organisation for Economic

Co-operation and Development (OECD), and Basel Committee on Banking Supervision, develop and encourage implementation of standards, principles, best practices, and economic architecture (Preston, 1996).

The Global Environment

The global environment encompasses the global climate, human use of resources (particularly resources that have become accessible only as a result of technological innovation and advances), and cross-border effects (the environmental concerns arising in different parts of the world involve more than one political jurisdiction) (Preston, 1996). Environmental problems entered public and political consciousness in the 1970s. In 1972, the United Nations Conference on the Human Environment, held in Stockholm, established a connection between economic growth and environmental degradation. The relationship between economic development, poverty, and environmental degradation has been researched in depth since the late twentieth century.

In 1992 the United Nation's Earth Summit brought environmentally sustainable growth into the public's consciousness. Sustainable development has been championed by many environmental organizations that recognize the importance or inevitability of worldwide economic growth. Traditional notions of sustainable development are being challenged by economic globalization. National environmental regulatory controls are increasingly ineffective when faced with increased trade integration, capital mobility, technological innovation, and changes in production.

Global environment stakeholders debate how best to protect the global environment in the context of economic globalization. Economic globalization, which challenges traditional regulatory approaches to environmental protection, requires new environmental governance approaches. Economic globalization empowers international economic and environmental organizations to create environmental policy rather than the local governments, where environmental efforts have traditionally been developed (Conca, 2001). In the global economy, the environment is managed and protected in three main ways: voluntary corporate environmental protection, national environmental regulation, and international governance by global policy regimes.

Voluntary Corporate Environmental Protection

Corporations are responding to stakeholder and shareholder concern for the environment by incorporating environmental ethics into their corporate activities and business practices. A form of corporate social responsibility, the most prominent and common voluntary efforts include life-cycle analysis, industrial ecology, design for disassembly, and strategic alliance. One study has found that voluntary corporate environmental protection does help increase profits for participating companies (Yu, 2012). Life-cycle analysis refers to the analytical tool used to calculate how much energy and raw material must be used and what quantity of solid, liquid, and gaseous waste is generated at every stage of a product's life span. Industrial ecology refers to the business practice of designing production and distribution facilities as closed systems that are dependent on recycling, reuse, and creative energy production. Design for disassembly refers to the environmentally friendly practice of designing a product that can be taken apart and reused in the manufacture of different products at the end of its useful life. Strategic alliance or partnerships refer to the practice of partnering businesses to share their resources and expertise in an effort to benefit the environment. Strategic alliances are part of a larger trend in corporate cooperation and research consortia. Corporations worldwide are increasingly practicing cooperative research. Companies, which remain competitors, may pool resources to undertake collaborative large-scale or highly technical research. Strategic alliances among competitors and government-business partnerships are becoming increasingly common. Critics of voluntary corporate environmental protection efforts argue that some of the most environmentally damaging business practices, such as land disposal, underground injection, and the transfer of wastes to other communities, are generally not reduced or addressed by voluntary environmental protection efforts of corporations (Harrison, 2003).

National Environmental Regulation

Environmental management has become a common feature of corporations. Environmental management, since its beginnings in the 1960s, has been characterized by the need to satisfy environmental regulations. Environmental regulation refers to state and federal statutes intended to protect the

North Seattle Household Hazardous Waste Collection Facility, Seattle, Washington. (Courtesy of Joe Mabel CC BY-SA 3.0 via Wikimedia Commons)

environment and wildlife, to prevent pollution, to save endangered species, and to conserve water. Environmental regulations often grant individuals and organizations the right to bring legal actions to enforce the law. Environmental regulation began in the United States with the Clean Water Act and the Clean Air Act. Regulation to address the problems of future and past hazardous waste disposal include the Resource Conservation and Recovery Act (RCRA) and the Comprehensive Environmental Response, Compensation, and Liability Act (CERCLA) or the Superfund program. Environmental regulation began in Europe with a common environmental protection policy built into the Treaty of Rome (1987) and extended and expanded by the Treaty on European Union (1992). Environmental regulation has been criticized by businesses for ignoring production processes, for being expensive, and for excessive oversight. Critics argue that environmental regulation has traditionally focused on "end-of-the pipe" solutions (such as emissions or waste control) rather than on addressing the basic processes that created the problem initially (Anderson, 1999).

Environmental regulation, both design and content, is evolving to create and promote "gains in corporate environmental performance through the creation of a hybrid system of public regulation, government-supervised corporate self-regulation, mandatory information disclosure, and green procurement or purchasing" (Eisner, 2004, abstract). In addition, the practice of managing environmental issues is transitioning from a regulatory phase to an increasingly common environmental management systems phase. Within corporations, environmental management practices are increasingly formalized into environmental management systems (EMSs). EMSs, as described by the U.S. Environmental Protection Agency, refer to a set of processes and practices that enable an organization to systematically assess and manage its environmental footprint. EMSs developed during the 1990s as the importance of environmental management increased in response to government and consumer pressure. EMSs complement and, in some cases, substitute for environmental regulations (Jayathirtha, 2001).

EMSs are characterized by proactive activities rather than reactive activities. EMSs, which can be used in factories, small businesses, service industries, and government agencies, come in many forms. Common corporate environmental management practices include clean production and ecologically sustainable development. Clean production refers to the initiatives undertaken by businesses to reduce the environmental impact of production activities. Examples of cleaner production approaches include the conservation of energy, reduction of raw material consumption, decreased use and production of hazardous materials, and the reduction of waste. Benefits of cleaner production approaches include improved community relations as well as reduced operating costs and liability risks. Ecologically sustainable development refers to the business practice of using, conserving, and enhancing the community's resources so that vital ecological processes are maintained for present and future generations. Ecologically sustainable development, which requires environmental, social, and economic cooperation, necessitates changes in the nature of production and consumption. Biodiversity (the maintenance and conservation of which is a main goal of ecologically sustainable development) refers to the variety of life forms and to the ecosystems in which they live.

Global Policy Regimes

In addition to voluntary environmental business initiatives, businesses and nongovernmental organizations are forming groups and coalitions to establish shared environmental principles. International governance, including environmental, political, and economic governance, is one of the most significant trends of economic globalization. The global economy and the global environment are managed and coordinated by international organizations or policy regimes. Policy regimes refer to the agreements that help to promote international harmonization and coordination of financial, ecological, and political matters. Policy regimes tend to be cooperative, mutually beneficial alliances.

There are four main types of international policy regimes. Global and comprehensive regimes refer to regimes that can surround the whole globe and any sphere of international activity. Regional and associative regimes refer to the acknowledging of less than global scope and with differing levels of comprehension within their geological boundaries. Functional financial regimes refer to preparations that might have worldwide geographical force but particularly restricted functional scope. Environmental regimes refer to arrangements that involve natural resources and surroundings.

Major international policy regimes that manage and control the global economy and global environment include the United Nations, the International Monetary Fund, the World Trade Organization, the World Bank, and the Organisation for Economic Co-operation and Development. Regional policy regimes, such as the North American Free Trade Agreement and the European Union, also have great control and influence over the global environment and global economy. Environmental regimes depend on compliance by all parties. The environment cannot be managed or tended to by one country and ignored by another. The responsibilities and effects of global environmental management are, by definition, global in nature.

Policy regimes are characterized by their scope, purpose, organizational form, decision and allocation modes, and strength. Scope refers to the domain of international economic or business activity covered by the administration. Purpose refers to the certain aims that are expected. Organizational form refers to the company structure and group members. Decision and allocation modes refer to the methods of voting or making decisions and the methods of allocating various costs and profits. Strength refers to the extent to which the membership conforms to the standards and rules of the regime (powers that allow for alteration).

The management of the global environment is based on economic analysis techniques and, to varying degrees, economic growth and development.

Environmental decision-making, including decisions involving permanent environmental modification, is based on economics that benefit modern society rather than long-term plans or projections. International policy regimes concerned with both economic and environmental activities tend to link these two global systems without sufficient long-term planning and thought about the future of the global environment. Ultimately, international policy regimes having to do with both economic and environmental activities must work against environmental irreversibility and toward its sustainability (Preston, 1996).

APPLICATIONS

Global Environmental Governance
The successful operation of the global economy requires the development and adoption of effective global environmental governance strategies. Environmental protection organizations, development organizations, business groups, corporations, and governments develop and implement environmental governance procedures. These stakeholders work together to create global environmental-use principles, recommendations, and tools for use worldwide. Examples of global environmental governance include the UN Earth Summit, Kyoto Protocol, and the Organisation for Economic Co-operation and Development's environmental efforts.

Earth Summit
In 1992, the United Nation's Earth Summit in Rio de Janeiro was held to help governments reconceptualize economic development and find ways to promote sustainable development in developing and industrialized countries alike. The 1992 Earth Summit produced a treaty called the Convention on Biological Diversity that specified conservation strategies, species protection, ecosystem oversight, environmental restoration, and economic incentives for environment-friendly policy and actions. The Convention on Biological Diversity gained rapid acceptance around the world (193 countries have signed and ratified the treaty into law in their home countries). The United States signed the treaty but has not ratified the treaty. The Convention on Biological Diversity requires each member government to develop a self-implemented strategy and plan of action

for the conservation and sustainable use of biodiversity in their country. In addition to the Convention on Biological Diversity, the Earth Summit had major impact on developing environmentally friendly strategies for patterns of production, alternative sources of energy, public transportation, and water sources. Follow-up meetings to the 1992 Earth Summit were held in 1997 at the UN General Assembly in New York and in 2002 in Johannesburg, South Africa.

Kyoto Protocol
In 1997, the Kyoto Protocol to the United Nations Framework Convention on Climate Change called for the creation of three mechanisms to effectively control global greenhouse gas emissions. The first mechanism was an emissions trading mechanism. The second mechanism was a clean development mechanism. The third mechanism was a financial mechanism that facilitated the transfer of income and technology from rich to poor countries. The United States, the world's biggest emitter of greenhouse gases, did not ratify the Kyoto Protocol (Caplan, 2003). Overall, the impact of the Kyoto Protocol on the climate is believed to outweigh the economic costs of implementation. The Kyoto Protocol has resulted in numerous associated environmental gains, including the creation of the European Climate Change Program in 2000 and the development of a pro-climate alliance across all decision-making levels of the European Union system (Hovi, 2003).

Organisation for Economic Co-operation & Development
The Organisation for Economic Co-operation and Development (OECD) is an international governance organization with thirty-four member nations and a commitment to democracy and market economies. The OECD produces internationally supported instruments, decisions, and recommendations intended to promote economic progress within the globalized economy. The OECD promotes sustainable development in developing and industrialized countries alike. Sustainable development refers to a wide view of human welfare, a long-term outlook regarding the effects of current activities, and worldwide cooperation to come to practical solutions.

The OECD produces and provides analytical tools and environmental indicators to national governments. The OECD encourages national governments

The main entrance to the Organization for Economic Co-operation & Development Conference Centre at 2 rue Andre Pascal in Paris. (Courtesy of Nick D via Wikipedia)

to develop environmental policies that are economically efficient and based on performance reviews, information collections, policy evaluations, and financial predictions. The OECD's corporate governance interests include the following fields:

- Biosafety
- Climate change, energy, and transport
- Chemical safety
- Economic policy and the environment in developing countries
- Environment and sustainable development: economic issues
- Consumption, production, and the environment
- Environment in emerging and transition economies
- Environmental country reviews
- Environmental-social interface
- Environmental indicators and outlooks
- Environmental policies and instruments
- Environment and trade
- Infrastructure into 2030
- Natural resource management
- Environment and development cooperation
- Waste (OECD, 2007)

CONCLUSION

Before the 1960s, there was no corporate or national accountability for the costs of environmental

damages. Environmental costs were externalized to national governments and local communities. The practice of environmental management began, as a legislated activity and requirement of corporate behavior, in the 1960s and 1970s in response to growing concern about environmental pollution highlighted and publicized by high-profile pollution stories. Beginning in the 1990s, economic globalization, and the global economy, created numerous problems for preserving the ecological health of the global environment. In particular, the relationship between the environment and global economic governance is complicated and contentious.

New configurations of power in the global economy have led to economic restructuring, spatial and social distancing between production and consumption, and a loss of traditional region-based approaches to environmental protection, such as sustainable development. These changes challenge global environmental protection efforts (Conca, 2001). Development policies and environmental policies are often at odds. For example, developing world metropolitan cities, such as Beijing and São Paulo, which struggle to enhance their own aggressive and ambitious edge in the global economy, are beginning to grow quickly and are enduring major urban-environmental forces. The growth of corporate districts, business headquarters, and global hotels is creating an immense verticalization and densification of land use. These emerging land-use patterns, which promote economic growth, are influencing the urban surroundings and foundation in many devastating ways (Melchert, 2005). In the final analysis, the future of the global environmental is intimately tied to the global economy and may depend on energy-efficient technologies, environmental legislation, and modest economic growth (Lejour, 2003).

BIBLIOGRAPHY

Anderson, D. (1999). "Incorporating risk management into environmental management systems." *CPCU Journal, 52,* 115.

Caplan, A. & Comes, R. (2003). "An ideal Kyoto Protocol: Emissions trading, redistributive transfers and global participation." *Oxford Economic Papers, 55,* 216.

Casey, M. (2014, September 20). "Why fighting climate change may help the economy, not hurt it." *Fortune,* 1.

Clapp, J. (1994). "The toxic waste trade with less-industrialized countries: Economic linkages and political alliances." *Third World Quarterly, 15*, 505–518.

Conca, K. (2001). "Consumption and environment in a global economy." *Global Environmental Politics, 1*, 53–71.

Eisner, M. (2004). *Corporate environmentalism, regulatory reform, and industry self-regulation: toward genuine regulatory reinvention in the United States.* Governance 17 : 145–167

Eskeland, G., & Xie, J. (1998). "Acting globally while thinking locally: Is the global environment protected by transport emission control programs?" *Journal of Applied Economics, 1*, 385.

Gunster, S. (2016). "This changes everything; Capitalism vs the climate." *Environmental Communication, 11*, 136–138.

Harrison, K., & Antweiler, W. (2003). "Incentives for pollution abatement: Regulation, regulatory threats, and non-governmental pressures." *Journal of Policy Analysis & Management, 22*, 361–382.

Hovi, J., Skodvin, T., & Andresen, S. (2003). "The persistence of the Kyoto protocol: Why other Annex I countries move on without the United States." *Global Environmental Politics, 3*, 1–23.

Howard-Grenville, J., et al. (2014). "Climate change and management." *Academy of Management Journal 57*, 615–623.

Jayathirtha, R. (2001). "Combating environmental repercussions through 'TQEM' and 'ISO 14000.'" *Business Strategy & the Environment (John Wiley & Sons, Inc), 10*, 245–250.

Lejour, A. (2003). "Globalization and the global environment: Four quantitative scenarios." *Transportation Planning & Technology, 26*, 9–40.

Melchert, L. (2005). "The age of environmental impasse? Globalization and environmental transformation of metropolitan cities." *Development & Change, 36*, 803–823.

Organisation for Economic Co-operation and Development. (2007). *Environment.*

Preston, L. (1996). "Global economy/global environment: relationships and regimes." *EarthWorks.*

The United Nations. (1997). *Earth Summit: UN conference on environment and development.*

Yang, C., Yang, K., & Peng, S. (2011). "Exploration strategies and key activities for the system of environmental management." *Total Quality Management & Business Excellence, 22*, 1179–1194.

Yu, F. (2012). "Participation of firms in voluntary environmental protection programs: An analysis of corporate social responsibility and capital market performance." *Contemporary Economic Policy, 30*, 13–28.

SUGGESTED READING

Basel Convention on the Control of Transboundary Movements of Hazardous Wastes and Their Disposal (2011).

Bergeson, L. (2005). "EPA considers how best to regulate nanoscale materials." *Environmental Quality Management, 15*, 81–89.

Bernstein, S. (2005). "Globalization and the requirements of "good" environmental governance." *Perspectives on Global Development & Technology, 4*(3/4), 645–679.

"Climage change is seen as a strategic threat to supply chains" (2013). *Corporate Board 34*, 26–27.

Wysokinska, Z. (2005). "Foreign trade in environmental products: The WTO regulations and environmental programs." *Global Economy Journal, 5*, 1–23.

—*Simone I. Flynn, PhD*

ENVIRONMENTAL AND NATURAL RESOURCE ECONOMICS

ABSTRACT

This article focuses on the complex interface between economic forces and social responsibility, in particular highlighting environmental resources: products of value to the whole as opposed to the individual. Natural resources, once considered limitless, face rapid depletion of substantial proportion as the roller-coaster of economic growth careens toward losses too great for the world to sustain. Businesses, like people, care most about things that directly impact their well-being, and they have less interest in things not directly affecting them. By nature, self-interest often supersedes what is right for the greater good. Air, water, and soil, all natural resources, are considered environmental capital even though they may not fit the conventional accounting definition of such. Because natural resources, like air and water, are "owned" by everyone, a conflict develops between our natural desire to meet self needs and the expectation to incorporate common goals for all. The reader of this essay will see, paradoxically, that the markets' economic growth relies on consumption and trade but contributes mightily to the destruction of our natural resources. Environmental resources improve humankind's well-being, but overconsumption and its by-products levy hefty costs to the environment.

OVERVIEW

Extent of the Environmental Issues

Humankind is leaving an irreversible footprint on the face of the home we call Earth. Economic growth, population expansion, financial incentives, entitlement, ignorance, greed, prosperity, and consumption are but a few of the contributing factors to the crisis we now face. Companies enjoying economic growth, financial gain, and prosperity are threatened not only by vocal environmentalists but also by their own consciences, recognizing that they are degrading the social welfare and are ethically responsible to mitigate the damage they are causing. Delayed action means a decreasing quality of life for the population. The United States, closely followed by China, is a major contributor to the world's environmental concerns. We must come face-to-face with the ramifications of ignoring our actions, economically painful though they may be. For many years already, economic development models have placed insufficient focus on environmental integrity and committed too few resources to incorporating natural resource support as a component of the same.

Greenhouse Gases—A Critical Resource in Danger

The Greenhouse Effect, warming of the air near Earth's surface, is a serious concern to the survival of the planet. Researches portend frightening increases in temperature, a key measure crucial to our very future. Although a good number of greenhouse gases are produced naturally, the dramatic increase in global average air temperature over the last 100 years is reported in the literature as being the direct result of human activities such as industrial

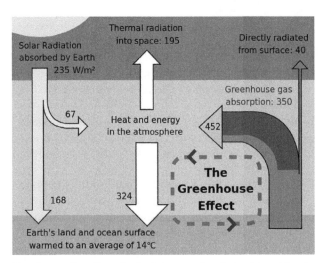

Greenhouse effect schematic showing energy flows between space the atomosphere and Earth's surface. Energy influx and emittance are expressed in watts per square meter (W/m2). (Courtesy of Robert A. Rohde GFDL 1.2 at Wikimedia Commons)

activities, human consumption activities, and tropical deforestation:

"Are we spending the world's natural capital in unsustainable ways? The answer is yes, according to the Millennium Ecosystem Assessment prepared by the Organisation for Economic Co-operation and Development (OECD) for the United Nations secretary-general. The report concluded that 'over the last 50 years, humans have changed the world's ecosystems more rapidly and extensively than at any comparable period in history.' And it's only going to get worse. The International Energy Agency estimates 'that China will overtake the U.S. as the major source of greenhouse gases by the end of the decade'" (Barnes, 2007).

APPLICATIONS

Economics & Externalities

Growth and production spell economic success; market activity strengthens the country's gross productivity. Growth of product in the market is typically assumed to enhance social welfare; however, society cannot disregard the destructive impact that increasing productivity is having on our ecology. Market transactions assume that the buyer and seller are both better off financially and socially when a mutually acceptable transaction has occurred. Believing that greater oil production and consumption are

Here southeastern China is covered by a thick grey shroud of aerosol pollution. The smog is so thick it is difficult to see the surface in some regions of this scene, acquired on January 7, 2002. The city of Hong Kong, the island of Taiwan, due east of mainland China, is also blanketed by the smog. This true-color image was captured by the Moderate-resolution Imaging Spectroradiometer (MODIS) sensor, flying aboard NASA's Terra satellite. (Courtesy of NASA via Wikimedia Commons)

beneficial to both the seller and the consumer is shortsighted; we must consider the environmental impact of the transaction. The harm caused by such a transaction—pollution—impacts more than just the two parties involved in the exchange. The economic term *externality* refers to the damage (cost) caused by any market transaction. When externalities occur, and unfortunately they are common, the outcome is considered a "market failure." Put simply, the transaction itself does not meet the criteria for enhancing social welfare; it is a human-driven transaction that causes harm to others. When market failure occurs, governmental intervention is commonly the route taken to improvement. Emitting pollutants is not against the law unless governmental regulation is set in place to make it so. Decreasing emissions per unit output is likely to cost the producer handsomely; business sense tells the company to continue financially beneficial production without emissions improvements until a sanction or incentive is imposed.

Economic Realities in Business

Companies understand their demand curve—how much of their product will be purchased at a given price. Every economist and business manager understands the relationship of cost to demand for product. Lower cost equals higher demand; conversely an increased price of a product leads to lower public demand. People find they can live with less of something when the price becomes too high for their pocketbook's comfort. Consumption and cost of public goods (commodities) behave differently than services and products regulated by standard market and economic behaviors. Purchasers of oil, for example, are not consistently responsive to increased cost, sometimes because they can't decrease their use (e.g., oil consumption is crucial to their survival) or because they are not impacted dramatically enough to make a behavior change.

So how do companies decide when and how to respond to emissions mandates in the most financially beneficial manner? Facing costly improvements to aging facilities is a concern for organizations, especially those with tight margins already. It is a difficult ethical and financial quandary at the very least.

Said Nobel laureate Eric Maskin, in an article highlighting his work on mechanism design theory, "Classical economic theory assumes buyers and sellers have complete knowledge of the available alternatives and therefore can make logical informed decisions. But in fact that's often not the case," (Maskin, 2007).

Paul Ormerod, author of *Why Most Things Fail*, comments that "…companies which use large amounts of energy and which participate in {the} trading scheme realize that they *can* make mistakes about their knowledge of how their own costs evolve" (Ormerod, 2005). Herein lays the obvious truth that companies are challenged in their ability to identify the monetary expenditure required to increase their production per unit in the face of mandated emissions controls. The decision to increase production, let's say for an oil-producing corporation, may result in diseconomies of scale when the cost of production per unit (including permit costs) advances upward, surpassing the point at which maximum economies have been recognized.

Discourse

Increased operating costs related to aging facilities, in combination with increasingly stringent regulatory mandates can lead to expensive capital upgrades. The challenge to corporations is to determine the optimal time to make these capital investments and to a certain extent make their best guess at uncertain future emissions mandates, which undoubtedly will become more stringent as social concerns grow. Cost and profit associated with continued production in an aging facility, including upgrading or retrofitting the facility to mitigate environmental impact, may not be well understood. The polluting conditions creating liability for some companies are difficult to place a price on; professionals are required to use their best discretion and business experience when reporting such liabilities.

Historical Perspective

In the 1970s, a number of pollution-emitting companies were grandfathered an exemption to the Clean Air Act (legislation that was passed to ramp up controls on pollution sources). Further expansion on the improvements related to this act will follow later in this essay. The incentive inherent in this grandfather clause allowed companies to expand, improve, and in fact increase production of product and pollution. Relatively speaking, it may be easier for a company to identify the costs it will incur when implementing improvements to decrease emissions; it is proven much more difficult for this same organization to identify the costs impacting others as a result of its actions, especially when costs are not measured in terms of dollars.

Governmental Response to Emissions "Command & Control"

Incentives affect the means people use to achieve a goal. Implementing incentives like the Clean Air Act was the government's reply to growing levels of air pollution in the 1970s. This "cap-and-trade" initiative offers a company an emissions permit—the value of which is neither a monetary fine nor cash incentive but a delineated amount of specific pollutants that a company can emit. The company has the option to sell its permits to other organizations; in this manner, the seller is able to continue producing at current levels without having to invest in costly facility improvements. The company is effectively putting a cap on its current productivity and presumably offering polluting capacity to another organization to enjoy higher production capacity. Companies emitting the highly worrisome gas sulfur dioxide (the cause of acid rain) employ the cap-and-trade system now; the long-term goal of this initiative is gradual reduction of permits available over time, thereby decreasing emissions—an improvement over maintaining the steady state.

Acid rain can have severe effects on vegetation. Here the effects of acid rain is obvious on these woods located in the Jizera Mountains in the Czech Republic. (Courtesy of Lovecz via Wikimedia Commons)

The incentive instruments do lead to lower social costs; however, companies take a greater financial hit because they are paying for the cost of abating the pollutants as well as paying a fee for ongoing pollution activity. Unless abatement costs, those that provide for existing infrastructure upgrades, are lower than pollution fines levied against emissions, abatement will be a second choice for the polluters.

Economic Impact of the Cap-and-Trade System

"In a cap-and-trade system, companies or entities that release more carbon emissions into the atmosphere than their allotment allows can buy credits from companies or entities that release fewer than their allowed amount of emissions." J. Drake Hamilton, the science policy director of St. Paul–based environmental group Fresh Energy, is a member of the cap-and-trade subgroup. Hamilton said a cap-and-trade system puts a price on carbon that can be traded in the marketplace. "What I especially like about it is that it lets the market kick in," Hamilton said. Ultimately, the Commerce Department will assemble the group's work into a report to the Legislature due Feb. 1, 2008 (Shaw, 2007).

Cap-and-trade is touted by some as the key to maximizing emission reductions while minimizing economic disruption. The House Energy and Commerce Committee is responsible for determining the allocation of caps and trades.

Judith McNeill and Jeremy Williams of U21 Global in Singapore submitted a working paper series, excerpts from which follow, expanding on carbon emission permits and the premises by which these mechanisms are likely to be successful.

"Putting aside theoretical difference, we {McNeill and Williams} believe the McKibbin-Wilcoxen scheme has many good features, not least of which is the potential for business to manage policy risk through the purchase or gift of long-term permits to emit carbon, thus lowering the cost of capital and encouraging investment in low-carbon alternatives. The long-term permits also offer a capacity to compensation impacts of a carbon price. The scheme also handles the difficult question of international competitiveness in a way that retains the incentive to invest in low-carbon technologies. It also incorporates some sound policy design principles such as gradualism, adaptability and micro-flexibility (among other features as recommended by ecological economists)" (McNeill, 2007).

Opposing Views to Cap-and-Trade Initiatives

"Some economists and financial managers vocally oppose the cap-and-trade recommendations of the federal government; concerns abound relating to clarity, enforcement, artificial markets, and potential for untoward financial gain. There are predictions that those who are on the front end of developing a market for carbon trading will be the winners financially from this inevitable and controversial debacle. Quoting an article from *Human Events*, some consider this argument sound: 'This system, which may sound market-friendly, is something only a bureaucrat could dream up. The twist is that the carbon market exists only because the government's imposition of a cap creates an artificial scarcity in the right to produce energy. In a cap-and-trade system, buyers will purchase their offsets from a broker or through an electronic trading platform. In Europe, carbon trading is already a reality. Since 2005, carbon offsets have been traded electronically on the European Climate Exchange'" (Barnes, 2007).

In summation the author predicts:

"Whatever its impact on the environment, the cap-and-trade carbon scheme is sure to boost the economic and political prospects of people and groups that are behind it. Before the company collapsed under the weight of financial scandal, Enron under CEO Ken Lay was a key proponent of the cap-and-trade idea. So was BP's Lord John Browne, before he resigned last May under a cloud of personal

scandal. In August 1997, Lay and Browne met with President Bill Clinton and Vice President Gore in the Oval Office to develop administration positions for the Kyoto negotiations that resulted in an international treaty to regulate greenhouse gas emissions" (Barnes, 2007).

In closing, the Barnes article follows with:

"But the president is unwilling to call for mandatory nationwide emissions rules and instead favors voluntary carbon-emission cuts in the private sector. This is deeply frustrating to all the brokers, wheeler-dealers, and interest groups that want to jump on the cap-and-trade bandwagon. There are billions of dollars to be made in trading emissions credits. But first the federal government must force everyone to play the game" (Barnes, 2007).

Case Study: Governmental Controls

"California Governor Arnold Schwarzenegger (R.) has signed into law the first statewide, cap-and-trade program for controlling greenhouse gas emissions. The law will cap the state's emissions at 1990 levels by 2020, an estimated 25% reduction. Facilities will be given emission allowances and be allowed to buy

Governor Arnold Schwarzenegger speaking at the lighting of the menorah at the California capitol building in Sacramento on December 13, 2008.

or sell surplus credits. The California Chamber of Commerce (Sacramento) opposes the bill, saying it will hurt the economy, and not help the environment.

The Global Warming Solutions Act also sets up an emissions reporting system to enforce the law, which will be administered through the state-run California Air Resources Board (Sacramento). Schwarzenegger said in an interview with the *Miami Herald* that the state hopes the federal government will follow suit with a nationwide greenhouse gas emissions cap-and-trade program" (Sissell, 2007).

Designing a Market-Based Mechanism for Climate Exchange

The Chicago Climate Exchange (CCX) is a voluntary greenhouse gas–reduction system. Companies participating with CCX benefit from the independent verification statistics the organization can offer. The exchange quantifies for participants their emissions of greenhouse gases and, like the governmental cap-and-trade system, trades greenhouse gas allowances. By joining, participating organizations commit to reducing their aggregate emissions by 6% by 2010.

"Today, with 300 members from multiple business sectors and emissions-offset projects around the world, CCX, along with the electronic, transparent trading concepts it has successfully extended into the emissions marketplace, is still very much in its infancy. Sandor {of CCX) has seen beginnings before. As an economics professor at University of California at Berkeley, Sandor thought up interest-rate futures as a way for banks and investors to hedge against possible shifts in rates" (Magee, 2007).

The Best Answer? Is it Governmental or Market Controls?

Emissions controls driven by the market, as opposed to governmental command and control systems, are likely a less costly means to the same end—decreased emissions. Companies involved in emissions trading are associated with each other in a collaborative mode, while the more punitive model tends to push companies into a "solo" position, responding independently to monetary fines. To that same end, companies subject to emissions penalties are likely to try and purchase more permits to produce. In this essay's earlier review of economic theory, the natural response to greater demand will concurrently drive up the price of the permits.

CONCLUSION

The world's economy becomes increasingly interconnected every day; the very nature of globalization leads to growth in production and consumption. Decisions to decrease overall pollution by regulation or controlling current levels through cap-and-trade or market trading are made by society. Planning for and participating in emissions control is the job of the companies that are involved. Complex economic and social decisions in the context of planning for our future will be the challenge for this generation and many more to come.

BIBLIOGRAPHY

Barnes, P. (2007). "Environmental update." *Business & Economic Review, 54*, 26–27.

Magee, J. (2007). "Exchanges for climate change." *Securities Industry News, 19*, 1–21.

Maskin, E. (2007). "A new Nobel laureate explains his path-breaking work." *njbiz, 20*, 15.

McNeill, J., & Williams, J. (2007). "The economics of climate change: An examination of the McKibbin-Wilcoxen hybrid proposal for a carbon price for Australia." *U21Global Working Papers Series*, 2–19.

Ormerod, P. (2005). *Why most things fayl. Evolution, extinction and economics.* Great Britain: Pantheon Books-Random House.

Shaw, C. (2007, October 6). "Capping and trading carbon." *Finance & Commerce (Minneapolis, MN)*.

Sissell, K. (2006). "California becomes first state to cap greenhouse gases." *Chemical Week, 168*, 53.

SUGGESTED READING

Lambro, D. (2007, October 9). "Obama's green goals aim to slash carbon emissions." *Washington Times, The (DC)*, A04.

Moorman, R. (2007). "Selling green." *Air Cargo World, 97*, 10–11.

Reinelt, P., & Keith, D. (2007). "Carbon capture retrofits and the cost of regulatory uncertainty." *Energy Journal, 28*, 101–127.

"Where things stand." (2007). *PA Times, 30*, 13. Retrieved from http://search.ebscohost.com/login.aspx?direct=true&db=buh&AN=23840725&site=ehost-live

—Nancy Sprague

EVOLUTION OF ECONOMIC THOUGHT

ABSTRACT

Economics as a discipline and body of theory goes back many centuries. Over the years, many ideas put forward have been discredited or downplayed by successors. Others have withstood the test of time, in part because they illuminate a fundamental economic process or mechanism and in part because no one has yet convincingly disproved them. Like most fields of human endeavor, brilliant minds over the course of centuries have shaped and reshaped our thinking on the workings of the marketplace. This evolution is most clearly evident in the changing views held about price central to the theory of value and the efficient allocation of resources.

OVERVIEW

Looking back at the evolution of economic thought, one cannot help but marvel at how concepts we consider patently obvious, like supply and demand, weren't always so. In point of fact, the laws of supply and demand were not formally articulated until the late nineteenth century. This does not mean, of course, that the fundamental dynamics of markets did not exist before then or that they were unknown but simply that they were not yet full-fledged ideas in their own right. Nor would they have been if not for the flash of insight and carefully reasoned arguments of a dozen brilliant minds: Smith, Ricardo, Cournot, Jevons, Menger, Walras, Marshall, and Keynes, chief among them. Keen observers all, each commented on the economic realities of his day. As historical documents then, each individual work mirrors the successive changes in the means and scale of production that have transformed economic life over the last two and a half centuries. Looking to the future, though, the true import of theirs and other innovative economists' work lies in the synthesis of ideas, new and old, confirmatory or contradictory, into a coherent understanding of economic forces that, when applied, will bring us and future generations good rather than ill fortune. To first appreciate the vitality of this synthesis we must go back in time thousands of years to the very beginnings of economic thought.

FURTHER INSIGHTS

STAGES OF THOUGHT
Ethical Living

Production and trade, investment and profits, poverty and wealth all, of course, predate the rise of capitalism by many, many centuries. Yet the intelligentsia of the ancient world paid scant attention to questions of supply and demand, capital accumulation and investment, and income distribution that would come to preoccupy classical and modern economics. Ethical rather than commercial considerations dominated the debate even as sea-faring Athens grew rich from trade. Some very modern-sounding business practices, what's more, were well established two thousand five hundred years ago. *In Ways and Means to Increase the Revenues of Athens,* the philosopher Xenophon chronicled how the supply of goods affected prices; how investment companies prorated earnings per share and paid out dividends, and how the sharing of risk lowered individual investors' exposure (Perrotta 2003). As long as commerce made the state more powerful, philosophers countenanced it. Yet their unease was equally evident in another of

Slavery played an important role in the economy of Ancient Rome. This is a Roman mosaic from Dougga, Tunisia (2nd century CE): the two slaves carrying wine jars wear typical slave clothing and an amulet against the evil eye on a necklace; the slave boy to the left carries water and towels, and the one on the right a bough and a basket of flowers. (Courtesy of Pascal Radigue CC BY 3.0 via Wikimedia Commons)

Xenophon's works, *Oeconomicus*, where he condemns the greed and excesses of those who seek wealth for its own sake.

Aristotle thought virtue and happiness came solely from being self-reliant and leading contemplative life. In so far as wealth furthers this end, it was natural and desirable. 'Chrematistic,' or wealth-getting, is neither; those in its thrall have unlimited appetites and are never satisfied. He took even greater umbrage at the idea of any man's gain coming at the expense of other men instead of from nature. All judgment aside, 'other men' of course excluded the slaves who labored in the fields and mines of ancient Greece and the Roman Empire, filling the granaries and supplying the metal armorers fashioned weapons from. It was, after all, the proceeds from both agriculture and conquest that fueled the consumption of goods that trade thrived upon.

Spiritual Salvation

Although war remained profitable for the victors and slavery morphed into serfdom, wealth still flowed primarily from the land well into the late middle ages. And Aristotelian thought suffused much of medieval philosophy. But the object now was spiritual salvation, not simply ethical living. St. Thomas Aquinas and other scholastics championed a just price, a just wage, and a prohibition against usury (interest) in the belief that what is taken should be equal to what is given (Pribram, 1953). Economic practices beyond the Christian pale were worse than unnatural; they were sinful. And it would take the Black Death, the rise of town, and the growing political influence of the commercial bourgeoisie, the Renaissance, and the Protestant Revolution to convince people otherwise.

Mercantilism

But convinced they were. Echoing classical philosophers, mercantilists from the sixteenth through the eighteenth century believed the power of the state paramount. At issue was the central question of how to finance the upkeep of very costly standing armies and naval fleets to fend off predatory neighbors. To defend the realm and further its interests, national governments, they argued, had to harness their national economies so that gold and silver flowed into their treasuries. The surest route to achieving a favorable trade surplus was to export more bullion-earning goods than one imports. Toward that end, sizable

tariffs should be levied on foreign-made luxury items, the moral virtues of thrift extolled to all, and, when all else failed, sales and excise taxes imposed. Since high-quality export products sold better and at higher prices, furthermore, governments should regulate manufacturing and require industry to reinvest the lion's share of profits. They should also forbid colonies from manufacturing goods, forcing them to import them from the mother country in exchange for cheap raw materials.

Agriculture

Ironically, it would take a courtier at the epicenter of absolute monarchy, Versailles, to challenge the mercantilist agenda by advocating a laissez-faire approach in its stead. Louis Quesnay, a physician attending King Louis XV of France and contributor to Diderot's *Encyclopedia,* called for an end to all government control of the economy. But Quesnay was no anarchist; he believed natural law would subsequently assert itself and the true productive capacity of the economy come to the fore (Pressman 1999). That, crucially, was not manufacturing, not trade in goods, but agriculture. For only there does the innate fecundity of the land create genuine surpluses; in the two other spheres of the economy—manufacturing and land ownership—all earned income is spent in full.

Outputs, in other words, equal inputs, so there is no net gain. Echoing Aristotle and Thomas Aquinas, the land then was the source of all national wealth. To prove this, Quesnay quantified the flow of funds among the three spheres in a rudimentary economic model, a first, in his *Tableau économique* of 1758. The proceeds, importantly, could be divvied up among landlords, church, and state only after enough was put aside to finance future production. Not all of the ideas like this elementary notion of capital put forth by Quesnay and his colleagues were as original: Their belief in a 'bon prix,' or fair price, differed little from Aquinas's 'just' price. And some of their ideas contradicted others: Though militantly opposed to government intervention, for example, they nonetheless wanted royal officials to set interest rates.

CLASSICAL ECONOMICS
Smith & the Invisible Hand

Political economics is said to have come into its own as a discipline with the publication of Adam Smith's *An Inquiry into the Nature and Causes of the Wealth of*

Portrait of the political economist and philosopher Adam Smith (1723-1790) by an unknown artist, which is known as the 'Muir portrait' after the family who once owned it. The portrait was probably painted posthumously, based on a medallion by James Tassie. (Courtesy of the Scottish National Gallery via Wikimedia Commons)

Nations in 1776. He draws praise to this day for recognizing the competitive marketplace as the preeminent engine of economic growth. It was, in truth, a brilliant insight convincingly articulated. As was his observation about the agency of the self-interest driving human behavior in the furtherance of economic order and ever greater prosperity. No great admirer of selfishness, the Scotsman nonetheless conceded its ubiquity and, crucially, argued that competition can transform this 'private vice' into a 'public virtue.' Everyone, he observed, typically considered his or her economic needs foremost and acts accordingly. Yet, serendipitously, out of this anarchy a robust, if unintentional, economic order materializes, one seemingly guided, as Smith famously put it, by an 'invisible' hand.

What distinguishes Smith's work from predecessors' is the scope of his inquiry and the systematic nature of his conclusions. Drawing on his and the

observations of other eighteenth-century philosopher-economists, Smith examined (Pressman, 1999)

- the central role played by prices in ensuring the efficient allocation of scarce resources;
- the way wealth was distributed;
- the productivity gains achievable through the division of labor;
- the perniciousness of monopolies; and
- the advantages of international free trade over mercantilism.

He seconded Roger Cantillon's earlier idea that every price has two components: a natural based on cost of production and a market determined by supply and demand (Groenewegen, 2002). The former suffices to pay the rents, wages, and interest incurred during production, no more, no less. In the long run, competition exerts a centripetal force on market prices, drawing them ever closer to their natural level. Any difference between the two in the short run, Smith observed, attracts or dissuades producers from entering a market. As such, price exerts tremendous influence, acting as an autonomous mechanism to allocate resources most efficiently. It acts as a proxy of that 'invisible hand' when it comes to the distribution of income as well: Landowner, laborer and investor earn that portion of an item's natural price commensurate with the value each one contributed to its production.

In a cruel irony, the very drive to better themselves eroded laborers' share, for by affording a higher standard of living, more of their children survived to adulthood and the ranks of the unemployed that producers cannot afford to hire. This demographic predicament, Smith reasoned destined workers in the long run to earn just enough to live and reproduce. No matter how dour the outlook became, the individual worker would continue to strive for a better life, which is why Smith believed a greater division of labor would be welcomed for the attendant increases in production and wealth it would bring. To realize such gains, sufficient funds, or 'stock,' had first to be secured to afford the necessary machinery and additional workers. Future wealth would come from reinvesting profits in manufacturing, not agriculture as Quesnay believed. Monopolies not governments, what's more, were a more endemic threat to the efficient functioning of a laissez-faire marketplace because they skewered prices, thwarting competition.

Mercantilism did much the same in Smith's view and was thus equally as pernicious.

David Ricardo & Comparative Advantage

Smith forever changed the line of inquiry future economic theorists would take. It would, however, be left to David Ricardo to formalize some of his seminal ideas about income distribution, free trade, and economic growth. In his *Principles of Political Economy and Taxation* of 1817, Ricardo proposed a theory to explain each of the constituent parts of national income alluded to by Smith: rent, wages, and profits. Agricultural production, or rather the lack thereof, figured prominently in Ricardo's differential theory of rent, citing Malthus's belief that famine is the natural consequence of unrestrained population growth. Ricardo reasoned that less and less fertile land would have to be cultivated at greater and greater expense, increasing in the process the value of the higher-yielding acreage. Landowners were thus destined to receive more and more national income at others' expense (Pressman, 1999).

Portrait of the British economist David Ricardo, by Thomas Phillips. This painting shows Ricardo, aged 49 in 1821, just two years before his relatively early death. (Courtesy of Thomas Phillips via Wikimedia Commons)

Scarcity, though, was hardly ever a problem with readily reproducible, manufactured goods; supply and demand therefore affected prices temporarily at best and mattered little compared to costs of production. Ricardo viewed the latter solely in terms of the quantity of labor expended directly and indirectly in making something. This labor theory of value inspired Ricardo to equate a worker's pay with the 'natural' price of the item he or she produced. Like Smith, then, Ricardo too believed laborers could only expect to earn a subsistence wage. As to profits, since higher-than-usual returns attract new competitors who push market prices down, over time a uniform profit rate will prevail across multiple industries. His ingenious argument in support of free trade between nations, the theory of comparative advantage, is Ricardo's most enduring contribution to economic thought. Unlike Smith, he considered the cost differential between producing countries far less important than the differential within countries. In purely economic terms, importing goods from a more efficient foreign producer, he reasoned, is preferable to purchasing them from a less efficient domestic one. No matter how noble the sentiment, economic self-sufficiency could not match what a country stood to gain by funneling all its investments into ultra-efficient export industries.

NEOCLASSICAL ECONOMICS
Cournot & the Demand Curve

Successors readily accepted the basic tenants of classical economics, most notably the preeminent importance of competition and the autonomous workings of the marketplace. They grew increasingly dissatisfied, though, with its theory of value. Missing in Smith and Ricardo's ideas, they felt, was an adequate explanation of pricing's role in the efficient allocation of resources. Simply put, the labor theory of value made no mention of demand per se much less of the fact that it varied proportionately with increasing or decreasing prices. The mathematician cum economic theorist who drew the very first demand curve was Antoine Augustin Cournot. Studying the French wine market, he observed that if there were more customers than goods, a bottle's price invariably rose. Conversely, if there were more goods than customers, it dropped (Pressman, 1999). Decisions on the size of firm's production runs, he therefore reasoned, are best made one additional 'unit' at a time.

Via this marginal analysis, Cournot examined the pricing behavior of monopolies: They stood to earn the most profits whenever their marginal revenues equaled their marginal costs. In marketplaces made up of many smaller producers, though, no one firm can control prices by withholding goods from the market; there 'perfect competition' existed.

Utility Theory of Value

But what exactly was demand? Why did people buy one thing and not another? Hitherto the focus of inquiry had been national economies, markets, and the firm. Mid- to late-nineteenth-century theorists realized demand arose from consumer choice. Separately, three economists—Jevons, Menger, and Clark—concluded that what truly mattered here was the benefit the individual consumer thought the purchase would derive. That almost everyone regularly made these calculated, rational decisions convinced them of the existence of a utility theory of value. Now, not only was this a subjective valuation but also, crucially, a private exercise in diminishing marginal analysis where the more of something one has, they observed, the more sated one becomes. Jevons went on to show how the utility of the goods paid for by their wages counterbalanced laborers' dislike of the inconvenience and unpleasantness of work, its 'disutility.' Surrounded by material plenty, consumers, Menger argued, rationally select some goods but not others, according to their needs and wants. These very personal preferences affect purchase decisions that collectively amount to market demand, a key constituent of any price.

Price Fluctuation

A much more expansive view about pricing came from another supporter of marginal utility theory and subjective valuation was taken by Léon Walras. A markup or markdown in one item, he maintained, rippled through the entire economy, potentially altering the price of every other item. A spectacular claim but one that simply took prevailing ideas to their logical conclusion. For, just as every price and every market balances and rebalances opposing forces, so too does the economy as a whole. Walras, what's more, marshaled some very sophisticated mathematics to support his notion of general equilibrium. Examining the behavior of individual markets in isolation instead, Alfred Marshall formalized the laws of supply and demand: The higher the price, the greater the quantity of goods produced; the lower the price, the greater the quantity of goods consumed. He also observed how the upward or downward movement in the price in some goods affected sales volumes more than in others: The larger the impact, the greater what he called an item's price elasticity of the demand; the smaller the impact, the greater its price inelasticity.

MODERN ECONOMICS

Inflation

With the mechanics of pricing now widely considered known, economists began to ask new questions, some related, others not. Inflation, the dysfunctional side of pricing, became one focal point of inquiry. The problem was caused by an overly abundant money supply, according to Fisher. To prove his assertion, he worked out a formula, the equation of exchange that showed how the quantity of goods produced multiplied by their prices had match as the amount of currency in circulation multiplied by the number of times each coin or bill was used per year. This became the central plank of latter-day monetarists' doctrine that calls for only very small, fixed year-to-year increments in money supply. A very different kind of monetary policy was advocated by Wicksell: since most business investment was financed through credit, interest rate fluctuations were much more likely to directly affect an economy. He is also remembered today for showing the important role economies of scale play in a firm's cost structure.

Keynes & Aggregate Demand

Given its legion of supporters and critics, the most far-reaching theoretical doctrine in modern economics, though, has been John Maynard Keynes's *The General Theory and Employment, Interest and Money*. Here, he challenged that prevailing notion that supply creates its own demand. If that is so, Keyes countered, everyone should have a job. (Pressman, 1999). Production and employment, he further argued, were largely determined by aggregate demand, a concept that revolutionized economics. Prior to Keynes, economists analyzed demand in terms of households, firms, and markets, not of the economy as a whole. Macroeconomics—the study of how national economies function—effectively began with Keynes. And his central thesis, that aggregate demand in turn is a function of consumer spending and business investment, has figured prominently in debates over both monetary and fiscal policy ever since.

Robinson & Imperfect Competition

A colleague of Keynes, Joan Robinson, meanwhile, challenged the prevailing microeconomic theory about market competition. Orthodoxy held a market was occupied by a sole supplier and therefore uncompetitive or by many small ones and purely competitive. But what happens, she asked, when larger firms compete against each other? Her real-world observations led her to conclude the result is often imperfect competition. That's because firms resort periodically to sales to rid themselves of unshipped inventory. In such instances, their marginal revenue declines. Or they could simply produce and sell fewer goods, giving competitors an opening. The outcome in either case is underutilized capacity.

British economist Joan V. Robinson. (Courtesy of Punt / Anefo CC BY-SA 3.0 via Wikimedia Commons)

CONCLUSION

Compared to what went before, contemporary economics seems riven by schisms: There are post-Keynesians, neo-Keynesians, New Keynesians, new classicals, monetarists, rational expectations theorists, real business cycle theorists, and supply-siders (Walker, 2002). History is like a glacier covering all but the highest peaks, however, in that it subsumes minor doctrinal disputes, so that, somewhat misleadingly, the past by contrast seems relatively free of controversy. And in the case of a general history of what are in fact at times opaque concepts, the illusion is even greater. There are a number of economic thinkers that the limits of time and space prevented any mention of. And the ideas of those that were can be and are gone into much greater detail. Rest assured, though, that past generations were equally as argumentative, and appropriately so. Economics is an observational, not an experimental, science. The proof of a theory here thus rests in how well it empirically withstands the counterarguments hurled at it: that and the test of time.

BIBLIOGRAPHY

Brander, J., Smith, G. (2017). "Economic research in Canada: Evolution and convergence." *Canadian Journal of Economics.*

Daniela, Z. (2013). ""New" and "old" in economic neoliberalism." *Annals of the University Of Oradea, Economic Science Series, 22*(1), 572–578.

Groenewegen, P. (2002). "Part I: Chapter 3: New light on the origins of modern economics." In *Eighteenth century economics* (pp. 76–96). Abingdon: Taylor & Francis Ltd.

Harrison, P. (1997). "A history of an intellectual arbitrage: The evolution of financial economics." *History of Political Economy, 29*(4), 172–187.

Jovanovic, F. (2008). "The construction of the canonical history of financial economics." *History of Political Economy, 40*(2), 213–242.

Perrotta, C. (2003). "The legacy of the past: Ancient economic thought on wealth and development." *European Journal of the History of Economic Thought, 10*(2), 177.

Polanyi-Levitt, K. (2012). "The power of ideas: Keynes, Hayek, and Polanyi." *International Journal of Political Economy, 41*(4), 5–15.

Pressman, S. (1999). "François Quesnay (1694–1774)." In *Fifty major economists* (pp. 13–17). Abingdon: Taylor & Francis Ltd.

Pressman, S. (1999). "Adam Smith (1723–90)." In *Fifty major economists* (pp. 20–26). Abingdon: Taylor & Francis Ltd.

Pressman, S. (1999). "David Ricardo (1772–1823)." In *Fifty major economists* (pp. 35–40). Abingdon: Taylor & Francis Ltd.

Pressman, S. (1999). "Antoine Augustin Cournot (1801–77)." In *Fifty major economists* (pp. 40–44). Abingdon: Taylor & Francis Ltd.

Pressman, S. (1999). "John Maynard Keynes (1883–1946)." In *Fifty major economists* (pp. 99–105). Abingdon: Taylor & Francis Ltd.

Pribram, K. (1953). "Patterns of economic reasoning." *American Economic Review,* 43(2), 243.

Walker, D. (2002). "Chapter 1: The relevance for present economic theory of economic theory written in the past." *Competing economic theories* (pp. 15–32). Abingdon: Taylor & Francis Ltd.

SUGGESTED READING

Groenewegen, P. (2002). "Part I: Chapter 3: New light on the origins of modern economics." In *Eighteenth century economics* (pp. 76–96). Abingdon: Taylor & Francis Ltd.

Heilbroner, R. (1980). "Modern economics as a chapter in the history of economic thought." *Challenge, 22*(6), 20.

Pressman, S. (1999). "Alfred Marshall (1842–1924)." In *Fifty major economists* (pp. 64–69). Abingdon: Taylor & Francis Ltd.

Pressman, S. (1999). "Joan Robinson (1903–83)." In *Fifty major economists* (pp. 128–132). Abingdon: Taylor & Francis Ltd.

Pressman, S. (1999). "Léon Walras (1834–1910)" In *Fifty major economists* (pp. 53–57). Abingdon: Taylor & Francis Ltd.

Thoben, H. (1982). "Mechanistic and organistic analogies in economics reconsidered." *Kyklos, 35*(2), 292.

—Francis Duffy, MBA

EXCHANGE RATE

ABSTRACT

This article focuses on exchange rate. It provides an overview of the ways in which governments and policy makers implement exchange rate policy to control and stabilize national economies. The main types of exchange rate regimes, including floating exchange rate regimes, managed exchange rate regimes, and pegged exchange rate regimes, will be described. The issues associated with exchange rate management will be discussed.

OVERVIEW

An exchange rate is a comparison between a national currency and a foreign currency. Exchange rates are flexible expressions that may serve as a multiplier, ratio, or price. There are multiple types of exchange rates: nominal, real, bilateral, and multilateral.

- Nominal exchange rates are reported daily in newspapers around the world and are based on financial markets called forex markets. Forex markets, also referred to as foreign exchange markets, are markets in which buyers and sellers conduct foreign exchange transactions. Nominal exchange rates may be fixed for a period of time by a central bank.

- Real exchange rates are nominal exchange rates that include adjustments based on inflation measures.

- Bilateral exchange rates are based on the comparison of two countries' currencies.

- Multilateral exchange rates are based on the comparison of multiple currencies. Multilateral currencies evaluate the dynamics of a country's currency toward the rest of the world and produce an effective country-specific exchange rate.

Some countries may choose to employ a system of multiple exchange rates. Different exchange rates may be used in commercial transactions, public transactions, consumer transactions, and investment transactions. Countries that do not have an explicit policy of multiple exchange rates may choose to unofficially have multiple exchange rates in the form of the official exchange rates *and* black market exchange rates. Exchange rate classifications are based, in part, on the number of currencies involved in comparisons.

Exchange rates and the global or macro-economy are closely related. A country's exchange rate influences exports, imports, job rates, working conditions, external purchasing power of residents abroad, and trade balances. For example, a rising exchange rate depresses exports, boosts imports, and depresses the trade balance (Piana, 2001). International capital markets respond to exchange rate fluctuations and exchange rate volatility. Exchange rate variability and volatility depress trade and the economy in general. In an effort to limit exchange rate variability, international governance organizations, such as Group of Seven (G7) industrialized countries and the European Union (EU), have explored the possibility of establishing informal target ranges for exchange rates. There is no international consensus on how currency relations among major regions should be approached or governed (Obstfeld, 1995); in the wake of the global financial crisis of 2008, in 2010, the G20 and the International Monetary Fund agreed to devise plans for global currency regulations, but, as of 2013, no such regulations have been put in place (Council on Foreign Relations, 2013). Variables that affect nominal exchange rates include exports, imports, and trade balances; the demand for currency; past and expected values of the financial market; and the interest rate on treasury bonds. Governments must carefully manage interest rates due, in part, to the effect that interest rates have on exchange rates. The following section provides an overview of the ways in which governments and policy makers implement exchange rate policy to control and stabilize national economies. This section serves as the foundation for later discussion of exchange rate regimes and the issues associated with exchange rate management.

Exchange Rate Policy
Governments employ exchange rate policies to control the economy. For example, in times of exchange rate devaluation or depreciation, a central bank may issue a fixed exchange rate as an anchor for the economy (Piana, 2001). Exchange rate policy, along with trade policy, monetary policy, and fiscal policy, is used to control economic transitions and

to achieve economic equilibrium. Governments and policy makers use two main approaches to exchange rate policy: the real targets and the nominal anchor approach.

- The real targets approach views the nominal exchange rate as a policy tool.
- The nominal anchor approach holds that a country's exchange rate should move toward fixity to introduce credibility, maintain financial discipline, and reduce inflation.

Currency convertibility is a central part of exchange rate policy. Currency convertibility is considered to be a central part of economic transitions. Currency convertibility imports a new price structure, creates competition, eliminates administrative allocation of foreign exchange, and serves as a symbol of openness and economic freedom. Economies in transition often undergo exchange rate reform. Exchange rate reform refers to a process of improving or removing administrative restrictions over exchange rate decisions as part of the larger goal of transition to a market economy.

The United States & China
The United States and China offer examples of exchange rate policy and exchange rate reform. Neither the United States nor China had effective explicit exchange rate policy in place until late in the twentieth century. Throughout much of the twentieth century, the U.S. economy continued its trade policy without explicit policy on exchange rates. The Chinese economy was undergoing a transition throughout the twentieth century and exchange rate policy, begun in 1980, facilitated the transition and strengthened the market-driven economy. China's exchange rate reform in the 1980s and 1990s directed the transition of the Chinese economy from a planned economy to a dynamic, market-driven economy. China adopted the real targets approach to exchange rate reform. Exchange reform in China occurred in four main stages: Reform Stage I (1981–1985); Reform Stage II (1986–1991); Reform Stage III (1991–1993); and Reform Stage IV (beginning in 1994). China unified multiple exchange rates in 1994 with a managed and market-determined floating rate while abolishing planning controls over the use of foreign exchange for imports (Zhang, 2000).

Chinese Vice Premier Wang Qishan, center, holds the autographed basketball given to him by President Barack Obama following their Oval Office meeting Tuesday, July 28, 2009, to discuss the outcomes of the first U.S.-China Strategic and Economic Dialogue. Looking on at left is Chinese State Councilor Dai Bingguo. (Courtesy of Pete Souza, White House, via Wikimedia Commons)

In contrast to China, the United States had no coherent policy on exchange rates until the late 1990s. The U.S. Treasury issued policy statement on exchange rate regimes in 1999. The U.S. Treasury announced that either floating or fixed exchange rates were acceptable in the U.S. economy and marketplace but pegged exchange rates were not (Hanke, 2002). In the United States, the economy is controlled primarily by fiscal policy. Fiscal policy refers to expenditures by federal, state, and local governments and to the taxes levied to finance these expenditures. Fiscal policy supports and funds the federal budget, aids the federal government's social policies, and promotes overall economic growth and stability. The history of the U.S. economy is full of economic expansion and economic contraction. Following the American Revolution, the individual economies of the states were faltering, paper money had little value, and there was conflict between borrowers and lenders. The original thirteen states came together to draft the U.S. Constitution, in part, to stabilize and strengthen the U.S. economy.

From the Civil War through the beginning of the Industrial Revolution, the U.S. economy was characterized by cycles of growing and contracting. In the 1930s, following the Great Depression, the United States government began a program and approach of mixed fiscal and monetary policies in an effort to produce sustained economic growth and stable

prices (for goods, services, and natural resources). The government, with a strong record in the latter half of the twentieth century for controlling cycles of expansion and contraction, remains challenged by inflation and the related problem of unemployment. Today, the U.S. dollar, despite its great volatility, is the predominant currency worldwide. For example, nearly 90 percent of all internationally traded commodities are valued, priced, and invoiced in U.S. dollars. Despite the prominence of the U.S. dollar, the U.S. government is reconsidering the role of exchange rate policy in economic operations. Economic globalization requires increased sensitivity to issues of exchange rate, interest rate, and trade policy (Hanke, 2002).

APPLICATION

Exchange Rate Regimes

Exchange rate regimes, also called currency institutional regimes, refer to specific institutional structures designed to produce specific exchange rate outcomes. The main exchange rate regimes, including floating, fixed, and pegged, are characterized by different levels of control and produce different results. Exchange rate regimes are closely connected to international economic policy. The field of international economic policy debates the merits of different exchange rate regimes and international financial architecture. The field of international economic policy is working to identify viable international exchange rate regimes for a wide range of markets. The increase in global capital flows between the 1970s and 1990s increased international trade, portfolio diversification, and risk-sharing. Countries invested in international trade are increasingly faced with the decision of whether or not to give up their nation's monetary-policy autonomy. Instability in foreign markets increasingly transmits instability abroad through a process of economic contagion.

Main Types of Exchange Rate Regimes

The main exchange rate regimes, including floating, managed, and pegged, are described below (Tavlas, 2003):

Floating exchange rate regimes have no commitment to a specific exchange-rate target. In floating exchange rate regimes, the exchange rate is determined

Examples of world banknotes. (Courtesy of Veronidae CC BY-SA 3.0 via Wikimedia Commons)

by market supply and demand rather than macroeconomic policy. The U.S. dollar and the euro tend to have floating exchange rates.

Managed exchange rate regimes have no constant exchange rate target. Instead, policy makers tweak interest rates to raise or lower the exchange rate as needed. Managed exchange rate regime refers to scenarios in which the central bank intervenes in the currency market to achieve a variable currency target. Policy makers make these adjustments on a daily, weekly, or monthly basis to counteract misalignments in the economy. Misalignments refer to a sustained departure of the exchange rate from what policy makers perceive to be its equilibrium value.

Pegged exchange rate regimes include a set exchange rate targets. Policy makers use monetary policy to maintain the established exchange rate target. Examples of pegged exchange rate regimes include soft peg, adjustable peg, and crawling peg. Adjustable peg regimes tend to include infrequent large adjustments in response to perceived differences between the target exchange rate and the equilibrium rate. Crawling peg regimes operate with a target exchange rate zone rather than a single exchange rate target and tend to include frequent small adjustments to the exchange rate.

These three competing exchange rate regimes have different strengths and weaknesses. Emerging market economies and long-established market economies will choose their exchange rate regime based on the

different economic needs of citizens and government and the established economic infrastructure. Both freely floating exchange rate regimes and managed floating exchange rate regimes experience depreciations. Depreciations refer to a loss in currency value. Stable fixed exchange rate regimes experience devaluations and revaluations. Devaluation refers to a loss of value forced by market or a purposeful policy action. Revaluation refers to an increase of international value. All exchange rate regimes may experience currency crisis. Currency crisis refers to a rupture of fixed exchange rates with an unwilling devaluation or even the end of that regime in favor of a floating exchange rate (Piana, 2001).

Other Means of Controlling Exchange Rates
In addition to exchange rate regimes, exchange rates can be controlled and directed through other means such as currency boards, dollarism, and monetary unions (Tavlas, 2003).

- Currency boards issue money that is convertible on demand at a fixed rate of exchange. Currency boards guarantee their commitment through the use of a foreign anchor currency and by establishing the exchange rate as a public law. Currency boards cannot extend credit or determine the amount of money in circulation.
- Dollarism, also referred to as euroisation, is a process in which a country formally adopts a foreign currency as it legal tender. Under this system, the country's monetary base is exchanged in total for the adopted foreign currency, and all contracts previously established in the local currency must be reconfigured in the adopted foreign currency.
- Monetary union, also called monetary unification, is a process in which a group of economies adopt a single currency and a common central bank. The community entity takes over control of exchange rate policy and the responsibility to oversee balance of payments of member economies with nonmember economies and countries. Individual member economies give up their individual rights to establish monetary policy for their economy.

International monetary organizations debate the strengths and weaknesses of extreme exchange rate control mechanisms such as floating exchange rate regimes and monetary unification. Emerging market economies may thrive with floating exchange rates but require inflation targeting. This system is called managed floating. Managed floating exchange rate is free to act as a market gauge for assessing policies and as a mode of conflict resolution. Countries analyze exchange rate regime choices based on the balance between internal price stability and external competitiveness (Klyuev, 2002).

ISSUES

Exchange Rate Management

Multinational corporations face exchange rate exposure or risk. In particular, multinational corporations face foreign currency risk. The exchange rate exposure of firms has potentially positive or negative impacts on the profitability and value of the firm (Jorion, 1990). Exchange rate variability affects firm operations, revenue, and valuation. For example, exchange rate variability creates cash flow risk for firms with foreign assets and liabilities. Exchange rate exposure refers to the sensitivity of its economic value, or stock price, to exchange rate changes. The major causes of increased foreign exchange risk include the following: "The adoption of a floating exchange rate regime; the rapid globalization of national economies; and the attempts by multinationals to seek investment opportunities and markets beyond their immediate borders" (Zubeiru, 2007, p.380). Due to the difficulty in predicting exchange rate movements, corporate managers and analysts have developed management and analytical strategies, such as the Jorion two-factor model, to neutralize exchange rate risks (Zubeiru, 2007). Exchange rate managers and analysts use the Jorion two-factor model to estimate the exchange rate exposure of a situation, group, or scenario (Jorion, 1990).

Exposure on an International Level

Risk managers are responsible for exposure management in general. Exposures refer to categories of risks faced by a firm. International financial managers protect the firms from exchange rate exposure, transaction exposure, economic exposure, and translation exposure. Risk managers work to reduce exposures faced by their firms.

- Exchange rate exposure reflects the extent to which currency exchange and exchange rate fluctuations will affect firm activities and profits.

- Transaction exposure refers to the degree to which future cash transactions are affected by exchange rate fluctuations. Risk managers control transaction exposure by analyzing extent and range of exposure by country for all activities of the organization. Risk managers are responsible for developing inflows and outflows of cash in multiple currencies. In scenarios in which the transaction exposure is high, risk managers may choose to use a hedging technique to reduce the risk.

- Economic exposure refers to the degree to which a firm's present value of current cash flows is affected by exchange rate fluctuations. International financial managers control economic exposure through the application of techniques such as debt restructuring, modified sales activity, adjusted orders with suppliers, and adjusted production volumes by country. International financial managers adjust their orders with suppliers and their production volume in different countries in an effort to reduce their economic risks.

- Translation exposure, also known as accounting exposure, refers to the risk that a firm's equities, assets, liabilities, and income will change in response to exchange rate fluctuations. International financial managers control translation exposure through the use of consolidation techniques and carefully chosen cost accounting evaluation procedures (Delk, 2000).

A firm's total exposure refers to economic effects resulting from exchange rate exposure, transaction exposure, economic exposure, and translation exposure.

Controlling Exchange Rate Exposure

Risk managers control exchange rate exposure, in part, by monitoring and managing the business cycle. Exchange rates are closely related to the business cycle. The business cycle, which includes a peak, recession, trough, and expansion, is a cycle of economic contraction and expansion. There are two types of business cycles: classical cycles and growth cycles.

- **Classical cycles** refer to hills and valleys in a series that represent the overall economic activity level.
- **Growth cycles** refer to repeating fluctuations in the growth rate of overall activity in relation to the long-run growth rate trend.

The measurement and analysis of business cycles is crucial for the economic health of the public and private sectors. Economic indicator analysis is one of the main tools used in measuring and analyzing business cycles. Economic indicator analysis involves using leading and coincident indexes of economic activity as strong forecasting factors or tools (Boehm, 1999).

Managing the Business Cycle

Managers often oversee exchange rate exposures and business cycle exposure simultaneously. Business cycles have a profound effect on business stakeholders owners, employees, investors, and society at large. The expansions and contractions of the economic business cycles create an environment of economic risks and uncertainties in the business sector. Firms use management strategies, tactics, and forecasting tools to survive through the economically challenging times during a business cycle. Business cycles must be managed by businesses to avoid economic collapse during periods of economic contraction. Executives with high levels of business cycle literacy may be referred to as master cyclist executives. There are three broad and general objectives that businesses use to manage the business cycle: evaluate the capabilities and resources that a firm may deploy to hedge or leverage business cycle risk; articulate strategies and tactics that companies may use to better manage business cycle volatility; and develop prescriptive measures in areas ranging from marketing, pricing, and human resources management in order to improve business cycle management. Risk managers perform two main tasks in business cycle management.

- First, risk managers hedge general business cycle risk by using tools such as business unit and geographical diversification.
- Second, risk managers hedge the specific risks potentially caused by movements in commodity and oil prices, interest rates, and exchange rates by using financial derivatives such as call options and futures (Navarro, 2006).

Savvy risk managers, who are aware of the relationship between exchange rates and business cycles, can often predict economic recession and prepare and protect their business accordingly.

CONCLUSION

In the final analysis, an exchange rate is a comparison between a national currency and a foreign currency. Exchange rates are flexible expressions that may serve as a multiplier, ratio, or price. There are multiple types of exchange rates: nominal, real, bilateral, multilateral, and multiple. Countries choose their exchange rate regimes based on the needs of their economy and the economic architecture and institutions available to direct and guide the exchange rate. Exchange rate fluctuations affect the strength of national economies and local businesses alike. Exchange rate management, as part of a larger system of exposure management and business cycle management, is vital for the success of most businesses.

BIBLIOGRAPHY

Avejiev, S., Bruno, V., Koch, C., & Shin, H. (2018). "The dollar exchange rate as a global risk factor: Evidence from investment." *BIS Working Paper No. 695.*

Bahmani, S. (2013). "Exchange rate volatility and demand for money in less developed countries." *Journal Of Economics & Finance, 37,* 442–452.

Bauer, C., & Herz, B. (2005). "How credible are the exchange rate regimes of the New EU countries?" *Eastern European Economics, 43,* 55–77.

Council on Foreign Relations. (2013, June 25). *The global finance regime.* Retrieved from "http://www.cfr.org/financial-regulation/global-finance-regime/p20177"

Delk, J. (2000). "International financial management concepts strengthen supply chain links." *Production and Inventory Management Journal, 41,* 59–64.

Grauwe, P., & Grimaldi, M. (2005). "The exchange rate and its fundamentals in a complex world." *Review of International Economics, 13,* 549–575.

Gray, P. & Irwin, T. (2003). *Allocating exchange rate risk in private infrastructure contracts.* The World Bank. Retrieved from "http://rru.worldbank.org/Discussions/Topics/Topic21.aspx"

Hanke, S. (2002). *On international economic and exchange rate policy hearings before the Banking, Housing and Urban Affairs Committee.* The Cato Institute. Retrieved from xlink:href="http://www.cato.org/testimony/ct-hanke050102.html"

Jorion, P. (1990). "The exchange-rate exposure of U.S. multinationals." *Journal of Business, 63,* 331.

Klyuev, V. (2002). "Exchange rate regime choice in Central and Eastern European transitional economies." *Economic Studies, 44,* 85–108.

Navarro, P. (2006) "Sustainable strategies for a world of economic shocks: we live in a time of sudden and severe economic and geopolitical shocks." *Financial Executive.*

Ndung'u, N. (2000). "The exchange rate and monetary policy in Kenya." *African Development Review, 12,* 24.

Nguyen, V. (2013). "How china to u.s. foreign exchange rate relates to U.S. interest rate and bank loans." *Global Journal of Business Research (GJBR), 7,* 101–108.

Obstfeld, M. (1995). "International currency experience: New lessons and lessons relearned." *Brookings Papers on Economic Activity,* 119–220.

Piana, V. (2001). "Exchange rate." The Economics Web Institute. Retrieved from xlink:href="http://www.economicswebinstitute.org"

Salifu, Z., Osei, K. & Adjasi, O. (2007). "Foreign exchange risk exposure of listed companies in Ghana." *The Journal of Risk Finance, 8,* 380.

Tavlas, G. (2003). "The economics of exchange-rate regimes: A review essay." *World Economy, 26,* 1215.

Taylor, M. (1995). "The economics of exchange rates." *Journal of Economic Literature, 33,* 13–47.

Zhang, Z. (2000). "Exchange rate reform in China: An experiment in the real targets approach." *World Economy, 23,* 1057.

SUGGESTED READING

Bonitsis, T. (2013). "Is the real U.S. dollar exchange rate neutral?" *Journal of Business & Economic Studies, 19,* 71–84.

ÉGert, B., Halpern, L., & MacDonald, R. (2006). «Equilibrium exchange rates in transition economies: Taking stock of the Issues.» *Journal of Economic Surveys, 20,* 257–324.

Jeanne, O., & Rose, A. (2002). "Noise trading and exchange rate regimes." *Quarterly Journal of Economics, 117,* 537–569.

Narayan, P., & Smyth, R. (2006). "The dynamic relationship between real exchange rates, real interest rates and foreign exchange reserves: Empirical evidence from China." *Applied Financial Economics, 16,* 639–651.

—*Simone I. Flynn, PhD*

EXPERIMENTAL ECONOMICS

ABSTRACT

Experimental economics creates a controlled environment in which many of the unanswered questions about economics may be given careful study. This paper provides a comprehensive analysis of experimental economics and its role in studying the ever-changing global economic system of the twenty-first century.

OVERVIEW

One of the most iconic scientific findings of the early twentieth century was Alexander Fleming's discovery of penicillin. As luck would have it, a tiny amount of mold floated up into Fleming's laboratory from a mycology lab one floor below and landed in an uncovered culture plate in 1928. When Fleming, who was on vacation at the time, returned to his workplace, he discovered the mold and its as-yet unrealized potential, and medical history was made. Years later, he visited another laboratory, one that was modernized and virtually free from contaminants. His host commented on the conditions in which Fleming had toiled and wondered aloud about what extraordinary discoveries Fleming could have made in such a facility. Fleming responded simply: "Not penicillin" ("Serendipity," 2009).

Indeed, science is often broken into two arenas: laboratory environments in which controlled experiments are conducted and "real-world" settings in which the processes or concepts being studied are allowed to play out in uncontrolled conditions. In the science of economics, the same generalization can be made. On the one hand are the trends that occur and systems that are in operation that are the focus

Alexander Fleming receives the Nobel Prize from King Gustaf V of Sweden on December 10, 1945 for his discovery of penicillin. (Courtesy of Wikimedia Commons)

of observant economists. These individuals take such data and establish theoretical frameworks to help explain what transpires. On the other hand are the concepts that may be compiled in theoretical constructs and then applied in real-world scenarios.

The latter of these two economic arenas is what is known as "experimental economics." Like Fleming's laboratory (as well as the modernized facility he visited later in life), experimental economics creates a controlled environment in which many of the unanswered questions about economics may be given careful study. This paper provides a more comprehensive analysis of experimental economics and its role in studying the ever-changing global economic system of the twenty-first century.

A Brief Overview of Experimental Economics
Economics is a science, complete with a wide range of analytical methods and theoretical frameworks. Of course, an arena as dynamic and multifarious as economics has largely been considered difficult to quantify or understand in a controlled environment. Many economists have therefore eschewed this approach, believing that the better avenue is to study economic trends in "real-world" settings.

Then again, much of economics focuses on the balance between supply and demand. Demand may be considered the preference of the consumer or, to put it in a psychological context, a matter of individual choice. In 1931, L. L. Thurstone first applied such an approach, employing utility theory (a psychological attempt to ascertain the value, or "utility," of choice)

to predict individual choice in consumerism. Several other studies, one in 1944 and two more in 1951 and 1953, supported Thurstone's theory. In fact, studies abounded over the next few decades, culminating in a series of studies in the 1990s that used utility theory to analyze irrational behaviors that could lend to rises in consumption and savings behavior (McKinney & Roth, 2006).

The Rules of the Marketplace
Part of what is being studied in experimental economics are the rules of the marketplace and how they impact the market itself. Over the course of the latter twentieth century, economist Vernon L. Smith

American professor of law and economics, Vernon L. Smith won the Nobel Memorial Prize in Economic Sciences. Here he is during a break in his lecture on Experimental Economics at the Nicholas Academic Centers I Annex on January 29th, 2011. (Courtesy of Dstringer71 CC BY-SA 3.0 via Wikimedia Commons)

conducted or oversaw thousands of experiments on social groups and the impact of consumer preference on the markets. He broke down the idea of market trading into simple interactions between individuals. In understanding the nature of consumer behavior, his laboratory studies of individual preference helped policy makers, industrialists, entrepreneurs and fellow economists better gauge consumer behavior. As Smith, a 2003 Nobel Prize winner, succinctly said, "The benefits of market exchange are easy to see in personal interactions, where you do something for me and I do something for you." He added, "Out there in 'markets,' though, they're not always clear. If the price goes up, the oil companies get more money and I have less. That's the average person's perception and experience. Experimental economics helps put a human face on markets" (Gillespie & Lynch, 2002).

Smith's approach stemmed from his experience working with Edward Chamberlin. Chamberlin had become cynical of the predictability of the markets during the Great Depression, an era in which such understanding was absolutely necessary. Chamberlin focused on three areas.

- The first was a streamlined version of the natural markets.
- The second was a laboratory interpretation of the markets, in which the various subcomponents could be separated and applied in a number of game experiments.
- The third of these areas consisted of individual experiments—putting a focus on a microscopic level and analyzing patterns of individual choice for re-application into market scenarios.

Through these market experiments (which entailed the employment of a number of test subjects—namely Chamberlin's graduate students, of whom Vernon Smith was one), Chamberlin constructed a number of early theories about consumer choice that would ultimately inspire Smith's later works (Davis & Holt, 1993).

Experimental economics is not employed to explain large, complex trends and systems in a given market. Rather, it is used to help analyze specific elements of a given system and, as a result, help explain how those elements contribute to the whole system in question. As California Institute of Technology professor Charles Plott said in a 2008 interview:

We create experiments that do not mirror the world around us because it is too complex ... Instead, we design very simple experiments that allow us to see the theory clearly, separating the accurate from the inaccurate, and then the question is: Does that theory that we have seen clearly in a simple case actually help us understand a more complex case?

Modeling

An important aspect of experimental economics is the use of modeling. Modeling entails placing elements of a given study area into a controlled framework in order to see how these parts interact. Models are general vehicles, to be sure, but have the potential to be flexible as internal elements are modified, supplemented, or reduced in number.

Modeling has become a popular form of experimental economic analysis, particularly among large companies and governments who seek to maximize returns on investments, business practices, or changes to policy-making strategies. In the modern era, computer technology has helped immeasurably to connect large quantities of complex and multifarious data into a working system whose parts' contributions can be studied individually or in the aggregate.

The use of models in experimental economics has caught on in many corporations who not only seek maximum return on investments and strategies but also want to locate flaws or loopholes in their current endeavors. Models could be used to determine the optimum time to introduce new products by taking into account mitigating factors such as manufacturing, marketing, and engineering. In big companies like Hewlett-Packard (HP), on-site economics labs are sometimes utilized to help predict and control business. For HP, such a lab meant the ability to predict demand from the company's distributors—forecasts that had previously been off by as much as 100 percent (Krakovsky, 2008).

Chamberlin used experimental economics and models to help make sense out of complex (and indeed daunting) economic circumstances. In periods in which cost-effective policies and strategies are paramount (particularly during recessions), studying and generating models of consumer behavior and supply-side management becomes critical. This paper next turns to a brief review of some of the forms of experiments used in experimental economics.

GAMES

The Prisoner's Dilemma

In 1950, mathematician Albert W. Tucker formalized a concept that he would call "The Prisoner's Dilemma." Within this theoretical design, a simple scenario was introduced that would ultimately play a tremendous role in the experimental economics arena by helping economists study the relationship between supply and demand.

In this "game," two hypothetical thieves are captured after they commit a crime. They could each get ten years in prison for being part of the crime. During their separate interrogations, each individual is given a simple choice: confess and implicate the other or refuse to confess. If Prisoners A and B both refuse to confess, they will only get one year in jail for a lesser crime (such as possession of a firearm). However, if Prisoner A confesses and implicates B while B does not confess or implicate A, A could be set free altogether while B gets put in jail for 20 years. If they both confess and implicate each other, each will get the ten-year sentence.

The key here is strategy—should Prisoner B refuse to confess, he or she could conceivably get one year instead of ten if his or her partner also refuses to confess. Then again, if he or she does not confess, B might also go to jail for 20 years if Prisoner A does confess and implicate him or her. Therefore, while the "rational" strategy would be for both to refuse to cooperate with the police, the temptation of getting away free for implicating the other means that both prisoners would likely be best served by confessing, even though the "irrational" course of action, bilateral silence, would in fact entail the best possible amount of jail time (McCain, 2008).

In experimental economics, games like the Prisoner's Dilemma help theorists determine dominant strategy equilibrium. Prisoner A, for example, must review all possible strategies for achieving the maximum gain for himself or herself (in other words, the least amount of jail time). If under the varying conditions that may become manifest Prisoner A maintains this strategy throughout the game, his or her course of action is known as the "dominant strategy." Of course, there is more than one player, and that adversary also seeks maximum gain from his or her interaction with A. With two competing strategies coming into contact with one another, the result is what is known as "dominant strategy equilibrium." In terms of the Prisoner's Dilemma, for example, the dominant strategy equilibrium of both prisoners confessing and implicating the other is both parties receiving 10-year sentences.

Games such as the Prisoner's Dilemma have implications and uses for a wide range of scientific study. These games allow individuals to make their own decisions and develop their own strategies; how well participants do in the game depends heavily on the choices and strategies of other players. Such conditions have particular use in experimental economics, as they often bear similarities to real economic situations and market conditions. In fact, economists experimenting with such games tend to do so to help form policy strategies and correct market or institutional issues as well as to validate economic theories (Shor, 2006).

Experimental economics, like any other form of scientific field, entails the study of certain elements of the subject matter in a relatively controlled environment. Games provide a vehicle for such study. Then again, there are those who believe that one of the great failings of economic theory is that it tends to emerge and return to textbooks without having a

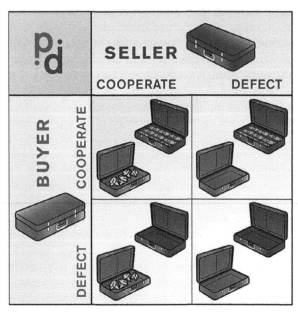

Using the exchange of briefcases (cash for diamonds) as an example of the Prisoner's Dilemma, this full-color info-graphic represents potential game outcomes in matrix (i.e. normal) form. (Courtesy of Christopher X Jon Jensen & Greg Riestenberg CC BY-SA 3.0 via Wikimedia Commons)

true basis in "real-world" settings (Bergmann, 2009). This argument is particularly evident in macroeconomics (the field of economics in which the workings of the overall, national economy are studied), where relevant public policy-making enters the picture. In these arenas, another manifestation of experimental economics, field experiments, comes into play. This paper next takes a look at field experiments and their value in addressing the perceived shortcomings of traditional economic study.

Field Experiments

Laboratory experiments in economics are important because they help verify existing assumptions and theories in a controlled environment. However, many of these assumptions and theories are offered in response to situations and trends that occur in the natural economic environment. It is therefore useful to the science of economics to conduct field experiments.

Field experiments have increased in popularity and effectiveness over the last century. In the 1920s and 1930s, such experiments were conducted in the agricultural sector to define the trends within the industry. In the mid-twentieth century, the field was expanded significantly to focus on government-sponsored social studies, assessing individual and group behaviors. The practice of field study in economic circles has continued to evolve and develop, most recently to such a level that a very broad range of experiments occur in controlled settings outside of the laboratory (Levitt & List, 2009).

Field experiments are often useful in studying the relationship between individual behavior and economic trends. One such experiment assessed the behavior of charitable donors. The author took interest in philanthropic giving when asked to assist in soliciting funds for a new economics department at the University of Central Florida. Dividing the pool of potential donors into several groups, the author determined that a donor would be more likely to contribute if he or she was informed by the solicitor that seed money had been invested by the University (List, 2008).

Whereas the Prisoner's Dilemma, for example, presents a scenario in which individual choices and strategies present a theoretical outcome, real-world situations do not always create such controlled settings. In a similar study of the philanthropic analysis

above, a 2007 essay looked into participant behavior in auctions. In a controlled laboratory setting, scientists would assume that there would be a fixed number of participants with predictable value based on the distribution of the materials on hand. They might even conclude that the revenue from that auction would be predictable based on a Nash equilibrium—a balance struck when two or more individuals' strategic decisions meet in such a way that the convergence of those strategies establish a common point.

Of course, such controlled circumstances lack an inclusion of a number of variables. For one, the rules of the auction might be such that individual strategies may differ or be adjusted, thereby effecting an alteration of bidding practices and revenue generation. Other factors may give rise to different predictive outcomes, such as increases in the number of bidders or a lack of information about the rules of the auction (Reiley & List, 2007).

As the above example suggests, field experiments should not be considered the alternative to laboratory studies within the experimental economics field. In fact, laboratory settings provide a strong theoretical foundation to a number of experimental subjects. Rather, field experiments are often seen as a valuable complement to the controlled environment of the laboratory, bringing to light previously unanticipated or variable elements that can have a significant impact on study outcomes.

CONCLUSION

Vernon L. Smith once commented on his inspiration for moving into the field of experimental economics. "I gradually became persuaded that the subjects, without intending to, had revealed to me a basic truth about markets that was foreign to the literature of economics" ("Vernon L. Smith quotes," 2009). Indeed, Smith and his mentor, Edward Chamberlin, saw that the constraints of traditional economics yielded useful theoretical information but fell short when the world evolved and economic systems grew more complex and less similar to those on which that literature was based.

As a result of this systemic evolution, Smith helped the study of economics evolve as well. He did not eschew theoretical or literature-based economics—he supplanted it and even helped validate much of it by fostering experimental economic methodologies. Over time, experimental economics techniques, such as the ones described in this essay, have demonstrated their worth not only for academic circles but for businesses and political leaders. Computer models and simulations and physical laboratories have created controlled settings for the careful study of the parts and subsystems that comprise larger issues. Additionally, the study of consumer choice and systemic operations is enhanced by the use of games and field experiments that help to predict trends and social developments for which the literature may not account. With the advent of a form of economic study that was considered radical as recently as the mid-twentieth century, economics has grown into a dynamic science that is as complex as the subject matter it studies.

BIBLIOGRAPHY

Bergmann, B.R. (2009). "The economy and the economics profession: Both need work." *Eastern Economic Journal, 35,* 2–9.

Charness, G., Gneezy, U., & Kuhn, M.A. (2013). "Experimental methods: Extra-laboratory experiments-extending the reach of experimental economics." *Journal of Economic Behavior & Organization, 91,* 93–100.

Davis, D.D. & Holt, C.A. (1993). *Experimental economics.* Princeton University Press. Retrieved from Google Booksxlink:href="http://books.google.com/books?id=mse-RpPIcc0C&printsec=frontcover"

Groves, V. (2008). "Interview with Charles Plott about experimental economics." California Institute of Technology. Retrieved from xlink:href="http://www.hss.caltech.edu/~cplott/interview08.pdf"

Koumparoulis, D. (2013). "Laboratory experimentation in economics." *Journal of Knowledge Management, Economics & Information Technology, 3,* 96–117.

Krakovsky, M. (2007, July 9). "Tech firms turn to experimental economics." *Wired.* Retrieved from xlink:href="http://www.wired.com/techbiz/it/news/2008/07/portfolio%5f0709"

Levitt, S.D. & List, J.A. (2009). "Field experiments in economics." *European Economic Review, 53,* 1–18.

List, J. (2017). "The past, present, and future of economics: A celebration of the 125-year anniversary of the JPE and of Chicago Economics." *Journal of Political Economy.*

List, J.A. (2008). "Using field experiments in the economics of charity. Retrieved from National Bureau of Economic Research." xlink:href="http://www.nber.org/reporter/2008number4/list.html"

Lynch, M.W. & Gillespie, N. (2002, October). "The experimental economist. *Reason* Online Version." Retrieved from xlink:href="http://www.reason.com/news/show/32546.html"

McCain, R.A. (2003). "The Prisoner's Dilemma." *Game Theory: A Nontechnical Introduction to the Analysis of Strategy.* Cincinnati, Ohio: South-Western College Publishing.

McKinney, C. N. & Roth, A.E. (2004). "Experimental economics." *Social science encyclopedia, 3rd edition.* London: Routledge.

Ouazad, A., & Page, L. (2013). "Students' perceptions of teacher biases: Experimental economics in schools." *Journal of Public Economics, 105,* 116–130.

Reiley, D.H. & List, J.A. (2007, May). *Field experiments in economics.* Retrieved from University of Arizona. xlink:href="http://econ.arizona.edu/downloads/working%5fpapers/Econ-WP-07-15.pdf"

Serendipity. (2009). Retrieved from Anecdotage. comxlink:href="http://www.anecdotage.com/index.php?aid=2308"

Vernon L. Smith quotes. (2009). Retrieved from Brainyquote.com xlink:href="http://www.brainyquote.com/quotes/quotes/v/vernonlsm289049.html"

SUGGESTED READING

Englebrecht-Wiggans, R. & Katok, E. (2007). "Regret in auctions: Theory and evidence." *Economic Theory, 33,* 81–101.

Fischbacher, U. & Stefani, U. (2007). "Strategic errors and audit quality: An experimental investigation." *Accounting Review, 82,* 679–704.

Samuelson, L. (2005). "Economic theory and experimental economics." *Journal of Economic Theory, 43,* 65–107.

Todd, K. (2007). "Beyond theory: Experimental economics." *Baylor Business Review, 25,* 40–41.

—Michael P. Auerbach

EXPORT-IMPORT OPERATIONS

ABSTRACT

Export-import operations are the actions and decisions necessary to take a product or raw material from a source in one country to a market in another. This article will discuss export-import operations as a three part process: pre-shipment, transport, and after-sale. Each of the three will be considered in turn from the perspective of business professionals attempting to expand their companies' interests across national boundaries. Export-import can be considerably more complex than doing business in a single, domestic market, but the realities of a globalizing economy are such that most companies and most people must increasingly deal across frontiers whether they wish to or not.

OVERVIEW

Export-import operations are in some ways a misnomer given that, in a globalized economy, the distinctions between domestic and foreign trade are ever more indefinite. However, for the purposes of this article, we can consider them to be the sum total of the tactical and strategic decisions and actions necessary to take a product from a source in one country to a market in another.

As such, export-import operations may be profitably considered a three-part process: 1) actions that occur before the actual shipment of the product, 2) those that relate to the shipment of the product to a customer, and 3) those that occur after the sale. For the sake of simplicity, this article will refer to them as pre-shipment, transfer, and after-sales.

Many businesses (particularly American) have historically avoided participation in international markets. However, the reality is that we dwell in an increasingly global economy. Even the smallest, most "domestic" transaction may involve suppliers of raw materials in one country, production in another, value-added remarketing in a third, and final consumption in a fourth. Ergo, every business professional must have some idea of the factors involved in international trade, simply because more and more business happens there (U.S. Department of Commerce).

APPLICATIONS

Pre-Shipment

While this taxonomy is in no way standard, export-import operations can be thought of as a three-part process. The first of these is *pre-shipment*—i.e., all operations that occur prior to the actual transport of the product or even prior to the sale. Thus, it is possible to regard as a legitimate part of pre-shipment operations even so fundamental a thing as determining a company's seriousness about entering the import/export business. Fortunately, one of the first tasks of pre-shipment is also an easy and effective way for managers to test their companies' ability and willingness to enter the import-export business. To wit, they must determine how willing their companies are to modify their products (or assist a supplier to do so) for foreign markets. It is useful, then, to keep in mind the (perhaps apocryphal but still instructive) story of the American automakers who complained of Tokyo's barriers to their imports but then declined to produce left-hand models of their cars when given a chance to enter the Japanese market.

If executives find that their companies and/or employers really are committed to import-export and get genuine buy-in from top management, then the next issue is channels. As in most other business

The Subaru Impreza was one of the first all-wheel drive cars on the market. Subaru is one of Japan's most popular car brands sold in the United States. (Courtesy of Tokumeigakarinoaoshima CC BY-SA 4.0 via Wikimedia Commons)

ventures, these boil down to just two—direct and indirect (Seyoum, 1998). The former is the option of companies that either have or are willing to invest in a sales force resident in the nations where they wish to do business. As such, it is often the best choice for larger companies with deeper pockets or that have some method of reaching individual consumers without a middleman. For example, the Internet, web-based sales, and direct package shipping companies (Federal Express, UPS, etc.) have given some companies the ability to directly address individual customers no matter how far away they might be.

If the exporting or importing company does not have a direct sales option, then indirect sales are the obvious alternative, and import-export sales channels range from the familiar to the quite exotic. The former consists of the distributors and resellers, not greatly different from those of any other indirect channel except that they may be based across national borders and must be handled with additional understanding of cultural differences. For example, a distributor located in a Muslim nation probably will not be available on Fridays, just as many American businesses do not operate on Sundays.

The more exotic, meanwhile, include specialist firms that do nothing but conduct international trade. The two most famed kinds of these, perhaps, are the export trading company (ETC) and export management company (EMC). An ETC, also called an international trade company (ITC), is a company that discovers customers in one nation, finds suppliers in another, purchases and takes title to products in the second country, and then arranges transport and sales to buyers in the first. EMCs are similar but do not take title to product and instead operate as a kind of outsourced export department for other companies (Seyoum, 1998). In addition, there are various modifications of these two models. For example, a number of manufacturers may band together to cooperatively export their products.

Until very recently, American exporters could also set up a foreign sales corporation (FSC), an export-oriented quasi-company based overseas. The benefit to the exporter was that the economic activity of the FSC was, in theory, conducted outside U.S. jurisdiction and therefore not as heavily taxed. However, the European Union objected on the grounds that this constituted an unfair trade advantage, the World Trade Organization concurred, and the U.S.

government finally abandoned the FSC ("FSCs agreement," 2006). In 2004, as part of the Jobs Act, a temporary measure to give a tax break to small and medium U.S. companies with foreign sales was introduced. The interest charge domestic international sales corporation (IC-DISC) federal tax incentive was extended for two more years in December 2010 but was allowed to expire at the end of 2012 (Thomas, 2012).

Lastly, the relative distance of customer from supplier means that managers doing international business need to be particularly careful about whom they sell to or buy from. It can be hard to collect an overdue account when the customer is not even on the same continent. Moreover, importers and exporters face a number of political problems. Americans, for example, cannot legally do business with a number of individuals or regimes around the world—those believed to be connected to terrorist organizations, for example. By like token, American businesses may be asked by some customers to honor boycotts against other buyers and sellers in third nations. Some nations, for example, have led a drive to boycott Israeli commercial interests. The U.S. government forbids its nationals to participate in such boycotts and, indeed, requires that requests to do so be reported to the proper authorities. For more on these and other issues regarding export controls, see the Department of Commerce's Bureau of Industry and Security website.

Transport

Transport is the actual process of moving a product from point A to point B as well as from country X to country Z. Transport across national borders is similar to any other problem in shipping. Indeed, most of the issues—logistics, deciding on proper modes of transport (bulk or piece, rail or air, etc.)—are identical. The major difference is that in international trade, goods cross frontiers, and the business professional has to consider a formidable host of additional documentation, tariff, and bureaucratic complexities.

Fortunately for the company that wishes to engage in transnational trade, there are many independent services and firms to assist navigating the logistical maze. These range from the ubiquitous package delivery services (which in recent years have added sophisticated logistics features to their core offerings)

Pictured are unloaded trucks on the right heading for the harbor cranes, while loaded trucks on left head out at Jawaharlal Nehru Trust Port in Navi Mumbai, India. The ship in the image is Xin Fu Zhou. (Courtesy of Jaxer at English Wikipedia CC BY 3.0 via Wikipedia Commons)

to more traditional freight forwarders. A freight forwarder is a firm or person who acts for the exporter or importer to ensure that shipments get from their sources to their destinations with a minimum of fuss. Forwarding is something of an arcane art, requiring its practitioners to be familiar with everything from the vagaries of international law to the mysteries of truck mechanics. As such, their services are invaluable, and even very large and very sophisticated corporations employ them rather than attempting to develop similar expertise in-house (Jones and Jones, 2004).

A similarly invaluable professional is the customs broker. A company employs the broker to manage a product's movement across national borders. The broker makes certain that the merchandise is properly classified, that taxes and duties are properly paid, and that any refunds owed to the company are remitted to it. Again, customs brokerage requires a unique set of skills—nothing that a company could not learn on its own but probably not worth the effort to obtain by a firm, whose core business is not customs brokerage.

However, the transnational executive does need to be aware of at least the broad outlines of international law and custom regarding international trade as well as American law on the subject. Since these all can change at the whim of parliaments and tax authorities, the executive must become a habitué

of the publications and websites of the relative parties. Regular visits to, for example, the websites of Export.gov, which works to link American companies to foreign partners, and the U.S. Department of Commerce's International Trade Administration, which provides information about investments that are worth making are suggested. Equally useful are subscriptions to various private information services, newsletters, and trade magazines that keep abreast of changing laws and situations.

In addition, the executive should keep in mind the grander scheme of things in international trade. This includes knowledge of the multinational organizations and regimes that tend to set the rules for the game—for example, the World Trade Organization (WTO). The WTO is perhaps the most important umpire in international trade today, but still executives must keep in mind regional trading and tariff zones. The North American Free Trade Agreement (NAFTA), which seeks to remove most tariffs and other trade barriers between Canada, the United States, and Mexico; the venerable European Union; the Association of Southeast Asian Nations (ASEAN); along with a number of other trade blocs can significantly impact a multinational's strategy. For instance, in the case of North America, selection of a vendor or subcontractor in a NAFTA member state can make all the difference between a profit and a loss to someone selling into another NAFTA member state.

After the September 11 terrorist attacks in 2001, security advocates pushed for tamper-proof shipping containers and more inspections at the ports of arriving cargo containers. Customs Trade Partnership Against Terrorism Guidelines were issued in November of that year, and all stakeholders in the importation business were invited to cooperate in a voluntary partnership to help reduce the inherent risk of terrorist violence being accomplished through more or less unsupervised ports. The Coast Guard instituted advance manifests for all containers bound for the United States, a measure that met opposition for slowing just-in-time shipping. By 2011, container traffic was still relatively free from regulation by national security agencies (Odoyo, 2011).

Equally important are finance and risk management. Transnational trade is, of course, inherently risky. When one sends merchandise overseas, they are to be subject to the whims of nature or foreign governments, and there is always a chance that ships will sink or cargo will be seized. As such, particularly smaller exporters and importers (but sometimes large as well) have had significant problems financing their operations. Banks and other lenders have simply not wanted to buy into the problems of international trade. Again, fortunately, governments have stepped in where private lenders have feared to tread or to trade. American exporters, for example, can take advantage of the Export-Import Bank (Ex-Im), which provides such things as working capital guarantees (pre-export financing); export credit insurance; and loan guarantees and direct loans. Ex-Im, in other words, does not compete with private lenders but will step in if there are none in sight and, preferably, assume enough of the risk of a failed transaction to make private lenders willing to become involved with exports.

After-Sale

After the sale, the chief concern of the importing company is to gain possession of the products it has bought. By contrast, the exporting company's chief concern is getting paid. Both can be somewhat less simple than might seem. For the company or individual importing goods into the United States, particularly after 9/11, moving products through customs can be time-consuming. Again, if the importer can afford it, then the services of a customs broker and/or freight forwarder are invaluable. If not, then the business professional must become proficient in the use of the Department of Homeland Security's Customs and Border Protection (CBP) webpage as well as the department's other publications and services. There, the reader can garner information on everything from the requirements for a customs broker's license to the wait times at major ports. Particularly important for the importer is the CBP website's section on import quotas—certain items, many textiles for example, are subject to import restrictions. As importantly, the individual who is moving cargo into the United States (or the other way) should make frequent visits to the U.S. International Trade Commission's (USITC) tariff database to determine the tariffs and other fees due on their products.

The exporter's goal of being paid, meanwhile, can also be complicated. A company based in the United States, for example, attempting to settle accounts with a firm located thousands of miles away in a nation with a radically different legal system that may or may

Tape used by U.S. Customs and Border Protection to reseal packages that they have searched, and to indicate that they have done so. (Courtesy of Tpdwkouaa CC BY-SA 4.0 via Wikimedia Commons)

not have special or even familial connections with the government, is not in an enviable position. However, there are resources at hand. First, of course, the American firm should not have done business without doing a diligent background and credit check on the potential partner ("Background," 2006). Second, even if it had, the exporting company might find considerable benefits in seeking ways of reducing its risk. Letters of credit (LOCs) are thus a mainstay of international trade. Also known as documentary credit, an LOC is issued by a bank or other financial institution as a guarantee that a debt owned by a client of that institution will, in fact, be paid. If the client can't make the payment, the institution provides the necessary funds. Thus, in a transaction backed up by an LOC, the seller can rest assured that, so long as the buyer's bank is solvent, its bill will be paid.

Also useful are the services of factors and forfeiters. These sorts of companies, in effect, purchase other businesses' accounts receivable at a discount. The exporter thus gets its money up front and off-loads any difficulties in the collection to the factor or forfeiter. (A factor and a forfeiter perform the same function. However, a factor tends to be a company that is in business to do nothing but factoring. A forfeiter may be, for example, a banker or another financial professional who puts together the resources for a one-time deal.)

Another middleman that importers and exporters may need to consult is the countertrade specialist. In recent years, multinational deals have been increasingly structured around barter or the premise that if a customer in country A is to buy something from an exporter in country B, then the exporter must also buy something from country A or at least take one of country A's products as payment. This means that an exporter of farm equipment, for example, may find itself in possession of large amounts of sugar or copper ore. The exporter can then attempt to market these materials itself or, as is rather more likely, will turn to one of the many countertrade management specialists who will handle the transaction for a fee or commission.

Currency value is yet another factor to consider. The transnational business professional faces the grim fact that a price negotiated yesterday in pounds or dollars may not be worth the same thing tomorrow in yen or euros. Again, fortunately, there are specialists who can offer some relief. Many banks and other financial institutes can offer access to hedging deals, whereby a set price for one currency can be locked in for a transaction to take place at some specified future date.

CONCLUSION

Thus, to restate, export-import operations can be defined as all those actions that are required to take goods and services from producers in one country to customers in another. These can be grouped into three distinct sorts of acts and decisions: pre-shipment, transfer, and after-sales. Pre-shipment is everything up to the actual transport of products and services. It includes even such fundamental things as determining the willingness and ability of a firm to export, learning the ins and outs of international trade, and deciding on the appropriate sales channel (viz., direct, indirect, etc.).

Transfer is, of course, the actual shipment of goods. This is almost identical to shipping in domestic sales except that the exporter-importer faces much additional documentation, tariff, and bureaucratic difficulties. To deal with these, the business professional may wish to turn to the host of independent services and firms that exist to make business across national frontiers less complex—freight forwarders, customs brokers, and so on. However, traders should also keep well informed of international regulations and practices, something they can do with regular visits to U.S. and other governmental websites dealing with international trade.

Finally, after-sales is everything that happens once an imported or exported good has arrived at its destination. For importers, this means gaining access to their purchases. Once again, the services of a licensed customs broker are invaluable. However, the importer who cannot afford one or who merely wishes to be well-informed about the process can go to the Department of Homeland Security's Customs and Border Protection webpage, as well as the Department's other publications and services, for additional information.

The exporter, meanwhile, is chiefly interested in being paid. Traditionally, international trading has been done with letters of credit (LOCs). However, factors and forfeiters (companies that purchase the accounts receivable of other companies) can also be important partners for any professional in the import and export business.

Quite simply, import-export is risky. The fact of the matter is that any time one does business across oceans or national boundaries, one faces dangers ranging from shipwrecks to civil wars. Yet, in an economy that is now worldwide, anyone in business anywhere is ever more doing business across borders. As such, it is no longer a question of whether or not one is going to enter the "international" market but rather how one may prosper in a "domestic" market that stretches from Siberia to Tasmania.

BIBLIOGRAPHY

"Background checks reduce risk of int'l partnerships." (2006). *Managing Exports & Imports, 2006*, 1–15.

A basic guide to exporting. (1998). U.S. Department of Commerce with the assistance of Unz & Co., Inc.

"FSCs agreement breaks out." (2006). *Accountancy, 137*(1354), 107–107.

Jones, D. and Jones, S. (2004). "Coping with licensing and customs." *Export Wise*, Spring 2004, 14–15.

Odoyo, S. (2011). "The effects of U.S. anti-terrorist laws on international business and trade." *Syracuse Journal of International Law & Commerce, 38*, 257–294.

Oliadnichuk, N., Pidlubna, O. (2017). "Accounting of export-import operations." *Ideas*, 1, 48–56.

Seyoum, B. (2000). *Export-Import: Theory, practices, and procedures*. New York: International Business Press.

Thomas, M. K. (2012). "IC-DISC offers tax advantages for closely held export companies." *Tax Adviser, 43*, 509–510.

United States Department of Commerce Spokesperson, Personal Communication, April 13, 2007.

Suggested Reading

Aristei, D., Castellani, D., & Franco, C. (2013). "Firms' exporting and importing activities: Is there a two-way relationship?" *Review Of World Economics, 149*, 55–84.

Fast. (2006). *Managing Exports & Imports, 2006*, 9.

Morris, L. (2007). "Shipping out." *Incentive*, 32–35.

Online trade resource: "Tradestats express." (2007) *Managing Exports & Imports, 2007*, 8.

—Michael Jay Tucker

F

FINANCIAL AND ECONOMIC TIME SERIES

ABSTRACT

In order to meet the ever-changing needs of the marketplace, industry, and other factors affecting the organization, managers need to estimate or predict future trends. This practice often involves the analysis of time series data—data gathered on a specific characteristic over a period of time. The goal of time series data analysis is to build a model that will allow managers or other decision makers to forecast future needs so that they can develop an appropriate strategy. There are a number of techniques available to forecast stationary time series data, but their application is part art and part science. Even in the simplest situations, one must determine which variables to include in the model and which variables to exclude. Several approaches are available for building time series models. These include moving average models, autoregressive techniques, and integrated techniques that incorporate both approaches in the manipulation and analysis of time series data.

OVERVIEW

American philosopher George Santayana said that those who cannot learn from history are doomed to repeat it. Although time and time again this truism is proven in political arenas, it has applicability in other areas, too. Certainly, businesses can learn from the past. Understanding the effects of trends, business cycles, seasonal fluctuations, and irregular or random events on the needs of the marketplace or the trajectory of the industry can help businesses better position themselves to leverage this knowledge into a better market position and enable themselves to predict coming needs and remain competitive in the marketplace. This process is called forecasting: the science of estimating or predicting future trends. Forecasts are used to support managers in making decisions about many aspects of the business including buying, selling, production, and hiring. Although there are purely judgmental approaches to forecasting available that depend on the expertise and experience of the manager, statistical techniques that build data-driven models and help forecast trends, seasonality, and patterns can help quantify the variables causing such fluctuations. Most of these techniques require the use of time series data.

Time Series Data

Time series data are data gathered on a specific characteristic over a period of time. Time series data are used in business forecasting to examine patterns, trends, and cycles from the past in order to predict patterns, trends, and cycles in the future. Time series methods include naïve methods, averaging, smoothing, regression analysis, and decomposition. These techniques are used in the forecasting of future trends or needs in decision-making about many aspects of the business including buying, selling, production, and hiring.

Time series data are data gathered on a specific characteristic over a period of time. To be useful for forecasting, time series data must be collected at intervals of regular length. In time series analysis, the sequence of observations is assumed to be a set of jointly distributed random variables. Unlike the ad hoc approach to forecasting where it is impossible to tell whether or not the formula chosen is the most appropriate for the situation, in time series analysis one can study the structure of the correlation (i.e., the degree to which two events or variables are consistently related) over time to determine the appropriateness of the model.

The primary reason for the analysis of times series data is to be able to understand and predict patterns. Time series analysis typically involves observing and analyzing the patterns of historical data in order to extrapolate past trends into future forecasts. To do this, most statistical analysis of time series data involves model building, which is the development of a concise mathematical description of past events. These models, in turn, are used to forecast how the pattern will continue into the future.

Deterministic & Stochastic Variables

There are two types of variables involved in time series data and analysis: deterministic and stochastic. Deterministic variables are those for which there are specific causes or determiners. These include trends, business cycles, and seasonal fluctuations. Trends are persistent, underlying directions in which a factor or characteristic is moving in either the short, intermediate, or long term. Most trends are linear rather than cyclic and grow or shrink steadily over a period of years. An example of a trend would be the increasing tendency to outsource and offshore technical support and customer service within many high-tech companies. Not all trends are linear, however. Trends in new industries tend to be curvilinear as the demand for the new product or service grows after its introduction and then declines after the product or service becomes integrated into the economy. A second type of deterministic factor is business cycles. These are continually recurring variations in total economic activity. Business cycles tend to occur across most sectors of the economy at the same time. For example, several years of a boom economy with expansion of economic activity (e.g., more jobs, higher

Super-storm Sandy caused widespread power outages in New York City. (Courtesy of Hybirdd via Wikimedia Commons)

sales) are often followed by slower growth or even contraction of economic activity. Business cycles may occur not only across one industry or business sector but also across the economy in general. A third type of deterministic factor is seasonal fluctuations. These are changes in economic activity that occur in a fairly regular annual pattern and are related to seasons of the year, the calendar, or holidays. For example, office supply stores experience an upsurge in business in August as children receive their school supply lists for the coming year. Similarly, the demand for heating oil is greater during the cool months than it is in the warm months.

Stochastic variables, on the other hand, are those that are caused by randomness or include an element of chance or probability. Stochastic variables include both irregular and random fluctuations in the economy that occur due to unpredictable factors. Examples of irregular variables include natural disasters such as earthquakes or floods, political disturbances such as war or a change in the political party in charge, strikes, and other external factors. Other unpredictable or random factors that can affect a business's profitability include situations such as high absenteeism due to an epidemic.

A simple example of a stochastic time series is the random walk process. This is based on an investment theory that claims that market prices follow a random path up and down and are not influenced by past price movements. This theory concludes that it is impossible to predict the direction of the market with any degree of accuracy, particularly in the short term. In the random walk process, each successive change

A Back-to-School sale at Walmart in Newburgh, New York, that always brings in more customers during the months of August and September. (Courtesy of Daniel Case CC BY-SA 3.0 via Wikimedia Commons)

is independently drawn form a probability distribution with a mean of zero. The simplest example of a time series is one that is completely random (i.e., has no recognizable pattern).

Forecasting in the real world typically involves many variables. Although in theory a purely deterministic model is possible, the complexity of real world problems usually results in situations involving both deterministic and stochastic variables. Business and economic problems usually involve unknown variables or uncontrollable factors. As a result, most time series in the business world are stochastic in nature.

Stationarity

Another characteristic of time series is stationarity. This condition exists when the probability distribution of a time series does not change over time. Stationarity is of interest to analysts because when one can assume that the underlying stochastic process is invariant with respect to time (i.e., stationary), then one can mathematically model the process with an equation with fixed coefficients that estimate future values from past history. If the process is assumed to be stationary, that probability of a given fluctuation in the process is assumed to be the same at any given point in time (i.e., invariant with respect to time). If, on the other hand, the process is non-stationary, it is difficult to mathematically model the process using a simple algebraic equation. Unfortunately, few processes of interest in business and economics are truly stationary. However, it is often possible to use a simple mathematical procedure to transform non-stationary processes into ones that are approximately stationary for purposes of analysis.

APPLICATIONS

Using time series data in econometric model building is part art and part science. Even in the simplest situations, one must determine which variables to include in the model and which variables to exclude. The goal of time series data analysis is to build a model that will allow managers or other decision makers to forecast future needs. There are several steps in developing time series models. First, one must specify the parameters of the model. Decisions to be made at this stage include the degree of homogeneity in the time series and the order of the moving average and autoregressive components of the analysis. After the model has been specified, it must be estimated. This is frequently done using nonlinear regression. The next step is to examine the autocorrelation function using a simple chi-square test to determine whether the residuals are uncorrelated. The parameter estimates should also be checked at this point to determine whether they appear to be stationary. The model must next be evaluated to determine whether or not it can be used to make accurate forecasts. This can be done through such methods as historical simulation starting at different points of time. Model building is an iterative process. If the model is not successful at this point, it can be manipulated to better represent the real-world situation.

Techniques for Forecasting Stationary Time Series Data

There are a number of techniques available to forecast stationary time series data (i.e., those that show no significant trend, cyclic, or seasonal effects). Different approaches, however, often yield different results. To help determine which forecast better models a given set of data, the forecaster needs to determine the amount of forecasting error produced by each technique. Error is the difference between the forecasted value of a variable and the actual value of a variable. Techniques for measuring error include mean error, mean absolute deviation, mean square error, mean percentage error, and mean absolute percentage error.

Naïve Forecasting Models

Several types of techniques are used to smooth out irregular fluctuation effects in time series data. Naïve forecasting models offer one approach to smoothing. These are simple models that assume that the best predictors of future outcomes are the more recent data in the time series. This assumption means that naïve forecasting models do not consider the possibility of trends, business cycles, or seasonal fluctuations. As a result, the naïve forecasting models work better on data that are reported more frequently (e.g., daily or weekly) or in situations without trends or seasonality. For example, if ten gross of widgets were sold last month, a naïve model would conclude that ten gross of widgets would also be sold next month. However, since naïve model forecasts are often based on the observations of one time period, they can easily become a function of irregular fluctuations in data (e.g., Acme corporation needed a one-time purchase of widgets to set up their new operations facility, which accounts for the one-time high demand for widgets in the previous month).

Averaging Models

Another approach to smoothing time series data uses averaging models. This approach helps neutralize the problem of naïve models in which the forecast is overly sensitive to irregular fluctuations as illustrated in the previous example. In averaging models, the data from several time periods are taken into account. In the simple average model, the forecast for the upcoming time period is the average of the values for a specified number of previous time periods. For example, the forecast of widgets sales for next month might be the average number of widgets sold per month over the past six months. Moving averages, on the other hand, not only use the average value from previous time periods to forecast future time periods but also update this average in each ensuing time period by including the new values not available in the previous average and dropping out the date from the earliest time periods. Although this approach has the advantage of taking into account the most recent data available, it can be difficult to choose the optimal length of time over which to compute the moving average. In addition, moving averages do not take in to account the effects of trends, business cycles, and seasonal fluctuations. To help overcome some of the problems inherent in moving averages, the analyst may use a weighted moving average that gives more weight to some time periods in the series than to others. For example, if three months ago Widget Corporation introduced their redesigned product to the marketplace, the analyst might believe that the past three months reflect the market's reaction to the new design and be better able to forecast the continuing reaction than if s/he did not have this information. In addition to naïve and averaging approaches to smoothing time series data, there are exponential smoothing techniques. The techniques use weight data from previous time periods with exponentially decreasing importance. In other words, the new forecast is a product of the current forecast and the current actual value.

Determining Trends Using Time Series Data

Although these approaches to time series modeling can be helpful for simple data sets, they do not account well for trends. However, there are several approaches to analyzing time series data to determine the influence of long-term changes in the business climate. Two of the simplest of these approaches are linear regression and regression using quadratic models. In order for these methods to produce accurate forecasts, however, the time series data cannot be influenced by seasonal fluctuations. If it is assumed that there is a seasonal effect influencing the time series data, other techniques must be used. One frequently used technique is decomposition, in which the time series data are broken down into the four component factors of trend, business cycle, seasonal fluctuation, and irregular or random fluctuation.

Time series models can produce spurious results when the error terms of the model are correlated with each other. This situation is referred to as autocorrelation or serial correlation. Autocorrelation causes problems in the use of regression analysis because regression analysis assumes that error terms are not correlated because they are either independent or random. When autocorrelation occurs, the estimates of the regression coefficients may be inefficient. In addition, both the variance of the error terms and the true standard deviation may be significantly underestimated because of their effect. Also, autocorrelation means that the confidence intervals and t and F tests are no longer strictly applicable. There are, however, a number of ways to determine whether or not autocorrelation is present in time series data (e.g., the Durbin-Watson test). Ways to correct for auto-correlated data include the addition of independent variables and by transforming variables.

Auto-Regression Time Series Modeling

Another approach to modeling time series data is auto-regression. This is a multiple regression technique used in forecasting in which future values of the variable are predicted from past values of the variable. Auto-regression takes advantage of the relationship of values to the values of previous time periods. In this approach, the independent variables are time-lagged versions of the dependent variable. In other words, one tries to forecast a future value of a variable from knowledge of that variable's value in previous time periods. This can be done for multiple previous time periods. This approach can be useful for locating both seasonal and cyclic effects.

Integrated Techniques

In addition to moving average and autoregressive models, times series data can be modeled using mixed or integrated techniques that utilize both approaches. One of these approaches to model fitting is the autoregressive integrated moving average (ARIMA) model (also called the Box-Jenkins model). This is an integrated tool for understanding and forecasting using time series data. An ARIMA model has both an autoregressive and a moving average component. Although ARIMA modeling techniques can be difficult to compute and interpret, they are powerful and frequently result in a better model than either the use of moving averages or autoregressive techniques alone. Specifically, ARIMA can be used to determine the length of the weights (i.e., how much of the past should be used to predict the next observation) and the values of these weights. Random walk, autoregressive models, and exponential models are special cases of ARIMA models.

BIBLIOGRAPHY

Arestis, P., Luintel, A. D., & Luintel, K. B. (2010). "Financial structure and economic growth: Evidence from time series analyses." *Applied Financial Economics, 20,* 1479–1492.

Black, K. (2006). *Business statistics for contemporary decision making* (4th ed.). New York: John Wiley & Sons.

Keho, Y. (2010). "Effect of financial development on economic growth: Does inflation matter? time series evidence from the UEMOA countries." *International Economic Journal, 24,* 343–355.

Nazem, S. M. (1988). *Applied time series analysis for business and economic forecasting.* New York: Marcel Dekker.

Pindyck, R. S. & Rubinfeld, D. L. (1998). *Econometric models and economic forecasts.* Boston: Irwin/McGraw-Hill.

Rodrigues, P. M., Rubia, A., & Valle e Azevedo, J. (2013). "Finite sample performance of frequency- and time-domain tests for seasonal fractional integration." *Journal of Statistical Computation & Simulation, 83,* 1373–1384.

SUGGESTED READING

Armstrong, J. S. & Collopy, F. (1998). "Integration of statistical methods and judgment for time series forecasting: Principles from empirical research." In Wright, G. & Goodwin, P. (Eds.). *Forecasting with Judgment.* New York: John Wiley & Sons.

Dauten, C. A. & Valentine, L. M. (1978). *Business cycles and forecasting* (5th ed.). Cincinnati: South-Western Publishing Co.

Di Giacinto, V. (2006). "A generalized space-time ARMA model with an application to regional unemployment analysis in Italy." *International Regional Science Review, 29,* 159–198.

Makridakis, S. & Wheelwright, S. C. (1982). "Introduction to management forecasting: Status and needs." In Makridakis, S. & Wheelwright, S. C. (Eds.). *The Handbook of Forecasting: A Manager's Guide.* New York: John Wiley & Sons.

Morrell, J. (2001). *How to forecast: A guide for business.* Burlington, VT: Gower.

Nelson, C. R. (1973). *Applied time series analysis for managerial forecasting.* San Francisco: Holden-Day.

Wynne, B. E. & Hall, D. A. (1982). "Forecasting requirements for operations planning and control." In Makridakis, S. & Wheelwright, S. C. (Eds.). *The Handbook of Forecasting: A Manager's Guide.* New York: John Wiley & Sons.

—*Ruth A. Wienclaw, PhD*

FINANCIAL GLOBALIZATION

ABSTRACT

This paper reviews the central themes and concepts of one manifestation of the globalization trend: financial globalization. In addition to casting light on its fundamentals, this article also provides insight into the positive and negative implications of financial globalization on the international community.

OVERVIEW

Beginning in the last two decades of the twentieth century, there has been a worldwide trend of international commercial activities operating beyond borders and the confines of national government-imposed regulations. Enterprises increasingly began looking for and establishing links to business partners in other countries. To be sure, international commerce has been a staple of human history, although intergovernmental trade agreements were considerably different than the business contracts of today.

Globalization has undergone an evolution of sorts, accelerating in growth and volume, particularly with the evolution of technologies that serve its needs and effectively make the notion of globalization's indefinite continuation inevitable. As former UN Secretary General Kofi Annan once said, "It has been said that arguing against globalization is like arguing against the laws of gravity" ("Kofi Annan quotes," 2009).

Indeed, the speed at which globalization has developed over a relatively short time corresponds with the suggestion that it is a powerful force of nature, one whose strength continues to build rather than subside. It is therefore important to understand the elements and trends that give it life. This paper reviews the central themes and concepts of one manifestation of this trend: financial globalization. In addition to casting light on its fundamentals, this article also provides insight into the positive and negative implications of financial globalization on the international community.

Understanding Financial Globalization

Financial globalization can be defined as the linkages created from cross-border financial flows.

Globalization is closely linked to another trend, financial integration, in which myriad national and regional markets merge into one single international entity (Prasad, et al, 2003). As has occurred in other studies, these terms shall be used interchangeably in this paper in light of their close connections. Such trends are significant, as they present a shift away from commerce on a nation-state basis and toward a more private, super-national network.

Super-national networks serve several important purposes:

- First, they make available and accessible the funds to be used for development loans (Arestis, Basu & Mallick, 2009). This is so because within such a large financial marketplace, greater opportunities exist for developing nations to tap into international development funds.
- The second purpose is akin to the first, in that the quality of living of developing nations, having been influenced by the same financial systems that strengthened industrialized countries, stands to improve as a result of this manifestation of globalization.
- The third of these purposes is one of global stability—by centralizing global financial systems, adverse systemic shocks may be mitigated (Federal Reserve Bank of New York, 2004).

This paper explores these three purposes in greater detail. However, it is first important to review the history of financial globalization in the modern world and how it led to the evolving system of financial integration prevalent in the twenty-first century.

A Brief History of Financial Globalization

Financial globalization is hardly a new concept in human history. During the latter nineteenth century, it was particularly commonplace because of the gold standard (the practice by which currencies were converted into gold at fixed prices per ounce), which was set by Great Britain and the United States. The fact that the British Empire was the dominant developer in the world also contributed to the centralization of various national financial systems: the Bank of England was the central lender in British

Headquarters of the Bank of England viewed from Lombard Street. (Courtesy of Diliff CC BY-SA 3.0 via Wikimedia Commons)

development efforts in Australia, India, Africa, the Americas, and other regions. As such, developing nations looked to the central, globalized British Empire to conduct any international financial business (Tobin, 1998).

The events of the early twentieth century turned this environment on its ear. The British central financial system was virtually destroyed during World War I and never returned to its pre–twentieth century form following the Great Depression and World War II. Instead, in the absence of a central banking authority for other countries, the international community fractured into a vast tapestry of independent nations, each developing its own currencies and converting against a myriad of other currencies. During the latter twentieth century, several regional economic powers grew to prominence, centralizing currency and gold exchanges based on three currencies: the U.S. dollar, the German mark, and the Japanese yen.

Coinciding with the nationalization (and later regionalization) of currency and financial transactions during the early to mid-twentieth century was the development of regulatory protections that were designed to promote stability of a given country's economic interests. Such measures, however, limited expedient growth, often isolated economies, and even created regional crises when exchange rates faltered (as was the case in Mexico and Southeast Asia during the 1990s and Argentina in the early 2000s).

Meanwhile, the three major regional currencies (the dollar, the mark, and the yen) began liberalizing their own exchange protocols, allowing for floating exchange rates rather than fixed ones. Doing so created greater stability among these currencies and

those countries that were linked to them. Continued liberalization of monetary regulatory schemes also proved enticing to those countries wishing to obtain development monies in order to build or rebuild their own economic infrastructures. As this paper next discusses, there are benefits as well as negative consequences to liberalized and globalized financial transactions—a trend that continues to grow in the twenty-first-century economic regime.

Development

In 1944, the European theater was devastated by war; the infrastructures of virtually every major country were crippled. The International Bank for Reconstruction (more popularly known as the "World Bank") was established at the Bretton Woods economic conference for the purposes of providing financing for those countries affected by this conflict. The bank would also serve a long-term purpose: provision of low-interest, long-term loans to developing countries around the world. Over time, the bank grew in membership, whose dues helped finance these loans (along with the sale of its securities), to more than 180 countries ("The World Bank," 2009).

As its name would suggest, the World Bank has worked to provide its loans worldwide but under a set of member guidelines subject to the bank's governance. Under a condition of such strict infrastructure and economic system management, the World

The view from the roof of St Paul's Cathedral towards the Old Bailey after the second Great Fire of London during WW II on January 3, 1941. The devastation is widespread. (Courtesy of H. Mason via Wikimedia Commons)

Bank's form of financial aid has proven very effective in aiding development since its introduction.

It is interesting to note that while the bank enables developing countries to rebuild their financial institutions and systems, globalization has spurred similarly developing countries and the regions to do so on their own. In fact, some experts argue, the economic development that has occurred naturally in a number of regions was done more quickly than was the development of World Bank–sponsored development.

Financial globalization has fostered this dynamic environment for two important reasons. First, whereas the World Bank and International Monetary Fund (IMF) have strict boundaries and regulations governing development, regional financial globalization tends to liberalize lending and development spending policies. Such liberalization means fewer administrative expenses and a greater degree of competition among financial lenders (as opposed to the singularity of the Bank and IMF). This means that securing development funds from a regional, nongovernmental organization equals less cost to the developing country in question.

The second reason for non–World Bank development is the fact that less regulation and restrictive policies have been shown to result in higher rates of regional integration and development. In one study, for example, the regions of East Asia and Latin America were analyzed in terms of their rates of development. Latin America, in its pursuit of regional development through integration, has engaged in formal intergovernmental treaties established under strict rules and guidelines. East Asia, on the other hand, did not employ as many formal agreements, largely due to the fact that its integrative efforts began before such regional agreements were the norm for distributing development loan monies.

The degree of informality and liberal monetary policy in the East Asian region activities has in fact allowed for financial market integration to occur at a faster rate, according to the study, than was the case in Latin America. Development, naturally, also occurred at a faster rate among these countries, as did political relationships. This latter point is important—with market integration already in place, political relationships are formed more readily and with greater strength because of the preexisting relationships (Aminian, Fung & Ng, 2009).

Of course, less formalized and structured development relationships have their risks in an era of financial globalization. At the 1997 Annual Meetings of the IMF, an economist presented to the participants his observations of the successes of financial globalization based on liberalized capital movement policy. Another economist, who had previously advocated for financial controls in international relationship building, commented on controls applied to capital transfers as "an idea whose time has passed," saying that the "correct answer to the question of capital mobility is that it ought to be unrestricted" (Rodrick & Subramanian, 2008).

Unfortunately, these comments were made shortly before the Asian financial crisis of 1997. The lack of governance of financial markets, the free flow of unregulated development money and a lack of market evaluation and risk assessment created widespread destabilization of both regional currencies and markets. Ironically, in an era of liberalized capital flow preferences, it was the IMF, whose mission it is to safeguard the international monetary system from such crises, that was called in to infuse approximately US$35 billion into the hardest-hit countries, while at the same time imposing new regulations and infrastructure redevelopments, in an effort to mitigate the crisis (IMF, 1999).

As shown above, the liberal policies attached to financial globalization do present great potential for fostering development. There are risks involved, to be sure, with eschewing the regulatory oversight of national economic systems. Striking a balance between the two regimes is a challenge that the international economic community strives to overcome as the trend of globalization continues in the twenty-first century.

Improving Quality of Life

Part of the pursuit of economic development entails the quest for a better way of life. Market integration is largely seen as a great opportunity to improve the quality of living for the developing nation's people. Such a development helps both parties involved, a point that becomes evident when one looks at the emerging market economy as a potential target for inclusion in a financially integrated relationship.

An emerging market economy can be defined as a system (or collection thereof) that is less than fully developed but contains the qualities that are enticing

The United Nations Commission of Inquiry on North Korea formally presented its report to the Human Rights Council March 17, 2014. The image shows the three commissioners: Michael Donald Kirby (Chair; Australia), Marzuki Darusman, (the existing Special Rapporteur on the situation of human rights in the DPRK; Indonesia), and Sonja Biserko (Serbia). The Commission of Inquiry found evidence of systematic, gross and widespread human rights violations in North Korea. (Courtesy of U.S. Mission Geneva/ Eric Bridiers via Wikimedia Commons)

to international investors. It has proven difficult for economists and policy makers to clearly identify such economies, as there are a great many factors that may play a role in enticing investment from foreign entities, such as natural resources, human capital, geography, and market stability.

A potential investor may be enticed by such factors and may, in the same vein, be turned away should any of these elements prove unsatisfactory or non-conducive to creating a palatable return. It is therefore optimal that the developing economic system (and the national system that supports it) demonstrates such systemic benefits. One study of the emerging market economy emphasizes two basic arenas.

- The first is that of the economic infrastructure: A system that does not contain overly intrusive or dominating regulatory precepts is less susceptible to corruption and/or has reasonable taxation laws and investment potential.
- The second is the human factor: A national system that has a demonstrated lack of emphasis on human rights or is enmeshed in conflict is less enticing for foreign-based developed financial systems (Das, 2004).

In this vein, a developing country with the potential to become an emerging market economy will tend to adopt policies and infrastructural frameworks that

are conducive to international market integration, allowing for more liberal regulatory systems as well as more emphasis on human rights, diplomacy, and social improvements (such as care for the poor and disenfranchised populations). There may also be increased investment in such arenas as environmental cleanup and protection, health care, workforce development, and modern technology (Watson, 2008).

Negative Implications & Perceptions

While it is clear that financial globalization is a trend of commerce that will likely continue to develop in the twenty-first century, there are aspects to its ongoing evolution that pose risks to those whose interests are merged with others. Additionally, there are perceptions of this trend that cite the negative aspects of globalization. It is to these issues that this paper next turns.

The first of these negative consequences is one that is quantifiable and finds its causes at the very foundation of globalization. In order to facilitate the linkage of systems beyond the parameters of national economic frameworks, financial globalization entails a more lax application of protocols than would be manifest in interstate commercial activities. The absence of such regulations facilitates higher quantities of monies to transfer between systems, enables the establishment of corporate development at a quicker rate, and even enables the companies themselves to operate with the potential to save on expenses (such as taxes and regulatory and licensing fees). On the other hand, such an absence of controls also means fewer market protections and safeguards should instability occur.

The case of the 1997 Asian financial crisis described earlier illustrates this issue. To be sure, Asian countries stood to benefit from the loosening of financial regulations, as integration and capital mobility (which can be defined as the degree to which investors may infuse or remove their money from a given system) more readily occurred as a result. Then again, the pressure to integrate in an expedited manner also raised risks based on the manner by which integration occurred. It is believed that institutional pressures for integration in East Asia led to disregard for the system-specific impacts such integration might have on the various developing and industrialized systems involved (Eichengreen, 1999). In fact, the crisis led to suggestions that financial globalization may undermine a country's ability to intervene during an economic downturn. At the very least, the issue underscored a perceived need for financial globalization to occur in such a way that allows the creation of safety nets to prevent market collapse.

The second of these issues is less tangible but nonetheless considered a viable risk posed by financial globalization. As stated earlier, market integration and capital mobility may be facilitated when the merging systems demonstrate a desire for social justice, environmental protection, and civil stability. However, the efforts of a given country to make such adjustments may seem, on the surface, innocuous but can have a significant impact on the society. For example, in the course of facilitating financial integration, countries may be selective in terms of the changes they make relative to human rights. Additionally, the benefits of financial globalization may be localized among a select social segment or geographic location rather than widespread.

The example of the Asian crisis again provides an illustration of this point. When the crisis occurred, unemployment surged, as did suicide rates and poverty. However, concurrent with these social issues was a diminished investment in social welfare programs (Ji, 2007). Such social services might have been in place if given a higher priority in the government modifications enacted prior to the crisis.

These two issues demonstrate that financial globalization and market integration, while clearly beneficial on a number of levels, also introduce risks, particularly for those systems that are ill-equipped to adjust accordingly.

CONCLUSION

Then UN secretary general Kofi Annan made a valid point when he suggested that the trend of globalization was akin to a force of nature. Indeed, globalization developed out of commercial interest and has continued to spread and evolve at a speed that even a series of financial crises could not halt.

Globalization has occurred in a number of areas, drawing together participants to address a wide range of issues in a forum that is framed outside of the governmental setting. As a result of this nongovernmental atmosphere, political and regulatory interference is less likely, thereby streamlining the efforts at hand. Because of this condition, information, ideas, and even money are more expeditiously (and sometimes in greater quantities) transferred between participants.

As demonstrated in this paper, financial globalization is no exception to this trend. With the absence of a number of interstate commercial controls, many relationships built under such a regime see strong economic returns at a faster rate. The notion of such returns is enticing for any participating country, from industrialized nations looking to develop resources and assets in systems with rich resources but onerous operating conditions to developing nations seeking aid monies to build their own market economies. The promise of market and economic integration, which is an important part of financial globalization, and the potential returns it represents only make globalization more of the seemingly "unstoppable" force suggested by Annan.

To be sure, there are risks involved with pursuing the transfer of capital across nongovernmental lines via liberalized protocols. As this paper has demonstrated, the East Asian financial crisis of 1997 provided an example of how a lack of regulatory oversight could create a market freefall. On the heels of that incident, a number of experts and leaders called for government bailouts and Keynesian policies designed to allow the government and/or the IMF to impose safeguards and regulatory measures so that such crises can be avoided in the future.

Financial globalization has reached a critical stage in its evolution. Few involved parties wish to see a return to the application of burdensome regulations, taxes, and policies, but situations like the Mexican peso crisis of the late 1990s and even the worldwide recession that began in 2008 have given rise to talk of revisiting financial globalization in its current form. Liang (2012) argues that financial globalization has been a major factor in both global imbalances and financial fragility. The ability of borrowers and lenders to shop among both foreign and domestic projects and funding sources resulted in the accumulation of cross-border debt, which Lane (2012) asserts was one of the major concerns in the run-up to the 2008 financial crisis.

BIBLIOGRAPHY

Aminian, N., Fung, K. & Ng, F. (2009). "A comparative analysis of trade and economic integration in

East Asia and Latin America." *Economic Change and Restructuring, 2*(½), 105–137.

Arestis, P., Basu, S. & Mallick, S. "Financial globalization: The need for single currency and a global central bank. University of Connecticut." Retrieved from xlink:href="http://ideas.repec.org/a/mes/postke/v27y2005i3p507-531.html"

Asongu, S. A. (2012). "Globalization, financial crisis and contagion: time - dynamic evidence from financial markets of developing countries." *Journal of Advanced Studies In Finance, 3*, 131–139.

Das, D. K. (2004). *Financial globalization and the emerging market economies.* Routledge. Retrieved from Google Booksxlink:href="http://books.google.com/books?id=5AVUxdfrYoYC&dq=globalization+"

Eichengreen, B.J. (1999). "The global gamble on financial liberalization." *Ethics and International Affairs, 13,* 205–226.

International Monetary Fund. (1999, January). "The IMF's response to the Asian crisis." Retrieved from xlink:href="http://www.imf.org/External/np/exr/facts/asia.htm"

Ji, Y.C. (2007). "Financial crises from the perspective of human rights." *Conference Papers—International Studies Association,* 1–28.

Kant, C. (2017). "Financial openness & inquisitions in developing countries." *SSRN.*

Kofi Annan quotes. Retrieved from Brainyquote.com xlink:href="http://www.brainyquote.com/quotes/quotes/k/kofiannan130999.html"

Lane, P. R. (2013). "Credit dynamics and financial globalisation." *National Institute Economic Review, 225,* R14–R22.

Liang, Y. (2012). "Global imbalances and financial crisis: financial globalization as a common cause." *Journal of Economic Issues (M.E. Sharpe Inc.), 46,* 353–362.

Prasad, E., et al. (2003, March 17). "Effects of financial globalization on developing countries." Retrieved from the International Monetary Fund Web site xlink:href="http://www.imf.org/external/np/res/docs/2003/031703.pdf"

Rodrick, D. & Subramanian, A. (2008, March). "Why did financial globalization disappoint?" Harvard University Kennedy School of Government.

Retrieved from xlink:href="http://ksghome.harvard.edu/~drodrik/"

Tobin, J. (1998, November 14). "Globalization of the world economy: Financial globalization. Autumn Meeting of the American Philosophical Society." Retrieved from xlink:href="http://www.globalpolicy.org/socecon/glotax/currtax/1114globalization.htm"

Watson, G. (2008). "The future of quality." *Journal for Quality and Participation, 31,* 4–10.

The World Bank. (2009). Received from Answers.com. xlink:href="http://www.answers.com/The%20world%20bank"

SUGGESTED READING

Artis, M.J. & Hoffman, M. (2008). "Financial globalization, international business cycles and consumption risk sharing." *Scandinavian Journal of Economics, 110,* 447–471.

Das, D.K. (2008). "Sovereign-wealth funds: Assuaging the exaggerated: Anguish about the new global financial players." *Global Economy Journal, 8,* 1–15.

Devereaux, M.B. & Sutherland, A. (2008). "Financial globalization and monetary policy." *Journal of Monetary Economics, 55,* 1363–1375.

Ferrari-Filho, F. & de Paula, L.F. (2008). "Exchange rate regime proposal for emerging countries: A Keynesian perspective." *Journal of Post-Keynesian Economics, 31,* 227–248.

Kargbo, J.M. (2009). "Financial globalization and purchasing power parity in the G7 countries." *Applied Economics Letters, 16,* 69–74.

Mosley, L. & Singer, D.A. (2008). "Taking stock seriously: Equity-market performance, government policy and financial globalization." *International Studies Quarterly, 52,* 405–425.

Preeta, G. & Debasis, M. (2009). "Covered interest parity and international financial integration: The case of India." *ICFAI Journal of Applied Finance, 15,* 58–74.

Sweeney, S.E. (2004). "Global economic transformations, national institutions, and women's rights: A cross-national comparative analysis." *Conference Papers—American Political Science Association,* 1–64.

—Michael P. Auerbach

Financial Strategies and Analysis: Insurance

ABSTRACT

This article provides an overview of the financial strategies and analysis that are a part of the insurance industry. The article provides an introduction to the financial management of insurance companies, including the definition of an insurance company, the most common types of insurers, and the unique financial considerations for insurance companies. In addition, this article also provides a financial analysis of insurance companies. This analysis includes explanations of the components of insurance company income, common insurance company dividend policies, and the modern development of dynamic financial analysis. Further, the investment strategies of insurance companies are described, such as the variables that are involved in investment strategies, risk management techniques, and the various investment portfolios held by insurance companies. Finally, this article explains some of the most important financial considerations facing insurance companies, such as the identification of loss exposures, contractual risk control measures, and the identification of security risks.

OVERVIEW

The central objective of insurance companies is to eliminate certain financial risks for businesses and individuals by transferring liability for the risk from businesses and individuals to the insurance company. To limit the scope of their liability, insurance companies specify the activities and events that they will insure and may even specify activities or events that they will not insure. Thus, insurance functions as a means by which certain known, probable, or potential risks are converted from an individual or business risk to an individual or business expense in the form of insurance premiums. The premiums, or payments, that the insurance companies charge insureds and the income received from investments held by the insurance company compose the reserves from which insurance companies pay benefits to insureds who suffer losses covered by a valid insurance policy.

In addition to underwriting insurance policies, insurance companies also act as financial intermediaries in other ways. Insurance company agents now market and sell various financial products such as mutual funds, individual retirement accounts (IRAs), annuities, money market funds, investment securities, and tax shelters. Insurance companies also manage large sums of money in the form of employee benefit, pension, retirement, and profit-sharing plans. Thus, insurance companies play an important role in today's financial world and, as a result, must be carefully managed for proper growth and profitability. The following sections provide an overview of the financial strategies and analyses that play a central role in the insurance industry.

Financial Management of Insurance Companies

Financial management involves implementing the techniques, research, and analysis necessary to provide a company's management team with sufficient information to make sound financial decisions on behalf of the company. At least three kinds of financial management decisions are essential in the development of successful insurance companies: investment decisions, financing decisions, and dividend decisions.

- Investment decisions involve the most efficient use and replacement of current and fixed assets and take into account the time value of money, cash flows, and the risks and returns of various investment and insurance underwriting options.

Photo of US Airways Flight 1549 after crashing into the Hudson River in New York City. The plane was written off after being ditched in the river. (Courtesy of Greg L. CC BY 2.0 via Wikimedia Commons)

Investment decisions are also referred to as capital budgeting.

- Financing decisions deal with identifying and selecting the sources of funds that will operate the insurance company and implement its various goals and projects. Financing decisions involve current liabilities, long-term debt, and equity.

- Dividend decisions refer to the percentage of earnings to be paid as dividends to stockholders. These decisions are closely related to financing decisions but are also concerned with the stability of dividends over time and the impact of periodic dividend payments on the company's net worth.

The combination of these decisions allows a company's management team to put in place the necessary changes to achieve the financial goals of the insurance company and its owners, which are often different than owners of a typical for-profit corporation. Many insurance companies are known as mutual insurance companies and are owned by policyholders, not stockholders. Regardless of the owners, a company's management team most likely has as its goal to create profit or economic surplus while sustaining a healthy level of growth and productivity for the organization. Like stock companies, insurance companies must grow at least as rapidly as inflation to maintain their profitability and service to policyholders. However, the insurance industry is governed by certain regulatory guidelines that establish certain financial requirements for insurance companies. Thus, for any type of insurance company, the goal of financial management is to maximize the surplus of policyholders while complying with regulatory guidelines.

The following sections provide a more detailed explanation of the financial management of insurance companies, including a definition of insurance companies, the most common types of insurers, and unique considerations for insurance companies.

Definition of Insurance Company
Insurance companies provide a medium through which individuals and businesses may transfer an element of risk in exchange for payments, called premiums. However, to actually form and maintain an insurance company, an organization must comply with special state statutes, regulations, and

9/11 was a major insurance loss, but there were disputes over the World Trade Center's insurance policy. (Courtesy of TheMachineStops (Robert J. Fisch) derivative work: upstateNYer via Wikimedia Commons)

common-law principles that govern insurance companies and insurance law. The insurance industry is largely regulated by state laws. Each state has a state insurance department that is charged with the power to oversee and regulate insurers. These insurance departments, among other things, certify that newly formed insurers comply with special statutes governing business organization and formation; license out-of-state insurers who satisfy certain requirements to operate in the state; require the filing of detailed annual statements showing the insurer's assets, liabilities, income, losses, and expenses; and supervise the general conduct of insurers. To support the administrative and regulatory costs of maintaining insurance departments, states levy premium taxes on insurers. At the federal level, Internal Revenue Service (IRS) regulations mandate that to be taxed as an insurer, the majority of a company's business must be issuing insurance. Key elements in the definition of an insurance company are the transfer of risk and the distribution of losses.

Transfer of Risk
An insurance policy transfers some risk from the insured to the insurer. To effectuate a legally cognizable transfer of risk, there must be a binding contract between two or more parties that states the terms of the risks that are transferred between or among the

parties and the consideration that supports the risk transfer. If these elements are not met, an activity that purports a transfer of risk may not fall within the scope of the definition of insurance. For instance, deposits that are made into a fund administered by another party would not constitute insurance if the insured entity was essentially paying toward its own losses because this arrangement does not involve a transfer of risk.

Distribution of Losses

The IRS also defines insurance as involving the pooling of exposure and the proportional sharing of losses. Traditional insurance companies distribute the costs of losses among a group of insureds exposed to such losses. Certain distribution arrangements are often made, however, to adjust the premiums paid by the insureds to reflect the individual losses. These arrangements are generally subject to maximum and minimum limits. Otherwise insurance companies would be acting as a type of financial organization in distributing and redistributing the flow of cash flows among insureds, and this activity would fall within the realm of banking rather than insurance. Thus, financial managers must pay careful attention to the activities of insurance companies to ensure that they continue to operate within the prescribed activities of insurers, or the companies may risk losing their tax status as insurance companies.

This tornado damage to an Illinois home on April 2, 2006, would be considered an "Act of God" for insurance reasons. Debris from this house also damaged neighboring houses. The insurance carrier declared this home a total loss. (Courtesy of Robert Lawton CC BY-SA 2.5 via Wikimedia Commons)

Types of Insurers

The legal form of organization of a company acting as an insurer is also an important factor in the financial management of insurance companies. The major types of insurers are stock companies, mutual companies, and reciprocal exchanges.

Stock Insurers

Stock insurers are corporations engaged in the insurance business and owned by stockholders, who are not necessarily policyholders. The stockholders elect the board of directors, which appoints the executive officers, who in turn hire the remaining managers and personnel. The stockholders share the gains or losses from operations through stock dividends established by the board of directors as well as through ups and downs in the market value of their shares of stock.

Stock insurers write almost three-fourths of the property and liability insurance premiums written by United States private insurers. Stock property and liability insurers range from small insurers writing only one line of insurance to large insurers writing practically all kinds of insurance.

Mutual Insurers

Mutual insurers are corporations owned by their policyholders. They elect the board of directors. The board of directors appoints the executive officers, who then hire the other employees. There are two types of mutual insurers: assessment mutuals and advance premium mutuals.

Assessment mutuals operate by taking a cash deposit, or premium, from members in exchange for insurance protection. If the company's losses and expenses exceed these deposits, the company can assess members for additional monies to cover losses. On the other hand, advance premium mutuals have no legal right to assess their policyholders. Some advance premium mutuals pay dividends at the discretion of the board of directors. Most of these insurers charge more than they expect they will need and thus return some of the excess premium as dividends on a regular basis. Others pay policyholder dividends only under certain specified circumstances. Instead they set a price that is close to their expected needs and the "dividend" takes the form of a lower initial premium. Advance premium mutuals write a significant portion of the life insurance and property and liability insurance policies in force today. Many of the nation's largest insurers are advance premium mutuals.

Reciprocal Exchanges

Unlike mutual insurers, reciprocal exchanges are not corporations but are unincorporated associations that involve individuals writing insurance as individuals, not as an organized business affiliation or as joint owners. Each subscriber agrees to insure individually all of the other subscribers in the exchange and is in turn insured by each of the other subscribers. Thus, there is a "reciprocal exchange" of insurance promises. Instead of writing a separate contract for each promise, the reciprocal exchange issues one contract to each subscriber that states the nature of the association and its business protections and operations.

Reciprocal exchanges write only a small fraction of the property and liability premiums today and they seldom write life insurance policies. Many reciprocal exchanges specialize in one type of insurance, such as auto insurance, although a few do offer multiple lines of insurance. Some reciprocal exchanges are affiliated with trade associations and write insurance only for members of the association.

Unique Financial Considerations for Insurance Companies

The financial statements prepared by insurance companies differ from those prepared by other corporations for audits or tax purposes. Insurance companies have relatively few fixed assets, and most of these do not appear on the balance sheet as admitted assets. In addition, on the liabilities side of a financial statement, insurance companies utilize minimal debt, so their liabilities generally consist primarily of reserves. The equity of insurance companies is generally identified as policyholders' surplus or, in the case of stock companies, capital and surplus.

The preparation of financial statements for insurance companies follows statutory accounting principles. These principles differ in several ways from the generally accepted accounting principles ("GAAP") used by other business entities. Most of the deviations from GAAP are due to requirements imposed by state insurance regulatory authorities or are accounting adaptations that have been created to accommodate

the special characteristics of the insurance business. These special accounting principles tend to be much more conservative than GAAP.

In order to focus on a company's solvency, insurance accounting procedures apply special rules for the valuation of assets. While GAAP recognize all assets, statutory accounting principles only recognize what are called admitted assets, or assets that are readily convertible to cash. Furniture and fixtures, automobiles, premiums due over 90 days, and other assets of an insurance company, which are referred to as nonadmitted assets, do not appear on the balance sheet. Unrealized capital gains or losses are recognized under the statutory system but not under GAAP.

Financial Analysis of Insurance Companies

Earning income is a major objective of all businesses that seek to attract and retain capital. This applies to all forms of insurance companies as well—stock, mutual, or reciprocal. Even though these organizations do not vie for funds in capital markets in the same manner as other businesses, their ability to increase insurance operations is dependent on their earning capacity.

Thus, insurance company managers face the same decisions as stock company managers and executives. They must set growth objectives and determine how desired growth will be financed. Even if an insurance company does not increase the number of policies it underwrites, it has to expand its insuring capacity simply to provide coverage to existing policyholders as their insured assets increase in value. The following sections explain the financial analysis performed by insurance companies in pursuit of their growth and profitability objectives.

Components of Insurance Company Income

Income determination rules have a wide influence on the financial and operating decisions of insurance companies. In measuring income, a distinction is drawn between accounting income and economic income.

- Accounting income is the total income established through the application of a certain set of accounting rules, such as GAAP, to the financial events affecting a company.

- Economic income is the variation in the total value of a company's net worth during a specific time period.

There are five sources of economic income for an insurance company: underwriting gain; net investment income; realized capital gains and losses; unrealized capital gains and losses; and other income. Income is obtained from underwriting gain if premiums earned in an accounting period are greater than the losses contracted during the same period. Net investment income is the excess of interest, dividends, and income earned from invested assets over expenses contracted while conducting investment activities. Insurers earn income through security investments. There are two main sources of funds insurance companies invest: the insurer's net worth and retained earnings and policyholder supplied funds, or reserves from premium payments.

Realized capital gains and losses function in much the same way as stock companies and have the same tax consequences. Net unrealized capital gains and losses are credited or charged directly to the insurance company's net worth and are not included as net income because these gains or losses might never be realized. Even though unrealized capital gains and losses are not included in accounting income, they do contribute to the total return earned by insurance companies because they affect the insurer's net worth. Any other income that an insurance company may generate consists of revenues and expenses that are not related to either underwriting or investment activities.

Insurance Company Dividend Policy

Financial management practices of insurers have important differences from those of nonfinancial companies and financial corporations that are not insurance companies. Creating dividend policies is complicated for insurers because of the unique aspects of insurance companies, such as the presence of stock, mutual, and reciprocal insurers; regulation and competition within the industry; special income measurement rules; and unique asset and capital structures. Because there is more than one way to measure income of an insurance company, there is some question as to which income measurement applies in setting an insurer's dividend policy.

In addition, capital gains and losses may have a significant effect on the dividends paid by property

and liability insurers due to the asset structures of insurers. Most assets of insurance companies are cash, securities, and real estate. Large capital gains and losses from these assets have a significant impact on the ability of an insurance company to distribute its equity in the form of dividends, especially since such a distribution would have an even greater impact on the company's net worth.

One alternative way insurance companies distribute their profits to owners is to repurchase their own shares of company stock, which results in a permanent reduction in the total future dividend payments and often leads to an increase in the market value of outstanding shares. A second alternative to paying cash dividends is to acquire ownership interests in other companies. Insurance companies are more likely to acquire other companies when investment opportunities within the scope of the company's current operations fail to justify the use of its reserves or surplus capital.

Dynamic Financial Analysis

Dynamic financial analysis (DFA) is a systematic approach that uses computer simulations of financial models to aid insurance companies in assessing the risks and benefits associated with strategic decisions. "DFA models an insurance company's cash flow in order to forecast assets, liabilities, and ruin probabilities, as well as full balance sheets for different scenarios. In the last years DFA has become an important tool for the analysis of an insurance company's financial situation. In particular, it is a valuable instrument for solvency control, which is now becoming important as regulators" (Eling, 2007, p.1) have taken a closer look at the role insurance companies play in responding to catastrophic or widespread losses.

Thus, DFA is an important tool insurance companies now use for risk management and strategic decision support. DFA functions as a type of flight simulator for the management team of insurance companies that helps them understand and analyze the potential impact of their decisions before making any actual financial changes or investments. Use of DFA, in particular, focuses on financial analysis and strategy involving issues insurance companies face, such as capital management, investment strategies, reinsurance strategies, and strategic asset-liability management. The financial models that are created using DFA technologies allow insurance companies to make informed decisions regarding growth, strategic investments, and overall profitability.

However, Yu, Tsai, Huang, and Chen (2011) found that while DFA is a useful decision-support system for the insurer, it lacks optimization capability. The authors applied a simulation optimization technique (a genetic algorithm) to a DFA system and used the enhanced system to search an asset-liability management solution for a property-casualty insurance company. "The optimization problem," they wrote, "is a constrained, multi-period asset allocation problem that takes account of insurance liability dynamics," and they found that coupling a DFA system with simulation optimization results in "significant improvements" over typical search methods. Applying simulation optimization to a DFA system "is therefore promising" (Yu, Tsai, Huang & Chen, 2011).

Investment Strategies of Insurance Companies

An important aspect of insurance company financial management is its investment strategy. The variables in common investment strategies are the expected return, the standard deviation, the mean-variance criterion, and the coefficient of variation. The following sections describe these concepts in greater detail.

Variables in Investment Strategy

Investment strategy attempts to balance several important variables, such as the expected return of an investment, the standard deviation, the mean-variance criterion, and the coefficient of variation. The

This oceanfront property is one of many left in shambles following Hurricane Irma in November, 2017 in Big Pine Key, Florida. (Courtesy of Howard Greenblatt/FEMA)

expected rate of return of an investment refers to the change in price of an asset, whether realized or unrealized, plus cash income divided by the price of the asset at the initial financial period. The rate of return of investments or asset acquisitions is one of the most important variables that is used to assess various investment strategies. Another important variable is the standard deviation of returns, which is a determination of the risk associated with an investment. Standard deviation measures the degree to which returns vary from a mean rate of return. If the returns show little fluctuation from the mean, there is a low level of risk.

Economic events, such as changes in the financial markets, can affect the standard deviation of risks and returns associated with an investment. In addition, external events can affect investment strategies for insurers. For instance, for property and liability insurers, a series of catastrophic events, such as a high number of fires, storms, or floods, may cause an increase in the number of claims filed, which could lead to reduced earnings and investment options for the insurers who must replace or cover damage to property affected by these events.

Another variable is known as mean-variance criterion, and this is a factor that is used by insurance companies in selecting investment options. When insurance companies choose investments on the basis of the average return and risk, this is known as the mean-variance criterion. Since many insurance companies prefer to minimize risk exposure, investment strategies with higher returns or lower risk are preferred to lower returns or higher risk.

The coefficient of variation is the standard deviation of return dividend by the expected rate of return and is a measure of risk per unit of return. This statistic is used by insurance companies when they are considering choosing the best investment strategy or opportunity. Thus, if an insurance company is considering investing in two different securities and in each case a higher return is associated with higher risk, choosing between the securities based on a return and risk assessment by calculating the coefficient of variation can help an insurance company select the right security for its investment strategy.

Risk Management

An effective risk management program depends on many factors. For instance, insurance companies must consider such factors as having a sound administrative framework and a clear understanding of the organization's overall strategy and goals in order to formulate solid risk management policies. Key elements and attributes of effective risk management include a formal, written, and widely disseminated risk management policy statement; a written manual that outlines business processes, procedures, responsibilities, systems, and documents that support the risk management program; and a risk management information system for tracking costs and trends and providing timely, accurate, and actionable information for management decision making.

Operational risk is increasingly important in the management and corporate governance of insurance companies (Martinez Torre-Enciso & Barros, 2013). The management and analysis of operational risk are necessary activities for insurers, presenting many opportunities for development and a "major field of study on conceptual and practical issues due to the particularity and complexity implied in this type of risk" (Martinez Torre-Enciso & Barros, 2013).

In addition, sound criteria for selecting brokers and other service providers and a structured process for collaborating with them are also important elements of good risk management. Finally, regularly scheduled audits to evaluate the effectiveness of the current risk management business processes are important in adapting an organization's ongoing risk management procedures.

Birchfield, referencing a KPMG report in 2013, contended that catastrophic events of the prior few years "shone a light" on risk management and insurance "like never before" (2013). The year was another challenging one in the insurance industry, Birchfield and KPMG stated, and more of the same was predicted for 2014. "Last year saw insurers re-examine their risk exposures and respond by revising geographic exposures, increasing premiums to match risk, and/or adapting their products with, for example, the emergence of fixed-sum cover for new homes rather than traditional open-ended replacement," according to Birchfield (2013). He and KPMG also predicted that insurers who embraced challenges posed by the "four megaforces" (products and markets, distribution and operations, regulation and capital management, and governance and people) would both "survive and thrive."

Investment Portfolios

Just as diversification is important for the portfolios of investors and financial advisors, the benefits of diversification also apply to the investment portfolios of insurance companies. To determine the ideal investment portfolio composition for insurance companies, the company's manager or financial advisor will examine the return and risk parameters for each investment option as it relates to the operating objective of the insurance company. Using this information, informed decisions can be made as to the best options and the ideal composition of investment alternatives. In addition to portfolio composition, investment strategies must also take into account the risk of interest-rate fluctuations and the duration, or maturity dates, of investment options. Ideally, an insurance company's portfolio should be balanced to match durations with interest rate changes.

APPLICATION

Financial Considerations Facing Insurance Companies
Insurance companies face unique financial considerations. For instance, since insurance involves the transfer of risk, insurance companies must continually identify the exposure they face to significant losses of covered assets. To minimize the impact of excessive losses, insurance companies can contractually assign various risk elements so that potential losses are diffused among a number of different parties. Finally, insurance companies must also remain vigilant about security risks that could cause harm to their own assets or to the assets owned by insureds that are covered by insurance policies. The following sections provide further explanations of these considerations.

Identification of Loss Exposures
The identification of loss exposure is an important element in the risk management process of an insurance company. Loss exposure involves three elements:

- The type of asset exposed to loss
- The peril causing loss
- The financial consequences that result from that loss

Insurance companies have to develop techniques that systematically identify the risks raised by each of these elements. Without a systematic approach, some loss exposures would not become evident until after they have occurred.

There are a variety of techniques that insurance companies can use to systematically identify loss exposures. These include surveys and questionnaires regarding the organization's operations, analysis of past losses, financial statement analysis, review of documents and other records, personal inspections, and consultations with experts inside and outside the organization. When these techniques are implemented, loss exposures can be more readily identified and categorized.

Typically, loss exposure assessments reveal that most losses occur in one of three categories.

- First, property losses generally occur where the assets of the organization are exposed to loss or damage, which may result in direct or indirect damage to the assets and/or loss of income to the company.
- Second, liability losses may arise when an organization's operations and activities cause injury or property damage to third parties.
- Finally, personnel losses may involve the negative effects to an organization from the loss or actions of its employees.

Once losses have been identified and categorized, techniques can be developed to prevent or minimize their occurrence. For instance, developing and practicing emergency plans or eliminating insurance coverage for certain high-risk activities are steps that insurance companies can take to minimize their loss exposure. Also, segregating or separating operations, activities, or assets can also help control potential losses. An example would be moving a plant that manufactures finished materials to a geographically different area than the company headquarters so that both facilities would not be subject to the same loss should a catastrophic event occur in that area. Finally, an ongoing monitoring program is an important part of identifying and managing loss exposure, as vigilant observation of trends and patterns may reveal the possibility of a potential loss before it occurs so that proactive steps may be taken to prevent its occurrence or the extent of its harm.

Contractual Risk Control

Insurance is a contractual transfer for risk financing. Other risk transfer techniques include indemnity agreements, requirements for other parties to provide insurance protection, surety and guarantee arrangements, and waivers and releases. Insurance companies use these options in drafting insurance policies to limit the degree of their exposure for certain events and to shift liability to other parties for activities or assets that fall outside of the scope of the insurance policy.

An indemnification agreement is an agreement to compensate, or indemnify, another party upon the happening of a particular set of circumstances. The type of indemnity language chosen will depend on the relative sizes and bargaining power of each of the parties and the subject matter of the contract. The indemnification obligation in a contract is paramount because it states which party must assume the risk and cost of losses. However, the indemnity agreement is only as good as the financial solvency of the party that has assumed the obligation, as an insurance company may be unable to seek indemnification from a party that is bankrupt or judgment proof.

Some insurance companies write policies that contain restrictions or requirements for others to provide insurance protection for specified activities. This may be because the activities fall outside the scope of coverage normally included in an insurance company's policies or because the activities are unusually dangerous, thus requiring additional insurance protections.

Surety and guarantee arrangements also minimize an insurance company's exposure through contractual transfer of risk. A surety is a person or organization that contractually guarantees to one party that another party will perform as promised. The surety mechanism is called a bond, and the surety is also known as the bonding company. While this arrangement is similar to insurance, the surety arrangement is a three-party contract. Unlike insurance, the surety does not anticipate that losses will occur, only that the party will perform as promised. If there are losses, the surety has the legal right to recover from the contractor that they have bonded. In addition, the surety's primary obligation is to perform as promised for the obligee, not to pay money to compensate the obligee for the principal's breach of contract.

Finally, insurance companies may use waivers and releases to manage risks contractually. A waiver is a relinquishment of a known right, such as the right to sue. After such a waiver has been given, the insurance company no longer faces an exposure to legal actions that were waived. However, to be effective, a waiver must be obtained fairly as waivers that are improperly obtained or contrary to public policy may be nullified by court. A release arises when the party granting the release agrees to absolve, or "release," the other party from future liability. To be binding, the release must be accompanied by legal consideration. Most insurance settlements offered by insurance companies will require that a release be executed as a condition of payment.

Identifying Security Risks

Breaches of security can cause substantial damage to an organization or a property. While insurance may cover these losses, some losses may fall outside the scope of the relevant insurance policy. Thus, both insurance companies and insurance policyholders have an interest in identifying and minimizing security risks. To combat security risks, an organization or individual may develop a security program that is designed to protect assets, income, employees or other individuals, and business operations and activities. Security risks may take the form of injuries, loss or damage resulting from theft, arson, fraud, malicious damage, and other dishonest or illegal acts. Effective security planning can result in the identification of an organization's vulnerabilities and the development and implementation of appropriate countermeasures to strengthen these vulnerabilities.

In order for a sound security program to be developed, an organization or individual will need to gather information regarding the location and security of physical assets and any current protective measures such as lighting, alarms, or access or egress controls. In addition, intangible assets must also be surveyed. This may involve determining what information each person or employee controls and how information flows through an organization. Certain internal practices, such as educational programs covering security and crime control topics, appropriate

hiring and training policies, and tough prosecution measures for offenders can minimize potential security risks from within an organization.

However, securing assets is an ongoing process. Although insurance coverage may be an important element of protecting vital assets, insurance policies may not be comprehensive or may contain certain provisions that limit their coverage in the event of security breaches or internal control failures. Thus, both insurance companies and insurance policyholders play important roles in creating and maintaining sound security programs for organizations, individuals, or assets that may be covered by insurance policies.

CONCLUSION

Insurance companies provide a medium through which individuals and businesses may transfer an element of risk in exchange for payments, called premiums. In order to operate efficiently and profitably, insurance companies use various methods of financial analysis to measure income, risk, loss, and growth. Insurance companies use specialized accounting techniques to prepare detailed financial statements and to track income and develop dividend policies that allow them to distribute profits to owners while maintaining the solvency and financial stability of the company. Increasingly, insurance companies are using dynamic financial analysis to create computer models of various financial strategies so that their impact can be assessed before any funds are actually transferred or invested. In addition, insurance companies employ financial strategies that enable them to grow in profitability without assuming excessive levels of risk. These strategies include measuring or tracking certain variables to assess investment options, developing sound risk management policies and diversifying their investment portfolios. Insurance companies face unique considerations in developing their financial strategies. Insurance companies must continuously monitor their loss exposure, contractually transfer risk levels where possible, and identify security risks to their assets and the assets of policyholders. Further, the investment strategies of insurance companies are described, such as the variables that are involved in investment strategies, risk management techniques, and the various investment portfolios held by insurance companies. By using a range of financial strategies and analysis tools, insurance companies are able to ensure their financial stability for the security of their policyholders and the profitability of their owners.

BIBLIOGRAPHY

Birchfield, R. (2013). "Managing risk - the four global megaforces impacting business risk." *New Zealand Management, 60,* 50–51.

Chen, C., Steiner, T. & White, A. (2003). "Risk taking behaviour and managerial ownership in the United States life insurance industry." *Applied Financial Economics, 11,* 165–171.

Cummins, J. & Grace, M. (1999). "Regulatory solvency prediction in property-liability insurance: Risk-based capital, audit ratios, and cash flow simulation." *Journal of Risk & Insurance, 66,* 417–458.

Eling, M. & Parnitzke, T. (2007). "Dynamic financial analysis: Classification, conception, and implementation." *Risk Management & Insurance Review, 10,* 33–50.

Feinberg, M., Shelor, R., Cross, M. & Grossmann, "A. (2006). A comparison of the solicited and independent financial strength ratings of insurance companies." *Journal of American Academy of Business, Cambridge, 10,* 37–43.

Kunreuther, H., Lyster, R. (2017). "The role of public and private insurance in reducing losses from extreme weather events and disasters." *Asia Pacific Journal of Environmental Law, 19,* 29–54.

Martinez Torre-Enciso, M., & Barros, R. (2013). "Operational risk management for insurers." *International Business Research, 6,* 1–11.

Miletsky, R. (2004). "Indemnification & additional insured clauses: What do you need to know?" *Financial Analysis, Planning & Reporting, 4,* 2–4.

Smith, B. (2001). "A financial analysis of the property and casualty insurance industry 1970–1999." *CPCU Journal, 54,* 134.

Staking, K. & Babbel, D. (1995). "The relation between capital structure, interest rate sensitivity, and market value in the property-liability insurance industry." *Journal of Risk & Insurance, 62,* 690–718.

Whitney, S. (2000). "Managing internal risks." *Best's Review, 100,* 141.

Yu, T., Tsai, C., Huang, H., & Chen, C. (2011). "Applying simulation optimization to dynamic financial analysis for the asset-liability management of a property-casualty insurer." *Applied Financial Economics, 21,* 505–518.

SUGGESTED READING

Lenckus, D. (2000). "Modeling tool gives USAA broad business picture." *Business Insurance, 34,* 261.

Rooney, S. & Brennan, K. (2006). "Securitization in the life insurance industry: Managing risk and capital requirements." *Journal of Structured Finance, 12,* 23–29.

Sclafane, S. (2006). "Rating firms take giant steps." *National Underwriter/Property & Casualty Risk & Benefits Management.*

—*Heather Newton, JD*

FOREIGN CURRENCY EXCHANGE AND RISK

ABSTRACT

This article focuses on the rise and fall of the Bretton Woods (agreement) system. There will be a discussion of the role of the U.S. dollar during this period as well as the role of the International Monetary Fund. The article will conclude with an explanation of how the Bretton Woods system ties into the study of international political economy.

OVERVIEW

Bretton Woods System

It was at the 1944 Bretton Woods international conference that a system of fixed exchange rates was adopted. In addition, the International Monetary Fund was established and charged with maintaining stable exchange rates at the international level. The Bretton Woods (agreement) system was concerned

The display case showing the flags of all the nations represented at the Monetary Conference at the Mount Washington Hotel resulting in the establishment of the International Monetary Fund in 1944. (Courtesy of Barry Livingstone CC BY-SA 3.0 via Wikimedia Commons)

with developing and implementing the rules and regulations for global commercial and financial transactions. The International Bank for Reconstruction and Development (now known as the World Bank) was established as a result. This was the first effort to create a system that would control monetary dealings between independent nation-states. The greatest accomplishments of the Bretton Woods (agreement) system occurred when each country agreed to implement a financial policy that would maintain the exchange rate of its currency as a fixed market price in terms of gold. The International Monetary Fund had the ability to create connections between momentary imbalances of payments. Unfortunately, the arrangement disintegrated in 1971 as a result of the United States' suspension of convertibility from dollars to gold. The system was dismissed, and in its place, a method of floating exchange rates was initiated.

When there is a reference to the Bretton Woods system, most are referring to the international monetary regime that existed between the 1940s and the early 1970s. This system set precedent. It was the first attempt at a "fully negotiated monetary order intended to govern currency relations among sovereign states. This regime was designed to combine binding legal obligations with multilateral decision-making conducted through an international organization, the IMF, endowed with limited supranational authority" (Cohen, n.d., par. 1). The approach was built on constant and changeable exchange rates. Three of the most significant points of the agreement were as follows:

- When a country signed the agreement, it was agreeing to submit its exchange rate to international disciplines, which implied that the country would surrender its national sovereignty to a global corporation.
- A nation wasn't required to deflate the domestic economy when it faced chronic balance of payments (BP) deficits.
- The dollar was the standard to which all other currencies were pegged. However, it should be noted that the United States "did not have the authority to set the exchange rate between the dollar and any other currency" (The Bretton Woods System, n.d., ¶ 4).

The Role of the U.S. Dollar

As mentioned in the third point above, the dollar became the dominant currency. In the 1950s, the United States became the foremost reserve nation, and the dollar replaced the worth of gold as a crucial and prominent global reserve advantage. However, it should be noted that this development was not planned; "all of the non-Communist countries maintained a stable relationship between their currencies and the dollar through the British pound; and the United States balance of payments was more important than those of other countries because other countries were holding the U.S. dollar

Federal Reserve Notes. (Courtesy of Hidro via Wikimedia Commons)

as the principal reserve asset" (The Bretton Woods System, n.d., "The Role of the U.S. Dollar").

During this period, the United States "was the dominant world power. As a result, over half of the international money transactions were financed in terms of the dollar. In addition, the United States produced more than half of the world output and owned about one third of the gold in the world. As the Bretton Woods system evolved, the reserves of most countries became a mixture of gold and dollars. Therefore, the U.S. dollar became increasingly more important. Unfortunately, the United States was unable to eliminate increasing trade deficits, which eventually undermined the Bretton Woods system" (The Bretton Woods System, n.d., "The Role of the U.S. Dollar").

APPLICATION

International Monetary Fund
The establishment of the International Monetary Fund (IMF) and the World Bank is probably one of the most important success stories for international economic cooperation. During the last sixty years, there have been many changes in terms of the political and economic climate on a global level, which have caused the world's top international financial institutions to shift in terms of how they operate their businesses. Given the number of financial crises that have surfaced during the last ten years, many scholars and practitioners in the field have called for a reform in how the international financial system is structured. These crises have exposed the weaknesses of the international financial system and highlight the fact that globalization has pros (benefits) and cons (risks).

Goals of the IMF
"The IMF was established to provide member countries with the necessary funds to cover short-term balance of payments problems. The Fund in turn received resources from members who were allotted quotas. Once a country enters the Fund, it receives a par value of its currency expressed in terms of gold or in terms of the U.S. dollar using the weight of gold in effect on July 1, 1944 ($35 per troy oz). All exchange transactions between member countries were to be effected at a rate that diverged not more than 1% (which approximates gold import/export

points) from the par values of the respective currencies" (The Bretton Woods System, n.d., "Contents of the Articles of Agreement").

The IMF continues to diligently work at providing continuous improvement in practices that affect many sectors. For example, this body continues to

- Encourage members to provide public press releases that would detail the IMF executive board's evaluation of a nation's finances and policies;
- Encourage members to provide information about the policies in place regarding the following and restoring of financial stability under the IMF regime;
- Help countries implement guidelines, such as the Reports on the Observance of Standards and Codes, that will evaluate a nation's development in practicing globally accepted standards;
- Address gaps in regulatory standards through the Basle Committee on Banking Supervision;
- Encourage members to put procedures in place when they are not experiencing any problems so that they are not responding to a crisis (it's an opportunity to be proactive versus reactive); and
- Help countries evaluate their obvious weaknesses and decide which exchange rate program is most appropriate for their needs.

VIEWPOINT

International Political Economy (IPE)
Many IPE researchers have highlighted the significance of the relationship between economic and political factors with regard to international relations. IPE scholars are interested in the Bretton Woods system because of its significance in providing the foundation for the development of formal regime theory. The Bretton Woods system was a well-designed regime that was negotiated and a part of the IMF. "The circumstances of the system's birth and life cycle offered scholars invaluable material for assessing the relative importance of diverse variables in promoting or inhibiting economic cooperation among governments"(Bretton Wood System, p. 10). The Bretton Woods system demonstrated that a social order could be durable at the international level. This factor provides the significance of the system to the IPE theory.

Influence of Political Factors on Economics

Many IPE scholars will argue that the international economic system and the international political system work in unison. Economic partnerships are determined by political and diplomatic relationships and vice versa. According to Spero (1990), political factors affect economic outcomes in three ways:

The political system shapes the economic system because the structure and operation of the economic system is determined by the structure and operation of the international political system. One could see the influence of the international political system on the international economic system by reviewing the political developments during three periods of time in history. The three periods are nineteenth-century imperialism, the post–World War II era of cold war between the Soviet Union and the Western free world led by the United States, and the post–Berlin Wall demolition and the demise of the Soviet Empire era (Phatak, Bhagat, & Kashlak, 2005).

Period 1: Nineteenth-century imperialism and mercantilism were driven by two major political factors: the powerful nation-states in Europe (i.e., the United Kingdom, France, Germany, and Holland), who had equal military power, and nationalism practiced by these nation-states. These countries encouraged their citizens to practice and participate in activities that enhanced national pride, national identity, self-sufficiency, wealth, and economic power. Cooperative relations between nations were not popular. Each country wanted to promote itself. Both of these two factors led these nation-states to pursue empire building, which encouraged colonialism in Asia, Africa, and Latin America. The objectives of the nation-states were to obtain raw material and minerals from the colonies, process the goods into finished products in their home countries, and market the products in the colony markets. The nation-states sought to accumulate wealth and power so that their citizens could have full employment at the expense of colonized countries whose markets and production were controlled by the nation-states. The European nation-states divided the world into parts that were controlled by each. The British controlled most of western and southern Asia and parts of Africa. The French controlled Southeast Asia and northwest Africa. The

Dutch controlled Indonesia and parts of Central and South America, and the Germans controlled parts of Western Africa. Wars broke out between the different nation-states as each attempted to take control of the others' territory. The British and French fought for control of India, and the British and Dutch fought for control over parts of Africa. European imperialism determined trade and investments. As a result, the political system was controlled by colonialism and empire building.

Period 2: As the imperialist system ended after World War II, the United Kingdom's dominance in the West came to an end. However, two other superpowers emerged—the United States and the Soviet Union. A new political and economic system developed as the result of the rivalry between these two countries. The new political system was bipolar and hierarchical. The United States led the West and Japan. The Soviet Union led the Soviet bloc in the East, which comprised of countries behind the Iron Curtain. The developing countries in the third world remained politically subordinate to their colonial mother countries. The United States and the Soviet Union battled in what was known as the Cold War. This political system determined the post–World War II international economic system. There were two different economic systems. The United States and the West supported a capitalist system,

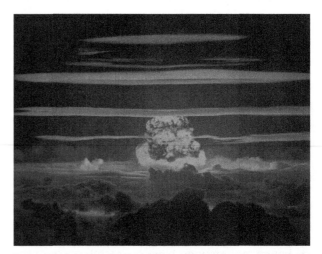

During the Cold War, the United States conducted approximately 1,054 nuclear tests by official count, between 1945 and 1992. This nuclear weapon test Dakota (yield 1.1 Mt) took place on Enewetak Atoll on June 26, 1956. (Courtesy of U.S. Department of Energy via Wikimedia Commons)

which encouraged free enterprise and free market economic systems. The Soviet Union and the East supported a Socialist/Marxist economic system, which called for a centralized economy controlled by the government where citizens were not allowed to have private property.

Period 3: There was another change in the late 1980s and 1990s as the post–World War II international economic system crashed. Poland and Hungary began to support a democratic state, the Berlin Wall fell, and the Soviet Union broke up. Countries that once supported the socialist model began to embrace capitalism. Russia became a democracy, and China, Vietnam, and India opened their markets to foreign investments and trade.

Political concerns often shape economic policy because economic policies are frequently dictated by overriding political interests. Internal political processes have a part in the determination of national economic policy. Economic policy is the outcome of the political bargaining process that is responsible for resolving the conflict over the outcomes preferred by different groups, each representing distinct and often conflicting interests. The overriding political and strategic interests of a nation help determine its international economic policy, which results in international economic policy becoming a

The Fall of the Berlin Wall, 1989. The photo shows a part of a public photo documentation wall at the Brandenburg Gate, Berlin. (Courtesy of Lear 21 at English Wikipedia CC BY-SA 3.0 via Wikimedia Commons)

tool to fulfill a nation's strategic and foreign policy objectives. International economic policy can sometimes be beneficial to multinational corporations (MNCs), especially if it is being driven by political considerations.

International economic relations themselves are political relations because both types of interaction are processes by which state and non-state players attempt to manage their conflicts and cooperate to achieve common goals. International economic relations may be viewed as the outcome of the political process involving the management of conflict and cooperation over the acquisition of scarce resources among the various members of the political system in the absence of a centralized world government. Both international and political interactions range from conflict to cooperation. The conflict among the members of the political system may be rooted in a struggle for greater power and national sovereignty. National sovereignty is associated with national wealth. A country that is not independently wealthy becomes dependent on others and loses some of its national sovereignty. Therefore, most countries seek wealth in a political system, and the pursuit of this goal in the presence of scarce resources frequently leads to conflict among the system members.

Foundations of International Political Economy

IPE is composed of a range of theoretical frameworks, and the foundations are established based on ideologies between states and markets. "The key difference between competing theoretical claims in IPE relates to the normative position that scholars adopt on the preferred mix of values to be embedded with the state-market nexus" (Murphy & Tooze, 1991, p. 2). Strange (1988) categorized these values into four domains, which were safety, affluence, independence, and justice. The most favored blend of these four values changes depending on the theoretical beliefs of the scholar (Watson, 2005).

CONCLUSION

It was at the 1944 Bretton Woods International conference that a system of fixed exchange rates was adopted. In addition, the International Monetary Fund was established and charged with maintaining stable exchange rates at the international level. The Bretton Woods system was charged with developing and implementing the rules and regulations for global commercial and financial transactions. The International Bank for Reconstruction and Development was established as a result. It was the first effort at creating a system that would control financial relations between independent nation-states.

The program was associated with stable but changeable exchange rates. Three of the most significant points of the agreement were as follows:

- When a country signed the agreement, it was agreeing to submit its exchange rate to international disciplines, which implied that the country would surrender its national sovereignty to an international organization.
- A nation wasn't required to deflate the domestic economy when it faced chronic BP deficits.
- The dollar was the standard to which all other currencies were pegged. However, it should be noted that the United States lacked the authority to establish the exchange rate between the dollar and other forms of currency (The Bretton Woods System, n.d.).

"The IMF was established to provide member countries with the necessary funds to cover short-term balance of payments problems. The Fund in turn received resources from members who were allotted quotas. Once a country enters the Fund, it receives a par value of its currency expressed in terms of gold or in terms of the U.S. dollar using the weight of gold in effect on July 1, 1944 ($35 per troy oz). All exchange transactions between member countries were to be effected at a rate that diverged not more than 1% (which approximates gold import/export points) from the par values of the respective currencies" (The Bretton Woods System, n.d., "Contents of the Articles of Agreement").

The Bretton Woods system was a well-designed regime that was negotiated and a part of the IMF. "The circumstances of the system's birth and life cycle offered scholars invaluable material for assessing the relative importance of diverse variables in promoting or inhibiting economic cooperation among governments"(Bretton Wood System, p. 10). The Bretton Woods system demonstrated that a social

order could be durable at the international level. This factor provides the significance of the system to the IPE theory.

BIBLIOGRAPHY

Cohen, B. (n.d.). "Bretton woods system." Retrieved from xlink:href="http://www.polsci.ucsb.edu/faculty/cohen/inpress/bretton.html"

Murphy, C., & Tooze, R. (1991). Introduction. In C. Murphy & R. Tooze (eds.), *The New International Political Economy*. London: Lynne Reener.

Niepmann, F., Schidt-Eisenlohr, T. (2017). "Foreign currency loans and credit risk: Evidence from U.S. Banks." *CESifo Working Paper Series No. 6700*.

Phatak, A., Bhagat, R., & Kashlak, R. (2005). *International management*. New York, NY: McGraw-Hill/Irwin.

Spero, J. (1990). *The politics of international economics relations*, (4th ed.). New York, NY: St. Martin's Press.

Strange, S. (1988). *States and markets: An introduction to international political economy*. London: Pinter.

The Bretton Wood System (n.d.). Retrieved from xlink:href="http://www.econ.iastate.edu/classes/econ355/choi/bre.htm"

Watson, M. (2005). *Foundations of international political economy*. New York, NY: Palgrave Macmillan.

SUGGESTED READING

Cross, J., Schwartz, M., & Gradwohl, C. (2004). "Inflation and foreign currency risks of placing debt in Mexico." *Tax Management International Journal, 33,* 426–427.

Dominguez, K. E., Fatum, R., & Vacek, P. (2013). "Do Sales of Foreign Exchange Reserves Lead to Currency Appreciation?" *Journal Of Money, Credit & Banking* (Wiley-Blackwell), 45, 867–890.

"Euro adoption to remain policy focus." (2007). *Emerging Europe Monitor: Central Europe & Baltic States, 14,* 8.

Iglesias, E. M. (2012). "An analysis of extreme movements of exchange rates of the main currencies traded in the Foreign Exchange market." *Applied Economics*, 44, 4631–4637.

Kai, S., & Li, N. (2012). "Adjusting the Currency Composition of China's Foreign Exchange Reserve." *International Journal Of Economics & Finance*, 4, 170–179.

Lustig, H., & Verdelhan, A. (2007). "The cross section of foreign currency risk premia and consumption growth risk." *American Economic Review, 97,* 89–117.

"Practical tips in an uncontrollable environment." (2007). *Government Procurement, 15,* 24–25.

Ramona, O. (2013). "The US Dollar, the Euro, the Japanese Yen and the Chinese Yuan in the Foreign Exchange Market – A Comparative Analysis." *Studies In Business & Economics,* 8, 102–107.

Sorensen, S. M., Zhaohui, X., & Kyle, D. L. (2012). "Currency Translation's Effects on Reported Earnings and Equity: An Instructional Case." *Issues In Accounting Education,* 27, 837–854.

Trevino, L., & Thomas, S. (2001). "Local versus foreign currency ratings: What determines sovereign transfer risk?" *Journal of Fixed Income, 11,* 65–77.

—*Marie Gould*

G

GEOGRAPHICAL ECONOMICS

ABSTRACT

Geographical economics takes a long-overdue look at the possible casual role location plays in the growth of productive capacity and wealth. More traditional economic theory has largely considered location irrelevant. Essentially, different regions enjoyed different natural endowments purely by accident, and regional economic growth was caused entirely by external market forces. But such dismissive explanations glossed over the ever-growing realities of spatial concentration and economic specialization, prompting some economists to ask whether the two were casually related. Economic growth in effect may well be an endogenous process after all. The challenge lies in not contradicting or undermining the basic tenets of modern economic theory while making the argument. Success here was deemed worthy of the considerable effort required since it would reapply existing concepts to the role of place in economic activity left languishing for want of a broader theory.

OVERVIEW

Globalization has caused neighboring countries to band together in super-regional trading blocs (most notably APEC, ASEAN, the EU, NAFTA and MERCOSUR) much more than it has turned the world into one gigantic trading bloc. The EU's economic integration is common knowledge. However, not many know that ASEAN member countries have agreed to form their own economic bloc—the ASEAN AEC—set to become effective in 2015. This integration is especially notable given the financial crisis in Europe that began in late 2009 (Volz, 2013). Location matters in economic activity far more than once thought. Such is the premise underlying geographical economics, which has shown that economic theory previously treated location as

an externality, a coincidental by-product of more fundamental economic forces. Growth occurred from exogenous causes. This conceptual bias dominated economic thought with few exceptions the last four centuries. In the final quarter of the twentieth century, a few economists began posing a radical question: Why were some goods and services being produced in some places more than in others? "Where," they contended, belongs beside "when, what and why" as a central line of inquiry. If everything existed everywhere, the material world would lack any and all distinctiveness. Yet, differences abound in kind, time, and distance. Why then was location ignored by economic theorists for centuries? Well, it seems place did not matter because, in the long run, all economic growth was either a function of the rate of savings or the rate of technological progress. The former provides capital, the latter more efficient modes of production. Both, significantly, are still considered by neoclassical economists to be near universal constants rather than the outgrowth of regional economic activity. Markets essentially were assumed to act the same wherever they were located.

FURTHER INSIGHTS

HISTORY OF ECONOMIC MARKETS & THEIR STUDY
Seventeenth Century

One has to go as far back as seventeenth-century mercantilism to find an economic theory in which the idea of place held any importance. The object during this time was to amass gold bullion by maintaining a surplus of exports over imports. Place mattered, then, but only as the demarcation line separating domestic and foreign markets. A particular locale was only important insofar as it proved a profitable foreign market to sell domestically produced items. Aside from cheap natural resources, imports from these very same markets, meanwhile, were kept to a

A picture from the gold vault of the Federal Reserve Bank of New York. (Courtesy of Federal Reserve Bank of New York via Wikimedia Commons)

minimum through the imposition of stringent tariffs. This "trade protectionism" also did much to promote a more self-sufficient domestic economy, a key political objective then as now.

Eighteenth & Nineteenth Centuries

Eighteenth-century laissez-faire economics, on the other hand, viewed markets as forums of "perfect" competition made up of numerous suppliers where individual buyers and sellers are free to enter or leave at will. Its first great theorist, Adam Smith, did state that locales differ in climate, availability of natural resources, and access to waterways. Crucially, though, such differences had to be accidental in nature and irrelevant to the actual workings of the marketplace. For, if it can shape the behavior of individual markets differently, they would no longer be structurally

alike. And that would mean in turn that competition was not perfect after all. But the entire theory of free-market capitalism rests on the assumption that it is perfect. Nineteenth-century Marxist theory likewise pitted capitalist against worker irrespective of place. Class struggle was inevitable everywhere given how the exploitive nature of the ownership of production inexorably forces virtually everyone to live at or below a subsistence wage.

Twentieth Century

When twentieth-century Keynesian economics came along, the focus of economic theory shifted to the relationship between aggregate demand and unemployment at the national level but, like earlier theories, posited that free market economies at this scale all functioned alike. Its counterpart, neoclassic theory, was built on more traditional notions about the ways price, output, and income were determined in the interplay of supply and demand in markets. Such notions gave rise to general equilibrium theory, which contends that a change in one item's price affects the prices of all other items, potentially upsetting the market equilibrium between the supply and demand of *all* goods and services *everywhere*. So, theoretically, at least, it is necessary to trace what the "knock-on effect" of every single price change will be on millions and millions of products worldwide—so daunting a prospect that theorists eventually began to assume that all other prices remained unchanged to isolate the effect on one item's price change on just one other item's price.

Endogenous Growth Theory

It is thus perhaps no coincidence that the one exception to this rule—the endogenous growth theory of the 1980s—tipped the scales in favor of including place as a factor of production. And this change happened only because such a theory considers economic growth to be driven primarily by internal factors like human capital that vary from one locale to another. Rather belatedly, then, the idea of place gained enough of a theoretical legitimacy to revisit the early work in location theory, which states that economic activities tend to spatially congregate of their own accord for explicit reasons. The clustering of productive capacity so readily apparent around the globe, across a continent, within the borders of a nation-state, inside a provincial region, and among

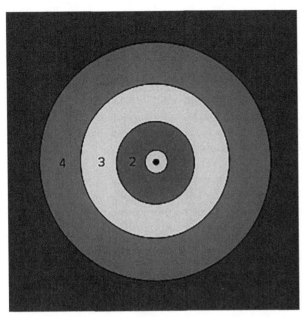

Johann Heinrich von Thünen's model of agricultural distribution around a city in concentric circles. The dot represents a city. The small area around it (1) represents dairy and market gardening; (2) the forest for fuel; (3) field crops and grains; (4) Ranching and livestock ;and the outer (dark green) region represents the wilderness where agriculture is not practiced. (Courtesy of Erin Silversmith via Wikimedia Commons)

different urban districts and rural areas counties alike might be modeled and explained.

And though scale itself does not play a determining role, distance does. This was the conclusion drawn in 1826 by Johann Von Thunen, who observed how crop production levels and distance to a central market were inversely related. The farther that farms were from population centers, the less intensive their cultivation. Conversely, the closer they were, the more intensive their cultivation. Von Thunen postulated that as this distance lengthened, transportation costs increased, which in effect depressed the farmers' locational rents and their profit from growing and selling surplus crops. Industrialization had yet to transform the economic landscape Von Thunen depicted; his identification of the pivotal role played by transportation costs nevertheless applies to plants and farms alike.

The Agglomeration Principle

People congregate in large numbers in a relatively small mass of land to take advantage of lower overall costs of transportation. Travel to and from work, local

marketplaces, religious institutions, and recreational outlets is cheaper, giving individuals spare income to spend on other goods and services. What is good for households is also good in a wider sense for firms and markets. Denser concentrations of customers generate greater demand for a wider variety of goods and services. High volume creates internal economies of scale that bring production costs down at the firm level. Critically, too, the broader the scope of products in demand, the more the incentive for firms to specialize their production processes. Over time, functional linkages between firms and shared infrastructure across industries in proximity also occasion external economies of scale. Agglomeration (as it is called) also facilitates collaboration and knowledge sharing between firms and industries instrumental to technological progress (Simonen, 2006).

Agglomeration, though, is a selective process that occurs in some places but not others, creating a de facto spatial hierarchy of densely and sparsely populated areas. Climate, access to waterways, and other factors play their part here. But none of these factors satisfactorily explains why some regions produce a greater number and diversity of goods and services than others. Geographer Walter Chandler hypothesized that the outcome here depends on two variables: the smallest possible market size by population and income where there's enough demand to warrant supply of a particular good or service and the longest distance a consumer is prepared to travel to acquire it. Decisions by individual buyers and sellers with respect to a particular location thus determine the size and scope of its market. So, the economic utility of a site attracts a proportional number of residents. As a consequence, some sites will grow larger and faster than others. This is the gist of Chandler's seminal central place theory.

Location & Revisionist Exogenous Growth Theories

On the other hand, economic base theory is more exogenous in nature. It tightly links regional economic growth to extraregional influences or "externalities," most notably worldwide exports. An offshoot, the regional business cycle theory, contends that intraregional economic instability is specifically triggered by export variability. Inter-regional differences in economic growth arise from inequalities in the relative performance of export-oriented industries from one region to the next. Leveraging export industries in a region that is stronger than in other regions reduces these inequalities.

A strategic determination first must be made about the relative efficiency of one region's export industries compared with other regions'. This is done through applying the principle of shift-share analysis. It is most often employed to examine the degree to which the change in employment rates for industrial workers in a given locale can be attributed to (Nazarra & Hewings, 2004)

- a rise or fall in the national manufacturing rate;
- a rise or fall in an industry-wide employment rate; and
- a strictly local factor of production like proximity to natural resources or a surplus in the supply of labor, in which case it has a competitive advantage.

Though quantitatively rigorous, shift-share analysis fails to adequately explain why, in the long run, some sectors grow and others do not and why some industries migrate into an area and others out of an area. Even so, its rich data-mining capabilities and straightforward calculations can and do yield information and insights about short-term conditions. Proponents of the theory of comparative advantage find shift-share analysis particularly useful.

Specialization & Regional Competitive Advantage

Specialization, a key component of modern-day trade theory, maintains that a given region has unique productive capacities that can be leveraged into a competitive advantage in one or more world markets. As contemporary-sounding an idea as this may seem, it can be traced directly to Alfred Marshall's early-twentieth-century observations of the pivotal importance location plays in the specialization of production processes. For more than thirty years, he studied the efficiencies brought about by the conglomeration of a skilled workforce, a diverse network of ancillary specialists to call upon, and the backward and forward integration of production between nearby firms. The theory of comparative advantage applies these principles on a truly grand scale. This theory was applied formally to international trade for the first time in Heckscher-Ohlin theory, which maintains that historical accident endowed various regions of the world with different natural resources and kinds of technological expertise that naturally lend themselves to a

comparative cost advantage in the production of certain goods and services. The resulting advantageous price differential in world markets fosters greater and greater local economies of scale.

Countries and transnational regions incur an opportunity cost every time they allocate resources to productive ends. Every investment made, moreover, could be put into some other activity. The amount that could be earned pursuing this alternative is its opportunity cost. Investing in an activity with lower expected returns than the opportunity cost of another option is not the most efficient use of funds (Clever, 2002). Every country therefore should concentrate on developing only those industries that promise it the highest returns in the global marketplace. Also, a country can readily and more cheaply import the goods and services it produces inefficiently from countries with complementary competitive strengths. Such, at least, is the theory. The realities of countervailing tariffs and import quota persist. Globally speaking, then, "free market" remains a relative concept. It is an entirely different matter, however, in large sections of the world belonging to regional custom unions and common markets where a greater parity in trade and transaction costs has been actively sought.

The New Growth Theory

The conceptual breakthrough that led to the reevaluation of spatial concentration as a cause rather than an effect of economic activity came in 1991. That year, Paul Krugman introduced a theoretical model that has since become synonymous with new growth theory. It is based on the premise that market competition is inherently imperfect, for at any given moment some markets will be in disequilibrium, others not. This puts the proposed model within the pale of the partial equilibrium theory. More important, it also means spatial concentration and increasing returns to scale can be linked. The latter occurs whenever a change in input in production leads to a proportionately greater change in output. This is essentially the driving force behind improving economies of scale.

One remaining connection had to be made for the model to pass theoretical muster. And that was to show how spatial concentration in and of itself creates advantages and opportunities that attract migrants. This necessitated a rethinking of what kinds of individual economic agents make location decisions. Firms alone were once thought to make this decision. But a given spatial concentration must generate enough local consumer demand to achieve increasing returns to scale in the first place. Such an outcome is much more likely economically when consumers, and firms, are free to migrate. Also, a person typically has to be a worker to be a consumer, so the spatial distribution of production and demand are two sides to the same coin. Krugman's model posits that both capital and labor are mobile, and both combined will accelerate the agglomeration principle more than capital mobility alone would.

To put this in layperson's terms, firms originate or migrate to a particular locale for the competitive advantages it affords. These firms attract additional workers seeking a better quality of life who quite naturally consume goods and services produced locally because of lower transportation costs and lower price structures. Once unleashed, the resulting centripetal forces fuel a cycle of local economic growth that, barring external shocks, continues until population outstrips available resources. The more these forces exert themselves, the more centralized and integrated the economic infrastructure and, consequently, the greater local economies of scale and scope achieved. And this, in turn, attracts more people, some of whom will bring technical expertise and innovative ways of thinking with them. All of which, significantly, can be accelerated by local investments in infrastructure and human capital. In the end, though, new growth theory's greatest single contribution may lie in the new lines of inquiry it has opened up. For at heart it asks two important questions:

- What identifiable advantages do spatial concentration create that cause it to subsequently grow and intensify?
- What exactly turns slight differences between locations into major ones?

Satisfactory explanations to one or both questions will further the possibility that if-then relationships do indeed exist between spatial concentration and productive capacity.

VIEWPOINTS

So how do all these theories relate to actual international trade? It is a fair question; unfortunately, there is no clear answer. Theory is just that—theory. It simplifies incredibly complex phenomena so we can better understand their governing principles. To do this satisfactorily, one has to generalize, and to generalize, one has to ignore exceptions to the rule. So, whereas international trade involves physical goods and services bought with real money on truly massive scales, trade theory debates the role externalities or returns to scale play in regional and global markets. These can seem maddeningly obtuse until you try to make some kind of sense of the minutiae of international trade. Be it exogenous or endogenous in origin, the economic consequences of the spatial concentration of economics are verifiable trends. Location theory and the like are useful because they suggest the most likely outcomes possible in policy decisions about economic development. It is fair to say that the custom unions and free trade zones cropping up all over the world owe their existence in part to the widespread acceptance of concepts such as agglomeration and central place theory. The question is not so much whether one or the other is economically tenable as it is the degree of influence over future globalization each may assert. Will it follow a more endogenous path and stabilize around regional trading blocs, or will it follow a more exogenous path and expand until the world is truly one enormous market?

BIBLIOGRAPHY

Bode, E., & Rey, S. (2006). "The spatial dimension of economic growth and convergence." *Papers in Regional Science, 85,* 171–176.

Clever, T. (2002). "Chapter 5: Free trade, regional agreements and strategic policies." In *Understanding the world economy* (pp. 91–107). Oxfordshire, UK: Taylor & Francis

Nazara, S., & Hewings, G. (2004). "Spatial structure and taxonomy of decomposition in shift-share analysis." *Growth & Change, 35,* 476–490.

Pike, A. (2013). "Economic geographies of brands and branding." *Economic Geography, 89,* 317–339.

Siegel, P., & Johnson, T. (1995). "Regional economic diversity and diversification." *Growth & Change, 26,* 261.

Simonen, J. (2006). "Regional externalities in the dynamic system of three regions." *Papers in Regional Science, 85,* 421–442.

Sunny, S. (2017). "Investments, incentives, and innovation: Geographical clustering dynamics as drivers of sustainable entrepreneurship." *Small Business Economics*, 1–23.

Volz, U. (2013). "ASEAN financial integration in the light of recent European experiences." *Journal Of Southeast Asian Economies, 30*, 124–142.

Werker, C., & Athreye, S. (2004). "Marshall's disciples: Knowledge and innovation driving regional economic development and growth." *Journal of Evolutionary Economics, 14*, 505–523.

SUGGESTED READING

Association of Southeast Asian Nations. (2013). *ASEAN Economic Community Chartbook 2012*. Retrieved from "http://www.asean.org/images/2013/resources/publication/2013%20-%20AEC%20Chartbook%202012.pdf"

Clever, T. (2002). "Chapter 6: Customs unions and common markets." In *Understanding the world economy* (pp. 108–124). Oxfordshire, UK: Taylor & Francis

Gleeson, B. (2003). "Learning about regionalism from Europe: "Economic normalisation" and beyond." *Australian Geographical Studies, 41*, 221–236.

Jayasuriya, K. (2003). "Embedded mercantilism and open regionalism: The crisis of a regional political project." *Third World Quarterly, 24*, 339–355.

Lopez-Bazo, E., Vaya, E., & Artis, M. (2004). "Regional externalities and growth: Evidence from European regions." *Journal of Regional Science, 44*, 43–73.

Phillips, N. (2003). "The rise and fall of open regionalism? Comparative reflections on regional governance in the Southern cone of Latin America." *Third World Quarterly, 24*, 217–234.

—Francis Duffy, MBA

GLOBAL MARKETING

ABSTRACT

This article will focus on how organizations can position themselves for successful global marketing. When entering the global market, social, economic, political, technological, and institutional factors are added into the equation as multinational corporations develop global marketing strategies. In order to be successful in global marketing, organizations will have to integrate their marketing initiatives into different countries. Given the changes that are occurring in the way business is conducted today, marketing professionals must be prepared to create campaigns that appeal to a global clientele. Global marketing is successful when there is coordination between the marketing policies for different countries and when the marketing equation for different countries can be adapted to the local market.

OVERVIEW

There is much activity between people, products, and organizations crossing over borders, which has led to the creation and growth of new global market segments. In addition, there are many forces that are transforming markets and changing the way that business is conducted. Factors that influence marketing include the marketing environment, the types of customers, and the competition in the market. When entering the global market, social, economic, political, technological, and institutional factors are added into the equation as multinational corporations develop global marketing strategies.

In most cases, global marketing generally manifests itself in two different phases (Caslione, 2003). The first phase is usually when an organization experiences rapid growth, high sales, and high profits. During this period, there tends to be an increased level of competition for limited resources. In addition, customers, suppliers and governments tend to be difficult to work with, and it is hard to develop relationships among these groups. However, "there is a specific infrastructure and unique behavioral mode of collective thinking and actions, which is referred to as the accelerated reactivity phase of globalization" (Caslione, 2003, p. 1).

The second phase occurs when an organization experiences slower economic growth, lower sales and profits, and reduced competition for limited sources. During this period, it is easier to gain access to customers, suppliers, and governments. Collaboration among these three groups is positive as all are attempting to find ways to improve the situation. Unlike the first phase, this period is categorized as a "decelerated proactivity phase of globalization due to a different type of infrastructure and behavioral mode dominating" (Caslione, 2003, p. 2).

Caslione (2003) believes that successful marketing professionals will be able to recognize and master the two different phases mentioned above by

- Measuring results within each country and region;
- Using a combination of marketing communication media;
- Using a globally centered mix of communications, marketing, and advertising;
- Building the corporate brand globally, country by country; and
- Appointing an experienced, highly motivated multicultural marketing team.

Marketing professionals will be required to understand the marketing concepts and practices needed to penetrate the political, economic, and social environments of potential markets (Kahle, Marshall & Kropp, 2003). In the era of global marketing, many organizations will be challenged to keep abreast of events affecting the marketing environment if they want to survive (Lin & Kao, 2004). In order to be successful in global marketing, organizations will have to integrate their marketing initiatives into different countries.

Preparing Marketing Professionals

Given the changes that are occurring in the way business is conducted today, marketing professionals must be prepared to create campaigns that appeal to a global clientele. Globalization is reshaping business strategy, especially marketing strategy, and marketing professionals will have to transition from a domestic focus to a global focus (Caslione, 2003). It will be imperative for marketing professionals to become well versed in the profiles of different segments that their organization plans to pursue. Unfortunately, many in the field are not prepared to make the transition. In a study conducted by the Massachusetts Institute of Technology, researchers found that 29% of the organizations surveyed did not have enough global marketing leaders in their organizations, 56% of the organizations believed that they did not have sufficient numbers of global marketing leaders to take their organization to the next level, and 80% were

Aerial view of the East Campus of the Massachusetts Institute of Technology (MIT) along the Charles River in 2015. (Courtesy of Nick Allen CC BY-SA 4.0 via Wikimedia Commons)

concerned that they lacked the global marketing professionals needed to staff their global marketing initiatives (Caslione, 2003). Therefore, marketers will need to upgrade their skill set in the field in order to be competitive in the market. As the marketing professionals become equipped for the challenge, they will be tasked to deal with the issues that have arisen in the field.

APPLICATION

Global Marketing Strategies

Globalization is not a new trend (IMF, 2002). With the prospect of conducting business on a global scale, global marketing professionals should create global strategies that will allow their organizations to reap the benefits instead of getting trapped by the pitfalls. In order to be successful in global marketing, organizations will have to integrate their marketing initiatives into different countries. Reddy and Vyas (2004) created a list of advantages and disadvantages of globalization as it pertains to marketing—information that is beneficial as global marketing professionals continuously improve upon their strategies in order to stay competitive.

Advantages

- Globalization leads to more economic growth. Economic growth is important to every country because it makes them feel strong, safe, and secure. Effective marketing approaches will lead

The CNN Headquarters is located in Atlanta, Georgia. (Courtesy of Josh Hallett from Winter Haven, Florida CC BY 2.0 via Wikimedia Commons)

to economic growth. Therefore, marketing is essential for economic growth and development (Reddy, 1996) and a major reason for globalization for multinationals, governments, and United Nation agencies.

- Globalization causes rapid technology transfer. Rapid technology transfers from one country to another are a result of increased globalization. Once there is a transfer of an organization's management and logistic expertise, there is potential for improvement in efficiency and reduction of costs for products and services across the world.
- Globalization is becoming effective as a result of more countries becoming democracies. There

McDonald's is an example of a successful multinational corporation. This is a McDonalds restaurant in Dukhan, western Qatar. (Courtesy of Vincent van Zeijst CC BY-SA 3.0 via Wikimedia Commons)

were many communist countries seeking a democratic state after the fall of the Soviet Union. In a globalized economy, democratization became easier than in a closed communist world where the information flow is restricted.

- The rapid spread of free enterprise system. Capitalism has been key in the success of the United States and Western countries, and many countries desired to pursue their model in order to own and operate business corporations.
- Unification of culture, living norms, and work ethic. Values and work ethics are becoming homogenous as a result of globalization, which has led to improved marketing effectiveness.
- Globalization will flourish as a result of increased communication through the Internet and other media. The Internet has provided many organizations with the ability to transmit media files quickly, which allows them to operate on an international level. Corporations can share who they are, what they market, and how customers may obtain their product.
- Instant news worldwide. Satellite and Internet communications, such as CNN and MSNBC, allow everyone to see news twenty-four hours in several languages. International media eliminates barriers to information flow.
- Worldwide improvement of health and living conditions. Globalization has brought improved quality of life throughout the world. Many products and services can be shared across the world with a mutual exchange of information.
- People are living longer. Life expectancy rates have increased across the world due to medical breakthroughs and new products that encourage health benefits. Globalization provides this type of information to an international audience.
- Multinational corporations are the greatest beneficiaries of the globalization trend. Corporations have the ability to use the same advertising themes and customize them for different countries by using marketing and distribution strategies to transfer the same message throughout the world.

Disadvantages

- Increasing unemployment in developed countries. Globalization has caused the unemployment rate to rise in developed countries because corpo-

Police close off the area around Brussels Central Train Station in Brussels, Belgium, after a bombing on June 20, 2017. (Courtesy of Romaine via Wikimedia Commons)

rations outsource and manufacture their products outside of their countries. According to Cateora (2002), there has been an increase in protests against global organizations such as WTO [World Trade Organization] and IMF [International Monetary Fund] because there is a perception that "globalization creates global worker exploitation, cultural extinction, higher oil prices, and diminished sovereignty of nations" (p. 51).

- Increasing trade deficit in developed countries. Increased imports of manufactured goods and services from other nations have led to trade deficits.
- Terrorism. Since people are able to migrate between countries so freely, there has been an increase in terrorism from other countries.

Fair Trade coffee beans being sorted by workers and volunteers, on an organic, fair-trade, shade-grown coffee plantation in Guatemala. (Courtesy of Wikimedia Commons)

- Loss of competitiveness in developed nations. Technology transfer has allowed underdeveloped countries to go from traditional manufacturing to modern manufacturing, which brings underdeveloped countries to the same level as the developed countries that provided them with the technology.
- Poorer nations feel that they are being taken advantage of by advanced nations. Poor countries have limitations in education, health care, and transportation, which keep them in a poor state (Kenny, 2002). Pirages (2000) believes that there are other issues (such as weakening of political authority without substitutions, increase of economic maladies, and destruction of culture) that create problems for poorer countries.
- Increasing economic gap between the rich and poor nations. Many poor countries believe that globalization has given the Western world more control over their economies. Rich countries tend to use cheap labor to get richer and do not help the poorer countries.
- Tradition- and religion-based countries feel that their norms and religious practices are violated. Some citizens believe that corporations will do anything to make a profit, even if it means violating some of their cultural practices and values.
- Comparison with rich nations makes poorer nations unhappy. With the increased use of satellites, citizens of the poorer countries have the opportunity to see the quality of living in the countries where corporations reside. When comparing the two ways of living, the citizens of the poorer countries perceive that they are being exploited in order to make the corporations and quality of life for their countries richer.
- Increasing pollution through manufacturing and transport worldwide. When corporations grow, there is an increase in manufacturing and traffic, which results in an increase in pollution. As a result, the pollution spreads globally.
- The spread of AIDS, West Nile virus, various kinds of flu and other diseases. Globalization increases the rate of diseases.
- As organizations develop their global marketing strategies, they will need to be mindful of the above-mentioned advantages and disadvantages of globalization as they relate to the countries that have been identified as their target markets.

Overseas Expansion

Licensing, franchises, and joint ventures that are undertaken overseas are sometimes referred to as global marketing.

- Licensing. Licensing occurs when a target country grants the right to manufacture and distribute a product under the licenser's trade name in a target country. The licensee pays a fee in exchange for the rights. Small and medium-sized companies tend to grant licenses more often than large companies. Since there is little investment required, licensing has the potential to provide a large return on investment. However, it is seen as the least profitable way to enter the market because most companies use licensing to supplement manufacturing and exporting. Licensing tends to be a viable option to enter a the market when the exporter does not have sufficient capital, when foreign government import restrictions forbid other ways to enter the market or when a host country is not comfortable with foreign ownership.

- Franchises. According to Edwards (2006), there are a number of reasons why a franchise may consider going global, and some of these reasons include opportunities to: "Build more brand and shareholder value, Add revenue sources and growth markets, Reduce dependence on the company's home market, Leverage existing corporate technology, supply chains, know-how and intellectual property, and Award more franchises in the home country by being global."

- Joint Ventures. Joint ventures occur when an organization enters a foreign market via a partnership with one or more companies already established in the host country. In most cases, the local company provides the expertise on the target market while the exporting company manages and markets the product. A joint venture arrangement allows organizations with limited capital to expand into international markets, and provides the marketers with access to its partner's distribution channels. According to QuickMBA.com, "Key issues in a joint venture are ownership, control, length of agreement, pricing, technology transfer, local firm capabilities and resources, and government intentions. Potential problems include conflict over new investments, mistrust over proprietary knowledge, how to split the pie, lack of parent company support, cultural clashes, and when and how to terminate the relationship" if it is necessary to take such action (2007).

VIEWPOINT

FAIR TRADE MARKETING

Fair trade marketing provides consumers with the opportunity to pay higher prices for imported goods so that producers in developing countries can have a decent standard of living (Witkowski, 2005). Supporters of this philosophy believe that prices need to be high enough so that multinational corporations in developing countries can have a living wage, safe working conditions and human dignity. In addition, there is a belief that trading has become unfair because the cost for developing global commodities has been undervalued when compared to commodities imported from industrialized countries.

When reviewing the concept of fair trade, it is important to analyze various ideological viewpoints. One could compare fair trade to antiglobalization; marketing management, ethical sourcing and ethical consumerism in order evaluate the different opinions and arguments on the topic. Witkowski (2005) has summarized some of the views by comparing and contrasting the positions.

CONCLUSION

Organizations that conduct business on a global level realize that it tends to be more complex, competitive, and difficult to manage. When entering the global market, social, economic, political, technological, and institutional factors are added into the equation as multinational corporations develop global marketing strategies. The companies that successfully master these challenges tend to be recognized for their best practices and excel in global marketing (Caslione, 2003).

Globalization is reshaping business strategy, especially marketing strategy, and marketing professionals will have to transition from a domestic focus to a global focus (Caslione, 2003). Unfortunately, many in the field are not prepared to make the transition. Therefore, marketers will need to upgrade their skill set in the field in order to be competitive in the market. As the marketing professionals become equipped for the challenge, they will be tasked to deal with the issues that have arisen in the field.

The Fair Trade Movement promotes trading partnerships, and there are organizations that work to make this effort successful. Common themes among these organizations include helping disadvantaged producers; promoting gender equity, transparent relations, and economic and environmental sustainability; reforming conventional international trade relationships; and creating consumer awareness of these issues (Witkowski, 2005, p. 24).

Witkowski (2005) presented the principles and goals of fair trade as defined by three organizations, and the results are listed below.

BIBLIOGRAPHY

Alden, D. L., Kelley, J. B., Riefler, P., Lee, J. A., & Soutar, G. N. (2013). "The effect of global company animosity on global brand attitudes in emerging and developed markets: does perceived value matter?" *Journal of International Marketing*, 21(2), 17-38.

Caslione, J. (2003). "Globalization demands new marketing skills." *Marketing News*, 37(14), 7-8.

Cateora, P. & Graham, J. (2002). *International marketing*, 11th ed. New York: McGraw-Hill.

Edwards, W. (2006). "Why go global?" Franchising World, 38(12), 38-40.

Ersun, A., & Karabulut, A. (2013). "Innovation management and marketing in global enterprises." *International Journal of Business & Management*, 8(20), 76-86.

Gao, T., & Shi, L. (2011). "How do multinational suppliers formulate mechanisms of global account coordination? an integrative framework and empirical study." *Journal of International Marketing*, 19(4), 61-87.

International Monetary Fund. (2000). "Globalization: Threat or opportunity? An IMF issue brief."

Kahle, L., Marshall, R., & Kropp, F. (2003). The new paradigm marketing model. Journal of Euromarketing, 12(3/4), 99-121.

Kenny, C. (2003). "Development's false divide." *Foreign Policy*, January/February, 76-77.

Kolk, A. (2014). "Linking subsistence activities to global marketing systems: The role of institutions." *Journal of Macromarketing*, 34(2), 186–98.

Lin, C., & Kao, D. (2004). "The impacts of country-of-origin on brand equity." *Journal of American Academy of Business*, Cambridge, 5(1/2), 37-40.

Pirages, D. (2000). "Globalization: A cautionary note." http://www.aaas.org/spp/yearbook/wooo/ch9.pdf"

Reddy, A., & Campbell, D. (1996). *Marketing's role in economic development*. Connecticut: Quorum Books

Reddy, A., & Vyas, N. (2004). "The globalization paradox: A marketing perspective." *International Journal of Management*, 21(2), 166-171.

Steenkamp, J.-B. (2014). "How global brands create firm value: The 4V model." *International Marketing Review*, 31(1), 5–29.

Witkowski, T. (2005). "Fair trade marketing: An alternative system for globalization and development." *Journal of Marketing Theory & Practice*, 13(4), 22-33.

SUGGESTED Reading

Field, A. (2007). "Breaking down barriers". *Journal of Commerce*, 8(16), 28-28.

Hult, G., Cavusgil, S., Kiyak, T., Deligonul, S., & Lagerström, K. (2007). "What drives performance in globally focused marketing organizations? A three-country study." *Journal of International Marketing*, 15(2), 58-85.

Laser, R. (2007). "BP takes global branding role away from marketing" *Marketing Week*, 30(5), 3-3.

Yung K. C. & Schellhase, R. (2014). "Exploring globalization and marketing performance at the 2012 Global Marketing Conference in Seoul." *Journal of Business Research*, 67(10), 2053–5

—Marie Gould

GLOBAL OUTSOURCING

ABSTRACT

This article discusses global outsourcing, the transfer of an organization's internal functions to a foreign country. Outsourcing is often undertaken as a way to procure skilled labor at a lower rate than it is available in developed economies. The transfer of manufacturing functions from developed nations like the United States to developing nations began in the 1950s. Technological advances have accelerated the ability of firms to procure and source products across the globe. Commonly outsourced functions include information technology tasks such as microchip development as well as many business services such as finance and accounting, human resources, data entry, and customer support centers. Global outsourcing has had a tremendous impact on how companies do business. This article examines the evolution of global outsourcing and its effect on business and labor.

OVERVIEW

The concept of outsourcing began when large companies decided to eliminate routine work that could be performed by third parties at a lower cost. Initially, many businesses started outsourcing everything but core business activities to other companies within the same national boundaries. But as the global economy started to evolve, businesses in developing countries began offering services to perform functions that companies had been outsourcing domestically. Transferring an organization's internal functions to a foreign country is known as "global outsourcing," while the entities that are set up to perform these functions are part of what's called "offshoring."

Growth of Outsourcing

Outsourcing continues to be a rapidly growing segment of the global economy; in 2014 it was an approximately $507 billion global industry. It is estimated that U.S. corporations outsourced more than 2.4 million jobs over the first decade of the twenty-first century, according to the Economic Policy Institute. Global outsourcing encompasses a variety of transactions including those focusing on both goods and services. A U.S. firm, for example, can outsource the production of goods, such as car parts, as well as services, including customer service positions. Companies that rely on outsourcing benefit from reduced labor costs and increased profits while the foreign countries that acquire outsourced jobs are enticed by the economic advancement. Another benefit to global outsourcing is that a company is able to focus more on its core responsibilities by transferring noncritical operations to a company that is better equipped to handle them. By outsourcing ancillary functions, businesses deliver products and services to the market more efficiently, thus enhancing their profits (Clott, 2004).

Outsourcing Strategies

Generally, there are two basic models used in outsource strategies: the outsource model and the captive model.

The Outsource Model

Within the outsource model, functions are transferred overseas and performed mostly by third-party providers. There are two subgroups within the outsource model: information technology outsourcing and business process outsourcing.

The MindSpace Campus in HITEC city, the hub of information technology companies, in Hyderabad, India. (Courtesy of Peculiar235 CC BY-SA 2.0 via Wikimedia Commons)

A Business Process Outsourcing hub in DLF Cyber City in Gurgaon, India. (Courtesy of Pithwilds CC BY-SA 3.0 via Wikimedia Commons)

- Information technology outsourcing, or ITO, is the transfer of the development and processing of information technology systems such as help desk functions, systems administration, network management, and web development.
- Business process outsourcing, or BPO, is the transfer of the management and processes of certain business operations like accounting, human resource functions (in particular payroll processing and health benefits management), and customer service call centers (Sen, 2005).

ITO transfers do not require an organization to establish a presence in a foreign country since third-party providers normally perform these functions. BPO transfers, however, sometimes require a company to establish an overseas subsidiary to control the functions being transferred. In addition to establishing a foreign subsidiary, some companies may opt to invest in an overseas company to which functions are being transferred. An investment of 10 percent or more in a foreign enterprise is considered direct foreign investment (Sen, 2005).

The Captive Model
BPO and direct foreign investments form the basis for yet another method—the captive model. Under this model, the outsourcing company establishes a foreign subsidiary, bypassing reliance on a third party. Under this model, a company maintains control of the operations being transferred, as well as

the hiring process and management of the workers performing the work. Because there is less risk for a company to establish a foreign subsidiary, a larger percentage of global outsourcing occurs following this method (Sinnett, 2006).

Global outsourcing has also caused a ripple effect on labor markets throughout the world. As jobs shift overseas, permanent jobs disappear, giving way to an increase in part-time, temporary, and freelance workers.

APPLICATIONS

Considerations
When a business decides to enter the global outsourcing market, there are a number of factors that contribute to that decision. These include, but are not limited to: risk, cost, and market opportunity.

Risk
Some of the risks involved in outsourcing are geopolitical and economic. In certain "hot spot" areas where there is a great deal of conflict and political turmoil, transferring functions to these regions can pose a threat to the health and safety of the employees as well as the economic well-being of the organization (Minevich, 2005). The terrorist attacks on certain subsidiaries of oil companies and service providers in Saudi Arabia is evidence of the geopolitical risks just as the nationalization of the oil industry in Venezuela is evidence of economic risk. Other risk factors that a business must consider are quality of service, loss of operations control, and security of data and stored information (Sinnett, 2006).

Cost
In addition to understanding the risks associated with a particular outsource market, organizations must also consider the cost of outsourcing and must be familiar with foreign wage structures. To be sure, there are skilled workers in many areas of the world who are willing to work for lower wages than workers in the United States, but as companies tap into these markets, competition eventually results in turnover as workers in those markets seek higher wages. Other costs include infrastructure costs, taxes, and regulatory fees. Finally, a company needs to determine market opportunity and identify those countries that provide workers in their particular industry. A skilled

workforce and established infrastructure will allow a company to expediently bring products and services to a market without sacrificing quality. Conversely, a company needs to also be ready to cease the operation in the event that the demand for the outsourced product or service declines (Minevich, 2006).

Market Opportunity

Before entering a global outsourcing market a business needs to determine what types of products and services are best suited for outsourcing. When global outsourcing first came into play, the production of labor-intensive products and manufactured goods was transferred abroad. At the time, labor-intensive products and manufactured goods were some of the only products that could be produced more efficiently in other countries. However, as time went on, advancements in the overseas economies and technologies made it possible to outsource products and services that required more advanced technology and know-how. This constant shifting and advancement allows for the creation and emergence of other outsource markets that specialize in different types of production. For example, consumer goods and textile manufacturing were some of the first products to be outsourced to China. However, as that market matured and economic development expanded, China as well as other Asian markets became outsource locations for products and services that required

Huawei Technologies Co., Ltd. is the largest telecommunications equipment manufacturer in the world. Its headquarters are locating in Shenzhen, China. (Courtesy of Brücke-Osteuropa via Wikimedia Commons)

more advanced technology. In particular, electronic components, telecommunications equipment, microchips, and computer boards were produced in China, Taiwan, and Hong Kong. This left the textile and other labor-heavy markets for other countries where such products could be produced in a similarly efficient manner.

Outsourcing & the Information Technology Industry

One industry that has been heavily affected by global outsourcing has been information technology. India has become a leader in this area because as demand for technology and its inherent complexities and costs grew, so did India's ability to provide low-cost, but capable assistance. During the 1990s, many U.S. corporations began to increasingly rely on data storage and retrieval systems, and this increased the demand for IT specialists that were capable of implementing and monitoring these systems. Eventually, the demand for these specialists exceeded the supply, and many firms sought out contract workers, consulting firms, and specialists throughout the world. Initially, many of these companies brought workers to the United States to work in their domestic information technology and engineering divisions. But over time, the number of skilled workers in foreign countries grew in conjunction with the establishment of offshoring businesses, and companies became more comfortable with using third parties abroad (Clott, 2004).

Policy Adjustments

In response to outsourcing, the U.S. government made adjustments to its policies on temporary work visas for immigrants. The goal of this policy was to assist businesses in meeting the demand for skilled workers. As more visas were issued, a greater number of workers were brought to America. Many of these workers came from India, because of its large pools of engineering and IT graduates who had the advanced technical skills, English language skills, and the willingness to work for lower wages than their American peers. At the same time, India had begun deregulating and modernizing its economy, and this spurred investment in its domestic telecom and computer industries. The combination of these events facilitated the growth of the information technology industry and its proliferation throughout the world markets during the 1990s (Clott, 2004).

Proliferation of Technological Advancement

This development eventually triggered further technological advances that transformed the nature of goods and services that could be sourced throughout the world. Because of vast improvements in telecommunications, many services that were considered non-tradable were transformed into services that were capable of being delivered electronically around the globe (Blinder, 2006). The confluence of these factors helped India to emerge as a leader in the outsource market for ITO and later on BPO. Initially, jobs outsourced to India included data entry and minor software development; however, these roles expanded into larger software projects, and even to running information technology departments for many organizations. Though over time it has lost some of its jobs to countries such as the Philippines (which has a more Americanized culture compared to India's heavy British influence) and Poland (which is more conveniently located for companies headquartered in Western Europe), India remains the world leader in outsourced jobs, especially in IT.

While information technology has been greatly transformed by global outsourcing, technological advances have also made it possible to have workers produce a variety of services from almost anywhere in the world. Because of these advances, business process outsourcing (BPO) is currently the most rapidly evolving model in the global outsourcing markets (Clott, 2004).

Initially, the types of jobs or business processes that were outsourced under this system were so-called "back office operations." These operations include payroll, accounts payable and receivable as well as accounting for financial services companies, insurance companies, and property management firms. As these operations were outsourced, workers in the source markets became more sophisticated and well trained, leading to further expansion of outsourced services. Initially, outsourced services included data entry, processing, and customer service call center support. In particular, many credit card companies and large consumer finance enterprises transferred their call centers abroad. Today, more complex tasks such as credit card collections, benefits

administration, and insurance-claims processing are being outsourced by U.S. businesses (Clott, 2004).

Development of the Global Marketplace

Although outsourcing has become an inevitable process for multinational businesses to effectively compete in the global marketplace, the rapid evolution makes it difficult to determine what effect increased globalization will have on business and labor because sufficient data is not currently available. Despite this lack of information, the changing nature of the global labor market does have significant implications for companies, workers, and countries, and there are some general conclusions that can be drawn. First, global outsourcing will continue to create a fluctuating worldwide labor market. Further, wage rates for some functions will be increased in low-wage countries while wage earners in wealthy nations like the United States, Great Britain, and Germany will find themselves competing with workers in developing countries. Finally, supply and demand for skilled workers in outsource markets is not efficiently matched. In some emerging outsource markets, the demand for available workers exceeds the supply while in well-established outsource markets the opposite holds true (Farrell, 2005).

One reason for the inefficiencies in the global outsource markets is the concentration of outsourced functions to a limited number of countries. By focusing on a few regions, many businesses have made investments that have limited their ability to establish themselves in other emerging markets. One possible result of this concentration will be that the demand for skilled labor will be greater than the supply, and this will force wages to rise. Of course, wages in these lower wage cost regions will not match wage rates in wealthy nations like the United States. However, increased wage pressures will have an effect on a company's profitability (Farrell, 2005).

In response to the concentration of global outsource markets in particular countries, there is another emerging trend in global outsourcing. As mentioned above, India has been a leader in the global outsourcing market. Today, in addition to jobs being transferred to India, jobs are also being sourced from India to other countries. Many staffing agencies based in India are establishing offices in other countries where global outsourcing markets are emerging.

In addition to this secondary outsourcing of jobs by India, other markets are emerging throughout the world. In North America, jobs from the United States have been transferred to Canada and Mexico, partially the result of the North American Free Trade Agreement of 1994. In Central and South America, outsourcing markets are rapidly developing in Costa Rica, Chile, and Brazil. The production of textile goods has contributed to the expansion of outsource markets in Chile, while Brazil has a large labor pool with solid technological skills. Eastern Europe also has some emerging outsourcing markets, with the top countries including Bulgaria, Lithuania, Estonia, Hungary, and Poland. Regardless of the specific methods that businesses employ in order to compete in the global marketplace, global outsourcing will continue as companies seek skilled workers at lower wages as well as new markets for their goods, products, and services.

VIEWPOINTS

Global outsourcing can be viewed as a natural progression from the increased connectivity of the world's economies, fostered by the expansion of free trade and technological advances. While there are proponents as well as critics, outsourcing of various functions will accelerate as the nature of work evolves. Essentially, more knowledge-based jobs will be subject to outsourcing. Information and knowledge are now the key assets of production in the world markets. As information becomes readily transferred via the global workforce, knowledge and expertise can be transported instantaneously around the world. In light of this transformation, a business can most effectively command comparative advantage through an ability to combine market and technological know-how with the creative talents of knowledge workers, such as those in the life sciences, logistics, and information technology (Clott, 2004).

Comparative Advantage
Comparative advantage is a fundamental economic theory that explains why it is beneficial for two parties—whether they are countries, regions, or businesses, to trade their goods and services. A key factor in determining comparative advantage is how readily the two regions can produce different goods that will subsequently be traded. If the United States can produce certain goods or services at lower cost than a foreign country, and if the foreign country can produce other goods and services at a lower cost than the United States, both countries may gain from trading each other's relatively inexpensively produced goods and services (Blinder, 2006).

Global Economic Growth
One result of continued outsourcing will be the expansion of global economic growth, and this has the potential to raise the standard of living in certain countries. Multinational businesses will derive benefits by continuing to rely on ITO and BPO, which will ultimately lower the cost of doing business and increase organizational productivity as goods and services are delivered to the global markets more efficiently. At the same time, outsourcing poses challenges and risks for both wealthy and developing nations, and there are labor and ethical issues that must be considered. As businesses in wealthy nations continue to seek lower wage markets, the availability of skilled labor markets in these outsource markets may not meet demand, and this will result in a larger wage gap between skilled and unskilled workers (Clott, 2004).

Further, the wage rates in wealthy nations will be suppressed because workers are competing with others in foreign nations who are willing to work at a lower rate. Also, to remain competitive many workers in wealthy nations are now performing functions on a part time or contract basis. This has resulted in a loss of job stability as well as traditional benefits such as health insurance. In addition to the challenges facing workers, businesses must also be able to respond to the challenges of globalization by changing the way that they are structured. Businesses that are not able to make innovative changes to the way they provide services and develop new products and services will not survive (Clott, 2004).

These challenges will require society to adapt. The United States, for example, currently enjoys a comparative advantage in knowledge-based jobs due to its well-established health and education services, professional and business services, and leisure and hospitality services. However, the United States will need to reorganize its workforce to maintain this advantage. These transformations, in turn, will require changes in the country's educational system to prepare workers for jobs that are available within the country (Blinder, 2006). Another possible development is a retreat from the free trade agreements that have been implemented over the last 50 years in an attempt by countries to maintain their position in the global markets and retain jobs by implementing protective tariffs (Clott, 2004).

In the end, global outsourcing will continue to be a method employed by multinational businesses in order to remain competitive in the world economy. The question remains as to how ready business, society, and governments are to respond to the challenges of the globalization of the world's economies.

BIBLIOGRAPHY

Bertrand, O., & Mol, M. J. (2013). "The antecedents and innovation effects of domestic and offshore R&D outsourcing: The contingent impact of cognitive distance and absorptive capacity." *Strategic Management Journal, 34*, 751–760.

Blinder, A. S. (2006, Mar/Apr). "Offshoring: The next industrial revolution?" *Foreign Affairs, 85*, 113–128.

Byrne, P.M. (2005). "Global sourcing: Opportunities and approaches for the 21st century." *Logistics Management, 44* 27–28.

Caruth, D. L., Pane Haden, S. S., & Caruth, G. D. (2013). "Critical Factors in Human Resource Outsourcing." *Journal Of Management Research (09725814), 13*, 1–9.

Clott, C.B. (2004). "Perspectives on global outsourcing and the changing nature of work." *Business and Society Review, 109*, 153–170.

Dolan, K. A. (2006). "Offshoring the offshorers." *Forbes, 177*, 74–76.

Farell, D., Laboissiere, M., & Rosenfeld, J. (2005). "Sizing the emerging global labor market." *Mckinzey Quarterly, 2005*, 92–103.

Frenkel, K. A. (2014). "The rise of no-location jobs." *CIO Insight,* 1.

Javalgi, R. G., Joseph, W., Granot, E., & Gross, A. C. (2013). "Strategies for sustaining the edge in offshore outsourcing of services: the case of India." *Journal Of Business & Industrial Marketing, 28*, 475–486.

Li, X. (2014). "Relational contracts, growth options, and heterogeneous beliefs: A game-theoretic perspective on information technology outsourcing." *Journal of Management Information Systems, 31*, 319–350.

Minevich, M.D., & Richter, F.J. (2005). "The global outsourcing report: Opportunities, costs and risks." *CIO Insight,* 55–58.

Rai, A., Keil, M., Hornyak, R., & Wüllenweber, K. (2012). "Hybrid Relational-Contractual Governance for Business Process Outsourcing." *Journal Of Management Information Systems, 29*, 213–256.

Relph, A., & Parker, D. (2014). "Outsourcing: A strategic risk?" *Management Services, 58*, 20–24.

Sen, R. & Islam, M.S. (2005/2006). "Southeast Asia in the global wave of outsourcing: Trends, opportunities and challenges." *Regional Outlook,* 75–79.

Sinnett, W.S. (2006). "Global sourcing for global markets." *Financial Executive, 22*, 46–48.

Verwaal, E. (2017). "Global outsourcing, explorative innovation and firm financial performance: A knowledge-exchange based perspective." *Journal of World Business, 52*, 1, 17–21.

SUGGESTED READING

Bean, M. & Meyer, M. (2005). "Career strategies for the age of global outsourcing." *Certification Magazine,* 7 16–44.

Gregory, R. W., Beck, R., & Keil, M. (2013). "Control balancing in information systems development offshoring projects." *MIS Quarterly, 37*, 1211–1232.

Han, K., & Mithas, S. (2013). "Information technology outsourcing and non-it operating costs: An empirical investigation." *MIS Quarterly, 37*, 315–331.

Manning, S., Larsen, M. M., & Bharati, P. (2015). "Global delivery models: The role of talent, speed and time zones in the global outsourcing industry." *Journal Of International Business Studies, 46(7)*, 850–877.

Murthy, S. (2004). "The impact of global IT outsourcing on IT providers." *Communications of AIS, 2004* 543–557.

Schwartz, E. (2006). "Salesforce goes to India." *Infoworld, 28*, 11.

—*Richa S. Tiwary, PhD, MLS*

GLOBALIZATION AND INTERNATIONAL ECONOMICS

ABSTRACT

This article focuses on globalization and how it affects the economic, political, and social frameworks of countries around the world. There is a discussion of the four aspects of globalization as well as the pros and cons of its implementation. In addition, the article discusses the impact of globalization on emerging markets.

OVERVIEW

Globalization, which can be defined as the growing combination of the economic and social aspects of the world, has been a point of contention in international economics. Although there has been rapid growth and reduction of poverty in countries such as China and India, there has been increasing antagonism over concerns that globalization has not improved matters of equality and environmental promotion (World Bank, n.d.). The concept of globalization has generated many different reactions. "Some view it as a process that is beneficial—a key to future world economic development—and also inevitable and irreversible. Others regard it with hostility, even fear, believing that it increases inequality within and between nations, threatens employment and living standards and thwarts social progress" (International Monetary Group, 2000, Section IV, ¶ 2).

Four Aspects of Globalization
The International Monetary Fund (n.d.) defined four aspects of globalization. These aspects were trade, capital movements, movement of people, and spread of knowledge and technology.

- Trade: Reports show that underdeveloped countries have started to up their portions of world trade, which can be shown through the increase in share from 19 percent in 1971 to 29 percent in 1999.
- Capital movements: Individuals, such as venture capitalists, elevated private capital flows to developing countries throughout the 1990s.
- Movement of people: It was found that many workers in developing countries tend to relocate from one country to another in an effort to gain work experience and job opportunities. Most of

The headquarters of the International Monetary Fund is located in Washington, D. C. (Courtesy of International Monetary Fund via Wikimedia Commons)

the migration was found to be between developing countries.
- Spread of knowledge: Exchanging information tends to be an overlooked aspect of globalization. Through the use of direct foreign investment, there could be opportunities for technical innovation as well as the expansion of physical capital stock.

Although globalization provides opportunities for development around the world, many believe the process has not been progressing evenly among all countries. It has been found that some countries (i.e., East Asia) are integrating into the global system at a faster pace than others. However, other countries, such as those in Latin America (other than Brazil) (Carranza Ko, 2013) and Africa, have not experienced the same level of change. Countries in these regions saw their economies stagnate or decline during the 1970s and 1980s. During the 1990s, the world experienced a crisis in the emerging markets, although the early 2000s saw robust growth in the BRIC nations. During the global financial crisis of 2008, Brazil, India and China were almost alone in the world in experiencing economic growth (Yao & Zhou, 2011; Carrasco & Williams, 2012).

Risks of Globalization
One of the lessons learned from the emerging market crisis in the 1990s was that there are risks when

attempting to integrate to a global economy. Two major risks are volatile capital movements as well as social, economic, and environmental degradation as a result of poverty. Some other risks include:

Political Risks

- Instability in national governments
- War, both civil and international
- Potential nationalization of an organization's resources
- Cancellation or non-renewal of export or import licenses
- Confiscation of the importer's company
- Imposition of an import ban after the shipment of the goods
- Imposition of exchange controls by the importer's country or foreign currency shortages
- Surrendering political sovereignty

Economic Risks & Political Risks

- Differences and fluctuations in the value of different currencies
- Differences in prevailing wage rates
- Difficulties in enforcing property rights
- Unemployment
- Insolvency of the buyer
- Failure of the buyer to pay the amount due within six months after the due date
- Non-acceptance
- Surrendering economic sovereignty

Emerging Markets

Although the 1990s was not a good time for emerging markets, there was a rebound during the next decade. According to a study of multinational corporations, "two thirds of the respondents believed investment in emerging markets is likely to continue to grow, with three quarters claiming to be actively investing in Central and Eastern Europe" ("Survey reveals," 2005, p. 43). Such optimism was borne out. Antoine van Agtmael, a senior executive at World Bank Group, was the first person to use the term "emerging markets" (Jana, 2007). Brazil, Russia, India, and China, which are known as the BRIC economies, were first identified as countries poised for large and rapid economic growth. Real gross domestic product (GDP) was expected to grow three times faster in these countries

over the next six years (Goldman Sachs, 2003). South Africa was later added to the list. In fact, between 2001 and 2010 the BRICs GDP per capita growth leaped as much as 10 percent, a staggering rate compared with the United States and Europe whose average over the same period was a mere 1 percent. In 2013, China was projected to be the largest economy in the world by 2027, while the BRICs were expected to equal the G7 in size by 2032 (Nelson, Maniam & Leavell, 2013). The significance of emerging markets has reached a point where corporations have recognized their influence on the corporations' bottom line.

The Altradius survey reported that the highest percentage of respondents from the multinational corporations was investing as follows: 74 percent invested in Central and Eastern Europe, 43 percent invested in China, and 35 percent invested in India and Southeast Asia. The countries that received the most funding in Central and Eastern Europe include Poland (60 percent), Czech Republic (46 percent), Russia (40 percent) followed by other EU accession countries. In Southeast Asia, India was the top choice followed by Malaysia, Thailand, and Indonesia ("Survey reveals," 2005).

Although the news appeared to be promising for emerging markets, there were some concerns that needed to be addressed. According to Olsen, Pinto, and Virji (2005), some potential pitfalls included:

- Organizations must deal with the same growth challenges that they face in other markets. Some of these challenges deal with: understanding what the customer wants, developing unique and cost-effective offers, creating an effective marketing strategy, and overcoming internal organizational barriers.
- Organizations must be prepared to cope with the changeability and imbalance of developing markets. Although venture capitalists are willing to fund these ventures, many seasoned venture capital managers are not willing to deal with fund management for these types of accounts.
- Corporate headquarter offices tend to take too much time when making decisions and communicating information, which hinders subsidiaries from reacting to problems in a timely manner. Organizations must eliminate the bureaucratic red tape and provide opportunities to respond quickly when solving problems. Another option would be to empower the subsidiaries to make decisions up to a certain level.

APPLICATION

Emerging Markets

According to the 1999 World Development Report, there was an increasing difference between the developed and developing countries (World Bank, 1999). Many had the perception that the international community should be doing more to close the gap since the aid per capita to developing countries was reduced by one-third in the 1990s. "As developing countries made strides to open their economies and expand their exports, they were faced with significant trade barriers with no aid or trade. To many in the developing world, trade policy in the more advanced countries seems to be more a matter of self-interest than of general principle" (Stiglitz, 2000, p. 438).

It appears that if there was a good economic analysis, it is used in favor of the advanced countries in order to support their self-interests. Given the number of opportunities for developing countries to be placed at a disadvantage, supporters of trade liberalization argue that standard economic analysis will benefit a developing country. Losses in one sector will be gained in another sector (i.e., job loss in one sector will be offset by job creation in another sector). However, there is an assumption that the markets are functioning properly, which is not always the case. As a result, the anticipated jobs may not be created in another sector, and the process becomes unbalanced. When situations such as this example arise, supporters of trade liberalization must be prepared to respond to the concomitant challenges.

One could argue that developing countries are at a disadvantage, and the scales are tipped against them. To address the different types of inequities that may arise, those in the international business arena must develop policies and procedures that address these issues and create a sense of fairness for everyone involved. Many believe that there should be standards for social responsibility and ethics to make sure that developing countries are not exploited. Having a formal global approach to these types of challenges can ensure a sense of fairness for everyone involved in the process.

Representational Approaches

Khan (2007) introduced an abstract framework that identified four representational avenues to comprehend how social inequities surface in developing countries as they attempt to venture into international business. When the model was created, it was established that there are many parties associated with the process. Since representation ranged from local workers to international mass media institutions, each party was defined in terms of geography. The two categories introduced are locals and foreigners. Locals were defined as individuals or entities that are primarily located in the developing countries. Locals are very diverse and have different perspectives and interests. Individuals falling into the "foreign" category are those that do not fit into the local category. Significant players in the foreign group would include international businesses that are directly involved in specific situations and their critics.

Both of these groups are considered to be "representers," as they work to resolve issues that arise. Each situation is analyzed and evaluated on the representers' role in the situation and the worldview of the situation. The approaches attempt to understand how the ethical issues regarding international business are represented in the underdeveloped world. The four different approaches are as follows:

Approach 1 (No-speak): Foreigners are the representers and the issue is expressed from a foreign world viewpoint. The local residents have no voice, and they have no input into the worldview. Local worldviews have no place in the development of issues, and the local experience is not considered relevant in social equity issues. Most of the international business research follows this approach (i.e., Hofstede's Culture's Consequence).

Approach 2 (Us-speak): The commonality between this approach and the first approach is that the foreigners are the representers. However, the difference is that the worldview incorporates the local experience. This approach attempts to represent local realities (local view) in a way that allows the local inhabitants to understand the situation. In many instances, the representer places himself in the local's position and attempts to articulate the viewpoint based on the local's perspective.

Approach 3 (Same-speak): The locals are the representers, and the worldview is the same as the foreigner's perception. Locals represent themselves based on one or more universal perceptions that originate from

The new headquarters of the Toyota Motor Corporation, opened in February 2005 in Toyota City, Japan. Toyota is one of the world's largest multinational corporations. (Courtesy of Chris 73 CC BY-SA 3.0 via Wikimedia Commons)

the West (i.e., modernism, post-structuralism, secular nationalism). Many of the most influential representations of ethical issues that affect global organizations in underdeveloped nations are based on this approach.

Approach 4 (Other-speak): Locals are the representers, and international business issues are explained in the

Nestlé's, a multinational corporation, has its corporate headquarters located in Vevey, Vaud, Switzerland. However, its presence is worldwide. Here the Brazilian president, Lula da Silva, inaugurates a factory in Feira de Santana (Bahia), in February 2007. (Courtesy of Ricardo Stuckert/PR (Agência Brasil CC BY 3.0 via Wikimedia Commons)

context of local viewpoints. When evaluating this approach, representation is being explained by locals using local concepts.

The above approaches provide an explanation as to how foreigners and locals perceive the severity of social issues, which is important to the interactions of the business community. Multinational corporations have to understand the culture and values of the countries in which they do business. Otherwise, the corporation may suffer as a result of conflict on social and business ethics issues. There has to be some sense of social responsibility on the part of the multinational corporation.

Integrative Justice Model
Santos and Laczniak (2013) suggest a normative ethics approach to constructing a framework for multinational corporations to use in order to avoid the tendency to exploit unsophisticated, low-income consumers while establishing a profitable new market.

- Engage impoverished consumers with nonexploitative intent.
- Work with customers to co-create value.
- Invest in long-term consumption while protecting the environment.
- Recruit representation by all stakeholders.
- Plan for long-term profit management instead of short-term profit maximization.

VIEWPOINT

Corporate & Local Leadership
Olsen, Pinto, & Virgi (2005) strongly believed that it was critical to develop a set of practices that would assist local and corporate leaders with achieving long-term success. Six practices were identified to aid these businesses with developing new models on how to make the process successful and profitable. The six practices were as follows:

- Establishing and Reviewing Long-term Direction
- Given the level of uncertainty in emerging markets, it is almost impossible to predict what the future will hold and many managers find it difficult to develop a long-term strategy about what direction the project should go. In lieu of a traditional approach to strategic management, the researchers have de-

termined that managers can develop some sort of direction by outlining:

- Opportunities for a future market as well as a SWOT analysis
- A broad, tangible plan that addresses financial, competitive, and operational needs
- A two- to four-year short-term plan that will allow the organization to obtain its short-term goals.

Once these objectives have been obtained, the organization can focus on developing strategies over a period of time. These plans should allow the organization to adjust its strategy to new conditions. As the business continues to grow and be responsible for addressing issues as they arise, it will be in a better position to develop long-term strategies. Long-term strategies "(a) serve as an anchor against which decisions can be tested, (b) align expectations between local and corporate leaders, (c) define the criteria for when local market change should trigger a change in the strategy" (Olsen, Pinto, & Virji, 2005, p. 39).

- Fitting the Emerging Market Business within the Organizational Structure
- Many multinational corporations hinder the decision-making process of their subsidiaries that function in the emerging markets. This type of problem may occur in three ways such as (a) grouping emerging market subsidiaries with subsidiaries in the larger developed markets, (b) units cannot learn from one another when the organizations allow the structure or a process to minimize opportunities of sharing information, and (c) the organizational structure is outdated for the current trends and there is a constant need to make adjustments in the organizational design.
- Defining Roles and Decision Rights between Headquarters and the Local Leadership

Many organizations may encounter problems when they attempt to divide decision-making rights regarding the corporate office and the local subsidiaries. The two extreme approaches are when the corporate office micromanages the subsidiaries and when the corporate office gives too much freedom to the subsidiaries and does not keep the senior management informed as to what is going on in the business. It is important for these organizations to create an organizational design and structure that will allow the

two entities to share and divide the different levels of responsibility and decision-making rights so that the emerging market can respond to the trends and conditions in the market.

- Prioritizing Local Decisions
- Subsidiaries must develop an agenda that prioritizes the different levels of strategies that need to be performed to reach long-term objectives. A potential process for the agenda may be to (a) place issues on the agenda list when they are recorded and described by local and corporate managers and (b) move the issues off the list when they have been dissolved.
- Making Resource Allocation More Flexible

Many multinational corporations do not have a resource allocation system that can meet the needs of the emerging market subsidiaries. Therefore, these organizations will need to define the criteria for emerging market subsidiaries and align them with the corporate standards. To meet this need, some multinational corporations are using the stage-gated funding method and linking it to specific performance indicators.

- Monitoring and Managing Performance

Performance needs to be measured based on the economic market conditions in the local nation.

To fully experience the emerging market growth experience, multinational corporations will be required to balance each of the areas mentioned above.

CONCLUSION

Trade liberalization should prove an asset to third world nations and the world at large. However, it must be "balanced in agenda, process, and outcomes, including not only sectors in which developed countries have a comparative advantage, like financial services, but also those in which developing countries have a special interest, like agriculture and construction services" (Stiglitz, 2000, p. 437). One could argue that developing countries are at a disadvantage and that the scales are tipped against them. To address the different types of inequities that may arise, those in the international business arena must develop policies and procedures that address these issues and create a sense of fairness for everyone involved.

Globalization can prosper when there is consideration for the whole package. According to the International Monetary Fund, the entire package should include strategies, rules, financial and technical aid, and help in erasing debt if possible and needed. Other factors within the package could include the following:

- Macroeconomic stability to create the right conditions for investment and saving
- Outward oriented policies to promote efficiency through increased trade and investment
- Structural reform to encourage domestic competition
- Strong institutions and an effective government to foster good governance
- Education, training, and research and development to promote productivity
- External debt management to ensure adequate resources for sustainable development (International Monetary Fund, 2000, "How can the poorest").

Khan (2007) introduced a conceptual framework that identified four representational approaches to understanding how social inequities surface in developing countries as they attempt to venture into international business. The approaches provide an explanation as to how foreigners and locals perceive the severity of social issues, which is important to the interactions in the business community.

BIBLIOGRAPHY

Carranza Ko, N. (2013). "Cementing class differences: Globalization in Peru." *Perspectives on Global Development & Technology, 12,* 411–426.

Carrasco, E. R., & Williams, S. (2012). "Emerging economies after the global financial crisis: The case of Brazil." *Northwestern Journal of International Law & Business, 33,* 81–119.

Darwis, Y. (2013). "Communication media (e-commerce) as a supporting factor in Indonesia's fashion industry in the international business competition." *International Journal of Organizational Innovation, 5,* 206–220.

International Monetary Fund. (2000, April 12). "Threat or opportunity?" Retrieved from xlink:href="http://www.imf.org/external/np/exr/ib/2000/041200.htm"

Jana, R. (2007, January 10). "Lessons from emerging-market leaders." *Business Week Online, 22.*

Khan, F. (2006). "Representational approaches matter." *Journal of Business Ethics, 73,* 77–89.

Nelson, G., Maniam, B., & Leavell, H. (2013). BRIC: "Overview and future outlook." *Journal of International Finance & Economics, 13,* 137–144.

Olsen, T., Pinto, M., & Virji, S. (2005). "Navigating growth in emerging markets: Six rules for improving decision making between corporate and local leadership." *Journal of Business Strategy, 26,* 37–44.

"Reforming policies for the business sector to harvest the benefits of globalisation." (2012). *OECD Economic Surveys: Netherlands, 2012,* 41–70.

Santos, N. C., & Laczniak, G. R. (2012). "Marketing to the base of the pyramid: A corporate responsibility approach with case inspired strategies." *Business & Politics, 14.*

Song, H., Li, G., Cao, Z. (2017). "Tourism and economic globalization: An emerging research agenda." *Journal of Travel Research.*

Stiglitz, J. (2000). "Two principles for the next round or, how to bring developing countries in from the cold." *World Economy, 23,* 437–455.

"Survey reveals major risks involved in trading with emergent markets." (2005). *Credit Control, 26,* 43.

The World Bank Group (n.d.). "Globalization." Retrieved from xlink:href="http://www1.worldbank.org/economicpolicy/globalization/World"

Yao, X., & Zhou, M. (2011). "China's economic and trade development: Imbalance to equilibrium." *World Economy, 34,* 2081–2096.

SUGGESTED READING

Driga, I. (2011). "FDI flows and host country economic development." *Annals of the University of Petrosani Economics, 11,* 101-108.

Eckhardt, G., & Mahi, H. (2004). "The role of consumer agency in the globalization process in emerging markets." *Journal of Macromarketing, 24,* 136–146.

Kaminsky, G. (2007). "Emerging markets and financial globalization sovereign bond spreads in 1870-1913 and today." *Journal of International Economics, 73,* 219–222.

Martin, P., & Rey, H. (2006). "Globalization and emerging markets: With or without crash?" *American Economic Review, 96,* 1631–1651.

—Marie Gould

H

HIGH-FREQUENCY TRADING

ABSTRACT

High-frequency trading refers to the popular practice of buying and selling stock through the use of sophisticated computer programs and increasingly larger volume trading platforms. In a volatile global financial market, high-frequency trading introduces the possibility of computer programs analyzing gigabytes of up-to-the-second financial data, including critical market information at very high speeds. However, given that the process virtually eliminates the human factor in stock purchasing, and given the vulnerabilities of even the most sophisticated computer systems, high-frequency trading has also sparked concerns over the risk of catastrophic financial panic as computerized trades become faster and faster.

OVERVIEW

For more than two centuries, the operating principle behind financial markets has been that the faster the sales and purchase of stock shares, the more liquid the financial marketplace, the better for both investors and companies. Information networks that link the principal stock trading centers—New York to London; New York to Tokyo; New York to Chicago; London to Hong Kong, for instance—have long sought to obtain accurate information quickly to maintain a healthy trading environment. Thus information has always been crucial—information about a company's health, earnings reports, all financial data gathered by government agencies, movement among both small investors and large investment firms, even information about personnel movements within individual companies, and even broader information about resource scarcity, weather interruptions of market activity, unexpected political and military events—all factor into the measuring of a market's health and in turn the viability of stock trading. Information, then, is at the heart of the trading transaction.

Securing such information quickly has always been the basis for shrewd market maneuvers that have routinely secured investors sizeable returns. The general premise, of course, has been for investors to buy below the trend prices and then sell when the market price for the share of stock pitches above trends. It is determining that moment that defines expert and successful trading.

For centuries, new communication networks have impacted the trading process. In a business that relied originally on a network of spies on horseback carrying secret information about new mineral reserves or potential trading routes opening on land or sea, the invention of the wireless telegraph and the subsequent introduction of telephone communication and then transatlantic communication through underwater cables created a frenzy for the increasingly rapid dissemination of crucial financial information and redefined trading as an industry onto itself. Speed and volume became the defining characteristics of the trading market.

A view from the Member's Gallery inside the NYSE in August, 2008. (Courtesy of Ryan Lawler via Wikimedia Commons)

The introduction in the mid-1980s of automation into the trading markets and the rapid evolution into digital information platforms (accomplished in less than 20 years) revolutionized the traditional conservative wisdom about the relationship between an investor and a broker and, in turn, the relationship between the trading market and the larger economic environment. The stock brokers, traditionally middlemen who gathered financial information and then advised their investors, seemed suddenly to embody antiquated, time-consuming, and even backward thinking. Traditionally, investors paid brokers for their insights, their market savvy and gut feelings, their ability to gauge and predict market activity, and to advise them when to buy and when to sell often huge volumes of stocks.

What if computers could do the thinking? "[High-frequency traders] are a natural outcome in a world in which trading is automated, and in which there is competition between lots of different exchanges and a need for someone speedily to knit together the prices they offer" ("Fast" 2012). By feeding massive amounts of data, raw financial information, into a software program and by devising algorithms that direct the computer to make the appropriate logical market moves, would it not be possible for an investor to sidestep the expense of the stockbroker and engage in market activity directly? Response time could be minimized to the point at which it is measured in millionths of a second, a far cry from the often time-consuming efforts of traditional stockbrokers to pore over financial information before deciding on purchase actions. By automating the middleman, of course, what would be lost would be the human factor, that uncanny insight and perceptions that stockbrokers can bring to their clients. But what would be gained would be higher sales volumes, stock shares bought and sold with such rapidity that by the time a stockbroker would receive the information, the information would already be obsolete and virtually useless. Machine talking to machine—that is the central vision of high-frequency trading.

APPLICATIONS

The evolution of high-frequency trading has redefined the stock market—if the conventional model centered on big-name firms with hundreds of high-priced financial analysts headquartered in multifloor office buildings in the financial heart of major international cities, the new model stressed smaller facilities in more remote areas, a smaller corps of younger, hipper financial advisers with computer science and mathematical backgrounds (known as quants), most digital natives born after 1980. Their job is to facilitate the movement of information, designing not only the information network systems whose effectiveness is measured by how many millionths of second the routing system can take off information transfer but also to design cutting-edge applications and code new algorithms that will, in turn, create computer systems more tuned to the meanings of fluctuations in the global market.

Of course, the rapid rise of these new stockbroker firms that manage high-frequency trading has raised security concerns. Unlike the established firms long in the financial market, these firms are not required to register with any government oversight or regulatory board, not even the Securities and Exchange Commission. In short, the volume of financial information and sales monitored by these high-frequency trading outfits is never scrutinized, books are never made public, and financial maneuvers are not subject to larger scrutiny to maintain a healthy larger economic environment. More problematic, there is no way to override the computer activities should the sales (and the volume is measured in millions of transactions per second) start to spin into some catastrophic meltdown.

A view from inside the Tokyo Stock Exchange on May 29, 2015. (Courtesy of Wpcpey CC BY 4.0 via Wikimedia Commons)

Undoubtedly high-frequency trading is cheaper and quicker to the point that investors, particularly those born entirely within the age of the Internet and computer accessibility, have begun to rely on the system (market analysts, many skeptical about the emergence of an entirely automated market dismiss that reliance as an addiction to the easy way, a way to avoid the hard work of market analysis and the human factor of assessing the market volatility and viability). Even conservative high-priced brokerage houses have begun to invest not merely in financial personnel to render experienced trading intermediation but now in trading infrastructure itself, investing billions in across-the-board revamping of computer systems, upgrading to high-speed servers, investing in the coding of increasingly more sophisticated programs to assess and even manipulate the market, and most importantly securing processing routes that provide efficient global links. In 2014, Matthew O'Brien, contributing editor for the *Atlantic*, termed this massive intra-business escalation of technology as a kind of "intellectual arms race." Clearly, high-frequency trading has become a defining and central reality—estimates agree on that. In 2013, for instance, about half of the billions of stock transactions were facilitated and executed using automation. That number will increase as the efficiency and security of machine-to-machine trading increases and as the speed of relayed information, sent along thousands of miles of fiber optic wiring, approaches the speed of light itself (see Adler, 2012).

It is perhaps difficult without a background in finance trading to appreciate the magnitude of the impact of high-frequency trading. Without the appropriate scale, the process and its potential advantage can seem more like picking up pennies in some infinitely large parking lot. If a stock in a shoe company trades at $2.00 a share and an investor purchases a volume of the stock through an automated purchase vendor and then, within seconds of the purchase, the stock price ticks up to $2.01, the same automated stock vendor will sell it, as it is programmed to sell at a margin of profit. Now if that stock price ticks up to a decimal higher, say $2.01, the same stock vendor will sell, programmed to sell at any margin of profit. For a stockbroker to peruse data and to horse-trade and quibble to that extent would be tedious, unrewarding, and time consuming—but a computer can do that evaluating effortlessly all day and all night.

For a computer, pursuing a fraction of one thousandth of a cent is a standard operating program.

Simultaneously, the program can process data regarding what to do with that stock at that price, whether to move it or hold it. Those decisions will be uncomplicated by the necessary caution of the human factor—the program will be fed a constant stream of international financial information, including market moves, international stock trading data, government data on world market health, even measures of cell phone upticks that might indicate hot spots in trading. It is more information than a stock broker could sift through in weeks. In milliseconds, the automated stock vendor measures patterns, assesses trends, tests prices, and logically makes the appropriate buy or sell move. To return to the example of that shoe company stock, if that apparently miniscule percentage of stock value increases across hundreds of shares traded thousands of time an hour, the impact of high-frequency trading starts to become evident. If one then multiplies that times the thousands of small and large companies that trade stock on the public market, the animation volume of trading becomes clearer. These automated investors are certainly not like old-school stockbrokers who were primarily committed to making their clients rich, hired to ensure their clients banked a profit at the end of the day through savvy observation of market movements. Rather, in high-frequency trading the goal for the program is to act logically, methodically, cleanly, and efficiently.

Given the industrywide interest in developing cutting-edge software applications that will facilitate and even manipulate stock market trading, and given the deep secrecy under which many investment firms cloak their software development divisions, cataloging the variety of software programs designed to work with trading is a challenge. As the industry moves toward being driven entirely by algorithms, perhaps the two best-known are the momentum algorithm and the mean-revision algorithm. The momentum algorithm buys stock expected to rise; the mean-revision algorithm sells stock expected to drop. Those expectations are shaped entirely by the constant stream of financial data. There is also an algorithm designed to weigh stock options in pairs, comparing activity in industries that are historically linked, for instance the fuel industry and the airline industry or the commodities market and the restaurant industry. These algorithms are designed to make financial moves by first weighing and comparing conditions in different industries. Another market maker algorithm looks for quick profit, the old-school conventional wisdom of buying low and then selling high, but this can be done increasingly rapidly and efficiently. "Stock exchanges can now execute trades in less than a half a millionth of a second more than a million times faster than the human mind can make a decision" (Baumann, 2013).

VIEWPOINTS

The larger question, of course, is whether high-frequency trading will render the current stock market obsolete. In high-frequency trading, computers operate without perceptions greater than the logic of the current negotiation and without regard for the health of the companies involved, much less the well-being of the greater economy. The traditionally accepted value of centralized financial institutions was to guarantee a smoothly operating economy, reassuring investors that stock transactions are conducted in stable and transparent ways. Traders "want the benefits of high-frequency traders' technology, but [they] need to make sure the technology is being deployed safely and responsibly because everyone has a stake in the outcome" (Chilton, 2014).

As the volume of high-frequency trading swells, as more stock brokerages commit resources to the strategies of automated trading, the risk grows of machine-to-machine error. Opponents of the trend toward high-frequency trading point out that given the volume of trading done in milliseconds, any financial perturbation or glitch in the information systems could render the market chaotic and vulnerable to precipitous collapse, and given the vastness of the automated systems, any kill button might be difficult to locate, much like running behind tipping dominos. Proponents of high-frequency trading have suggested batching trading orders in sequential stock folders, thus preventing continuous trading and minimizing the possibility of snowballing (Budish et al., 2012).

Indeed the so-called Flash Crash on May 6, 2010, in which the Dow Jones industrial average plummeted more than 600 points in just under five minutes, triggering a massive global panic, was initially blamed by conservative financial experts on the untrackable high-frequency trading. The initial explanation centered on computer systems acting on false information, most likely leaked into the global network at some portal point, which led to programs beginning to sell and buy their own unwanted stocks, bouncing the volume back and forth in a kind of vacuum loop. However, much later, financial forensics indicated that the programs actually prevented the sales loop from escalating into a major global meltdown, that the system actually corrected itself, patched across its own misinformation, and halted the accelerating sales spiral. The algorithm shut itself off from compounding its own error (Goldfarb, 2010).

At any rate, old-school investment advisers are reluctant to concede the implications of the computer-driven market. "High-frequency traders tend to narrow the bid-ask spread by protecting the market makers from bad news while they help their positions. Thus, trading costs get lower" (Conerly, 2014). The potential profits from high-volume, high-speed transactions position high-frequency trading as a kind of inevitability for the stock market and for the global economy.

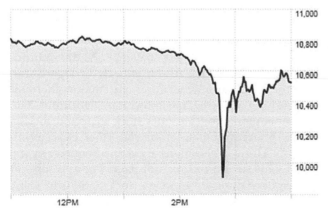

The Dow Jones Industrial Average on May 6th, 2010 (11:00 AM - 4:00 PM EST) during the 2010 Flash Crash. (Courtesy of CNN, PM3 via Wikimedia Commons)

BIBLIOGRAPHY

Adler, J. (2012, August 3). "Raging bulls: How Wall Street got addicted to light-speed trading."

Bauman, N. (2013, January/February). "Too fast to fail: Is high-speed trading the next Wall Street disaster?" Mother Jones

Budish, E., Cramton. P., & Shim, J. (2012). *The high-frequency trading arms race: Frequent batch actions as a market design response.* University of Chicago Booth School of Business publications.

Chilton, B. (2014, July 7). "No need to demonize high-frequency trading." *New York Times.*

Conerly, B. (2014, April 14). "High frequency trading explained simply." *Forbes.*

"The fast and furious." (2012, February 25). *Economist.*

Goldfarb, Z. (2010, October 1). "Report examines May's 'flash crash' expresses concern over high-speed trading." *Washington Post.*

Kirilenko, A., Kyle, A., Samadi, M., Tuzun, T. (2017). "The flash crash: High-frequency trading in an electronic market." *The Journal of Finance, 72,* 3, 967–998.

O'Brien, Matthew. (2014, April 11). "Everything you need to know about high-frequency trading." *The Atlantic.*

SUGGESTED READING

Brogaard, J., Hendershott, T., & Riordan, R. (2014). "High-frequency trading and price discovery." *Review of Financial Studies, 27,* 2267–2306.

Clarke, T. (2014). "High-frequency trading and dark pools: sharks never sleep." *Law & Financial Markets Review, 8,* 342–351.

Lewis, Michael. (2014). Flash boys. New York, NY: Norton.

Manahov, V., & Hudson, R. (2014). "The implications of high-frequency trading on market efficiency and price discovery." *Applied Economics Letters, 21,* 1148–1151.

Patterson, Scott. (2013). *Dark pools: The rise of the machine traders and the rigging of the U.S. stock market.* New York, NY: Crown.

—Joseph Dewey

HUMAN RESOURCE ECONOMICS

ABSTRACT

When firms hire workers they are, knowingly or unknowingly, acquiring human capital. The idea is far from new but only recently has it acquired enough stature to be considered a factor of production in its own right. Human capital theory and the resource-based view of the firm maintain that to prosper, a business must create value in ways that rivals cannot. The wellspring of innovative thinking this requires is the knowledgeable worker capable of 'learning by doing.' Such at least is the current economic thinking that drives the more traditional human resource function of screening, selection, training and development.

OVERVIEW

We live in a 'post-industrial' age where our individual and collective prosperity increasingly depends on how well or ill we acclimate to the 'knowledge' economy. But in order to succeed at this, we will have to see ourselves as more than just hardworking members of the labor force. High wages and steady employment will increasingly go to those of us who think of themselves as an investment in 'human' capital.

We must, in a word, build a sophisticated 'skills-set' that adds value to prospective employers' products and services. The alternative is to become a casualty of the onward rush of technology and globalization and eke out an uncertain living at a succession of low-paying jobs. It's a grim choice with a decidedly

Educated, skilled labor is becoming increasingly important in this technological age. Here are some students at the Massachusetts Institute of Technology. Team Codex is solving a puzzle during the 2007 MIT Mystery Hunt. (Courtesy of Madcoverboy at English Wikipedia CC BY-SA 2.0 via Wikimedia Commons)

contemporary edge to it. Actually, though, the idea of people as 'human' capital was discussed in 1776 by the 'father' of classical economics, Adam Smith, in *An Inquiry into the Nature and Causes of the Wealth of Nations.*

Any worker who invests time and effort into mastering a skill, Smith maintained, has a right to a wage over and above a common laborer's. To Smith, this higher wage was just compensation not only for the years of grueling apprenticeship the worker endured to become a tradesman but also for the immediate gratification of other needs that he willingly postponed (Wößmann, 2003). Over the next two centuries, then, economists considered learning a form of consumption driven by a particular individual's utility function—the sum of goods, services, and activities afforded by working that each of us finds uniquely satisfying. To this day, ambitious people forgo income and leisure time to undertake years of demanding academic training to maximize their long term utility. But today, pivotally, this is seen as an investment in 'human capital' rather than a household purchase-decision.

Human Capital

What exactly is 'human capital'? The formal concept arose in the 1960s out of the work of two American economists, Theodore Schultz and Gary Becker. Schultz had observed how parents in rural households willingly chose to sacrifice their own material comfort in order to finance their children's college educations, so convinced were they that the improved earning powers a degree would bestow on their offspring. Both Schultz and Becker were struck by how their decisions were no different than a firm's forward-looking decision to reinvest profits in a new plant and equipment. The two, in fact, were so similar, they further concluded, that intangible knowledge and concrete physical capital actually mirrored each other in key respects. That very idea was the centerpiece of Becker's groundbreaking 1962 book, *Investment in Human Capital: a Theoretical Analysis.*

It was a timely introduction, for the traditional factors of production—land, labor, and physical capital—added together no longer accounted for all the yearly growth in gross domestic product recorded for the U.S. economy in the 1950s. Initially at a loss to explain the growing discrepancy, economists assigned it the nondescript label, the 'residual' factor.

Human capital proved a far more satisfying theoretical explanation (Nafukho, Hairston & Brooks 2004). One that, in hindsight, correctly assessed the pivotal importance technology would assume in production, service delivery, and information processing in the coming decades (Iacob & Andrei, 2011).

Human Capital Theory

Crucially, though, human capital theory, as it became known, was applied only to the household and the nation as a whole. The firm, the source of all the productive capacity and most of the employment in a national economy, was yet to be incorporated. Still, as originally formulated, it did bridge the labor-capital divide prevalent in previous economic thinking on the subject. Education and training no longer necessarily belonged in the broader definition of labor, which stemmed from the axiom that work could be both mental and/or manual. Knowledge gleaned from a firm's direct experience with production processes, alternatively, no longer had to necessarily be considered a form of physical capital.

Amendment to the Theory of Production

Before the construct could be applied to the firm, though, one of the most basic models in all of microeconomics—the theory of production—would first have to be amended. It conceives the firm strictly as a production 'function' where profits are maximized by turning raw materials, labor, and fixed capital goods (its 'inputs') into goods and services (its 'outputs'). Whether a business succeeds or fails depends on its ability to simultaneously minimize short-run costs and maximize both short- and long-run profits. To do this, it has to decide the price it will charge and how much to produce. These decisions, in turn, are heavily influenced by the rents, wages, and interest it must pay out and the quantities of each productive factor it will require to meet its output quota.

The Resource-Based View

It would take another twenty years for a successor model, the resource-based view of the firm, to come along. Here, a firm is the sum of the strategic resources available to it. And, significantly, many of these are decidedly less tangible forms of assets than the usual plant, equipment, financial capital, etc. Resources like organizational processes, knowledge, and technical expertise, in fact, contribute more toward building a sustainable competitive advantage, provided, that is, they are rare, inimitable, and non-substitutable. So the morphing of the traditional personnel department into its modern human resources reincarnation is more than just cosmetic. For, fundamentally, the processes, knowledge, technical expertise, and other strategic resources vital to the survival of today's firm are the product of its human capital (Crook, Combs, Todd, Woehr & Ketchen, 2011). A company has to either make or buy it and retain and encourage it thereafter. And therein lies the reason for the name change.

FURTHER INSIGHTS

Compared to human capital theory, marginal analysis, the prevailing neoclassical construct of its day, comes across as mechanistic and one-dimensional. As well it might, considering how simple the basic idea behind it is: The amount of output created by one additional unit of input of labor or capital is a very useful measure. And that's because all a firm has to do to maximize its profits is ensure its marginal costs equal its marginal revenues. Formulated at the turn of the twentieth century, it bears all the hallmarks of the era of mass industrialization when most of the labor employed in manufacturing was unskilled and, therefore, homogeneous. The labor force since then, of course, has grown ever more heterogeneous and the attendant wage differentials among workers more pronounced (Teixeira, 2002). Although not as quantitative perhaps, human capital theory acknowledges this changed reality. Firms that embrace it, moreover, do so because by investing in human capital, a firm is better able to increase its productivity while keeping its wages relatively constant, a sure route to profitability in the twenty-first century.

The Valuation Problem

Still, human capital is an intangible product of the mind and, therefore, cannot be quantified as easily as rents, wages, or investments in plants and equipment. Yet, if it is a full-fledged factor of production as its supporters contend, it must have monetary value, like land, labor, and physical capital. But how exactly do you go about this? Economists have been grappling with the larger question of how to determine the intrinsic net worth of the individual since 1694, but at the national not the firm-level. For centuries,

The John F. Ross Collegiate Vocational Institute is an institution of vocational learning in Guelph, Canada, considered one of the first in the country. (Courtesy of Tabercil CC BY 3.0 via Wikimedia Commons)

the preferred method relied on calculating the net present value of an individual's lifetime earnings net his living expenses. Applied across an entire population, income-based valuation assays the monetary worth of a nation's stock of 'human' capital. One such exercise conducted in 1914 estimated the stock of 'human' capital in the United States was six to eight times that of conventional capital (Kiker, 1966).

An alternate, cost-based method of valuation first proposed in the nineteenth century simply tallied up the expenses incurred in raising a child from birth to age 25. Subsequent refinements have veered from this original formula only in so far as drawing a distinction between the costs of someone's physical maturation on the one hand and the enhancement of the quality or productivity of his or her labor on the other. This latter category, it must be said though, is rather expansive: Besides education and training, outlays for health, transportation, and other so called 'social' costs are included. More recently, attention has turned to the more focused valuation of a country's educational stock: The aggregate sum of all the costs of every citizen's formal schooling and vocational training. Included here is taxpayer spending on public education, tuition paid to private academic and trade schools, company outlays for in-house training programs, etc.

Although individual or national in scope, each valuation method can also be applied more narrowly to the firm. So, for example, a firm's aggregate spending on training is one measure of its investment in human capital. But by the same token, so is its spending on finding qualified new hires or its total expenditures on human resources. A separate set of income measures might include productivity per employee, return on investments in new products, licensing fees earned from patents held by the company, etc. It's fair to say, though, that no one figure completely captures the total value of a firm's human capital. Nor will there likely be one until accounting practices standardized the requisite balance sheet line items.

Human Capital in Perspective

Should knowledge in all its form be considered an asset or just some specialized subset germane to the firm's business or its industry? As far as Becker was concerned, the terms *education* and *human capital* were more or less interchangeable. He did, however, draw a distinction between 'general' and 'specific' education—the former being traditional schooling, the latter on-the-job training—yet considered each a part of a greater whole. Firms, needless to say, have long relied upon academic performance to gauge the innate cognitive abilities of prospective employees. Moreover, the reasoning, writing, numeracy, and problem-solving skills honed during the most general of liberal arts educations is thereafter at the firm's disposal. This kind of screening, though, ignores other forms of human capital—mechanical, technical, artistic, interpersonal, and leadership aptitudes—firms can readily take advantage of.

Theorists since Becker have thought long and hard about how best to properly weigh the economic importance of different levels of knowledge and skill. One widely accepted pyramidal hierarchy parses knowledge and skill according to whether it's specific to an individual, an industry, or a firm. Here, the more generic the knowledge and skill, the less it contributes directly to a firm's competitive advantage. Companies always benefit from hiring people with a good academic grounding in a particular vocational field like accounting or electronics and/or prior managerial or entrepreneurial experience. Although specialized to a degree, academic and vocational knowledge or functional skills of this sort can be put to use across a wide spectrum of industries. More importantly from a cost-benefit perspective, new entry-level hires generally have already acquired

the requisite knowledge and skills at their own or others expense, not the company's.

Still, successful careers in any line of business are predicated on a lifetime's worth of learning about its evolving technology platforms, manufacturing processes, product benefits, customer needs, etc. As rational economic agents, then, we have a vested interest in industry-specific knowledge. For, the more one knows about these relatively arcane subjects, the greater an asset one becomes to any firm competing in a particular market space. Too specialized for the general public yet not proprietary in nature like the firm-specific variety, industry-specific knowledge lies halfway between the two (Dakhli & De Clercq, 2004). Sometimes, though, the boundary lines become blurred: companies occasionally exchange firm-specific knowledge when unsolved problems with enabling technologies stand in the way of developing a new class of product. At other times, the enthusiasm of most technical specialists for their work being what it is fosters informal, intermittent communication among colleagues at rival firms.

Firm-Specific Human Capital

At the pinnacle of the pyramid sits the nontransferable, firm-specific knowledge. Few would dispute that the highly specialized knowledge instrumental to creating competitive advantage is much more of an asset to a firm than the general knowledge individuals use every day or industry-specific knowledge: Enough of an asset in fact to be the centerpiece of the resource-based view of the firm that puts a premium on rare, hard-to-imitate 'core' competencies a firm develops internally. Purists further argue that the costs directly related to their development constitute the sum-total of a firm's human capital. If other firms have access to the same knowledge and skill sets, they do not in and of themselves create competitive advantage (Lin & Wang, 2005). Perhaps not the firm's sole form of human capital, it nonetheless may well be its single most important, ongoing investment. To prosper, a firm has to be better at providing customers with a unique benefit and/or reducing production costs. For, over time, more conventional bulwarks—branding, market share, capitalization, and the like—are less unassailable; competitors can and will respond in kind. Be it product design, manufacturing processes, marketing plans, etc., the only durable defense is to continually innovate—something talented, knowledgeable, and technically skilled employees excel at (Youndt & Snell 2004).

Indeed, it has become almost an article of faith that a firm can successfully fend off any competitor by leveraging knowledge it alone possesses. The resource-based view of the firm stresses the value of human capital for a reason. Innovation comes about through complex social interactions involving the informal exchange of tacit knowledge between co-workers on an ongoing basis (Hatch & Dyer, 2004). That value is created via these undocumented, often spontaneous, knowledge transfers is a widely accepted premise even though the evidence to support this claim is still largely qualitative and anecdotal. In the workplace, as in the rest of the real world, learning and creative collaboration takes many forms and flows through many channels; some obvious, others not. Existing cost accounting practices, simply put, do not and perhaps cannot itemize such sub-rosa exchanges. For its importance notwithstanding, how exactly do you assess the amount of a firm's profits flowing directly from something so ephemeral and episodic? That's not the same as saying human capital plays little or no role in creating value, but just that it is very difficult to isolate and quantify (Gallié & Legros, 2012).

CONCLUSION

Individuals continue to invest time and money today to acquire marketable skills on their own, much like the artisan of Adam Smith's day. Spurred on by the prospect of mutual gain, moreover, high-tech firms and knowledge-workers seek each other out in much the same way as buyers and sellers in any marketplace have done for centuries. What's changed is the extent to which a firm's success today, tomorrow and five years from now increasingly hinges on the organizational processes that supply the knowledge and skills it needs to carve out a defensible competitive position. Screening, selection, training and development of the firm's human resources are strategically vital tasks. Without the complimentary funding of extensive in-house training and compensation packages commensurate with the value an individual creates, and the indirect costs of structuring and perpetuating an organization where information flows freely and workers 'learn by doing,' these efforts will be for naught. Human capital is fast becoming as

important as physical capital, and any firm that fails to adjust accordingly does so at its peril.

BIBLIOGRAPHY

Basdevant, O. (2004). "Some perspectives on human capital and innovations in growth models." Compare: A Journal of Comparative Education, 34, 15-31.

Crook, T., Combs, J. G., Todd, S. Y., Woehr, D. J., & Ketchen Jr., D. J. (2011). "Does human capital matter? A meta-analysis of the relationship between human capital and firm performance." Journal of Applied Psychology, 96, 443-456.

Dakhli, M., & De Clercq, D. (2004). "Human capital, social capital, and innovation: A multi-country study." Entrepreneurship & Regional Development, 16, 107-128.

Gallié, E., & Legros, D. (2012). "Firms' human capital, R&D and innovation: A study on French firms." Empirical Economics, 43, 581-596.

Hatch, N., & Dyer, J. (2004). "Human capital and learning as a source of sustainable competitive advantage." Strategic Management Journal, 25, 1155-1178.

Iacob, A., & Andrei, A. (2011). "Human capital and organizational performance." Managerial Challenges of the Contemporary Society, , 130-136.

Kiker, B. (1966). "The historical roots of the concept of human capital." Journal of Political Economy, 74, 481.

Le, T., Gibson, J., & Oxley, L. (2003). "Cost- and income-based measures of human capital." Journal of Economic Surveys, 17, 271-307.

Lin, K., & Wang, M. (2005). "The classification of human capital according to the strategic goals of firms: An analysis." International Journal of Management, 22, 62-70.

Nafukho, F., Hairston, N., & Brooks, K. (2004). "Human capital theory: Implications for human resource development." Human Resource Development International, 7, 545-551.

Teixeira, A. (2002). "On the link between human capital and firm Performance: A theoretical and empirical survey." Working Papers (FEP) — Universidade do Porto, , 1-38.

Wößmann, L. (2003). "Specifying human capital." Journal of Economic Surveys, 17, 239-270.

Youndt, M., & Snell, S. (2004). "Human resource configurations, intellectual capital, and organizational performance." Journal of Managerial Issues, 16, 337-360.

SUGGESTED READING

Henderson, D., & Russell, R. (2005). "Human capital and convergence: A production-frontier approach." International Economic Review, 46, 1167-1205.

Hitt, M., Biermant, L., Shimizu, K., & Kochhar, R. (2001). "Direct and moderating effects of human capital on strategy and performance in professional service firms: A resource-based perspective." Academy of Management Journal, 44, 13-28.

Monteils, M. (2004). "The analysis of the relation between education and economic growth." Compare: A Journal of Comparative Education, 34, 103-115.

-Francis Duffy, MBA

I

INFORMATION, STRATEGY, AND ECONOMICS

ABSTRACT

This article examines the relationship between the management of information, business strategy, and economics. Levels of business strategy are explained along with the various types of information systems that business executives need to either stay on course or modify their strategies. These information systems include enterprise resource planning systems, decision support systems, and competitive intelligence systems. Factors that drive corporate change, including economic downturns, are also reviewed, and the impact of severe simultaneous changes is examined. How corporate executives manage change and create change is also reviewed.

OVERVIEW

Business Strategy

A business strategy guides a company's product, marketing, and sales efforts. Company executives and managers use information to direct operations, forecast sales, and respond to customer needs. Information generated by corporate systems and competitive intelligence obtained from outside the company help executives respond to changing economic conditions. Actions can include adjusting manufacturing output, modifying pricing, or revamping marketing campaigns (Moran, 2009) (Sull, 2009). These basic managerial functions and activities have remained relatively unchanged over time. However, what has changed over time is how managers have viewed and executed these functions (Hill & McShane, 2008). As businesses work to survive in poor economic conditions, the relationship between strategy development and the information to make good business decisions has become critical.

Grand Strategy

Developing and supporting a business strategy is both a challenging and complex process. The grand strategy, or master strategy, is developed by analyzing a company's operating environment. The grand strategy provides the guidelines necessary for the different branches of a firm to develop strategies, operational plans, and resource requirement documents. According to Novack, Dunn, and Young,

The implementation of the grand strategy allows the firm to achieve its long-term objectives (quantifiable measures of mission achievement) and should take the firm on the path to mission accomplishment. As such, the grand strategy and resource requirements must be developed with input from all other areas of the firm that will be responsible for its implementation (1993).

Functional Strategy

Novack, Dunn, and Young go on further to mention,

Once formulated, the grand strategy can be translated into what can be called functional strategies. This method of plan development is called the "bottom up, top down" approach because it begins with inputs from within the organization that rise to the top of the organization and then flow down again for implementation. Functional strategies take the form of marketing, manufacturing, and logistics strategies. Support strategies might take the form of accounting, finance, legal, and research and development strategies. If resource planning for the functional strategies is developed in coordination with the grand strategy, then the implementation of the functional strategies will in turn implement the grand strategy. Functional strategies must be consistent with the grand strategy as well as consistent with one another (1993).

The resource planning process assures that the acquisition of resources is planned in a manner that facilities efficient work flow across functions (Novack, Dunn & Young, 1993).

Strategy & Business Processes

Strategies are accomplished through the execution of business processes. Business processes comprise the inputs and activities required to produce an output that is desirable to the customer. Each business process is a collection of activities that combine different inputs to create an output that is of value to the customer. Businesses generally engage in three main processes: acquiring and paying for resources, converting resources into goods/services, and acquiring customers, delivering goods and services, and collecting revenues (Klamm & Weidenmier, 2004). Successful implementation of strategies requires that business processes are properly timed and appropriate resources are available when and where they are needed. Both the timing and availability of resources are accomplished through well-managed resource planning (Yukl & Lepsinger, 2007).

Information Systems

Corporate investment in information systems can enable mangers to maintain strong control over operations and have a positive impact on revenue (Oh & Pinsonneault, 2007). Managers obtain information from both internal systems and outside sources.

Internal systems provide executives with information on administrative functions, sales activities, manufacturing, quality control, logistics, and customer support. Most corporate information systems are

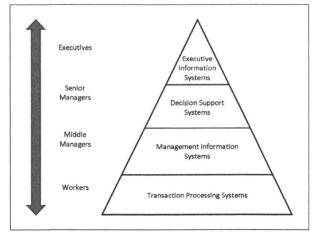

A four level pyramid model of different types of Information Systems based on the different levels of hierarchy in an organization. (Courtesy of Compo CC BY-SA 3.0 via Wikimedia Commons)

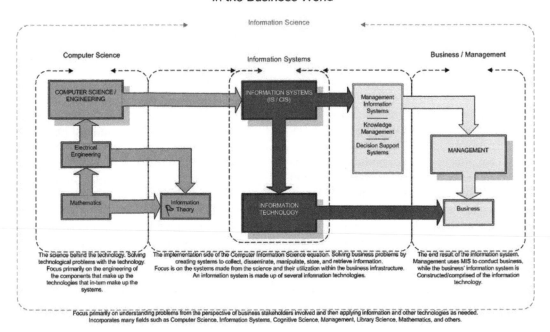

The relationship between Information Science, Computer Science, Information Systems and Management. (Courtesy of Dbmesser CC BY-SA 3.0 via Wikimedia Commons)

designed to support these essential business-to-business (B2B) applications and play a key role in the modern supply chain structure. Supply chain management systems (SCMS) are digitally enabled interfirm processes that integrate information flow, physical flow, and financial flow. Such systems require reliable networks capable of spanning the globe.

Supply Chain Systems

According to Kumar (2001),

Supply chain systems support entire networks of manufacturers and distributors, transportation and logistics firms, banks, insurance companies, brokers, warehouses and freight forwarders, all directly or indirectly attempting to make sure the right goods and services are available at the right price, where and when the customers want them.

Implementation of IT-based supply chain management systems has been shown to have a "positive effect on procurement of materials for production as well as distribution, marketing, and sales after production" (Richardson, 2006).

Microcomputer-Based Software

Many corporate executives rely on microcomputer-based software and systems to analyze business data. Spreadsheets, for example, can aid in analytical tasks that range from the simple to the very complex. Many of these decision support systems involve the analysis of business intelligence using problem-specific

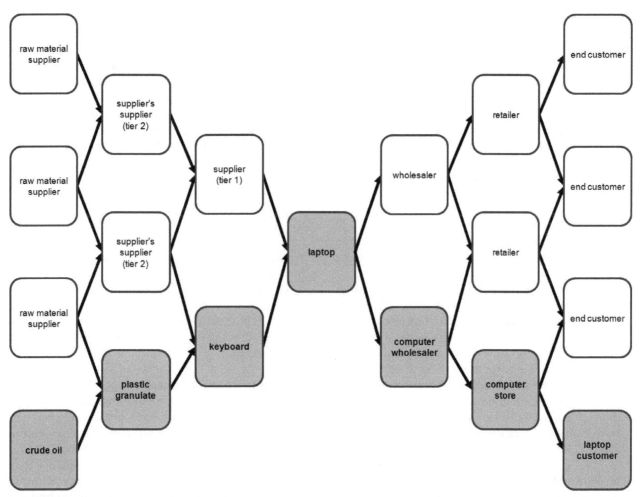

A supply chain is actually a complex and dynamic supply and demand network. (Courtesy of Andreas Wieland CC BY-SA 3.0 via Wikimedia Commons)

methodologies. The purpose of such systems is to solve an unstructured problem in the business environment. Therefore, knowledge of procedures for problem-solving is critical for executives as is an understanding of the decision-making process (Chou & Gensler, 1993).

Internet & Intranet

Both Internet and intranet applications provide support for business strategy planning and operations management. The use of intranets in organizations has become a vital tool for information exchange, knowledge creation, and sharing and allows the possibility of communicating horizontally and vertically (Nystrom, 2006). Internet applications ranging from information dissemination, customer support, web-based sales, and the support of remote workers have been successful for many organizations in Europe and North America (Johnston, Wade & McClean, 2007).

Business & Competitive Intelligence

Obtaining information about markets, competitors, and social or political influences on the economy has long been of interest to corporate managers (Jourdan, Rainer, & Marshall, 2008). The field of business intelligence and competitive intelligence has changed considerably over the last several decades. In the past, intelligence and information were often confused. In contemporary terms, intelligence is focused on helping corporations develop and sustain competitive advantages that set them apart from other companies in their markets or geographical region (Calof, 2007). To qualify as intelligence, material must provide not only insight but also a basis for action on the part of corporate management.

Competitive intelligence can cover many business areas, geographical regions, or activities that may impact business in the future. Most large companies around the world have expended considerable effort to better understand or verify what they know about their competitive environment. This includes profiles of companies in direct competition for market share or resources. It also includes analysis of organizations that drive business trends such as investment banks, venture capitalists, industry associations, and lobbyists (Richardson & Luchsinger, 2007).

The Bottom Line

When all is said and done (strategy developed, information management systems in place, and competitive intelligence systems activated and tuned), to achieve long term sustainability, corporate managers must still cope with sometimes unanticipated economic shifts. During 2008 and into 2009, the economy turned more than sour. Corporate failures, bankruptcies, foreclosures, sales declines, drastic drops in consumer spending, and, of course, layoffs were in the news daily (Alleven, 2009). Many predicted that more declines in spending were on the way (O'Leary, 2009). Losses for corporations as well as individual retirement plans, family incomes, state treasuries, and local funding sources for schools and public services were all suffering declines. Recession seemed to be on the horizon (Gopal, 2009).

APPLICATIONS

In Search of the Corporate Control Panel

What information is required to navigate and pilot a large corporation? How do managers create and manage the information they need? These are big questions with lots of little answers. However, to date, the super-duper corporate control panel that all starship captains dream of has not been developed. But corporate executives do have a wide range of tools available. How well the tools work and how capable managers are of using the tools are issues that are rather widely debated.

Three types of systems are currently in widespread use:

- Enterprise resource planning systems
- Decision support systems
- Competitive intelligence systems

Each of these systems serves as a tool to help managers plan activities and control processes in their organizations.

Enterprise Resource Systems

During the last twenty years, enterprise resource planning (ERP) systems have helped support corporate operations across all administrative, manufacturing, and logistics functions. ERP systems have also helped interconnect different companies in a supply chain environment. However, implementing an ERP system is a long and complex process and not all systems have readily fulfilled their promise as an

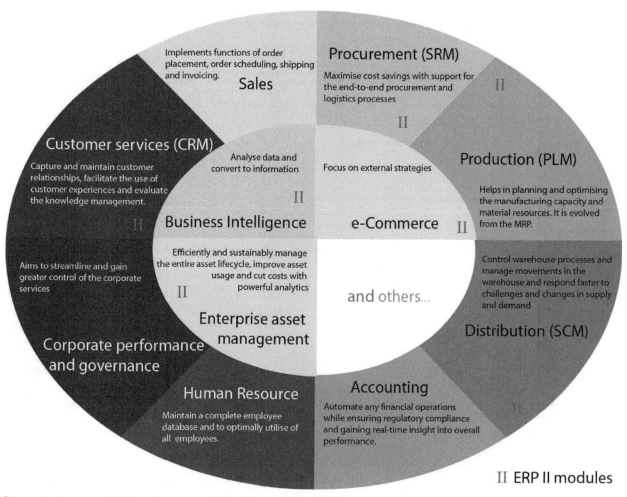

Diagram showing some typical Enterprise systems modules. (Courtesy of Shing Hin Yeung CC BY-SA 3.0 via Wikimedia Commons)

integral part of the corporate control panel (Garcia-Sãnjchez & Perez-Bernal, 2007).

Implementing an ERP system is also a very expensive process (Peslak, Subramanian, Clayton, 2007). The cost of the ERP software is just the beginning of the expenses. Data preparation, application migration, customization, and training are also part of the implementation costs. As the costs of projects get out of hand, many organizations end up cutting the training budget. This often results in underutilization of the system and a lower-than-desired return on investment for the ERP system. Some studies have also noted that even when training employees was vigorously executed, many still did not learn the systems well enough to operate independently (Barrett, 2007).

Business intelligence software applications have been developed by many companies to help extract or mine data from internal ERP systems that can aid in making marketing or pricing decisions. These applications are generally designed for specific industries or business areas. Managers can optimize the use of capacity, schedule supply orders, and project human resource needs. This can help to maximize profitability on an ongoing basis (Rus & Toader, 2008).

Decision Support Systems

Decision support systems (DSS) are software applications that are designed to support managerial decision-making in a specific environment. A DSS can be a simple and straightforward application designed to provide, extract, collect, and perform basic data

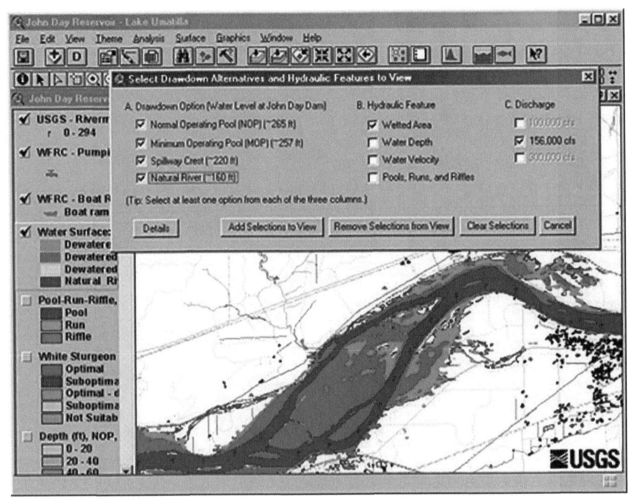

This is an example of a decision support sytem for the John Day Reservoir in Oregon. This set of tools, in conjunction with 2-dimensional hydraulic modeling, is being used to estimate the effects of reservoir level and water discharge fluctuations on aquatic and terrestrial habitats in John Day Reservoir. Different scenarios are being studied now that range from typical reservoir levels at high and low discharges to a simulation of what things might be like if the river were to return to natural conditions. (Courtesy of Project contact Michael J. Parsley, U.S. Geological Survey, via Wikimedia Commons)

analysis functions. However, many contemporary DSS applications also have the ability to apply business rules that are modeled after the managerial decision-making process. This can save time by providing managers with recommended actions or directions that should resemble the human-based thinking process (Mateou & Andreou, 2008). In many cases some of the data used in the DSS can be extracted from ERP systems.

Competitive Intelligence Systems
Competitive intelligence systems provide a different type of support for managers than ERP and DSS

applications can provide. First, competitive intelligence systems generally rely on external data whereas ERP and DSS applications generally provide analyses of internal data. Second, the internal data that is analyzed using ERP and DSS applications is far more structured, focuses mainly on internal operations, and needs less interpretation than that analyzed with competitive intelligence systems. Finally, to benefit from competitive intelligence, mangers must have a far greater understanding of industry trends as well as general business trends and how those trends can impact their business.

Competitive intelligence comes from many different sources and in many different forms. In most sectors, there are research and consulting firms that provide annual or periodic reports about the state of an industry and provide some background on major players in the industry. Many sectors also have industry associations that compile reports about business conditions while also providing background information about process, sales, or marketing trends. In the case of regulated industries, there are also government reports that may provide some insight into trends and conditions.

Larger companies with more money to spend often establish internal competitive intelligence units or hire external consultants to gather and analyze competitive intelligence. The internal unit usually develops a list of areas or topics that require ongoing intelligence. These could include pricing, packaging, strategic marketing plans, and strategic relations development of competitors.

External consultants can operate in a similar fashion to that of the internal unit but most often are hired when specific questions need to be answered in a short period of time. External consultants often market themselves based on their personal or staff backgrounds and knowledge in specific industries. The overall goal of competitive intelligence activities or systems is to provide knowledgeable and actionable information as opposed to just reams of data (Brown, 2007).

The combination of competitive intelligence about the marketplace, internal operations data, and business intelligence generated from business activity provides corporate executives with complex sets of data and analysis. Once these systems are in place, it is still up to the executive to make adjustments to corporate strategy and to plan for production needs or develop marketing campaigns. When business is flowing at a steady pace, this may be relatively easy. However, when changes are rapidly occurring on multiple fronts, the skills and knowledge of executives are essential regardless of how much data and analysis is at their fingertips.

ISSUE

Keeping Pace with Change at the Speed of Light

In the business environment, change is constant. Shifts in global relationships, the introduction of new technology, and economic booms and downturns are among the most powerful catalysts for change (Oakland & Tanner 2007). Business can be steady for years to the point where many things are predictable. The velocity of change, however, can be greatly accelerated when several unfavorable simultaneous events or trends converge. This occurred in 2008 during a serious economic crisis. In a short period of a few months, the less-than-sound business practices of the previous several years took their toll on almost every industrial and business sector.

The complexity of global markets, technology innovation, economic interconnectedness, and the volume of information necessary to manage organizations have all increased over the last twenty years. The interrelationships between all of these factors sometimes make it difficult to identify the source of change and the impact that various changes will have on a corporate strategy (Freda, Arn, & Gatlin-Watts, 1999). Thus, it is important to establish and manage a company's capacity and capability to adapt to change (Chirico & Salvato, 2008).

Implementing Change

Change is often difficult for individuals as well as corporations. Executives often struggle with implementing changes to production processes, human resource management, or marketing approaches. Resistance can come from managers themselves, employees, labor unions, or even customers. When the economy is booming and financial resources are plentiful, change efforts can be accelerated through incentives, buyouts, or programs designed to ease the change process and reinforce the importance of new goals. In addition, corporate executives have the opportunity to retune their change management efforts until they can achieve greater levels of implementation (Holt, Dorey, Bailey, & Low, 2009).

When the economy is in a downturn and financial resources are tight or even nonexistent, executives usually do not have the luxury of implementing incentive programs or hiring consultants to help with change management. The key to survival in a rapidly changing world or a sudden economic crisis is an organization's indigenous ability to forecast coming changes, plan for contingencies, and develop change strategies in advance (Evenson, 2009).

Even with all of the advanced notice possible and the best laid plans in place, change during an economic downturn is difficult for people to accept and thus difficult for managers to implement. Since superheroes are few and far between, organizations faced with difficult changes often turn to the next best thing a champion of change (Warrick, 2009). Keep in mind that the economic downturn in 2008 was not the first that has ever occurred, nor is it likely that it will be the last. Managers as well as students of business may do well to look to the past in order to help deal with the present and plan for the future.

IBM as a Model of Change

One case that is repeatedly commented on is International Business Machine's (IBM) efforts to restructure and realign business practices after the economic downturn of the early 1990s. As the economy worsened, stock prices fell, the bottom fell out of the real estate market, and 401k plans plummeted in value. There was also increasing competition in the computer industry and the margins on all of IBM's product lines were taking a nosedive. Commentaries on the causes of IBM's woes were endless. The facts were clear that IBM was simultaneously facing multiple changes on multiple fronts and facing them at the speed of light ("Gerstner's jury is still out," 1994) (Hayes, 2009) (Khermouch, 1994).

Enter the champion. Louis Gerstner Jr. was hired to bring life back to IBM and establish a sustainable business model. Gerstner's background included being at the helm of RJR Nabisco. It took several years and both insiders and outsiders will tell you that it was not a pretty sight. There were massive layoffs in

IBM is headquartered in Armonk, New York. (Courtesy of Treesmittenex CC BY-SA 4.0 via Wikimedia Commons)

the name of downsizing. New sales approaches were implemented through a system of channel partners. Advertising efforts and advertising agencies were cut, redesigned, and relaunched. Excess real estate holdings were sold off, and, in a move that shocked many old time executives inside and outside of the company, IBM closed its three private golf courses that had been used to entertain customers and the upper management of IBM.

IBM survived. The company returned to profitability in the fourth quarter of 1993. The commentaries continued and still do even today. Was Gerstner good? Did he make the right choices? Is IBM better or worse for the experience? These questions are all difficult to answer. One thing for sure: IBM is not the same company it was before the experience.

CONCLUSION

Corporate management can be a financially rewarding career with perks, bonuses, and a wide range of benefits. It is also challenging and perhaps never more challenging than during an economic downturn. The skill set and knowledge base to become and remain a successful executive is constantly growing. Among the most complex areas in which executives must be fluent are strategy, information, and change. Executives must also be aware of global business trends and global economics. They must also be very good futurists and not be afraid of the many changes that the future brings.

What the downturn of the last year and the many downturns of the past have shown is that corporate executives need to embrace change. They need to love change and be strong enough to stand during turmoil. Not just stress, but real turmoil. Economic shifts can sometimes ripple through sectors and impact a company in a manner that was completely excluded from a corporate strategy. At other times, economic shifts can roll through multiple sectors like a tsunami washing away the past in mere moments.

The adage of the survival of the fittest is often applied to life, business, and civilizations. The definition of "fit" changes with each new wave of challenges. Strength may have worked well in the past. Adaptability has served many well. But survival also requires agility, knowledge, insight, and speed of response.

BIBLIOGRAPHY

Alleven, M. (2009). "Making sense of tumultuous times." *Wireless Week, 15,* 4.

Amcoff Nystrom, C. (2006). "Demands on intranets viable system model as a foundation for intranet design." *AIP Conference Proceedings, 839,* 381–387.

arrett, J. (2007, March 27). "Big and small face same SAP hurdles." *Computer Weekly,* 28.

Brown, M. (2007). "'Don't give me more data; give me more knowledge!'" *Hydrocarbon Processing, 86,* 19.

Calof, J. (2007). "Competitive intelligence and the management accountability framework." *Optimum Online, 37,* 3.

Chirico, F., & Salvato, C. (2008). "Knowledge integration and dynamic organizational adaptation in family firms." *Family Business Review, 21,* 169–181.

Chou, D., & Gensler, P. (1993). "Using spreadsheets to teach decision support systems in business schools." *Journal of Education for Business, 69,* 116.

Clemons, E. K. (2008). "How information changes consumer behavior and how consumer behavior determines corporate strategy." *Journal of Management Information Systems, 25,* 13–40

Clemons, E. K., Kauffman, R. J., & Weber, T. A. (2009). "Special section: Competitive strategy, economics, and information systems." *Journal of Management Information Systems, 26,* 7–13.

Evenson, R. (2009). "Prepare yourself: Like it or not, change is coming!" *Supervision, 70,* 8–11.

Freda, G., Arn, J., & Gatlin-Watts, R. (1999). "Adapting to the speed of change." *Industrial Management, 41,* 31.

"Gerstner's jury is still out." (1994). *Economist, 330*(7848), 67.

Gopal, P. (2009, January 23). "Rents drop nationwide as vacancies spike." *Business Week Online,* 17.

Hayes, F. (2009). "The pain begins." *Computerworld, 43,* 32.

Hill, C. & McShane, S. (2008) *Principles of management.* McGraw-Hill

Holt, D., Dorey, E., Bailey, L., & Low, B. (2009). "Recovering when a change initiative stalls." *OD Practitioner, 41,* 20–24.

Johnston, D., Wade, M., & McClean, R. (2007). "Does e-business matter to SMEs? A comparison of the financial impacts of internet business solutions on European and North American SMEs." *Journal of Small Business Management, 45,* 354–361.

Khermouch, G. (1994). "At Gerstner's IBM: All for one." *Brandweek, 35,* 1.

Klamm, B., & Weidenmier, M. (2004). "Linking business processes and transaction cycles." *Journal of Information Systems, 18,* 113–125.

Kumar, K. (2001). "Technology for supporting supply chain management: Introduction." *Communications of the ACM, 44,* 58–61.

Mateou, N., & Andreou, A. (2008). "A framework for developing intelligent decision support systems using evolutionary fuzzy cognitive maps." *Journal of Intelligent & Fuzzy Systems, 19,* 151–170.

Moran, G. (2009). "Five great -and necessary- marketing makeovers." *Entrepreneur, 37,* 49–53.

Novack, R., Dunn, S., & Young, R. (1993). "Logistics optimizing and operational plans and systems and their role in the achievement of corporate goals." *Transportation Journal, 32,* 29–40.

Oakland, J., & Tanner, S. (2007). "Successful change management." *Total Quality Management & Business Excellence, 18*(½), 1–19.

Oh, W., & Pinsonneault, A. (2007). "On the assessment of the strategic value of information technologies: Conceptual and analytical approaches." *MIS Quarterly, 31,* 239–265.

O'Leary, N. (2009). "Just the start for consumer cutbacks." *Adweek, 50,* 8.

Peslak, A., Subramanian, G., & Clayton, G. (2007). "The phases of ERP software implementation and maintenance: A model for predicting preferred ERP use." *Journal of Computer Information Systems, 48,* 25–33.

"The power of patterns and pattern recognition when developing information-based strategy." (2010). *Journal of Management Information Systems, 27,* 69–95.

Richardson, L., & Luchsinger, V. (2007). "Strategic Marketing implications in competitive intelligence and the Economic Espionage Act Of 1996." *Journal of Global Business Issues, 1,* 41–45.

Richardson, V. (2006). "Supply chain IT enables coordination." *Industrial Engineer: IE, 38,* 10.

Rus, V., & Toader, V. (2008). "Business intelligence for hotels' management performance." *International Journal of Business Research, 8,* 150–154.

Sull, D. (2009). "How to thrive in turbulent markets." *Harvard Business Review, 87,* 78–88.

Warrick, D. (2009). "Developing organization change champions." *OD Practitioner, 41,* 14–19.

Yukl, G., & Lepsinger, R. (2007). "Getting it done: Four ways to translate strategy into results." *Leadership in Action, 27*, 3–7.

Suggested Reading

Alhashmi, S., Siddiqi, J., & Akhgar, B. (2006). "Staying competitive by managing organisational knowledge." *Engineering Management, 16*, 43–45.

Andersson, G., Flisberg, P., LidÃn, B., & RÃ¶nnqvist, M. (2008). "RuttOpt a decision support system for routing of logging trucks." *Canadian Journal of Forest Research, 38*, 1784–1796.

Daneva, M., & Wieringa, R. (2006). "A requirements engineering framework for cross-organizational ERP systems." *Requirements Engineering, 11*, 194–204.

Garcia-Sanchez, N., & Perez-Bernal, L. (2007). "Determination of critical success factors in implementing an ERP system: A field study in Mexican enterprises." *Information Technology for Development, 13*, 293–309.

Grant, G. (2003). "Strategic alignment and enterprise systems implementation: The case of Metalco." *Journal of Information Technology, 18*, 159.

Hamm, S. (2009, January 12). "Is Silicon Valley losing its magic?" *Business Week*, (4115), 28–33.

Hubbard, G. (2009). "Measuring organizational performance: Beyond the triple bottom line." *Business Strategy & the Environment (John Wiley & Sons, Inc), 18*, 177–191.

Jourdan, Z., Rainer, R., & Marshall, T. (2008). "Business intelligence: An analysis of the literature." *Information Systems Management, 25*, 121–131.

Pather, S., Remenyi, D., & De La Harpe, A. (2006). "Evaluating e-commerce success—a case study." *Electronic Journal of Information Systems Evaluation, 9*, 15–26.

Schwarz, J. (2007). "Competitive intelligence: a field for futurists?" *Futures Research Quarterly, 23*, 55–65.

Singh, M., Singh, P., & Singh, S. (2008). "Decision support system for farm management." *Proceedings of World Academy of Science: Engineering & Technology, 29*, 346–349.

Thornlow, C. (2009). "Technology's seat at the strategy table." *Law Office Management & Administration Report, 9*, 2–5.

Verma, A. (2009). "Navigating the financial crisis." *Communication World, 26*, 4–7.

Vowler, J. (2008, December 9). "Take the wheel of business change." *Computer Weekly*, 18–20.

—*Michael Erbschloe*

International Banking

ABSTRACT

This article will focus on the practices of international banking and its position in the world economic system. As more financial institutions begin to participate in the global economic system, process improvement has led to the reduction of communication and information costs as a result of technology. One of the focal points for many multinational corporations is to have the ability to perform financial transactions outside of the United States. There tends to be a variety of information problems in the financial markets and those responsible for overseeing the processes attempt to find different ways to address the issues that arise. One such attempt explores long-term relationships between firms and banks. The purpose of the Basel Committee on Banking Supervision will be examined.

OVERVIEW

As more financial institutions begin to participate in the global economic system, process improvement has led to reduced communication and information costs as a result of technology (Baldwin & Martin, 1999). "One variable that has been used in the international finance literature to proxy information costs is the (geographical) distance between two markets" (Buch, 2005, p. 787). Many have attempted to determine if there is a correlation between international asset holding and distance. Unfortunately, there has not been much research on the effect of distance on international financial relationships over a period of time. Although researchers (Portes & Rey, 2001) have found that some investors seek out nearby businesses in markets that exhibit correlation in business cycles, Petersen and Rajan (2002) reported that there has been an increase in the business being conducted between banks and their credit customers. What is important is the fact that international banking is a key factor in the way organizations, such as multinationals, conduct their business today.

One of the focal points for many multinational corporations is to have the ability to perform financial transactions outside of the United States. It is important for these corporations to have the ability to participate in the international trade process. Some of the key banking services that are needed include letters of credit, wire transfers, collections, and foreign exchange (Teller Sense, 2003). It is important for organizations to have the ability to wire deposits in a timely manner, have the credibility for banks to provide a letter of credit on its behalf, and collect payments quickly and easily.

In March 2004, the International Banking Federation was established when the banking associations from Europe, the United States, Australia, and Canada united. The headquarters for the group was London. The purpose of this consortium was to provide an international forum to address issues such as legislation, regulations, and other issues that affected the countries and the global banking system. One of the main objectives of the group was to increase the effectiveness of how the banking industry responded to national and international issues (Teller Vision, 2004).

One issue that this group may discuss is the ability for the market to absorb shocks in times of financial crises such as the crash of 1987, the Asian crisis of 1997, and the Russian crisis of 1998. One of the effects of globalization in the financial industry is that the banking sectors across the world have become interdependent across borders (Elyasiani & Mansur, 2003). Given the fact that the banking systems in different countries are not the same in structure and regulatory constraints, it is important that the international financial community is responsible and collaborates on what type of plan should be in place for the global financial market. Organizations such as the International Banking Federation need to develop a plan of action to address these types of events so that the members are not adversely affected when a crisis happens. They are responsible for minimizing the risk of a domino effect occurring.

APPLICATION

Banking Supervision

"The present international, regional, and national rules on banking supervision are strongly permeated by a high degree of fluidity directly descendent both from the revolution of principles and techniques steering the global financial markets, and from the connected difficulty of the nation States to face the new technological challenges" (Ortino, 2004, p. 715). Policy makers, experts, and scholars will need to analyze and evaluate the level of fluidity when attempting to implement policies and regulations to govern global financial markets. The changes in information technology have challenged the European states by requiring them to evaluate the political and economic systems that they have in place.

According to Ortino (2004), there are two specific features of the institutional order as it relates to banking supervision at an international level. First of all, national legislators are responsible for setting up the legal norms and developing the foundation for the proper power structure and procedures. Second, the powers of the banking supervision authorities

The headquarters for the Basel Committee on Banking Supervising is located in Basel, Switzerland. (Courtesy of Taxiarchos228 via Wikimedia Commons)

are assigned by the banking sector. These features are encouraging banking supervision authorities to work together as well as with supervisory authorities in other financial sectors.

One entity that works at the international level is the Basel Committee on Banking Supervision. This entity was set up in December 1974 by the central bank governors of the Group of 10 (G-10) nations and meets four times a year. The membership includes representation from countries such as Belgium, Canada, France, Germany, Italy, Japan, the Netherlands, Sweden, Switzerland, the United Kingdom, and the United States. The countries meet in order to consult on economic, monetary, and financial matters. The purpose of the committee is to discuss how to handle supervisory problems, such as global financial crises. Although the committee coordinates the supervisory responsibilities among the national authorities and monitors the effectiveness of supervision of banks' activities, it does not have formal status as an international organization (Ortino, 2004). However, the establishment of the Basel Committee was a significant point in the history of international banking supervision.

G-10
In 1999, there was a section that was added to the Gramm-Leach-Bliley Act, which broadened the range of activities that banking institutions in the United States could participate in, especially those institutions that elected to become financial holding companies. Although this was a significant step, financial institutions in the United States still had a narrower range than most of the other countries that were members of the G-10 group. What are some of the differences between some of the countries?

As a rule, most G-10 countries have allowed their banks to provide a full range of securities market activities (i.e., underwriting, brokering, and dealing) versus performing the transactions through a subsidiary. Also, there are a few G-10 countries that will allow a full range of insurance activities. However, the main restrictions tend not to be on the types of insurance activities. Rather, many of the restrictions tend to focus on where the activities are performed (i.e., some of the activities are required to be performed via a subsidiary). In addition, there are also restrictions on real estate activities for banks based on the range of activities, whether or not the activities are

performed at a subsidiary or bank or both. Nolle (2003) provided research that compared which G-10 country banks were allowed to own nonfinancial firms and which nonfinancial firms were allowed to own banks. The results showed that most G-10 countries were allowed to own nonfinancial firms, and nonfinancial firms were allowed to own banks. However, the United States is one of the countries that has greater restrictions on the above-mentioned combination of activities. Japan was the only country to have a greater level of restrictiveness than the United States.

"The United States supervisory system has the most complex structure in the G-10, and in several key respects its banking supervisory structure puts it among the minority of G-10 countries. However, in one key respect—the funding of bank supervision as practiced by the OCC—the U.S. is similar to the majority of G-10 countries" (Nolle, 2003, par. 10). Nolle's report (2003) "shows that nine of the 11 G-10 countries assign banking supervision to a single authority." The United States and Germany were the only two countries that had more than one federal level bank supervisor. In addition, the United States is "one of four G-10 countries that assigns bank supervisory responsibility to the central bank. The majority of G-10 countries' bank supervisory authorities have responsibilities beyond the banking industry, either for securities firms, insurance firms, or both" (Nolle, 2003).

Importance of Supervision
The type of supervision is important because the type of funding received could have an effect on how bank supervisors make decisions, especially if there is an opportunity for some type of political influence. For example, "supervisory agencies that receive funding from the institutions they supervise may have less pressure to pursue a political agenda than supervisory agencies that are dependent on general government revenues" (Nolle, 2003). Nolle's report showed that the United States tends to have a hands-on approach in performing the bank supervision role. They tend to conduct on-site exams on an annual basis and have a good ratio of total supervisory organizational staff to the number of banks as well as a good ratio of banking system assets to the banking system. The United States' ratio of banking assets per supervisory staff member is

the lowest among the G-10 countries. This finding indicates that there is a significant amount of coverage on the banking system activities on a per staff member basis. With the exception of Italy, all of the G-10 countries require an external audit as part of the bank supervision role. However, the United States does not require external auditors to report bank misconduct to the supervisory authorities, but there is a commitment to the external auditing process.

Contributions of the Basel Committee

The Basel Committee has made two major contributions since its inception. The first contribution occurred in 1975 when the committee took a lead role in making sure that countries share responsibilities when making international banking transactions. The Basel Concordat was an agreement that established the foundation for this process. The first stipulation was that the parent and host authorities shared responsibility for the supervision of the foreign banking establishments. The second stipulation stated that the host authorities had primary responsibility for supervision of liquidity. The third stipulation indicated that the solvency of foreign branches and subsidiaries was the primary responsibility of the home authority of the parent and the host authority. The second major contribution was a standard that would assist in adequately measuring a bank's capital and establishing minimum capital standards.

VIEWPOINT

Firm-Bank Relationships

There tends to be a variety of information problems in the financial markets and those responsible for overseeing the processes attempt to find different ways to address the issues that arise. One such attempt explores long-term relationships between firms and banks. Some believe that these types of relationships are crucial to the structure of credit markets. As a result, Degryse and Ongena (2002) reviewed the firm-bank relationship and the structure of banking markets on a global level.

A firm-bank relationship is established when the two entities have a close interaction and the banker is allowed to observe and collect a variety of information about the firm. The banker has the opportunity to evaluate whether or not the firm can meet future financial obligations. Although the banker has a chance to observe how the relationship will benefit the lender in the long term, there are some advantages for the firm as well. For example, the firm can increase its access to credit at a lower cost and with less collateral if it has established a relationship with a bank. Also, the firm may have the opportunity to enter into complex and high-risk projects as a result of having an established relationship with a bank. Finally, a firm's reputation and image may be seen as favorable due to an established and credible relationship with a bank.

The Down Side to Firm-Bank Relationships

Although this is seen as a positive endeavor, there is a down side. There may be some individuals who will become concerned with the type and amount of information a bank knows about a firm. "The ability for a bank to privately observe proprietary information and maintain a close relationship with its customer can also impose costs on the customer" (Degryse & Ongena, 2002, p. 404). For example, a bank can devise a campaign that will lock customers into maintaining a relationship with it and prevent customers from receiving competitive financing from another bank. This will lead to the original bank having a monopoly over the market as a result of having privileged client information. One solution to this type of problem would be for firms to enter into more than one bank relationship. The banks will offer competitive services, which will minimize the possibility of any one bank getting the upper hand and creating a monopoly situation.

Firms can diversify their financial portfolio by entering into relationships with banks across the world. There will be opportunities for banks to form consortiums and market to a variety of firms. The banks could come together and establish rules and regulations for different types of organizational projects around the world. The Second European Banking Directive and the 1994 United States Riegle-Neal Act created large international banking markets. "Established bank-firm relationships are very important in the current development of the financial system across the world" (Degryse & Ongena, 2002).

CONCLUSION

Many have attempted to determine if there is a correlation between international asset holding and distance. Unfortunately, there has not been much research on the effect of distance on international financial relationships over a period of time. Some of the key banking services that are needed include letters of credit, wire transfers, collections, and foreign exchange (Teller Sense, 2003). It is important for organizations to have the ability to wire deposits in a timely manner, have the credibility for banks to provide a letter of credit on their behalf, and collect payments quickly and easily.

In March 2004, the International Banking Federation was established when the banking associations from Europe, the United States, Australia, and Canada united. The purpose of this consortium was to provide an international forum to address issues such as legislation, regulations, and other issues that affected the countries and the global banking system. One issue that this group may discuss is the ability for the market to absorb shocks in times of financial crises such as the crash of 1987, the Asian crisis of 1997, and the Russian crisis of 1998. One of the effects of globalization in the financial industry is that the banking sectors across the world have become interdependent across borders (Elyasiani & Mansur, 2003).

BIBLIOGRAPHY

Baldwin, R., & Martin, P. (1999). "Two waves of globalization: Superficial similarities, fundamental differences, in Horst Siebert" (ed.), *Globalization and Labor*. Tubingen: Mohr Siebeck.

Botis, S. (2013). "Mergers and acquisitions in the international banking sector." *Bulletin of the Transilvania University of Brasov. Series V: Economic Sciences, 6*, 119–126.

Buch, C. (2005). "Distance and international banking." *Review of International Economics, 12*, 787–804.

Cetorelli, N., & Goldberg, L. S. (2012). "Banking globalization and monetary transmission." *Journal of Finance, 67*, 1811–1843.

Dietz, M., Härle, P., & Nagy, T. (2013). "A new trend line for global banking." *Mckinsey Quarterly,* 18–19.

Elyasiani, E., & Mansur, I. (2003). "International spillover of risk and return among major banking institutions: A bivariate GARCH model." *Journal of Accounting, Auditing & Finance, 18*, 303–330.

Degryse, H., & Ongena, S. (2002). "Bank-firm relationships and international banking markets." *International Journal of the Economics of Business, 9*, 401–417.

"International banking federation established." (2004). *Teller Vision,* (1321), 5–6.

Levin-Koningsberg, G., Lopez, C., Lopez-Gallo, F., Martinez-Jaramillo, S. (2017). "International Banking and Cross-Border Effects of Regulation: Lessons from Mexico." *International Journal of Central Banking, 13,* 2, 249–271.

Nolle, D. (2003, June). *Bank supervision in the U.S. and the G-10: Implications for Basel II.*

Petersen, M., & Rajan, R. (2002). "Does distance still matter? The information revolution in small business lending." *Journal of Finance, 57*, 2533–2570.

Portes, R., & Rey, H. (2001). *The determinants of cross-border equity flows.* Center for International and Development Economics Research, University of California, Department of Economics, Berkeley, CA.

"The world of international banking." (2003). *Teller Sense,* 1–8.

Ortino, S. (2004). "International and cross-border co-operation among banking supervisors: The role of the European central bank." *European Business Law Review, 15*, 715–734.

SUGGESTED READING

Comford, A. (2007). "Trade, investment and competition in international banking." *Journal of Banking Regulation, 8*, 195–197.

Frierson, R. (2006, July 13). "Orders issued under international banking act." *Federal Reserve Bulletin,* C128–C130.

Ingves, S., & Lind, G. (2007). "Using international sound practices as a basis for banking reforms." *Sveriges Riksbank Economic Review,* 5–20.

—*Marie Gould*

INTERNATIONAL BUSINESS LAW

ABSTRACT

This article discusses the sources and content of international business law. Trading nations have entered into a series of treaties and organizations to promote free trade and end discriminatory or isolationist practices. The WTO is the premier organization that negotiates and regulates agreements among nations. This article will take look at the processes that establish international business law and the general features of the law.

OVERVIEW

International business is a critical part of the world economy that shapes the fortunes of individuals and entire nations. This article provides an overview of the sources, content, and consequences of the "international business law" that regulates business across borders. The goal is to identify major themes, mechanisms, and institutions that govern international business. International business law embraces many specific fields of practice that relate to a wide array of business transactions. Each type of international commerce (export and import of goods and services,

The Peace Palace in The Hague, Netherlands, which is the seat of the International Court of Justice. This is the principal judicial organ of the United Nations. It settles legal disputes between members of the United Nations, including issues concerning treaties. (Courtesy of International Court of Justice via Wikimedia Commons)

foreign direct investment, joint ventures, research and development arrangements, franchising, sale and distribution arrangements, and licensing of intellectual property) has a distinct body of law.

To introduce the idea of international law, it helps to start by contrasting it with domestic law. Domestic laws are law because a legislature has the power,

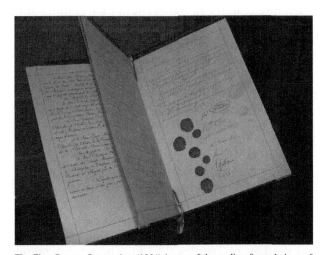

The First Geneva Convention (1864) is one of the earliest formulations of international law. This is the original document of the first Geneva Convention from 1864, on loan to the International Red Cross and Red Crescent Museum in Geneva, Switzerland. (Courtesy of Kevin Quinn, Ohio, US CC BY 2.0 via Wikimedia Commons)

The headquarters of the World Trade Organization is located in Geneva, Switzerland. (Courtesy of E. Murray CC BY-SA 3.0 via Wikimedia Commons)

under our political system, to pass legislation binding people within its jurisdiction. Accordingly, a court has the authority to apply the law. The power to do so comes from the sovereignty of the nation. A sovereign has supreme and ultimate authority over affairs and individuals within its borders and does not have to answer to any higher authority. Each nation is sovereign.

On the other hand, international law involves an arrangement between sovereign nations. As a matter of theory, it may seem strange that law could operate on sovereigns, when neither sovereign state has to account to any higher power and can ultimately behave as it wishes. Law that does not have to be followed is no law at all, some would argue. However, despite this theoretical problem, nations do, in practice, obey international law.

International law arises from the willingness of each nation to bind itself. A nation will do so because adherence to the law is in its best interest. Generally, nations have a self-interest in promoting a systematic rule of law to foster predictability and stability in international affairs over the long term. While other nations and international bodies often lack the authority to compel compliance, if a nation decides to behave contrary to an international law, there still may be consequences. The violating nation's image may be tarnished both at home and abroad, economic sanctions may be imposed; in short, the country could lose the benefit of reciprocal treatment from other nations.

When violations do occur they are rarely flagrant and not usually tolerated silently by others. Protest often breaks out due to perceived violations of international law. Violators themselves concede the authority and importance of the law by usually trying to explain their actions on legal grounds.

International law largely arises from three categories: general principles, customary international law, and treaties. General principles are fundamental understandings common to the world's great legal systems. When an advocate can show that almost every nation agrees on a principle, then that principle can be elevated to a binding rule of international law. An example of a general principle would be the rule of good faith in international obligations. Of course, the more abstract a principle is, the easier it would be to find consensus, but the less useful it would be in practice to resolve a specific problem. This paradox limits the practical use of general principles to situations in which a party cannot find a more concrete alternative.

Customary international law arises from the persistent conduct of international actors including nations, international institutions, and international business organizations. A court may consider a practice international law if the advocate can show that the practice has been followed generally and also has been accepted by those actors as law as opposed to courtesy or convenience. Proving a customary international law is very difficult and requires extensive evidence.

While courts may recognize international law based on the methods noted above, the bulk of international business law comes from written agreements between nations called treaties. As a practical matter, treaties are international business law. As opposed to general principles and customary international law, treaties are specific and negotiated to address particular conduct. There are a huge number of treaties on a huge number of topics and are sometimes called a pacts, protocols, conventions, covenants, or declarations. Treaties are divided into two general categories. Agreements between two countries are called bilateral treaties, and agreements among three or more countries are called multilateral treaties. International institutions can also enter into treaties with other organizations or with nations. A treaty, once signed and ratified by the government of each host country, becomes law in each country and an agreement between the countries. For example, in the United States, the executive branch negotiates and signs and the Senate must then approve it. This is called "advice and consent." Once the treaty is ratified, it becomes federal law. In that way, international law is not an entirely distinct body of law that acts upon nations from the outside; it is also part of domestic law that operates within a country. Therefore, the degree of enforcement depends, in part, on the strength of a given country's legal system.

Another factor in the enforcement of international law is treaty interpretation. A leading authority on interpretation and procedure related to treaties is the multilateral treaty called the Vienna Convention on the Law of Treaties (VCLT). The interpretation of treaties determines how a country observes international law. It is very difficult, if not impossible, to draft legal documents that clearly determine the outcome of every set of facts that may occur in the future.

Circumstances may arise that the drafter of a relatively simple legal document, e.g., a will or contract, may not have foreseen that cause ambiguity or vagueness as to its application. Treaties are no different, and the problem is often compounded because treaties are political compromises that sometimes defer resolution of contentious issues in order to achieve some current agreement (Bederman, 2001).

The interpretation of treaties has a couple of default rules and three general perspectives. The default rules are, first, that treaties are applied prospectively, to future events, unless the parties expressly agree otherwise. Second, treaties are normally assumed to apply to the entire territorial sovereignty of a nation, unless expressly agreed otherwise. Determining how a treaty is to apply to a specific set of facts can be done with a textual approach, an intentionalist approach, or a teleological approach and can involve all three. The textual approach looks to the plain meaning of the text in a specific section and throughout the document. For example, whether a treaty section that uses the word "airplane" also applies to a "glider" can turn on whether the document uses the more general term "aircraft" in other sections suggesting that "airplane" should be a more inclusive term. Under the VCLT, treaty interpretation begins with the "plain language"—a textual approach that is limited by shades of meaning in language particularly when a treaty is translated into different languages (Bederman 2001).

Under the VCLT, the intentionalist approach can be used to fill in the text where the text is ambiguous or leads to an absurd result. The intentionalist approach employs an understanding of the original parties that drafted the treaty in order to determine what the treaty means. To understand the intent of the drafter, the negotiating history, or travaux préparatoires, is often consulted. The intentionalist approach is somewhat disfavored, in part, because many nations join a treaty regime after drafting is over, and it seems unfair to bind a nation to negotiating history they did not participate in. Further, negotiating parties often have different reasons for their involvement, and negotiating history can often be contradictory and difficult to establish for someone claiming its use.

The teleological approach looks to the object and purpose of a treaty as opposed to slavishly following the text or attempting to determine the intent of the

drafters. For example, a written agreement can produce results counterproductive to the stated goals of the treaty; the teleological approach allows interpretations of the treaty to depart from the "plain meaning" of the text. The VCLT endorses the teleological approach by requiring that treaties be viewed in light of their object and purpose (Bederman 2001). The important point for the international trader to remember about treaty interpretation is that there are sometimes several ways to read the same words, and care should be taken to fully understand the meaning and consequences of the often complex international law.

In addition to bilateral and multilateral treaties, nations join international organizations that produce rules relating to business and trade. For example, the North American Free Trade Agreement (NAFTA) is a trading block composed of the United States, Mexico, and Canada, whereby the members have made a number of agreements designed to promote trade within their collective borders. Many other areas of the world have likewise engaged in such agreements, for example, the Association of South East Asian Nations (ASEAN), MERCOSUR includes many South American cone nations, and the Asia Pacific Economic Cooperation (APEC). The European Union (EU) is probably the most aggressive and integrated agreement between nations to encourage free trade. The EU employs a common currency, the euro, and super-governmental institutions, like the European Central Bank, the European parliament and the Court of Justice of the European communities.

With 150 member nations, the World Trade Organization (WTO) is the largest and most comprehensive international organization related to international business law. The WTO was created in 1995, to implement and institutionalize a collection of multilateral agreements known as the General Agreements on Tariffs and Trade (GATT). Negotiations began on the GATT in 1948 and continued for eight successive rounds that each produced new agreements to liberalize world trade. The WTO intends to regulate most all areas of trade law and permits organizations such as those mentioned above provided they do not interfere with the WTO's rules. Because the substantive rules of the WTO are composed so heavily of the agreements negotiated during the GATT rounds, the WTO is sometimes referred to as WTO/GATT;

reference to one should be taken as reference to the other.

The motivation for the global move to free trade was the theory of comparative advantage. It is widely held that free trade enhances the wealth of all trading partners because it takes advantage of each county's comparative advantage. A comparative advantage is the increased effectiveness a particular nation has in producing specific goods as opposed to others. Those efficiencies may arise for many reasons including the nation's people, natural resources, or climate. Accordingly, every nation should concentrate on producing the product that they can produce most effectively. Nations then trade with other nations for all other goods. In that way, the overall production of the world increases and all nations benefit.

In accord with the theory of comparative advantage, the stated objectives of the GATT are to raise living standards, ensure full employment, raise real income and effective demand, develop full use of the world's resources, and expand the production and exchange of goods. The GATT seeks to achieve those goals by adhering to certain principles. Prior to entering the WTO, nations must enter into mutually advantageous agreements to reduce tariffs and other barriers to free trade, eliminate discriminatory treatment in international commerce, and agree to the general elimination of quantity restrictions like duties, taxes, or other charges that restrict the import or export of goods.

The WTO regulatory regime rests on what are called the "Four Pillars" of WTO membership. First, when a nation joins the WTO, it gets the benefit of, and is bound to extend, "most favored nation" (MFN) status. MFN prohibits discriminatory trade practice by requiring that a trade privilege granted to one nation must also be granted to all WTO members. Second, each country is entitled to "national treatment" of its goods, services, and intellectual property. After a product enters into a country, that host country must treat and protect the imported product as if it were a domestic product. Third, each country must agree to tariff bindings. Tariff bindings are agreements to limit, reduce, or eliminate tariffs over a given period of time. Predictable and decreasing tariffs provide stability for traders. Fourth, every nation must commit to eliminate or reduce nontariff barriers that impede free trade. Nontariff barriers include quotas, excessive paperwork requirements,

and undisclosed trade rules. To encourage transparency and discourage restrictive policies, the WTO has a dedicated committee to examine trade policies. In addition to the "Four Pillars," the WTO has other agreements that take aim at the goal to liberalize and promote fair world trade. Some of those areas include laws related to dumping, countervailing duties, subsidies and initiatives to systemize procedures for customs administration, and valuation (Friedland, 2002).

Dumping is when a particular company exports goods at a lower price than it normally charges at home. Dumping effectively eliminates competition and, as a result, causes governments to take action in order to protect their domestic industry. Because the WTO is an agreement among nations, it does not regulate individual businesses. Therefore, the WTO anti-dumping agreement regulates how governments respond to dumping. The anti-dumping agreement allows a government, in certain circumstances, to act contrary to the normal WTO principles of binding a tariff or not discriminating between trading partners. Governments may impose a duty on specific products if the government can show genuine injury to domestic industry from dumped goods. The extra duty seeks to equalize the price of the dumped products with the price normally charged. However, before a government may impose those duties, the price difference must be calculated based on WTO rules, and a detailed investigation must show that domestic industry is actually being harmed by dumped products. Anti-dumping prevents potentially unfair competition injurious to a nation's economy and limits the restrictive effect of duties on international trade by controlling the reaction a government may employ.

A countervailing duty protects domestic industry by offsetting subsidies given by foreign governments to manufacturers of the goods for export. For example, a company in country X receives assistance from its domestic government in the form of interest-free loans and is therefore able produce an item at a lower price for sale in country Y. Country Y may want to impose a countervailing duty so that country Y manufacturers do not have to compete with that lower-priced product. A subsidy is a grant made by the government to an enterprise that is judged to be in the public interest. Subsidies put industries or enterprises at a competitive advantage with respect to foreign producers. One often hears of farm subsidies, whereby a farmer is paid by the government to help produce or in some cases not produce, certain products. Subsidies can damage the trade of other nations by hurting competing exporters from another nation, by hurting foreign exporters trying to compete in the subsidized market, and by hurting domestic industry in the importing country.

The WTO agreements on countervailing duties and subsidies control the use of subsidies and regulate the measures a government can take to offset the effect of a particular subsidy with countervailing duties. The WTO sets out rules whereby countries can challenge subsidies and have them judged harmful and immediately repealed. If the offending country does not repeal the subsidy, the complaining country is allowed to take countervailing measures themselves. The rules with regard to countervailing duties and subsidies are similar to the anti-dumping agreement. Dumping and subsidies are very similar in effect, in that each artificially lowers the price that goods are offered for sale, and the permissible governmental responses are likewise similar. Some subsidies are important to developing countries and least developed countries, and the WTO has special provisions and exceptions in certain circumstances to promote those interests.

The WTO has several agreements that address bureaucratic or legal issues with the potential to hinder trade. These agreements cover import licensing, rules for the valuation of goods at customs, pre-shipment inspections, rules of origin, and investment measures. The Agreement on Import Licensing Procedures calls for import licensing to be simple, transparent, and predictable. The agreement requires countries to notify the WTO of new or changed procedures and offers guidance to countries on how to evaluate applications for licenses. The agreement also sets up procedures and criteria for licenses to issue automatically in certain cases.

The objective of the WTO customs agreement is to set up a fair, uniform, and neutral system to allow traders to accurately estimate the value of their goods. Standard Industrial Classification (SIC), Standard International Trade Classifications (SITC), Harmonized Tariff Schedule of the United States (HTSUS), and North American Industry Classification System (NAICS) are all examples of systems designed to promote stability and ease the administrative burden of international trade.

Some developing governments use pre-shipment inspection to check the shipment details (like price, quantity, and quality) to help safeguard their financial interests (like fraud and duty evasion). The WTO agreement has an independent review procedure and obligates governments that engage in pre-shipment inspection to nondiscrimination, transparency, protection of confidential business information, the avoidance of undue delay, and the use of specific guidelines for price verification.

Rules of origin determine where a product was made. Origin is an important part of trade because some WTO policies involve countervailing duties, quotas, and preferential treatment that discriminate by exporting country. Additionally, trade statistics are also compiled by country of origin. The rules of origin must be transparent, must not have a disruptive effect on trade, must be applied consistently, impartially, and reasonably, and must state a standard that describes what confers origin as opposed to what does not.

Trade-Related Investment Measures (TRIMS) apply to investment policies that discriminate against foreigners or foreign goods or lead to quantity restrictions. TRIMS include a list of illustrative practices that are inconsistent with the WTO/GATT principles.

Going forward, the WTO promises to figure even more prominently in the global business environment. The GATT focused on trade rules for products and commodities. With the formation of the WTO, two new agreements were created in response to the changing landscape of the world's economy. First, the service industry become increasingly important as countries began to trade more heavily in industries such as financial services, transportation, telecommunication, construction, information technology, and tourism. The WTO introduced the General Agreement on Trade in Services (GATS). In response to concerns about the piracy of patents, trademarks, and copyrights, the WTO introduced the Trade-Related Aspects of Intellectual Property Rights (TRIPS). In 2001, the WTO began new negotiations called the Doha Development Agenda, which was aimed at multilateral agreements between developed and developing economies. Stalemated in 2008, non-WTO negotiated preferential trade agreements (PTAs) and free trade agreements (FTAs) have proliferated (Hartman, 2013). It has been argued, however, that members are now better able to define their strategic objectives and usefully participate in negotiations to defend national trade interests (Smeets, 2013).

TRIPS were negotiated during the final round of GATT negotiations between 1986 and 1994, called the Uruguay Round, and introduced the first intellectual property rules to multilateral trade regulation. "Intellectual property rights" refers to the right of a creator to prevent others from using a creation and the right to negotiate payment for its use. TRIPS cover copyrights, trademarks, service marks, geographical indications (like Cognac, Champagne, Scotch), industrial designs, patents, layout designs of integrated circuits and trade secrets, and other undisclosed information. The TRIPS agreement establishes a minimum amount of protection that a government must extend to intellectual property and a systematic dispute resolution mechanism in addition to the basic principles of MFN and national treatment of intellectual property rights.

GATS, also negotiated during the Uruguay Round, is the first and only multilateral agreement on the trade in services. GATS covers all internationally traded services: services supplied from one country to another (like international phone calls), consumers making use of a service in another country (like tourism), foreign companies that set up branches or subsidiaries to provide services in another country (like foreign banks), and individuals that travel to a foreign country to provide services (like consultants). Under GATS, if a nation allows competition in an area, MFN requires that all WTO members be treated alike, although some temporary exceptions are allowed where a nation had existing bilateral or small multilateral agreements. GATS also requires governments to publish all relevant laws and notify the WTO of any changes (called transparency). GATS includes rules in a number of other areas relevant to trade in service including international payments and transfers, reasonableness of domestic regulation, recognition of qualifications, and provision for further negotiations.

The Doha Development Agenda refers to a collection of negotiations conducted in several ministerial conferences. The Doha agenda was largely focused on the problems developing countries are having in implementing current WTO Agreements and involves many topics.

CONCLUSION

International business law has taken aim at a free trade, or at least freer trade, as opposed to the protectionist approach of the past that some maintain contributed or caused the Great Depression (Forbes 2006). Protectionism as a general theory has been abandoned in favor of the theory of comparative advantage and an effort to maximize global production and wealth. So far, this practice has produced profound effects on the world economy. As a general matter, mature economies like the U.S. are becoming more service-based, and U.S. companies are expanding their operations abroad to capitalize on new markets and opportunities. Emerging economies like China, Brazil, and Mexico are taking on manufacturing. India is a leader in technology and service outsourcing. From a historical perspective, these changes are coming fast, and many more seem to be on the way (Mehring 2007).

However, the global shift to unrestricted trade has not been without challenges and opponents. Many people have seen their jobs move abroad and have been forced to adapt. Russia's membership in the WTO, or accession as it is called, has been stalled. The Doha Round of talks, mentioned earlier, has met with serious setbacks (Scott, & Wilkinson, 2010). The implementation and effectiveness of some WTO rules has been criticized (Zuckerman 2006). Despite these growing pains, more people are more prosperous in more parts of the world. International business law does not just regulate business among nations; it shapes the business within nations as well.

BIBLIOGRAPHY

Bederman, D.J. (2001). "Concepts and Insights Series," *International Law Frameworks.*

China Trade: "WTO membership and most-favored-nation status: T-NSIAD-98-209." (1998). *GAO Reports.*

Doh, J., Rodrigues, S., Saka-Helmhout, A., Makhija, M. (2017). "International business responses to institutional voids." *Journal of International Business Studies, 48*, 3, 293–307.

Eglin, M. (2004). "Part 1: The origins and nature of the world trade organization: The development of multilateral trade agreements." *Handbook of World Trade.*

Engardio, P., Yang, C., Roberts, D., Byrnes, N., & Arndt, M. (2006). "The runaway trade giant." *Business Week, 3981*, 30–33.

Hartman, S.W. (2013). "The WTO, the Doha round impasse, PTAs, and FTAs/RTAs." *International Trade Journal, 27*, 411–430.

Pearlman, R. (2007). "Bridging the gap...globally." *Smart Money, 16*, 19–20.

Forbes, S. (2006). "Ridiculously retarding trade." *Forbes, 178*, 28.

Friedland J. (2002), *Understanding International Business and Financial Transactions.* Dayton, Ohio: LexisNexis.

Scott, J., & Wilkinson, R. (2010). "What happened to Doha in Geneva? Re-engineering the WTO's image while missing key opportunities." *European Journal of Development Research, 22*, 141–153.

Smeets, M. (2013). "Trade capacity building in the WTO: Main achievements since Doha and key challenges." *Journal of World Trade, 47*, 1047–1090.

SUGGESTED READING

Fishman, T. (2005).*China Inc. How the Next Superpower Challenges America and the World.* New York: Scribner.

U.S. Dept of Commerce (1998). *A Basic Guide to Exporting.* UNZ & Co.

Engardio, P (Editor) (2006). *Chindia: How China and India are Revolutionizing Global Business.* New York: McGraw Hill.

Mehring, J. (2007). "Expanding abroad—and growing at home." *Business Week,* March 06, 2007.

Zuckerman, M. (2006, January 23). "A giant's growing pains." *U.S. News & World Report,* pp. 68, 66.

—*Seth M. Azria, JD*

INTERNATIONAL BUSINESS OPERATIONS

ABSTRACT

This article focuses on how corporations make the decision to operate on an international level and the types of systems and processes that they put in place so that the business operations of the international entity run smoothly. The world has changed significantly since World War II. Organizations have been challenged to duplicate their success in other countries. In order to accomplish this task, the management team must devise a plan that will bring them the same level of success that they experienced in their home country. After a company has decided on what strategy would benefit the organization, it will move to the next step, which is the development of an approach to manage its global business operations. One approach that has been explored is the international trade theory. Once an organization has defined its international strategy, the next step would be to develop a process for implementing the strategy.

OVERVIEW

The world has changed significantly since World War II. "Countries that were previously separated by thousands of miles, and by historical enmities, are now closer together, thanks mainly to the impact of globalization and the lifting of trade barriers" (McLean, 2006, p. 1). Organizations have been challenged to duplicate their success in other countries. In order to accomplish this task, the management team must devise a plan that will bring them the same level of success that they experienced in their home country.

International business strategy provides corporations the opportunity to expand and manage business operations in many locations across the world. Many organizations are weighing the pros and cons of starting operations overseas. However, it is imperative that the decision makers identify opportunities, explore resources, and assess core competencies before implementing a plan to move forward. These three factors may provide a foundation for many corporations as they implement an international strategy. According to Hoskisson, Hitt, and Ireland (2003), each factor should be evaluated when determining whether or not to move forward.

AREAS FOR CONSIDERATION
Identify International Opportunities

   a.   Increase market size—If a domestic market's size is unable to support needed manufacturing facilities, it may make more business sense to start an operation abroad.

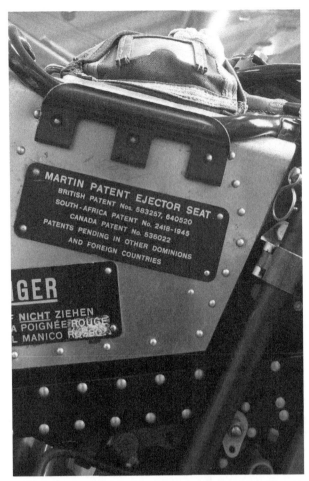

The top of the military airplane ejector seat with plate, stating that this design is covered by multiple patents in the United Kingdom, South Africa, Canada and pending in "other" jurisdictions. This is found in the Dubendorf Museum of Military Aviation. (Courtesy of Audrius Meskauskas CC-BY-SA-3.0 via Wikimedia Commons)

b. Return on investment—There are two issues that decision makers may consider when determining the effect on the organization's finances. First of all, global markets may be necessary to support and enable the large capital requirements of substantial investment projects. Secondly, some countries have weak patent laws. Therefore, an organization may have to expand overseas in order to stay ahead of competitors who may attempt to market similar products.

c. Economies of scale or learning—Economies of scale can increase profit per unit and spread costs over a larger sales base. In addi-

tion, moving into the international market allows the organization to expand the size of its market, which leads to economies of scale for departments such as marketing, manufacturing, distribution, or research and devolvement.

d. Advantage in location—Organizations can develop a competitive advantage by moving into markets that have low costs. These types of markets would provide the organization with better access to raw materials, lower labor costs, energy, and a key customer base.

Explore Resources and Capabilities (International Strategies)

e. International business-level strategy—If an organization wanted to develop an international strategy at the business level, the management team should evaluate the four determinants of national advantage. These determinants include

   i. demand conditions (the nature and size of buyers' needs in the home market for the industry's goods or services);

   ii. related and supporting industries (the supporting services, facilities, and suppliers);

   iii. firm strategy, structure, and rivalry (the pattern of strategy, structure, and rivalry among firms); and

   iv. factors of production (the inputs needed to compete in any industry).

f. International corporate-level strategy—In certain international business situations, corporate strategies allow for the individual overseas operation centers to control their own procedures. In other situations, the strategy is to homogenize procedures across the entire organization, regardless of location. Whatever method the organization decides upon, the way that business level strategies are selected and implemented will be impacted. There are three types of corporate level strategies that an organization can choose from.

   i. Multi-domestic strategy—The products are tailored to meet the needs of local preferences, and the organization is isolated from global competition by competing in industry segments that are most affected by differences among local countries.

ii. Global strategy—The products are standardized across the national market. Business-level strategy decisions are made by the headquarters office. This type of strategy is prominent among Japanese firms.

iii. Transnational strategy—The combination structure has characteristics that emphasize both geographic and product structures. Global efficiency and responsiveness are the goals of this type of strategy.

Assess Core Competencies (Modes of Entry)

g. Exporting—high cost, low control
h. Licensing—low cost, low risk, little control, low returns
i. Strategic alliances—shared costs, shared resources, shared risks, problems of integration
j. Acquisitions—quick access to new market, high cost, complex negotiations, problem of merging with domestic operations
k. Establishment of a new subsidiary—complex, often costly, time-consuming, high-risk, maximum control, potential above-average returns

After a company has decided on what strategy would benefit the organization, it will move to the next step, which is the development of an approach to manage its global business operations. One approach that has been explored is the international trade theory.

International Trade Theory

Classical economics was created as a response to the economists who supported the mercantilism school of thought. The concept was introduced in the late eighteenth century and focused on economic growth and freedom, laissez-faire ideas, and free competition.

Three Key Principles of Mercantilist Thought

There were three key principles to the mercantilist thought:

- Exporting is good, but importing should be avoided.
- When a merchant exports, he will receive payment.
- It is best to export as much as possible in order to maximize the amount of money one can receive.

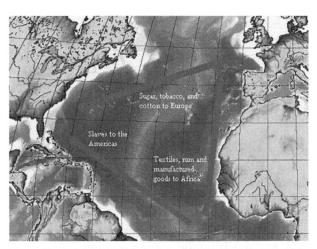

Mercantilism helped create trade patterns such as the triangular trade in the North Atlantic, in which raw materials were imported to the metropolis and then processed and redistributed to other colonies. (Courtesy of SimonP CC BY-SA 2.0 via Wikipedia Commons)

The downside to this theory is that it does not recognize the positive effects of importing. Therefore, if the country does not import, it will have to sacrifice the consumption of certain items.

Economists Adam Smith & David Ricardo

Adam Smith wrote a book titled *The Wealth of Nations*, which highlighted the significance of specialization. His work was in response to the mercantilist thought that was popular in Britain since the sixteenth century. This book established a foundation for the concepts and principles of classical economics. Smith believed that free competition and free trade were the best ways to promote a country's economic growth. According to his theory, international trade was considered a type of specialization. Specialization advocates that each country should specialize in the production of goods that it is equipped to produce (i.e., absolute advantage). The countries should export part of their production and use the other part to barter for products that they cannot produce. Smith believed that communities would grow if the members were allowed to pursue their own interests, and these members would make a profit by producing goods that other people were willing to buy. The members would use the profits to purchase the products that they needed. Unfortunately, the concept of absolute advantage is not realistic. It tends to only work in those markets where geographic and economic environments are simple.

David Ricardo expanded on this concept by introducing the principle of comparative advantage. Ricardo's theory was based on the labor theory of value, which makes labor the only factor of production. He proposed that the value of goods produced and sold under competitive conditions were proportionate to the labor costs incurred in producing them. However, he acknowledged that there would be periods during which the price would be dependent on supply and demand. He argued that if one country had the ability to produce everything more efficiently than another country, it was not a hindrance for international trade. Rather, the theory of comparative advantage provides a strong argument in favor of free trade and specialization among countries.

Political & Economic Risks of International Trade

Although both of these economists support the concept of international trade, there are some risks, and they can be broken down into two categories—political and economic risks.

Political risks include the follwing:

- Instability in national governments
- War, both civil and international
- Potential nationalization of an organization's resources
- Cancellation or non-renewal of export or import licenses
- Confiscation of the importer's company
- Imposition of an import ban after the shipment of the goods

- Imposition of exchange controls by the importer's country or foreign currency shortages
- Surrendering political sovereignty

Economic risks are interdependent with political risks and include the following:

- Differences and fluctuations in the value of different currencies
- Differences in prevailing wage rates
- Difficulties in enforcing property rights
- Unemployment
- Insolvency of the buyer
- Failure to pay the amount due within six months after the due date
- Nonacceptance
- Surrendering economic sovereignty

APPLICATION

Operations

Once an organization has defined its international strategy, the next step would be to develop a process for implementing the strategy. According to Ball, McCulloch, Frantz, Geringer, and Minor (2005), the process of strategic planning provides a formal structure for managers to

- "Analyze the company's external environments;
- Analyze the company's internal environment;
- Define the company's business and mission;
- Set corporate objectives;
- Quantify goals;
- Formulate strategies; [and]
- Make tactical plans."

Situational Analysis & Forecasting

Companies should analyze the variables that they can control, and this analysis should include a situational analysis and a forecast. After the analysis has been completed, the management team is ready to proceed with the examination of the business, vision, and mission statements. Once the statements have been defined, the company may proceed to setting corporate objectives. After everyone agrees on the objectives, the organization is ready to formulate the corporate strategies. These corporate strategies will assist the company in determining what types of goals it wants

The Anglo-Dutch Wars were fought between the English and the Dutch for control over the seas and trade routes. The title of this painting is the Battle of Terheide, 10 August 1653: episode from the First Anglo-Dutch War (1652-54). (Courtesy of Willem van de Velde the Elder via Wikimedia Commons

to accomplish in the global market. Contingency and tactical plans are developed in order to complete this process. Contingency plans are developed to address best- and worst-case scenarios that could have an impact on the company. The tactical plans, also called operational plans, are designed to be specific and spell out the objectives that need to be reached. Tactical planning is specific and short term.

Factors Affecting Strategic Planning

Some of the factors affecting a strategic plan are time horizon, plan implementation facilitators, and sales forecasts and budgets. The time horizon addresses the timeline for the process. Strategic plans can be short-, medium-, or long-term. The timeline is dependent upon the age of the organization and the stability of the market. Plan implementation facilitators are responsible for developing and implementing the policies and procedures that will govern the process. In most cases, the policies and procedures are

- Broad guidelines approved by the senior management team and the board;
- Designed to assist operational managers with handling daily business transactions, including potential problems; and
- Developed to efficiently use the operational managers' time as well as provide consistency and uniformity across operating units.

Planning Methods for Operations

Each organization has the opportunity to decide which type of planning process it should pursue. The three main planning methods are top-down planning, bottom-up planning, and iterative planning, and the features of each are as follows:

a. Top-down planning—Planning process that starts at the top (i.e., senior management team) and flows down to the different levels of the company. In this model, "corporate headquarters develops and provides the guidelines that include the definition of the business, the mission statement, company objectives, financial assumptions, the content of the plan, and special issues" (Ball, McCulloch, Frantz, Geringer, and Minor, 2005). An advantage of this method is that the corporate headquarters should be able to develop global plans that effectively utilize the organization's resources. A disadvantage is it may restrict motivation and initiative at the lower

levels of the organization and be insensitive to local conditions.

b. Bottom-up planning—Planning process that starts at the lower ranks of the organization and proceeds to the top. In this method, the workers on the floor inform the management team about what they think will work. These recommendations become the organization's goals. An advantage to this method is that all employees feel empowered and that they have made a valuable contribution to the success of the organization. A disadvantage of the method is that some employees may have too much freedom to influence the operations of the organization, and there may be hidden personal agendas.

c. Iterative planning—This method is a spin-off of the two methods mentioned above. Each method continues to refine its process until all of the differences have been resolved. This type of approach is becoming more popular as international corporations seek a single global plan when operating in many diverse foreign environments.

Some top-level managers believe that they spend too much time on issues, strategies, and implementation. Some thought should be given to the organizational design of the company. When designing the structure of an organization, managers need to be concerned with finding the most effective way to departmentalize in order to take advantage of the efficiencies gained from specialized labor and coordinating the activities of departments that assist the organization with meeting its overall objectives.

The international division is at the same level of the domestic division but is responsible for all host country activities. Product divisions are responsible for global operations such as marketing and have the production of products under their control. Each division is assigned regional experts. Geographic regions are formed and are responsible for all of the activities in their designed areas. Area managers oversee the operations and report to the CEO. Few organizations are designed to function from the top level. Those reporting to the CEO tend to be senior-level functional executives.

VIEWPOINT

Legal Framework for International Operations

As international businesses continue to grow, many organizations in the United States will shift from exporting their products to establishing a business operation abroad. In order to set up a business at a global level, organizations will need to address issues such as setting up the office, hiring employees in the host country, and acquiring property in foreign countries. When establishing a foreign presence, organizations must tackle the different legal, tax, and commercial issues in both countries. According to McVey (n.d.), organizations must decide on the type of legal form in which they plan to do business overseas.

Direct Forms of Foreign Presence

Some of the direct forms of foreign presence include foreign subsidiary, branch office, representative office, and joint venture. A foreign subsidiary is formed when the corporation establishes a separate legal entity (i.e., corporation, limited liability company, or equivalent entity) in the host country. Another option is for the corporation to establish an office, distribution center, or manufacturing facility in the host country, without establishing a separate entity. In this type of scenario, the office is still a part of the main corporation and is responsible for conducting business in the host country. On the other hand, the corporation may establish an office in another country for special projects. There are no business transactions, but special projects such as preliminary marketing analysis and promotional campaigns are developed. A final form of direct presence is the joint venture. The corporation may form a partnership with a business in the host country.

Indirect Forms of Foreign Presence

Some of the indirect forms of foreign presence include distributor, agency, and marketing representative licensing/franchising. In the distributor model, the corporation finds an independent party in the host country and conducts business with that party or other members in the chain of distribution. Some corporations may appoint an independent party to act as their legal representative in the foreign countries, and the agency has the authority to negotiate on behalf of the corporation. This is an example of the agency model. Transactions performed by the agency are legally binding for the corporation. However, some corporations may decide to appoint independent representatives but not give them the power to enter into any legal agreements. This model has been classified as the marketing representative approach. Contracts are sent back to the corporation's legal

department. Licensing/franchising involves the assignment of an independent party to use proprietary assets such as trade secrets, copyrights, trademarks, patents, software, data, and business systems.

There may be a time when the organization decides that it does not want a foreign presence. In this type of situation, the organization will either export directly from the United States or transmit the information itself. Sometimes, it is advantageous for the organization to sell products directly to the customer.

CONCLUSION

"An increasing number of U.S.-based associations are facing an urgent need to create a successful strategy for international programs and activities" (Barkan, 2006). According to Barkan (2006), this trend is being driven by one or more of the following factors:

- "Globalization has encouraged organizations to demand more international reach from their trading opportunities as they are faced with international issues."
- "Corporations may have been trading at the international level for a number of years, but the results have not met expectations and a new approach is needed."
- "In the search for growth, international markets offer the best untapped or underdeveloped opportunities for programs and services."
- Many corporations will develop a specific strategy to address these factors. Although this type of approach could work in the corporation's favor, there are potential pitfalls such as:
- The organization's established core strategy does not fit the needs of international organizations and a conflict is created.
- There is potential of a silo or split being created as a result of the organization's international strategy taking on a life of its own.
- If an organization wrongly assumes that most American corporations have the same needs and those needs are different from the needs of international corporations.
- It is therefore beneficial for the organizations to consider the following suggestions when developing their international business strategies to successfully run their operations abroad. Barkan (2006) believes that organizations should:

- Make sure that the common mission is clear to all involved, especially partners that are at the international level.
- "Adopt a global governance policy that defines the roles and responsibilities of the board, staff, and volunteers."
- "Identify global strategic objectives/key performance indicators and balanced scorecard measurements that will assist the organization in defining success."
- "Develop regional structures and strategies mapped to the global governance and strategy structure."
- "Gather input and feedback on a local/regional level and at the same time, collect and validate input gathered globally."
- "Identify those issues that are common universally versus those that are specific and of high importance to a region."
- "Develop an implementation strategy based on the information collected."

BIBLIOGRAPHY

Ajmal, M., Helo, P. (2017). "Conceptualizing trust with cultural perspective in international business operations." *Benchmarking : An International Journal, 24,* 4, 1099–1118.

Ball, D., McCulloch, W., Frantz, P., Geringer, J., & Minor, M. (2005). *International business* (10th ed.). New York: Irwin McGraw-Hill.

"Classical economics." (2007). In *Encyclopedia Britannica* from Encyclopedia Britannica Online:

Hoskisson, R., Hitt, M., & Ireland, R. (2003, January). *International strategy.*

International trade theories. (n.d.).

McLean, J. (2006). Globalization is here to stay. *British Journal of Administrative Management,* 16.

McVey, T. (n.d.). *Structuring international operation—A legal framework for companies operating abroad.* Williamsmullen. com.

SUGGESTED READING

"International codes and multinational business: Setting guidelines for international business operations." (1986). *Sloan Management Review,* 27, 90.

Kumar, S., & Chase, C. (2006). "Barriers and success factors in the management of international operations: Mexico and China overview." *International Journal of Management & Decision Making, 7,* 525–537.

McNeil, M., & Pedigo, K. (2001). "Western Australian managers tell their stories: Ethical challenges in international business operations." *Journal of Business Ethics, 30,* 305–317

Milani, K., & Rivera, J. (2004). "The rigorous business of budgeting for international operations." *Management Accounting Quarterly, 5,* 38–50.

—Marie Gould

INTERNATIONAL ECONOMIC DEVELOPMENT

ABSTRACT

International economic development must somehow find a way to bring world trade's zero-sum game to a close. The idea that someone gains only at someone else's expense makes the prospect of globalization far less appealing. Yet for better and for worse, that's exactly what happened from the sixteenth century onward. We live today in one of two worlds—the developed and the developing—as a consequence. Such is the nature of seemingly intractable dilemmas economists specializing in development grapple with. Daily they ask themselves: How exactly can we ensure a more equitable sharing of wealth between countries and continents through the workings of competitive markets? Should developing countries invest in domestic or export industries? Is capital investment proper or the technological innovation it affords the true engine of growth? Must the agricultural poor seeking a better life make due indefinitely as subsistence-wage earners in nascent manufacturing industries to speed the domestic accumulation of capital? Can everyone win, albeit some perhaps more than others, without anyone necessarily losing?

OVERVIEW

Fairly or unfairly, wealth is unevenly distributed among people and places. Be it between classes, countries, or whole continents, the gulf between rich

Buildings in Rio de Janeiro, Brazil, demonstrating economic inequality. (Courtesy of Leandro Ciuffo from Rio de Janeiro, Brazil CC BY 2.0 via Wikimedia Commons)

and poor goes as far back as recorded history itself. We live with its global consequences today. Some of us are fortunate to live in the twenty or so highly industrialized countries that collectively hold most of the world's wealth. The poverty endemic in the remaining hundred or so countries is so abject it must be seen firsthand to be believed. Yet it is all too real for *billions* of people who, until recently, had absolutely no hope of bettering themselves. That some now do is largely a planned outcome achieved by leveraging macroeconomic fundamentals to good effect. Greater aggregate output and the income it generates finances improved standards of living. This situation only happens in theory when all available labor, capital, and land are actively utilized in the production of goods and services. Anything less than the 'full' employment of all these factors of production brings about scarcity—the root cause of economic underdevelopment.

Economic Growth
Growth by definition involves going beyond existing limits. In macroeconomics, the boundaries being pushed outward are the production possibility frontier and long-term aggregate supply. The first concept comes from microeconomics and refers to the range of maximum output of one good versus another in the short run, when technology and capital remain unchanged. Aggregate economic growth entails the maximization of innumerable 'paired-goods' outputs in the long run; however, it can also serve to demark the outer boundary of the trade-off

in productive capacity between the manufacturing and agricultural sectors in general. The more capital and more efficient technology brought to bear over time in both sectors, the more the two's production possibilities frontiers expand. Aggregate supply and demand are macroeconomics concepts and manifest themselves in both the short and long term. They differ, however, in one critical respect: Prices of some resources are assumed to be inflexible in the short term but flexible in the long term. A price change in one resource, essentially, throws other, interdependent resources markets into temporary disequilibrium, for said rise signals an imbalance in supply and demand that must be redressed by the marketplace. Eventually, the full effect of a price change ripples through the economy as a whole, and a general equilibrium reasserts itself. Whatever scarcity or surplus occasioned by the initial price change disappears. This is what is meant by price flexibility.

Trends in Economic Growth/Recession
What in theory seems a relatively straightforward distinction in practice, however, soon falls apart because there's widespread disagreement about the amount of time that must expire before the short run turns into the long run. Some say several months, others a year, and still others several years. In the case of economic development in poor countries, the more appropriate time span might be five to ten years. Then, too, maintaining general equilibrium at full employment for any length of time has proven next to impossible in 'have not' economies where 'variable' resources like labor and raw materials largely determine the extent of achievable productive capacity. Unlike more 'fixed' resources like capital and new technology, these factors of production can change fairly quickly. The minute output outstrips any of these available resources, scarcities arise, and price hikes invariably follow.

If sufficiently steep and/or swift, said price hike's knock-on effect unleashes inflationary pressures. A vicious cycle often develops that takes on a life of its own as producers begin to pass along supplier price rises to customers. As rises in income rarely come as quickly, the purchasing power of the individual consumer shrinks. Offsetting wage increases often only leads to even greater inflation and the value of the affected currency depreciates even further. Real economic growth slows as appreciating prices decrease demand which, in turn, pushes unemployment higher as suppliers respond by cutting back production. Resources go unused until prices stabilize again. When such a downturn occurs in the most advanced economies, existing productive capacity shrinks for a time. No matter how long a recession lasts, however, the expectation remains that a recovery will follow. In underdeveloped economies, there is no such expectation because nonexistent productive capacity simply doesn't get built in the first place. Here setbacks in the short run stymie a more efficient *allocation* of resources in the long run where, in more developed economies, a more efficient *reallocation* is simply delayed. Fundamentally, then, successful 'development' hinges on the answer to this paradoxical question: How does one create something out of virtually nothing?

FURTHER INSIGHTS

Since the mid-twentieth century, economists have put forth formal economic models as possible answers noteworthy for both their number and their conceptual diversity. All of them involve investment of one sort or another. In the strict sense of the term, of course, this means funds raised by stock flotations, joint ventures, bonds, and other kinds of loans as well as direct aid or debt forgiveness. Whatever its source, these funds go toward the acquisition of capital goods, the equipment and plant used in production processes. In the broader context of economic activity per se, the term refers to any resource—labor, land, technical know-how, entrepreneurship—dedicated to one economic purpose instead of another where the payoff might be more immediate but not as great. Any sacrifice of short-term gains for the sake of potentially larger long-term gains thus constitutes an investment in this broader sense of the word.

EARLY FORMAL MODELS
Harrod-Domar Model

One rather influential early theory of economic growth, the Harrod-Domar model, was built around the narrower sense of the term. Gross domestic product, or GDP—the sum of all goods and services sold in a year—grows at a rate proportionate to the national savings ratio and inversely proportionate to the national capital to output ratio. The latter signifies the amount that must be invested in order to

produce a certain amount of something, the former the percentage of total household income left in interest-bearing accounts. By setting a targeted rate of growth in GDP, fiscal and monetary policy makers can calculate the exact amount of investment funds required to meet it by first empirically determining the capital to output ratio. Should savings recycled by domestic banks as loans not cover the required amount, the difference can be made up by borrowing from foreign banks and governments. The exactness of the relationship stems from the model's clear-cut identification of three different types of growth: the warranted, the natural, and the actual. All three concepts stem from Keynes's groundbreaking General Theory of Employment, Interest and Money, which states that at full employment, income—not interest—sets investment levels. So, the actual rate of growth here is defined as the general population's propensity to save and invest. The warranted growth rate, meanwhile, is the amount of planned savings it will take to match planned investments. Meanwhile, the natural rate is the growth in population and thus the labor forces along with the rate at which new technologies improve national productivity. When these two rates are the same, the resulting equilibrium creates a steady rate of growth at full employment.

Rostow's Five Stages of Growth

Other models are more descriptive than normative. The earliest synthesis of development as a multiphase progression came with Rostow's Five Stages of Growth, a model gleaned from an exhaustive analysis of economic history (Clever, 2002). It traced national

Walt Rostow at a meeting in the Cabinet Room in the White House. (Courtesy of Wikipedia)

economic and investment activity back to its origins in subsistence farming over two thousand years. Lack of any surpluses to speak of undermines nascent savings and investment to this day in some traditional societies. In barter economies, where resource allocation decisions are guided by custom and obligation, production capacity and standards of living remain mired at low levels. A transitional stage emerges as the division of labor encourages greater efficiency in production, yielding more substantial surplus for trade. This in turn occasions improvements in transportation and the evolution of a merchant class. The preconditions now exist for a 'takeoff' by the economy as a whole, the third stage. Here growing income in the primary product sector stimulates demand and investment in other emerging product sectors. One or two manufacturing industries gain traction and establish themselves, giving agricultural laborers and other laborers more attractive employment alternatives. More importantly, perhaps, investment rises to as much as 10 percent of GDP. Diversification ensues, and technology comes to play a leading role in expanding productive capacity thereafter, creating new investment opportunities and more higher-paying jobs as the so-called 'drive to maturity' gathers pace, leading eventually to the fifth and final stage: the 'age of high mass consumption.'

Lewis-Ranis-Fei Model of Surplus Labor

A third theory to gain currency in the two decades immediately after World War II has the distinction of being the only to start from the premise that underemployment was the major obstacle to development, not underinvestment. In the Lewis-Ranis-Fei model of surplus labor, the engine of economic growth is, ironically, the subsistence wage. At the stage in economic development when traditional agriculture and modern industrial manufacturing coexist, workers migrating from farm to factory end up receiving the same subsistence wage because of the huge untapped reserve of labor readily available in the countryside. Unskilled workers, in effect, have no real bargaining power. And the lower the manufacturing overhead, the greater the profits available for interest-free investment, the ideal means of stimulating further economic growth. The manufacturing workforce's fortunes eventually improve, too, but only after industrialization has absorbed all of the excess agricultural workforce. At that point,

workers in both sectors would begin to be paid their marginal product of labor. A follow-up on development theory, the Lewis dual-sector surplus model calls upon governments to actively shape policies to encourage structural changes that foster the migration from the rural, agricultural sector to the urban, manufacturing one.

Policies Inspired by Early Models

These three theories were quickly put to the test in the 1960s and 1970s as sovereign independence replaced colonial rule in Africa and industrialization increasingly topped national economic agendas in Asia and Latin America. With perhaps the exception of oil, economic planners and policy makers in the emerging world saw little future in remaining solely suppliers of commodities and/or raw materials. Attention turned to the very real problem of how to transition quickly from a traditional to a modern economy, the goal in Lewis-Ranis-Fei model, from Rostow's 'takeoff' through the 'drive to maturity' in effect, using capital drawn from domestic savings whenever possible as the Harrod-Domar model proscribes. Promoting the domestic production of capital and consumer goods, of course, was the obvious solution. The problem quickly became how to do this most effectively in the shortest amount of time.

Import Substitution

Given that manufactured goods were already being imported, one ready-made solution was to impose tariffs and quotas and finance domestic production of these goods to satisfy demand. Import substitution as a development plan would create much-needed infrastructure, expand productive capacity, generate income that, as 'savings,' could provide further investment-capital, and promote economic self-sufficiency in one fell-swoop (Lauterberg, 1980). Compelling arguments all, import substitution in practice had unintended consequences that proved its undoing in the long run. Foremost among these was that the tariffs and quotas made it much more expensive to acquire the capital goods abroad that domestic producers relied upon and were not manufactured locally. Heavy industry's development in particular suffered from a lack of modern equipment. And without heavy industry to cost effectively supply intermediate products to end-product manufacturers, consumer goods prices remain high. Restricting the flow of consumer goods through preexisting import channels, what's more, invariably leads to temporary scarcities, pushing high prices even higher and triggering inflation. Worse still, import substitution turns a national economy into a de facto protected market, stifling competition.

Export Orientation

In short, import substitution failed to live up to expectations. Yet, its underlying objective—industrialization—remained sound, so the focus shifted to finding another, far less problematic means to the same end. Export orientation proved the most promising candidate. As opposed to turning their backs on world markets, domestic industries should be actively encouraged to produce manufactured goods tailor-made for them. Underemployment, the curse of the developing world, now becomes a strength, for foreign manufacturers seeking cheap labor will invest in local production plants, finance the acquisition of capital goods, and greatly accelerate specialization of the local workforce. Producers, moreover, have to turn out truly competitive goods to gain a share of world markets. Domestic capital accumulation benefits too as workers have wages to put into savings accounts and businesses have operating profits to reinvest (Holt, 1996). Hong Kong, Singapore, Taiwan, and South Korea, known collectively as the East Asian 'tigers,' implemented this strategy with spectacular success in the 1960s and 70s. Results elsewhere proved mixed.

The Port of Hong Kong is one of the busiest container ports in the world. (Courtesy of Baycrest CC BY-SA 2.5 via Wikimedia Commons)

REVISIONIST THINKING
International Dependency Theory

Interestingly, the most vocal criticism of export orientation policies came from the developing countries themselves. Adherents of international dependency theory argued that in most developing economies, primary products, not locally manufactured goods, made up the bulk of exports. These rarely earned enough to cover import purchases. But, without import substitution policies in place, there was no other ready source of manufactured goods. So, developing countries gain little beyond mounting debts from this uneven exchange. Developed countries, what's more, had no real incentive to change this, making it very hard indeed for developing countries to break free of a deepening dependency. Export-driven development was, in a word, really just colonialism in a different guise.

Neoclassical Theory

A contrarian view, neoclassical theory, soon emerged inspired by the work of early proponents of 'laissez-faire' capitalism, Adam Smith and David Ricardo. For developing countries, it argues that the surest, fastest route to development lay in unrestrained market competition. Government intervention in any form—tariff restrictions, low-cost loans to export industries, etc.—hindered rather than helped. Championed by leading lender countries in the 1980s and 1990s, neoclassical theory's ascendancy as the dominant model of development was swift and its application widespread. Both the International Monetary Fund and the World Bank saw to this by making free-market reforms a precondition for further development assistance. By then, export-driven economies of the Asian 'tigers,' Mexico, Brazil, and Argentina urgently needed financial bailouts and were in no position to argue. In each case, currency devaluations had eroded their terms of trade, bringing about soaring inflation and/or prolonged economic recession. Some, like Argentina and Mexico, could not meet short-term debt obligations. Reeling from higher oil prices, many other lesser-developed countries found it necessary to borrow to replenish energy stocks, adding to already high debt burdens. Additional loans, restructured repayment schedules, and debt forgiveness were extended to developing countries that put free-market 'stabilization' policies in place.

This renewed emphasis on classical economic theory's role in development led to the reevaluation of the importance of technology that Adam Smith assigned to fostering growth. Investment's singular virtue might well be the reorganization of workflows around the ever more efficient production processes it facilitates (Kregal, 2004). Such, at least, was the conclusion drawn by Robert Solow, who estimated technology singlehandedly accounts for almost all of the economic growth the industrialized world experienced before and after the turn of the twentieth century. This insight forms the core of the exogenous growth model that extols the developmental virtues of technology as an agent of change and, by implication, the value of investing in human capital. Without the funding or the infrastructure to support education, in effect, no country can expect to harness human capital successfully. And, if technology is in fact the engine of growth, any country that fails to adequately educate its people will stagnate economically.

ISSUES

Much progress has thus been made on the theoretical front. Much less progress alas has been made on the practical front. There are, of course, notable successes like Brazil, China, and India. But unlike most developing countries, all three are geographically enormous and teeming with so-called 'surplus' labor. Progress measured in material improvements has been uneven at best. Even successful development has its ugly side: massive population dislocation, squalid urban slums, tremendous income disparities separating rich from poor, environmental pollution, etc. Where there are expectations of future improvements, these conditions, fortunately, are tolerated. But in many places such expectations remain wishful thinking because development there is moving afoot at a snail's pace, if at all. Theory does not factor in corrupt governments nor rent-seeking local industrialists, trade barriers erected by developed countries denying developing countries access to profitable markets for agricultural exports, or world capital markets' reluctance to refinance the majority of 'third world' debt on terms more favorable to less-developed countries.

BIBLIOGRAPHY

Clever. T. (2002) "Chapter 11: Development, growth and Asian dragons." *Understanding the world economy* (pp. 209–235). United Kingdom: Taylor & Francis Ltd.

Diamond, L., & Mosbacher, J. (2013). "Petroleum to the people." *Foreign Affairs, 92,* 86–98.

Hafer, R. W. (2013). "Economic freedom and financial development: International evidence." *CATO Journal, 33,* 111–126.

Hout, W. (1996). "Development strategies and economic performance in third world countries, 1965-92." *Third World Quarterly, 17,* 603–624.

Hughes, H. (2003). "Trade or aid? Which benefits developing countries more?" *Economic Papers, 22,* 1–19.

Kregel, J. (2004). "Two views on the obstacles to development." *Social Research, 71,* 279–292.

Lauterbach, A. (1980). "The erosion of the development concept: Prospects for a new international economic order." *ACES Bulletin, 22,* 53.

Marangos, J. (2012). "The post Keynesian retort to "After the Washington Consensus"." *Journal of Post Keynesian Economics, 34,* 583–610.

SUGGESTED READING

Gopinath, M., & Upadhyay, M. (2002). "Human capital, technology, and specialization: A comparison of developed and developing countries." *Journal of Economics, 75,* 161–179.

Parker, D., & Kirkpatrick, C. (2005). "Privatisation in developing countries: A review of the evidence and the policy lessons." *Journal of Development Studies, 41,* 513–541.

Shafaeddin, S. (2005). "Towards an alternative perspective on trade and industrial policies." *Development & Change, 36,* 1143–1162.

Sen, S. (2005). "International trade theory and policy: What is left of the free trade paradigm?" *Development & Change, 36,* 1011–1029.

Weisbrot, M., Baker, D., Kraev, E., & Chen, J. (2003). "The scorecard on globalization 1980-2000: Twenty years of diminished progress." *Social Policy, 33,* 42.

—Francis Duffy, MBA

International Financial Markets

ABSTRACT

The term *International Financial Markets* is generally, albeit not always, applied to the various exchanges of foreign currency and currency-linked derivatives, plus the international bond market. These markets emerged after the Bretton Woods System collapsed in the early 1970s. The Bretton Woods System had pegged most free market currencies to the U.S. dollar, which in turn had been linked to gold. However, once currencies were allowed to float in value relative to one another, it was possible to trade them and derivatives based on them (futures, spots, etc.) in much the same way that other commodities may be traded. These new international markets include the Foreign Exchange (FX) Market, the Eurocurrency Market, and International or Eurobond Market (among others). Basic knowledge of these markets is, thus, vital to anyone doing business either international or, given the increasingly globalized nature of commerce, within a single nation.

OVERVIEW

The term *International Financial Markets* is generally applied to the various exchanges of foreign currency and currency-linked derivatives, plus the international or Eurobond market. It should be noted, though, that this nomenclature, while common, is not universal, and some writers will use the term to mean anything from the world's stock exchanges to the money changers of third world villages. That said, *International Financial Markets* will be used in this article to mean the global Foreign Currency Exchange (FX), Eurocurrency, and Eurobond Markets.

Foreign Currency Exchange

The *Foreign Currency Exchange (FX)* market can be broadly defined as the decentralized network in which currency traders located across the world buy and sell the money of different nations.

Eurocurrency Market

The *Eurocurrency Market* is the similarly decentralized market for "Eurocurrency," that is, deposits in a bank

Bureau de Change of Siam Commercial Bank PCL, seen at Suvarnabhumi International Airport in Thailand. (Courtesy of Mattes via Wikimedia Commons)

in one country which are denominated in the currency of another country.

Eurobond Market

The *Eurobond Market*, finally, is the market for Eurobonds, that is, bonds denominated in the currency of a particular nation, but which are not sold in that nation. Thus, a Eurobond might be issued in American dollars, but by a bank outside the United States, and sold exclusively in Asia.

These markets are vitally important to anyone doing business anywhere in the world today. In an age when raw material suppliers and final customers are almost certainly located in different nations, and when a "single" product may contain parts from many different countries, the reality is that all trade is multinational trade. The price of any one item in any one location will then be dependent on the purchasing power of the currency used to pay for it. That purchasing power, in turn, will depend on the currency's standing in the International Financial Markets.

Discussion

While International Financial Markets have existed in some form since merchants discovered there was a profit to be made in buying and selling the coinages of different weights and purities issued by different princes, they developed their present form only quite recently literally less than two generations ago, with the demise of the Bretton Woods system in the early 1970s. The Bretton Woods system was brought into existence in the aftermath of World War II by the Western Allied powers, chiefly the United States and the United Kingdom. At that time, the world's major powers, or at least those involved in the free market economy, were particularly concerned with stability. The recent world war and the Great Depression before it seemed to prove that some form of currency regulation was necessary to keep national economies from spiraling into debt, crisis, inflation, and ultimately, dictatorship and war.

Bretton Woods Agreement

The Bretton Woods agreements (so called because they were drawn up at a conference held in Bretton Woods, New Hampshire, in 1944) specified that free market world currencies would be pegged to the dollar, which in turn would be pegged to gold. In effect, this allowed British pounds, U.S. dollars, West German marks, Japanese yen, and so on, to be freely convertible with one another, thus facilitating international trade. But, because these were all ultimately linked to gold, their value was more or less stable (Cohen, 2001).

The Bretton Woods system worked chiefly because at the time, the U.S. economy was enormously strong compared to every other on the planet, raw

The Bretton Woods agreements were drawn up at a conference held at the Mount Washington Hotel in Bretton Woods, New Hampshire in 1944. (Courtesy of Rickpilot 2000 from Hooksett, USA CC BY 2.0 via Wikimedia Commons)

materials (and particularly oil) were relatively cheap, and the volume of international trade was relatively small. In the late 1940s and early 1950s, no one could have possibility foretold that German and Japanese cars and electronics, Chinese textiles and South American low-cost labor would someday compete with America's factories and mills. Moreover, if anyone had suggested that gasoline would be more costly than distilled water, that person would surely have been dismissed as an alarmist.

Failure of the Bretton Woods System

In the 1970s, all those things had come to pass. The American dollar was under enormous inflationary pressure, oil prices had skyrocketed, and international trade was now far too large for any one economy to act as a sort of world lender of last resort. Thus, by 1973, the Bretton Woods system had been largely dismantled. The dollar was no longer pegged to gold, and individual currencies floated in value against one another.

Development of the Foreign Currency Exchange Market

As a result, de facto market mechanisms soon took the place of those official mechanisms of Bretton Woods. The *Foreign Currency Exchange (FX)* market was perhaps the first to draw the attention of the public. Roughly defined, it is the large (not to say enormous), decentralized, amorphous, high-risk, and high-volume market in which currency traders located across the world buy and sell the money of different nations. It has no one central point and no one predominant physical location. In other words, it has no equivalent to Wall Street or the City of London, but rather exists chiefly in what might be called economic cyberspace. In effect, it is the Internet of the financial world, which makes a certain sense, given that both the Internet and the modern FX market developed at roughly the same time and were similarly based on electronic communications. However, if the FX market has no one location, it does have geographic capitals where the participants are more often based than not– i.e., the traditional banking centers, such as the United States, the United Kingdom, Germany, Japan, Singapore, Hong Kong, Switzerland, and so on. In addition, China and India have become ever more aggressive players in the market.

The FX market can be thought of, then, as a network whose individual nodes are traders, brokers, banks, governments, pension funds, multinational corporations, speculators and more. All of these may also be "market makers," i.e., people or companies who offer to buy currencies at one price and to sell them at another (Grabbe, 1996, p. 88). Such market makers, who attempt to profit from the difference between the bid and the offer, tend to be the predominant players in FX, and these are the people one usually thinks of when someone says "currency trader."

In theory, traders could deal in any of the world's many currencies and, to a certain extent, they do. However, the reality is that there is relatively little trade in the less well-known currencies. It is a rare trader who will, for example, specialize in the North Korean *won*. Thus, while almost all of the world's currencies are traded, the currencies that are traded the most are the Euro, the German mark, the British pound, the Swiss franc, the French franc, the Canadian dollar, the Australian dollar, the Dutch guilder, the Belgian franc, the Italian lira, and the U.S. dollar (Grabbe, 1991, p. 86). These currencies may be treated directly, as they are, or may be traded in a variety of other forms, that is, as derivatives.

Indeed, the FX market was revolutionized in the 1980s by the discovery that currency could and perhaps should be thought of as simply one more commodity among many. As a result, trading tools and concepts from Chicago's commodity pits were soon transferred successfully to FX. Perhaps first among these was "futures," which here means the sale and purchase of some item (in this case, money) at a specific price today for delivery at some point in the future, even though at that time the actual market of the commodity may have risen or fallen. A speculator in futures is, obviously, either buying on the assumption that prices will rise in the near term so that today's price is a bargain, or selling on the assumption that they will fall, so that today's price is inflated. Either way, there is a profit to be had and a loss to be avoided.

There are several future-oriented devices in FX. In a *spot* transaction, for example, the buyer and seller agree on a price for currency with delivery scheduled within a very short period, usually two days at most. In a *forward* transaction, delivery is scheduled for a later date, say, two weeks after the purchase. In a *swap* agreement, meanwhile, the buyer will agree to purchase a certain amount of currency at a certain time, but to then sell it back to the seller at another specified price. The buyer might do this if he or she had a short-term need for a specific currency—such as a unique project in a particular country—but did not need that sum in the long run, and might indeed believe that the value of the currency in question might soon decline. In addition, there are FX options, in which traders exchange the right to buy or sell specific currencies at some time in the future, though they are not *required* to do so when that time comes. Again, all these derivatives have their direct analogs in other financial markets (stocks, commodities, etc.), and more are being constantly invented, refined, and revised.

The Eurocurrency Market

Beyond the FX market is the *Eurocurrency Market*. This, too, is a large, potent, high-value, high-risk, and amorphous entity *sans* a geographic center. The term "Eurocurrency" refers to a deposit in a bank in one country that is denominated in the currency of another country. Thus, a U.S. dollar denominated account in a Swiss bank would be a Eurocurrency account. But, the term "euro" here does not mean that the bank is necessary in Europe. Rather, it is a holdover from the 1950s, when some European banks developed the practice of foreign currency denominated accounts. Ergo, *Eurocurrency* means here simply that there is a difference between the nationality of the bank and the nationality of the cash it contains, and an account denominated in Turkish Lira in a bank in Hong Kong would still, technically, be Eurocurrency.

The Eurocurrency Market, in turn, is the business of using the FX stored in the various banks. For example, a company in Russia may need dollars for some purchase. Perhaps, it attempts to get them from U.S. sources, but finds that difficult for reasons ranging from price to politics. So, it can turn to a bank in Hong Kong, which already has dollars available, and is perhaps willing to loan them at a lower rate than the Russian company can get in New York. Thus, Eurocurrency becomes a kind of stateless money, easily accessible, fluid, and largely beyond the controls (however feeble) of the governments and central bank that minted the cash in the first place.

The Eurocurrency Market is important because it is a vital source of much-needed capital for the funding of projects the world over. However, it is has been the subject of some concern in Washington (and most Eurocurrency accounts remain, for the moment, also Eurodollar accounts) as well as in other capitals. Given that Eurocurrency is so fluid, and so far removed from central bank controls, many a government has begun to wonder exactly what its yen, pounds, or dollars are doing beyond its borders. There have long been, therefore, calls for some form of international regulation of the Eurocurrency Markets (Putnam, 1979). However, to date, those calls seem to have elicited few responses.

The Eurobond Market

The *Eurobond Market*, meanwhile, has likewise raised a few red flags. A Eurobond, like Eurocurrency, is something of a misnomer. It is a bond, like any other, that happens to be denominated in the currency of a particular nation, but which is not sold in that nation, nor is it subject to the controls of that nation (Giddy 1975). Thus, a Eurobond might be issued in Japanese yen but by an agency outside of Japan and sold exclusively in, for example, Africa or the Arab World.

Again, Eurobonds are important to finance worldwide and are increasingly seen as an important tool to fund all manner of projects. The Eurobond Market (that is, the trade in Eurobonds by individuals and institutions) have made them accessible to investors and companies. But, again, the fact that they tend to be beyond the control of the central banks has made governments a bit uneasy. The United States, beset with problems of drug smuggling and money-laundering, has been particularly concerned by the fact that they have traditionally been bearer bonds, and so have given a distressing anonymity to their owners.

Still, the world's appetite for Eurobonds seems insatiable and they continue to be issued by the score. Thus, in 2007, Brazil, China, India, and Russia were all four moving eagerly into the Eurobond business, and bankers were more than happy to be of service (Attwood, 2007). Meanwhile, Ireland, a more traditional source of Eurobonds, has been offering American lawmakers some satisfaction by moving its offerings away from the bearer model (Hurley and Heuston, 2007).

Quite simply, then, the Eurobond Market joins the Eurocurrency and FX markets as permanent fixtures on the international scene. There is every reason to believe that they will be as much a part of the financial future as are stock and commodity exchanges.

Yet, one should exercise at least a little caution in the matter. The three International Markets are not universally loved. In particular, third world and developing nations have felt that the three have put their currencies at the mercy of traders in places far away and in nations with very different cultures. As a result, particularly outside the West, various governments have attempted to impose renewed currency controls from time to time. Often, such attempts yield mixed results, but in the 1997 currency crisis, the government of Malaysia did seem to successfully defend its currency against foreign traders. Indeed, after 1997, many Islamic nations considered a Bretton Woods-like joint trading currency, the Gold Dinar, which would be based on precious metals, and so beyond the reach of the FX market (Evans, 2007).

CONCLUSION

The International Financial Markets include the Foreign Currency Exchange (FX) market, the Eurocurrency Market, and the Eurobond Market. These markets developed in the ruins of the Bretton Wood system in the 1970s. In effect, all three exploit the concept of currency as a commodity, which can be traded and sold like any other.

These markets are relevant not only because of their size, but also because they affect *anyone* buying or selling *anything* in the world today. No matter how small the purchase, nor how local the transaction, any commercial exchange is governed by the purchasing power (or lack thereof) of a currency. In a globalized and globalizing world, any currency's purchasing power is directly impacted by its standing on world markets. Thus, whether the customer is a multinational corporation making a trillion-dollar investment or a child buying a gum ball from a machine, the cost of the purchase is at least partly governed by the movements of bonds and valuations of traders, in offices and suites that may be half a world away.

BIBLIOGRAPHY

Ahmed, S., Coulibaly, B., Zlate, A. (2017). "International financial spillovers to emerging market economies: How important are economic fundamentals?" *Journal of International Finance and Money, 76,* 133–152.

Attwood, M. (2007, January 12). "Brazil, Russia, India, China the currencies to watch." *Euroweek*, pp. 130–131.

Cohen, B.(2001). "Bretton Woods system." In R. J. B. Jones (Ed.), *Routledge encyclopedia of international political economy*. London: Routledge.

Evans, A. (2003, July 8). "Evolving a Gold Dinar trade bloc." *Malaysian Business.*.

Grabbe, J. O. (1996). *International financial markets.* Englewood Cliffs, NJ: Prentice Hall.

Giddy, I. (1975). "The blossoming of the Eurobond Market." *Columbia Journal of World Business, 10,* 66–76.

Hurley, C., & Heuston, A. (2007). "The future is green for finance." *International Tax Review, 18,* 33–35.

"New European regulations to fight market manipulation." (2013). *FOI: Future & Options Intelligence, (1832),* 89.

Putnam, B. (1979). "Controlling the Euromarkets: A policy perspective." *Columbia Journal of World Business, 14,* 25.

Resnick, B. G. (2012). "Investor yield and gross underwriting spread comparisons among U.S. dollar domestic, Yankee, Eurodollar, and global bonds." *Journal of International Money & Finance, 31,* 445–463.

"SSAs look to euros as basis swap move eliminates arbitrage." (2013). *Euroweek, (1327),* 71.

SUGGESTED READING

Glattfelder, J. B., Dupuis, A. A., & Olsen, R. B. (2011). "Patterns in high-frequency FX data: discovery of 12 empirical scaling laws." *Quantitative Finance, 11,* 599–614.

John, A. (2013). "The market with the FX factor." *Fundweb,* 16.

Kwaw, E. (2004). "The evolving law on Eurobank-Customer relationship and the Common Law: The need for clarity." *Syracuse Journal of International Law & Commerce, 32,* 87–131.

"Gazprombank brings trouble Eurobond, Ursa set to follow." (2007, February 9). *Euroweek* , 21.

"Living by their wits." (2007). *Economist, 382*(8514), 6–9.

Ramsaran, R. F. (1998). *An introduction to international money and finance.* New York: St. Martin's Press.

—*Michael Tucker*

INTERNATIONAL POLITICAL ECONOMY

ABSTRACT

This article will focus on how globalization influences the international political economy. International political economy (IPE) evolved into an international studies approach as the result of the 1973 oil crisis and the breakdown of the Bretton Woods system. Many IPE researchers have highlighted the significance of the relationship between the economic and political factors in regard to international relations. The international economic system and the IPE work in unison. IPE is composed of a range of theoretical frameworks, and the foundations are established based on ideologies between states and markets.

OVERVIEW

"Globalization has become a particularly fashionable way to analyze the changes in the international economy and in world politics. Advances in technology and modern communications are said to have unleashed new contacts and relationships among people, social movements, transnational corporations, and governments" (Woods, 2000, p.1).

The term, "political economy" is used to describe different events and situations in political science and international relations. Sometimes, the term is used to explain the "relationship between political systems and economic forces" (Devetak & Higgott, 1999).

Within the trend toward globalization, there are two aspects of change. The quantitative position has been around for a while, but the qualitative approach is fairly new. When referencing quantitative globalization, one is referring to an increase in trade, capital movement, investments, and interdependence. These concepts have been buzzwords since the nineteenth century. The most recent changes in globalization have occurred as a result of qualitative changes in international politics. These changes have occurred in the way people think and identify themselves and in the way states and firms perceive and pursue their goals.

There are three elements of globalization and they are interconnected. All three theories work together to provide different perspectives of globalization. The three elements are the expansion of markets, the transformation of politics, and the emergence of new social and political movements (Woods, 2000).

The expansion of markets. This element highlights the "transformation of global economic activity. Technological change and government deregulation have encouraged the growth of transnational networks in production, trade, and finance" (Woods, 2000). Production refers to organizations such as multinational corporations who use advanced technology and new production techniques to promote their products across the world. Trade refers to an organization's ability to increase the quantity and speed of goods and services that are distributed around the world, increase the impact trade has on domestic economic arrangements, and strengthen a firm's ability to facilitate trade. Finance refers to the creation of a global financial system in which a broad range of goods and services can be sold across the world in a timely manner.

The transformation of politics. This element highlights a global political economy in which a country's

A clean-up crew working to remove radioactive contamination in the auxiliary building after the Three Mile Island accident. This incident took place in reactor number 2 on March 28, 1979. Three Mile Island is located near Harrisburg, Pennsylvania. (Courtesy of John G. Kemeny via Wikimedia Commons)

Greece-based Lawyer Electra Leda Koutra at the Athens Pride on June 8, 2013, in a public place on the Korai Square at her human rights organization's stand, informing Athens Pride visitors about her organization's activities. She was the subject of nationwide and international press attention when she claimed she was harassed by the police while she was visiting a transgender client and she is also known for her work at TED Academy. (Courtesy of Cogiati via Wikimedia Commons)

borders become less important. If one were to compare the old system with the new system, the old system would be defined as the process of sovereign states working together based on the rules that they agreed upon. The new system is based on how political power and political activity work together across sovereign states (Held, McGraw, Goldblatt & Perraton, 1999). Global issues require sovereign states to make policies at levels above the individual level. Some issues that require a joint effort among nations are human rights, environment degradation and nuclear safety. Global warming and the armed weapons race are two such issues (Clapp & Helleiner, 2012; Wangler, Altamirano-Cabrera & Weikard, 2013).

With every good deed, some type of turmoil may be created. While the technological advances and cooperation of nations has been hailed as a positive step toward world harmony and growth, some negative aspects exist such as transnational crime, weapons, drugs, and illegal immigrants. Therefore, globalization requires new forms of regulation since individual states cannot overcome these issues on their own.

The emergence of new social and political movement. Globalization not only affects the markets and states but also affects people's lives. The new communication systems have produced a global culture. However, the effort to bring everyone together has not always been welcomed. For example, some citizens in Russia and the Middle East have rejected Westernization.

International political economy (IPE) evolved into an international studies approach as the result of the 1973 oil crisis and the breakdown of the Bretton Woods system. During the 1970s, scholars

A man at a service station reads about the gasoline rationing system in an afternoon newspaper during the 1973 oil crisis; a sign in the background states that no gasoline is available. (Courtesy of David Falconer via Wikimedia Commons)

started to understand the importance and weaknesses of the economic base for the world order. Many IPE researchers have highlighted the significance of the relationship between the economic and political factors with regards to international relations.

Theories & Perceptions of the Global Political Economy
Many scholars have made contributions to the field of IPE. Highlights of their contributions include the following:

APPLICATION

International Economics & International Politics = International Political Economy
The international economic system and the international political system work in unison. Economic partnerships are determined by political and diplomatic relationships and viceversa. According to Spero (1990), political factors affect economic outcomes in three ways:

1. The political system shapes the economic system because the structure and operation of the economic system is determined by the structure and operation of the international political system.

One could see the influence of the international political system on the international economic system by reviewing the political developments during three periods of time in history. The three periods are (a) nineteenth-century imperialism, (b) the post-World War II era of cold war between the Soviet Union and the Western free world led by the United States, and (c) the post-Berlin Wall demolition and demise of the Soviet Empire era (Phatak, Bhagat, & Kashlak, 2005).

Period 1: Nineteenth-century imperialism and mercantilism were driven by two major political factors: (1) the powerful nation-states in Europe (i.e. the United Kingdom, France, Germany and Holland) that had equal military power and (2) nationalism practiced by these nation-states. These countries encouraged their citizens to practice and participate in activities that enhanced national pride, national identity, self-sufficiency, wealth, and economic

The Congress of Vienna by Jean-Baptiste Isabey (1819). The congress was actually a series of face-to-face meetings between colonial powers. It served to divide and re-appropriate imperial holdings. (Courtesy of Jean-Baptiste Isabey via Wikimedia Commons)

power. Cooperative relations between nations were not popular. Each country wanted to promote itself. Both of these factors led these nation-states to pursue empire building, which encouraged colonialism in Asia, Africa, and Latin America. The objectives of the nation-states were to obtain raw material and minerals from the colonies, process the goods into finished products in their home countries, and market the products in the colony markets. The nation-states sought to accumulate wealth and power so that their citizens could have full employment at the expense of colonized countries whose markets and production were controlled by the nation-states. The European nation-states divided the world into parts that each controlled. The British controlled most of western and southern Asia and parts of Africa. The French controlled Southeast Asia and northwest Africa. The Dutch controlled Indonesia and parts of Central and South America, and the Germans controlled parts of Western Africa. Wars broke out between the different nation-states as each attempted to take control of the other's territory. The British and French fought for control of India, and the British and Dutch fought for control over parts of Africa. European imperialism determined trade and investments. As a result, the political system was controlled by colonialism and empire building.

Period 2: As the imperialist system ended after World War II, the United Kingdom's dominance in the West came to an end. However, two other

The Cuban Missile Crisis was a critical moment in the Cold War between the U.S. and the U.S.S.R. This is a U.S. aerial reconnaissance photograph of a medium range ballistic missile launch site at San Cristobal in Cuba, on November 1, 1962. (Courtesy of the National Archives)

superpowers emerged—the United States and the Soviet Union. A new political and economic system developed as the result of the rivalry between these two countries. The new political system was bipolar and hierarchical. The United States led the West and Japan. The Soviet Union led the Soviet bloc in the East, which was comprised of countries behind the Iron Curtain. The developing countries in the Third World remained politically subordinate to their colonial mother countries. The United States and the Soviet Union battled in what was known as the Cold War. This political system determined the post-World War II international economic system. There were two different economic systems. The United States and the West supported a capitalist system, which encouraged free enterprise and free market economic systems. The Soviet Union and the East supported a Socialist/Marxist economic system, which called for a centralized economy controlled by the government where citizens were not allowed to have private property.

Period 3: There was another change in the late1980s and 1990s as the post-World War II international economic system crashed. Poland and Hungary began

"Signing the Agreement to eliminate the USSR and establish the Commonwealth of Independent States". Ukrainian President Leonid Kravchuk (second from left seated), Chairman of the Supreme Council of the Republic of Belarus Stanislav Shushkevich (third from left seated) and Russian President Boris Yeltsin (second from right seated) during the signing ceremony to eliminate the USSR and establish the Commonwealth of Independent States at Viskuly Government House in the Belorusian National Park, "Belovezhskaya Forest," on December 8, 1991. (Courtesy of RIA Novosti archive, image #848095 / U. Ivanov / CC-BY-SA 3.0 via Wikimedia Commons)

to support a democratic state, the Berlin Wall fell, and the Soviet Union broke up. Countries that once supported the socialist model began to embrace capitalism. Russia became a democracy, and China, Vietnam, and India opened their markets to foreign investments and trade.

The Organization for Economic Cooperation and Development (OECD) was founded in 1961, though its roots extend to an earlier Europe centered organization. Market-based and West leaning, this partnership of thirty-four nations "closely mirrored major phases in the post-war international political economy" according to Clifton & Díaz-Fuentes (2011). In the twenty-first century, however, the OECD's dependence on Western countries may leave the organization out of step with non-Western powers.

2. Political concerns often shape economic policy because economic policies are frequently dictated by overriding political interests.

Internal political processes have a part in the determination of national economic policy. Economic policy is the outcome of the political bargaining process that is responsible for resolving the conflict over

the outcomes preferred by different groups, each representing distinct and often conflicting interests. The overriding political and strategic interests of a nation help determine its international economic policy, which results in international economic policy becoming a tool to fulfill a nation's strategic and foreign policy objectives. International economic policy can sometimes be beneficial to MNCs, especially if it is being driven by political considerations.

3. International economic relations themselves are political relations because both types of interaction are processes by which state and non-state players attempt to manage their conflicts and cooperate to achieve common goals.

International economic relations may be viewed as the outcome of the political process involving the management of conflict and cooperation over the acquisition of scarce resources among the various members of the political system in the absence of a centralized world government. Both international and political interactions range from conflict to cooperation. The conflict among the members of the political system may be rooted in a struggle for greater power and national sovereignty. National sovereignty is associated with national wealth. A country that is not independently wealthy becomes dependent on others and loses some of its national sovereignty. Therefore, most countries seek wealth in a political system, and the pursuit of this goal in the presence of scarce resources frequently leads to conflict among the system members.

VIEWPOINT

Models of International Political Economy (IPE)
IPE is composed of a range of theoretical frameworks, and the foundations are established based on ideologies between states and markets. "The key difference between competing theoretical claims in IPE relates to the normative position that scholars adopt on the preferred mix of values to be embedded with the state-market nexus" (Murphy & Tooze, 1991, p. 2). Strange (1988) categorized these values into four domains, which were security, prosperity, freedom, and justice. The preferred combination of these values differs according to the theoretical beliefs of the scholar (Watson, 2005).

CONCLUSION

There are positive and negative attributes of globalization. States, markets, and other groups work together to ensure that policies and practices to promote globalization are in place. Although some forms of state sovereignty have been minimized, new areas of power and competition have surfaced. These include regional organizations, international agencies, and competition among currencies. Some groups are embracing the Western value system, whereas others are identifying alternative identities and values.

BIBLIOGRAPHY

Bretton Woods agreement. (2007). *Investopedia.*

Clapp, J., & Helleiner, E. (2012). "International political economy and the environment: Back to the basics?" *International Affairs, 88,* 485–501.

Clifton, J., & Díaz-Fuentes, D. (2011). "The OECD and phases in the international political economy, 1961–2011." *Review of International Political Economy, 18,* 552–569.

Devetak, R., & Higgott, R. (1999). "Justice unbound: Globalization, states and transformation of the social bond." *International Affairs, 75,* 483–500.

Held, D., McGraw, A., Goldblatt, D., & Perraton, J. (1998). *Global transformations: Politics, economics and cultures.* Cambridge: Polity Press.

Murphy, C., & Tooze, R. (1991). Introduction. In Craig Murphy & Roger Tooze (Eds.), *The new international political economy.* London: Lynne Reener.

Phatak, A., Bhagat, R., & Kashlak, R. (2005). *International management.* New York, NY: McGraw-Hill/ Irwin.

Spero, J. (1990). *The politics of international economics relations* (4th ed.). New York, NY: St. Martin's Press.

Sovacool, B. (2017). "Advancing the international political economy of climate change adaptation: Political ecology, political economy and social justice." *Handbook of the International Political Economy of Energy and Natural Resources.*

Strange, S. (1988). *States and markets: An introduction to international political economy.* London: Pinter.

Wangler, L., Altamirano-Cabrera, J., & Weikard, H. (2013). "The political economy of international environmental agreements: a survey." *International Environmental Agreements: Politics, Law & Economics, 13,* 387–403.

Watson, M. (2005). *Foundations of international political economy.* New York, NY: Palgrave Macmillan.

Woods, N. (2000). *The political economy of globalization.* New York: St. Martin's Press.

SUGGESTED READING

Bucur, C. (2006). "Foundations of international political economy." *Journal of International Relations & Development, 9,* 216–219.

Dickins, A. (2006). "The evolution of international political economy." *International Affairs, 82,* 479–492.

Ikes, A. (2006). "The international political economy of making consumption sustainable." *Review of International Political Economy, 13,* 340–358.

Thurston, C., & Bowen, K. (2011). "U.S. domestic politics and international political economy: an introduction to the special issue." *Business & Politics, 13,* 1–4.

—*Marie Gould*

INTERNATIONAL TRADE ECONOMICS

ABSTRACT

Economics is the study of reconciliations between unlimited wants and limited resources. Those reconciliatory attempts extend across geographic boundaries. A central issue in international trade is whether gains accrue to citizens in the global market place due to their exchanges. Theoretically, larger quantities and wider choices of goods are available with international trade than without it. Exchanges include both goods and currencies because of the interactions among firms, households, and governments located around the globe. In this essay, students will learn economic concepts and philosophical differences that allow them to examine policies affecting the prices and the quantities of items traveling between nations. We will focus some initial attention on the production possibilities model, the opportunity cost concept, and the foreign exchange market. Afterwards, readers will gain a better understanding about the processes and content of payments between trading partners. Those exchanges take into account how much of one currency is worth in terms of another currency, which is something that continues to captivate many people's attention. Readers will find that international trade is a rather odd concoction of free-trade practices and trade restrictions. Across time and space, international leaders and their countries come together in an attempt to lessen trade restrictions in some instances and increase them in other instances. The essay closes by providing readers with some insight into various arguments and rationales for trade restrictions.

OVERVIEW

Readers may come to understand economics as a study of reconciliations between unlimited wants and limited resources. Reconciliation is an attempt to find some optimal middle ground in problem-solving. The economic problem arises due to resource scarcity and prompts decision makers to make rational choices from amongst all the alternative solutions. Each and every choice involves a sacrifice because it is very difficult, if not impossible, to avoid tradeoffs.

International trade is an interesting topic and lends itself to being one of the most controversial topics in economics. Getting to the conceptual foundations of international trade, the main purpose of this essay is to inform undergraduate students about the economic context in which exchanges of physical quantities of products and currencies occur between countries. To some extent, the author assumes readers are familiar with the principles of economics. Nonetheless, the information found in this essay appeals to those unfamiliar with economics, but engages all readers in pondering and attempting to answer some important initial questions.

Where do you stand regarding the issue of international trade? Do you favor protecting domestic jobs? If so, what cost attachments are there to job preservation measures? To what extent are you willing to make sacrifices in terms of accepting fewer choices in the marketplace and paying higher prices for them? Where does product quality and safety fit into all this? Perhaps recent news reports about recalls of foreign-made products diminishes the concern about higher prices. One could reasonably argue that consumers

realize that high quality is available at a high price though some major retailers of imported goods claim quality is available at a low price.

Basic Economic Concepts & International Trade Components

At issue is whether benefits or gains accrue through international trade. Economists tend to believe that international trade does provide benefits to consumers, producers, and workers. However, their views fall short of being universally acceptable due, in part, to the various dimensions of any international trade issue. Free trade may be an ideology given the existence of constraints such as trade barriers, international politics, and isolationist strategies. All those issues and concerns provide a rich backdrop against which to learn the major tenets of international trade theory as the reader may find in an introductory economics course.

International trade theory fits well with a basic understanding of how a country progresses through various stages of an economic maturation process. As countries move from an economy primarily based on hunting and gathering through manufacturing, services, and information heading toward and beyond a knowledge-based economy, a larger portion of domestic production becomes available for exchange with a trading partner. Opportunities arise to trade that excess production for other goods, which are the excess production of another country. In accordance with theory, specialization in production creates those opportunities (Razmi & Refaei, 2013).

Absolute Advantage

For varied reasons some countries are better at producing specific items than are other countries. As a case in point, the United States is better at growing wheat and Columbia is better at growing coffee beans. In essence, each country will specialize in producing those goods best suited to its resource bases. Specialization arises from the discovery and acknowledgement that one country in the absolute sense is better suited at producing more of one specific item than is another country. Absolute advantage by definition is the ability of one country to produce more of something than another country. However, maximizing the gains from trade is reliant upon a country's ability to produce more than another, doing so in a most efficient manner.

Coffee plantation in Quimbaya, Quindío, Colombia. View from the road to La Union (Quimbaya), looking south towards Montenegro. (Courtesy of Shaun McRae via Wikimedia Commons)

Opportunity Cost

The gains from trade are observable when a country's citizenry attains a combination of goods that consists of larger amounts of each good than would be possible in the absence of trade. Comparative advantage by definition is specializing in that product for which the country's sacrifice in terms of other goods is minimal. The value of the foregone alternative is, by definition, an opportunity cost. In essence, finding solutions to the economic problem of scarcity involves minimizing opportunity costs. In brief, the gains from trade accrue through specialization, which in turn, reflects a country's recognition of what it can and should produce at a lower opportunity cost than another country.

Opportunity costs sometimes take the form of sacrifices that are linear in their relationship, which translate into the correspondence of a benefit with some given or constant amount of cost. However, economists tend to view the equation as one involving increasing amounts of cost in the form of a curvilinear relationship. The illustration of the opportunity cost concept is most effective when one attempts to consider all the possible choice combinations whether the opportunity costs are increasing as in the case of a curved-line concave-shaped arrangement or are constant as in the case of a straight-line downward-sloping arrangement. A study of international trade introduces students to both forms within a larger model of production, specialization, and exchange often in the context that the world contains only two countries. Furthermore, students and other

readers should think of a model as a tool that simplifies reality and remain cognizant of the fact that a key component in any economics model is the ceteris paribus assumption, which in translation from Latin into English means "all else held constant."

Under this and some other assumptions, Country A will eventually purchase products from Country B and vice versa by virtue of their being trading partners within the population of countries around the globe. At any given moment, for the sake of simplicity if for no other reason, there is an immediate need to hold constant the state of technology, the availability of resources, and the level of productivity. This constraint limits production possibilities to an initial set of specific combinations. With a view toward a nation's current ability to produce two items, say goods X and Y, there is some precise point at which a specific combination of X and Y is possible in equal amounts, but any attempt to produce more of one essentially translates into the production of less of the other. In brief, the opportunity cost associated with producing one unit of X is the sacrifice of one unit of Y. This situation illustrates the opportunity cost concept while holding all else constant.

Marginal Analysis

Economics, in general, involves applying the opportunity cost concept to decisions made at the margin; in other words, how a change in one variable results in a change in another variable. As an introduction to the orientation of economics toward marginal analysis, the production possibilities frontier is a model that portrays all those combinations that a country's entire economy can produce. It is a macroeconomic concept, which effectively conveys the interdependencies among scarcity, choices, and tradeoffs. The difference between those economic divisions resides in their scope. Macroeconomics is a study of economics using models of the whole economy whereas microeconomics is a study of the behaviors of consumers and producers as they interact through price mechanisms in models we can refer to as a market.

Microeconomics & Macroeconomics

International trade is a topic that spans microeconomics and macroeconomics. The foundation of microeconomics emphasizes consumers and demand as integral components. With regard to the consumer or demand side, students learn very early in their coursework that an inverse relationship exists between price and quantity demanded in accordance with the Law of Demand. Relatively speaking, smaller amounts are in demand at higher prices and vice versa. On the producer or supply side, they learn that a positive relationship exists between price and quantity supplied according to the Law of Supply.

Positive & Normative Economics
International trade is also a topic that spans positive economics and normative economics. A call for governmental policies or interventions suggests that something should occur in order to alleviate a problem. That call would fit the classification of normative economics, which is one of two types of economic analysis. The other type is positive economics, which occurs when analysts deal strictly with data or facts centering their attention on whether that information is accurate. For example, individuals are more likely to agree on matters regarding the accuracy of data than they are on matters regarding what ought to occur in response to their interpretations of the data. In sum, differences exist in the content of a statement containing the word "is" versus others containing the word "ought" or "should." Macroeconomics is more normative than microeconomics due primarily to its orientation toward policies promoting economic growth, employment, and price stability.

Expenditures
Students in macroeconomics courses receive an introduction to how the total expenditures of the household sector, the business sector, the public sector, and the trade sector provide an aggregate numeric estimate of a county's annual production. The last sector is comprised of national expenditures on imports and exports. Subtracting import expenditures from export expenditures yields a mathematical difference, which defines the term net exports. The value of net exports may be negative (known as a trade deficit), zero (balanced trade), or positive (trade surplus). Expression of trade balances and expenditures are in terms of the importing country's own unit of currency; for instance, the U.S. dollar or the Japanese yen.

The aforementioned set of clarifications, distinctions, and assumptions provide a foundation with which readers can form an understanding of the way economists view the world. In the pages ahead, readers will also gain a better sense of international trade theory and receive suggestions for learning reinforcement. As they move through this condensed essay, readers are encouraged to consult textbooks and other sources for additional details, examples, and cases because those omissions help achieve brevity.

APPLICATIONS

Any study of international trade will hone student abilities to apply microeconomics and macroeconomics. In addition, they will find it integrates normative and positive economics by examining policies that affect the prices and the quantities of items exchanged on a global scale. Furthermore, students will recognize value in applying the production possibilities model and opportunity cost concept. However, Pearce (1992) and others point out that the essential difference between domestic or internal trade and international or foreign trade is the use of different currencies in payment for the exchanges between and among countries.

Prices of Exports: The Need to Convert Currencies
It is prudent to begin by taking note that each trading partner pays in the currency of the country from which it is acquiring the product. Most countries

The U.S. International Trade Commission provides the president and Congress with information and analysis on matters of tariffs and international trade and competitiveness. Its headquarters is located in Washington, D. C. (Courtesy of Toytoy CC-BY-SA-3.0 via Wikimedia Commons)

have foreign currencies on hand in addition to their own currency. For example, most banks in the United States contain deposits of the Japanese yen and other currencies along with the U.S. dollar. In order for a buyer located in the United States to purchase a motor vehicle made in Japan, for instance, the buyer needs to convert dollars into yens as part of the payment processes. Likewise, purchases of U.S.-made products by foreigners require payment in some amount of dollars equivalent to the agreed-upon price of that item.

Prices in a global context usually reflect international marketplace situations whether left to free trade or artificial sanctions. Sometimes governments restrict trade through regulations or impose a tariff or tax on an import thereby raising the item's price. The tariff becomes revenue for the government of a country that purchases the imported item. An import is by definition an item received by one country from another country; whereas an export is an item sent from the providing country to the purchasing country. Price increases can also result from the imposition of a quota, which by definition is a limit on the quantity of an item imported into a country. An import quota effectively reduces the amount of an item available for purchase or the quantity of that item supplied.

Exchange Rates

Exchange rates are, by definition, the price of a domestic currency in terms of foreign currency. As they examine exchange rates, which are readily available through daily publications, students will find the U.S. dollar as a standard against which to compare foreign currencies. In general, there are a variety of perspectives on exchange rate determination, but two are worthy of brief mention at this juncture.

- One perspective holds that exchange rates originate from supply-and-demand conditions that exist in the foreign exchange market. For instance, a trade surplus will generate a greater demand for the currency of the exporting country than would a trade deficit as trading partners seek to convert their currencies into that of the exporter. If the supply of its currency remains constant, then the domestic price of its currency will rise affecting the exchange rate.
- Another perspective, which takes into account actual and expected changes in the domestic

supply of money, holds that exchange rate is a direct function of fluctuations in the value of a nation's currency. According to this perspective, the value of a unit of currency depends on its relative scarcity. Therefore, any increase in the supply of a currency while holding demand for the currency constant will then decrease its price and affect the exchange rate.

Currency Demand & Supply: The Foreign Exchange Market

Whether one emphasizes the supply side or the demand side of the foreign exchange market, any exchange rate is an expression of how much of one currency it will take for the conversion into or the purchase of another currency. Certainly, it will take more foreign currency to acquire a U.S. dollar when there is an increase in the latter's value. This situation represents an increase in the price of exports from the United States to a trading partner because it has to convert more of its currency to obtain the dollar amount required in payment for that export or import. By extension, a higher price may spark a chain of events increasing the likelihoods of a decrease in the quantities sold, a lower amount of expenditures on exports, a smaller level of national output, higher unemployment rates, and/or a lower rate of economic growth; immediately, the reader may see the value of holding other things constant. In essence, the volume of goods traded internationally is partly a function of comparisons between the world price and the domestic price (Yutaka, 2013). A country selling at a price that is lower than most other countries may increase its volume of exports. That is the situation when free trade occurs on a global level.

Free Trade, Restricted Trade, or Both?

International trade is an odd combination of free-trade practices and trade interventions. From a historical standpoint, countries banded together with their trading partners and established the parameters through which they engaged in and promoted free exchange in the global marketplace. Evidently, that undertaking was and is a formidable challenge. In 1948, the General Agreement on Trade and Tariffs (GATT) came into existence in which a number of countries set out to find ways to resolve trade problems, eliminate tariffs, and reduce barriers to trade. A series of rounds occurred during the course of almost five

President George W. Bush explains the history of his desk during a meeting with Central American presidents in the Oval Office on April 10, 2003. From left are: Presidents Francisco Flores of El Salvador, Ricardo Maduro of Honduras, Abel Pacheco of Costa Rica, Enrique Bolanos of Nicaragua, and Alfonso Portillo of Guatemala. (Courtesy of Paul Morse via Wikimedia Commons)

decades with mixed results prompting other agreements and sub-agreements, all with mixed results. In a concise summary of more recent agreements directly involving the United States, Guell (2007) refers to the World Trade Organization (WTO) as an organization that arbitrates trade disputes; the North American Free Trade Agreement (NAFTA), which involves the United States, Canada, and Mexico; and the CAFTA, which involves the United States and five other countries in Central America.

The International Monetary Fund (IMF)
About the same time that GATT came about, the International Monetary Fund (IMF) began its pursuits encouraging international cooperation among monetary authorities or central banks, facilitating a balanced expansion in international trade, and promoting stability in foreign exchange markets. Consequently, exchange rates became both constant, but indexed to allow for a slight deviation around the value of the U.S. dollar; at that time, the dollar was directly convertible into gold according to a fixed rate. Readers who have an interest in learning how international trade stabilization relates to the manipulative exchange of currencies in detail are encouraged to examine the IMF and the so-called "Bretton Woods" system.

Tariffs
The international trade literature contains a great deal of material describing various organizational attempts to orchestrate free trade by reducing barriers to trade. Tariff and non-tariff barriers form a useful dichotomy. By way of a review, as we head toward this essay's closure, a tariff is like a tax as it effectively raises the price of import. Non-tariff barriers are of different types. A quota is one type and limits the amount of imports. Other methods of limiting trade include government regulations, which may arise from politics and/or address issues of safety or quality, and voluntary export restraints. The latter, as the name implies, will likely occur in the absence of and/or as a precursor to official regulations or sanctions.

Arguments for Trade Limitations
The final section of this essay lists six reasons and arguments for limiting trade. It draws from the presentations in introductory economics textbooks authored by Arnold (2005), Guell (2007), and McConnell & Brue (2008) and many others.

- First, the national-defense argument designates some industries as being vital to homeland security.
- Second, the infant-industry protection argument, as introduced long ago by Alexander Hamilton, encouraged a level playing field and protected the colonies from potential abuse by Europe.
- Third, the anti-dumping argument is used to prevent foreigners from selling exports below cost in order to drive domestic competitors out of business.
- Fourth, the foreign-export subsidies argument discourages the negotiation of below-market interest rates that could favor trade with specific organizations or countries.
- Fifth, the low-foreign-wages argument addresses the lower costs of, and wages paid by, offshore producers and calls into question the quality of exports and the regulatory and safety orientations of foreign governments.
- Lastly, the saving-domestic-jobs argument is an attempt to protect domestic jobs and to promote full employment.

CONCLUSION

International trade as a topic of study in economics certainly exhibits a dynamic tension between free trade and restricted trade. Perhaps those dynamics alone explains why it is so fascinating yet challenging at the same time. Nonetheless, this essay presents a conceptual framework that allows students and others to realize how the gains from international trade are the consequence of scarcity-induced choices, opportunity cost minimization, and product specialization. In closing, this essay aims to shed some light on the complexities and the components in an exchange of goods and services that happen to cross a nation's geographical boundaries.

BIBLIOGRAPHY

Arnold, Roger A. (2005). *Economics* (7th ed.) Mason, OH: Thomson South-Western.

Awad, A., Yussof, I. (2017). "International trade and unemployment: Evidence from selected ASEAN+3 coutnries." *DSLU Business and Economics Review, 27,* 1, 124-144.

Guell, R. C. (2007). *Issues in economics today* (3rd ed.). Boston, MA: McGraw-Hill Irwin.

McConnell, C. R. & Brue, S. L. (2008). *Economics* (17th ed.). Boston, MA: McGraw-Hill Irwin.

Razmi, M., & Refaei, R. (2013). "The effect of trade openness and economic freedom on economic growth: The case of Middle East and East Asian countries." *International Journal of Economics & Financial Issues (IJEFI), 3,* 376–385.

Yutaka, K. (2013). "Effects of exchange rate fluctuations and financial development on international trade: Recent experience." *International Journal of Business Management & Economic Research, 4,* 793–801.

SUGGESTED READING

Crenshaw, E., & Robison, K. (2006). "Globalization and the digital divide: The roles of structural conduciveness and global connection in internet diffusion." *Social Science Quarterly (Blackwell Publishing Limited), 87,* 190–207.

Fuller, D., & Geide-Stevenson, D. (2003). "Consensus among economists: Revisited." *Journal of Economic Education, 34,* 369–387.

Gawande, K., & Hoekman, B. (2006). "Lobbying and agricultural trade policy in the United States." *International Organization, 60,* 527–561.

Gilbert, J., & Oladi, R. (2011). "Excel models for international trade theory and policy: An online resource." *Journal of Economic Education, 42,* 95.

Hainmueller, J., & Hiscox, M. (2006). "Learning to love globalization: Education and individual attitudes toward international trade." *International Organization, 60,* 469–498.

Hira, A. (2003). "The brave new world of international education." *World Economy, 26,* 911–931.

Thurow, L. (2004). "Do only economic illiterates Argue that trade can destroy jobs and lower America's national income?" *Social Research, 71,* 265–278.

Winchester, N. (2006). "A classroom tariff-setting game." *Journal of Economic Education, 37,* 431 –441.

—Steven R. Hoagland, PhD

L

LABOR DEMAND

ABSTRACT

This article focuses on labor demand. This article provides an analysis of the major U.S. labor demand policies. The relationship between labor markets, labor demand, labor supply, and wages is described. The U.S. Bureau of Labor Statistics' program to measure labor demand, through the Job Openings and Labor Turnover Survey, is discussed. The issues associated with forecasting labor demand across industries are addressed.

OVERVIEW

Labor economists, also referred to as demographic economists, study the relationship between labor supply and demand, wage distribution across industries, and changing demographic trends in an effort to explain and predict economic activity and business cycles. Labor economists argue that the aggregate labor, or productive work, of the population drives the economy and economic growth. Economic growth, the quantitative change or expansion in a country's economy, is measured as the percentage increase in a nation's gross domestic product (GDP) during one year. Gross domestic product refers to the market value of goods and services produced by labor and property in the United States. The United States government, recognizing the importance of a strong labor market, develops and implements labor demand policies to promote the creation of new jobs and work industries. Labor demand refers to both the total labor costs for a particular skill level and total output the firm is capable of producing to meet customer needs for profit maximization as well as the aggregate need for labor in a given region or sector. Increased labor demand will theoretically draw more workers into the workforce and increase productivity and economic growth.

Importance of Labor Demand

The public and private sectors, and economic stakeholders in general, rely on labor market information, economic analysis, and short- and long-term forecasting for effective economic planning. For example, information about forecasted labor demand in different sectors and industries allows individuals to strategically plan their education and training to capitalize on labor demand. In addition, information about forecasted labor demand in different sectors and industries allows organizations to make strategic hiring decisions and investigate technology to lessen the burden of forecasted employee shortages. Businesses, industries, and occupations generally have differing levels of labor demand.

Labor Demand in Microeconomics

The concept of labor demand is a fundamental building block in microeconomics. Microeconomics, in contrast to the large-scale inquiry of macroeconomics, studies the behavior of small economic units including households, organizations, and individual consumers. The concepts of labor demand and labor supply are based on the economic theory of supply and demand that refers to the relationships between a product's place in the market and the market's valuing of the product. The theory of supply and demand is a fundamental economic theory applied to multiple businesses, industries, and issues. Labor economics, which refers to the area of economics concerned with labor markets, adopted the theory of supply and demand to help explain how labor markets function. Labor economists often represent demand and labor supply in a graphical way as supply-demand curves. These curves, which are common conceptual tools in economics, are two lines on a graph representing people's willingness to buy or sell a product depending on its price. The labor supply curve is likely to be different for different individuals and the labor demand curve will be different for various businesses, industries, and sectors.

Factors Affecting Labor Demand & Supply in the United States

The following factors and variables affect labor demand and labor supply in the United States: Budget constraint, rate of substitution, income effect, substitution effect, and opportunity cost. Budget constraint refers to the consumption options available to someone with a limited income to allocate among various goods. The rate of substitution refers to the least-favorable rate at which a business is willing to exchange units of one good or service for units of another. Income effect refers to the influence that a change in income will have on consumption decisions. The substitution effect is a price change that changes the budget constraint but leaves the consumer on the same indifference curve. Opportunity cost refers to the cost of passing up the next best choice when making a decision. Labor economists consider labor demand to be a derived demand. The demand for labor is dependent on or derived from the demand for particular goods in a particular market. A business's overall labor demand is determined by its marginal physical product of labor (MPL). The marginal physical product of labor refers to the additional output that results from an increase of one unit of labor. Ultimately, the demand for labor is an important economic indicator for the health of the labor market and the economy in general.

The following section provides an overview of U.S. labor demand policy. This section serves as the foundation for later discussion of how and why the U.S. government measures labor demand with the Job Openings and Labor Turnover Survey. The issues associated with forecasting labor demand across industries are addressed.

U.S. Labor Demand Policies

The federal government, recognizing the importance of a strong labor market, develops and implements labor demand policy to promote the creation of new jobs and work industries. The U.S. government creates policies and programs to increase labor demand. Labor demand policies are developed to increase the number of poor and disadvantaged persons hired into gainful employment. Significant labor demand policies of the twentieth century included the public

works programs of the 1930s, public service jobs of the 1970s that were funded by the Comprehensive Employment and Training Act (CETA), and tax credits for employers hiring poor and disadvantaged individuals (Bartik, 2001).

Labor Demand Policies & Public Problems

Economists and government stakeholders in general debate the development and use of labor demand policy as a solution for the public problem of poverty and unemployment. Labor economists in favor of the use of labor demand policies to eradicate poverty argue that an increase in the number and scope of labor demand policies is necessary for several reasons. First, America's poor need significantly more jobs made available to them. The U.S. labor market would need at least 9 million additional full-time jobs to provide each poor, non-elderly U.S. household with one full-time worker. Second, labor supply policies alone may be insufficient to solve job shortages. Labor supply policies, such as welfare reform, are generally a costly way to increase employment opportunities for the poor. For example, welfare reform, which has brought millions of workers into the labor force, has required the development and implementation of extensive job and workforce training programs. Third, aggregate labor demand policies are necessary but insufficient to eradicate poverty and its related conditions. For example, in 1999, the U.S. unemployment rate was 4.2 percent and the poverty rate was 11.8 percent. As a result of the difference between poverty and unemployment rates, lowering unemployment to zero would not fully eliminate poverty. Fourth, targeted labor demand programs, such as programs that hire targeted low-employment groups for public service jobs or subsidized jobs with private employers, can be effective in addressing poverty and its related conditions.

Recommended Labor Policies

Labor economists generally recommend three types of labor demand policies: tax credits, wage, subsidies, and wage redistribution. First, a tax credit program can be implemented to provide subsidies to all employers who expand their labor force. Second, a wage subsidy program can be implemented that awards wage subsidies to selected employers who hire selected individuals from disadvantaged groups (Bartik, 2001). Third, a wage redistribution program can be implemented to redistribute and equalize wages. The main types of wages manipulated in labor demand policies include reservation wage, market clearing wage, real wage, minimum wage, and nominal wage. A reservation wage refers to the lowest possible real wage that makes workers indifferent between consumption and leisure. Market clearing wages are the wages necessary to clear the labor market of all surpluses and shortages. Real wages refer to wage amounts, useful for economic analysis and comparisons, that have been adjusted for inflation. Minimum wage refers to the lowest hourly wage, determined by the Fair Labor Standards Act (FLSA), that may be legally paid to full-time and part-time workers in the private sector and in federal, state, and local governments. Nominal wages are wages written down in contracts between the employee and the organizations that are unadjusted for inflation.

Criticisms of Government Labor Demand Policies

There are numerous criticisms of government labor demand policies. Critics of labor demand policies argue that the federal government negatively impacts the private sector's ability to create new jobs. Critics argue that the federal government, through legislative mandates and employer or business regulation, weakens the demand for labor and the supply of labor. The increasingly large presence of government in the employment process can, in some instances, slow down the growth of employment rates in the United States, raise the cost of the hiring process, and discourage the creation of new jobs (Weidenbaum, 1994).

APPLICATIONS

Measuring U.S. Labor Demand through the Job Openings & Labor Turnover Survey

The U.S. Bureau of Labor Statistics (BLS) of the U.S. Department of Labor collects statistics on job openings and job turnover in the United States. The U.S. Bureau of Labor Statistics is the primary federal government body in the field of labor economics and statistics. The U.S. Bureau of Labor Statistics gathers data relevant to the social and economic conditions of U.S. workers and their families. The public and private sectors use data gathered by the U.S. Bureau of Labor Statistics to assess the health of the economy and adjust wages. The Bureau of Labor Statistics,

The Frances Perkins Building of the U.S. Department of Labor headquarters in Washington, D.C. (Courtesy of Ed Brown via Wikimedia Commons)

in 1999, developed the Job Openings and Labor Turnover Survey (JOLTS) to "assess the excess demand for labor in the U.S. labor market." The JOLTS measures labor demand and provides a thorough analysis of the U.S. labor market. The JOLTS, along with the monthly unemployment rate, serves as a measure of labor market activity, general economic conditions, and labor supply and demand (Clark & Hyson, 2000).

Categories of JOLTS Statistical Data

The JOLTS provides demand-side economic indicators of labor shortages at the local and national levels. Its statistical data categories include the following: total employment, job openings, hires, and separations. The Bureau of Labor Statistics describes the JOLTS' statistical data categories in the following ways:

Employment: The JOLTS' employment data categories, which refer to all persons on the payroll who worked during or received pay for the pay period that includes the 12th of the month, include the following people: full-time and part-time employees; permanent, short-term, and seasonal employees; salaried and hourly workers; and employees on paid vacation or other paid leave. The JOLTS' employment data categories do not include proprietors and partners of unincorporated businesses; unpaid family workers; employees on strike for the entire pay period; employees on leave without pay for the entire pay period; and employees of temporary help agencies, employee leasing companies, outside contractors, or consultants (JOLTS, 2007).

Job Openings: The JOLTS' job opening data category refers to all positions that are open, or not filled, on the last business day of the month. A job is considered open if it meets all three of the following conditions: First, a specific position exists and there is work available for that position. Second, the position can be full-time or part-time and can be permanent, short-term, or seasonal. Third, the job could start within 30 days whether or not the establishment finds a suitable candidate during that time. The JOLTS' job opening data category does not include positions open only to internal transfers, promotions or demotions, or recall from layoffs; openings for positions with start dates more than 30 days in the future; positions for which employees have been hired but the employees have not yet reported for work; and

Monster is primarily used to help those seeking work to find job openings, for lower to mid-level employment, that match their skills and location. This is Monster's office in Hyderabad, India. (Courtesy of Bssasidhar CC BY 3.0 via Wikimedia Commons)

positions to be filled by employees of temporary help agencies, employee leasing companies, outside contractors, or consultants (JOLTS, 2007).

Hires: The JOLTS' hires data category refers to all additions to the payroll during the month. The category includes the following people: newly hired and rehired employees; permanent, short-term, and seasonal employees; full-time and part-time employees; on-call or intermittent employees who returned to work after having been formally separated; workers who were hired and separated during the month; transfers from other locations; and employees who were recalled to a job at the sampled establishment following a formal layoff lasting more than seven days. The JOLTS' hires data category does not include transfers or promotions within the sampled establishment; employees returning from strikes; and employees of temporary help agencies, employee leasing companies, outside contractors, or consultants working at the sampled establishment (JOLTS, 2007).

Separations: The JOLTS' separations data category refers to all employees separated from the payroll during the calendar month. The JOLTS' separations data category includes quits, layoffs, and discharges. Quits refers to employees who left voluntarily. Layoffs and discharges, which refer to involuntary separations initiated by the employer, include layoffs with no intent to rehire; discharges because positions were eliminated; discharges resulting from mergers, downsizing, or plant closings; firings or other discharges for cause; terminations of seasonal employees; and layoffs lasting or expected to last more than seven days. Other forms of employment separations include retirements, transfers to other locations, deaths, or separations due to employee disability. The JOLTS' separations data category does not include job transfers within the sampled establishment; employees on strike; employees of temporary help agencies; employee leasing companies; and outside contractors or consultants working at the sampled establishment (JOLTS, 2007).

Geographic Regions Studied in the JOLTS Survey
The JOLTS survey includes labor statistics on job openings, hires, total separations, quits, layoffs and discharges, and other separations for four geographic regions: Northeast, South, Midwest, and West.

- Northeast: Connecticut, Maine, Massachusetts, New Hampshire, New Jersey, New York, Pennsylvania, Rhode Island, and Vermont.
- South: Alabama, Arkansas, Delaware, District of Columbia, Florida, Georgia, Kentucky, Louisiana, Maryland, Mississippi, North Carolina, Oklahoma, South Carolina, Tennessee, Texas, Virginia, and West Virginia.
- Midwest: Illinois, Indiana, Iowa, Kansas, Michigan, Minnesota, Missouri, Nebraska, North Dakota, Ohio, South Dakota, and Wisconsin.
- West: Alaska, Arizona, California, Colorado, Hawaii, Idaho, Montana, Nevada, New Mexico, Oregon, Utah, Washington, and Wyoming (JOLTS, 2007).

Relevancy of JOLTS Survey Data

The data for JOLTS are gathered, through collaboration between the Bureau of Labor Statistics and the Atlanta JOLTS Data Collection Center, from a sample of 16,000 U.S. businesses. According to the Bureau of Labor Statistics, the JOLTS survey is relevant for all nonagricultural industries in the public and private sectors currently in operation in the United States. The Job Openings and Labor Turnover Survey publishes industry estimates based on the North American Industry Classification System (NAICS). The NAICS, established in 1997, is a common classification system shared by the United States, Canada, and Mexico that facilitates direct comparison of economic data across borders in North America. The JOLTS program publishes unadjusted estimates for the following NAICS sectors: natural resources and mining; construction; durable goods manufacturing; nondurable goods manufacturing; wholesale trade; retail trade; transportation, warehousing, and utilities; information; financial and insurance; real estate rental and leasing; professional, scientific, and technical services; management of companies and enterprises; waste management and remediation services; educational services; health care and social assistance; arts, entertainment, and recreation; accommodation and food services; federal government; and state and local government.

Purposes of JOLTS Survey Data

The JOLTS s data, which is released on a monthly basis in the media and online, is used for the following purposes: "National economic policy; business cycle analysis; industry retention rates; economic research

and planning; industry studies, and education and job training" (JOLTS, 2007). The data provided by the JOLTS, in particularly the availability of unfilled jobs or the job openings rate, provides a measure of the tightness of job markets. The JOLTS is the first economic indicator that provides information about of the unmet demand for labor. The public and private sectors use JOLTS data to assess where and when labor shortages occur in the United States.

ISSUES

Forecasting Labor Demand

The public and private sectors, and economic stakeholders in general, rely on labor market information, economic analysis, and short- and long-term forecasting to provide the information necessary for successful economic planning. For example, information about forecasted labor demand in different sectors and industries allows individuals to strategically plan their education and training to capitalize on demand. In addition, information about forecasted labor demand in different sectors and industries allows organizations to make strategic hiring decisions and investigate technology to lessen the burden of potential employee shortages. Economists and businesses make both short- and long-term job and labor forecasts. Businesses, industries, and occupations generally have differing levels of labor demand. In short-term forecasts, job growth is tied to price changes or supply-and-demand shocks such as rises or drops in oil prices. In long-term forecasts, economists work to show the overall trends in job growth and structural changes in the economy.

Changes in the U.S. Labor Market

In the United States, the labor market changed significantly at the end of the twentieth century. Labor market changes included "increased overall wage inequality and shifted wage and employment opportunities in favor of the more-educated and more-skilled" workers (Katz, 1996). The overall balance of labor demand shifted from less-educated manufacturing jobs toward more-educated workers, with half of all jobs created between 2010 and 2012 being in such fields as nursing, computer technology, and high-skill manufacturing, which require post-secondary education and training (Kochan, Finegold & Osterman, 2012). The demand for this type of labor outmatched the supply and wages rose significantly. Increasing wage inequality was and continues to be tied to the increasing demand for labor that is educated and technologically savvy. The demand for skilled labor has been reinforced by the business sector. Reinforcements include "new pay-setting norms, increased competition in many product markets, increased immigration of less-educated workers, and the weakening of institutions" such as labor unions that have historically offered job protection to non-educated workers (Katz, 1996). Labor economists debate whether substantial shifts in labor demand between sectors, such as that seen between manufacturing and information technology (IT) industries at the end of the twentieth century, are a result of the business cycle or permanent sector or industry specific events. Labor economists, and the U.S. Bureau Labor of Statistics, collect statistics on labor demand to track patterns and provide analytical labor demand forecasts (Haltiwanger & Schuh, 1999).

CONCLUSION

In the final analysis, labor demand is an important economic indicator for the health of the labor market and the economy in general. The federal government, recognizing the importance of a strong labor market, develops and implements labor demand policy to promote the creation of new jobs and work industries. The U.S. government creates policies and programs to increase labor demand across business sectors and industries. Increased labor demand will theoretically draw more workers into the workforce and increase productivity and economic growth. Labor economists debate the best strategies for bringing poor and uneducated persons into a labor market that has increasing demand for educated and technologically savvy workers. In the twenty-first century, public and private sector stakeholders must address labor issues, such as labor demand and wage determination, the economics of wage policies, and occupational wage differentials, to create effective and balanced labor markets.

BIBLIOGRAPHY

Bartik, T. (2001). *Fighting poverty with labor demand policies.* W.E. Upjohn Institute for Employment Research. Retrieved August from "http://www.upjohninst.org/publications/newsletter/tjb%5f701.pdf"

Belfield, C. (2005). "The teacher labour market in the US: Challenges and reforms." *Educational Review, 57*, 175–191.

Brambilla, I., Tortarolo, D. (2018). "Investment in ICT, productivity, and labor demand." *Open Knowledge Repository.*

Clark, K. & Hyson, R. (2000). "Measuring the demand for labor in the United States: The job openings and labor turnover survey." The U.S. Department of Labor. Retrieved from xlink:href="http://www.bls.gov/ore/abstract/st/st000120.htm"

Craig, B. (1997). "The long-run demand for labor in the banking industry." *Economic Review, 33*, 23–33.

Crihfield, J. (1989). "A structural empirical analysis of metropolitan labor demand." *Journal of Regional Science, 29*, 347–371.

Foster-McGregor, N., Stehrer, R., & Vries, G. (2013). "Offshoring and the skill structure of labour demand." *Review of World Economics, 149*, 631–662.

Haltiwanger, J., & Schuh, S. (1999, Mar/Apr). "Gross job flows between plants and industries." *New England Economic Review*, 41–64.

Hyclak, T. (1996). "Structural changes in labor demand and unemployment in local labor markets." *Journal of Regional Science, 36*, 653–663.

Kochan, T., Finegold, D., & Osterman, P. (2012). "Who can fix the "middle-skills" gap?" *Harvard Business Review, 90*, 81–90.

Katz, L. (1996, May/Jun). "Shifts in labor demand and supply." *New England Economic Review*, 179–181.

Palley, T. (2002). "The child labor problem and the need for international labor standards." *Journal of Economic Issues, 36*, 601–615.

The Job Openings and Labor Turnover Survey (JOLTS). (2007). U.S. Department of Labor, Bureau of Labor Statistics. Retrieved from xlink:href="http://www.bls.gov/jlt/home.htm#overview"

Rothstein, J. (2012). "The labor market four years into the crisis: assessing structural explanations." *Industrial & Labor Relations Review, 65*, 467–500.

Weidenbaum, M. (1994). "How government reduces unemployment." *Society, 31*, 72–77.

SUGGESTED READING

Graham, D., & Spence, N. (2000). "Manufacturing employment change, output demand, and labor productivity in the regions of Britain." *International Regional Science Review, 23,* 172–200.

Henderson, W. (1976). "Measuring the supply and demand for dentists in a population." *American Journal of Public Health, 66,* 70–72.

Puhani, P. (2003). "Relative demand shocks and relative wage rigidities during the rise and fall of Swiss unemployment." *Kyklos, 56,* 541–562.

—*Simone I. Flynn, PhD*

LABOR ECONOMICS

ABSTRACT

The fundamental dynamics of supply and demand apply as much to labor as they do to markets for goods and services. Unemployment, the bane of white and blue collar workers alike, occurs whenever there are more people seeking a particular job than there are employers looking to fill such positions. Thus, unemployment is a constant that varies only in degree and kind. How employers determine the number of workers they require at any given time and the number of hours workers are willing to spend on the job at a given wage rate are both micro-economically quantifiable. No less important (but harder to precisely pin down) is the microeconomic impact of unemployment. Consumer spending accounts for almost two-thirds of all purchases in developed economies, and the vast majority of consumers here are wage earners. So, higher unemployment rates slow or cause negative economic growth that can lead to more layoffs.

OVERVIEW

All wealth stems from a nation's productive capacity; the harnessing of land, raw materials, capital and

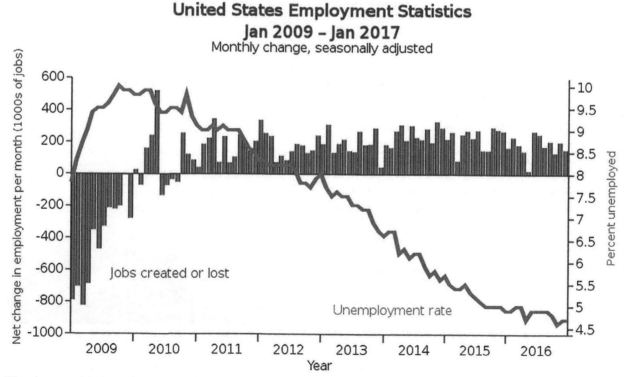

US employment statistics (unemployment rate and monthly changes in net employment), 2009–2016. (Courtesy of Ben Moore CC BY-SA 3.0 via Wikimedia Commons)

labor for the express purpose of creating saleable goods and services. Collectively, the earnings garnered through labor amount to some three-quarters of an industrially developed country's total national income. Consequently, the earnings fund much of the consumer spending that typically makes up some two-thirds of a country's overall economic activity. No wonder, then, that public anxiety quickly mounts when the national unemployment figure exceeds a certain level and why the goal of government economic policy is full employment. The more people working, essentially, the more money they have to spend on discretionary items like electronics, cosmetics, etc. This increased demand leads suppliers to ramp up production and eventually hire additional workers. Alas, the converse also holds true: If demand for too many goods drops appreciably, producers lay off workers. And their subsequent belt-tightening causes demand to drop further, triggering more lay-offs and even sharper drops.

Even the most penny-pinching industrialist has a long-term vested-interest in paying more than a subsistence wage. But exactly how much should a given employer pay its hourly workers? When exactly should it hire or lay off additional ones? Can a firm maximize its profits *and* compensate its workers with a fair and living wage or are the two objectives in the final analysis incompatible? And what about the worker: Does he or she economically benefit from many years of schooling or from joining a union? Questions like these are the focus of inquiry in labor economics, a field that draws heavily on the microeconomic principles of supply and demand (Cleaver, 2002). Laborers basically sell services that employers are willing to buy. The greater the demand for a particular service, the higher the price or wage. However, this is not true past a certain point, as few producers can afford to pay out more in costs than they earn in sales revenue for very long. This very real constraint tempers union demands made of employers during contract negotiations. Employers face the countervailing constraint of a strike; a strong union can leverage its sole supplier status to its advantage just like a business monopoly can.

APPLICATIONS

Microeconomic theory presupposes perfect competition and perfect information—ideal conditions that rarely (if ever) occur in real-world markets.

Competition is said to be perfect when every market participant can enter and exist at will and none face outside restraints on how he or she conducts business. Similarly, information is said to be perfect when every participant knows the range of prices on offer for a good or service it supplies and the identity of all its competitors. Much is gained, though, by suspending disbelief and buying into this simplified model, for several of its fundamental concepts and principles can now be applied to very good effect. Indeed, market equilibrium, marginal analysis, opportunity costs, price elasticity, the utility function, and the substitution effect, as we are about to see, add to and deepen our understanding of how labor markets function.

Supply of Labor

The labor force is made up of everyone either employed or seeking employment. Children and the stay-at-home parents who care for them are excluded, as are the institutionalized. Market-wise, moreover, atypical constraints are built into the labor force: Namely, that there is an upward limit to the number of employable people at any given time and not one of them is capable, much less willing, to work twenty-four hours a day. In fact, in developed countries, in-kind payments by governments to the indigent and unemployed effectively eliminate the threat of starvation; not necessarily everyone has to work and earn his or her keep. In industrialized nations, then, the particular utility function of the individual, the

Mo Willems is an American writer, animator, and creator of children's books. He is also famous for being a stay-at-home dad. Here he is at the Mazza Fall Conference in 2012 promoting one of his books. Courtesy of Alvintrusty CC BY-SA 3.0 via Wikimedia Commons)

sum of goods, services and activities that satisfies him or her, causes people to seek work. That, after all, is what economists expect any rational person to do. An individual exhibits utility-maximizing behavior whenever he or she both works and regularly enjoys a certain amount of leisure time.

Marginal Utility of the Individual

But no two people are exactly alike. Some enjoy material goods more than others and are willing to work longer hours to afford them. Conversely, some enjoy leisure for leisure's sake more and are not willing to work longer hours. When plotted on a graph, the line connecting different degree points of preference for income measured in hours worked versus leisure time curves up and inwards to a point, and then outwards again above that point. Apparently, people are prepared to sacrifice only so much leisure time to earn added income and vice versa; only so much income to enjoy added leisure time. The point where leisure time and income converge is referred to as an individual's marginal utility. Of course, the availability of work affects both decisions as Larson (1981) documents; people simply have fewer choices overall during periods of recession. During periods of economic growth, by contrast, employers come under increasing pressure to raise wages. If they do not, workers will migrate to employers who do. Higher production volumes presumably generate greater profits for the company as well as more work for employees, so the latter feel they truly deserve a raise.

The often unasked question for both then becomes: How will a wage increase affect the existing range of employee preferences for work over leisure? Having more money to spend, after all, enhances one's utility function; by rights, then, the balance should either tip more toward leisure or remain largely unchanged, shouldn't it? Actually, as it turns out, the preference shifts decidedly toward working more hours to earn a higher income. As workers factor in the higher wage, the prospect of missing out on the chance to earn more by pursuing leisure activities instead is simply too onerous. The opportunity cost in potential wages lost by not working additional hours here supersedes the more intrinsic value the employee assigns to leisure activities. And thanks to labor economists, employers know all about this seemingly paradoxical effect. Indeed, they have determined that the cost of hiring new workers exceeds the cost of a raise and wisely opt for the latter.

Price Elasticity of Supply

The preceding example illustrates how the price elasticity of supply can trigger the substitution effect. A higher price (wage per hour) in this instance resulted in a greater number of units of output (hours of labor) from existing employees willing to forgo leisure time. An actual value can be calculated for this index by dividing the percent change in output by the percent change in price. Just how elastic this supply is, though, differs in the short and the long run. Generally speaking, the farther out the time horizon, the greater the amount of production capacity on stream, the more the number of established providers and the greater the likelihood of available product substitutes. Labor's elasticity of supply tends to be more elastic in the long run for skilled workers but not for unskilled ones (Acemoglu, 2001). It takes much time to train and season skilled workers. Barring their migration from other locales, demand will likely exceed supply, necessitating higher wages that will attract enough trainees eventually to reestablish market equilibrium. Unskilled laborers, on the other hand, are always available and require little or no training, so the price-supply relationship here is much more inelastic and wages rise slowly if at all.

Waste Elasticity

Wage elasticity, what's more, tends to be higher in industries and markets where there are an ample number of competitors. The more firms vying to hire workers, in fact, the more "perfectly" elastic the wage rate becomes; the fewer the more inelastic. In the extreme case where a monopoly controls an entire market, one company effectively sets the going price for a good or service by deliberately limiting its production volume. Given the lack of alternative employers, workers are reduced to the status of price-takers when it comes to wages and hours. They can and do resort to form unions to gain bargaining power; challenging one monopoly by banding together to create another (Moroney & Allen, 1969). In oligopolies, workers can at least seek alternate employment at two or three other major competitors and thus theoretically enjoy greater price elasticity in their wage package. Oligopolies are creatures of maturing markets, however, where profits come as much if not more from cost-containment as from sales growth. Firms also leverage economies-of-scale wherever and whenever possible, and substitute technology for labor to further trim costs. Realistically, these combined factors tend to lessen such elasticity.

Demand for Labor

Both skilled and unskilled laborers have jobs to begin with because the firms that employ them earn enough income from sales in the long term to stay in business. But as any businessperson can tell you, sales fluctuate from year to year. And so, invariably, does production, necessitating adjustments in the size of a firm's workforce. Demand for labor is thus said to be a derived demand, so every firm periodically adjusts its labor requirements to respond to changing market conditions using a series of calculations to arrive at an exact figure. A firm must first determine the wage rate it is prepared to pay. Knowing this allows it to come up with a rough approximation of its labor needs since every job market has a supply curve.

Marginal Physical Product of Labor

While approximations can be helpful, a firm's interests are better served by coming up with an exact figure. This can be done by calculating the Marginal Physical Product of Labor; the number of additional units of output one extra worker produces. When multiplied by the selling price of a unit, an employer can ascertain the unit's Value of Marginal Physical Product of Labor, which in competitive markets equals the Marginal Revenue Product of Labor, or, the total revenue earned when the output of one additional worker is sold. A firm maximizes its profits when its marginal cost, the added expense incurred to produce one more unit of output, equals its marginal revenue. By extension, then, the maximum amount of labor needed lies at the point where a firm's Marginal Resource Cost of Labor, the additional cost incurred to hire one more worker, equals its Marginal Revenue Product.

Law of Diminishing Returns

Employers who disregard this seemingly arcane calculation end up regretting their decision. Curiously, though, more problems arise when employers hire too many new workers as opposed to too few. This can be explained by the Law of Diminishing Returns, which states that steadily increasing one variable factor of production while holding the others constant will eventually cause a decline in productivity. When that variable is labor and there isn't a corresponding increase in equipment and plant, overcrowding on the factory floor can begin to take its toll on production. Thereafter, the amount of additional output the latest new hire produces will be less than the amount the preceding new hire produces.

Unemployment

The term "unemployment" evokes all sorts of dire connotations. Anyone who has experienced it knows why. Economically speaking, though, it's a constant and considered as inevitable as a naturally occurring phenomenon. As odd as this sounds, unemployment even exists in times of "full employment" when, theoretically, everyone who can work has a job that makes the most efficient use of his or her skills. This is because information regarding job availability is never "perfect." It takes time to find openings, be interviewed, and the like. Job-seekers, as economists are fond of saying, incur transaction costs. But they have every expectation of finding work and usually do in time. This kind of unemployment is thus relatively benign and so much a part of economic life that it is dubbed "fictional." People are constantly entering the workforce for the first time, re-entering it after retraining or raising a child, or else simply keen to find a better job.

As the auto industry declined in cities like Detroit due to the economy and automation eliminated even more of those factory jobs, abandoned homes like this one in the Deray neighborhood of Detroit became more and more common. (Courtesy of Notorious4life via Wikimedia Commons)

Structural Unemployment

"Structural" unemployment is a completely different matter. Essentially there are far more workers looking for employment in a particular occupation or industry than there are openings for them (Wood, 1988). Sometimes a major shock to the economic system as a whole is to blame. Over time there's usually a rebound and a return to previous levels of employment, so the dislocation is not permanent. More often, though, it is because an irreversible shift has occurred either in derived demand or in the production process. The goods and services workers once produced have either fallen out of favor, been replaced by substitutes, or their jobs are now done better, faster and cheaper by technology. Laid-off workers with skills not easily transferable to other industries face bleak economic futures only partly ameliorated by unemployment benefits, welfare, and other in-kind government payments. Indeed, unless they are willing to invest time, effort, and money in learning a more marketable skill of equal value, the earning power of these displaced workers will never be as great again. Herein lies one major reason why the idea of human capital has gained so many adherents.

Human Capital

The "post-industrial" age, the "knowledge" economy and other familiar buzz words underscore the importance put these days on human capital. But what exactly does the term mean? In theory and practice, the idea of human capital revolves around one central idea: The more skills a worker accrues, the more his or her value to employers and the greater his or her earnings potential and long-term job security (Acemoglu, 1996). Firms here have vested interest in providing training and education that improves the skill sets of their workers. One benefit of such practices is improved productivity and cost-efficiency, both of which increasingly depend upon leveraging technology. Another benefit is worker retention: The higher the employee turnover rate, the higher the transaction costs of hiring replacements and the higher the opportunity costs of failing to keep experienced workers. Individuals, like firms, have a vested interest in improving their skill sets with or without their company's help. Capitalism, as a famous economist once pointed out, continually engages in a process of "creative destruction" where the only real

constant is change. Increasingly, too, that change is driven by advances in technology that workers must keep abreast of to have "marketable" skills. Investing in training, education, and the like is thus as important to the individual as investing in mutual funds to build a retirement nest egg and to the firm as investing in new equipment and plants.

Unions

Mention the word "labor" and most people immediately think "union." Unions are formed by and for workers for the express purpose of safeguarding and furthering their members' interests and welfare through collective bargaining and mediation. Their public image as the champion of the worker belies, economically speaking, how strikingly similar a union's organizational agenda and desired outcomes are to those of a business (Oswald, 1982). Its membership dues in this respect are its sales revenue, its product favorable contract terms for its rank and file, and its overriding strategic consideration for its own survival and growth. Contrary to its "militant" roots, today's union typically resorts to confrontational tactics only when compromise and cooperation fails. And it will more than likely tone down its rhetoric and relent on its threats of work stoppages and strikes the minute management puts an acceptable offer on the table. This is due, in part, to the fact that union leaders are aware that their relationship

Duncan West speaking with union organizer Cesar Chaves at the Delano UFW rally in Delano, California in June of 1974. Duncan represented the Teamsters who were supporting the United Farm Workers - UFW, and condemning their IBT union leadership for working as thugs against a fellow union. Duncan and his wife Mary were the branch organizers of the LA IS. (Courtesy of Joel Levine CC BY 3.0 via Wikimedia Commons)

with company management is ultimately symbiotic. The specter of wholesale lay-offs in the smokestack industries of the United States in the 1980s and 1990s and the result of irreversible structural shifts in the economy as a whole have not been forgotten. Nor can it be, for globalization, the root cause of these shifts, is now an ever-present factor.

Some would go so far as to argue that the union movement in the developed world is in decline. It certainly has been steadily losing membership and thus bargaining power in the U.S. manufacturing sector over the last four decades. Countervailing organizing efforts in the growing service-industry sector have met with only limited success primarily because the pool of labor drawn on here is unskilled. Greater mobility in the workforce, declining demographics, and automation have all eroded the traditional base of support for unions. In Europe, the traditions of trade union militancy and social democratic politics run deeper and have made the labor movement more resilient. Nonetheless, the industrial workers who once swelled unions' ranks in the developed world are now much more likely to be found in the developing world. And the prevailing political climate and economic development policies there often do not countenance union organizing to any great degree.

Discourse

Labor may not have as high a public profile as it once did. Its importance as a key variable factor of production nonetheless remains undiminished. Labor runs the machines, builds both the components–parts and plant infrastructure instrumental to the production of saleable goods and does the work required to provide marketable services. The earnings workers make fuel consumer spending and are thus an integral part of the circular flow of money at the heart of all economic activity. Demand for and supply of labor has been, is, and will always be, a central concern of microeconomics.

BIBLIOGRAPHY

Acemoglu, D. (1996). "A microfoundation for social increasing returns in human capital accumulation." *Quarterly Journal of Economics, 111*, 779–804

Acemoglu, D. (2001). "Good jobs versus bad jobs." *Journal of Labor Economics, 19*, 1–22.

Clever, T. (2002). "Chapter 3: Microeconomics and macroeconomics." In *Understanding the world economy* (pp. 53–67). United Kingdom: Taylor & Francis Ltd.

Dobbs, R., Lund, S., & Madgavkar, A. (2012). "Talent tensions ahead: A CEO briefing." *Mckinsey Quarterly, ,* 92–102.

Hamermesh, D. (2017). "Replication in labor economics: Evidence from data, and what it suggests." *American Economic Review, 107*, 5, 37-40.

Larson, D. (1981). "Labor supply adjustment over the business cycle." *Industrial & Labor Relations Review, 34*, 591–595.

Mitton, T. (2012). "Inefficient labor or inefficient capital? Corporate diversification and productivity around the world." *Journal of Financial & Quantitative Analysis, 47*, 1–22.

Moroney, J., & Allen, B. (1969). "Monopoly power and relative share of labor." *Industrial & Labor Relations Review, 22*, 167–178.

Osterman, P. (2011). "Institutional labor economics, the new personnel economics, and internal labor markets: a reconsideration." *Industrial & Labor Relations Review, 64*, 637–653.

Oswald, A. (1982). "The microeconomic theory of the trade union." *Economic Journal, 92*, 576– 95.

Wood, A. (1988). "How much unemployment is structural?" *Oxford Bulletin of Economics & Statistics, 50*, 71–81.

SUGGESTED READING

Baily, M., Bartelsman, E., & Haltiwanger, J. (2001). "Labor productivity: Structural change and cyclical dynamics." *Review of Economics & Statistics, 83*, 420–433.

Brown, A. (1971). "Further analysis of the supply of labour to the firm." *Journal of Management Studies, 8*, 280.

Edwards, E. (1959). "Classical and keynesian employment theories: a reconciliation." *Quarterly Journal of Economics, 73*, 407–428.

Gowler, D. (1969). "Determinants of the supply of labour to the firm." *Journal of Management Studies, 6*, 73–96.

—*Francis Duffy, MBA*

LABOR RELATIONS LAW

ABSTRACT

This article explores the reasons and justifications for current American labor law and provides a history of the federal statutory schemes that have affected business and business-related labor relation practices. A survey of federal labor laws such as the Railway Labor Act and the Labor Management Reporting and Disclosure Act (LMRDA) is included to give the reader a comprehensive overview of labor-relations law and the implications of present labor relations.

OVERVIEW

Labor-relations laws exist to protect workers' labor-relations rights. Since the 1930s, a body of federal statutes has been implemented in the United States to promote successful and amicable labor-management relations. Modern U.S. federal law regulating labor-management relations is largely a product of the New Deal era. While Congress has acted to raise the minimum wage and has considered labor-law reform affecting both private and public employees, no major statutes or revisions of labor laws have been enacted over the past several decades ("Federal Labor Laws," 1993). In light of this, it is important to understand the history and significance of these laws to gain a full understanding and appreciation of their present-day applications.

Early Labor Laws

Labor laws began to be instituted in the United States shortly after the Civil War, the result of public pressure placed on the federal government to manage the growing country's labor force. During this period, the Industrial Revolution was in full swing, and it transformed the United States from a relatively agricultural society into an industrial one that was manned by laborers who were mostly immigrants with little to no rights or legal protections from unfair practice.

Railroads became the epitome of this early industrialized age. The railway system "expanded from about 30,000 miles of track before the Civil War to nearly 270,000 miles by 1900. The industrial labor force nearly tripled between 1880 and 1910 to about 8 million. Large factories, which had existed only in the textile industry before the Civil War, became commonplace in a variety of industries" (Illinois Labor History Society, 2000).

During this time, the population of the United States was growing at a staggering rate, from 31,443,321 in 1860 to 76,212,168 in 1900 and then

The New Deal programs were enacted by the federal government in response to the Great Depression of the 1930s. Top left: The Tennessee Valley Authority, part of the New Deal, being signed into law in 1933. Top right: President Franklin Delano Roosevelt was responsible for the New Deal. Bottom: A public mural from one of the artists employed by the New Deal's WPA program. (Courtesy of LordHarris via Wikimedia Commons)

Child laborers work in an Indiana glass works factory. Trade unions have an objective interest in combating child labor. This photograph is from a series of photographs of child labor at glass and bottle factories in the United States by Lewis W. Hine, for the National Child Labor Committee, New York. (Courtesy of Lewis Wickes Hine, restored by Michel Vuijlsteke (Library of Congress) via Wikimedia Commons)

92,228,496 by 1910 (Illinois Labor History Society, 2000). "Labor was in high demand to run the new industries. Unfortunately, the continued high population growth spurred by immigration helped to keep the value of individual workers low as there was a ready supply of people to fill the positions" (Illinois Labor History Society, 2000).

This was an active and fascinating period in the United States' labor history. It was during this time that workers began to organize and resist when their health or way of life was being threatened. These actions, coupled with worker organization, laid the groundwork for unions and union organization.

The events that led to the public's demand for labor legislation and laborer recognition can be viewed as separate and individually unique occurrences, but placed together, one can get a sense of the necessity and urgency for such laws. In the late nineteenth and early twentieth centuries, various events conspired to influence labor legislation.

Timeline of Labor-Related Events, 1878–1913

1878

Greenback Labor Party organized by a merger of the Workingmen's Party and Greenback Party.

1879

Knights of Labor elect Terrence Powderly as Grand Master Workman.

1881

Federation of Organized Trades and Labor Unions, forerunner of the American Federation of Labor, formed in Pittsburgh.

The Haymarket Affair was the aftermath of a bombing that took place at a labor demonstration on May 4, 1886, at Haymarket Square in Chicago, Illinois. (Courtesy of Harper's Weekly via Wikimedia Commons)

Author Sinclair Lewis wrote about the horrible conditions in the meat industry. Here workers are shown working in a typical stockyard in Chicago, Illinois, in 1923. (Courtesy of Suhling & Koehn Co., Chicago, Ill. via Wikimedia Commons)

1882

First Labor Day celebration held in New York City.

1883

Brotherhood of Railroad Trainmen organized.

1885

Immigration of laborers on contract is outlawed by the Foran Act.

1885–6

Period of greatest influence by Knights of Labor.

1886

In Columbus, Ohio, the American Federation of Labor (AFL) is formed with Samuel Gompers as the first president. Violence erupts following a mysterious explosion at Haymarket Square in Chicago during a rally in support of the 8-hour day.

1887

Seven accused in the Haymarket explosion are sentenced to death. Five are later executed.

1888

First federal labor relations law passed, but it only applies to rail companies.

1890

The AFL, at its annual convention, announce its support for women's suffrage. United Mine Workers of America (UMWA) formed.

1892

Homestead Strike in Pennsylvania. The Amalgamated Association of Iron, Steel, and Tin Workers (AAISTW) lose the fight over Carnegie Steel's attempt to break the union.

1893

Business depression.

1894

Strike by the American Railway Union (ARU) against the Pullman Palace Car Company near Chicago is defeated by the use of injunctions and federal troops.

1898

Erdman Act passed, which provides for mediation and voluntary arbitration on the railroads. This law replaces the 1888 law.

1900

International Ladies' Garment Workers' Union (ILGWU) founded.

1901

United States Steel defeats the AAISTW after a strike that lasted three months. United Textile Workers of America founded.

1902

Coal miners in Pennsylvania end a five-month strike and agree to arbitration with a presidential committee.

1903

At the annual AFL convention, blue-collar and middle-class women unite to form the National Women's Trade Union League (NWTUL). This organization is created to help organize women. Mary Morton Kehew is elected president, while Jane Addams is elected vice-president. The Department of Commerce and Labor is formed. Mother Jones (Mary Harris Jones) leads the March of the Mill Children to President Roosevelt's home in New York. Many of the children are victims of industrial accidents.

1905

In Chicago, the Industrial Workers of the World (IWW) is founded. U.S. Supreme Court in *Lochner v. New York* declares a New York maximum hours law unconstitutional under the due process clause of the 14th Amendment.

1906

Upton Sinclair publishes *The Jungle*, which exposes the unsafe and unclean aspects of the Chicago meat-packing industry. The International Typographical Union (ITU) struck successfully for the eight-hour day, which helped pave the way for shorter hours in the printing trades.

1908

In *Muller v. Oregon*, the Supreme Court rules that female maximum hour laws are constitutional due to a woman's "physical structure and ...maternal functions." Section 10 of the Erdman Act, which deals

with "yellow dog" contracts and forbids a person from being fired for belonging to a union, was declared unconstitutional (*US v. Adair*).

1909

Two-month strike by the International Ladies Garment Workers' (ILGW) Union was settled by providing preferential union hiring, a board of grievances, and a board of arbitration.

1911

Supreme Court upheld an injunction ordering the AFL to eliminate the Bucks Stove and Range Co. from its unfair list and to cease to promote an unlawful boycott. (*Gompers v. Bucks Stove and Range Co.*) One-hundred-forty-six workers, mostly women, die in the Triangle Shirtwaist Company fire in New York City. This leads to the establishment of the New York Factory Investigating Commission to monitor factory conditions.

1912

Massachusetts adopts the first minimum wage law for women and minors. Textile strike led by the Industrial Workers of the World in Massachusetts wins wage increase.

1913

U.S. Department of Labor established. Secretary of Labor given power to "act as a mediator and to appoint commissioners of conciliation in labor disputes." (Illinois Labor History Society, 2000)

This series of events led Congress to pass a number of federal mandates for the purpose of addressing these issues in a comprehensive manner.

EARLY LABOR LAWS
The Clayton Act

The first of this series of early labor-relation laws was the Clayton Act of 1914. This legislation was a direct response to the growing public pressure on the federal government to clarify the position of labor under antitrust law. The Clayton Act "included several major provisions protective of organized labor" ("Federal labor laws," 1993). It stated, "The labor of a human being is not a commodity or article of commerce," and went on to assert that nothing in the federal antitrust laws "shall be construed to forbid the existence and operation of labor...organizations...nor shall such organizations, or the members thereof, be held or construed to be illegal combinations or conspiracies in restraint of trade, under the antitrust laws" (15 U.S.C. §17).

Railway Labor Act

In 1926, Congress passed the Railway Labor Act (RLA), which established procedures for collective bargaining and prohibited discrimination against emerging unions. The act originally only applied to interstate railroads and their related undertakings. In 1936, with the advent of the airline industry, the act "was amended to include airlines engaged in interstate commerce" ("Federal labor laws," 1993).

Davis-Bacon Act

The Davis-Bacon Act of 1931 required "that contracts for construction entered into by the Federal Government specify the minimum wages to be paid to persons employed under those contracts" ("Federal labor laws," 1993).

Reforms in Labor Law

Traditionally, labor law opposed concerted activities by workers, such as strikes, picketing, and refusals to deal, to obtain higher wages and better working conditions. At various times, such activities were found to constitute criminal conspiracy, tortuous conduct, and violations of antitrust law. As subjecting workers to criminal sanctions became publicly unpopular, employers began resorting to civil remedies in an attempt to halt unionization. The primary tool in this campaign was the injunction. Eventually, public opposition to such actions forced Congress to intervene.

Norris-LaGuardia Act

One of the most significant laws with regard to modern labor relations was the Norris-LaGuardia Act, passed in 1932. It "was the first in a series of laws passed by Congress in the 1930s which gave Federal sanction to the right of labor unions to organize and strike, and to use other forms of economic leverage in dealings with management" ("Federal labor laws," 1993). This was in direct response to the growing criticism of the use of injunctions in peaceful labor disputes. The act "specifically prohibited Federal courts from enforcing so-called 'yellow dog' contracts or agreements (under which workers promised not to join a union or promised to discontinue membership in one)" ("Federal labor laws," 1993). It also withdrew from the federal government the power to legally prevent, via injunction or restraining order, either labor unions or individuals from participating

Senator George W. Norris of Nebraska and Representative Fiorello H. La Guardia of New York, both Republicans, were the chief sponsors of the Norris-La Guardia Act. (Courtesy of George W. Norris & Fred Palumbo via Wikimedia Commons)

in or providing various forms of nonviolent aid to workers in a labor dispute.

In the act, the term "labor dispute" is broadly defined to include any controversy concerning terms or conditions of employment or union representation, regardless of whether the parties had an employer-employee relationship or not. More significantly, the act made the statement, albeit indirectly, that under U.S. law, labor was to have full freedom to form unions without employer interference. This set in motion the development of federal agencies that would enforce workers' rights and entitlements schemes, as well as government supports and mandates that would further protect the American workforce.

NEW DEAL–ERA REFORMS

National Industrial Recovery Act

Congress passed the National Industrial Recovery Act (NIRA) in 1933. The NIRA "sought to provide codes of 'fair competition' and to fix wages and hours in industries subscribing to such codes" ("Federal labor laws," 1993). In other words, it essentially established the minimum wage.

Under title 1 of the NIRA, "all codes of fair competition approved under the Act should guarantee the right of employees to collective bargaining without interference or coercion of employees" ("Federal labor laws," 1993). In 1935, the U.S. Supreme Court found this provision to be unconstitutional due to 10th Amendment violations. Congress reconvened on the issue of collective bargaining and devised an act that would not violate constitutional rights.

National Labor Relations Act

"By far the most important labor legislation of the 1930s was the National Labor Relations Act (NLRA) of 1935, more popularly known as the Wagner Act, after its sponsor, Sen. Robert F. Wagner (NY-D). This law included reenactment of the previously invalidated labor sections of the N[I]RA as well as a number of additions.

"The NLRA was applicable to all firms and employees in activities affecting interstate commerce with the exception of agricultural laborers, government employees, and those persons subject to the Railway Labor Act. It guaranteed covered workers the right to organize and join labor movements, to choose representatives and bargain collectively, and to strike.

"The National Labor Relations Board (NLRB), originally consisting of three members appointed by the President, was established by the Act as an independent Federal agency. The NLRB was given power to determine whether a union should be certified to represent particular groups of employees, using such methods as it deemed suitable to reach such a determination, including the holding of a representation election among workers concerned.

"Employers were forbidden by the Act from engaging in any of the five categories of unfair labor practices. Violation of this prohibition could result in the filing of a complaint with the NLRB by a union or employees. After investigation, the NLRB could order the cessation of such practices, reinstatement of a person fired for union activities, the provision of back pay, restoration of seniority, benefits, etc. An NLRB order issued in response to an unfair labor practice complaint was made enforceable by the Federal courts.

"Among those unfair labor practices forbidden by the Act were:

1. Dominating or otherwise interfering with the formation of a labor union, including the provision of any financial or other support.
2. Interfering with or restraining employees engaged in the exercise of their rights to organize and bargain collectively.

3. Imposing any special conditions of employment which tended either to encourage or discourage union membership. The law stated, however, that this provision should be construed to prohibit union contracts requiring union membership as a condition of employment in a company—a provision which, in effect, permitted the closed and union shops. (In the former, only pre-existing members of the union could be hired; in the latter, new employees were required to join the union.)
4. Discharging or discriminating against an employee because he had given testimony or filed charges under the Act.
5. Refusing to bargain collectively with unions representing a company's employees.

"The NLRA included no provisions defining or prohibiting as unfair any labor practices by unions. The Act served to spur growth of U.S. unionism—from 3,584,000 union members in 1935 to 10,201,000 by 1941, the eve of World War II. The 1941 figure represented more than 25 percent of the nonagricultural workforce in the U.S." ("Federal labor laws," 1993).

Anti-Strikebreaker Law

"The Byrnes Act of 1936, named for Sen. James F. Byrnes (SC-D) and amended in 1938, made it a felony to transport any person in interstate commerce who was employed for the purpose of using force of threats against non-violent picketing in a labor dispute or against organizing or bargaining efforts" ("Federal labor laws," 1993).

Walsh-Healy Act

"Passed in 1936, the Walsh-Healy Act stated that workers must be paid not less than the 'prevailing minimum wage' normally paid in a locality; restricted regular working hours to eight hours a day and 40 hours a week, with time-and-a-half pay for additional hours; prohibited the employment of convicts and children under 18; and established sanitation and safety standards" ("Federal labor laws," 1993).

Fair Labor Standards Act

"Known as the wage-hour law, this 1938 Act established minimum wages and maximum hours for all workers engaged in covered 'interstate commerce'" ("Federal labor laws," 1993).

POST-WORLD WAR II LAWS
Labor-Management Relations Act

"It was not until two years after the close of World War II that the first major modification of the National Labor Relations Act was enacted. In 1947, the Labor-Management Relations Act—also known as the Taft-Hartley Act, after its two sponsors, Sen. Robert A. Taft (OH-R) and Rep. Fred A. Hartley, Jr. (NJ-R)—was passed by Congress, vetoed by President Truman (on the basis that it was anti-labor), and then reapproved over his veto. This comprehensive measure:

- established procedures for delaying or averting so-called 'national emergency' strikes;
- excluded supervisory employees from coverage of the Wagner Act;
- prohibited the "closed shop" altogether;
- banned closed-shop union hiring halls that discriminated against non-union members" ("Federal labor laws," 1993).

The Labor-Management Relations Act "retained the Wagner Act's basic guarantees of workers' rights to join unions, bargain collectively, and strike, and retained the same list of unfair labor practices forbidden to employers. The Act also added a list of unfair labor practices forbidden to unions" ("Federal labor laws," 1993). This was revolutionary, since until this point, union practices had not been formally regulated. The list of banned union practices included:

- the use of "restraint or coercion of workers exercising their rights to bargain through representatives of their choosing";
- the use of "coercion of an employer in his choice of persons to represent him in discussions with unions";
- "refusal of unions to bargain collectively";
- "barring a worker from employment because he had been denied union membership for any reason except non-payment of dues";
- "striking to force an employer or self-employed person to join a union";
- the use of "secondary boycotts";

- the use of "various types of strikes or boycotts involving interunion conflict or jurisdictional agreements";
- "levying of excessive union initiation fees";
- the use of "certain forms of 'featherbedding' (payment for work not actually performed)" ("Federal labor laws," 1993).

Other provisions of the Labor-Management Relations Act included:

- "authorization of suits against unions for violations of their economic contracts";
- "authorization of damage suits for economic losses caused by secondary boycotts and certain strikes";
- "relaxation of the Norris-LaGuardia Act to permit injunctions against specified categories of unfair labor practice";
- "establishment of a 60-day no-strike and no-lockout notice period for any party seeking to cancel an existing collective bargaining agreement";
- "a requirement that unions desiring status under the law and recourse to NLRB protection file specified financial reports and documents with the U.S. Department of Labor";
- "the abolition of the U.S. Conciliation Service and establishment of the Federal Mediation and Conciliation Service";
- "a prohibition against corporate or union contributions or expenditures with respect to elections to any Federal office";
- "a reorganization of the NLRB and a limitation on its power";
- "a prohibition on strikes against the government"; and
- "the banning of various types of employer payments to union officials" ("Federal labor laws," 1993).

The Labor-Management Reporting & Disclosure Act

"The Labor-Management Reporting and Disclosure Act of 1959, also known as the Landrum-Griffin Act, made major additions to the Taft-Hartley Act, including:

- definition of additional unfair labor practices;
- a ban on organizational or recognition picketing;
- provisions allowing State labor relations agencies and courts to assume jurisdiction over labor

disputes the NLRB declined to consider, at the same time prohibiting the NLRB from broadening the categories of cases it would not handle" ("Federal labor laws," 1993).

Modern Labor-Relations Law

Beginning in the 1970s, the legal landscape surrounding labor-relations legislation began shifting its focus. Labor law no longer stood alone; instead, it became an arm of a new and emerging area called employment law, the purpose of which was to address not only labor issues but also unfair and discriminatory employment practices. This broader area of laws reflected society's demand to both protect the skilled worker and address discriminatory practices that affected all professions, including those not afforded the benefits of union representation. Some of the best known of these anti-discrimination laws are the Equal Pay Act (EPA) of 1970, the Sex Discrimination Act of 1975, the Disability Discrimination Act (DDA) of 1995, the Protection from Harassment Act of 1997, the Public Interest Disclosure Act (PIDA) of 1998, and the Employment Equality (Age) Regulations of 2006. These laws reflected a new outlook on employment and employment practices, at the same time making a clear statement to an American public that had become disheartened by legislative emphasis on labor unions and labor-union issues. These laws

Labor issues remain important today. People have campaigned for a $15 an hour minimum wage, because the real minimum wage has fallen by more than 33% compared to 1968. In "tipped" jobs, some states still enable employers to take their workers' tips for between $2.13 and the $7.25 minimum wage per hour. Here people rally in New York City on April 15, 2015, to encourage such a raise of the minimum wage in America. (Courtesy of The All-Nite Images from NY, NY, USA, CC BY-SA 2.0 via Wikimedia Commons)

would address a larger societal issue: equity and equality in the American workforce.

CONCLUSION

As American society looks toward the future, what will be the next steps to fulfill society's need to recognize and protect workers' rights? Are the labor laws established in the first part of the twentieth century going to be upheld in the twenty-first? Will unions and unionization continue to be as applicable as they were when those laws were first instituted? Laws and legal schemes are like many other aspects of society: they reflect public sentiment and the needs of the times. Perhaps society will see a resurgence of labor-relation laws, either in the United States or abroad. Whatever the case may be, those involved in business, whether national or international, will need to be aware of labor-relations law in the relevant countries and its implications for successful business practices.

BIBLIOGRAPHY

Balsmeier, B. (2017). "Unions, collective relations laws and R&D investment in emerging and developing countries." *Research Policy, 46,* 1, 292-304.

Bernhardt, A., Spiller, M. W., & Theodore, N. (2013). "Employers gone rogue: Explaining industry variation in violations of workplace laws." *Industrial & Labor Relations Review, 66,* 808–832.

Brill, E. A., Fant, L. M., & Baddish, N. M. (2013). "2012–2013 US Supreme Court wrap-up: Hot topics in labor and employment law." *Employee Relations Law Journal, 39,* 3–8.

Carrell, M., & Heavrin, C. (2006). *Labor relations and collective bargaining: Cases, practice, and law.* New Jersey: Prentice Hall.

Cihon, P. J. & Castagnera, J. O. (2001). *Employment and labor law.* Mason, Ohio: South-Western Educational Publishing.

Federal labor laws. (1993). *Congressional Digest,* 72(6/7), 164–166.

Illinois Labor History Society. (2000). A curriculum of United States labor history for teachers.

Katz, H. C. (2013). "Is US public sector labor relations in the midst of a transformation?" *Industrial & Labor Relations Review, 66,* 1031–1046.

Twomey, D. (2006). *Labor and employment law: Text and cases.* Boston, Massachusetts: Thompson.

SUGGESTED READING

Godin, K. & Palacios, M. (2006, May). "Comparing labour relations laws in Canada and the United States." *Fraser Forum*, 5–7.

Gross, J. A. (1999). "A human rights perspective on U.S. labor relations law." *LaborLaw Journal, 50*, 197–203.

Koeniger, W., Leonardi, M., & Nunziata, L. (2007). "Labor market institutions and wage inequality." *Industrial & Labor Relations Review, 60*, 340–356.

Marshall, S. & Mitchell, R. (2006). "Enterprise bargaining, managerial prerogative and the protection of workers' rights: An argument on the role of law and regulatory strategy in Australia under the Workplace Relations Act of 1996." *International Journal of Comparative Labor Law & Industrial Relations, 22*, 299–327.

Warner, K. (2013). "The decline of unionization in the United States: Some lessons from Canada." *Labor Studies Journal, 38*, 110–138.

—*Sara Rogers, JD*

LABOR SUPPLY

ABSTRACT

This article focuses on the theory of labor supply. The relationship between labor markets, labor supply and demand, labor force, and wage rate are discussed. The article explores why and how the U.S. government measures labor supply and unemployment rates. The issues associated with child labor and labor policies are addressed.

OVERVIEW

The health and demographics of a nation's labor force effects the nation's productivity and potential for economic growth. National economies rely on steady and, in most instances, growing labor supply and demand. Economic growth is often created by increased productivity from a larger labor supply. Individual and aggregate labor supply is determined by individual and aggregate appetite for leisure and consumption as well as wage rates. The public sector can manipulate wage rates and institute labor policies that control work-related issues such as child labor and work visas, to raise or lower the labor supply. Labor supply policies are often developed to address the public problem of intractable poverty. Labor supply policies, such as welfare reform, job training, and the Earned Income Tax Credit (EITC), are developed to increase the labor supply, job skills, or wages of the poor (Bartik, 2001).

Labor Economics

Labor economics considers labor supply and demand to be a central factor in the health of the labor market and the economy as a whole. Labor economics is concerned with the relationship between markets and labor. Labor markets are the markets that form from the interaction of employers and workers. Labor markets differ from the market for other public goods in the finite nature of human labor, energy, and productivity; human workers can work a finite number of hours. In addition, reproduction rates and global resources limit the growth in the overall population of workers. The scope of labor economics extends to the following areas: Labor supply, labor demand, income, wages, and employment patterns and trends.

Labor Supply

The concept of labor supply is a fundamental building block in both microeconomic and macroeconomic theory. In microeconomics, labor supply is directly linked to the theory of income-leisure choice. In microeconomic theory, the labor supply increases or decreases in response to changes in real wages (Morris, 2001). The overall labor supply includes employment and unemployment rates. Employment and unemployment, in microeconomic theory, are viewed as alternative uses of time. People are believed to choose the type and duration of their work based on their preferences for leisure and wage requirements. This perspective does not explain or account for involuntary unemployment (Spencer, 2005).

Labor Supply & Economic Fluctuations

In macroeconomics, labor supply is studied as a means of understanding large cyclical fluctuations in the economy. Economists debate the role of labor supply and demand in causing economic booms and slumps. Economists agree that workers expend greater work effort during times of economic boom than in times of economic slumps but cannot fully explain and predict individual labor supply decisions. Individual and aggregate labor supply decisions are affected by variables and factors such as wages, availability of work, and preference for leisure over consumption. In the United States, households make individual decisions about labor market participation. In most instances, economists find that wage amounts affect labor market participation more than a laborer's preference for leisure (Change & Kim, 2005). Labor supply is managed in most industrialized nations through labor supply and wage policies that promote full employment and labor market equilibrium.

The following section provides an overview of the neoclassical theory of labor supply. This section serves as the foundation for later discussions of how and why the U.S. government measures labor supply and unemployment rates in the United States. The issues associated with labor supply and child labor are addressed.

THE THEORY OF LABOR SUPPLY

Neoclassical Theory of Labor Supply

The neoclassical labor supply theory conveys the largest amount of hours a worker will be willing to contribute to the economy over the course of a certain span of time at each wage rate. The neoclassical theory of labor supply is used to analyze employment and unemployment patterns in labor markets. Neoclassical economic theory argues that employment and unemployment are two alternate ways to spend time. Individuals are believed to choose whether or not to work based upon their preference for work or leisure and the wage rate available to them. Unemployment, in this theory, can be interpreted as a form of voluntary leisure. Economist John Keynes developed the idea of involuntary unemployment in his book, *The General Theory of Employment, Interest, and Money* (1936). Involuntary unemployment is believed to exist due to an insufficiency in aggregate, or total, labor demand. Involuntary unemployment is generally addressed by government intervention and labor policies.

The neoclassical model of labor supply and demand, often represented as a curve, is based on the idea that participating in the labor market is a voluntary choice more than an economic necessity. Unemployment in the neoclassical theory of labor supply is considered to be a labor-leisure choice (Spencer, 2005). The following factors and variables affect labor supply and demand: utility function, budget constraint, rate of substitution, income effect, and opportunity cost. The neoclassical theory of labor supply is directly connected to the neoclassical theory of labor demand. While the labor supply theory, often represented as a curve, conveys the largest amount of hours a worker will be willing to contribute to the economy over the course of a certain span of time at each wage rate; the theory of labor demand illustrates the most hours an employer will demand at each wage rate.

Labor Market Equilibrium

When labor demand and labor supply are balanced, labor market equilibrium occurs. The neoclassical theory of labor equilibrium argues that when labor supply and demand are equal, the economy is in equilibrium. Neoclassical economists argue that the supply and demand for labor will be equal to one another in the absence of fixed or static wages. In labor equilibrium, the labor supply is balanced. Workers give their time to work in a manner that balances the utility of their wages with the utility of leisure time. In labor equilibrium, the labor demand is also stable and balanced. Businesses hire workers based on business productivity needs and estimations. Businesses can entice workers to forgo leisure by offering wages above the worker's reservation wage. A reservation wage refers to the minimum real wage that causes workers to become indifferent when faced with consumption and leisure choices.

Understanding & Predicting Labor Patterns

Ultimately, the theory of labor supply is one-half of the labor supply and demand model used to understand and predict employment and unemployment patterns. The theory of labor supply is often equated with a labor-leisure tradeoff or choice. In practice, economic factors such as wages and income needs, possibly more than leisure preferences, affect individual labor supply choices. Labor supply and labor force participation rates are tracked by the government as part of the overall project of promoting and facilitating economic growth for the nation. The following section describes how and why the federal government measures the U.S. labor supply and the unemployment rate.

APPLICATIONS

MEASURING THE U.S. LABOR SUPPLY & THE UNEMPLOYMENT RATE
Measuring Labor Supply
In the United States, the labor supply is measured through the national unemployment rate. The labor supply and demand rates control local labor markets. As wages increase, businesses seek lower cost alternatives to increasingly more expensive labor. For example, businesses may invest in productivity-enhancing technology and ultimately reduce the number of workers required to do the work. At the same time, as wages increase, workers are drawn into the labor force. The overall quantity or supply of labor is increased. Ultimately, the demand for labor is a decreasing function of wages while the supply of labor is an increasing function of wages.

In a balanced labor system, labor equilibrium and full employment will exist at the intersection of labor supply and demand. For example, all those workers wishing to work at a certain wage will be employed, and labor demand will be met. In most labor markets, labor equilibrium and full employment are rarely achieved. In most local and national labor markets, there are more persons willing to work at the prevailing wage than there are businesses willing or able to hire at the prevailing wage. The unemployment rate refers to the number unemployed as a percentage of the total labor force. The total labor force is the number of unemployed persons in addition to the number of employed persons.

Unemployment

- Economists debate whether or not all labor markets have an inherent or natural rate of unemployment. Unemployed people are generally grouped into three unemployment categories: frictional, cyclical, and structural unemployment.
- Structural unemployment: unemployment caused by changes in technology or the structure of the economy.

On June 1, 2009, General Motors declared bankruptcy. On July 10, 2009, General Motors, backed by the federal government, was allowed back in business under a Chapter 11 reorganization plan. This is GM's headquarters located in Detroit, Michigan. (Courtesy of James Marvin Phelps CC BY 2.0 via Wikimedia Commons)

- Cyclical unemployment: unemployment caused by downturns in the aggregate economy.
- Frictional unemployment: unemployment caused by changing jobs, reentering the job market, or searching for their first job.

Additionally, there is a "shadow" labor supply that the U.S. government refers to as "discouraged" workers because they have stopped actively looking for jobs but claim to want employment. The shadow labor supply increased greatly in the aftermath of the 2008 financial crisis and continued to grow even after the recession ended in 2009. By early 2013, there were approximately 6.7 million discouraged workers—7.5 percent of the non-employed (Davig & Mustre-del-Río, 2013).

Unemployment of all kinds is affected by wages. If the wage rate falls below the much-debated full employment wage rate, the labor supply will diminish. If the wage rate rises above the full employment wage rate, the labor demand will increase. The public and private sectors adjust wages in response to labor supply and demand (Deller, 1999). Unemployment generally impacts the economy negatively by diminishing rates of national productivity and consumption.

A rise in unemployment almost inevitably accompanies economic recession. During the Great Recession of 2007–2009, the United States experienced extensive job losses as even very large companies, such as General Motors, closed or contracted and reduced their workforces. As with the earlier 1980 recession, economic recovery was slow and unemployment remained high. By the end of 2012, the official employment level was 3.6 million below the pre-recession level. Because the labor supply grew during this same period, owing largely to younger adults entering the job market and others returning to it, the U.S. economy needed to add an additional 5.2 million jobs to achieve full employment (Kochan, 2013).

The Bureau of Labor Statistics

he Bureau of Labor Statistics (BLS) of the U.S. Department of Labor collects statistics on the unemployed in the United States. The BLS is the main federal agency in charge of labor economics and statistics. The BLS gathers data relevant to the social and economic conditions of U.S. workers and their families. The BLS announces, on a monthly basis, the total number of employed and unemployed persons in the United States for the preceding month along with the demographic characteristics of all those counted. Unemployment rates are considered vital information to business and industry and, as a result, are generally widely reported in the media.

The Current Population Survey

The government gathers monthly unemployment statistics from a monthly sample survey called the Current Population Survey (CPS). The CPS, which began in 1940 as a Work Projects Administration project, generally samples 60,000 households each

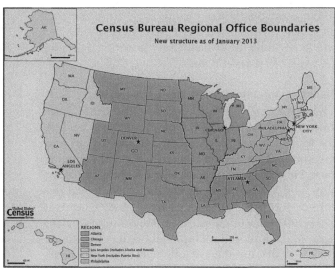

U.S. Census Bureau Regional Office Boundaries. (Courtesy of US Bureau of the Census via Wikimedia Commons)

month from a total of 3,141 counties and 1,973 geographic areas in the United States. Fifteen-hundred Census Bureau employees interview persons by telephone and in person in the 60,000 sample households to gather data on labor force happenings and the non-labor force designation of the members of these households.

Classifications Used in the Current Population Survey (CPS)

The Census Bureau, as part of the CPS, has clear criteria for classifying a person as employed or unemployed. Employed persons are those people who performed any work at all for either pay or profit over the course of the survey week or persons who performed a minimum of 15 hours of unpaid work at a family-operated enterprise. Work includes part-time work, temporary work, and full-time year-round employment. People who are absent from work for any of the following reasons are still considered by the U.S. Census Bureau to be employed: on vacation; ill; experiencing child-care problems; taking care of some other family or personal obligation; on maternity or paternity leave; involved in an industrial dispute; or prevented from working by bad weather. Unemployed persons are all persons who do not have a job; who have not proactively searched for work during the last four weeks; and who are presently available for employment. Employment and unemployment figures include only those persons currently in the labor force. The labor force, as a whole, includes the civilian, non-institutional population aged 16 years and up.

Data Gathered by the U.S. Census Bureau

The employment data gathered by the U.S. Census Bureau, for use by the Bureau of Statistics, include the following: employment status of the civilian non-institutional population 16 years and over by age, sex, race, Hispanic origin, marital status, family relationship, and Vietnam-era veteran status; employed persons by occupation, industry, class of worker, hours of work, full- or part-time status, and reasons for working part time; employed multiple jobholders by occupation, industry, numbers of jobs held, and full- or part-time status of multiple jobs; unemployed persons by occupation, industry, class of worker of last job, duration of unemployment, reason for unemployment, and methods used to find employment; the labor force status of particular subgroups of the population such as women maintaining families, working women with children, displaced workers, and disabled veterans; work experience, occupational mobility, job tenure, educational attainment, and school enrollment of workers; and weekly and hourly earnings by demographic group, occupation, education, union affiliation, and employment status (How the government measures unemployment, 2001, "Where do the statistics come from?")

Use of Data Gathered by the U.S. Census Bureau

The BLS data are used in the following ways: economic indicators; measures of national employment and unemployment; sources of information on employment status and labor force characteristics, developing patterns, and changes; quantifying the possible labor supply; and establishing factors that impact the labor force participation of various demographics. In additional to the labor supply indicator of the monthly unemployment rate, the BLS also releases a labor demand indicator. The BLS, in 1999, developed the Job Openings and Labor Turnover Survey (JOLTS) to evaluate surplus labor demand in the U.S. labor market. The unemployment rate, released every month by the BLS, along with the JOLTS are intended to serve as a marker of labor market activity, overall economic conditions, and labor market supply and demand (Clark & Hyson, 2000).

ISSUES

Labor Supply & Child Labor

The workforce or labor force in most industrialized countries refers to all persons designated as employed or unemployed in the civilian, non-institutional population aged 16 years and up. In many nations, particularly developing nations, the workforce includes extensive child labor. How do nations and global governing organizations solve the problem of child labor? Governments can work to control the labor supply of and labor demand for child workers through the manipulation of wages, regulations, and labor policies. Child labor is an economic problem with an economic solution. Economic problems refer to factors that hinder the functioning and growth of an economy. Economic problems of all kinds, including structural, fiscal, and cultural, impact economic development efforts by national governments, corporations, and international development organizations. Economic development encompasses a wide range of programs and strategies aimed at promoting growth in a part or whole of an economy. Developing countries with limited economies or economies in transition are particularly sensitive to the economic problem of child labor.

International Labor Organization (ILO) Statistics on Worldwide Child Labor

Exploitative child labor, which refers to any economic activity done by a person under the age of fifteen, is a major economic and social problem in developing countries. The International Labor Organization (ILO) estimates that there are roughly 250 million children between the ages of five and fourteen involved in at least part-time labor. The ILO approximates that there are 120 million involved in hazardous and exploitative full-time work. Child labor by region suggests that child labor is a global problem: Asia has 152.5 million child laborers, Africa has 80 million child laborers, and Latin America has 17.5 million child laborers (Palley, 2002). The ILO reports that child labor is used in multiple industries and sectors including agriculture, fishing, forestry, hunting, manufacturing, retail, trade, community and personal services, transport, storage, communications, construction, mining, and quarrying (Tierney, 2000).

Girls and women were the most common employees of the garment industry in Bangladesh. Pictured is a female beneficiary under one of USAID's Global Climate Change (GCC) programs sewing clothes at a training center, as a part of Income Generation Activity. (Courtesy of USAID via Wikimedia Commons)

Addressing Child Labor in Developing Countries

Child labor is deeply connected to the economic life and prosperity of many developing countries. Child labor in developing countries cannot be eradicated without resolving problems that plague developing labor markets. Dysfunctional labor markets and under-development are believed to be key factors that result in the exploitation of child labor in developing regions of the world. The eradication of exploitative child labor practices needs the development and implementation of economic development programs that strengthen the economies of developing countries. International development organizations, national governments, and corporations debate whether voluntary practices or required labor rules should be used to solve the problem of child labor in developing countries. Corporations are increasingly adopting voluntary practices, such as private labeling schemes, as part of corporate social responsibility (CSR) efforts, which let global consumers know that a product has been created without the use of child labor. While voluntary efforts by corporations to use adult labor rather than child labor is a positive step, voluntary practices alone are not believed to be sufficient to eradicate child labor in developing countries. International labor standards, which address the underlying causes of child labor such as labor market dysfunction and under-development, will likely succeed better than voluntary practices alone.

International Labor Organization (ILO) Standards for Reducing Child Labor

The ILO, as described in the 1998 Declaration of Fundamental Principles and Rights at Work, promotes five main international labor standards which, if adopted by developed and developing countries alike, would likely significantly impact the problem of child labor (Palley, 2002):

Freedom of Association: The ILO Freedom of Association and Protection of the Right to Organize Convention (No. 87) establishes the right of workers to form and join organizations, including unions, of their own choosing.

Effective Recognition of the Right to Collective Bargaining: The Right to Organize and Collective Bargaining Convention (No. 98) protects unions from outside interference.

The Elimination of All Forms of Forced or Compulsory Labor: The Forced Labor Convention (No. 29) and the Abolition of Forced Labor Convention (No. 105) require governments to suppress all forms of forced and compulsory labor in their territories.

The Effective Abolition of Child Labor: The Minimum Age Convention (No. 138) sets a baseline minimum working age of fifteen.

The Elimination of Discrimination in Respect of Employment and Occupation: The Discrimination Convention (No. 111) requires governments to establish national policies that eliminate discrimination on the basis of race, color, sex, religion, political opinion, and national origin (Palley, 2002, p.5–6)

Ultimately, a labor market dependent on child labor is out of balance and, unfortunately, self-reinforcing. Labor market conditions in developing countries, characterized by low wages and a large labor pool, provide families with few options for subsistence and survival other than sending their children to work. Basu (1998) argues that to eliminate child labor supply, governments must raise adult wages. Wage changes in developing labor markets will decrease and possibly eliminate the need for child labor. Doran (2013), however, looked at data from a Mexican farm labor experiment and concluded that adult wages rise in response to demand as child labor is removed from the supply. National governments, and global governing organizations, can institute anti-child labor policies as part of an economic effort to restore equilibrium or balance in labor supply and demand. Government changes may include higher wages, new technologies, and active brainstorming and participation of employers, workers, and policymakers (Basu & Van, 2003).

CONCLUSION

In the final analysis, the concept of labor supply is central to microeconomic and macroeconomic theory. Labor supply, which is half of the labor supply and demand model, affects national productivity and economic growth. Economists are increasingly aware that labor supply, and the decision to enter the workforce, is more affected by external variables such as economic need and wage rates than on preference for leisure over consumption. Labor supply can be controlled by the manipulation of wages and the development of labor supply policies that address issues such as child labor and intractable poverty.

BIBLIOGRAPHY

Altman, M. (2001). "A behavioral model of labor supply: Casting some light into the black box of income-leisure choice." *Journal of Socio-Economics, 30,* 199–219.

Bartik, T. (2001). Fighting poverty with labor demand policies. W.E. Upjohn Institute for Employment Research. Retrieved from "http://www.upjohninst. org/publications/newsletter/tjb%5f701.pdf"

Basu, K. (2003). "The economics of child labor." *Scientific American, 289,* 84–91.

Basu, K. & Van, P. (1998). "The economics of child labor." *American Economic Review, 88,* 412–427.

Chang, Y., & Kim, S. (2005). "On the aggregate labor supply." *Economic Quarterly, 91,* 21–37.

Clark, K. & Hyson, R. (2000). Measuring the demand for labor in the United States: The job openings and labor turnover survey. The U.S. Department of Labor. Retrieved from xlink:href="http://www. bls.gov/ore/abstract/st/st000120.htm"

Davig, T., & Mustre-del-Río, J. (2013). "The shadow labor supply and its implications for the unemployment rate." *Economic Review,* 5–29.

Deller, S. (1999). *The wage curve.* University of Wisconsin-Extension Center for Community

Economic Development Community Economics Newsletter. Retrieved from "http://www.aae.wisc. edu/pubs/cenews/docs/ce277.txt"

Doran, K. B. (2013). "How does child labor affect the demand for adult labor?" *Journal of Human Resources, 48,* 702–735

Dustmann, C., Schonberg, U., Stuhler, J. (2017). "Labor supply shocks, native wages, and the adjustment of local employment." *The Quarterly Journal of Economics, 132,* 1, 435-483.

Glossary. (2007). U.S. Department of Labor, Bureau of Statistics. Retrieved from "http://www.bls.gov/ bls/glossary.htm#L"

Grootaert, C. & Kanbur, R. (1995). "Child labour: An economic perspective." *International Labor Review, 134,* 187–203.

How the government measures unemployment. (2001). The U.S. Department of Labor. Retrieved from "http://www.bls.gov/cps/cps%5fhtgm.htm"

Kochan, T. A. (2013). "The American jobs crisis and its implication for the future of employment policy: a call for a new jobs compact." *Industrial & Labor Relations Review, 66,* 291–314.

Palley, T. (2002). "The child labor problem and the need for international labor standards." *Journal of Economic Issues, 36,* 601–615.

Shack-Marquez, J. (1991). "Issues in labor supply." *Federal Reserve Bulletin, 77,* 375–387.

Spencer, D. (2006). "Work for all those who want it? Why the neoclassical labour supply curve is an inappropriate foundation for the theory of employment and unemployment." *Cambridge Journal of Economics, 30,* 459.

SUGGESTED READING

Kogan, I. (2006). "Labor markets and economic incorporation among recent immigrants in Europe." *Social Forces, 85,* 697-721.

Neumark, D., Powers, E., & Zimmermann, K. (2006). "Supplemental security income, labor supply, and migration." *Journal of Population Economics, 19,* 447–479.

Noonan, K., Reichman, N., & Corman, H. (2005). "New fathers' labor supply: Does child health matter?" *Social Science Quarterly (Blackwell Publishing Limited), 86,* 1399–1417.

—*Simone I. Flynn, PhD*

M

MATHEMATICS IN ECONOMICS

ABSTRACT

Economics is the study of how resources are used as well as an analysis of the decisions made in allocating resources and distributing goods and services. Mathematics is the language of numbers and symbols that can be used to logically solve problems and precisely describe size, quantity, and other concepts. Some complex problems could not be described and complicated problems could not be acted upon without the language of mathematics and its support of logical processes to solve problems. Mathematical modeling is used in economic analysis to study existing economic relationships and helps economists study what-if scenarios to see what might happen to the economy if a certain action is applied. Economic concepts and relationships can be measured in mathematical indexes, formulas, and graphs. Several areas of mathematics can be utilized in economic analysis, including linear algebra, calculus, and geometry. Since economic concepts can be complex, it is important to use care in representing data and relationships in isolation. Results can be misinterpreted based on the representation of data.

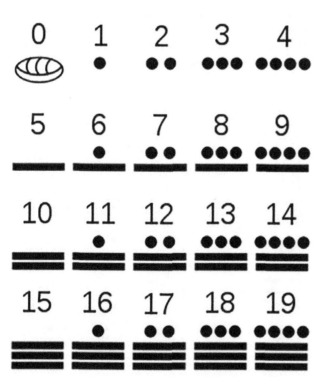

Mayan numerals. (Courtesy of Bryan Derksen CC-BY-SA-3.0 via Wikimedia Commons)

OVERVIEW

Economics

Economics is "the study of how people choose to use resources which can include land, labor, money, equipment, taxes and investments" ("What Is economics?", n.d.). The broad field of economics has many descriptions each trying to discover a way to make clear what the field covers. De Rooy (1995, xiii) states that economics is about people and "…the things they do." Decisions have to be made in life and people are constantly making decisions about resources at the individual, company, and government levels. Gottheil (2007, p.1) describes economics as "an important branch of the social sciences" that is all about resources. This discussion of resources surrounds the fact that resources are limited and people have needs and wants. Scarcity is a term used to explain these limited resources. Typically, resources have to be distributed to people in the form of goods and services. Gottheil notes that resources are limited but the wants of people are not. The three main problems which Gottheil ascribes to economic study are:

- The problems related to scarce resources and unlimited wants of humans;
- The problem of making choices about allocation of resources to produce goods and services;

- The problem of distributing completed goods and services to people.

Gottheil points to distribution of goods and services as a way to understand the economy. Investorwords. com (n.d.) defines economy as "Activities related to the production and distribution of goods and services in a particular geographic region."

Mathematics

Large (2006, p.2.) describes the field of mathematics as "the study of the relationship between size, shape and quantity, using numbers and symbols." These numbers and symbols convey meaning in a clear, concise, and consistent way. Mathematics is a way to explain, explore, decipher, and analyze complex concepts that otherwise might be resistant to synthesis. Math can also demonstrate whether or not a theory is true. The logical process of problem solving using mathematics can give precise answers to complicated, compound and multi-faceted problems.

Mathematics in Economics

Mathematics is helpful in economics because it can help quantify or provide measurement and meaning to economic concepts. Mathematics also plays a large role in the area of economic analysis. Economics uses modeling to describe certain states of being and to analyze economic scenarios. Modeling suggests what will happen if certain actions are taken. Simulation of real-world situations is possible with economic analysis and modeling and would not be possible without mathematics. Barnett, Ziegler & Byleen (2008, p. 210) describe mathematical modeling as "the process of using mathematics to solve real-world problems." The authors further break mathematical modeling into three steps:

- Constructing the model. This step provides the basis for understanding the problem or question being asked. Once an answer is given to a question asked by the model, it can be used to apply the information learned to a real-world problem.
- Solving the mathematical model.
- Interpreting the solution to the mathematical model in the context of the real-world problem that needs to be solved.

These steps are repeated over and over again as long as information is needed to solve the real-world

problem. Gottheil notes that modeling in economics helps "to understand cause-and-effect relationships in the economy." Lim (2001, p.2) calls mathematics "a useful tool for the analysis of all economic problems" and says it is "practically indispensable for many." Lim lists the following mathematical concepts as important to economics:

- Calculus;
- Linear algebra;
- Differential equations.

Micro- & Macroeconomics

There are sub-branches of economics. Two important ones are microeconomics and macroeconomics. Each branch covers different types of decisions. Microeconomics is the study of economic relationships and decisions of the individual. Macroeconomics looks at the economy as a whole. Economists utilize models to analyze both micro- and macroeconomics using supply and demand as the foundation (Baumol & Blinder, 2001). "Supply and demand are the most fundamental tools of economic analysis" (McAfee, p. 14). Macroeconomics looks at measures that affect the whole economy including inflation, unemployment, Gross Domestic Product, and prices. Aggregate demand and supply are macroeconomic measures that provide "a way

Circulation in Macroeconomics

Circulation in macroeconomics. (Courtesy of Beyond silence /svg by LadyofHats via Wikimedia Commons)

of illustrating macroeconomic relationships and the effects of government policy changes" (Riley, 2006). Every part of the economy has an interrelationship with other parts of the economy. As an example, if the population increases, the demand for certain goods will increase. Similarly, as goods become obsolete, demand will decrease. Various economic measures are represented as mathematical variables. Mathematics is a way to track variables under consideration and to model changes in variables.

Mathematics in Practice

Math can be used in economics in many ways. For example, Cooper (2009) discusses the importance of an increase in housing starts and draws a direct relationship between the decline in homebuilding and the sluggish and declining financial markets. At the current rate of decline, housing starts will fall to zero by November of 2009. In an additional example, Magner (2000, para. 2.) discusses Markus Mobius, a Harvard economics professor, who used his skills in mathematics and economics to study social problems. In his thesis, Mobius "used economic theory to explore the formation of ghettos." Mobius found that economics was inconsistent since it relied on human behavior, but purported that mathematics can compensate for these changes and variations. Mobius's strength in math helped him to become an excellent economist. Successful economists are those able to master economic concepts and mathematics at the same time (Magner).

Chicago ghetto on the South Side in May of 1974. (Courtesy of John H. White via Wikimedia Commons)

Donald Trump speaking at a rally in Fountain Hills, Arizona, on March 19, 2016. During the presidential campaign he often referred to global warming as a "hoax" and that it was "created by and for the Chinese in order to make U.S. manufacturing non-competitive." (Courtesy of Gage Skidmore CC BY-SA 3.0 via Wikimedia Commons)

Math's Limits

Scrubbing the Skies (2009) looks at a traditional problem of costs in attempting to reduce carbon emissions from global warming. Interestingly enough, part of the economic problem in this case is the politics involved in getting action on carbon-dioxide reductions. Politics is inextricably related to economics because economics is tied to behavior, and politics influences behavior. Math helps us measure, monitor, and predict behaviors but cannot help to completely overcome political issues. Many industries and powerful companies may be reluctant to make costly changes to comply with tougher carbon emission regulations and there may be little 'political will' to force anyone's hand. Powerful companies can afford lobbyists to forestall change efforts and have the wherewithal to persuade politicians to adopt a position since many will need campaign contributions to remain in office. McAfee (p.7) calls the controlling interest of politics in government "political economy" or "the study of allocation by politics."

Economic Literacy

Many people and groups care about economics including governments and economists. However, economics affects individuals as well. De Rooy introduces a concept called economic literacy in which an individual understands the economic environment and how the environment affects the individual. Some people may be frightened away from economic data because of mathematics. Economically literate people can interpret how economic metrics and news affects them and what economic relationships will create a successful environment for them as individuals. As a result, economically literate people will be interested in when conditions signal a recession or when prices rise along with unemployment, for example. Individuals might care about inflation because purchasing power declines with rising inflation. All of these economic concepts are represented in mathematical terms.

Economic Concepts & Measures

Mathematics can help in visualizing and quantifying economic concepts. Formulas and graphs can be used to describe and display such concepts. Mathematics is also a way to deal with uncertainty in a problem. Many economic terms can be represented mathematically. The terms are used to describe values and behaviors concerning supply and demand, the U.S. economy, producer and consumer theory, imperfections in the market, and strategic behavior. The national economy is very complex, so it is impossible for one single number or measure to accurately represent it whether as snapshot in time or over a period of time (De Rooy).

Mathematics in Price & Cost Measurements

Mathematics can be used to show relative size or whether something is high or low or large or small. A basic economics concept related to scarcity of resources is price or cost. Price is "the exchange of goods and services for money" (McAfee, 2006, p.7). However, the true cost or opportunity cost is based on what must be given up or what cannot be purchased because funds are allocated elsewhere. McAfee (p.9) calls opportunity cost "the value of the best foregone alternative." Price-related economic measures include the consumer price index (CPI) and personal consumption expenditures (PCE). Both CPI and PCE are indexes. An index is "a number or ratio (a value on a scale of measurement) derived from a series of observed facts; and can reveal relative changes as a function of time" (WordNet). Baumol and Blinder (p.522) define index as a number that "expresses the cost of a market basket of goods relative to its cost in some base period." The CPI is weighted over several years while the PCE compares the current period to the preceding period. CPI and PCE

play "important roles... in guiding economic policy" (McCully, Moyer, & Stewart, p. 26). De Rooy (p.100) says prices "are at the center of a market economy because they make things happen." Price levels and changes directly impact the economy.

Econometrics

Economics has grown because of the ability to use statistical models on 50+ years of data to "test the accuracy of economic models." Econometrics is the name used for the sub-branch of economics using "statistical methods to analyze economic data" (Gottheil, p.1). An application of statistics can be seen in the measurement of inflation ("the overall general upward price movement of goods and services in an economy"). A few of the indexes that are used by the Bureau of Labor Statistics(BLS) (2008) to look at different components of inflation are:

- Consumer Price Index: "Produces monthly data on changes in the prices paid by urban consumers for a representative basket of goods and services." Two categories of consumer are measured: urban consumers, and urban wage earners and clerical workers.
- Producer Price Indexes: Measures "changes in the selling prices received by domestic producers of goods and services."
- Import and Export Prices: Measures non-military trade to and from the United States.
- Employment Cost Trends: Changes in employment and compensation costs over time.

Gross Domestic Product

The U.S. Department of Commerce has a Bureau of Economic Analysis (BEA). The BEA tracks major economic trends and makes available current information about the U.S. economy. One of the measures tracked by the BEA is Gross Domestic Product (GDP). GDP is the "broadest measure of the economic activity that goes on in the nation during the year" (De Rooy, p. 3). GDP is also described as the total market value of final goods and services produced in a year. Final goods are those that reach the end-user and are not components in other products. Mathematically, GDP reports are made in percentages and typically describe either an increase or decrease in GDP. Reports will also indicate where the changes are coming from; for example, a decrease due to a decline in software.

Demographic Information

Many of the statistics that reflect information about the United States and its economy have to do with people. Tracked demographic information includes the number of people, ethnicity, gender, education, place of habitation, household type, earnings, and spending. Statistics regarding production are also gathered. McAfee (p. 62) gives an example of the mathematical formula for production:

$$Y = C + I + G$$
$$WY = \text{Income}$$
$$C = \text{Consumption}$$
$$I = \text{Investment and}$$
$$G = \text{Government}$$

The formula shows how income is divided based on what we spend, save, or give to the government.

ECONOMIC ANALYSIS

Government Analysis

TA country or government might want to track and analyze information related to the national or regional economy for many reasons. Analysis can determine the general health of the economy and highlight trends of growth or decline. Economic analysis is "analysis that is undertaken using economic values, reflecting the values that society would be willing to pay for a good or service" (European Union funds, n.d.). Economies are driven by the production of goods and services.

The Food and Agriculture Organization of the United Nations describes economic analysis as "...a way of looking at the worth of a development from the viewpoint of the whole economy, i.e. the general public interest or public good. These costs are adjusted to account for any distortions, such as subsidies, taxes and transfer payments."

It is the responsibility of a government to work for the common good. Governments analyze the economy to determine how fiscal policy might impact the growth and health of the economy.

Individual & Company Analysis

Individuals and companies can engage in economic analysis as well. McAfee gives the example of a company, British Petroleum, engaging in economic

The Deepwater Horizon oil spill in the Gulf of Mexico on April 20, 2010, brought British Petroleum into the news worldwide for reasons other than their economic analysis capabilities. Here platform supply vessels battle the blazing remnants of the off shore oil rig Deepwater Horizon. A Coast Guard MH-65C dolphin rescue helicopter and crew document the fire aboard the mobile offshore drilling unit Deepwater Horizon, while searching for survivors. Multiple Coast Guard helicopters, planes and cutters responded to rescue the Deepwater Horizon's 126 person crew. (Courtesy of United States Coast Guard via Wikimedia Commons)

analysis by using a demand model that estimates the demand of oil refineries and individual gasoline consumers. The anticipated demand from both refineries and customers impact the decisions British Petroleum makes. "Stock market analysts use economic models" to predict stock prices and company profits while governments use modeling to forecast budget deficits. Changes in "laws, rules and other government intervention in markets" can be suggested by economic analysis (McAfee, p. 8).

Mathematical Graphing

Mathematical graphing can be used in economic analysis to represent economic concepts and measures. Baumol and Blinder (p. 18) note "Economic graphs are invaluable because they can display a large quantity of data quickly and because they facilitate data interpretation and analysis." The authors continue to note that it would not be possible to take a lot of information and immediately see the relationships in the data without graphs. But, they also warn against graphs that are poorly constructed that can lead to confusion and misinterpretation. Baumol and Blinder (p.18) use an example of a misleading graph of exploding unemployment between 1990 and 1992 possibly indicating a collapse of the U.S. economy that showed only partial information. Baumol and Blinder caution against the overexposure of a single metric or isolated statistics in this way, something they decry as common in print media.

McAfee states that economic analysis serves two purposes: positive analysis and normative analysis. Positive analysis evaluates existing economic relationships (Gottheil). McAfee (p.8) calls positive analysis the "scientific understanding of how allocation of... scarce resources" is decided. Normative analysis is "the study of what ought to be in the economy" (Gottheil, p.1). A central figure or star in economic analysis modeling is *homo economicus*—representing people acting in their own self-interest. An assumption when examining the behavior of people such as consumers is that they always make decisions based on what is in their own self-interest. In an economy, everyone demonstrates "maximizing behavior" as in companies wanting to maximize prices and consumers wanting to maximize value (McAfee).

VIEWPOINT

A Look at the Current Economic Crisis

Economic analysis is a "systematic approach to determining the optimum use of scarce resources..." Mathematics can support this process but cannot achieve an ideal result. Nor can mathematics overcome the influence of politics on an issue. A good example of this is the economic stimulus efforts in the United States and other countries attempting to resolve the global economic crisis. There are many disagreements as to what the appropriate action should be for government, financial institutions, and other private sector companies. Coy (2009) examined the varying views of economists on whether or not government intervention helps, hurts, or is necessary. Although everyone may have access to the same information, it may not be interpreted the same way. "Is the economy in a dangerous downward spiral, or is this a painful but ultimately healthy adjustment leading to a sustainable growth path?" (Coy, para.1). Misdiagnosing the situation could be a significant problem just as overreacting might increase the problem. Mathematics can help quantify the problem but can only be used as one tool in the decision-making process. Similarly, the economic problems have trickled down to the individual who may be facing foreclosure on a home or

job loss. Economic analysis can describe the situation for the individual and model alternatives but cannot assure the success of any particular path.

In early 2008, the federal government passed the Economic Stimulus Act of 2008, which provided tax rebates in an effort to stimulate the economy. Experts are divided on the benefit of the act. Later in 2008, the U.S. Senate approved a government rescue plan called the Emergency Economic Stabilization Act that has a provision called TARP—Troubled Asset Relief Program. The economy had suffered due to an overabundance of risky mortgage loans. TARP is considered to be a tool the government can use to repair the economy through support for financial institutions. TARP allows the federal government to purchase up to $700 billion in troubled assets as relief to financial institutions. In 2009, a second bailout or stimulus bill was passed. The American Recovery and Reinvestment Act of 2009 is a $789 billion compilation of tax cuts, additional federal spending and bolstering of social programs. Stimulus packages are controversial because the added spending will increase the national debt since the government is borrowing or creating money that does not exist. Stimulus packages are also controversial because they usually contain provisions that some see as unnecessary but were politically necessary to get votes to pass the bill. Mandel (2009) suggests that education and health have to be the focus of any economic stimulus because he views them as the most needed items that provide the best results. Mandel criticizes prior efforts to give money directly to people or banks because he does not feel that has stimulated the economy in the way funding for health and education would. McGregor (2009) reports on the companies grabbing stimulus work opportunities as private sector ones dry up. The downside is being under government control and rules. Davis (2009) also warns against accepting government support that could lead to a loss of autonomy in a business.

While money does not solve every problem, it can help. Garber (2009) reports that the Department of Energy's Energy Information Administration (EIA) is struggling because of funding. EIA is falling short because of an inability to provide up-to-date and accurate statistics about energy production, usage, and availability. In addition to stimulus money allocated for energy, EIA is seeking an increase in federal budget allocations.

The current economic stimulus plan may be a plan that does not add up. The global economic crisis puts countries like the United States in an untenable position. Something has to be done. Since the economy has so many interrelated parts, impact in one part of the economy creates a ripple effect in another part of the economy. If people are unemployed, they will spend less, if they spend less, business will sell fewer items and have to lay off people, and the cycle continues. Many areas of the economy are showing decline and the U.S. government has a responsibility to not allow the economy to fail. Countries holding U.S. debt are requesting assurances that they will be paid while they deal with their own economic problems.

Mathematics can measure the debt and count the size of the stimulus package. It can help create impressive graphs that map economic relationships, revenues, output, and spending. It can support arguments on both sides with economic analysis and models. However, mathematics cannot guarantee that the funds will reach the intended targets with the intended results.

BIBLIOGRAPHY

Barnett, R.A., Ziegler, M.R., & Byleen, K.E. (2008). *College algebra (8th ed.).* Boston: McGraw-Hill.

Baumol, W. J. & Blinder, A. S. (2001). *Economics: principles and policy (8th ed.).* Orlando: Harcourt, Inc.

Congressional Budget Office. (2009). A preliminary analysis of the President's budget and an update of CBO's budget and economic outlook. Retrieved from xlink:href="http://www.cbo.gov/ftpdocs/100xx/doc10014/03-20-President-Budget.pdf"

Cooper, J.C. (2009). "Job one: build a floor under housing." *BusinessWeek,* (4122), 10.

Coy, P. (2009). "A dogfight over the rescue plan." *BusinessWeek,* (4124), 18–19.

Davis, K.L. (2009, March 24). "Warning to executives: Prepare for business regulation crackdown."` *The Journal Record.*

De Rooy, J. (1995). *Economic literacy: What everyone needs to know about money and markets.* New York: Three Rivers Press.

Economic analysis [definition]. (2009). Retrieved from BusinessDictionary.com xlink:href="http://www.businessdictionary.com/definition/economic-analysis.html"

European Union funds. (n.d.). *Glossary.* Retrieved from xlink:href="http://www.strukturalni-fondy.cz/csf%5fCD/documents/2%5fManagMonit/"

FAO Corporate Document Repository. (n.d.). *Glossary.* Retrieved from xlink:href="http://www.fao.org/DOCREP/006/Y4851E/y4851e0f.htm"

Garber, K. (2009). "The trouble with numbers." *U.S. News & World Report, 146,* 40.

Gottheil, F. (2007). *Study guide to accompany principles of economics.* Mason, OH: Thomson Custom Solutions.

Economy. (2009). Retrieved from Investorwords.com. xlink:href="http://www.investorwords.com/1652/economy.html"

Index [definition]. (n.d.). Retrieved from WordNet Database xlink:href="http://wordnetweb.princeton.edu/perl/webwn?s=index"

Large, T. (2006). *The Usborne illustrated dictionary of math.* London: Usborne Publishing Ltd.

Lim, C.P. (2001). "The art of using an economics hypermedia learning package." *Educational Media International, 38*(2/3), 183–197.

Magner, D. (2000). "Social deconstructor: Using math and economics to explore real-world problems." *Chronicle of Higher Education, 47,* A16.

Mandel, M. (2009). "The two best cures for the economy." *BusinessWeek,* (4124), 23.

McAfee, R.P. (2006). *Introduction to economic analysis.* Retrieved from xlink:href="http://www.mcafee.cc/Introecon/IEA.pdf"

McCully, C.P., Moyer, B.C., & Stewart, K.J. (2007). "Comparing the consumer price index and the personal consumption expenditures price index." *Survey of Current Business, 87,* 26–33.

McGregor, J., Boyle, M. & Burrows, P. (2009). "Your new customer: the State." *BusinessWeek,* (4124), 66.

Miller, L., & Bertus, M. (2013). "An exposition on the mathematics and economics of option pricing." *Business Education & Accreditation, 5,* 1-16.

Palasca, S. (2013). "Mathematics in economics. A perspective on necessity and sufficiency." *Theoretical & Applied Economics, 20,* 127–144.

Pear, R., Phillips, K., & Zelaney, J. (2009, February 11). "Deal reached in Congress on $789 billion dtimulus plan." *New York Times.* Retrieved xlink:href="http://www.nytimes.com/2009/02/12/us/politics/"

Riley, G. (2006). *AS macroeconomics / international economy.* Retrieved from xlink:href="http://tutor2u.net/economics/revision-notes/"

Rogers, J.E. & Haney, B.F. (2000). *Mathematics of business.* Upper Saddle River, NJ: Prentice-Hall.

Sarukkai, S. (2011). "Complexity and randomness in mathematics: philosophical reflections on the relevance for economic modelling." *Journal of Economic Surveys, 25,* 464–480.

Scrubbing the skies. (2009). *The Economist, 390*(8621), 22–24.

U.S. Department of Commerce, Bureau of Economic Analysis. (n.d.) *U.S. economic accounts.* Retrieved from xlink:href="http://www.bea.gov/"

U.S. Department of Labor, Bureau of Labor Statistics. (2008). *Overview of BLS statistics on inflation and prices.* Retrieved from xlink:href="http://www.bls.gov/bls/inflation.htm"

U.S. Department of Treasury. (2009). *Emergency Economic Stabilization Act.* Retrieved from xlink:href="http://www.ustreas.gov/initiatives/eesa/"

"What is economics?" (n.d.). *Undergraduate economics.* Retrieved from Vanderbilt University xlink:href="http://www.vanderbilt.edu/AEA/students/WhatIsEconomics.htm"

SUGGESTED READING

Aastveit, K.A. & Trovik, T. (2008). "Estimating the output gab in real time: A factor model approach." *Norges Bank: Working Papers,* (23/24), 2–4.

Gotibovski, C. & Kahana, N. (2009). "Second-degree price discrimination: A graphical and mathematical approach." *Journal of Economic Education, 40,* 68–79.

Hrygorkyv, V.S. (2009). "Some approaches to modeling prices in an ecological-economic system." *Cybernetics & Systems Analysis, 45,* 1–7.

Pippenger, J. (2008). "Freely floating exchange rates do not systematically overshoot." *Journal of International Finance & Economics, 8,* 37–56.

Sohel Azad, A.S.M. (2009). "Efficiency, cointegration and contagion in equity markets: Evidence from China, Japan and South Korea." *Asian Economic Journal, 23,* 93-118.

—Marlanda English, PhD

MICROECONOMIC THEORY

ABSTRACT

Microeconomic theory prepares individuals for analyzing demand, supply, and equilibrium under certain assumptions. A study of economic theory involves recognizing explicit forms of assumptions and elevating our sensitivity to other assumptions encountered in our daily pursuits at work, play, and/or study. Far beyond the simplicities afforded by assumptions, however, are the Law of Demand and the Law of Supply. As the reader of this essay will see, both laws inform us of a specific relationship between price and quantity. More importantly, supply and demand when taken together help describe equilibrium and portray the dynamics between equilibrium price and quantity. This essay attempts to convey a vast array of concepts, models, and views that undergraduate students will encounter in a study of microeconomics. The essay also recognizes some obstacles to learning that students are likely to encounter during their studies of the discipline.

OVERVIEW

Microeconomic theory provides a conceptual foundation for analyzing demand, supply, and equilibrium in addition to other interrelated topics. Let us begin with a brief overview of how those concepts fit together from within an overarching theoretical framework. Consider first that theory is a mental abstraction consisting of a set of principles, methods, and models. In general, those models of economic theory and behavior contain an array of variables and interrelationships. In essence, variables and relationships set forth by a theory help us to simplify reality by breaking it down into manageable pieces and by subscribing to some key underlying assumptions.

A discussion of assumptions will follow in the section ahead. Models present us with a framework for organizing key pieces of information. Keep in mind that a model, moreover, is a tool that enables us to simplify reality and to summarize key hypotheses and relationships. Theories provide a basis with which to formulate those hypotheses. By nature, hypotheses convey information about what we can expect to observe in terms of how one or more variables relate to a key variable in accordance with theory. Scientists and researchers use theories and test hypotheses in order to generate knowledge and information from a limited amount of data. Some hypothesized relationships become truths after a long period of confirmation and/or of acceptance by a profession; eventually, they become laws. Two laws central to the study of microeconomic theory are the Law of Supply and the Law of Demand, which will receive ample attention in the text ahead.

Textbooks also devote a considerable amount of content to these two laws, expanding them into several hundred pages on demand and supply. Readers of this essay will find references to economics textbooks for which the essay author is most familiar (Arnold, 2005; Guell, 2009; McConnell & Brue, 2008) given their use in introductory courses. The reader of this essay may find benefit in knowing that the first eight or so chapters of most principles of economics textbooks provide a firm foundation for the study the economic theory. Specifically, *Issues in Economics Today*, the text book authored by Guell, is a valuable resource to any introductory level course in economics; particularly those courses designated for the non-business major or individuals in the major exploration phase of their academic pursuits.

Guell (2009) defines microeconomics as "[t]hat part of the discipline of economics that deals with individual markets and firms." This essay, which takes the form of a scholarly application and integration of theory, extends that definition and describes how individuals and firms create and interact in markets. Consider another yet deeper, perhaps more salient description of microeconomics, as found in Pearce (1992, pp. 276–277). According to Pearce, the term microeconomics is engaged to "describe those parts of economic analysis whose concern is the behaviour of individual units, in particular, consumers and firms" and that analysis "of individual behaviour concentrates on consumer demand theory" and "analysis of firm behaviour concentrates on production decisions and price theory." In other words, theories of consumer demand and prices coupled with analyses of individual and firm behavior comprise microeconomic theory.

The reader should have a sense by now that consumers and firms are two groups about which we can offer some generalizations. Microeconomic theory comprises a theory on consumers and a theory on firms from which we can simplify reality and deal with most of its complexities. In addition, the reader should be mindful that economic models consist of three highly interactive components: Consumers, businesses, and markets. The next section begins with a set of assumptions that are necessary in covering and learning economics.

APPLICATION

ASSUMPTIONS
Ceteris Paribus
Assumptions are sometimes implicit and at other times are explicit; elevating sensitivity to either form is beneficial in a life of work, play, and study. A number of assumptions are applicable to an in-depth study of economics. Foremost among those three assumptions is the *ceteris paribus* assumption. Its literal translation from Latin into English means "all else is held constant." Anyone examining economics will discover that a wide array of relationships exists, which makes it necessary to consider as few as possible.

Rational Actors
Next is the assumption in microeconomic theory that individuals (primarily consumers and producers) behave rationally and choose to maximize their own self-interest. As strange as this may sound, those behaviors and choices serve a major function in the betterment of society according to an economics perspective. This second assumption means that consumers and producers have full and immediate access to perfect information relevant to their decisions.

Collective Implications
A third assumption is that those agents engage in transactions through which no individual or group brings an inordinate amount of influence to an exchange decision. In essence, this assumption carries the notion that an exchange between a buyer and a seller yields benefits and/or costs to them whereby third parties incur the same set of benefits and/or costs. Actions of individuals can affect the larger society whether in a good or a bad manner; for the sake of brevity, this author invites those who want to learn more about that societal dimension to explore topics

such as welfare economics and macroeconomics by considering the entries found in the suggested readings list near the end of this essay.

The Economic Problem

The aforementioned assumptions enable us to study economics and recognize some key tenets of an economic perspective on the world with which we interact. Economics is all about scarcity. In terms of our own behaviors, most of us truly have unlimited wants and face limited resources. Our attempt to reconcile between those wants and resources gives rise to a major problem: The economic problem. A reason for studying economics is to alleviate that problem.

Opportunity Cost

Scarcity forces us to make choices, and each decision presents us with a trade-off or an opportunity cost. We can measure the value of our decisions in terms of the value of the forgone alternative. For example, the opportunity cost of reading this essay is the value you place on whatever it is that you might prefer to be doing when it is the next best alternative to reading this essay. Economic valuations of opportunity costs help consumers decide how to allocate scarce resources (time, money, etc.). Likewise, business owners and entrepreneurs usually have a minimum profit rate in mind for the enterprise they operate, which typically coincides with that for the industry in question. If the actual profit rate fails to meet expectations, those operators can choose another industry where they can pursue whatever may be considered a normal rate of profit.

Price

By extension, the costs of conducting business include the normal rate of profit. This means that an enterprise must receive a price for its goods and services that covers profit and explicit costs. Price needs to become an agreement between a seller and a buyer of those goods and services. The seller or supplier will provide some amount at each price within a given range of prices, and the buyer or consumer will purchase some amount at each price within a given range. In essence, price is a mechanism that is said to clear the market because buyers and sellers arrive at a price that is agreeable between them.

Let us begin with the demand or consumer side of the situation. This article and many economists subscribe to the view that a good or service becomes available because of consumer demand. In brief, suppliers provide and offer goods and services, but the consumer ultimately decides whether to pay the asking price. The next two sections describe the relationships between prices and quantities beginning with the demand side and ending with the supply side.

DEMAND

The Law of Demand

The Law of Demand informs us that an inverse or negative relationship exists between price and quantity demanded. In other words, consumers demand less (more) of a good or service when its price rises (falls). Individual demand schedules are estimates of how many units of that good or service a specific consumer is willing and able to purchase over a period at a given price. On a graph, price is plotted on the vertical axis and quantity on the horizontal axis. In addition, a change in price corresponds with a change in quantity demanded. Note that a change in demand is movement along the demand curve.

Willingness & Ability to Pay

In terms of whether there is an increase or a decrease in demand and a corresponding shift in the demand curve, keep in mind that willingness and ability to pay the price are key considerations. The hypothetical amount of benefit or utility that originates from a quantity creates a willingness on the part of a consumer to buy; discussion of utility is forthcoming. Likewise, income level translates into a consumer's ability to pay the price. As one considers various price-quantity combinations comprising a demand schedule, willingness and ability run through the set of five factors. Furthermore, it is important to keep in mind that we hold constant willingness and ability to pay and several related factors unless specific information suggests otherwise.

Determinants of Demand

Known as determinants, a change in one or more of five factors will influence whether a consumer wants greater or smaller amounts of units at any given price. The difference between a change in demand and a change in quantity demanded bears worth repeating because it is a major stumbling block that is common amongst students in introductory economics courses. The five factors or determinants that shift a demand curve are as follows: the number of buyers; the prices of related goods; consumer income; consumer expectations; and consumer tastes and preferences. It is worthwhile here to summarize each item in that list of five.

- First, population size determines the number of buyers.
- Second, goods for which quantities demanded change when the price of another good changes or when incomes change are considered related goods; for example, one can really compare apples and oranges in terms of the effect of relative prices on the quantities demanded of fruit.
- Third, a change in consumer income can directly influence the purchase quantity at any given price.
- Fourth, consumer expectations, perspectives, or views about the present or future economic situation will influence whether they make a purchase or postpone it.
- Last, consumer tastes and preferences determine popularity of a good or service; all the variations in today's caffeinated beverages serve as one example.

Before entering a discussion of utility for which consumer preferences and willingness to pay are foundational, brief coverage of how individual-level demand translates into market-level demand is necessary. Taking into account the aforementioned set of factors, an individual consumer will have a demand schedule that illustrates the various price and quantity combinations for any good or service under consideration. Furthermore, those individual schedules are brought together to construct the market demand for a specific good or service. This entails aggregating the quantities in those individual-level demand schedules or curves, which again correspond with prices, for all consumers in the market for a specific good or service. Economists refer to that process as horizontal summation across demand schedules. Now that we understand the mechanics in constructing market-demand schedules from individual schedules and the five factors in shifting the demand curve, our attention shifts to a few more details represented by a demand curve.

Theory of Consumer Choice & Behavior

Incomes, budgets, prices, quantity, and utility woven together are the essential ingredients in a demand recipe. First steps in the process require a draw from many of the basics introduced above. Let us start by acknowledging consumer tastes and preferences as a factor that tends to forge market trends; the want of diversity in caffeinated beverage consumption, for instance. It is important to note that a difference exists between wants and needs; food, clothing, and shelter are the most basic needs and are readily identifiable.

Two questions for which answers, aside from being elusive, will likely vary among individuals: What is it that you want? How much of it is enough? When, where, and why do you want whatever it may be? Satisfaction from having the good or service is a plausible answer to the why question, but all the other questions and more remain. In the study and the practice of economics, an attempt to resolve the problems stems from these questions and from unlimited wants and limited or scarce resources.

Consumer Equilibrium

Consumers must make choices in the context of those wants and resources. Preferences suggest what the consumer wants to do, with income going only so far within that set of choices. Budget constraints suggest what is affordable. Crude economic rationality reminds us that we strive to maximize benefits subject to the budget constraint. In other words, as economic agents, consumers do the best with what they have at any given moment; arrival at consumer equilibrium is imminent.

Consumer equilibrium is a point at which consumers achieve the greatest benefit in the face of current budget constraint. The underlying assumption is that more is better than less whether concerning an income level and/or a physical quantity. Consumers can get more of something with higher incomes and more of that something translates into greater satisfaction levels in an absolute sense.

Marginal Utility

Total satisfaction increases to certain level that corresponds with each unit consumers are able and willing to attain. However, it is necessary to depart from examining the total amount by taking into consideration the incremental amount of a change in that total. At issue is the precise change in an amount of satisfaction that results from consuming one more physical unit; note that economists use satisfaction and utility interchangeably. Marginal utility is the

Pizza is universally loved. Here the White House staff join a pizza tasting gathering on April 10, 2009, in the Roosevelt Room at the White House. (Courtesy of Pete Souza, White House, via Wikimedia Commons)

change in utility that comes from consuming one more unit.

Consider a favorite beverage or food item. Maybe it is pizza. That first slice of pizza tastes so good, the second almost as fine, and the third or fourth or fifth is probably a little less satisfying than the previous slices. Somewhere along the way in consuming that pizza, the consumer is likely to encounter regrets; eat one slice too many. At that point of saturation, economists report that marginal utility drops to zero. Before then, however, marginal utility increases but at a decreasing rate. That is the Law of Diminishing Marginal Utility in operation, upfront and real. Perhaps we have reached the saturation point regarding the demand side of microeconomic theory, its laws, and now we find ourselves with a thirst for knowledge on the other side of that theory. The next section of this essay summarizes laws and key relationships relevant to supply.

Supply

The Law of Supply dictates that a direct or positive relationship exists between price and quantity supplied. In other words, producers supply less (more) of good or service when its price falls (rises). Supply schedules are estimates of how many units of that good or service a specific producer is willing and able to supply over a period at a given price. As is the case with demand, a graph of that schedule plots price on the vertical axis and quantity on the horizontal axis. Likewise, changes in quantity supplied are movements along the supply curve.

Willingness and ability also influence whether there is an increase or decrease in supply and a corresponding shift in the supply curve. In this instance, willingness to supply given quantities at a given price is a function of the expected level of profit and ability to supply is a function of costs. Furthermore, five factors or determinants can influence the price-quantity combinations comprising a supply schedule:

The number of sellers;

- The prices of resources or inputs;
- Productivity;
- Technological state;
- Expected future price of product.

Profit levels typically determine the number of sellers in a market. When those actual levels rise above (fall below) the normal level, new firms will enter (exit) the market thus increasing (decreasing) the supply of that good or service. One will notice openings of new stores or retail outlets in a geographic area when profit exceeds the normal level; caffeinated beverages are illustrative again. An increase (decrease) in the price of raw inputs such as wages for labor will raise (lower) the costs of doing business thereby prompting a decrease (increase) in supply. Productivity represents the amount of output that a worker can provide in any given work day or eight-hour period. An increase (decrease) in productivity will result in an increase (decrease) in supply. The amount and/or state of technology also influences the supply curve and worker productivity. State-of-the-art machines, computers, and so forth will boost worker productivity and company output levels; antiquated, obsolete, and worn-out technology detracts from output and productivity. Producer pessimism and optimism come to bear on the supply level as well. When business leaders expect prices to rise (fall), they will take actions to increase (decrease) current supply levels thereby indirectly effecting unemployment levels.

Taking into consideration all those determinants, readers need to know there is a point at which businesses will cease or continue. To be a viable operating entity, a business must be able to cover payroll and make payments on its buildings and equipment. It will shut down if prices are too low to cover payroll. Consequently, the market supply curve is an aggregation of individual supply schedules, but only for those quantities corresponding with prices higher than the level of insolvency; again, production will cease when price fails to cover payroll costs. For the sake of brevity, this author needs to refer students and other interested parties to textbooks for detailed coverage of several cost types (as well as their mathematical and graphical natures) and of revenues. Speaking in terms of basic theory, when price is above the level of business failure, horizontal summation applies just as it does on the demand side of a market. The essay will now shift attention to microeconomic theory.

Market Equilibrium

This section brings together supply and demand for an initial brief description of equilibrium and a subsequent portrayal of changes in equilibrium price and quantity; the latter requires a change in demand and/or supply. The supply and demand model is an essential component in economics, especially in economic systems driven by capitalistic market forces.

A market in this context is a place in which consumers and producers come together to exchange a specific good or service; the market for caffeinated drinks, for instance. The supply curve intersects the demand curve creating a market equilibrium point. The market price is what economists refer to as "clearing the market," which means buyers and sellers agree to exchange dollars and quantities. The quantity associated with that market or equilibrium price is the equilibrium quantity. Recall the five determinants of demand and of supply; we are holding them constant for the moment by assumption.

For sake of examination, let us relax the *ceteris paribus* assumption and imagine that consumers become more optimistic about the future status of our nation's economy. In essence, they become more willing to purchase more at prevailing prices. This results in an increase, or a rightward shift in demand. Consequently, equilibrium price and equilibrium quantity arrive at a level higher than the previous level.

A sketch of this increase in demand would result in a graph or model featuring a new demand curve, parallel to the old curve that intersects the supply curve at a higher point. By altering any one determinant at a time, it would be possible to view the changes of graphic results in comparison to those above.

Microeconomics covers a lot of ground given its focus on markets and the integral roles of producers, consumers, and organizations. This essay attempts to convey a vast array of concepts, models, and views that undergraduate students will encounter in a study of microeconomics.

BIBLIOGRAPHY

Arnold, Roger A. (2005). *Economics* (7th ed.) Mason, OH: Thomson South-Western.

Astroza, S., Pinjari, A., Bhat, C., Jara-Diaz, S. (2017). "A microeconomics theory-based latent class multiple discrete-continuous choice model of time use and goods consumption." *Transportation Research Record, 2664.*

Caballero, R.J., Cowan, K.N., Engel, E.A., & Micco, A. (2013). "Effective labor regulation and microeconomic flexibility." *Journal of Development Economics,* 10192–104.

Guell, R.C. (2009). *Issues in economics today* (5th ed.). Boston, MA: McGraw-Hill Irwin.

Irmak, C., Wakslak, C.J., & Trope, Y. (2013). "Selling the forest, buying the trees: The effect of construal level on seller-buyer price discrepancy." *Journal of Consumer Research, 40,* 284–297.

McConnell, C.R. & Brue, S.L. (2008). *Economics* (17th ed.). Boston, MA: McGraw-Hill Irwin.

Pearce, D.W. (Ed.). (1992). *The MIT dictionary of modern economics.* Cambridge, MA: MIT Press.

SUGGESTED READING

Colander, D. (2009). "In praise of modern economics." *Eastern Economic Journal, 35,* 10–13.

Colander, D. (2005). "What economists teach and what economists do." *Journal of Economic Education, 36,* 249–260.

Milgrom, P. & Strulovici, B. (2009). "Substitute goods, auctions, and equilibrium." *Journal of Economic Theory, 144,* 212–247.

Pashigian, B., & Self, J. (2007). "Teaching microeconomics in wonderland." *Journal of Economic Education, 38,* 44–57.

Pressman, S. (2011). "Microeconomics after Keynes: Post Keynesian economics and public policy." *American Journal of Economics & Sociology, 70,* 511–539.

Pyne, D. (2007). "Does the choice of introductory microeconomics textbook matter?" *Journal of Economic Education, 38,* 279–296.

—Steven R. Hoagland, PhD

MICROECONOMICS AND PUBLIC POLICY

ABSTRACT

This essay provides a frame of reference for objective approaches to complex political and legal public policy environments typically found within a market-system context. In contrast to other economic systems, the market-system orientation of the United States' economy subscribes to and protects the notion of free enterprise. This essay covers two intertwined theories: the microeconomic theory and the public-interest theory of regulation. With its focus on firm and consumer behaviors, microeconomic theory encompasses production decisions and determinations of price, output, and profit levels and presents a foundation for crafting and analyzing public policies. Public-interest theory of regulation contends that the need for regulation arises to protect the consuming public from abuses by producers. Antirust, industrial, and social regulations demonstrate the value of microeconomic theory to public policy. The essay introduces an array of methods and ideologies that economic analysts employ.

OVERVIEW

The information presented in this essay provides a frame of reference within which to describe the perpetual need for economists and other social scientists to lend objective mindsets to complex political and legal public-policy environments. Though this essay provides a foundation for developing future analysts and effective navigators who can moderate these environments, its main purpose is to help undergraduate students and other readers develop their knowledge of economic theory, demonstrate their understanding of its relevance to public policy, and apply their skills in serving the public interest. In general, this essay will generate a better understanding of the interdependent relationships between market economics, industrial and social regulation, and government policy. More specifically, it will convey information about the role of the federal government in encouraging industrial stability, protecting citizens' well-being, and maintaining competitive exchanges of goods, services, and scarce resources.

In contrast to a command- or a plan-based economic system in which the government or a few powerful individuals determine the nature and scope of domestic economic activity, the market system that the United States operates is built upon the notion of free enterprise. Though some flaws exist in this system, its essence merely requires voluntary involvement between those who pay a price in exchange for goods and services that bring satisfaction and those who incur costs and earn profits while providing the goods and services that satisfy the other party's needs and wants. In other words, consumers and producers come together in product markets to exchange dollars for goods and vice versa. Those markets often vary

American Electric Power is a major investor-owned electric utility with its headquarters located in Columbus, Ohio. (Courtesy of Tysto via Wikimedia Commons)

to some extent in terms of the degree and nature of competition between and among producers. Perfect competition, as a reference point, is analogous to an auction-house scenario and is a natural element in a market-based system. In essence, the general intent of public policy in terms of microeconomics is to manage the level of competition. The government laws and policies covered in this essay include protecting vulnerable industries, moderating noncompetitive prices, and addressing market power.

This essay conveys the tenets of two intertwined theories. One is microeconomic theory, which will be discussed below in detail before we turn our attention to its applications to public policy. Public-interest theory of regulation presents the notion that industrial regulations protect the consuming public from abuses by producers who hold market power (McConnell & Brue, 2008). Market power usually occurs whenever a few firms are the dominant suppliers of a product, whether by design or coincidence. Electric power, natural gas, and communication companies serve as examples of natural monopolies. Like any monopoly, market power accrues because rival firm entry is nearly impossible and profit maximization occurs at a low level of output, resulting in costs and prices that are higher relative to firms operating in highly competitive markets. Consistent with this theory, the imposition of regulations benefits consumers through reduced costs and higher outputs while allowing producers to cover production costs and earn a fair return. We will return to this perspective and its application, but first we need to cover microeconomic theory and gain an understanding of its relevance.

Microeconomic Theory: A Perspective on Markets, Behaviors, & Interventions

With its focus on firm and consumer behavior, microeconomic theory focuses partially on production decisions and price derivations. On the one hand, firm behavior analyses focus on production decisions and pricing, usually with an eye toward the type of market in which the firm supplies an item. Microeconomic theory also focuses on analyses of individual behavior and market demand for an item.

Microeconomic Assumptions

Studies in microeconomics usually begin by accepting a set of assumptions, which forms the parameters for additional inquiry.

- First and foremost is the *ceteris paribus* (all else is held constant) assumption.
- The second assumption is that consumers and producers behave as rational agents who have access to full, perfect information relevant to their decisions.
- A third assumption is that when those agents engage in transactions, no individual or group brings an inordinate amount of influence to an exchange decision.
- The fourth and last assumption of interest here is that item prices reflect only the direct private value of an exchange between a buyer and a seller; in other words, the system of exchange omits or ignores the indirect benefits or costs incurred by other members of larger society.

Problems arise in the marketplace when any of the last three assumptions become unrealistic or fail to hold true. Policy analysts and economists refer to such a situation as a market failure. Its occurrence may establish a rationale for governmental intervention, such as the formation and implementation of public policies; for more information on these and other concepts found in this essay, consult the economics dictionary as edited by Pearce (1992).

Supply & Demand

In addition to learning about market failures and public policies, students of microeconomics often begin by focusing their attention on relationships between the possible prices of an item, the quantities consumers are willing and able to purchase at each price, and the quantities suppliers are willing and able to produce.

Demand Side

On the consumer or demand side, an inverse relationship exists between price and quantity in accordance with the law of demand. Relatively speaking, smaller amounts are in demand at higher prices and vice versa.

Prices generally reflect an agreement between sellers and buyers, who exchange goods and services as they interact in the marketplace. Most sellers take the price dictated by market forces, and very few sellers are able to set the market price. In terms of demand, typically the higher the price for any item, the more sensitive consumer purchases become.

Elasticity is a concept that measures consumer sensitivity to price hikes. Calculations of the price elasticity of demand allow economists to determine precisely, in percentage terms, how much a consumer's purchases of an item will decrease in response to an increase in its price. Guell (2007, p. 41) summarizes a few studies on the price elasticity of demand; for instance, the evidence with respect to airline travel informs us that any given 10 percent increase in the airfare will result in an 18 percent decrease in the number of tickets sold. Keep in mind that the ratio varies according to whether the travel is for business or leisure and that business travelers are less responsive to price hikes than leisure travelers. We will return to this concept and the questionable practice of segmenting a market according to buyers' price elasticity of demand.

Supply Side

On the producer or supply side, a positive relationship exists according to the law of supply. The price at which producers can sell their goods and services is only one constraint. The relationship between market prices and producer costs often influences whether item production will occur. Firms incur a variety of costs in their production of goods and services. The following sections provide a short discussion and description of those costs and some direction regarding their applicability to public policy and analysis.

Costs

Total costs are the sum of fixed and variable costs. Fixed costs are those that exist even without any production and do not vary with the scale of production. Some examples of fixed costs are monthly fees paid for machinery, buildings, and land. Variable costs are those that vary with production. Some examples of variable costs are wages, materials, and supplies.

The allocation of costs across larger scales of production results in a variety of cost curve shapes. Graphs depicting these functions show cost on the vertical axis and quantity on the horizontal axis. Average total cost and average variable cost form important U-shaped curves. Their calculation involves dividing them by the production quantity. The lowest points on those curves are significant. At those points is where the marginal cost curve, which is J-shaped, intersects them. Marginal cost is the change in total costs that arises from producing one additional unit.

Revenue

Firms produce and sell items and receive a price for each one sold. Total revenue is the mathematical product of price times the quantity sold at each price. Marginal revenue is the change in total revenue that arises from selling one additional unit. Price is equal to marginal revenue in competitive market structures and greater than marginal revenue in monopolistic market structures. Though graphs can become quite confusing with each addition of a line or curve, keep in mind that the marginal revenue line is horizontal in perfectly competitive market structures and downward sloping in monopolistic structures.

A key relationship exists where marginal revenue equals marginal cost and where these two curves intersect. The intersection determines the profit-maximizing amount of output. Most, if not all, firms attempt to set production to that amount as they exhibit profit-maximizing behaviors. Now, let us bring prices back into the analysis for a short discussion of the rules of production. These rules help gauge whether a firm may continue its operation as a competitive, viable entity.

Rules of Production

To comply with the first of two rules, firms must produce at the profit-maximizing output, which is, again, where marginal revenue equals marginal cost. The second rule is that firms must receive a price that is equal to or greater than average variable cost. Their sales must cover, at the least, average variable costs and contribute something toward average fixed costs. In other words, they must cover their variable inputs, such as labor costs, and make payments on their plants and machinery. Moreover, they must operate at or above the shut-down point, which is where the marginal cost curve intersects the average variable cost curve, at the latter's lowest point.

Break-Even Point

Another key reference point is the break-even point. This point is where the marginal cost curve intersects the average total cost curve, at the latter's lowest point. The break-even point also marks the location at which those costs are equal and the firm earns a normal profit. The term is misleading, as it seems to indicate an absence of profit. However, profits become part of an operating cost if the owner is to be consistent with the notion of opportunity costs, which is the value the decision maker assigns to the best foregone alternative.

Market Structure

Depending on the market structures in which they operate, some firms can influence the market price, while others merely accept the market price for their outputs. Market structure reflects whether a firm makes the market price or takes the market price. Structures at the extreme ends of a continuum refer to the presence or the absence of competition in a market for a specific output or item. The bookends of that continuum are perfect competition and monopoly or imperfect competition. In addition to whether firms are price makers or price takers, market structure descriptors often include the number of sellers and buyers, the ease with which firms can enter or exit a market, and the level of profit.

Highly Competitive Market Structures

One example of a highly competitive market structure is agriculture. In this instance, there are numerous buyers and sellers of an agricultural product such as corn. Farmers usually take the price dictated by the market, and almost anyone can obtain enough resources to grow corn. In contrast, the production of computer-operating systems serves as an example of a noncompetitive market structure. In this instance, there are numerous buyers of the system but only a very few sellers. Microsoft and Apple are two firms that often come to mind with reference to operating

The birthplace of Apple Computer. In 1976, Steve Jobs co-founded the company in the garage of his childhood home on Crist Drive in Los Altos, California. (Courtesy of Mathieu Thouvenin CC BY-SA 2.0 via Wikimedia Commons)

The Commons, located on the campus of the Microsoft's headquarters in Redmond, Washington. (Courtesy of Ayoleol CC BY-SA 3.0 via Wikimedia Commons)

systems for personal computers. Consequently, these system developers make the market price, as they are essentially the only producers, and virtually no one else can obtain the legal or intellectual resources required for producing and developing their software. Furthermore, these firms generate lower quantities and charge higher prices than perfect competitors would, due in part to their market power. Those prices are much higher than the break-even point, a tactic that provides monopolists with a profit greater than the normal level. Economic profit accrues when prices are higher than average total cost, inviting new firm entry into a market. However, entry into the market for operating-system software as a producer is virtually impossible, mostly due to legal constraints such as licenses and patents.

Entry barriers and economic profit suggest the presence of market power. They also represent the existence of an inordinate influence in the marketplace that tends to favor the seller over the buyer. In response to market failures, governments may intervene by establishing price controls. These controls come in two forms: price ceilings and price floors. In an effort to protect an industry subject to intense competition, such as dairy farming, a price floor will prevent the price from falling below a specified amount, so that nobody can charge below a minimum price for products such as a gallon of milk or a pound of cheese. Conversely, in an effort to emulate a competitive situation, a price ceiling will prevent the price of a product, such as a unit of electricity or natural gas, from rising above a specific amount. Price controls are one application of public policy to microeconomics.

APPLICATIONS

This section applies microeconomic theory to regulatory interventions. Forms of public policy covered in this essay are antitrust regulation, industrial regulation, and social regulation. The first two are interrelated in addressing product markets and constitute the first part of this section. The last part is more general in nature, addressing environmental concerns, product and worker safety, and some items straddling the resource and labor market. The common thread that weaves all these parts together is the role of government in maintaining competition, promoting industrial and societal stability, and providing a legal framework within which to conduct economic and policy analyses.

Antitrust & Industrial Regulations

These regulations serve to limit the amount of potential or actual market power held by a small number of firms. Price fixing and predatory pricing are illegal activities. In order to gain market power, two or more rival firms may conspire to fix the price of an item at a specific amount. This action effectively diminishes competitiveness between and among these firms and erodes the benefits consumers receive from paying a low price instead of a high price. Furthermore, the firms preserve their market share. Another illegal tactic to gain market power is when one rival firm temporarily lowers its price to below cost in order to force its competitor to lower its prices. In predatory pricing schemes, a few rounds of price cuts can force a competitor into a shut-down situation crafted by the actions by the predator firm. Once the rival exits the market, the surviving firm will gain share and market power, raising its price and realizing economic profit, especially when entry into the market is difficult.

Market-Structure Evaluation

One feature that defines market structure is whether entry into or exit from a market is easy or difficult. By way of review, additional features include the size of the producing or consuming population and the ability of a small number of firms to set prices. Competition may occur on the basis of price

or through advertising that creates an image with which a buyer identifies or perceives as a dimension of quality. Soft-drink manufacturers are famous for concocting differences between their carbonated caramel-colored sweetened beverages through massive expenditures on advertising and marketing. In reality, the amount of product differentiation frequently masks the degree of competition. Sometimes the delineation of market power is in terms of the portion of total market sales held by the largest firms.

Monopolies/Oligopolies

Analysts have a set of measures available to them by which to estimate market power. Farthest from perfect competition on the market-structure continuum, a monopolist is one firm that supplies an item to an entire market. One step closer along that continuum is an oligopolistic market structure, *oligo*- meaning "few," in which a few firms sell most of the product. Two common measures of market power include the concentration ratio and the Herfindahl index (HI). Calculating the concentration ratio for the four largest firms (the CR4) involves dividing the dollar amount of their sales by the total dollar amount of market sales. For example, the CR4 in the soft-drink market could be somewhere around a 95, after multiplying the result by 100, meaning that the four largest firms sell 95 percent of the product in a given market. For a monopolist, the CR1 would be 100 percent, which is the maximum possible value of a concentration ratio. Calculating the HI involves squaring the market share of each firm in the market and adding them together; the maximum possible value, in the case of a monopolist, would be 10,000.

Monopolists face a downward-sloping market demand curve. Their prices usually place at the higher end of the curve, which is in the elastic region. Though this means that consumer purchases are responsive to changes in price, there is an absence of competitors who offer close substitutes for the good or service provided, partly due to significant barriers to entry. Furthermore, price discrimination, which is charging buyers different prices by segmenting them according to their individual price elasticities of demand, occurs when airlines impose restrictions on leisure travelers' fares, recognizing that their sensitivities to price are greater than those of business travelers, who usually require maximum flexibility in their travels. Moreover, the high price is the result of the profit-maximizing output being lower than it would be in other market structures. Usual monopoly behavior entails restricting output, which in turn forces prices upward, and generating unemployment and lower incomes because they produce less and employ fewer workers than do firms operating within other types of market structures. For these reasons, many economists, public-policy analysts, and other individuals consider monopolies bad for society.

Regulations of Monopolistic Behavior

Regulations and laws are enacted due to those unfavorable perceptions, analyses, or behaviors. Regulators typically concentrate on manipulating price-output combinations. The price controls imposed by regulators on natural monopolies such as utilities take one of two forms. First, regulators may pursue the socially optimal price, which is equal to marginal cost. This type of pricing generates the largest amount of output and the lowest price, which is characteristic of a perfectly competitive market structure. Second, regulators may pursue a fair return price, which is equal to average total cost. This pricing strategy forces firms to accept a normal profit, which eliminates any economic profit. The strategy also generates higher outputs and lower prices, but it provides a return on the capital investment. Utility providers usually depend on generators, transmission lines, and other equipment in supplying electric power and transporting natural gas. Both pricing schemes are consistent with the public-interest theory of regulation.

Several antitrust laws exist for controlling economic behaviors and monopolistic inclinations. The

Kraft Heinz

When Heinz merged with Kraft Foods on March 25, 2015, they completed a horizontal merger to become known as Kraft Heinz Company, one of the largest food companies in the world. Above is the new logo for the company. (Courtesy of Wikimedia Commons)

key pieces of federal legislation are the Sherman Act, the Clayton Act, the Federal Trade Commission Act, and the Celler-Kefauver Act. Some of these are instrumental in examining potential market power when firms propose to merge.

Concentration ratios and the HI as well as levels of profit, price, and output are useful in examining merger proposals. A vertical merger occurs when a firm buys one or more of its suppliers, such as when a soft-drink manufacturer buys an aluminum-can producer. A horizontal merger occurs when a firm buys a competitor, such as when a restaurant owner buys another restaurant. A conglomerate merger occurs when a firm buys another firm in a separate but related industry, such as when a soft-drink manufacturer buys a fast-food restaurant. Industrial and antitrust regulations focus on market power and define markets according to product and/or geographic location. They attempt to protect consumers from high prices and restricted choices while also pursuing stability for firms facing intense competition. For more detail regarding the latter, readers should consult chapters in microeconomics textbooks on farm policy, healthcare policy, international trade policy, and labor markets.

Oil companies, like ExxonMobil, often adopt a vertically integrated structure whereby they are involved with the processes of locating, drilling, transporting, refining and distributing oil for sale to consumers. On June 14, 2012, The Baton Rouge refinery in Louisiana (above) experienced a naphtha spill into the neighborhood where people began reporting health issues soon afterwards. (Courtesy of Adbar CC BY-SA 3.0 via Wikimedia Commons)

Social Regulation

As McConnell and Brue (2008) point out, industrial regulation concerns itself with regulating rates or prices of natural monopolies. In contrast, social regulation is described as an emergent field that focuses on the conditions in which production occurs, the societal impact of production, and the physical attributes of outputs. In brief, this form of regulation deals with safety and environmental issues and employment practices.

Policy analysts in this domain of regulation generally must be skilled in examining the benefits and the costs associated with decisions. They tend to concern themselves with net benefits as they compare private gains against societal losses. These policy analysts use optimization analyses to determine whether marginal benefits are greater than or equal to marginal costs. At first glance, costs are usually easier to identify and quantify than are benefits. Nonetheless, the rewards may be a fair match given those challenges.

The same may be said for the areas that social regulation targets. As a backdrop, social regulation is more comprehensive than antitrust and industrial regulation. In addition, it addresses matters that affect consumers and producers on a daily basis. The growth of social regulation since its inception has generated numerous tasks and public agencies and continues to provide ample opportunities for economic analysts. Among the list of possible areas of study, as referenced in McConnell and Brue (2008, pp. 592–95), are the effectiveness of food, drugs, and cosmetics; industrial health and safety of workers and products; recruitment, promotion, and outplacement of human resources; cleanliness of air and water; and noise abatement. Additional opportunities may arise from reviewing the positions of those who defend or critique social-regulation policy and the articles listed as suggested reading.

In conclusion, this essay demonstrates the value of microeconomics to public policy and describes many concepts and terms relevant to public-policy analysis. It also extends an invitation to undergraduates to develop and refine their skill sets for possible service in an area of public policy, having introduced them to a limited array of methods and ideology of economists.

BIBLIOGRAPHY

Apgar, W. C., and Brown, H. J. (1987). *Microeconomics and Public Policy*. Glenview, IL: Scot, Foresman and Co.

Arnold, Roger A. (2005). *Economics*(7th ed.) Mason, OH: Thomson South-Western.

Campos, R. G., Reggio, I., & García-Píriz, D. (2013). "Micro versus macro consumption data: The cyclical properties of the Consumer Expenditure Survey." *Applied Economics, 45,* 3778–3785.

Guell, R. C. (2007). *Issues in economics today*(3rd ed.). Boston, MA: McGraw-Hill Irwin.

Haidar, J. (2011). "A note on the social costs of monopoly and regulation." *IUP Journal of Financial Economics, 9,* 76–79

McConnell, C. R. & Brue, S. L. (2008). *Economics*(17th ed.). Boston, MA: McGraw-Hill Irwin.

Pearce, D. W. (Ed.). (1992). *The MIT dictionary of modern economics.* (4th ed.). Cambridge, MA: MIT Press.

Pressman, S. (2011). "Microeconomics after Keynes: Post Keynesian economics and public policy." *American Journal of Economics & Sociology, 70,* 511–539.

SUGGESTED READING

Appelbaum, E. (1982). "The estimation of the degree of oligopoly power." *Journal of Econometrics, 19,* 287–299.

Bariloche, R. (2011). "A critical view of innovation in the context of poverty, unemployment and slow economic growth." *Modern Economy, 2,* 228–258.

Blank, R. (2002, Winter). "What do economists have to contribute to policy decision-making?" *Quarterly Review of Economics & Finance, 42,* 817.

Bonner, J. (1990). "Microeconomics for public policy: Helping the invisible hand." *Economic Journal, 100,* 671–671.

Cheung, S. (2004). "The microeconomics of public policy analysis" (Book). *Economic Journal, 114,* F367–F368.

Chidmi, B., Lopez, R., & Cotterill, R. (2005). "Retail oligopoly power, dairy compact, and Boston milk prices." *Agribusiness, 21,* 477–491.

Keating, B. (1997). "Essential microeconomics for public policy analysis" (Book). *Social Science Quarterly (University of Texas Press), 78,* 246–247.

Kinoshita, J., Suzuki, N., Kawamura, T., Watanabe, Y., & Kaiser, H. (2001). "Estimating own and cross price elasticities and price-cost margin ratios using store-level daily scanner data." *Agribusiness: An International Journal, 17,* 515–525.

Lucas Jr., R., Krueger, A., & Blank, R. (2002). "Promoting economic literacy: Panel discussion." *American Economic Review, 92,* 473–477.

Microeconomics for public policy: "Helping the invisible hand." (1990). *Journal of Economic Literature, 28*, 125.

Veal, A. J. (2017). "Public policy making." *CAB Direct, 4*, 119–140.

Zaleski, P., & Esposto, A. (2007, September). "The Response to Market Power: Non-Profit Hospitals versus For-Profit Hospitals." *Atlantic Economic Journal, 35*, 315–325.

—*Steven R. Hoagland, PhD*

MICROECONOMICS AND TECHNICAL CHANGE

ABSTRACT

This article focuses on microeconomics and technical change. It provides an overview of the connection between technical change, productivity, and economic growth as well as the economic theory and history of technical change. The main processes of technical change, including technical evolution and technical innovation, are described. The main actors involved in promoting technical change are discussed. The issues associated with measuring technical change in the global market are addressed.

OVERVIEW

The field of economics, and microeconomics in particular, has an established history of studying the relationship between technical change and capitalist economies. Economists argue that technical change drives economic growth, productivity growth, and social change. Understanding the microeconomics of technical change is important in an increasingly global and technological world. Technical change refers to a change in the amount of output produced from the same inputs. Technological change is characterized by a change in a set of existing production plans and procedures. While technical change may occur in any area, including organization, production, or technology, economists generally consider technical changes in the technology field to be the primary engine of economic growth and social change.

Technical change occurs through two different processes: technical innovation or technical evolution.

- Technological innovation (TI) refers to the process by which industry generates new and improved products and production processes. Technical innovation is characterized as a goal-directed activity. A technical change is one that has been chosen from amongst a set of feasible changes. Karl Marx considered technical innovation to be one of the main forces of history.

- Technical evolution is generally conceived of as a process of trial and error or the culmination of small modifications to the production process (Brotherton, 1988). Despite the similarity in names, technical evolution differs from biological evolution. Technical evolution can be directed and managed while biological evolution is a slow, self-generating process (Parayil, 1999). In addition, technical evolution is much more rapid than biological evolution. Human beings, with the capacity for memory, expression, recording, teaching, and communication, may guide technical evolution by changing production techniques and social organization. Technical knowledge is cumulative and builds on what comes before (De Bresson, 1987).

The following section provides an overview of the economic theory and history of technical change. This overview serves as the foundation for later discussion of the process of promoting technical change and the issues associated with measuring technical change in the global market.

ECONOMIC THEORY & HISTORY OF TECHNICAL CHANGE

Microeconomics vs. Macroeconomics

Economists have studied and debated the economics of technical change since the eighteenth century. The debate about the economics of technical change has tended to divide economists. Economists tend to favor explaining technical change as either a macroeconomic or micro-economic process. Microeconomics is a subfield of economics that studies how small economic groups, including households, individuals, and firms, make economic decisions. Microeconomics is concerned with the relationship between price, supply and demand, and small economic group decision-making.

In contrast, the field of macroeconomics is concerned with large-scale economic activity, including inflation, unemployment, and national growth. Macroeconomic studies of technical change or progress tend to be concerned with the rate of technical progress or change in a market or society. In addition, macroeconomic studies tend to equate technical progress and advances in knowledge. Macroeconomic studies of technical change consider "pure" technical progress the single most important determinant of the growth of living standards. In contrast, microeconomic studies of technical change examine the process of technical change in a disaggregated way. For example, microeconomic studies of technical change studies production functions as separate subjects (Kennedy & Thurlwall, 1972).

Development of Technical Economic Growth Theories

Economic study of technical change was led by Karl Marx in the nineteenth century and Joseph Schumpeter in the twentieth century. Marx's viewpoints characterized the classical economic position on technical change. Marx argued that the forces of production and technology determine social change. Schumpeter, following Marx, saw that technological change was the key factor behind economic development. Modern economists are building on Schumpeter's work to develop new theories of economic growth with technical change at their center. Schumpeter prioritized the importance of innovation process in the technical change process. According to Schumpeter, technological change is led by entrepreneurs and connected to the business cycle. The destruction of existing modes of production and exchange in the marketplace creates economic evolution and economic growth (Parayil, 1999).

Memorial to Karl Marx in Moscow. The inscription reads "Пролетарии всех стран, соединяйтесь!" (Proletarians of all countries unite!) (Courtesy of Wikipedia)

Joseph Schumpeter. (Courtesy of Volkswirtschaftliches Institut, Universität Freiburg, Freiburg im Breisgau, Germany, via Wikimedia Commons)

Original model of three phases of the process of Technological Change – Schumpeter's Trilogy. (Courtesy of Joost.vp via Wikimedia Commons)

Schumpeter's Trilogy

Schumpeter argued that technological change occurs in three distinct steps or stages: invention, innovation, and diffusion. Invention refers to the "generation of a new idea or new concept that may lead to a new product or process" (Curlee & Goel, 1989, p.5). Innovation, which follows invention, occurs when the "idea from an invention is developed into a new product or process and the new product or process is commercially transferred. Diffusion refers to the process in which the new process or product spreads across firms within and across markets" (Curlee & Goel, 1989, p.5). Schumpeter's theory of technical change, also referred to as the Schumpeter trilogy, argues that technical change occurs most rapidly and successfully in concentrated industries. Concentrated industries refer to industries in which a small number of companies sell a large percentage of an industry's product.

Modern Economics Theories of Technical Change

Modern economic theories of technical change tend to be based on neoclassical economics. Neoclassical economic theory argues that new creation occurs due to the drive to maximum profits. Neoclassical economic theory argues that individual firms and whole industries produce technical innovation in response to two types of market forces: demand-pull and technology-push. The demand-pull market force approach argues that firms employing larger marketing research facilities have an advantage over firms that have smaller marketing research facilities. The technology-push market force approach argues that technical change originates within a firms' research and design department (Curlee & Goel, 1989).

APPLICATIONS

Promoting Technical Change

Economists, businesses, and governments recognize that technical change increases economic growth and productivity. As a result, businesses and governments actively promote technical change at the corporate and industry level. Governments actively diffuse new technologies into society and industry in an effort to increase productivity in their nations and increase their level of international competition. Economists encourage the public and private sectors to cooperate and work together to promote technical change. Governments and firms work together to promote the expansion of new technological capabilities in an effort to counteract and address market failures that inhibit the invention, innovation, and diffusion of new technologies (Curlee & Goel, 1989).

Promotion of Technical Change by Firms

Firms and governments promote technical change. Individual firms and whole industries make frequent technological choices. Economists argue that firms engage in ongoing cost-minimizing technical choices. Firms choose from a wide variety of feasible production techniques based on their relative prices of production. Firms are moving toward technical progress characterized by increased optimization. Technical progress requires that firms embrace a technical strategy characterized by technical innovation or technical adoption. Economists argue that firms self-select into one of these two categories. Firms that prioritize technical innovation, such as biotechnology and pharmaceutical firms, tend to focus on discovering new techniques of production or consumption. These firms tend to have large research and development (R & D) budgets. In contrast, firms that prioritize the adoption of existing techniques of development and consumption, such as agricultural firms, tend to be motivated by their profit objective. Both firms have rates of technical progress. A firm's rate of technical progress refers to the "plant size and equipment decisions together with the relative prices of inputs and outputs under different technical possibilities" (Caputo & Paris, 2005).

Promotion of Technical Change by Government

While firms work from within to promote technical change, governments promote technical change through microeconomic reform and policy reform (Adams & Parmenter, 1994). The U.S. government's science and technology policy program and infrastructure is composed of the Office of Science and Technology Policy, the National Science and Technology Council, and the President's Council of Advisors on Science and Technology (PCAST). In the

President Gerald R. Ford signing H.R. 10230, establishing the Office of Science and Technology Policy. (Courtesy of White House via Wikimedia Commons)

United States, the Office of Science and Technology Policy oversees science and technology policy. The Office of Science and Technology Policy was established in 1976 by Congress to advise the president and other policymakers on the effects that scientific and technological advancements have on domestic and international affairs. The National Science and Technology Policy, Organization, and Priorities Act of 1976 (Public Law 94-282) authorizes Office of Science and Technology Policy to accomplish the following tasks: provide scientific and technological analysis and make decisions regarding the research for the president regarding important policies, plans, and programs of the federal government; "lead an interagency effort to develop and implement sound science and technology policies and budgets; work with the private sector to ensure federal investments in science and technology contribute to economic prosperity, environmental quality, and national security; build strong partnerships among federal, state, and local governments, other countries, and the scientific community; and evaluate the scale, quality, and effectiveness of the Federal effort in science and technology" (Stine, 2009, p.8).

Executive Order 12881
In 1993, Executive Order 12881 established the National Science and Technology Council (NSTC) as the principal agency working with the executive branch to equalize science and technology policies between the various entities that carry out federal research and development efforts. The National Science and Technology Council is composed of the president, the vice president, the directors of various agencies, including the Office of Science and Technology Policy, and the cabinet secretaries. The National Science and Technology Council is organized under five main committees, including the Committee on Environment, Natural Resources, and Sustainability and the Committee on Homeland and National Security. The National Science and Technology Council's main responsibility is to develop national goals for federal science and technology investments in a wide range of areas representing all the mission areas of the executive branch.

Executive Order 13226
In 2001, Executive Order 13226 established the President's Council of Advisors on Science and Technology (PCAST) to allow private sector and academic community members to advise the president on technological and scientific matters as well as math and science education efforts. The President's Council of Advisors on Science and Technology includes members from industry, education, and research institutions and other nongovernmental organizations. The council considers issues such as technology and the role of emerging companies, U.S. research and design investment, and energy efficiency. The federal government's approach to science and technology initiatives and policies is based on the belief in the benefits of interagency efforts.

President Barack Obama meets with the President's Council of Advisors on Science and Technology (PCAST) in the State Dining Room, on August 7, 2009. (Courtesy of Pete Souza, White House, via Wikimedia Commons)

The Public Sector

The public sector is actively involved in promoting technical change as part of its larger effort to create economic strength and stability. The public sector addresses multiple types of market failure scenarios through the diffusion and promotion of technical innovation and change. Examples of market failures include "(l) the lack of competitive markets, the existence of market externalities, and the lack of contingent commodity markets or failures with respect to information and uncertainty" (Curlee & Goel, 1989, p.13). "Lack of competitive markets refers to situations in which some of the producers and consumers of goods and services have market power" (Curlee & Goel, 1989, p.13). "Externalities refer to costs or benefits that result from the production and use of a good or service and which are incurred by individuals or firms that are not directly involved in the economic transaction" (Curlee & Goel, 1989, p.14). Failures of information or confidence occur when producers and consumers do not have perfect information or the opportunity to insure against the market risk.

Public policies that result in the diffusion of new technologies into these market failure scenarios create increased research, development, spending, confidence, and employment. Public policy responses to market failures include indirect policy instruments or direct policy instruments.

- Indirect policy instruments refer to "public sector measures that alter the incentive structure of the private sector with respect to technical change such that the pursuit of invention, innovation, and diffusion is made more attractive" (Curlee & Goel, 1989, p.15).
- Direct policy instruments trigger research and development in the knowledge and technology sectors. The public sector uses direct policy instruments to guide the invention, innovation, and diffusion of new technology.

Market Structure & Technical Change

Ultimately, firms, industries, and governments study the relationship between market structure, innovation, and diffusion activities to gather the information necessary for making technical choices. Market structures refer to the number of firms and the power of those firms in the market place. The relationship between market structure and technological change is nonlinear and complex. The influence of innovation on market structure depends on the type of innovation, type of market, and timing of introduction. Policy issues and technical change are complex. Technology policy must assess the relationship between market structure and technological advances. For example, Schumpeter realized that rapid technical change is most appropriate for and successful in concentrated industries. In addition, monopolies are considered by economists to be better suited to bearing the risks associated with research and advancement and have the resources to take new technologies to market (Curlee & Goel, 1989).

ISSUE

Measuring Technical Change in Global Markets

In the twentieth century, technical change created economic growth and the competitive advantage in the global marketplace for firms and national economies. The rate of technical change is an important indicator of current and future economic health. Measuring the rate of technical change is complicated by numerous factors. Technical change is heavily influenced by changes in corporate business practices and the development of global markets. Factors in firms and markets that influence technical change include increases in competition, pace of development, and labor productivity (Ahlstrom, 2004).

Increased competition: Technical change is influenced by increased competition in the marketplace. Economic growth in the marketplace increases competition between local and foreign firms. Trade agreements, such as the North American Free Trade Area (NAFTA) and the single European market in the early 1990s, created new opportunities and new competitors. The interdependent global economy creates new levels of competition among foreign and multinational corporations. The modern trend of globalization, and resulting shifts from centralized to market economies in much of the world, has created both the need and opportunity for economic development in developing countries and regions of the world. Open markets and foreign development aid have created new competitors in business sectors. Corporations around the world are adopting new management practices and building their brands to compete in global markets.

Increased pace of development: Technical change is influenced by increased pace of development in industry. The development of global markets has spurred the development of high-tech businesses. Global markets emphasize fast growth facilitated through new business procedures and new technologies such as the Internet and other networking technologies. Increased spending in research and design has yielded a wide range of profitable new products and services. The profits from economic growth provide funds for further technological development and investment. Both public and private sector interests have invested and driven the pace and direction of technological development in global markets. High-tech firms, with fast-paced product development tracks, depend on equity funding by venture capitalists, market investors, stock options, brand-building, and corporate reputation to establish themselves as competitors in global marketplace.

Increased labor productivity: Technical change is influenced by increased labor productivity in industry. The rate and pace of labor productivity is used by economists as a measure of the economic health of a country. Labor productivity refers to a business's output divided by the number of employees. Increased labor productivity, resulting from expanded global markets and new technologies, increases profits, spending, product development, and the overall economic health of a country.

Firms and governments consider the type and rate of technical change to be a strong economic indicator. Firms, industries, and governments work to estimate a general index of technical change for every given production technology. The general index serves as the basis for analysis of the determinants of technical change (Baltagi & Griffin, 1988). Despite the importance and usefulness of generating data about the rate of technical change, firms, industries, and governments face numerous challenges gathering such data. Ambiguity in economic research on technical change is generally believed to be caused by a lack of data on research-and-development processes. Measurement issues are related to a lack of research on technical change across businesses and industries.

CONCLUSION

In the final analysis, economists consider technical change to be one of the main forces driving capitalist economies. The microeconomics of technical change is a lens with which to examine the small-scale economic processes that influence technical change. Microeconomic theories of technical change, including demand-pull market force, technology-push market force, technical innovation, and technical evolution, offer explanations about how and why technical change occurs in firms and industries (Freeman, 1994). Technical change affects the pace and growth of firms, national economies, and markets. Technical change drives economic development. Historical examples of technical change that altered business practices include the nineteenth-century railroad and twentieth-century mass production manufacturing technologies. In the 1990s, new information and communication technologies began a business revolution with new products, services, business models, and economic markets. Information and knowledge have become both the means and the product of many businesses around the world. Terms such as the information society became popular descriptors of modern life for Westernized countries. Ultimately, technical change drives the economy and shapes history.

BIBLIOGRAPHY

Acemoglu, D. (2002). "Technical change, inequality, and the labor market." *Journal of Economic Literature, 40,* 7–72.

Adams, P., & Parmenter, B. (1994). "Microeconomic reform and employment in the short run." *Economic Record, 70,* 1.

Ahlstrom, D., Young, M., Ng, F., & Chan, C. (2004). "High technology and globalization challenges facing overseas Chinese entrepreneurs." *SAM Advanced Management Journal, 69,* 28–37.

Baltagi, B., & Griffin, J. (1988). "A general index of technical change." *Journal of Political Economy, 96,* 20.

Bariloche, R. (2011). "A critical view of innovation in the context of poverty, unemployment and slow economic growth." *Modern Economy, 2,* 228–258.

Brotherton, C. (1988). "Technological change and innovation: Setting the agenda for occupational psychology." *Journal of Occupational Psychology, 61,* 1–6.

Camagni, R. (2017). "Technological change, uncertainty and innovation networks: Towards a dynamic theory of economic space." *Seminal Studies in Regional and Urban Economics*, 65–92.

Caputo, M. & Paris, Q. (2005). "An atemporal microeconomic theory and an empirical test of price-induced technical progress." *Journal of Productivity Analysis*, 24, 259–281.

Conlisk, J. (1967). "A modified neoclassical growth model with endogenous technical change." *Southern Economic Journal, 34*, 3.

Curlee, T. & Goel, R. (1989). *The transfer and diffusion of new technologies: A review of the economics literature.* A U.S. Department of Energy Technical Report.

De Bresson, C. (1987). "The evolutionary paradigm and the economics of technological change." *Journal of Economic Issues, 21*, 751.

Deutch, J. (2005). "What should the government do to encourage technical change in the energy sector?" MIT Joint Program on the Science and Policy of Global Change.

Färe, R., Grosskopf, S., & Tremblay, V. (2012). "Market power and technology." *Review of Industrial Organization, 40*, 139–146.

Kennedy, C., & Thurwall, A. (1972). "Surveys in applied economics: technical progress." *Economic Journal, 82*, 11–72.

Kraft, J., & Kraftova, I. (2012). "Innovation—Globalization—Growth (Selected relations)." *Engineering Economics, 23*, 395–405.

Mankiw, N. (1995). "The growth of nations." *Brookings Papers on Economic Activity, 6*, 25–29.

Parayil, G. (1999). *Conceptualizing Technological Change: Theoretical and Empirical Explorations.* New York: Rowman & Littlefield.

Stine, D. (2009). "The president's office of science and technology policy: issues for congress." Congressional Research Service. Retrieved from xlink:href="http://fpc.state.gov/documents/organization/120584.pdf"

SUGGESTED READING

Barcenilla-Visús, S., Gómez-Sancho, J., López-Pueyo, C., Mancebón, M., & Sanaú, J. (2013). "Technical change, efficiency change and institutions: Empirical Evidence for a sample of OECD countries." *Economic Record, 89*, 207–227.

Intriligator, M. (1992). "Productivity and the embodiment of technical progress." *Scandinavian Journal of Economics*, 94, S75–S87.

Nemoto, J., & Goto, M. (2005). "Productivity, efficiency, scale economies and technical change: A new decomposition analysis of TFP applied to the Japanese prefectures." *Journal of the Japanese & International Economies, 19*, 617–634.

Ruttan, V. (1997). "Induced innovation, evolutionary theory and path dependence: sources of technical change." *Economic Journal, 107*, 1520–1529.

Tavani, D. (2013). "Bargaining over productivity and wages when technical change is induced: Implications for growth, distribution, and employment." *Journal of Economics, 109*, 207–244

—*Simone I. Flynn, PhD*

MONETARY THEORY

ABSTRACT

Monetary theory explores the root economic causes shaping the demand for currency. The amount of money in circulation at any given moment, some contend, is largely determined by total spending across the economy. Because the speed at which this money changes hands rarely changes and there's a lead time involved in more goods and services, increasing the money supply only causes inflation. Another major school of thought emphasizes individual preference in the use of money as the major determinant. Consequently, the money supply, output, prices and the rate at which money is spent can all fluctuate over time. Third theory views money as really just another commodity and demand for it is subject to supply, prices, inflation, and preference for substitutes.

OVERVIEW

Its symbols vary—$, £, €, ¥—but they all identify the most useful device ever created: money. Just how useful it is becomes painfully clear when you don't have any; then nothing else matters but acquiring

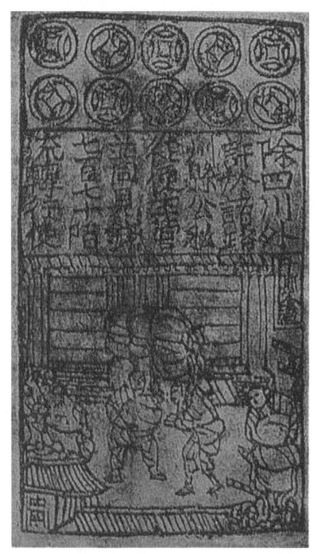

Song Dynasty Jiaozi, the world's earliest paper money. (Courtesy of Wikimedia Commons)

service. Using money as a standard unit of account permits us to represent this relative worth numerically as a price. The fact that virtually everything can be assigned a price makes money a universal medium of exchange (Zijlstra, 1979).

In all, then, money may well be the most versatile tool every invented. Its adoption and use proved instrumental to the economic specialization and division of labor that sped the production of an ever-widening number of goods (Clever, 2002), just as its concentration and use as investment capital made the industrial revolution possible. These historical facts, along with money's utter centrality to modern economic life, have led economists for some time now to wonder what, if any, the exact relationship might be between the supply of available money and the amount of aggregate demand and output. Their reasoned conclusions collectively make up what's known as monetary theory. Arestis and Mihailov (2011) define monetary theory as "rationalizing and microfounding money itself as well as its demand by economic agents" (p. 772). On the whole, it is a fairly abstract body of work that explores a very historical phenomenon, so our surest route to understanding the essentials of the former lies in reprising the major developments of the latter first.

A Brief History of Money

For centuries, gold and silver cast along with baser metals into coins physically stored a set amount of value. Their scarcity made them 'precious' metals ideally suited to the task, just as the widespread need for a food preservative made salt a much earlier form of "exchange currency." Crucially, both could be easily divided into smaller portions when the need arose. More to the point, perhaps, each was scarce and widely in demand; as such, each made for viable medium of exchange. Population growth and economic expansion, however, increases demand for currency, straining the available supply of the scarcer forms of exchange currency like gold and silver. When this happened, royal mints diluted the silver content per coin to put more in circulation. But the population's valuation of goods and services remained largely unchanged. It thus took more of the debased coins to provide the same amount of gold or silver as before, effectively driving up prices.

In the quantities needed for large transactions, what's more, silver coins were bulky and heavy; bars

some. To get anything of economic value, we must be prepared to give something of like value. In-kind exchanges of tangible goods or services involve the transfer of readily apparent value. However, barter on a large scale isn't very efficient. Bulk items are too cumbersome and the demand for most specialty items too sporadic to trade either with enough frequency to stimulate economic growth. Money solves this problem rather ingeniously: By design, it's a very portable substitute for all kinds of barter. It also assigns value. Every good and service, you see, has a particular worth relative to every other good and

A 640 BC one-third stater electrum coin from Lydia, an ancient kingdom in Anatolia. (Courtesy of Wikipedia)

The oldest bank in the world is Banca Monte dei Paschi di Sience, founded in 1472. Its headquarters is located in Siena, Italy. (Courtesy of Lucarelli CC-BY-SA-3.0 via Wikimedia Commons)

of gold bulkier and heavier. One way around the problem was to leave precious metals with a trustworthy party who, in return, would issue a certificate of ownership redeemable at any time. The practice dates back to the goldsmiths of medieval times; the distant forerunners of today's commercial banks. Traveling merchants found they could often pay for goods with the certificates themselves. Commercial banks in the eighteenth century followed suite on a much wider scale, issuing promissory notes with face values redeemable by the bearer in gold or silver coins from their vaults. Bankers were pleased to discover most bearers were just as content conducting transactions solely via these notes, so banks as a rule had only to keep enough gold and silver on hand to cover a portion of the notes they had issued.

Yet, any transaction made with these notes was in the final analysis an act of faith on the part of the buyer and seller. The notes themselves had to be genuine, the buyer had to have purchased them via a deposit at the issuing bank, and the bank itself had to be able to convert the note into gold or silver on demand. Banks with trustworthy reputations and very large asset and customer bases helped popularize the concept of a paper currency. Over time, though, problems arose that forced changes. "Bank notes" could be counterfeited much more easily than coinage. As much as a third of all the early bank notes circulating in the United States were forgeries. Any bank or merchant could issue its own paper currency.

In fact, well over a thousand did in the United States in prior to the reforms of 1861.

With so many different sizes, colors, and designs of bank notes passing through their hands, it's little wonder consumers and shopkeepers alike remained skeptical about their value. The only effective way to end this chaos was to make a national government or a single bank of its choosing the sole issuer. By the second half of the nineteenth century, this responsibility fell to the U.S. Treasury Department; the Bank of England, the U.K.'s largest private bank; and a semi-autonomous central bank in Japan. Each, significantly, stockpiled the necessary reserves of precious metals to redeem any bank note it issued. Other countries followed suit and, within decades, the base value of most currencies was set by assigning each an equivalent fixed weight in gold, which greatly facilitated trade between nations.

Eventually, though, the amount of currency required to sustain the growing volume of cash transactions surpassed the world's stock of gold and silver. A continued preference for a commodity-backed currency was no longer economically tenable. As populations rose, a fixed money stock would invariably lead to disinflation and a reemergence of barter exchanges on a large scale and overall economic activity would suffer. The only solution lay in a "fiat" currency. Here, essentially, the government declares a currency to be "legal tender." Its base value equals the amount of physical goods it can be exchanged for at the point in time when the public comes to accept and believe this assertion. From then on, monetary authorities expand or contract the money supply to maintain this common perception of its nominal value. As a medium of exchange, it works because we all willingly suspend our disbelief. In the final analysis, though, it's just paper or, in the case of demand-deposit checking accounts, entries in a bank ledger.

Insights

All monetary theory flows from two key concepts: the money stock and the velocity of money.

- The money stock is the sum of all the coin, currency, and demand-deposit funds in circulation along with the vault cash held by banks and, in the last seventy-five or so years, the reserve requirements these banks must deposit with their central bank.
- The velocity of money is a measure of how quickly on average the money stock turns over or changes hands as transactions take place. Its inverse, $1/V$, thus represents the amount of cash in circulation that is not spent.

Multiplying the stock of money by its velocity gives us the total value of expenditures across the entire economy. Now, crucially, the very same aggregate can also be calculated by multiplying the physical quantity of goods sold by their average price. Economists call this inherent parallelism the Equation of Exchange; it in turn gave rise to the Quantity Theory, an idea with roots that go back as far as the seventeenth and eighteenth centuries (Glasner, 2002).

The Quantity Theory

In formal terms, the Quantity Theory hypothesizes that an increase or decrease in the money stock will cause proportional increases or decreases in prices. Now this sounds like nothing more than a restatement of Quantity Equation, so why has it warranted

the separate and, as we shall see, considerable attention of economists? Because of the way the terms are defined, the first is treated as a given and true in all cases: it's thus a logical expression. Proving the validity of the second essentially required a more explicit form of economic reasoning. Here, the underlying principle of market equilibrium is just as inviolate as the rules of deductive reasoning. Any proof of the Quantity Theory therefore must be derived from the basic precepts of classical macroeconomic analysis: that full employment is a condition of general equilibrium, and that, because markets compensate so quickly to any change, any disequilibrium is temporary and transitory (Handa, 2000).

It follows then that the velocity of money and the total physical amount of goods sold, outcomes associated with general equilibrium at full employment, must be independent variables. They must, what's more, remain fairly constant relative to each other. That being the case, the way is open to treat the amount of the money stock and the average price level, the other term on each side of the Equation of Exchange, as dependent variables. And since there are year-to-year fluctuations in total expenditures, finally, said treatment is reasonable and warranted. More simply put, the theory states that increasing the money supply will only end up pushing the inflation rate higher. Such at least was the seminal conclusion of Fisher's 1911 mathematical proofs establishing a formal relationship between the two dependent variables.

Monetary theorists from the Cambridge School subsequently examined the role played by an individual's preference to spend or invest in this process. The more of one's resources earmarked for consumable items, the greater the demand for cash and demand deposits. Conversely, the more of one's resources put into time-deposit accounts and like financial instruments, the greater the supply. How much of each we individually elect depends on the rate of return on investment and the amount of immediate gratification the consumer in us is prepared to forgo. Critically, furthermore, since the rate of return mirrors the marginal productivity of capital, it is an independent variable much like the velocity of money is. For there to be equilibrium, then, the remaining variable on either side of the equation—the money stock and the average price level—must be dependent, rising or falling in lock-step with each other.

Keynes' Demand for Money

John Maynard Keynes, a member of the Cambridge School, questioned the basic assumption underlying classical and neo-classical monetary theory. Perhaps equilibrium at full employment is not nearly as universal or as inevitable as previously thought. Indeed, the empirical evidence supporting the contrarian view that unemployment, not full employment, was frequent and systemic enough for equilibrium to be the norm. In the short-run, moreover, the velocity of money and the output of goods were not independent variables. Both could and were affected by changes in the money supply, leading Keynes to reject the Quantity Theory outright (Davidson, 1978).

Expanding on the idea that individuals made conscious choices about the types and amounts of money they hold, Keynes theorized that the demand for money arose from its actual use, the most rudimentary of which is the need to make cash purchases. This he labeled the "transaction motive." A second, more forward looking use was to cover unexpected expenditures. It requires that some cash be held onto as opposed to spent. Keynes called this the "precautionary motive." The more daring profit-seekers were recognized in his third functional category, the "speculative motive." Given the likelihood of a future profit, essentially, many of us will elect to invest rather than spend. The price of money, i.e. the interest rate, figures prominently in this decision: the higher the rate, the more attractive investing seems. Thus, aggregate demand for money in Keynesian economics is a composite figure, the sum of funds we pay out in transactions, the funds we keep hold of as a cash reserve and the funds we are prepared to invest given the prevailing rate of return.

Monetary Theory After Keynes

Keynes' overall approach was more descriptive than prescriptive and recognized the possibility that less quantifiable factors may influence the demand for money. It was a seminal contribution and still relevant to theorists today (Harcourt & Kriesler, 2011). However, some economists after Keynes still found aspects of the Quantity Theory appealing in principal. By scaling back some of its underlying assumptions, they believed, it might still prove a serviceable model of monetary demand. Milton Friedman led the way in this by jettisoning the ideas that prices and the money stock changed in unison. He still

Professor Milton Friedman wins the Nobel Prize for Economics in 1976. (Courtesy of UPI via Wikimedia Commons)

maintained, however, that the velocity of money over time changed very little if at all. Likewise, he still resolutely believed that the size of the money stock played no real role in determining aggregate output.

His ideas on the root cause of the demand for money were more original. This he likened to the demand for any other kind of consumer or capital good. And, as a commodity, it had a utility that varied in degree from one individual or firm to the next. Only the goods money acquires holds value, not money itself (Brunner & Meltzer, 1972). This, in turn, makes the real rather than the nominal value of money important. Inflation erodes its face value; the real harm comes from its diminished purchasing power. So, monetary demand proper, Friedman postulated, depended on the real and nominal values of current cash balances, price levels, inflation, the amount of wealth held in other assets, the yields of these other assets, and expected future earning power.

VIEWPOINTS

Monetary theory deals in abstractions, while money itself deals in goods and services. Using money day-in and day-out may be second nature to us, but thinking about it as a distinct economic entity is not. We all experience money changing hands but few of us assign it a rate and even fewer argue that this rate is stable over time. Certainly many of us do not regularly contemplate the intrinsic worthlessness of fiat currency unless we're caught up in an inflationary spiral. Mostly, though, we tend to take money for granted—it runs through the economy much as blood flows through the body. Monetary theorists do not. To them, it's much more an observable phenomenon to be analyzed and perhaps harnessed in some way. Yet it is a subject that defies ready explanation. Theories are proposed, accepted, reevaluated, and revised or rejected. There is as of yet no one universally accepted theory that fully explains how the demand for money works.

A hundred years ago, monetary demand was pictured mechanistically. The espoused Quantity Theory seemed straightforward enough: in a full-employment economy, increases in the money stock resulted in inflation, not greater economic output. But subsequent real-world events undermined the Quantity Theory's basic premise. The economic status-quo was often less than full employment. Keynes considered the reason why people used money a more pertinent theoretical spring-board and rejected the Quantity Theory. His analysis of the behavioral roots maps out a more fluid and complex process where investment plays a much bigger role than previously thought. Friedman subsequently attempted to reconcile the two opposing views and, in the process, showed how the supply and demand for money is no different than for any other commodity. Some theorists posit that the factors underlying any monetary theory are so context dependent that no one theory can be used to explain all economies (Rashid, 2012). It will be interesting, then, to see what the next great conceptual leap forward will be.

BIBLIOGRAPHY

Arestis, P., & Mihailov, A. (2011). "Classifying monetary economics: Fields and methods from past to future." *Journal of Economic Surveys, 25,* 769–8 00.

Brunner, K., & Meltzer, A. (1972). "Friedman's monetary theory." *Journal of Political Economy, 80,* 837.

Clever, T. (2002). Chapter 7: Money, banking and international finance. In *Understanding the world economy.* Oxfordshire, UK: Routledge.

Davidson, P. (1978). "Why money matters: Lessons from a half-century of monetary theory." *Journal of Post Keynesian Economics, 1,* 46.

Glasner, D. (2000). "Classical monetary theory and the quantity theory." *History of Political Economy, 32,* 39–59.

Handa, J. (2000). Chapter Two: The analysis of money and prices: The heritage. In *Monetary economics.* Oxfordshire, UK: Routledge.

Harcourt, G. C., & Kriesler, P. (2011). "The enduring importance of the general theory." *Review of Political Economy, 23,* 503–519.

Rashid, S. (2012). "Importing the unusable: The Quantity theory and the LDC's." *Journal of Developing Areas, 46,* 385–396.

Rossner, P. (2018). "Monetary theory and cameralist economic management, c. 1500–1900 A.D." *Economic Thought.*

Zijlstra, J. (1979). "Monetary theory and monetary policy a central banker's view." *De Economist, 127,* 3–20.

SUGGESTED READING

Moore, B. (1978). "A post-Keynesian approach to monetary theory." *Challenge, 21,* 44.

Salerno, J. (2006). "A simple model of the theory of money prices." *Quarterly Journal of Austrian Economics, 9,* 39–55.

White, L. (1999). "Hayek's monetary theory and policy: A critical reconstruction." *Journal of Money, Credit & Banking, 31,* 109–120.

—*Francis Duffy, MBA*

MULTINATIONAL BUSINESS FINANCE

ABSTRACT

This article will focus on capital budgeting as it applies to multinational corporations. Capital budgeting could be the result of purchasing assets that are new for the organization or getting rid of some of the current assets in order to be more efficient. Capital budgeting for the multinational corporation presents many problems that are rarely found in domestic capital budgeting. There will be a review of recommendations that could assist financial analysts with conducting a cost-benefit analysis and reviewing cash flow from the perspective of the parent corporation and its subsidiaries.

OVERVIEW

Many organizations charge the finance department with overseeing the financial stability of the organization. The chief financial officer (CFO) may lead a team of financial analysts in determining which projects deserve investment. To do this, an organization undertakes capital budgeting; a process that frequently involves conducting a cost-benefit analysis. A cost-benefit analysis comprises a comparison between the cash inflows (benefits) and outflows (costs) to determine which is greater. Capital budgeting could result in the purchase of assets that are new for the

Starbucks is an American multinational corporation. Pictured is one of its coffee shops located in Dortmund, Germany. (Courtesy of Sven2512 at German Wikipedia CC BY-SA 2.0 via Wikimedia Commons)

organization or the removal of some of the current assets in order to be more efficient. The finance team is charged with evaluating which projects would be good investments, which assets would add value to the current portfolio, and how much the organization is willing to invest into each asset.

To answer the questions about potential assets, a set of components must be considered in the capital budgeting process. The four components are initial investment outlay; net cash benefits (or savings) from the operations; terminal cash flow; and the net present value (NPV) technique. Most of the literature discusses how the capital budgeting process operates in the traditional, domestic environment. However, as the world moves to a more global economic environment, consideration needs to be made as to how multinational corporations will conduct the capital budgeting process when operating in countries outside of their home base.

International capital budgeting refers to when projects are located in host countries other than the home country of the multinational corporation. Some of the techniques (i.e. calculation of net present value) are the same as traditional finance. However, "capital budgeting for a multinational is complicated because of the complexity of cash flows and financing options available to the multinational corporation" (Booth, 1982, p. 113). Capital budgeting for the multinational corporation presents many problems that are rarely found in domestic capital budgeting (Shapiro, 1978; Ang & Lai, 1989).

Financial analysts may find that the analysis of foreign projects is more complex than domestic projects due to the need to do the following:

Distinguish between parent cash flow and projects cash flow. Multinationals will have the opportunity to evaluate the cash flow associated with projects from two approaches. They may look at the net impact of the project on their consolidated cash flow or treat the cash flow on a stand-alone or unconsolidated basis. The theoretical perspective asserts that the project should be evaluated from the parent company's viewpoint since dividends and repayment of debt is handled by the parent company. This action supports the notion that the evaluation is actually based on the contributions that the project can make to the multinational's bottom line.

Some organizations may want to evaluate the project from the subsidiary's (local) point of view. However, the parent company's viewpoint should supersede the subsidiary's point of view. Multinational corporations tend to compare their projects with the subsidiary's projects in order to determine where their investments should go. The rule of thumb is to only invest in those projects that can earn a risk-adjusted return greater than the local competitors performing the same type of project. If the earnings are not greater than those of the local competitors, the multinational corporation can invest in the host country's bonds since it will pay the risk-free rate adjusted for inflation.

Although the theoretical approach is a sound process, many multinationals tend to evaluate their projects from both the parent and project point of view because of the combined advantages. When looking from the parent company's viewpoint, one could obtain results that are closer to the traditional net present-value technique. However, the project's point of view allows one to obtain a closer approximation of the effect on consolidated earnings per share. The way the project is analyzed is dependent on the type of technique utilized to report the consolidated net earnings per share.

Recognize money reimbursed to parent company when there are differences in the tax system. The way in which the cash flows are returned to the parent company has an effect on the project. Cash flow can be returned in the following ways:

Dividends—It can only be returned in this form if the project has a positive income. Some countries may impose limits on the amount of funds that subsidiaries can pay to their foreign parent company in this form.

Intrafirm debt—Interest on debt is tax deductible and helps reduce foreign tax liability.

Intrafirm sales—This form is the operating cost of the project and helps lower the foreign tax liability.

Royalties and license fees—This form covers the expenses of the project and lowers the tax liability.

Transfer pricing—This form refers to the internally established prices where different units of a single enterprise buy goods and services from each other.

Anticipate the differences in the inflation rate between countries given that it will affect the cash flow over time:

Analyze the use of subsidized loans from the host country since the practice may complicate the capital structure and discounted rate. The host country may target specific subsidiaries in order to attract specific types of investment (e.g., technology). Subsidized loans can be given in the form of tax relief and preferential financing, and the practice will increase the net present value of the project. Some advantages of this practice include adding the subsidiary to project cash inflows and discounts; discounting the subsidiary at some other rate, risk free; and lowering the risk adjusted discount rate for the project in order to show the lower cost of debt.

Determine if the political risk will reduce the value of the investment. Expropriation is the ultimate level of political risk, and the effects of it depend on when the expropriation takes place; the amount of money the host government will pay for the expropriation; how much debt is still outstanding; the tax consequences of expropriation; and the future cash flow.

Assess the different perspectives when assessing the terminal value of the project. Estimating the salvage value or terminal value depends on the value of the project if retained, the value of the project if purchased by outside investors, and the value of the project if it were liquidated. The corporation would use the assessment that yields the highest value.

Review whether or not the parent company had problems transferring cash flows due to the funds being blocked. An example would be when a host country limits the amount of dividends that can be paid. If this were to occur, the multinational corporation would have to reexamine its reinvestment return and other methods in which funds could be transferred out of the country. The blocked funds can be used to repay bank debt in the host country and allow the organization to have open lines of credit to other countries.

Make sure that there is no confusion as to how the discount rate is going to be applied to the project:

Adjust the project cash flow to account for potential risks. One must assume that every project has some level of risk, which is usually seen as part of the cost of capital. International projects tend to have more risk than domestic projects. Therefore, it is advantageous to review the risk based on the parent's and project's perspective. Each perspective has a different way of adjusting risk. For example, the parent company may propose to treat all foreign risk as a single problem by increasing the discount rate applicable to the foreign projects or incorporate all foreign risk into adjustments to forecasted cash flows of the project. The first option is usually not recommended because it may penalize the cash flows that are not really affected by any sort of risk and may ignore events that are favorable to the organization. The four components are initial investment outlay; net cash benefits (or savings) from the operations; terminal cash flow; and net present value (NPV) technique.

APPLICATION

Given the complexities experienced by most multinational corporations when evaluating foreign investments, researchers in the field have indicated a need for a better way to evaluate the investments. One proposal was to establish operational foreign investment criteria that are consistent with the behavioral theory of the corporation. Stonehill and Nathanson (1968) conducted a survey to see what methods were utilized by organizations when making multinational financing investments. The researchers used Fortune's list and selected 219 American firms and 100 foreign firms. The results of their research revealed that most foreign and domestic investment alternatives use the same capital budgeting procedures. However, there was a difference in the way that organizations viewed foreign income. More than 64 percent of the organizations did not vary cost or capital for foreign investments. Nearly all the organizations indicated that they made allowances for risk and consolidated majority-owned foreign subsidiaries with domestic divisions.

Oblak and Helm (1980) conducted a similar study to see if there had been any significant changes since the study conducted by Stonehill and Nathanson.

Their survey was sent to 226 Fortune 500 organizations that operated wholly owned subsidiaries in twelve or more foreign countries. There was a 26 percent response rate and the capital budgets of the respondent firms ranged from $10 million to $2 billion annually with a median of $200 million. The results of the survey indicated that multinational corporations conducted more detailed analyses of their foreign projects. Compared to the results found by Stonehill and Nathanson in 1966, Oblak and Helm reported that a higher percentage of multinational corporations used discounted cash flow methods and adjusted for risk in foreign project evaluations. However, the corporations had not made a significant change in the way in which they measured the returns from foreign projects or determined the appropriate discount rate.

VIEWPOINT

"Capital budgeting is a financial analysis tool that applies quantitative analysis to support strong management decisions" (Bearing Point, n.d.). Capital budgeting seeks to provide a simple way for the finance department to see the "big picture" of the benefits, costs and risks a corporation planning to make short-term and/or long-term investments may experience. Unfortunately, many of the leading methods for capital budgeting resulted in problems; especially when an organization is using a standardized template. Examples of potential problems include:

- The benefits, costs, and risks associated with an investment tend to be different based on the type of industry (i.e. technology versus agricultural).
- A corporation may highlight the end results of the return on investment model and the assumptions that support the results versus a balanced analysis of benefits, costs, and risks.

If an organization does not account for the above-mentioned scenarios, there is a possibility of skewed results, which would make the data unusable. This type of error could keep a project from being approved. Therefore, it is critical for financial analysts to have a more effective and efficient technique to use. Bearing Point (n.d.) identified several leading practices that organizations are using in order to avoid reporting faulty information. The theme in all the techniques is that capital budgeting is not the only factor considered. Other quantifiable factors are utilized in order to see the big picture.

Consider the nature of the request—The type of benefit obtained by the investment will determine the nature of the request. Therefore, it may be beneficial to classify the benefit types into categories such as strategic, quantifiable, and intangible.

All benefits are not created equal—Benefits should be classified correctly in order to properly analyze. There are two types of benefits: hard and soft. Hard benefits affect the profit- and-loss statement directly, but soft benefits do not have the same effect.

Quantify risk—Make sure that the risks are properly evaluated. In most cases, risks are neglected. Also, it would be a good idea to build a risk factor into whatever model is utilized.

Walmart is an American multinational corporation. Here shoppers browse in the toy department at a Walmart store in Hangzhou, China. (Courtesy of Alexmar983 CC BY-SA 4.0 via Wikimedia Commons)

Be realistic about benefit periods—Make sure that the expectations are realistic. In the past, corporations have created unrealistic goals for the benefits period by anticipating benefits to come too early and reusing models that reflect the depreciation period for the capital asset.

CONCLUSION

Capital budgeting could be the result of purchasing assets that are new for the organization or getting rid of some of the current assets in order to be more efficient. The finance team will be charged with evaluating which projects would be good investments, which assets would add value to the current portfolio, and how much the organization is willing to invest into each asset. International capital budgeting refers to when projects are located in host countries other than the home country of the multinational corporation.

International capital budgeting can be a very complex process as the financial analysts carefully conduct a cost-benefit analysis comparing cash inflow and outflow. Stonehill and Nathanson (1968) recognized that there could be potential problems when applying the "pure" capital budgeting theory to a multinational corporation, and made the following recommendations when performing the techniques:

- Incremental cash inflow from the viewpoint of the parent corporation should include dividends, know-how payments, interest and loan repayments, export profits, any intangible gains, and the "cash out" value of the subsidiary at a time horizon that allows capital budgeting to reflect the value of reinvested earnings. Cash outflow should include both equity and loan capital provided to the subsidiary.
- Incremental cash inflow from the viewpoint of a foreign subsidiary should include net earnings after local taxes but before depreciation interest and "know how" payments. Cash outflow should be the original investment in assets.
- The parent corporation should discount the cash flows by its normal weighted average cost of capital under an "optimal" capital structure.
- The foreign subsidiary should discount its cash flow by its own weighted average cost of capital under an "optimal" capital structure. The optimal

capital structure may be different than other local firms because of the financial backing of the parent corporation (p. 52).

Bibliography

Ang, J., & Lai, T. (1989). "A simple rule for multinational capital budgeting." *Global Finance Journal, 1,* 71-76.

Bearing Point (n.d.). Improve your capital budget techniques. Retrieved from xlink:href="http://office.microsoft.com/en-us/help/HA01155 3851033.aspx"

Booth, L. (1982). "Capital budgeting frameworks for the multinational corporation." *Journal of International Business Studies, 13,* 113–123.

Guillén, M. F., & García-Canal, E. (2009). "The American model of the multinational firm and the "new" multinationals from emerging economies." *Academy of Management Perspectives, 23,* 23–35.

Lutz, S. (2012). "Determination of market values and risk premia of multi-national enterprises and its application to transfer-pricing." *International Business Research, 5,* 1–7.

Maria, M. (2009). "Operational risk in international business: Taxonomy and assessment methods." *Annals of the University Of Oradea, Economic Science Series, 18,* 195–201.

Oblak, D., & Helm Jr., R. (1980). "Survey and analysis of capital budgeting methods used by multinationals." *Financial Management (1972), 9,* 37–41.

Shapiro, A. (1978). "Capital budgeting for the multinational corporation." *Financial Management (1972), 7,* 7–16.

Stonehill, A., & Nathanson, L. (1968). "Capital budgeting and the multinational corporation." *California Management Review, 10,* 39–54.

Suggested Reading

Dotan, A., & Ovadia, A. (1986). "A capital-budgeting decision-The case of a multinational corporation operating in high-inflation countries." *Journal of Business Research, 14,* 403–410.

Edmunds, J., & Ellis, D. (1999). "A stock market-driven reformulation of multinational capital budgeting." *European Management Journal, 17,* 310–316.

Stanley, M. (1993). "Multinational capital budgeting, emerging markets and managerial agency: A proposal for an ethically constrained capital budgeting model." *Business & Professional Ethics Journal, 12,* 87.

—*Marie Gould*

N

NORTH AMERICAN FREE TRADE AGREEMENT (NAFTA)

ABSTRACT

This article concerns the North American Free Trade Agreement (NAFTA) that became effective in 1994. This is an agreement signed by the United States, Canada, and Mexico aimed at eliminating trade barriers among the three nations. Essentially, NAFTA is an extension of the Free Trade Agreement (FTA) between Canada and the United States that was established in 1989. There are a number of other considerations beyond free trade under the scope of NAFTA, including, but not limited to, intellectual property, telecommunications, and environmental protection. This article will provide an overview of the history of NAFTA and its impact on trade and labor in North America. There will also be a discussion of the agreement's effect on certain industries in each signatory country as well as issues related to NAFTA.

NAFTA members: from left: Mexican President Enrique Pena Nieta, Canadian Prime Minister Justin Trudeau and U.S. President Barack Obama at the North American Leaders' Summit in Ottawa, Ontario, Canada, on June 29, 2016. (Courtesy of Presidencia de la República Mexicana CC BY 2.0 via Wikimedia Commons)

OVERVIEW

History of NAFTA
In January of 1994, the United States, Canada, and Mexico entered into the North American Free Trade

Log driving near Vancouver, British Columbia, Canada. British Columbia is a major exporter of soft lumber to the United States. Such trade is governed under NAFTA. (Courtesy of Tony Hisgett CC BY 2.0 via Wikimedia Commons)

Agreement (NAFTA or the Agreement), and in so doing created the largest free trade zone in the world. At that time, NAFTA was the most comprehensive free trade agreement implemented by friendly nations. Moreover, the Agreement marked the first time that a developing nation entered into such a trade relationship with developed nations (Hirsch, 1995).

NAFTA was essentially an expansion of the Free Trade Agreement (FTA) entered into between the United States and Canada in 1989. Canada and the United States were already each other's largest trading partners, and the FTA was aimed at eliminating tariffs between the two countries. Even though the United States and Canada had long established trading relations, there were numerous disputes over tariffs imposed on certain products. This was particularly the case with respect to trade of softwood lumber.

Softwood lumber is the largest product that Canada exports to the United States and is used extensively by U.S. homebuilders. Softwood lumber is produced from pine, spruce, firs, and other "softwood" trees. In addition to softwood lumber, Canada also supplies the United States with oil and natural gas while the United States exports significant amounts of beef as well as a broad array of agricultural products to Canada. So the FTA was aimed at eliminating barriers to trade between the two nations, and ultimately making the agreement multilateral.

Prior to the enactment of NAFTA, goods traded between Canada and the United States received most favored nation treatment. This is the manner in which nations must treat each other's goods and services. Most favored nation status provides equal levels of "preferential" treatment to products manufactured in countries that are signatories to the General Agreement on Tariffs and Trade (GATT), an agreement initially negotiated in 1947 among twenty-three countries including the United States, Canada, and those in Western Europe. Over the ensuing years, GATT was expanded to include many of the developing nations. The so-called Uruguay Round of negotiations during the 1980s resulted in the establishment of the World Trade Organization (WTO) in 1995. The purpose of this organization is to oversee the further implementation of GATT and the agreements established by the Uruguay Round. Included in those agreements were the elimination of duty restrictions and a timetable to eliminate tariffs on certain products. These are important developments to consider as the expansion of world trade has affected trade among the United States, Mexico, and Canada.

In addition to goods and services traded between the United States and Canada being granted most favored nation treatment, under the terms of the FTA, Canadian manufactured goods that were made from products imported from the United States and were subsequently exported back to the United States were entitled to the return of duty that had been imposed on the imported products. A duty is essentially a tax on an imported good or service, and in some ways is similar to a tariff. A tariff, moreover, is a fee imposed on imported goods that gives locally produced goods a price advantage over similar goods that are produced abroad. Essentially, there are two types of tariffs:

- An ad valorem tariff is a fee calculated as a percentage of the value of the imported good.
- A specific tariff, on the other hand, is a set dollar amount applied to each imported unit of a product.

With respect to products that were exported from Mexico to Canada, duty rates were decreased because Mexico is considered a developing country (Hirsch, 1995).

Including Mexico in a free trade agreement was a natural progression of the FTA since both the United States and Canada were trading with Mexico under separate bilateral agreements. Further, the fact that disputes still remained between Canada and the United States required revisions to the FTA. The main objectives of NAFTA were to eliminate trade barriers and expedite the shipment of products among the nations; allow for fair competition and enhanced investment opportunities; establish effective implementation procedures and a system to resolve disputes; and finally, create a framework for the expansion of the Agreement to establish greater multilateral trade and cooperation (Hirsch, 1995).

Effects of NAFTA

NAFTA effectively eliminated duty rates for products flowing through the three nations and requires the importer to verify the origin of the goods. Since NAFTA was initially limited to the three signing nations, there was a need to establish strict controls to verify the country of origin of imported products.

This was an especially sensitive issue for Canada, since certain wood products from the United States are manufactured with wood from other countries. Therefore, NAFTA established a system that places the burden on manufacturers and importers to verify the country of origin. The administrative procedures put into place require the completion of a certificate of origin. This is a statement provided by the supplier of a good or service that the product is in compliance with the rules of origin requirements of the agreement (Hirsch, 1995).

At the time NAFTA was being negotiated, it was a hot-button political issue that played a role in the presidential campaigns in all three nations. However, since the Agreement was signed in 1994, there has been an increase in free trade among Canada, Mexico, and the United States. Trade is considered "free" or open when goods or services can be delivered into markets without duty restrictions and, therefore, prices are ultimately determined by supply and demand. One of the objectives of free trade is to provide consumers expanded choices for goods and services. This increased competition should result in lower prices and improved quality of products and most importantly economic stability in the North American marketplace.

While each of the signatory nations to NAFTA has benefited from the pact, there have been complications. The establishment of the WTO in 1995 and the agreements of the Uruguay Round contained provisions for eliminating tariffs that replaced or superseded those established by NAFTA. Moreover, after China was granted most favored nation status by the United States and eventually admitted into the WTO, increased trade between China and the United States affected trading levels with Mexico and Canada. In fact, for a time, China became America's largest trading partner and American manufacturing jobs that many claimed would be lost to Mexico were actually lost to China; however, as of 2013, Canada and Mexico are again the largest trading partners with the United States (Bury, 2004; US Census, 2013).

APPLICATIONS

Benefits

Notwithstanding the foregoing impediments to the success of NAFTA, the Agreement has been positive for all three signatories. In addition to the benefits

that have arisen for consumers, there have also been benefits for certain North American businesses and industries. From the perspective of the United States, many businesses gained access to a greater market throughout North America and have been the beneficiaries of new export and investment opportunities. For Mexico, all products imported from the country became duty free by 2008, as all of the act's provisions became vested in January of that year. Canada has also benefited because the Agreement established procedures to resolve trade disputes that were not as extensive as the provisions originally set forth in the FTA. Ultimately, these procedures prompted the United States and Canada to resolve the longstanding dispute over the tariffs imposed by the United States on Canadian softwood lumber (Howard, 2006).

Canadian Furniture Industry

On a corollary note, the Canadian wood furniture industry has seen an increase in trade with the United States. Increased exports to the United States of Canadian-produced wood furniture has helped provide Canada with the opportunity to invest in modern technology, which ultimately led to more efficient and productive companies. On the other hand, in connection with rules and requirements for certificate of origin mentioned above, some Canadian manufacturers now use wood or other products that are manufactured in China and other Asian countries. In addition, these countries are also producing wood furniture at a lower cost than the Canadian producers, some of whom claim that the Asian nations are not competing fairly. Despite this development, there is still a great deal of opportunity for Canadian manufacturers, particularly those that emphasize the quality of their products (Howard 2006).

American Manufacturing

Some of the other industries that have benefited from NAFTA include those involved with agricultural trade, the automotive industry, and the textile and apparel industry. For the United States, NAFTA has enhanced the production and efficiency of the agricultural sector as the market has become more integrated. Moreover, vehicles and automotive parts that are manufactured in America have become more competitive and efficient. While some of these manufacturing jobs have been displaced from Midwestern states, there has been a net gain of manufacturing jobs in this sector in the Southeast. There has also been improvement in the American textile and apparel industry. Prior to NAFTA, America faced stiff opposition from Asian markets, and this sector saw many textile market job losses. However, the effect of the Agreement has been enhanced efficiency and productivity and manufacturing investment in the United States' textile and apparel industry (Field 2006).

North American Markets

One of the effects of increased international trade and competition has been the need for foreign businesses to establish a presence in North America. Moreover, one of the most significant impacts of NAFTA has been the effect the Agreement has had on the North American labor market. This is being manifested in the integration of a bi-national labor market particularly in the United States and Mexico; a result of the dramatic influx of Mexican citizens into the United States. Between 1994 and 2004, 10 million Mexicans moved to America. However, since that time, Mexican immigration to the United States has dropped off considerably. From 2005 to 2010, 1.4 million Mexicans immigrated to the United States (Passel, Cohn, & Gonzalez-Barrera, 2012). The influx of Mexican immigration from 1994 to 2004 correlates to the implementation of NAFTA, while its decline in subsequent years is attributable to the financial crisis that began in 2008 as well an

President Donald J. Trump signing Border Security and Immigration Enforcement Improvements Executive Order 13767 calling for the immediate extension of the border wall at the Department of Homeland Security on January 25, 2017. (Courtesy of the U.S. Department of Homeland Security via Wikimedia Commons)

increased spotlight on border security (Passel, Cohn, & Gonzalez-Barrera, 2012).

One factor contributing to the influx of migrant workers into the United States is the increased need for low-skilled labor, especially in the hospitality, construction, and agricultural industries. In this regard, the Mexican government has not been successful in establishing economic policies to create these jobs in their own country. In addition to the increased need for low-skilled workers, however, the United States and Mexico have also established programs for the recruiting, training, and seasonal allocation of managers, technicians, and skilled professionals. These developments have far-reaching implications for both countries (Quan, 2005).

American Economy

Overall, the Agreement has had a positive impact on the United States' economy. For example, during the 1990s, U.S. exports to Mexico increased 400 percent while exports to Canada increased by more than 200 percent. Further, exports from these two countries to the United States and each other also rose dramatically. This trend continued in the first decade of the twenty-first century. However, other world developments have tampered the positive effects of NAFTA. While China, as a most favored nation, became the largest exporter of goods to the United States and the integration of the European

A small fence separates densely-populated Tijuana, Mexica, right, from the United States in the Border Patrol's San Diego Sector. Construction is underway to extend a secondary fence over the top of this hill and eventually to the Pacific Ocean. (Courtesy of Sgt. 1st Class Gordon Hyde via Wikimedia Commons)

Union has resulted in increased global competition for the North American trading partners, another significant event had an effect on the early promise of NAFTA was the September 11, 2001, terrorist attacks on the United States. The ensuing war years have prompted America to partially turn its attention away from trade relations with Mexico to focus attention on the Mideast and Central Asia (Field, 2004).

Calls for Free Trade

In response to these world developments, however, have been increasing calls for the NAFTA members to reinvigorate the potential of free trade. Achieving this goal, however, will require North American companies, businesses, and industries to produce and trade goods more efficiently in order to be able to compete more effectively on a global scale with China, Asia, and the European Union. With respect to the latter, some have suggested looking at initiatives taken in Europe as a way forward for NAFTA. One idea has been to create the development of a North American customs union that would establish a common tariff for similar products that are manufactured in all three countries. The proceeds from this tariff could then be used to finance economic development in Mexico, particularly in areas other than the northern states (Field, 2004). Such a proposition is no longer part of mainstream discussion, though it remains a possibility.

In Mexico, funds from a common tariff could be used to develop the infrastructure of regions in central Mexico where there are isolated communities and insufficient roads connecting these communities. Developing the infrastructure would create construction jobs, which would also lead to the development of other service occupations in that region. Moreover, by developing this region, natural resources could be tapped, produced, and manufactured and ultimately traded. This would stimulate economic growth in Mexico and benefit the United States since many of the migrant workers coming to America have fled this region of Mexico because of the lack of jobs (Field, 2004).

VIEWPOINTS

Political, Economic & Environmental Issues

Many political, economic and environmental issues are related to trade relations. In particular, the "Doha Round" of negotiations in WTO has contemplated the elimination of all tariffs for products manufactured and traded among WTO members by 2018, which has the potential to mitigate possible future benefits of NAFTA and could also result in increased global trading competition. However, the WTO members participating in the Doha Round reached an impasse in 2008 over the issues, and no significant progress has been made since. Notwithstanding the concerns of global trade agreements, NAFTA has benefited the three signing countries, albeit in different ways and to different degrees.

Benefits of a Common Tariff for Mexico

All three countries have seen increased volumes of trade which, in turn, have led to the evolution of programs designed to expedite customs release and duty elimination. As trade grew, border patrol along the United States-Mexican border began to evolve and systems were put into place to track and expedite the movement of labor. Initially, the goal was to enhance trade efficiency; however, the events of 9-11 shifted the emphasis from trade efficiency to security. Further, the slowdown in the Mexican economy contributed to the influx of immigrants from Mexico to the United States. Despite the problems facing free trade in North America, there has been a push for renewed emphasis on NAFTA.

Central American Free Trade Agreement

In addition to the aforementioned initiatives, the provisions of NAFTA were expanded by the signing of the Central American Free Trade Agreement (CAFTA) in 2005. This is an agreement based on the principles of NAFTA that was entered into among the United States and its new Central American trading partners: Costa Rica, the Dominican Republic, El Salvador, Guatemala, Honduras, and Nicaragua. CAFTA eliminates most of the duties on certain U.S. products exported to those countries and has potential benefits for the chemical, environmental, and transportation equipment industries. At the same time, this agreement calls for investment by the United States in each of these countries. The aim of this investment is to develop infrastructure and create jobs (Field 2006).

By reinvigorating NAFTA and following through on the implementation of CAFTA, the Americas may become more efficient producers, manufacturers, and trading partners. The ultimate goals are to compete globally and enhance the economic prosperity of the developing countries.

BIBLIOGRAPHY

"Bordering on reform." (2005). *Latin American Monitor, 22,* 1–3.

Bury, S. (2004). "NAFTA: 10 years after." *Wood & Wood Products, 49,* 46–50.

Business Mexico, 15, 46–47. Retrieved from "16499557" xlink:type="simple">http://search.ebscohost.com/login.aspx?direct=true&db=buh&AN=16499557&site=ehost-live

Carlson, J. (2014). "NAFTA's legacy." *Baylor Business Review, 32,* 26–28.

Field, A.M. (2004). "A new vision for NAFTA." *The Journal of Commerce, 5,* 16–17.

Field, A.M. (2006). "CAFTA's payoff." *The Journal of Commerce, 7,* 38–39.

Hirsch, J. (1995). "The real day-to-day business of NAFTA." *CMA Magazine, 69,* 11.

Morton, R. (2006). NAFTA: Twelve years after. *Logistics Today, 47,* 10.

Prina, S. (2013). "Who benefited more from the North American free trade agreement: small or large farmers? Evidence from mexico." *Review of Development Economics, 17,* 594–608.

Quan, M., Chelini, E., Fanning, K., Mohar, G. & Fanning, K. (2005). *A silent integration.*

Passel, J.S., Cohn, D., & Gonzalez-Barrera, A. (2012, Apr 23). "Net migration from mexico falls to zero—and perhaps less." *Pew Research Center.*

Rothlisberger, L. (2012). "Nafta, labor, and the recovery project." *WorkingUSA, 15,* 67–86.

US Census Bureau. (2013, Nov 14). Top trading partners—September 2013. Retrieved from http://www.census.gov/foreign-trade/statistics/highlights/top/top1309yr.html

Villareal, M., Fergusson, I. (2017). "The North American free trade agreement (NAFTA)." *Digital Commons.*

SUGGESTED READING

Carpentier, C.L. (2006). "NAFTA Commission for Environmental Cooperation: Ongoing assessment of trade liberalization in North America." *Impact Assessment and Project Appraisal, 24,* 259–272.

Field, A. M., Szakonyi, M., & Cassidy, W. B. (2014). "NAFTA at 20." *Journal Of Commerce, 15,* 10–17.

Frickel, B.J., Kotcherlakota, V.V., Tenkorang, F.A., & Elder, B.R. (2011). "The effect of NAFTA on trade and investment between member countries." *International Business & Economics Research Journal, 10,* 1–8.

Hakim, P. (2006). "Is Washington losing Latin America?" *Foreign Affairs, 85,* 39–53.

Ley-Borras, R. (2005). "A decision analysis approach to policy issues: The NAFTA case." *Review of Policy Research, 22,* 687–708.

—*Richa S. Tiwary, PhD, MLS*

OPERATIONAL COST

ABSTRACT

Operational costs are those recurring costs incurred in the operation of a business. Seemingly simple in concept, the identification, allocation, and control of these costs are complex and have generated a plethora of management practices. This article clarifies what constitutes operational costs, including the distinction between direct, indirect, variable, and fixed costs. It then looks at some of the most common practices of accounting allocation, including absorption costing, marginal costing, activity-based costing, throughput accounting and target costing. Finally, it explores lean manufacturing, total quality management, and the theory of constraints as methods companies have used to control costs.

Operational costs are the recurring costs incurred by a company in the course of running its business. They encompass virtually all the expenses incurred by a company, except the costs of financing (interest), income tax, and depreciation. Thus, on the income statement, operating income is identified as remaining monies after the cost of revenue and other expenses are deducted from revenue.

Categories of Operational Cost

As an example, Dell Inc.'s 2005 income statement is shown below in Table 1 for illustration purposes. The two broad areas of operational costs are the cost of revenue and the operating expenses.

Direct & Indirect Costs

Operational costs include direct costs and indirect costs.

- Direct costs are those that can be directly attributable to specific products the company produces

	(In thousands)
Revenue	55,908,000
Cost of Revenue	45,958,000
Gross Profit	9,950,000
Operating Expenses	
Research & Development (R&D)	463,000
Selling, General & Administrative Expenses (SG&A)	5,140,000
Nonrecurring	
Other Operating Expenses	
Operating Income	4,347,000
Income from Continuing Operations	
Total Other Income/Expenses Net	255,000
Earnings before Interest & Taxes	4,602,000
Interest Expense	28,000
Income before Tax	4,574,000
Tax Expense	1,002,000
Net Income	3,572,000

and typically include materials and production labor.
- Indirect costs are not directly allocated to specific products or directly impacted by the level of production (at least over a short term).

The cost of revenue is generally comprised of direct costs, though certain manufacturing overhead is generally included through cost allocation, as we'll see later. Operating expenses are indirect costs.

Variable & Fixed Costs

This all seems relatively straight forward, but things get a little more complex beneath the surface. In addition to thinking of costs as direct and indirect, we must also consider whether they are variable or fixed.

- Variable costs vary in direct proportion to the volume of product being produced. For instance, if a widget factory produces 10,000 widgets per day and demand suddenly increases by 5,000 per

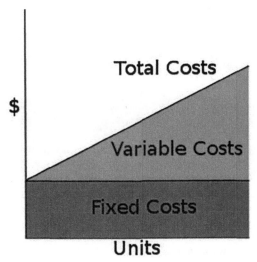

Decomposing total costs as fixed costs plus variable costs. Along with variable costs, fixed costs make up one of the two components of total cost: total cost is equal to fixed costs plus variable costs. (Courtesy of Nils R. Barth via Wikimedia Commons)

day, there are correspondingly immediate costs incurred by the factory, including an increase in raw materials being purchased and added production-line labor. Variable costs appear on the income statement in the cost of revenue.

- Fixed costs, on the other hand, relate to manufacturing and general overhead costs that cannot easily be allocated to specific production units. These costs are not immediately impacted by increases or decreases in production, and are therefore "fixed." On the income statement, fixed costs are included in both the Cost of Revenue (manufacturing overhead – a direct cost) and Operating Expenses (indirect costs).

There are two variations of fixed and variable costs worth noting. The first, "step" costs, are those that will change once certain levels of production are reached. For instance, as the production in the factory grows, at some point it will overcome the capacity of the janitorial staff to support it, and the factory will need to add more staff.

Another variation is a cost that includes a mix of direct and indirect costs. An example might be electricity to the factory. While the factory as a whole uses a baseline of electricity, each production unit also uses a portion of electricity to power its own equipment.

This is not simply an exercise in accounting mania, but has real implications for organizations because fixed costs are very often the larger percentage of overall costs. You can see from Dell's income statement that the cost of revenue (which includes an unknown amount of manufacturing overhead, a direct, fixed cost) consumes a whopping 82 percent of revenue, and operating expenses consumes another 56 percent. Once these are paid for, Dell is left with a mere 7.8 percent of revenue in operating profit. In fact, manufacturers (and many other industries) consider 10 percent operating profit to be quite good.

This then, is why cost accounting is such an important topic. From pricing product to capacity planning to profitability analysis, an understanding of the true costs of products is vital to a company's financial health.

Identification of Operational Costs in Manufacturing

There is an old adage in business – "you can't control what you don't measure." The first step in accounting for and controlling costs, then, is to understand what they are. The following provides more detail on the costs involved with manufacturing companies:

Cost of revenue represents the direct costs incurred to produce the products sold by the company. The primary costs include:

- Direct labor (production line staff)
- Materials (used in producing the products)
- Manufacturing overhead (e.g. non-production-line staff, general supplies, heat/light/power, freight)

R&D expenses are the costs associated with developing new products and improving existing products. They include:

- Labor
- Supplies
- Royalties & patents

Selling expenses are the costs associated with selling the products offered by the company. They include:

- Labor & commissions
- Market research

- Advertising
- Sales promotions
- Account management
- Travel & entertainment

Administration expenses are general overhead costs incurred by every company running a business:

- Financial functions – accounts payable and receivable, collections, payroll, budgeting, financial reporting, etc.
- Human resources administration – recruiting, training, compensation and benefits administration, etc.
- Information systems management – new systems implementations, systems maintenance, etc.
- Facilities management – lease management, janitorial functions, landscaping, etc.

In a typical accounting system, accounts are set up that reflect the above categories, and costs are allocated into these accounts as they are incurred. However, reports derived from these accounts are not very helpful in managing operational costs, except for comparing the costs over time and against budget. For instance, they do not tell us anything about how much direct labor is being spent on different products. Which products are contributing the most margin? Which might actually be unprofitable?

With all this, it becomes clear that the company's management is making important decisions for the firm with too little information. We need another way to identify and control costs.

Cost Allocation

There was a simpler time when a factory generally made a single product and most of the costs were directly allocated to that product. Indirect costs were limited to simple management and administrative functions and comprised a small percentage of overall costs.

However, over time factories became more diversified and began producing more varied product lines. The companies became more complex and factory overhead increased in size to accommodate these changes. Ancillary functions, such as human resources, accounting, compliance staff, facilities management and information systems, also became larger to deal with the increasing complexity. Pretty

As a marketing expense, Dell Inc. sponsors Dell Diamond, the home stadium of the Round Rock Express, the AAA minor league baseball affiliate of the Texas Rangers major league baseball team. Shown is the southwest entrance to the Dell Diamond in Round Rock, Texas. (Courtesy of Larry D. Moore CC BY-SA 4.0 via Wikimedia Commons)

soon, as we saw in the Dell example, indirect costs comprised a hefty portion of operating costs.

In order to track and control these costs, a number of methodologies, philosophies, and practices have been developed over the years to allocate costs in a more meaningful way. Some of the most prominent are discussed briefly here.

Absorption Costing

The earliest and still widely used method for allocating these costs is referred to as absorption costing. Also called standard cost accounting and full costing, it allocates manufacturing overhead evenly across products, thus providing a somewhat truer picture of what a product is actually costing the company to produce.

However, this blanket approach poses problems as the fixed costs become a larger part of the operational costs. It does not take into consideration that some products consume more overhead than others. Further, this method makes the "cost" of the product vary with production levels. If we produce 1,000 widgets this month and only 800 next month, the allocation of fixed costs produces a higher cost-per-unit in the second month. While this is seemingly meaningful and "correct," it makes pricing, among other things, difficult.

Marginal Costing

Marginal costing (also called contribution margin costing and break-even costing) is focused on pricing and profitability planning. Rather than trying to allocate fixed costs to production units, the company determines the cost of a production unit using only its variable costs (i.e. materials and direct labor). This cost is subtracted from the unit's selling price to determine its contribution margin – that is, the amount left over that is available for paying fixed costs.

The total annual fixed costs for the manufacturing cell where the unit is produced is then calculated and divided by the contribution margin to determine the number of units that need to be produced (and sold) to cover the fixed costs – or, in other words, the break-even point. The manufacturer would obviously want to produce more than this number to achieve profitability.

Activity-Based Costing (ABC)

In 1987, Robert Kaplan and Thomas Johnson introduced Activity-Based Costing (ABC) in their book *Relevance Lost – The Rise and Fall of Management Accounting*. They claimed that traditional cost accounting (i.e. financial reporting) was not timely enough nor detailed enough, and focused on cost reduction rather than on identifying how those costs were contributing to profitability.

ABC involves identifying activities associated with specific cost objects (e.g. a product). An activity could be, for example, a purchasing function for reordering parts. The resources (time or labor, paper, phone, etc.) associated with this activity are assigned a cost and that cost is associated to the cost object (the consumer of the activity) when it needs that activity performed. A cost driver (what triggers the activity to be executed) is identified that links the activity with the cost object to determine when an allocation is required.

This method of cost accounting certainly enables companies to identify their operational costs and make well-informed decisions regarding product and company strategies, but it is a complex and costly system to implement and maintain. Many firms abandoned their attempts at it and Kaplan himself noted that the adoption rate was low and the cost too high in many cases.

His improved version came in April 2007, with the co-authored book *Time-Driven Activity-Based Costing*. Kaplan recognized that the practice of assigning costs to activities was the primary cause for the complexity and cost of ABC, and replaced this core aspect of ABC with a much simpler model. In time-driven

ABC, the company need only estimate the cost rate of supplying capacity for each department or process and then determine how much of that capacity is used by each transaction, product, or customer.

Another update on ABC has been the development of Resource Consumption Accounting (RCA), which is a blend of activity based costing and Germany's cost management system, Grenzplankostenrechnung (GPK).

These approaches all focus on the resources that are consumed by activities or cost centers to determine the profitability of specific products, set pricing, and identify wasteful practices.

Throughput Accounting

Throughput accounting (TA) was developed in response to the application of the Theory of Constraints (discussed later). In this accounting, only total variable costs (TVC) are allocated as cost of revenue. TVCs are those costs that truly vary with the addition of each product unit. Thus, these are generally just the material costs, though in certain cases, direct production labor may be included if it is truly piece-based labor. In TA, all other costs are operating expenses.

The advantage of this method is that it allows management to more easily identify the impact to unit costs (How much more money will we generate?), fixed costs (How much more in operating expenses will it cost us?), and captured costs (What do we need to make it happen – e.g. equipment?) when making decisions about production.

Target Costing

Target costing (TC) is a unique approach to costing that is preemptive rather than reactive. That is, instead of analyzing costs to set pricing, the market is used to determine the best competitive price of the product. After deducting a desired profit margin from the price, the remaining amount becomes the target cost for the production of the unit. The manufacturing process is then defined to produce the unit at that cost and continuous improvement efforts are aimed at keeping the costs at that target.

This method is used most often in conjunction with lean manufacturing (discussed below).

Controlling Costs

The next step after allocating and understanding unit costs, of course, is controlling them. Numerous methods have been developed over the years to do just this, from focusing on the intricacies of the manufacturing process to enterprise solutions dealing with such decisions as the physical location of the plant and the efficiencies of administrative overhead. Some of these approaches are explored here.

Lean Manufacturing

Lean manufacturing arose out of Toyota's Total Production System (TPS), particularly for its focus on eliminating waste. The book *Lean Thinking* by James Womack and Daniel Jones, released in 2000, resulted in a growing popularity in manufacturing for lean practices.

Lean manufacturing focuses on the elimination of muda, the Japanese word for waste. Taiichi Ohno, Toyota's Chief Engineer and later CEO, identified seven wastes in the context of the TPS:

- Overproduction – Producing more than the customers need.
- Waiting – Idle time of people waiting for something.
- Transportation – Moving materials from one place to another without adding value.

The new headquarters of the Toyota Motor Corporation opened in February 2005 in Toyota City, Japan. (Courtesy of Chris 73 CC BY-SA 3.0 via Wikimedia Commons)

- Inventory – Holding too much inventory (raw materials, work-in-progress, and finished goods.
- Motion – Inefficient people movement.
- Over-processing – Making to a higher standard than is needed by the customer.
- Defects/Correction – Time spent detecting, correcting, disposing of, and preventing defects.

TA myriad of lean tools have been developed to tackle these wastes. A few of the more notable are:

- 5S – Basic workplace housekeeping. Seiri (Sort – put things in order), Seiton (Straighten – arrange things so that they're easily accessible), Seiso (Shine – keep things clean), Seiketsu (Standardize – consistency in how things are done), Shitsuke (Sustain – commitment to keeping to these practices).
- Total Productive Maintenance (TPM) – A system to ensure that machines and equipment are in top condition, thereby reducing or eliminating emergency and unscheduled down time.
- Kanban – A "pull" system using signals to communicate the need for more material. Materials should not be stockpiled, but made available as they are needed.

Lean manufacturing, unlike TOC, focuses on reducing costs by eliminating waste. It is not concerned, per se, with maximizing throughput like TOC, but achieves that as a natural outcome of waste reduction.

Total Quality Management (TQM)

Another management practice arising out of the TPS is total quality management (TQM). TQM focuses on continuous improvement of the quality of products produced and eliminating the costs associated with poor quality. The philosophy behind TQM is that it is much more expensive to deal with the repercussions of poor quality (detecting, fixing, customer complaints) than to prevent their occurrence in the first place.

A key measure for this practice is the Cost of Quality (COQ). This includes prevention costs (avoiding quality issues), appraisal costs (inspecting for errors or defects), internal failure costs (fixing/ rework), external failure costs (customer returns and other issues associated with defective items that were shipped) ("Strategic cost management," 2000). Thus, TQM focuses on reducing costs by improving quality.

The Theory of Constraints

Physicist Eliyahu Goldratt in his best-selling novel *The Goal* introduced the Theory of Constraints (TOC), in 2004. The core principle of TOC is that companies exist to make money and should do whatever is needed to enable its processes to generate more money. Dr. Goldratt proposed that constraints in those processes inhibited companies from maximizing this goal, and organizations should focus on those constraints. There are five steps to achieving this:

Identify the system's key constraint. This would be the one thing in the organization that most impacts the achievement of the goal. It might be specialized equipment that has limited capacity relative to the capacity of other equipment in the chain, or a specialized skill set, or even an insufficient number of customers (if the capacity of the operations is greater than the demand).

Exploit the constraint. Determine how the organization is going to enable the constraint to maximize its throughput.

Subordinate everything in the organization to this constraint. The organization puts in place processes that ensure the constraint is exploited to the fullest to achieve maximum throughput. Everything is focused on optimizing the constraint. The constraint or control point becomes the "drum" for the entire organization, setting the pace for production, and is driven by demand.

Elevate the constraint. Enlarge the constraint to achieve more capacity. If the constraint is the equipment, add more equipment. If the constraint is insufficient customers, enlarge the marketing and sales force.

Constraint shift. In the course of these activities, the key constraint may shift. For example, if the equipment is optimized, the shipping process may become a bottleneck. This, then, becomes the new constraint, and requires moving back to Step 1.

The interesting thing about TOC is that it moves always from the traditional practice of focusing on costs and instead improves the company's ability to optimize its moneymaking capabilities. In the course of this, relevant cost reduction naturally takes place.

The strength of TOC is in its simplicity (in concept, if not in implementation) and the focus it creates within an organization to streamline its value-chain processes. Unlike ABC, which focuses on allocating overhead costs to identify inefficiencies, TOC lumps all overhead costs into one bucket and doesn't worry about allocation at all. It's theory surmises that those inefficiencies that matter will be addressed through the 5 steps, and those that aren't identified don't matter anyway.

Enterprise Level Cost Approaches

Of course, cost control doesn't stop on the factory floor. Companies have implemented a variety of cost-control measures over the years to keep down manufacturing and administrative overhead, including

Israeli scientist Eliyahu M. Goldratt. (Courtesy of Wikipedia)

outsourcing, relocation, compressed workweeks, safety practices to reduce claims, and even outsourcing the human resources function.

CONCLUSION

While the various approaches outlined above resolve the issues of allocation and control in theory, in practice they are very difficult and complex to implement, and therefore costly. So, ironically, companies are spending more money to control costs. And they are often failing to get these systems in place. In fact, about 60 percent of U.S. firms started ABC projects, but only 20 percent were able to complete them (Shaman, 2003).

Some approaches, like throughput accounting, attempt to get around the complexity by shifting focus away from the tedious analysis of costs. But they have all had their successes and failures. It may be that the nature of business best dictates the approach that works best. It remains to be seen if there will be a clear winner.

BIBLIOGRAPHY

"Activity-based costing" (2005, May 1). *A to Z of Management Concepts & Models*, 7–9.

Ando, M., Upfal, E. (2017). "Minimizing operational cost for zero information leakage." *Communications (ICC)*.

Baxter, W.T. (2005). "Direct versus absorption costing: A comment." *Accounting, Business & Financial History*, 15(1), 89–91.

"Business Recordkeeping" (n.d.). Retrieved xlink:href="http://www.tenonline.org/art/bsr/9803.html"

Chen, R.C., & Chung, C.H. (2002). "Cause-effect analysis for target costing." *Management Accounting Quarterly*, 3(2), 1–9.

Carmen, P.D. (2004). "Legal solutions for reducing your labor costs." *Business Journal* (Central New York), 18(12), 7–10.

Chapter 8: Section 1: "Costing for planning" (1998, October 20). *Finance & Accounting Desktop Guide*, 246–253.

Corbett, T. (2006). "Three-questions accounting." *Strategic Finance*, 87(10), 48–55.

Crain, W. M., & Johnson, J. (2001, December 1). "Compliance costs of federal workplace regulations: Survey results for U.S. manufacturers."

Retrieved from xlink:href="http://www.mercatus.org/publications/pubID.1220/pub%5Fdetail.asp"

Dell, Inc. (2005). "Fiscal 2005 in review." Retrieved from xlink:href="http://i.dell.com/sites/doccontent/corporate/financials/en/Documents/ar%5Ffy2005%5Fannual.pdf"

Hashmi, K. (2000-2007). "Introduction and implementation of total quality management (TQM)." Retrieved from xlink:href="http://www.isixsigma.com/library/content/c031008a.asp"

Hoffman, W. (2007). "Automatic productivity." *Journal of Commerce* (15307557), 8(21), 18–18.

Husby, P. (2007). "Becoming lean." *Material Handling Management*, 62(8), 42–45.

Kaplan, R.S. (2007). "The Speed-Reading Organization." *Business Finance*, 13(6), 39–42.

Lansing, T. (2013). "Regulation of exchange traded funds as part of ESMA guidelines implementation: Operational costs and requirements for exchanges." *Journal of Securities Operations & Custody*, 6(1), 19–24.

Myrick, M. (2007, August 23). "Lean, Six Sigma prove cost effective for business operations." ARMY.MIL/NEWS. Retrieved from xlink:href="http://www.army.mil/-news/2007/08/23/4554-lean-six-sigma-prove-costeffective-for-business-operations/"

Rickards, R.C. (2005). "Management perspectives on problems in controlling and cost accounting." *Investment Management & Financial Observations*, 2(3), 109–1271.

Sharman, P.A. (2003). "The case for management accounting." *Strategic Finance*, 85(4), 1.

Spanos, M. (2012). "Controlling operational cost and risk." *Money Management Executive*, 20(45), 9.

Strategic cost management (2000). *Bulletpoint*, 69, 7–10.

Tulabandhula, T., & Rudin, C. (2013). "Machine learning with operational costs." *Journal of Machine Learning Research*, 14(7), 1989–2028.

SUGGESTED READING

Caplan, D., & Melumad, N. D., & Ziv, A. (2005). "Activity-based costing and cost interdependencies amount products: The denim finishing company." *Issues in Accounting Education*, 20(1), 51–62.

Goldratt, E. M., & Cox, J. (2004). *The goal*. Great Barrington, MA: North River Press.

Johnson, H. T., & Kaplan, R. S. (1987). *Relevance lost, the rise and fall of management accounting.* Boston: Harvard Business School Press.

Moore, R., & Scheinkopf, L. (1998). "Theory of constraints and lean manufacturing: Friends or foes?" Retrieved from xlink:href="http://www.tocca.com.au/uploaded/documents/Lean%20and%20TOC.pdf"

Womack, J. P., & Jones, D. T. (2003 New Ed edition). *Lean thinking.* New York: Free Press.

—*Joyce Gubata, MBA*

OPERATIONS AND BUSINESS PROCESS MANAGEMENT

ABSTRACT

Operations managers are increasingly concerned with the management of business processes in organizations. These processes are any of a number of linked activities that transform an input into the organization into an output that is delivered to the customer or other member of the supply chain. Emphasizing business processes enables the organization to be more flexible, optimize the responsiveness of the organization to the demands of the marketplace, reduce costs, and address issues of quality, consistency, and capability. Some of the most well-known approaches to business process management include business process reengineering, Total Quality Management, and Six Sigma programs. When applied correctly, these tools can be invaluable for optimizing the effectiveness of the organization.

Operations management comprises those areas of management that are concerned with productivity, quality, and cost in the operations function (i.e., the activities necessary to transform inputs such as

Entrance to Texas Instruments North Campus facility in Dallas, Texas. (Courtesy of Texas Instruments via Wikimedia Commons)

business transactions and information into outputs

Hewlett-Packard headquarters in Palo Alto, California. (Courtesy of LPS.1 via Wikimedia Commons)

such as completed transactions) as well as strategic planning for the organization. The discipline of operations management covers not only manufacturing processes, but also support processes that add value to the product or service and the management of the entire supply chain. Increasingly, operations managers are looking at this function in terms of business processes. These are a number of linked activities that transform an input into the organization into an output that is delivered to the customer or other member of the supply chain. Business processes include management processes, operational processes (e.g., purchasing, manufacturing, marketing), and supporting processes, (e.g., accounting, human resources). These processes are typically interrelated and cross-functional boundaries with both inputs and outputs. Business process management is the process of managing these processes on a continuing basis. A number of businesses have successfully implemented business process management, including Rank Xerox, Nortel, Texas Instruments, and Hewlett-Packard.

Operations managers are increasingly concerned with the management of business processes for a number of reasons. First, viewing the operations of an organization as a series of business processes allows organizations to be more flexible in meeting the changing demands placed upon them by the marketplace. Second, conceptualizing an organization's operations in terms of business processes can help optimize the speed of bringing new products and services to market and the responsiveness of the organization to the needs of the marketplace. Further, the emphasis on business processes that cross functional lines can also facilitate the reduction of costs as well as the increased reliability of delivery. Finally, an emphasis on business processes helps the organization address product and service quality issues by focusing on their consistency and capability.

Business processes have been categorized in a number of different ways. As shown in Figure 1, one empirically based approach divides business processes into four types: operational, support, direction-setting, and managerial. Operational processes include those processes that enable work to get done; in particular, the production of products or services including product development and order fulfillment. Operational processes are also integral to integrated supply-chain management and just-in-time manufacturing. It is operational processes that are most often targeted in business process reengineering efforts (see below). Support processes within the organization comprise those processes that enable the

operational processes to run smoothly. Support processes may provide support technology (e.g., information technology and systems), personnel-related processes (e.g., human resources management), and accounting skills (e.g., billing) to enable the effective performance of the organization. Direction-setting processes are those processes concerned with organizational strategy, marketing, and change management. Managerial processes comprise the decision-making and communication activities of the organization. In this categorization, direction-setting and management are broken into separate processes for two reasons: Not only has this approach proven a successful strategy in many practical models, but the literature tends to regard strategy as a process in its own right and not just a subset of management processes. It should be noted, however, that although this categorization – like most models – may not be a perfect fit for all instances in the real world, it does present a worthwhile framework for considering business process management research.

One of the most well-known aspects of business process management is business process reengineering. This is a management approach that strives to improve the effectiveness and efficiency of the various processes within an organization. Business process reengineering is intended to be a radical rethinking and redesign of business processes so that they achieve dramatic improvements in critical organizational performance criteria such as cost, quality, service, and speed. To do this, organizations need to reexamine the assumptions underlying their business operations and to question why they do things the way that they do. Frequently, this analysis reveals obsolete, erroneous, or inappropriate practices or procedures that do not add value to the product or service being offered by the business. Once the root of any business process problems that the organization is experiencing has been determined, the process can be reinvented – not just modified – to meet the needs of the organization to make it more effective, efficient, and flexible.

Since business process reengineering requires a total revamping of business processes, it is appropriate where more traditional methods fail or where there is a major discrepancy between where the organization is and where the organization needs to be. There are three types of organizations that can benefit from this type of major change effort. Businesses

(from Armistead & Machin, p. 893)

that are in serious trouble (e.g., have costs that are significantly higher than the competition's, customer service that is causing the organization to lose a significant number of customers, or failure rates that are significantly above those for the industry) often need a major retooling of their business processes. Organizations that find themselves in this situation have little choice than to perform a major overhaul of their business processes if they want to be viable. In addition, organizations that are not yet in such dire straits but headed on such a trajectory can often profit from business process reengineering. This situation can arise from any number of factors, like: increased competition; competitors that have significantly improved their offerings; or new customer needs that cannot be adequately met by the current business processes. Business process reengineering may make it possible for such organizations to avoid falling into the first category where reengineering is mandatory for the organization to survive. Another category of organization that can benefit from business process reengineering comprises top performing organizations with aggressive management who wants to take the organization farther. Business process reengineering can help such organizations further consolidate their position in the marketplace and create additional barriers to their competitors.

Another strategy often utilized in business process management that has been widely adapted in recent years is Total Quality Management (TQM). TQM attempts to increase the quality of goods, services, and concomitant customer satisfaction by raising awareness of quality concerns across the organization. This business process management strategy emphasizes developing an organizational environment that supports innovation and creativity as well as taking risks to meet customer demands using such techniques as participative problem solving that includes not only managers, but employees and customers as well.

TQM is based on five cornerstones: the product, the process that allows the product to be produced, the organization that provides the proper environment needed for the process to work, the leadership that guides the organization, and commitment to excellence throughout the organization. A successful TQM program needs to consider all five of these primary emphases. To help optimize the effectiveness of a TQM implementation in an organization, it is necessary to foster an environment of quality within the organization. This should include emphases on qualities such as consistency, integrity, and other positive interpersonal relationship skills. To enable the success of a TQM program, the organizational culture should also foster pride in the product and professionalism among the all team members through all levels of the organization. TQM also encourages organizations to implement a decentralized authority structure where decisions are made close to those affected and all have a chance to participate in the process. This helps to foster the teamwork necessary to bring about high quality. In this type of organizational culture, employees can be made to feel part of the system as well as a vital part of the organization, not just hirelings. Ownership of team members in the product can also be fostered by increasing the flow of communication across all levels of the organization and providing each employee the training that he or she needs to successfully add value to the product.

Six Sigma is a spin-off of TQM that is also an important element of many business process management implementations. The term "six sigma" refers to how far (i.e, the number of standard deviations, symbolized by the Greek letter sigma, s) a data point is from the middle of the normal curve. At six sigma above "normal," a product reaches its quality goal 99.9999997 percent of the time, or has only 3.4 defects per million. This is the goal toward which manufacturing and quality-control efforts in the organization are focused. The Six Sigma process can also be targeted toward improving non-manufacturing processes and functions within the organization.

The goal of Six Sigma programs is to reduce costs by making changes before defects or problems occur. To help reach the six sigma goal, employees and managers are trained in statistical analysis, project management, and problem-solving methodology so that they can use these skills to reduce defects in their products. By getting it right the first time and reducing costs for having to redo work previously done, most organizations that have implemented Six Sigma programs find that it increases their profitability and lowers their production costs.

APPLICATIONS

Although business process reengineering is still successful in many organizations and is a sound approach to organizational change and effectiveness, it is not as popular as it was when originally introduced. This is because in some instances, it was used as a code word to excuse making unpopular decisions such as layoffs or reductions in force without truly addressing the underlying problems or processes of the organization. However, business process re-engineering and business process management are both valuable concepts if correctly applied. For example, using qualitative methodology, Armistead and Machin examined business process management in four large organizations. These organizations were at various stages in their implementation of business process management, but were all considered excellent against various criteria of success as discussed above. The results of the study showed six clusters of attributes: organizational coordination, process definition, organizational structuring, cultural fit, improvement, and measurement.

Typically, business processes are characterized in part by the fact that they cross functional lines within the organization, starting with inputs from outside the organization and ending with outputs to the marketplace. One of the implications of this characteristic is that business process management is cross-functional in nature. Therefore, to be optimal, it is necessary to coordinate functions across the entire organization. Managers of organizations that have effectively implemented business process management tend to discuss how they run their entire organization rather than isolated pieces or processes. Processes are also described in layers from a top-level view down to an individual task-level view. To coordinate across the entire organization effectively, it is important to also manage the borders of the processes. This can be done, for example, by establishing networks around each process to formulate and implement strategy as well as to liaise with other processes with which there might be issues. In this way, not only can one business process be improved, but the other processes that impact or are impacted by it can be improved in a ripple effect throughout the organization.

As shown in Figure 2, when initially approaching business process management, most organizations tend to first address operational processes. Once these have been improved, organizations typically move on to also consider the support processes while maintaining their emphasis on operational processes. Direction-setting is then added to the mix while continuing to address the needs of the other two types

(Adapted from Armistead & Machin, p. 895)

of processes. Typically, management is considered a superordinate to the other categories of processes. This "sandcone" model of business processes has additional implications. First, as organizations develop their approaches to business process management, their techniques will change. In addition, as organizations move through the process of refining their business processes, there will be an increasing impact on the organizational structure. This means that structural changes (i.e., the design of an organization including its division of labor, delegation of authority, and span of control) will also need to be addressed in order to optimize the benefits of business process management. Finally, as the organization moves through the stages of emphasis in business process management, coordination throughout the organization will need to be concomitantly increased.

Another aspect of successful business process management is process definition. Although much of the literature deals specifically with business process improvement, empirical research has found that the real value of business process management does not come from focusing on the details of improving tasks at the task or team levels, but by defining and improving processes at a higher level. This often proves a difficult task, with much of the effort focusing on the defining procedures. However, communication across different levels of the organization can help overcome this problem by increasing a common understanding and definition of the processes of the organization.

In addition, another aspect that needs to be considered in the optimization of business process management is the structuring of the organization. Organizational structure is the design of an organization including its division of labor (i.e., the way in which work in an organization is divided into separate jobs assigned to different people), delegation of authority (i.e., authorization for a subordinate to make certain decisions in place of the supervisor), and span of control (i.e., number of employees who are directly supervised by the person one level above in the organizational hierarchy). Although some theorists propose that the best organizational structure for business process management revolves around the processes themselves, in practice, optimal structure is usually matrixed. In a matrix structure to organizational design, employees report both to a functional or departmental supervisor and to a project supervisor. Matrix structures in organizations that have implemented business process management matrix the organizational structure between processes and functions. Again, processes provide a framework for the relationships and help the organization build understanding and common approaches to processes across the organization. Although in theory these matrices may tend to be unstable and move toward a process-centric structure, in practice they are both stable and desirable and enable the organization to remain flexible so as to be more successfully responsive to various demands.

Business process management also needs to take into account the culture of the organization if it is to be effective. Organizational culture is the set of basic shared assumptions, values, and beliefs that affect the way employees act within an organization. Although in the long-term it may be necessary to address and change the organization's culture , to be successful, business process management needs to work within the parameters of organizational culture – at least within the short-term. This is as opposed to some approaches to business process reengineering that unsuccessfully attempt to implement change while running rough-shod over the organizational culture. Organizational culture often changes as the implementation of business process management techniques is successful and a drive to constantly improve processes builds within the organization. Finally, business process management can only be successful if measurement techniques are set in place. Organizations need to be able to objectively determine whether or not their change efforts and new processes are effective. In addition, they need to be able to continually identify trends, determine marketplace requirements, and assess the stability of the organization. This can be done through measuring performance against predetermined goals and objectives, collecting measures of customer satisfaction and loyalty, and looking at the efficiency of processes in addition to the effectiveness.

BIBLIOGRAPHY

Armistead, C. & Machin, S. (1997). "Implications of business process management for operations management." *International Journal of Operations & Production Management*, 17(9/10), 886 – 898.

Creech, B. (1994). *The five pillars of TQM: How to make total quality management work for you.* New York: Truman Talley Books/Dutton.

Grossman, T., Mehrotra, V., Sidaoui, M. (2018). "Alternative spreadsheet model designs for an operations management model embedded in a periodic business process." *Software Engineering.*

Hammer, M. & Champy, J. (1993). *Reengineering the corporation: A manifesto for business revolution.* New York: HarperBusiness.

Levis, J. (2012). "Seeing the forest and the trees." *Industrial Maintenance & Plant Operation,* 73(7), 34–35.

Saad, G. H., Greenberg, R. H., & Greenberg, P. (2012). "Using business process and operations management concepts to improve transparency and to protect stakeholder interest." *Journal of Accounting & Finance* (2158–3625), 12(1), 11–19.

Škrinjar, R., & Trkman, P. (2013). «Increasing process orientation with business process management: Critical practices.» *International Journal of Information Management,* 33(1), 48 – 60.

Vonderembse, M. A. & Marchal, W. G. (2001). "Operations management." In Saul I. Gass, S. I. & Harris, C. M. (eds.). *Encyclopedia of Operations Research and Management Science* (pp. 585– 588). New York: Wiley.

SUGGESTED READING

Austerberry, D. (2012). "Business process management." *Broadcast Engineering,* 54(10), 10–12.

Gershon, G. (2006). Service oriented architecture and business processes. AIIME-DOC, 20(3), 24–28.

Gomez, K. (2013). "The future is here now." *Process & Control Engineering (PACE),* 66(7), 10– 11.

Lambert, D. M., García-Dastugue, S. J., & Croxton, K. L. (2005). "An evaluation of process-oriented supply chain management frameworks." *Journal of Business Logistics,* 26(1), 25–51.

Liu, Y., Müller, S., & Xu, K. (2007). "A static compliance-checking framework for business process models." *IBM Systems Journal*, 46(2), 335–361.

McClure, M. (2006). "A case of automating the workflow." *EContent*, 29(8), 45–47.

Piller, G. (2005). "Process first, technology second." *Canadian Underwriter*, 72(2), 42–45.

—*Ruth A. Wienclaw, PhD*

OPERATIONS AND COMPETITION

ABSTRACT

In many industries today, one not only needs to be concerned about competition on a local or national level, but also with competition on an international level. To be viable in this increasingly competitive environment and maintain or increase market share, businesses need to be more concerned than ever with those areas of management that are concerned with productivity, quality, and cost in the operations function as well as strategic planning for the organization. This requires an emphasis on improving various aspects of operational functioning including the development of a sound strategy that will allow the organization to increase its competitive advantage, development of a value chain that will effectively and efficiently distribute inputs to and outputs from the organization while adding value to the product or service that is delivered to the customer, various performance variables including the implementation of a solid infrastructure that supports the business processes, the processes themselves, quality assurance mechanisms, and various human resource considerations including motivation.

Cargo planes make transport of goods fast and economical. Shown here is a FedEx McDonnell-DouglasMD-10-30F. (Courtesy of Wikipedia)

In many ways, today's global marketplace offers businesses many more opportunities than ever before. With the relative ease of transportation, it is significantly easier to provide goods and products to customers across the globe than it was once to provide them to customers across the country. Further, improvements in information technology mean that an increasing number of organizations are trafficking in information and services rather than in tangible products. These things are even better suited to the global marketplace since transportation and storage are typically not issues. In addition, the global economy not only means that there are more customers for an organization's goods and services, but also means that there are more opportunities to outsource offshore processes or functions in order to take advantage of cheap labor and production rates in other countries.

On the other hand, globalization also means that there is stiffer competition in many industries. Many organizations no longer need to be concerned only about competition on a local or national level, but about competition on an international level as well. This is true for a wide spectrum of industries. High-tech equipment is more likely to be made abroad than it is domestically. The call for technical help with a software problem may be answered in Manila. The X-ray taken in a local emergency room may be read in Delhi. Local microbrews must compete against the established products of large German breweries.

Importance of Operations Management

To be viable in this increasingly competitive environment and maintain or increase their market share, businesses need to be more concerned than ever with operations management. This discipline comprises those areas of management that are concerned with productivity, quality, and cost in the operations function (i.e., activities necessary to transform inputs such as business transactions and information into outputs such as completed transactions) as well as strategic planning for the organization. To successfully compete in the global marketplace, an increasing number of organizations are placing emphasis on becoming high-performing organizations that consistently outperform their competitors. As shown in Figure 1, this approach requires an emphasis on improving various aspects of operational functioning. These include the development of the following: a sound strategy that will allow the organization to increase its competitive advantage; a value chain that will effectively and efficiently distribute inputs to and outputs from the organization while adding value to the product or service that is delivered to the customer; various performance variables including the implementation of a solid infrastructure that supports the business processes; the processes themselves; quality assurance mechanisms; and various human resource considerations including motivation.

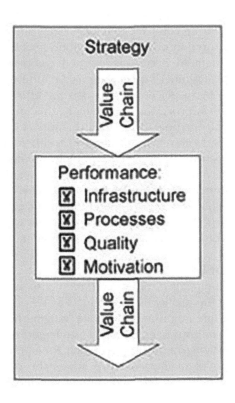

Strategic Planning

The first step to be taken in order to become or remain competitive in today's marketplace is to develop a strategic plan that will help clarify the organization's goals and objectives and develop an approach and processes to achieve these. Strategic planning allows the organization to determine and articulate its long-term goals and develop a plan to use the company's resources – including materials, equipment and technology, and personnel – in reaching these goals. Developing clear goals is essential to achieving and maintaining a competitive advantage in the marketplace. For example, for years, Domino's Pizza tried to differentiate itself from the competition by advertising that it would deliver its pizzas in 30 minutes or less or the pizza was free. Over time, however, Domino's found that the incentive of fast delivery was insufficient to stay ahead of the plethora of competition from pizza delivery restaurants ranging from

While no longer guaranteeing 30-minute deliveries, Domino employees still strive to make and deliver their pizzas as soon as possible while also maintaining their quality. Here an employee works the line at a local shop. (Courtesy of Apatzi CC BY-SA 3.0 via Wikimedia Commons)

other large chains to local mom-and-pop businesses. When a new CEO took over, the reason became clear. Although Domino's did meet its objective of delivering pizza quickly, the new head of the corporation found that not only was the pizza that was delivered not very good, it was also not hot. Steps have been taken to correct this situation so that Domino's can remain competitive in the marketplace.

Approaches for Developing Competitive Strategy

There are a number of approaches to developing a competitive strategy – a plan of action by which a business attempts to increase its competitive advantage. Typically, this is done in one of three ways. Businesses may achieve a competitive advantage by providing products or services at a lower cost than their competitors. This is the approach used by Walmart, for example. Another approach to achieving a competitive advantage is through differentiating one's product or service from that of the competition. The Domino's example cited above illustrates this approach. A third approach to developing a competitive advantage is by focusing on niche marketing – a sub-segment of a particular market where the consumers' needs are not being met and on which an organization focuses its efforts. A management consultant who only works with telecommunications companies would be an example of this approach.

Sam Walton's original Walton's Five and Dime store in Bentonville, Arkansas, now serving as The Walmart Museum. Walmart bases its business on the model of cheaper prices than the competition. (Courtesy of Bobak CC BY-SA 2.5 via Wikipedia Commons)

Aligning Business Processes with Goals & Objectives

Strategy alone, however, is insufficient to ensure the competitiveness of the organization. Business processes need to support the achievement of the organization's goals and objectives, and an infrastructure needs to be in place that supports the efficiency of the processes. Business processes are any of a number of linked activities that transform an input into the organization into an output that is delivered to the customer. Business processes include management processes, operational processes (e.g., purchasing, manufacturing, marketing), and supporting processes, (accounting, human resources). Business processes take one or more inputs such as data, raw materials, or components parts, and transform them into something that is of value to the customer. For example, a business could take raw demographic data concerning the people who live within a ten-mile radius of a retail store, analyze it, and create a report that tells the store management who lives in the area, what kind of products they need or want, and how to better target their inventory or displays. Another example of a business process would be a computer manufacturing company that takes chips and boards manufactured in other businesses and puts them together to build a custom-designed computer that meets the customer's specifications. An infrastructure needs to be in place that supports the efficiency of the business processes. Increasingly, this means the use of information technology to support business processes. However, investments in technology tend to be expensive. Therefore, technology should be put into place only for those processes in the organization that can increase its effectiveness and deliver added value to the customer. To merely automate processes that add nothing of value to the customer or to the product or service is not a sound investment.

Quality of Products & Services

To be competitive, an organization also needs to consider the quality of its products or services. This can be done in a number of ways, ranging from traditional industrial engineering strategies to Total Quality Management (TQM), which attempts to raise awareness of quality concerns across the organization. In addition, increased competition means that an organization needs to place increased emphasis on customer satisfaction. Efforts to do this can include

L.L. Bean, a mail-order and retail company that has its headquarters in Free-port, Maine, is known for its customer service. Pictured is their L.L.Bean shoe car (Bootmobile) driving along the streets in Freeport, Maine, on July 7, 2012. (Courtesy of Dirk Ingo Franke CC BY 3.0 via Wikimedia Commons)

the organization's intentional attempts at improving customer satisfaction through the institution of such things as around-the-clock customer service lines or email rebate systems; positioning itself to be perceived as environmentally or socially aware by lessening the environmental impact of a product or instituting a recycling plan; improving quality-control methods; or reducing the number of defects per group of products.

Employee Motivation

No matter how well-designed the organization's strategy, business processes, and infrastructure, if the employees are not motivated to implement these in such a way as to enable the development of a high-performing organization, these things will be insufficient to ensure competitiveness. One thing that can be done to help motivate employees to contribute to the company's high performance is to link the desired performance to rewards. This is frequently done through an approach called "pay for performance." In this approach, employees are rewarded financially for high performance and contributing to the organization's goals. Pay for performance can be effectively applied not only for workers at the bottom of the organizational structure such as production workers, but also to workers all the way up to the chief executive officer (CEO).

Value Chain Consideration

Development of a competitive strategy, however, requires not only an analysis and understanding of the organization itself, but of its entire value chain. This chain is the network of businesses working together to bring a product or service to the market. Value chains typically comprise one or a few primary suppliers supported by many secondary suppliers, each of whom adds value to the product or service before it is offered to the customer. A chain member can add value to a product or service by adding information (e.g., writing a user's guide or technical manual), inventory or warehousing the product, convenience for the customer (e.g., delivering the product to the customer's door, or making it available in a retail outlet where the customer can examine or compare products), and so forth.

Value chains comprise both primary and support activities. Primary value chain activities are the basic business processes that are foundational in any industry. These include inbound and outbound logistics, operations, marketing and sales, and service. Support value chain activities support the primary value chain activities, including procurement activities that acquire raw materials, supplies, equipment, facilities, or other items necessary for the business to do its work. Support value chain activities can also include technology development. Human resource management is another support activity that supports the organization in its work through policies and procedures related to managing human beings employed in an organization. These include recruitment and placement, training and development, compensation, and employee relations.

APPLICATIONS

Business Process Reengineering

Business process reengineering is a management approach that strives to improve the effectiveness and efficiency of the various processes within an organization. According to Hammer, one of the first practitioners to tout this practice in print, business process reengineering is much more than a cosmetic fix to refine current business practices and procedures within an organization so that they are more effective. It is a radical reconstruction of business procedures so that they achieve significant improvements in vital organizational performance criteria including cost, quality, service, and speed. Business process reengineering requires organizations to reexamine the assumptions underlying their business operations and question why they do things the way that they do. In many situations, this analysis will reveal obsolete, erroneous, or inappropriate practices or procedures that do not add value to the product or service being offered by the business. The purpose of this analysis is to get at the root of any business process problems that the organization is experiencing in order to reinvent the way that things are being done as opposed to modifying current practices in a way that is somewhat more effective.

Types of Organizations that Benefit from Business Process Reengineering

Of course, not every organization requires a major overhaul. Business process reengineering is appropriate when more traditional methods fail or there is a major discrepancy between where the organization is and where the organization needs to be. In general, there are three types of organizations that can benefit from business process reengineering. The first of these are businesses that are in serious trouble. Symptoms of this situation include having costs that are significantly higher than the competition's, customer service that is causing the organization to lose a significant number of customers, or failure rates that are significantly above those for the industry. Organizations that find themselves in such difficulties have little choice than to perform a major overhaul of their business processes if they want to be viable. The second type of organization that can benefit from business process reengineering are those organizations that are not yet in such dire straits but that are headed on a trajectory to that condition. This situation can arise from any number of factors, including increased competition or competitors that have significantly improved their offerings or new customer needs that cannot be adequately met by the current business processes. If business process reengineering is undertaken by organizations in this situation, it may be possible to avoid falling into the first category where reengineering is mandatory if the organization is to survive. The third category of organization that can benefit from business process reengineering comprises top performing organizations with aggressive management that wants to take them further. Business process reengineering in these organizations can help further consolidate their position in the marketplace and create further barriers to their competitors.

Common Results of Business Process Reengineering

TA number of recurring themes occur across organizations that reengineer their business processes. First, reengineering frequently results in several jobs being consolidated into one. For example, at IBM Credit, reengineering resulted in several specialist jobs (e.g., credit checker, pricer) being combined into one position. This reduced the need for communication and time delays (as tasks were handed off from person to person), and resulted in a single specialist who better understood the case. In addition, engineering the process in this way gave customers a single point of contact to call when they needed a problem resolved without endlessly repeating the details of their situation. Business process reengineering also often changes processes so that workers who better understand the situation can make decisions rather than submitting these up the line for a supervisor to consider. This results in fewer delays, lower overhead costs, and higher job satisfaction for employees. In addition, this reengineered process can help improve customer satisfaction by allowing quicker resolutions to problems. Similarly, business process reengineering often ends up with work being performed where it makes the most sense.

Another frequent result of reengineering a business process is that steps in the process are performed in a natural order rather than an artificial order that does not add value to the product or service. One of the principal tenets of business process reengineering is that tasks and activities associated with the process need to add value to it. For example, in a manufacturing company, a process might analyze the customer requirements and then translate these into internal product codes, transmit this information to various plants and warehouses, receive the various components, assemble the components into a finished product, and deliver and install the equipment, requiring the involvement of a different organization for each step in the process. These steps might traditionally be performed sequentially. However, if, for example, some of the data collected are not needed until delivery, time could be saved by not waiting until all of these steps were completed before starting the rest of the process. In addition, reengineered processes frequently have different versions. Standardization of business processes works fine in an assembly line, but many jobs today do not need this degree of structure. For example, many technical support agencies have a script for their technicians that helps them walk through the troubleshooting process with their callers step by step. Most of these procedures, however, are based on the assumption that the caller knows little or nothing about computers or troubleshooting. Therefore, if an experienced user calls for technical support he or she is forced to repeat the steps he or she has already performed in the troubleshooting process. This situation often ends up with an irritated customer who is determined at a minimum to never call for technical assistance again (which harms the profitability of the call center) or to never buy from the hardware manufacturer again. Allowing the technician more flexibility, however, could potentially avoid both these possibilities and ensure continuing customer loyalty instead.

BIBLIOGRAPHY

Eboreime, O. F., & Adedoyin, S. (2013). "Strategies for making competition irrelevant in the global market for developing economies." *Journal of Emerging Trends in Economics & Management Sciences,* 4 (3), 297–301.

Hammer, M. & Champy, J. (1993). *Reengineering the corporation: A manifesto for business revolution.* New York: HarperBusiness.

Jackson, E. (2013). "Operations is key to success." *MEED: Middle East Economic Digest,* 9.

Kittilaksanawong, W. (2016). "Catch-up strategies of emerging market firms: Lessons learned from India and China." *International Manufacturing Strategy in a Time of Great Flux,* 63–84.

McShane, S. L. & Von Glinow, M. A. (2003). *Organizational behavior: Emerging realities for the workplace revolution* (2nd ed). Boston: McGraw-Hill/Irwin.

Piercy, N. (2012). "Business history and operations management." *Business History,* 54 (2), 154–178.

Senn, J. A. (2004). *Information technology: Principles, practices, opportunities* (3rd ed.). Upper Saddle River, NJ: Pearson/Prentice Hall.

SUGGESTED READING

Banker, R. D., Khosla, I., & Sinha, K. K. (1998). "Quality and competition." *Management Science,* 44(9), 1179–1192.

Boyaci, T. & Gallego, G. (2004). "Supply chain coordination in a market with customer service competition." *Production & Operations Management,* 13(1), 3–22.

Colquitt, J., LePine, J. A. & Wesson, M. J. (2011). *Organizational behavior: Improving performance and commitment in the workplace.* 2nd ed. New York, NY: McGraw-Hill Irwin.

Fynes, B., De Búrca, S., & Voss, C. (2005). "Supply chain relationship quality, the competitive environment and performance." *International Journal of Production Research,* 43(16), 3303–3320.

Kumar, N. (2006). "Strategies to fight low-cost rivals." *Harvard Business Review,* 84(12), 104–112.

McGovern, G. & Moon, Y. (2007). "Companies and the customers who hate them." *Harvard Business Review,* 85(6), 78–84.

McShane, S. L., & von Glinow, M. A. Y. (2013). *Organizational behavior: Emerging knowledge, global reality.* 6th ed. New York, NY: McGraw-Hill Irwin.

Niederkohr, T. (2007). "How the race is won." *Aftermarket Business,* 117(5), 20–26.

Reddy, S. B. (2006). "Strategic flexibility and information technology properties: Competitive advantage and asset specificity." *Advances in Competitiveness Research,* 14(1), 16–43.

Tsay, A. A. & Agrawal, N. (2000). "Channel dynamics under price and service competition." *Manufacturing & Service Operations Management,* 2(4), 372–391.

—Ruth A. Wienclaw, PhD

P

POLITICAL ECONOMY OF SOCIAL POLICY

ABSTRACT

This article will focus on the political economy of social policy. The history, policymaking, and funding of social policy in the United States will be discussed. Areas of study include social welfare, social welfare provisions, the war on poverty, and the concept of a social safety net. The use of social indicators and social reports as the basis for policy choices will be analyzed. In addition, the strengths and limitations of problem-based and strength-based approaches to social policy will be described.

OVERVIEW

Social policy, like all public policy, is an expression of the values held by both citizens and their government. Social policy is an expression of moral and economic values and viewpoints. In the United States, social policies, enacted through social welfare programs and serving as a social safety net, regulate

Clara Donney, (right), a Meals on Wheels recipient of a Thanksgiving dinner sponsored by the Great Falls Community Food Bank, is all smiles as Airman 1st Class Courtney Taylor, customer service technician with the 341st Comptroller Squadron, delivers her meal. (Courtesy of U.S. Air Force photo/Airman 1st Class Katrina Heikkinen via Wikimedia Commons)

and govern human behavior in areas such as general morality and quality of life.

Social policy is created, in part, to respond to pressing social needs such as poverty, social exclusion, unemployment, aging, children, mental illness, learning disabilities, and physical disabilities. Social policy is developed, enacted, and implemented to create self-sufficiency, equity, and social cohesion for all members of a society. Examples of significant social policy created in the United States during the twentieth century include the Social Security system, welfare, public housing, hunger and nutrition programs, childcare and child support, health care for people on low incomes, public education, and the social and health services of the Veterans' Administration (Spicker, 2006). All of these social policies, and social policies in general, reflect moral, political, and economic choices.

The focus of this article is on the political economy of social policy. Political economy, a subfield of economics dating back to the eighteenth century, refers to the interactions between political processes and economic variables such as economic policies. Political economy describes how political institutions, the political environment, and market forces and structures, such as capitalism, influence each other. Thus the political economy of social policy is an examination of the relationship between politics, economics, and social policy (moral and value-based policy choices for citizens).

One of the main realms and purposes of political economy is the formulation of public policy. Political economy of social policy is a form of social economics that examines the ways in which market principles resolve social problems. Political economy of social policy is a tool for understanding social inequalities that exist in society due to policy choices, enduring structures, and status-quo power and economic relations. Political economy of social policy describes how the public welfare is connected to public access to public services and social programs (Klein, 1998).

In the United States, the political economy of social policy refers to the efforts of federal and state government to address the economic insecurity and inequality that result from lapses in regular income. Social policies tend to focus on maintenance of incomes, healthcare for sick, and basic services to those in crisis due to loss of income. In the United States, social policy is interconnected with economic policy (Amenta & Bonastia, 2001).

The following sections provide an in-depth description and analyses of social policy history and funding as well as an explanation of the American government's policymaking process. The policymaking section, with its focus on the U.S. Government Accountability Office's production of social indicators and social reports, will serve as a foundation for a later discussion of the complex issues concerning the problem-based approach of U.S. social policy.

The United States: Social Policy History & Funding
Social policy in the United States serves and functions as a social safety net for citizens. The United States has a welfare state that serves, protects, and provides for its members through social welfare provisions, social policy, social programs, and social welfare initiatives. Public sector (or governmental) social policy and support became common practice in the twentieth century. The twentieth century was

President Bill Clinton and Vice President Al Gore talk while walking through the Colonnade at the White House. While in office Clinton increased the work requirements in an attempt to curb welfare dependence. (Courtesy of Wikimedia Commons)

characterized, in part, by a switch in national perspective from individualism to interdependence. The social safety net switched from private sector (family, charity, community) to public sector (social policies such as welfare). The government became a source for social welfare provisions, such as public education, welfare payments, pensions, and Social Security for disadvantaged groups such as the poor, the elderly, the disabled, and students.

Significant social policy of the twentieth century includes Social Security, welfare, Medicare, Medicaid, and public housing. America's welfare system, the cornerstone of much U.S. social policy, began in 1935 with President Franklin D. Roosevelt's enactment of a social welfare program called Aid to Dependent Children (ADC) and expanded in the 1960s when President Lyndon B. Johnson added Medicare, Medicaid, and public housing programs. In 1996, President Bill Clinton reformed the social policies that structure the American welfare state or system to increase work requirements and reduce overall welfare dependence.

The twentieth-century economic expansion and transition to industrialized production created the reasons and means to finance social policy and programs in the United States. The needs of populations change as society's transition from small-scale production to industrialized production. Economic development, created by industrialization, increases work force, wage labor, the prevalence of isolated nuclear families, and creates the need for social policy. The new work force, dependent on income rather than agriculture or small business, is at risk from problems associated with income loss. The government (along with citizen self-support paid through taxes) subsidizes or insures the risk that citizens take by joining and working in industrialized economies and societies, through social policy. An industrialized society can afford (and desperately needs) social policy. This perspective is known as the modernization argument for social policy (Amenta & Bonastia, 2001).

Public sector social policy and the welfare state is funded through provisions established by Congress. Congress established the modern system of grants-in-aid to support state and local governments in the early twentieth century. Grants-in-aid refer to the federal funds appropriated by Congress for distribution to state and local governments. Congress awards four kinds of fiscal grants (Canada, 2003):

- Categorical grants: federal funds that can only be used by states for a pre-determined purpose.
- Block grants: federal funds given automatically to state and communities to support community development and social services programs and needs.
- Project grants: federal funds awarded on the basis of the merits and strengths of an application.
- Formula grants: federal funds awarded based on a set legislative or regulatory formula.

The funds for state and local budgets, which support social programs and enact social policies, come from federal grants, as described above, as well as indirect taxes and personal income taxes. Trends in government grants to state and local governments have followed social policy interests over the past few decades. State and local spending during the latter half of the twentieth century was characterized by the need to finance and support public education and Medicaid. Federal grants supported the economic burden and social responsibilities of these two social policy initiatives. Public education and Medicaid expenditures were responsible for 60 percent of the gross domestic product growth from 1952 to 1975 both locally and statewide. For example, between 1952 and 1976, grant increases were related to education, training, employment, and social services. The need to educate a growing population helped to create a peak in federal education grants in the late 1970s. Since that time, education grants have stabilized. Health grants increased significantly with the beginning of Medicaid in 1965 and then leveled off after 1976 (Penner, 1998).

The federally financed social policy program of Medicaid established a strong program and channel of grants to state and local governments. Medicaid characterized an era of big government. The size of grants-in-aid to state and local governments is declining (in areas such as education, training, transportation, and community development) as the federal government works to avoid a budget deficit. The decline in federal support has caused states and local governments to become more fiscally self-reliant in their efforts to finance the budget categories of public education, income support, Social Security, and welfare.

Making Social Policy: Social Indicators

Modern social policy is made based on the information provided through social indicators and social reporting. Social indicators refer to a social statistic that has significance for quality of life. Social report refers to an organized collection of social indicators. Social indicators are quantifiable tools used for evaluating social policies. Common social indicators include family characteristics, employment, working mothers, poverty persistence, social expenditure, healthcare expenditure, subjective well-being, and suicides. Social indicators, created and developed by economists, psychologists, sociologists, and politicians, are the link between social policy and economic theory and analyses (Michalos, 2004).

Social indicators are tools used to assess the impact of social policy as well as continued or emerging social needs. The social indicators movement of the 1960s corresponded with a boom in social policy initiatives and programs around the world. In the United States, the social policy focus centered on poverty. The anti-poverty agenda (typified by the 1960s "War on Poverty" campaign of the federal government) continued to direct current social policy choices (Kalimo, 2005).

The Organization for Economic Cooperation and Development (OECD), which was established in the 1960s, promotes the use of social indicators to evaluate

Rates of suicides are one social indicator used in evaluating social policies. This is the suicide prevention message on the Golden Gate Bridge in San Francisco California. (Courtesy of Miskatonic CC-BY-SA-3.0 via Wikimedia Commons)

President Lyndon B. Johnson, in his "war on poverty," signs the Poverty Bill (also known as the Economic Opportunity Act) while press and supporters of the bill watch on August 20, 1964. (Courtesy of the U.S. Government, LBJ Library, via Wikimedia Commons)

social trends and policy developments. The OECD social indicators serve as a widely adopted tool for planning, decision-making, and international comparisons of social policy (Kalimo, 2005). The OECD uses five main categories of social indicators. The 2011 categories include general context indicators, self-sufficiency indicators, equity indicators, health indicators, and social cohesion indicators (OECD, 2011).

- General context indicators: household income, age-dependency rates, fertility rates, migration, and marriage and divorce.
- Self-sufficiency indicators: employment, unemployment, education spending, student performance, and pensionable years.
- Equity indicators: income inequality, income difficulty, poverty, and public social spending.
- Health indicators: life expectancy, infant mortality, healthcare expenditure, water and air quality, and health inequalities.
- Social cohesion indicators: voting, confidence in social institutions, trust, tolerance, and pro- and anti-social behavior (OECD, 2011).

Numerous national governments and international aid and development organizations compile and

distribute sets of social indicators, in part, to meet the demand for quantifiable data about social progress and social need. Governments around the world, in particular Australia, New Zealand, Canada, and the United Kingdom, use social reporting to inform social policy. International organizations that depend on and produce social indicators include the United Nations and the World Bank.

The United States: Social Policy & National Indicators

The historical origins of social indicators in the United States date back to the early twentieth century when there were at least two major periods of use and dependence on social indicators. During the 1930s, statistics from National Income and Product Accounts were routinely used for public policymaking. The 1930s were characterized by postwar efforts to resolve and end economic recession. Planning associations, with work and social programs, developed to solve social and economic problems. During the 1950s and 1960s, social indicators were used primarily by governments committed to social activism. New social programs (such as welfare and Medicare) needed social indicators to monitor and evaluate their effect and progress. The motives for social policy indicators during the twentieth century focused on developing a grand social accounting scheme. Governments and aid organizations created social indicators as a means to use quantitative information to solve public policy problems (Michalos, 2004).

In the United States, social policy, such as those policies described above, is made at the federal level.

The General Accounting Office Building is the headquarters of the U.S. Government Accountability Office. It is located at 441 G Street NW in Washington, D.C. (Courtesy of AgnosticPreachersKid CC BY-SA 4.0 via Wikimedia Commons)

The U.S. government, specifically the Government Accountability Office (GAO) (formerly known as the General Accounting Office), begins the social policymaking process by gathering information about current federal programs, federal expenditures, and social needs. The gathering of information is a precursor to Congress's review and creation of its annual social policy agenda. (The policymaking process is known as a policy cycle, with four main stages: agenda setting, policy development, policy implementation, and policy review.) The Government Accountability Office is Congress's investigative arm. The information the GAO gathers and analyzes is used by Congress to make policy decisions that affect U.S. society and culture as well as the economy and the environment. The Government Accountability Office describes its purpose in the following way:

The U.S. Government Accountability Office (GAO) is an independent, nonpartisan agency that works for Congress. Often called the "congressional watchdog,:"

> "GAO investigates how the federal government spends taxpayer dollars. . . . Our mission is to support the Congress in meeting its constitutional responsibilities and to help improve the performance and ensure the accountability of the federal government for the benefit of the American people. We provide Congress with timely information that is objective, fact-based, nonpartisan, nonideological, fair, and balanced." (About GAO, 2013)

The information provided by the GAO that most directly influences social policy is national indicators. National indicators, including economic indicators and social indicators, enable the government to evaluate current programs and expenditures and determine their impact. In addition, the GAO uses social indicators to plan future programs and expenditures that reflect government values and goals. The GAO's national indicators are comprised of statistics, statistical series, and other forms of evidence.

The federal government researches and produces a portfolio of national indicators for multiple reasons:

- National indicators serve as a framework for related strategic planning efforts.

- National indicators enhance performance and accountability reporting.
- National indicators inform public policy decisions, including baseline review of existing government policies, programs, functions, and activities.
- National indicators facilitate public education and debate as well as informed electorate.

Nearly all the reasons that the federal government, as represented by the GAO, produces social reports and social indicators, as well as economic indicators, can be connected to the government's role as a policymaker and policy educator.

ISSUES

Problem-Centered vs. Strength-Centered Approaches to Policy

Social policies are viewed as societal responses to social problems. Social policy is often characterized as a social goal, enabling objective, or social solution. The social policy process is a problem-solving activity that solves or resolves a problem or conflict in society. Social policy, requested by society and enacted by government, unites and mediates the relationship between society and government. Chapin argues that effective social policy is built on the cornerstone of careful problem definition (1995). The political economy of social policy, as described in this article, illustrates that the American social policy system is predominated by "pathology oriented" policy. The

President George H. W. Bush signs the Americans with Disabilities Act into law on July 26, 1990. The act prohibited employer discrimination on the basis of disability. Pictured from left: Evan Kemp, Rev Harold Wilke, President Bush, Sandra Parrino and Justin Dart. (Courtesy of Wikimedia Commons)

"pathology" affecting society is more often than not viewed by the U.S. government (i.e. public policy-makers) to be poverty.

The economic development model or argument for social policy, which seeks to ameliorate risk caused by loss of income, was the impetus for a "war on poverty" approach to policy. The U.S. government announced a "war on poverty" in 1964. Poverty-related topics dominate government-sponsored research and programs (Haveman, 1988) and antipoverty strategies continue to characterize U.S. family policy (Ozawa, 2004).

Ultimately, the political economy of social policy illustrates that the American welfare state influences the majority of social policies. The post-1970 trajectory of the American welfare state has been characterized by efforts to combat poverty. Social policy of the twentieth and twenty-first centuries has been characterized by a problem-centered approach to policy formulation. Governments have used social and economic indicators to evaluate and assess social health. The focus on problem definition and assessment has largely ignored assessment of the strengths of the people and the environment that social policy target.

While American social policy is characterized by the problem-centered approach, strength-centered approaches to policy have an important role to play in empowering people within society and promoting social cohesion. These two approaches to policy-making—strengths-centered and problem-centered approaches—are based on different understandings of social need.

- Strengths-centered approach: The strengths-centered approach to social policy argues that social policy should emphasize the strengths and resources of individuals and their surroundings rather than their problems.
- Problem-centered approach: The problem-centered approach to social policy argues that social problems, which appear as deficits in people and environments, can be addressed and resolved through social programs and policies.

Critics of American current social policies, characterized by problem-centered approach, argue that by emphasizing individual pathologies and deficits, policies ignore structural barriers to social and economic participation (Chapin, 1995).

There are numerous challenges to integrating the strengths perspective into social policy. In fact, the economic development model and argument for social policy in industrialized nations that influenced social policy throughout the twentieth century continues today with very few exceptions. One example of a social policy that successfully integrates the strength-based approach to social policy is the Americans with Disabilities Act (ADA) of 1990. The ADA requires *reasonable accommodations* for people with disabilities that make it possible for them to participate in the workplace and community. The ADA emphasizes the need for development of structural supports that enable the individual to achieve social and economic inclusion rather than rely exclusively on social services (Chapin 1995).

CONCLUSION

Governments create public policies—the basic guidelines that serve as the foundation for public laws—for their citizens. There are numerous types of public policy including fiscal policy, monetary policy, national policy, urban policy, environmental, and social policy. In the final analysis, the development of social policy is complex due to finite resources, growing need, and debates about the purpose and scope of social policy and the welfare state. The economic development model of social policy has structured and influenced the majority of U.S. social policy. In the United States, social need, as measured by social indicators, is almost always transmuted and defined as an economic need. Ultimately, social policy in the United States is problem-based approach to solving the social and economic problem of poverty and its many related conditions.

BIBLIOGRAPHY

About GAO. (2013). Government Accountability Office.

Amenta, E., Bonastia, C., & Caren, N. (2001). "U.S. social policy in comparative and historical perspective." *Annual Review of Sociology, 27,* 213.

Canada, B. (2003). "Federal grants to state and local governments: A brief history." *Report for Congress.*

Chapin, R. (1995). "Social policy development: The strengths perspective." *Social Work, 40,* 506–515.

Daguerre, A. (2011). "US social policy in the 21st century: The difficulties of comprehensive social reform." *Social Policy & Administration, 45,* 389–407.

Guzman, T., Pirog, M. A., & Seefeldt, K. (2013). "Social policy: What have we learned?" *Policy Studies Journal, 41*, S53–S70.

Haveman, R. (1988). "Facts vs. fiction in social policy." *Challenge, 31*, 23.

Kalimo, E. (2005). "OECD social indicators for 2001: A critical appraisal." *Social Indicators Research, 70*, 185–229.

Klein, D. (1998). "Who is the practitioner of political economy?" *Challenge, 41*, 113.

Margalit, Y. (2013). "Explaining social policy preferences: Evidence from the Great Recession." *American Political Science Review, 107*, 80–103.

Michalos, A. (2004). "Social indicators research and health-related quality of life research." *Social Indicators, 65*, 27–72

OECD. (2011). *Society at a glance 2011—OECD social indicators.*

Ozawa, M. (2004). "Social welfare spending on family benefits in the United States and Sweden: A comparative study." *Family Relations, 53*, 301–310.

Penner, R. (1998). *A brief history of state and local fiscal policy.* The Urban Institute.

Spicker, P. (2006) *An introduction to social policy.* The Robert Gordon University.

Strauss, J., & Thomas, D. (1996). "Measurement and mismeasurement of social indicators." *American Economic Review, 86*, 30.

SUGGESTED READING

Bagenstos, S. (2004). "Has the Americans with Disabilities Act reduced employment for people with disabilities?" *Berkeley Journal of Employment & Labor Law, 25*, 527–563.

Eyraud, C. (2001). "Social policies in Europe and the issue of translation: The social construction of concepts." *International Journal of Social Research Methodology, 4*, 279–285.

Kioukias, D. (2003). "Reorganizing social policies through social partnerships: Greece in European perspective." *Social Policy & Administration, 37*, 121–132.

Lewis, J. (2006). "Work/family reconciliation, equal opportunities and social policies: The interpretation of policy trajectories at the EU level and the meaning of gender equality." *Journal of European Public Policy, 13*, 420–437.

Thurston, C., & Bowen, K. (2011). "U.S. domestic politics and international political economy: An introduction to the special issue." *Business & Politics, 13*, 1–4.

—Simone I. Flynn, PhD

PRICING STRATEGIES

ABSTRACT

This article will focus on how marketing professionals develop pricing strategies for their organizations. There will be a review of the guidelines that these individuals process in order to determine the optimal pricing structure for each product or service. The different types of potential pricing strategies (i.e., entrepreneurial, penetration, premium) will be explored. The concept of international countertrade as it relates to pricing will also be introduced.

OVERVIEW

Pricing is one of the four aspects (product management, pricing, promotion, and place) in the marketing mix and directly affects how a product is positioned in the market. Pricing should take into consideration fixed and variable costs, competition, organizational objectives, proposed positioning strategies, target groups, and consumer willingness to pay the price. When an appropriate price is selected, it should assist the organization in reaching its financial goals, be a realistic price for the target market, and be cohesive with other marketing mix components as well as with product positioning. Many organizations have utilized various factors when determining the pricing strategies for their products and services. However, all share some general guidelines. For example, the marketing representatives may go through a series of steps such as:

- Create a marketing strategy: This entails conducting a market analysis, product segmentation, targeting, and positioning. The team will have to determine each aspect of the marketing mix formula. The first step will be to develop a marketing strategy for the product or service. At this point, a decision is made as to who the target market will be and how the product will be positioned. Another factor will be based upon whether pricing is going to be a key point of the positioning.
- Determine the proper marketing mix. This involves product definition, distribution, and promotion. There will be trade-offs between the variables in the marketing mix. Pricing will be based on other decisions that have been made in the areas of distribution and promotion. For example, is the expectation to sell a small number of luxury items at high prices so that the product becomes a rare, unique commodity?
- Be aware of the demand curve: Determine how price affects the quantity demanded. There tends to be a relationship between price and quantity demanded. Therefore, the marketing team will attempt to estimate the demand curve for the product or service since pricing directly affects sales. The first step will be to conduct market research to find out how a particular price point will affect the demand for the product. If the product already exists, the marketers may want to survey whether the market will accept prices above the current price. The results will give the marketing team an idea of the price elasticity of demand for the product.
- Determine the cost of the product: Calculate a product's associated fixed and variable costs. Once it has been determined that the product will be launched, the marketing team will need to understand all the costs involved. Therefore, it will need to calculate the fixed and variable costs associated with the product or service, which is referred to as the total unit cost. The unit cost of the product determines how much is needed in order to break even. Any price set higher than this will help set the profit margin.
- Understand environmental factors: Evaluate potential responses from competitors and understand legal constraints. The marketing team should find out if there are any legal restraints on pricing. For example, offering different prices to different consumers can lead to cases of price discrimination. In some markets, legislation may dictate how high prices can go. Also, there are laws that prevent predatory pricing, especially in the international trade market.

Set pricing objectives. Pricing objectives can be set in a variety of ways. Some of the most popular include:

Profit maximization—By taking into consideration revenue and costs, this objective seeks to maximize current profits.

Revenue maximization—This objective does not take profit margins into consideration when attempting to maximize current revenue.

Maximize quantity—The reduction of long-term costs can be achieved by maximizing product or service sales.

Maximize profit margin—In a situation where quantity of sales will be low, unit profit margins can be increased to foster greater returns.

Differentiation (quality leadership)—This objective looks at the difference in price when determining the target market. While some companies may seek to be the low-cost leader, others will highlight quality as the justification for higher prices. For example, consumers expect to pay a high price for a high-end, name-brand designer handbag.

Survival—This objective is successful when there is a crisis in the marketplace. For example, the market may be experiencing a price war, market decline, or market saturation. Therefore, the company may be forced to temporarily set a lower price that will cover costs and allow the business to continue to operate in order to survive. In this type of situation, survival is more important than profits.

Partial cost recovery—An organization may seek only partial cost recovery if it has other sources of income.

Some of the most classical pricing strategies are:

Price skimming: When the product is introduced, the organization will set a high price in order to attract customers who are not sensitive to price. However, the prices will eventually fall due to an increase in supply, especially from competitors. This strategy is most appropriate when customers are not sensitive to price, there is no expectation of large cost savings at high volumes, and the organization cannot produce high volumes of its product at low profit margins.

Penetration pricing: When the product is introduced, the price is set low in order to gain market share. Once market share has been obtained, the prices are increased. This strategy tends to be used by companies attempting to enter a new market or desiring to build a small market share. A penetration strategy may also be used when a company wants to promote complementary products. The main product is set at a low price in order to get customers to buy the accessories, which are sold at higher prices.

Economy pricing: This strategy is considered the "no frills" approach. The cost of marketing and manufacturing are kept low. An example is store-brand products or generic drugs.

Premium pricing: When the product is unique and the company has a competitive advantage, a high price can be set.

Determine pricing: Using the information acquired through the steps above, define a pricing method, pricing structure, and discounts.

Once the prices have been set, the marketing team may employ one or more of the following pricing methods in order to achieve its goals.

Cost-plus pricing—The price arrived at by adding the production costs and a selected profit margin.

Target return pricing—The price is set to recognize a certain return on investment.

Value-based pricing—A price is set based on the notion that a customer will pay in accordance to the perceived value to the customer versus the cost of an alternative product. Caminal's and Vives' (1996) research showed that "a higher current market share can be interpreted by future consumers as a signal of higher relative quality and will tend to increase future demand" (p. 222).

Psychological pricing—A price is set based on factors such as product quality and perceived consumer value. The company perceives that the customer will respond based on emotion versus logic. For example, the price may be $1.99 versus $2.00.

The list price is usually the price that is quoted to the target market. However, discounts may be given to distributors and a select group from the target market. Examples of discounts include:

Quantity discounts—Discounts that are awarded to customers based on the quantity purchased.

Cumulative quantity discounts—The discount offered increases as the cumulative purchase increases. This is a good approach for resellers who make large purchases over time versus purchase large quantities at one time.

Seasonal discounts—Discounts offered based on the time of year that the purchase is made. The purpose is to offset seasonal variations in sales.

Cash discounts—Discounts offered to customers who pay before the due date.

Trade discounts—Discounts offered to distributors who successfully perform their responsibilities to the organization.

Seasonal Sales promotion. (Courtesy of Henning Schlottmann CC BY 4.0 via Wikimedia Commons)

Promotional discounts—Discounts offered to generate sales. This type of discount is usually set up for a short, specified period.

APPLICATION

Entrepreneurial pricing. Although pricing represents one of the most visible decision factors for marketing teams, it tends to be one of the least creative parts of the marketing strategy (Pitt & Berthon, 1997). Many marketers look at pricing from a functional point and view it only as a means to cover costs and generate revenue. Others have wrongly assumed that they could not be creative in pricing due to competitor pricing or legal constraints. Basically, many marketing managers have not conducted much research into how they price a product because they "did not really understand how to price and were insecure about the adequacy of the pricing approach they employed" (Pitt & Berthon, 1977, p. 344).

However, this approach may change as many organizations use modern approaches in developing their pricing formulas. The change is being driven by environmental factors such as international legislation forcing firms to open up markets and consumer preference for quality over brand image. For instance, companies such as Coca-Cola and Pepsi experienced a backlash from consumers as they decided to purchase store-brand cola over their respective products (Hulbert & Pitt, 1986).

Some researchers have looked to the field of entrepreneurship as a way to add life and creativity to the pricing process. Miller and Friesen (1983) assert that entrepreneurship is based on three dimensions—innovativeness, assumption of risk, and proactiveness. Innovativeness implies that an organization's vision is designed around a unique product, service, or process. Risk-taking infers that the organization is willing to pursue opportunities even if it loses money and takes calculated risks. Miller (1987) defined proactiveness as an organization's willingness to be assertive and take bold risks (i.e., acting versus reacting to market conditions).

As mentioned in the Overview, developing a pricing structure for a product or service requires decision making on a number of topics. The marketing department must come to a consensus on issues such as price objectives, price strategy, pricing method, promotions, and discounts. In each category, there

are a number of options in which the appropriate selection can be made. However, there is evidence that organizations still need to review their pricing strategy based on four key dimensions. The four dimensions are:

- **Cost-based versus market-based.** Cost-based strategy occurs when the marketing team focuses on covering its own costs more than any of the other determinants (e.g., demand conditions, competitive market structures, company marketing strategies). It tends to rely on formulas such as cost-plus, keystone, or target return (Pitt & Berthon, 1997). Market-based strategy values the consumer's opinion. The pricing structure is based on the perceived value that the customer receives from the product or service.
- **Risk-averse versus risk-assumptive.** Risk-averse strategy is the conservative approach. Prices are kept in line with competitors and only changed when necessary and the process is kept simple. Risk-assumptive strategy is more uncertain because the managers go into uncharted territories with less concern over potential loss in revenue.
- **Reactive versus proactive.** Reactive strategy refers to when a company copies the pricing patterns of its competitors. In most cases, there will not be an adjustment in price if the market does not warrant a change. On the other hand, the proactive approach assumes that the organization is the leader and initiates changes in the market. It will introduce the new pricing schemes and tends to be more aggressive in pricing as well as quick in making adjustments.
- **Standardization versus flexibility.** Standardization is self-explanatory. There is a universal price set regardless of the situation. However, flexibility implies that the organization may fluctuate prices based on "segment or user elasticities, time and place of purchase, as well as in response to opportunities for product or service unbundling or bundling, and anticipated or actual moves by competitors" (Pitt & Berthon, 1997, p. 346).

These are the major dimensions in which organizations must make decisions when analyzing and evaluating factors that are important to the pricing strategy. When participating in the entrepreneurial pricing strategy, the dominant factors in the pricing formula are market based, risk assumptive, proactive, and flexible. To combat threats and capitalize on opportunities, organizations are encouraged to design pricing structures based on the entrepreneurial pricing strategy. Organizations have to be ready to respond and adapt to a global economy that constantly changes. Pitt and Berthon (1997) created a checklist for marketing departments to assess whether or not they are positioned to transition to an entrepreneurial pricing system.

VIEWPOINT

International countertrade. During the Clinton administration, the United States experienced high trade deficits. To combat the trend, the administration identified ten emerging markets and committed to assisting American corporations with winning contracts in these areas. The American government created a national exporting strategy that had components such as lowering obstacles to U.S. exports, developing a responsive trade finance strategy, improving access to trade information, and focusing on key markets and sectors (Paun, Compeau & Grewal, 1997). Unfortunately, these efforts had "no clear and consistent policy stance on international

countertrade" (Park, 1990, p. 38). Countertrade occurs when "a seller provides a buyer with products and agrees to take some or all of the payment in a form other than money" (Paun, Compeau & Grewal, 1997, p. 69). As the buyer pool decreases and competition among sellers in the global market increases, sellers will participate in countertrade in order to gain a competitive advantage over noncountertrade bids (Cavusgil & Ghauri, 1990).

Research has shown that countertrade transactions can be very complex, especially when selecting a pricing strategy (Kublin, 1990). Therefore, it is critical for marketing departments to understand pricing strategy as it relates to countertrade (Yoffie, 1984). Pricing is considered to be the primary factor in determining whether or not a countertrade transaction is processed (Cho, 1987). Although exporters wanted to use price as a competitive tool in countertrade, they did not know how to perform this task effectively (Kublin, 1990).

Nagle and Holden (1995) believed that once an organization determined its marketing objectives, it could utilize three potential pricing strategies: sell at premium price, sell at a going-rate or neutral price, or sell at a discount price. Countertrade results are based on the contributions of the buyer and seller on

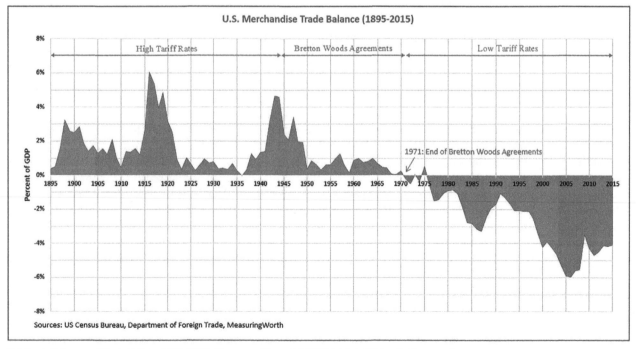

U.S. Trade Balance and Trade Policies (1895–2015). (Courtesy of James 4 CC BY-SA 4.0 via Wikimedia Commons)

the pricing process. The success of a countertrade transaction occurs when there is an intersection between the seller's and buyer's pricing strategies or expectations. Based on the model that Paun, Compeau, and Grewal (1997) introduced, "a countertrade transaction is more likely to occur when a buyer is willing to pay a price that matches or exceeds the seller's asking price for the countertrade products and less likely to occur when a seller's asking price exceeds what the buyer is willing to pay" (p. 70). To close a deal, the difference between the price the seller is seeking and the price the buyer is offering must be minimized. This can occur if the seller lowers the asking price, the buyer raises the offering price, or a combination of both options occurs.

CONCLUSION

Pricing is one of the four aspects (product management, pricing, promotion, and place) in the marketing mix and directly affects how a product is positioned in the market. It should take into consideration fixed and variable costs, competition, organizational objectives, proposed positioning strategies, target groups, and consumer willingness to pay the price. Many organizations have utilized various factors when determining the pricing strategies for their products and services. However, all share some general guidelines.

Although pricing represents one of the most visible decision factors for marketing teams, it tends to be one of the least creative parts of the marketing strategy (Pitt & Berthon, 1997). Many marketers look at pricing from a functional point and view it only as a means to cover costs and generate revenue. Others have wrongly assumed that they could not be creative in pricing due to competitor pricing or legal constraints. Miller and Friesen (1983) assert that entrepreneurship is based on three dimensions—innovativeness, assumption of risk, and proactiveness.

The marketing department must come to consensus on issues such as price objectives, price strategy, pricing method, promotions, and discounts. In each category, a selection can be made from a number of options.. However, there is evidence that organizations still need to review their pricing strategy based on four key dimensions. When participating in the entrepreneurial pricing strategy, the dominant factors in the pricing formula are market based, risk

assumptive, proactive, and flexible. Pitt and Berthon (1997) have created a checklist for marketing departments to assess whether or not they are positioned to transition to an entrepreneurial pricing system.

BIBLIOGRAPHY

Calandro, E., & Chair, C. (2016). "Policy and regulatory challenges posed by emerging pricing strategies." *Information Technologies and International Development, 12*(2), 13–28.

Caminal, R., & Vives, X. (1996). "Why market shares matter: An information-based theory." *RAND Journal of Economics, 27*, 221–239.

Cavusgil, S., & Ghauri, P. (1990). *Doing business in developing countries.* London, England: Routledge.

Cho, K. (1987). "Using countertrade as a competitive management tool." *Management International Review (MIR), 27*, 50–57.

Danziger, S., Hadar, L., & Morwitz, V. G. (2014). "Retailer pricing strategy and consumer choice under price uncertainty." *Journal of Consumer Research, 41*, 761–774.

Ellickson, P., Misra, S., & Nair, H. (2012). "Repositioning dynamics and pricing strategy." *Journal of Marketing Research (JMR), 49*, 750–772.

Hellofs, L., & Jacobson, R. (1999). "Market share and customers' perceptions of quality: When can firms grow their way to higher versus lower quality?" *Journal of Marketing, 63*, 16–25.

Hulbert, J., & Pitt, L. (1996). "Exit left centre stage? The future of functional marketing." *European Management Journal, 14*, 47–60.

Kimpel, M., & Friedrich, C. (2015). "The right pricing strategy for offline retailers when expanding into the online sales channel." *Journal of Business and Retail Management Research, 9*(2), 54–67

Kublin, M. (1990). "A guide to export pricing." *Industrial Management, 32*, 29.

Merry QR coding!. (2012). *Chief Marketer, 3*, 52.

Miller, D. (1987). "Strategy making and structure: Analysis and implications for performance." *Academy of Management Journal, 30*, 7–32.

Miller, D., & Friesen, P. (1982). "Innovation in conservative and entrepreneurial firms: Two models of strategic momentum." *Strategic Management Journal, 3*, 1–25.

Miniard, P. W., Mohammed, S., Barone, M. J., & Alvarez, C. O. (2013). "Retailers' use of partially comparative pricing: From across-category to within-category effects." *Journal of Marketing, 77,* 33–48.

Nagle, T., & Holden, R. (1995). *The strategy and tactics of pricing* (2nd ed.). Englewood Cliffs, NJ: Prentice Hall.

Naughton, K., & Light, L. (1997). "Taurus may tumble from the top." *Business Week,* (3510), 4.

Park, J. (1990, April). "Policy response to counter-trade and the U.S. trade deficit: An appraisal." *Business Economics, 25,* 38–44.

Paun, D., & Compeau, L. (1997). "A model of the influence of marketing objectives on pricing strategies in international countertrade." *Journal of Public Policy & Marketing, 16,* 69–82

Pitt, L., & Berthon, P. (1997). "Entrepreneurial pricing: The Cinderella of marketing strategy." *Management Decision, 35*(5/6), 344–351.

Rohani, A., & Nazari, M. (2012). "Impact of dynamic pricing strategies on consumer behavior." *Journal of Management Research, 4,* 143–159.

Schade, J. (2017). "Brief review about the public acceptability of road pricing strategies." *Reflets et Perspectives de la Vive Economique,* 164.

Yoffie, D. (1984). "Profiting from countertrade." *Harvard Business Review, 62,* 8–16.

Farrell, C. (2015). "Global pricing strategies." *Global Marketing: Practical Insights and International Analysis* (pp. 156–176). London: Sage Publications.

Farrell, C., & Fearon, G. (2005). "Renting goodwill in international marketing channels: An analysis of pricing strategies and bargaining power." *Atlantic Economic Journal, 33,* 285–296.

Jobber, D., & Shipley, D. (1998). "Marketing-oriented pricing strategies." *Journal of General Management, 23,* 19–34.

Nagle, T. (1998). "Make pricing a key driver of your marketing strategy." *Marketing News, 32,* 4.

Nicholas, III, A. (1965). "Apply value analysis to your own product: Some guides to pricing and marketing strategy." *Management Review, 54,* 4–16.

Nagle, T. T., Zale, J., & Hogan, J. E. (2011). *The strategy and tactics of pricing: A guide to growing more profitably.* 5th ed. New York: Routledge.

Petersen, C. D. (2011). "Defense and commercial trade offsets: Impacts on the U.S. industrial base raise economic and national security concerns." *Journal of Economic Issues, 45,* 485–492.

Sharma, S. (2016). "Pricing strategy adopted by small-scale entrepreneurs." *IUP Journal of Entrepreneurship Development, 13*(3), 7-24.

—*Marie Gould*

SUGGESTED READING

Abhik, R., & Walter, H. (1995). "Special issue on pricing strategy and the marketing mix." *Journal of Business Research, 33,* 183–185.

PRIVATE-SECTOR ECONOMIC DEVELOPMENT

ABSTRACT

This article will focus on the practice of private-sector economic development. Three models of economic development organizations—private sector, public sector, and public-private sector—will be introduced and serve as the foundation for the discussion of economic development partnerships. Development partnerships between corporations and development agencies, a strong and growing practice in private-sector economic development, allow groups to combine staff, technology, and the funding of resources to achieve development goals such as reducing poverty, improving infrastructure, and providing job training. Barriers to private-sector development, including inhospitable business climates and the need for policy reform in developing countries, will also be analyzed to see how they undermine local businesses and alienate foreign investment.

OVERVIEW

Private-sector economic development, often referred to simply as private-sector development, is a strategy for promoting economic development by private industries that benefits the poor in developing countries and regions of the world. The private sector comprises all the micro, small, medium, and large

President Donald J. Trump has made improvements in the United States' infrastructure part of his legislative agenda for 2018. Here he is speaking to auto workers at the American Center for Mobility in Ypsilanti, Michigan on March 15, 2017. (Courtesy of Shealah Craighead, the White House, via Wikimedia Commons)

enterprises that are outside of government ownership and control.

Modern private-sector economic development involves numerous private-sector stakeholders, such as development agencies, corporations from industrialized countries, businesses from developing countries, community agencies, and populations in need, who are committed to ending poverty and related conditions in developing countries. The World Bank estimated that in 2013, more than one billion people in the world suffered from extreme poverty, with nearly that number suffering from hunger as

Heads of State at the Millennium Summit at the United Nations headquarters in New York City on September 6, 2000. (Courtesy of Kremlin.ru CC BY 3.0 via Wikimedia Commons)

well. The World Bank defines extreme poverty as living on less than $1.25 a day. Private-sector economic development efforts are based on the argument that poverty reduction is tied to economic growth.

Combating global poverty is a goal that unites international development organizations and national governments around the world. For example, in 2000, the United Nations Millennium Summit was held to create time-bound and measurable goals for combating poverty and related conditions. The millennium development goals, known as MDGs, have become a blueprint of sorts for national governments, development agencies, and corporations committed to aiding the world's poorest people. The millennium development goals include:

- Eradicate extreme poverty and hunger.
- Achieve universal primary education.
- Promote gender equality and empower women.
- Reduce child mortality.
- Improve maternal health.
- Combat HIV/AIDS, malaria, and other diseases.
- Ensure environmental sustainability.
- Develop a global partnership for development.

While contemporary forms of private-sector economic development are focused primarily on eradicating extreme poverty and related conditions, private-sector economic development has existed in one form or another since the end of World War II. The modern era of sending aid to developing countries began in the 1940s as World War II ended. After the war, world leaders and governing bodies put structures such as the World Bank, the United Nations, the World Trade Organization, and the International Monetary Fund in place to prevent the economic depressions and instability that characterized the years following World War I.

The modern trend of globalization, and the resulting shifts from centralized to market economies in much of the world, has created both a need and an opportunity for economic development in developing countries and regions of the world. International development organizations, national governments, and corporations are coming together to focus on building frameworks for private-sector development as the basis for achieving sustainable economic growth. The following is an analysis of the three main models of economic development used to aid developing countries.

APPLICATIONS

Three Models of Economic Development Organizations

There are three distinct models of economic development organizations: the private-sector model, the public-sector model, and the public-private partnership model. Economic development organizations of all three kinds tend to share a similar structure, consisting of a governing board, which makes policy decisions, goals, and objectives, and an administrative work force, which carries out the board's instructions. What varies between economic development organizations is the level of participation and funding from either the private or public sector. Private-sector development is increasingly characterized by partnerships between these three different models, described below (Whitehead & Ady, 1989).

Private-Sector Model

Private-sector economic development organizations are funded by contributions from business, industry, and private individuals. Economic development functions include activities such as creating, attracting, and retaining jobs and capital investments. Board members may come from a wide range of nongovernmental organizations, such as banks or small businesses. Operational advantages of private-sector development organizations may include freedom from political boundaries or restrictions, freedom to maintain confidentiality about important issues, and knowledge of the business sector's interests and needs. Organizational disadvantages include lack of control over development issues requiring government involvement, such as investment incentives and infrastructure planning. Private-sector economic development organizations may choose the legal form of a nonprofit organization, otherwise known as a 501(c) corporation.

Public-Sector Model

Public-sector economic development organizations are funded by local and national governments. The public-sector model is often referred to as the government-agency model. While the governing body of private-sector organizations is usually a board of directors, the governing body of the public-sector organization is most often an elected or appointed government official, such as a mayor or city council member. Economic development functions, similar to those of the private-sector development organizations, include creating, attracting, and retaining jobs, and capital investment. Operational advantages may include control and direct access to investment incentives, such as tax abatements, and control over infrastructure planning, such as roads and utilities. In addition, the public-sector model invites, and sometimes requires, input and participation from all sectors of the community. Public-sector economic development organizations are legally defined as government agencies for tax-reporting purposes.

Public-Private Partnership Model

Public-private economic development organizations are funded by both the private and public sectors. Policy direction, objectives, and goals are determined through collaboration between public and private interests. Governing boards include members from business and government posts. Public-private partnership organizations are often called balanced organizations. Reasons for the growing number of public-private partnership organizations include the burdensome and escalating costs of economic development activities. In many instances, those involved in economic development combine public- and private-sector resources to build sufficient funds and staff to accomplish development projects and goals. Public and private sectors combine their respective operational advantages to benefit their communities and service areas.

Two important organizational issues should be considered when choosing a model of economic development. First, there are numerous benefits gained from combining a new economic development organization with an existing agency, either nonprofit or governmental. This practice is called piggybacking. The public-private partnership often allows the new organization to use the legal status of the established organization, thus saving time and money. Second, economic development organizations must choose the legal form and tax status most suited and advantageous to their organization. For example, the legal designation of a nonprofit organization allows for tax-exempt status, which means that organizational revenues are not taxed and donations are tax deductible for the donor. Economic development organizations usually apply for and are approved for tax-exempt status under sections 501(c) and 501(c) of the Internal Revenue Service (IRS) tax code. The former section applies to a variety of religious, educational, charitable, and scientific organizations. The latter section applies to business endeavors such as chambers of commerce.

Clearly, the organizational structure of an economic development enterprise has the potential to influence the performance and success of economic development organizations and projects. Private-sector development programs, as described in the following section, are an example of the partnership model. The following section analyzes the private-sector development programs and partnerships that have formed between development organizations and businesses in the interest of eradicating poverty in developing countries.

Private-Sector Development Programs

The world's largest and most influential international development agencies, including the World Bank and the Asian Development Bank, endorse private-sector economic development as the best strategy for reducing poverty and improving the quality of life for poor populations worldwide. In 2012, over one-third of the World Bank's "approximately 1000 pieces of analytical and advisory work" being done at the time "support[ed] a critical aspect of private sector development, such as investment climate, competition policy, consumer protection, property rights, or

Asian Development Bank headquarters is located in Mandaluyong City, Metro Manila, Philippines. (Courtesy of AndreaADB CC BY-SA 4.0 via Wikimedia Commons)

market reforms" (World Bank, 2012). Private-sector development programs are a natural extension of the World Bank's efforts to stabilize and strengthen economies around the world.

The development of the private sector in low-income countries and regions of the world requires cooperation, trust, and partnership between all parties involved in promoting economic development. International development agencies are increasingly turning to corporations for partnership. Development agencies solicit and partner with corporations from industrialized nations to fund, staff, and direct private-sector development programs in developing countries.

Private-sector development programs are interventions that aim to stimulate the development of an economically, socially, and environmentally sustainable private sector in developing countries (Pedersen, 2005). Development agencies encourage corporations to demonstrate corporate social responsibility—the private sector's commitment to improving social and environmental issues—through participation in and funding of private-sector development programs.

Private-sector development programs cover a wide range of economic and environmental support programs and business partnership programs that are introduced by development agencies to stimulate growth in the private sector. Examples of private-sector development activities include liberalizing world trade, investing in physical infrastructure, strengthening the labor market, and offering training and technical assistance to individuals and companies.

Private-sector development programs involve numerous stakeholders. Examples of these stakeholders include the program administrators, companies from industrialized countries that want to invest in a developing country, companies from developing countries that are interested in building a commercial partnership, human-rights organizations, job-training institutions, community-based organizations, and local populations. The stakeholders join together to offer and pool advisory services and financial support.

Private-sector development programs are considered win-win situations for all stakeholders. Development agencies receive benefits from additional funding, staff, and technology resources. Companies are compensated for some of the risks associated with investing in markets in developing countries. Developing countries benefit from private-sector investment in their economies.

Corporate investment in private-sector development programs is growing, but many corporations do not invest in development programs or refuse to invest in certain regions. Understanding the obstacles to private-sector investment in certain regions of the world is crucial to reaching the development goal of eradicating poverty and its related conditions. The following section analyzes the problems with the business climate in many developing countries.

ISSUES

The Business Climate

Private-sector investment drives job creation and income growth, providing poor populations with the opportunity to improve their living standards. Unfortunately, obstacles exist in some developing countries that prevent private-sector investment. Inhospitable business climates with red tape, weak legal systems, aggressive licensing regulation, and inefficient banking systems are part of the experience of doing business in many developing nations. A business climate, also known as an investment climate, is the combined factors that affect the profitability and experience of conducting business in a particular country or region of the world, such as tax structure, public services, government regulations, labor force, and infrastructure.

According to the World Business Environment Survey, conducted in 2000, labor regulations, tax administrations, and customs administration were considered to be the top regulatory constraints of business operations in Latin America, Africa, developing East Asia, South Asia, and the Middle East and North Africa. Why do such business obstacles exist when corporations are eager to invest in developing countries?

Administrative and policy reform is occurring in developing countries to make business climates more hospitable to private-sector investment, but the pace is slow. While attracting foreign direct investment is at the top of the agenda for most countries, there is still much debate about which factors and policies— e.g., rule of law, corruption, legal and regulatory stability, market size, taxes, or infrastructure services— most influence corporate investment decisions.

Developing countries wishing to attract foreign private-sector investment may choose to reform policies to make their business environment more hospitable to investment (Sullivan, 1998). Common policy reform issues in developing countries wishing to benefit from private-sector economic development include:

- Privatization
- Bankruptcy and liquidation law
- Tax system
- Labor laws
- Pension system
- Arbitration and mediation
- Financial system reform
- Stock exchanges
- Access to credit
- Trade
- Corporate governance
- Sound accounting systems on internationally accepted principles
- Preventing insider trading
- Regulating conflicts of interest
- Bank-corporation relationships
- Share registries and custodial arrangements
- Property rights reform
- Feedback and participation mechanisms

Countries are increasingly aware of the investment criteria that multinational corporations use to determine investment. The US-Brazil Business Council surveyed multinational companies to discover what factors they regarded as being important in making long-term investment decisions. Common factors included:

- Strong internal market
- Freedom of access to the market
- Available labor force and raw materials
- Protection from currency devaluation
- Remittance of dividends, interest, and royalties payments
- Property-rights protection
- Export potential
- Manageable regulatory burdens
- Favorable taxation and tax incentives
- Low political risk
- Reliable infrastructure support

Policy reform may be a voluntary choice made by the developing country or region in an effort to build a better business climate or may be a condition imposed from the outside business sector interested in investing and others engaged in building a better business climate. International donor agencies are increasingly making funding conditional on the country's monitoring of a small set of quantifiable indicators or eliminating the obstacles to doing business. In addition to the need for policy reform to attract private-sector investment, policy reform in developing countries is needed to support small-scale indigenous or local businesses in these areas.

Small & Medium Enterprises

Small and medium enterprises—the official term used by international development agencies and governments for a small business—make up more than half of all economic activity in many developing countries. Small and medium enterprises in developing countries are often informal firms with no official legal status. While unofficial firms often remain outside of the tax system and regulatory requirements, these firms are disproportionately burdened by a poorly defined or administered business environment. For example, small firms are often overwhelmed by flat-rate registration fees, the difficulty of securing loans and infrastructure services, and the need to pay bribes.

Economists argue that small and medium-sized enterprises in many nations around the world are regenerating many declining economies. Small-scale entrepreneurs, with great flexibility and simple business structures, are thought to be one of the main agents of change in the economy of many developing nations (Ivy, 1996). Clearly, small and medium enterprises are an important economic resource and stabilizing force in developing countries. The World Bank policy solutions for addressing the business problems facing small and medium enterprises include reducing administrative and regulatory barriers, implementing innovative methods of reducing the costs of regulation, and developing competition policy.

Individual countries are addressing the problems faced by small and medium enterprises (SMEs) in an inhospitable business environment in numerous ways. For example, China passed the SME Promotion Law of 2003 to support the small SMEs operating in the private sector, which is becoming an increasingly important part of the Chinese economy. The law creates enabling institutions and support systems for SMEs at the municipal level (Atherton & Fairbanks, 2006).

The success, and the anticipated economic and social benefits, of private-sector development requires the existence or creation of certain economic market conditions. In particular, private-sector development requires competition in the marketplace between providers and vendors of goods, products, and services. Competitive market conditions, almost always present in industrialized countries, are often absent in developing countries and must be created through the development and implementation of competition law and policy (Cook, 2002). Many national governments of developing countries realize the economic and social benefits of competitive markets and are reforming their economic policies to allow for privatization, support small business, and attract foreign private-sector investment.

CONCLUSION

The scope of private-sector economic development is vast, encompassing actors from all areas and levels of corporate, non-profit, and government entities. In particular, those engaged in the business sector, whether as entrepreneurs, corporate employees, or staff members of business associations, have the potential to use corporate resources to influence the economies and populations living in poverty in developing countries. Understanding how and why private-sector economic development operates is vital for all those engaged in corporate, government, or non-profit enterprises.

The three models for economic development organizations described in the this article—private-sector model, public-sector model, and public-private partnership model—have real-life applications in the private-sector development work of international development agencies, multinational corporations, and small-scale businesses. While discrete sector models of economic development worked post–World War II to stabilize economies, the current global problems of extreme poverty and related conditions require the shared creativity and pooled resources of public-private development partnerships.

All models of development organizations and all economic development stakeholders will be faced with obstacles to meeting development goals. Obstacles to private-sector development investment include inhospitable business climates in developing countries and extensive program requirements regarding monitoring, reporting, and evaluating. Overcoming these obstacles is crucial to achieving the shared development goals of strengthening world economies and combating poverty.

BIBLIOGRAPHY

Atherton, A. & Fairbanks, A. (2006). "Stimulating private sector development in China: The emergence of enterprise development centers in Liaoning and Sichuan Provinces." *Asia Pacific Review, 12,* 333-354.

Basu, P. K. (1994). "Demystifying privatization in developing countries." *The International Journal of Public Sector Management, 7*(3/4), 44–56.

Benneh Mensah, M., & Nyadu-Addo, R. (2012). "Juxtaposition of the role of small businesses and the state in Ghana's economic development." *International Business & Management, 5,* 75–82.

Cook, P. (2002). "Competition and its regulation: key issues." *Annals of Public & ICooperative Economics, 73,* 541–558.

"Current developments in the private sector." (2013). *CPA Journal, 83,* 38–41.

Ivy, R. L. (1996). "Small scale entrepreneurs and private sector development in the Slovak Republic." *Journal of Small Business Management, 34,* 77–83.

Leurs, R. (2000). "The role of the state in enabling private sector development: an assessment methodology." *Public Administration and Development, 20,* 43–59.

McEwan, C., Mawdsley, E., Banks, G., Scheyvens, R. (2017). "Enrolling the private sector in community development: Magic bullet or slight of hand?" *Development and Change, 48,* 1, 28–53.

Pedersen, E. R. (2005). "Guiding the invisible hand." *The Journal of Corporate Citizenship, 20,* 77–91.

Sullivan, J. D. (1998). "Institutions and private sector development." *The China Economic Review, 9,* 85–96.

Whitehead, W. T. & Ady, R. M. (1989). "Organizational models for economic development." *The Economic Development Review, 7,* 8–13.

World Bank. (2012). *World Bank Group innovations in leveraging the private sector for development: A discussion note.*

Zhang, Q., & Liu, M. (2013). "The political economy of private sector development in Communist China: Evidence from Zhejiang Province." *Studies in Comparative International Development, 48,* 196–216.

SUGGESTED READING

Carter, R. C. & Danert, K. (2003). "The private sector and water and sanitation services policy and poverty issues." *Journal of International Development, 15,* 1067–1072.

Hameed, S., & Mixon, K. (2013). *Private-sector development in fragile, conflict-affected, and violent countries: CSIS working group on private-sector development in fragile states.* Washington, DC: Center for Strategic and International Studies.

Randolph, R. S. (1994). "Economic reform and private sector development in Russia and Mexico." *CATO Journal, 14,* 109–125.

Rondinelli, D. A. (1991). "Developing private enterprise in the Czech & Slovak Federal Republic." *Columbia Journal of World Business, 26,* 26–36.

—*Simone I. Flynn, PhD*

Q

QUANTITATIVE APPLICATIONS IN ECONOMICS AND FINANCE

ABSTRACT

The business manager's tool kit is filled with common tools to manage the financial performance of an organization, among them financial ratios, variance analyses, and budget projections. Capital-budgeting tools assume that decision makers have access to remarkably complete and reliable information, yet most strategic decisions must be made under conditions of great uncertainty (Courtney, Lovallo, & Clarke, 2013). A core function of financial oversight is having intimate knowledge of strategies to effectively manage changing environments, shrinking operating margins, and increasing accountability. Managers are being held to specific performance goals by their organizations and stakeholders. It is readily apparent that quantitative analytic skills, or the ready access to these skills, are necessary to maintain a secure position in the industry. Historically, finance and economics experts' tools tended toward tried and true empirical models, long accepted in the business sector. One must ask, however: How successful would a manager be with access to the tools of measurement and inference that are necessary for market and business processes? Common trajectories can be uncovered from where they are hidden behind the coevolution of a large array of indicators (Du & Kamakura, 2012). This essay offers a snapshot of several economic and financial modeling techniques that organizations are using successfully to decrease variance and error. The models develop a hypothesis, apply analytic tools, and strengthen analysis and projection positions. Some industries are further ahead than others in the statistical analysis playing field, and they are finding remarkable benefits to being on the cutting edge. It is not within the scope of this essay to instruct the reader in the science of statistics, rather to deliver the concept and its relevance to business and economics today.

OVERVIEW

Quantitative analysis, the process of applying mathematics to business, suggests that operational success can be enhanced beyond current systems, which look very much like an "applied intuition" method of management. The literature suggests that the setting of budgets, assessing changes in the marketplace, forecasting, and strategy can be improved with the use of econometrics, the business of mathematically studying the underlying causes of varying outcomes. Variance is often poorly understood, and is always inefficient, wasteful, and costly.

APPLICATIONS

Case Study Number One: Initial Public Stock Offering

Who: The seller of common or preferred stock often enlists the services of an underwriter to determine pricing and timing of an initial public offering (IPO) of stock to investors. In the September 2007 *Journal of Financial Analysis*, a study by Binay, Gatchev, and Pirinsky hypothesized that there is a predictable impact on IPO's sales related to the IPO underwriter's relationship with known investors (Binay et al., 2007). The group defined the event (the element to which a probability can be applied) in terms of a relational participation of the investor and the underwriter to determine the relationship's impact on future investment tendencies.

What: Sales of an IPO present a risky investment option because the stock offering is usually brand new to the market and provides no historical performance with which the investor can compare. Uncertainty for the investor is the hallmark of an IPO; these offerings are commonly sold by newer companies in an early

The social networking company Facebook held its initial public offering (IPO) on May 18, 2012. An electronic billboard on the Thomson Reuters building welcomes Facebook to the Nasdaq. (Courtesy of ProducerMatthew CC BY-SA 3.0 via Wikimedia Commons)

growth phase. To the casual observer, it would appear that there is much unpredictability in how well the stock will sell in its first days of going public. Given factors like market volatility, investor confidence, and risk perception, predictions are primarily speculative. Intuitively, the underwriter considers the question: Is there method, a model for predicting the relative success of the early offering; what investors should be approached early? It would appear very difficult to find any predictability in the answer to this question. History suggests that empirical experience drives the underwriters' assumptions. However, the following example just goes to show that where predictability seems unlikely, conditional probability analysis can provide a more robust prediction. Probability is simply the measure of the chance that an event will occur, given that another event has already taken place; the outcome of this type of study can support the analyst's prediction using inferential analysis.

How: Analysis is a process, and the deliverable is the recommendations for change and improvement. What Binay and others were searching for follows: "Despite the importance of underwriter-investor relationships, empirical research provides little evidence on the role of regular investors in the equity issue process in part because data on actual IPO allocations are proprietary and rarely disclosed by investment banks. [In this paper] we empirically examine the role of underwriter-investor relationships in the IPO process by examining institutional positions in IPO's as disclosed in quarterly 13F filings with the SEC. We construct a measure of relationship-based participation by institutional investors in IPOs as the difference of two probabilities—the probability that an institution investor participates in an IPO conditional on that investor's past participation in the same lead underwriters' IPO's, and the unconditional probability that an institutional investor participates in the IPO" (Binay et al., 2007). The writers hypothesized the following: "In this paper we investigate the role of regular IPO investors in the going-public process. IPO allocation practices often leave the impression that underwritings unfairly reward favorite clients and neglect other investors. Economic theory, however, predicts that favoritism toward regular investors is an efficient way to extract information relevant for IPO firms" (Binay, 2007). The reader can examine in more detail, from the EBSCO Online Research Database (see bibliography) how the study was derived and administered, as well as the statistical strength of its findings.

Why: Refined and innovative analysis is costly: Time, experience, and knowledge are required. The organization that makes the investment of enhancing its managers' skills or bringing in expertise is positioning itself to an advantage.

Where: The study on relational impact revealed that "We further find that regular institutional investors are more likely than casual investors to participate in IPO's with higher underpricing" (Binay, 2007). This is but a snapshot of quantitative analysis at work, validating and verifying predictive behaviors in the market clearly can prove instructive to underwriters and sellers. Absent statistically significant findings, the exercise may still be of value due to the inquiry and opportunity it brings to the investigators.

Case Study Number Two: Entrepreneurial Benefit of Storytelling

Who: Martens, Jennings, and Jennings published in the *Academy of Management Journal* a qualitative and quantitative study on the effects that storytelling has on potential investors' behavior response; for this research, they used the statistical method of regression analysis. The reader will recall that some quantitative analyses involve developing a hypothesis, running the experiment, and gauging the effect of the independent variable on the outcome. For purposes of this essay, the quantitative work (not the qualitative component) of Martens et al. will be discussed. The group developed three distinct hypotheses surrounding resource acquisition, the premise of which is described by Jennings and Jennings in a subsequent paragraph.

Why: Applying logical (statistical) techniques to compare data can be a powerful means to support strategic initiatives in an organization. The adage that time is money supports businesses' efforts to improve their forecasting and predictions. Read further about the statistical study that identifies several dependent variables and measures their behavior in response to an independent action and the exciting outcomes of this design.

"Adopting a narrative approach to resource acquisition research, we examine the effects of storytelling on a firm's ability to secure capital. We argue that narratives help leverage resources by conveying a comprehensible identity for an entrepreneurial firm, elaborating the logic behind proposed means of exploiting opportunities and embedding entrepreneurial endeavors within broader discourses. Qualitative analyses of all 1996–2000 initial public offering prospectuses in three high-tech industries reveal how identity constructions, story elaboration, and contextual embedding are invoked within narratives. Our quantitative findings show how these aspects of an entrepreneurial narrative impact resource acquisition net of previously emphasized factors. To our knowledge, this paper offers the first systematic, large-sample test of the overarching claim that effective storytelling can facilitate external resource acquisitions. Integrating theory and research on the resources acquisition process with work by narrative scholars, we develop and test three arguments about how narratives (stories) help entrepreneurs attract capital" (Jennings, 2007).

How: The Martens, Jennings, and Jennings group's three hypotheses were (Martens et al., 2007):

Hypothesis #1 The identity constructed for a firm in an entrepreneurial narrative has an influence on resource acquisition that is net of the influence of factual information about the firm's existing resource endowments.

Hypothesis #2 Elaborating the rationale behind a firm's intended actions in an entrepreneurial narrative has a positive but diminishing effect on the firm's resource acquisition ability.

Hypothesis #3 Embedding both contextually familiar and contextually unfamiliar elements in an entrepreneurial narrative has a positive but diminishing effect on resource acquisition ability.

What: The degrees of statistical strength in the results were varied, showing some correlation between the independent and dependent variables. Inference is determined by the strength of the findings; however, the experimenters' involvement in the process and any partial evidence of correlation is valuable nonetheless. The take-home message from this experiment is that further exploration is warranted. The authors close with the following words: "With respect to future research, we can envision a host of other intriguing directions for further work adopting a narrative approach to entrepreneurial phenomena. One of the most obvious is triggered by the dot.com scandals (Lowenstein, 2004): the need to investigate the nature, prevalence and effects of *inauthentic* entrepreneurial narratives" (Marten et al., 2007).

Case Study Number Three: Sawmill Industry

Who: Rudolf Beran from the University of California applied multivariate analysis (observation and analysis of more than one variable at a time) to the processes of board-cutting at a sawmill that was experiencing too many random errors in cut boards' thickness. As we discuss the test itself and the findings, the reader should recall that for statistically significant, meaningful tests and results, statisticians are a primary resource for advising on the actual study technique.

Why: What is the business case for embarking on a costly statistical analysis, might shareholders or owners ask? To what benefit, since aren't the majority of the boards at our sawmill good enough for

Workers are cutting big timbers into planks in a sawmill in the Seguntor Industrial Area in Sandakan, Sabah, Malaysia.
(Courtesy of CEphoto, Uwe Aranas / via Wikimedia Commons)

processing? Beran offers the answer to this question in his introduction: "The increasing scarcity of top quality lumber in the western United States provides an economic incentive for strengthening process control in the sawmill industry" (Beran, 2007). The market is looking for quality and price all in one; and the market drives the demand.

What: What are the variables known to be contributing to error; is there more than one? Can it be identified? Among the multiple variables listed in the analysis were various stages through which the wood was processed and cut. Because the board product is subjected to so many processes throughout its preparation, the cumulative effect of all these processes would provide little insight into the variation; what is needed is a multivariate analysis.

How: How was the analysis performed? As a standard, baseline data were collected, analyzed for relations to errors, and recorded. Identification of individual variable(s) impacting quality was the goal.

Where: Where were the opportunities found? Managing the saw's performance, identifying the impact of cumulative re-sawing, and setting specific size targets were key findings in the analysis. As the author states, "The main finding of this paper is that fitting a physically based statistical model to measured board thicknesses provides sound quantitative

insight into the propagation of thickness error through lumber resawing. The model thereby enables effective quality control of individual saws, determination of target mean thickness by sawing code and setting priorities for sawmill improvements" (Beran, 2007). Discussion at the end of the Beran article can offer the reader a fuller understanding of not only the power but also the process of statistical process improvement.

Case Study Number Four: Decision Analysis Tools for Marketing Investment

What: What is the best use of our organization's resources? If the demand for product is there, but not realized, should the company invest in more advertising? How will we know if it is worth the cost, if it is where our best return resides?

Why: No manager favors uncertainty in decision-making. Facts lay the groundwork for success, yet much decision-making continues to be made with limited data. Stanford University professor Chip Heath said, "The analogy I like is how we handle problems with memory. The solution isn't to focus harder on remembering; it's to use a system like a grocery-store list. We're now in a position to think about the decision-making equivalent of the grocery-store list" (Heath, 2013). There is truth to the theory that the efficacy of a system within a larger system inevitably impacts other subgroups; the larger the organization, the more complexity and ambiguity. Understanding how related systems interact and their overall contribution is paramount in today's environment, especially with the reality of globalization and interconnectivity. Companies are looking for recommendations from their units that are defensible, while leaders are being held accountable for their actions. Errors in forecasting occur for many reasons, some of which include the challenge of additive error processes, conditional forecasting whose values are for an incorrect time period, inaccurate assumptions, or the silo phenomenon within organizations.

How: Some organizations are relying on simulation models, those that take a big picture view of where the organization or system is expected to be. Statistical forecasting has recognized value in capital and other resource budgeting, while more recently it has been employed as a primary tool for assessing return on marketing investments.

Who: How does econometrics bring value to decision makers? Laura Bogomolny of the *Canadian Business Journal* writes, "Managers used to just throw money at their marketing department and hope for the best. Nowadays, they want proof that they are getting a return on their investment. There's an old saying familiar to anyone in the marketing biz: 'Half the money I spend on advertising is wasted— I just don't know which half.' However, a growing number of managers are convinced that they can unravel the mystery. Metrics, long embraced by almost all other business divisions, are finally grabbing hold in the marketing world—and many on the front lines report that innovative new methods for determining advertising's effectiveness are helping them get more bang for their buck. Tracking return on marketing investment, advocates argue, is now a real option, and as a result companies big and small are leaping at the chance to end the tradition of wasting huge sums on useless promotional campaigns before finding one that works" (Bogomolny, 2004).

In the business sector, some believe that for far too long, forecasting (budgeting and projecting) has been mostly intuitive, speculative, and lacking numerical grounding. Bogomolny goes on to say, "Even CEOs of small, private companies are now at least open to the idea that there may be proof the money they pour into marketing isn't going down the drain." And those willing to follow a marketing officer's advice on a "trust me" basis are a dwindling breed. Many executives have begun to demand that the efficiency and effectiveness of marketing expenses be carefully and scientifically tracked—and they are modifying budget decisions according to the results (Bogolmony, 2004).

VIEWPOINT

Contrasting View on the Utility of Quantitative Analysis

Few analysts would argue that the measurement of tangible data is easier than factoring a return on investment in something more nebulous, like marketing. Again from the *Canadian Business Journal*,

Huntsman Hall is the Wharton School's main building. The Wharton School is part of the University of Pennsylvania. (Courtesy of WestCoastivieS via Wikimedia Commons)

Bogolmony says some public affairs and marketing professionals are not sure that scientifically measuring their efficacy is playing fair.

Amid the converts, however, skeptics still abound. Teasing out the impact of individual marketing projects requires advanced statistical modeling, and many question the accuracy of these techniques. Can you really capture the excitement created by a first-rate ad campaign with a numerical calculation? Some professional marketers remain unconvinced that you can accurately assess the influence of a specific initiative on an individual's purchase patterns. And many creative types—who insist that products survive on "buzz" and are loath to see advertising fall prey to corporate homogenization—are especially put off by the whole return-on-marketing-investment (ROMI) concept. Supporters counter that questioning marketing metrics is simply an excuse. As they see it, the naysayers are merely afraid to track how effective their work is because they fear it may highlight bad decisions made in the past.

Leonard Lodish, a professor of marketing at the Wharton School of business at the University of Pennsylvania and a leading expert in the field of return on marketing investment, certainly falls into that camp. He argues that "although there are some things that are notoriously variable in terms of measuring," ROMI analyses are "pretty accurate." Lodish says the real roadblock to getting companies on board is that measuring "pushes the egos of a lot of managers, because it sometimes will show you that your prior judgments didn't work very well. You have to be a very confident manager to do this kind of stuff" (Bogolmony, 2004).

The Shortage of Operational Managers with Quantitative Analytic Skills

In forward-moving sectors, employees are being "trained up" to enhance their analytic skills. In effect, bringing operational high performers to a higher level is the process of re-recruiting from within. Managers today are expected to manage quality processes such as those in lean manufacturing, continuous service and product improvement, innovation, solving problems by examining them, synthesizing measurable and defendable data, and leading development to solutions. Last but not least, growing professionals from within an organization means providing the development opportunities to produce the next generation of multitalented financial, operational managers whose tool kit is much broader than that of their predecessors. Internal resources commonly provide the best investment a company has.

CONCLUSION

There should be no doubt in the reader's mind, after reviewing this essay, of the strength inherent in merging quantitative analytic skills into routine operational processes of business. Business degree programs teach quantitative financial analysis; these financial experts are excellent at what they do, and they can assess a process from afar with remarkable facility. However, the challenge for graduates is in gaining the real-world experience, the lack of which decreases the robust results possible from multitalented managers facile in both econometrics and operations. Why are business managers not universally enjoying dramatic success in financial performance measures, given what we know? Sticking with business as usual comes at a cost; the savvy manager must understand that striking out ahead of the competition means challenging oneself and increasing his or her skills to the next level.

BIBLIOGRAPHY

Beran, R. (2006). "Statistical modeling for process control in the sawmill industry." *Applied Stochastic Models in Business & Industry, 22*(5/6), 459–481.

Binay, M., Gatchev, V., & Pirinsky, C. (2007). "The role of underwriter-investor relationships in the IPO process." *Journal of Financial & Quantitative Analysis, 42*, 785–809.

Bogomolny, L. (2004). "Do you measure up?" *Canadian Business, 77*, 93–103.

Courtney, H., Lovallo, D., & Clarke, C. (2013). "Deciding how to decide." (cover story). *Harvard Business Review, 91*, 62–70.

Du, R., & Kamakura, W. (2012). "Quantitative trendspotting." *Journal of Marketing Research (JMR), 49*, 514–536.

Heath, C., & Sibony, O. (2013). "Making great decisions." *McKinsey Quarterly, 66*–76.

Martens, M., Jennings, J., & Jennings, P. (2007). "Do the stories they tell get them the money they need? The role of entrepreneurial narratives in resource acquisition." *Academy of Management Journal, 50*, 1107–1132.

Olkhov, V. (2017). "Quantitative wave of macrofinance." *International Review of Financial Analysis, 50*, 143–150.

RECOMMENDED READINGS

McColloch, A.C. (1986). "Institute for quantitative research in finance." *Financial Analysts Journal, 42*, 10–11.

Terui, N., & Imano, Y. (2005). "Forecasting model with asymmetric market response and its application to pricing of consumer package goods." *Applied Stochastic Models in Business & Industry, 21*, 541–560.

Sreenivasan, R. (2004). "Applied quantitative finance: Theory and computational tools." *Journal of the Royal Statistical Society, 167*, 191–192.

—Nancy Sprague

QUANTITATIVE ECONOMIC ANALYSIS

ABSTRACT

Economists are interested in interpreting data to better understand and predict the behavior of economies and economic variables. To do this, they need to be able to quantitatively analyze data to determine the effect of changes on variables of interest, or to weigh the relative merits of econometric models. Quantitative analysis techniques used in economics include many of the tools of inferential statistics as well as various tools for building empirical, testable models. Through the use of quantitative analysis, economists can test and validate their theories and revise them so that they better reflect the realities of real-world economies.

Economists can be found working in a wide spectrum of situations: From academicians who work in universities and develop and test theoretical models of various aspects of economies; to economists working in government and industry who apply those models to the real world in an attempt to forecast future trends based on past and current data. The application of economic theory is the stuff of headlines. In the government, economists may analyze the pros and cons of various alternative economic

President Barack Obama confers with Federal Reserve Chairman Ben Bernanke, a notable economist, following their meeting at the White House on April 10, 2009. (Courtesy of Pete Souza, White House, via Wikimedia Commons)

policies under consideration based on various facts and figures. Economists working in banks may evaluate whether or not interest rates should be changed. In the private sector, economists may be called upon to forecast the change in various economic variables such as exchange rate movements and their effect on the exports of their organization. In all these situations, it is important that the economist is able to quantitatively analyze data to determine the effect of changes on variables of interest or to weigh the relative merits of econometric models. Having a theory based on one's observations of historical trends or current conditions is a good start in understanding the realities of an economy. However, such observations on their own are insufficient for reliably forecasting the future. Economists must be able to quantify the facts known about various economic conditions and analyze these in order to test the validity of an economic model and forecast trends (Koop, 2009).

APPLICATIONS

MATHEMATICAL STATISTICS & ECONOMIC STUDY
Descriptive Statistics

Mathematical statistics give economists a number of quantitative tools that enable them to develop and test theories that help them better understand and predict economic behavior. These tools range from ways to organize and summarize data so that they are more easily understandable, to methods for predicting future trends using data and models. At the simpler end of this continuum, descriptive statistics help economists to clearly describe large amounts of data using pie charts, histograms, and frequency. Other methods of descriptive statistics include measures of central tendency (i.e., mean, median, and mode) that give the "average" for a particular variable of interest as well as measures of variability (i.e., range and standard deviation) that help one understand how widely dispersed the values of the variable are.

Inferential Statistics

In addition to such descriptive tools, mathematical statistics also offer economists tools that allow them to make inferences about data. These techniques, called inferential statistics, allow one to draw conclusions about a population from a sample and test hypotheses to determine if the results of a study occur at a rate that is unlikely to be due to chance (i.e., have statistical significance). For purposes of hypothesis testing, the hypothesis is stated in two ways. A null hypothesis (H0) is the statement that there is no statistical difference between the status quo and the experimental condition. In other words, the treatment being studied made no difference on the end result. The alternative hypothesis (H1) states that there is a relationship between the two variables and that the intervening variable did make a difference in the outcome. To determine whether one should accept or reject the null hypothesis, one must first determine how the data are to be statistically analyzed. This decision is made during the design of the experiment so that the appropriate statistical tool can be chosen and the necessary data collected. One frequently used class of statistical tests used in hypothesis testing is the family of tools known as t-tests. These tests are used to analyze the mean of a population or compare the means of two different populations. (In other situations where one wishes to compare the means of two populations, a z statistic may be used.)

Correlation Techniques
Correlation techniques are another classification of techniques that can be used by economists. These techniques help economists better understand the degree to which two variables are consistently related. For example, correlation can help one understand the relationship between various economic indicators and purchasing behavior. Correlation coefficients show the degree of relationship between the two variables, and vary between 0.0 and 1.0. A correlation of 1.0 shows that the variables are completely related: A change in the value of one variable will signify a corresponding change in the other variable. A correlation of 0.0, on the other hand, shows that there is no relationship between the two variables: Knowing the value of one variable tells nothing about the value of the other variable. A correlation coefficient also signifies how the two variables are related. If the correlation coefficient is positive, then as the value of one variable increases so does the value of the other variable. A negative

correlation, on the other hand, means that as the value of one variable increases the value of the other variable decreases.

Analysis of Variance
Another family of inferential techniques that is used for analyzing data in applied settings is analysis of variance (ANOVA). This family of techniques is used to analyze the joint and separate effects of multiple independent variables on a single dependent variable and to determine the statistical significance of the effect. Multivariate analysis of variance (MANOVA) is an extension of this set of techniques that allows economists to test hypotheses on more complex problems involving the simultaneous effects of multiple independent variables on multiple dependent variables. The work of Kureshi, Sood, and Koshy (2009) offers an example of how analysis of variance can be meaningfully used on economic data. The authors were interested in developing a profile of customers of a single brand sport store in an emerging market to assist retailers in identifying revenue-generating customers. The authors used a survey research technique to collect data. Based on their shopping patterns at the store, the customers were classified as purposive patrons, purposive nonpatrons, and browsers. The authors used analysis of variance to analyze the survey results and determine differences in demographic and psychographic characteristics, media habits, and ownership of personal lifestyle products or services. The results of that analysis indicated that the purposive patrons differed significantly from other store visitors on eighteen characteristics, information that can be useful in identifying and targeting potential customers.

Regression Analysis
Another frequently used quantitative technique for analyzing economic data is regression analysis. This is a family of statistical tools that can help economists better understand and predict economic behavior. Regression analysis allows researchers to build mathematical models that can be used to predict the value of one variable from knowledge of another. There are a number of specific regression techniques that can be used by sociologists to model real-world behavior.

Linear Regression

Simple linear regression analysis allows the modeling of two variables. Although correlation techniques, as discussed above, can indicate the degree of relationship between two variables, this knowledge alone does not necessarily provide sufficient information to predict behavior. In situations in which one needs to be able to predict the value of one variable from knowledge of another variable based on the data, simple linear regression is often used. Simple linear regression is a bivariate statistical tool that allows the value of one dependent variable to be predicted from the knowledge of one independent variable. For example, simple linear regression might be used to predict one's income based on the level of education that the person had attained. The pairs of data used in linear regression analysis are typically graphed on a scatter plot that shows the values of the points for two-variable numerical data. A line of best fit is superimposed on the scatter plot and used to predict the value of the dependent variable based on different values of the independent variable.

Standard regression analysis techniques make several assumptions including that the model is correct and that the data are good. Unfortunately, the real-world situations of interest to economists frequently do not follow these assumptions. For example, the variables themselves may be correlated, thereby inflating the value of the correlation (e.g., intelligence often being related to both income and educational level), the sample data may contain outliers (i.e., observations in which the value is abnormally large or small) that pull the distribution in the direction of the skew, or multicollinearity among subsets of the input variables such that they exhibit nearly identical linear relations, can all influence the validity of the results. Unfortunately, there are few indications in standard statistics to indicate that these problems have been incurred.

Multiple Linear Regression

Simple linear regression can be very useful for building models and predicting the value of one variable from the knowledge of the value of another variable. However, the type of problems investigated by economists in the real world are often more complex and include multiple variables. For many such situations, multiple linear regression can be used to model the data. As opposed to simple linear

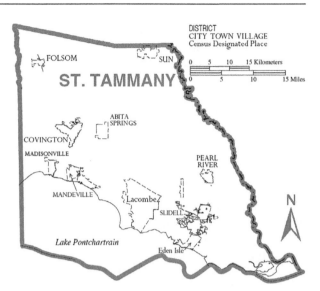

Map of St. Tammany Parish, Louisiana, with municipal labels in July of 2007. (Courtesy of Ruhrfisch CC-BY-SA-3.0 via Wikimedia Commons)

regression, multiple linear regression analysis allows the modeling of two or more independent variables to be used in the prediction of a dependent variable. By using multiple linear regression analysis instead of simple linear regression, an economist can potentially take all the important independent variables into account to determine their effect on the dependent variable of interest.

Henderson, Willson, Dunn, and Kazmierczak (2009) used regression to investigate the impact of forestry-related ordinances on timber harvesting in St. Tammany Parish, Louisiana. The authors observed that local government regulations regarding forestry practices on private land in the parish were often made without a sufficient understanding of the potential economic consequences of the ordinances. Using regression analysis to determine the size of this effect, the authors found a significant negative relationship between certain classifications of forestry-related ordinances and the level of timber harvest. These results had economic implications for the regions in which the ordinances were instituted.

Forecasting

In addition to looking at relationships between variables in the present, economists are also interested in making predictions about future values of various economic variables based on past data. To this end, economists frequently take existing (i.e., secondary) data regarding current and past economic behavior to extrapolate trends and predict future behavior. This type of quantitative analysis allows organizations to better position themselves to leverage knowledge into profits. This process is known as forecasting. Forecasting is the science of estimating or predicting patterns and variations, and is a technique that is frequently used in economics. Forecasting is based on the observation that there are a number of causes of variation in economic activity: trends, business cycles, and seasonal fluctuations as well as irregular and random fluctuations. Trends are persistent, underlying directions in which something is moving in either the short, intermediate, or long term. Many trends tend to be linear rather than cyclic, steadily growing (or shrinking) over a period of years. On the other hand, trends in new industries tend to be curvilinear as the demand for the new product or service grows after its introduction, and then declines after the product or service becomes integrated into the economy.

Structural Models

Economists frequently use quantitative methods for forecasting through the development of models, including structural, time series, and deterministic models. Structural models are sets of mathematical functions that are designed to represent the causal relationships between variables within an economy. Another approach to modeling uses time series data. In this approach, data are gathered on a specific characteristic over a period of time. To be useful, time series data must be collected at intervals of regular length. In time series analysis, the sequence of observations is assumed to be a set of jointly distributed random variables. Time series analysis allows one to study the structure of the correlation of variables over time to determine the appropriateness of the model. The model can then be adjusted as needed to make it more representative of the real-world situation. Deterministic models assume that the variable of interest is a deterministic function of time and does not include the effects of any underlying data uncertainty or variability in the time series.

CONCLUSION

The use of quantitative analysis is essential to helping economists better understand the way that economies

work and how economic variables are related as well as to predict changes in one variable based on changes in another variable or variables. Although like most social scientists, economists are often limited to secondary data, they still have a wide range of quantitative techniques available for analyzing not only simple economic behaviors and relationships but also for modeling complex systems. Quantitative analysis allows economists to test and validate their theories and to revise them so that they better reflect the realities of real-world economies.

BIBLIOGRAPHY

Bagwell, K., Staiger, R., Yurukoglu, A. (2018). *The National Bureau of Economic Research.*

Black, K. (2006). *Business statistics for contemporary decision making* (4th ed.). New York: John Wiley & Sons.

Du, R., & Kamakura, W. (2012). *Quantitative trendspotting. Journal of Marketing Research (JMR), 49(4),* 514–536.

Henderson, J. E., Willson, T. M., Dunn, M. A., & Kazierczak, R. F. Jr. (2009). "The impact of forestry-related ordinances on timber harvesting in St. Tammany Parish, Louisiana." *Contemporary Economic Policy, 27(1),* 67–75.

Koop, G. (2009). *Analysis of economic data* (2nd ed.). New York: Wiley.

Kureshi, S., Sood, V., & Koshy, A. (2008). "An in-depth profile of the customers of single brand store in emerging market." *South Asian Journal of Management, 15(2),* 81–99.

Lee, G. & McGuiggan, R. (2008). "Understanding small- and medium-sized firms' financial skill needs." *Journal of International Finance and Economics, 8(3),* 93–101.

Özkaynak, B., Adaman, F., & Devine, P. (2012). «The identity of ecological economics: Retrospects and prospects.» *Cambridge Journal of Economics, 36(5),* 1123–1142.

Wieland, V., Cwik, T., Müller, G. J., Schmidt, S., & Wolters, M. (2012). "A new comparative approach to macroeconomic modeling and policy analysis." *Journal of Economic Behavior & Organization, 83(3),* 523–541.

Witte, R. S. (1980). *Statistics.* New York: Holt, Rinehart and Winston.

Suggested Reading

Framingham, C. F. & MacMillan, J. A. (1971). "Some comments on the treatment of problems of the inadequate statistics in the United States: Precept and practice." *Journal of Economic Literature, 9(1),* 64–68.

Jagric, T. (2003). "A nonlinear approach to forecasting with leading economic indicators." *Studies in Nonlinear Dynamics and Econometrics, 7(2),* 1–18.

Jagric, T. (2003). "Business cycles in central and east European countries." *Eastern European Economics, 41(5),* 6–23.

Jagric, T. (2003). "Forecasting with leading economic indicators – A neural network approach." *Business Economics, 38(4),* 42–54.

Miller, T. W. (2011). "Active management of real options." *Engineering Economist, 56(3),* 205–230.

Tseng, J., & Li, S. (2012). "Quantifying volatility clustering in financial time series." *International Review of Financial Analysis,* 2311–19.

—*Ruth Wienclaw*

R

RESEARCH METHODS IN ECONOMICS AND BUSINESS

ABSTRACT

With statistics, economists can study the intricacies of real-world markets, forecast future business conditions and, most importantly, test the applicability of their models to the real world. Before statistics was introduced, economics was a strictly theoretical exercise. People accepted its principles because they made sense or "seemed" right. But the all-important objective corroboration of theory with fact was missing. That bothered economists keen on making their discipline more scientific. They went on to found the field of econometrics that has since become a mainstay of economic analysis.

OVERVIEW

As Adam Smith famously noted over two centuries ago, self-interest and competition collectively act like an "invisible hand" to shape the efficient allocation of resources in free and open markets. Ever since then, economists have sought to flesh out the way these forces are naturally harnessed and manifest themselves in mechanisms of exchange. Much of the work here has been, by necessity, descriptive. Observation in turn leads to the formation of intuitive models to explain otherwise random events. Scientists follow the exact same methodology. But economists cannot take the next all-important step and experimentally validate their theories as scientists do. For no amount of ingenuity, alas, will successfully re-create real-world economic activity in a laboratory.

A hypothesis cannot be proved or disproved unless it is tested in controlled conditions free from outside influences. Depending on the premises, the most patently absurd propositions can be successfully argued logically. No matter how brilliant the reasoning employed, then, a theory is treated as a fact only when

A plaque commemorating the house in which Adam Smith wrote *The Wealth of Nations* in his hometown of Kirkcadly, Scotland. (Courtesy of James Eaton-Lee CC-BY-SA-3.0 via Wikimedia Commons)

it has been substantiated objectively. Barring that, it remains an assumption regardless of how elegant, insightful, or useful it might be. As such, its applicability to real-world phenomena is problematic, and any forecast based on it susceptible to unintentional error. Whereas businesses might lose money when predictions prove inaccurate, model builders lose something much harder to recoup: credibility. In the absence of objective proof, the next best thing is a track record of accurate predictions (Wallis, 1984).

What Adam Smith could not have foreseen was how intricate and complex these models could be when formulated as equations. Mathematics provides the means not only to build complex models of macroeconomic theory but also, crucially, to test their accuracy and statistical robustness. Econometrics in fact came about as a separate discipline when an enterprising economist in 1933 used the formulae describing harmonic oscillation to investigate and explain the business cycle (Bouhmans, 2001). Meanwhile, pure mathematics has proved a much suppler means of expressing economic concepts than words alone. So much so, in fact, that much of today's economic theory is elucidated using algebra, logarithms, calculus, group theory, and symbolic logic, just as mathematical rules governing the manipulation of symbols and the advancement of formal proofs in general have given economists new ways to argue the legitimacy of their constructs ("Theoretical assumptions and nonobserved facts," 1985).

Moreover, Silvia PALASCA writes, in the twenty-first century, one must pay attention to the use of software in economics, since software is built based on mathematical tools. The difference lies in the fact that the mathematics is hidden and is not directly accessible to the user, who often forgets the substrate of such software and makes use of it without fully understanding the results produced or ignoring the possible problems raised by the mathematical model behind the program (2013).

Only observable data can prove or disprove the veracity of their claims, and how can one ensure the accuracy and reliability of this data? What's to say the events in question are actually random in nature or an unrepresentative subset of the phenomenon under study? In other words, assuming your experimental design is sound, how do you know the data you've collected isn't just random? The short answer is statistics: the branch of mathematics specializing in the collection, assessment, and analysis of large amounts of numerical data. And its roots interestingly lie in analytical geometry.

FURTHER INSIGHTS

Econometricians gather, collate, and interpret real-world macroeconomic data (yearly figures on national output, employment, inflation, the money supply, etc.) going back over 60 years. Among all economists,

then, they are perhaps the most outwardly oriented and, due largely to statistics, the most "scientific." Their counterparts in the business world employ the very same statistical techniques to solve production problems, maximize customer service functions and plan and evaluate marketing campaigns. The tools of their trade are time series data, cross-sectional data, panel data, and multidimensional panel data. In each case, a sample of the larger population is examined and the findings extrapolated. How this sample is collected is crucial: It must be selected indiscriminately from a large data set that encompasses the full range of possible outcomes. Time series data is measured periodically over an extended duration while cross-sectional data is measured all at once, much like a camera takes a photograph. Panel data combines both for purposes of analysis, and multidimensional panel examines the potential impact on the resulting findings that the introduction of another variable might have. The mathematics employed includes single- and multiple-equation modeling, hypothesis testing, statistical significance assessment, regression analysis, and analyses of variance and covariance.

Modeling

To yield useful insights, models must take certain liberties with reality. For, a cause-and-effect relationship cannot be corroborated as long as any other possible influence might be in play. Economists would be particularly hard-pressed to provide any insight into the fundamental dynamics of the marketplace, in fact, if they could not avail themselves of the principle of *Ceteris paribus,* or "all other things being equal." It is a necessary presumption but one that nonetheless entails the deliberate oversimplification of complex processes. Model builders are prepared to live with this trade-off because their primary concern is how faithfully they represent the phenomenon under study. Everything else is secondary. As such, bias-based error can and sometimes does creep unobserved into the model. Usually, however, it is tolerated because the risk and impact of any such error pales in comparison to the usefulness of the correlation demonstrated.

Advantages of Mathematical Models

Mathematical models have certain built-in advantages. Data by its very nature is numerical. Equations or inequalities, moreover, can more precisely state the nature of the relationship between two or more types of events than words or diagrams. Using both, econometricians can build very sophisticated multi-variable models of macroeconomic activity. Now, the variables, or symbols, denote a range of possible values for the events being studied. They can be either a discrete set of numbers or a continuous function or equation stating the probable distribution of future values. When a cause-and-effect relationship is being modeled, any change in an independent variable triggers a change in its dependent variable. Critically, though, a change in the dependent variable does not cause a change in the independent variable. A model is said to be deterministic, moreover, only when prior values and its equations account for all the change. Eliminating randomness entirely, though, is very hard to do. So, the values of most econometric variables are expressed differently, as a continuous probability function that only gives the odds on a particular quantity occurring. A dynamic model, finally, factors in the passage of time and thus frequently employs differential equations from calculus, a static model does not and generally employs linear equations from algebra.

The Accuracy of Models

Curiously, though, testing the accuracy of any real-world model is not a straightforward affair, not at least when the burden of proof rests on statistics. For important reasons, in fact, the working hypothesis must first be turned into a negative statement called the null hypothesis. It asserts that there is no relationship even though the object is to show that there is one. This indirect approach has one very big advantage: The working hypothesis is rejected only when the ensuing statistical analysis confirms the random nature of the data. Otherwise, the working hypothesis is accepted. Yes, it is a roundabout way of doing things, but it has its merits. Foremost among these is how a negative assertion is far easier to statistically substantiate than a positive one. Indeed, all that has to be shown is that the results are not random; something statistics does very well. But, the only logical inference this form of analysis supports is that the data does not refute the working hypothesis. That is not the same as declaring outright that the data supports the original proposition or even that there is the reasonable likelihood that an underlying relationship exists. As conclusions go, it is rather circumscribed.

Yet it nonetheless better reflects the general limitations of experimental inquiry, where a theory holds up only as long as the data supports it.

Statistical Significance

Any set of observed values captures a tiny fraction of the set of total values generated in the real world. How do we know if the historical data is not in fact just coincidence? In other words, how confident are we that the trend extrapolated from this limited amount data actually exists (McCloskey & Ziliak, 1996)? Of course, randomness exists to one degree or another in virtually everything. So how do you quantify it, and how much is acceptable? Without a satisfactory answer, inferential statistics itself is fatally undermined. Much thought has therefore gone into the question of statistical significance: What it is, and how it can be established? If we study a completely random process such as flipping a coin or throwing dice, the results on a scatter graph after a very large number of tries invariably resemble a bell-shaped curve. Here, slightly over two-thirds of all random results fall in relatively close proximity to each other, within one standard deviation of the mean of distribution; the apex of the bell. Any graph can be divided horizontally into equal intervals on the other side of the samples mean via a measure of central tendency called the standard deviation. The fewest random events, between 0.5 percent and 2.5 percent, take place at the farthest reaches of the bell-shaped curve, at a standard deviation of plus or minus 2.5 and beyond.

For any "normally" distributed set of data to be significant, then, only a certain number of sample observations can fall beyond its standard deviation of plus or minus 2.5. And the sample's standard deviation can be readily calculated. First comes the basic arithmetic value where, by convention, the mean or average of the sample is subtracted from each value. Given how the result here, called a deviate, can be positive or negative, each result is then multiplied by itself, or "squared" to avoid unnecessary complications. The product of a negative number multiplied by itself is always positive. All of these values, what is more, can vary except the last. It must be fixed so the others can fluctuate; the total of all the deviations divided by the number of observations must equal the sample mean. That last value, when added or subtracted, ensures this. So the degree of freedom of a given sample is one less than its total number of observed events. And the mean of the sum of deviates is always divided by its sample's degree of freedom. All that remains now to arrive at the standard deviation is to return it to positive and negative values, which is done by taking the square root.

Regression Analysis

Regression analysis figures prominently in econometric and operations research. Given that it measures the extent to which an independent variable directly affects a dependent one, one can see why. The existence and extent of this causal relationship is determined mathematically by examining comparable data sets for both variables. By plotting each known data point along an X and Y axis, the resulting scatter graph shows an overall pattern that suggests a line that is either a line or curved or else simply a hodge-podge of dots. The so called regression line here is what is most important, be it barely decipherable or readily apparent. Two factors now need to be assessed: How many and how closely the data points cluster around an imaginary straight line or curve. The greater the number and the nearer the proximity of each, the more likely changes in the independent variable(s) will occasion changes in the dependent variable. Conversely, the fewer the number and the farther the proximity, the less likely there is a direct cause-and-effect relationship. Thanks to analytical geometry, what is more, when the regression line is linear, the nature of the relationship can be expressed algebraically in a "regression equation," and its robustness by a constant within it called "the correlation coefficient." The latter is a number between -1 and 1, where 1 signals a direct correspondence between variables, -1 an inverse correspondence and 0 none. Most of the time, though, this correspondence is partial and this constant is a decimal less than 1 or -1.

Noting the predominant role of linear regression analysis in empirical economics, Soyer and Hogarth (2012) asked 257 academic economists to make probabilistic inferences based on different presentations of the outputs of this statistical tool. The questions concerned the distribution of the dependent variable, conditional on known values of the independent variable. The answers based on the standard presentation mode demonstrated "an illusion of predictability"; the outcomes were perceived to be more predictable than could be justified by the model.

In particular, the authors noted, many respondents failed to take the error term into account. The implications of the study are that economists need to reconsider the way in which empirical results are presented and consider the possible provision of "easy-to-use simulation tools" that would help readers of empirical papers make accurate inferences.

Analysis of Variance & Covariance

Linear regression analysis is a relatively straightforward form of one-way analysis of variance (ANOVA) for two variables. What exactly, though, is variance? Basically, it measures the degrees of difference between observed events, or "signal," and the randomness, or "noise," lurking in the background. ANOVA essentially assesses how spread out the dispersion pattern of individual data points is both within and between these variables. When only two variables are being examined, this ratio's calculation is relatively straightforward and is known as the t-test (Evans, 1999). First, the differences between variables, the signal, must be measured and summarized quantitatively by subtracting one mean from the other. When the sample is very large and the events normally distributed, the randomness of the overall phenomenon is said to be "known," so degrees of freedom are not needed in this equation. Each sample's variance is thus computed by dividing its sample size directly into the sum of its squared deviates. The standard error in the difference between the two sample's means is the square root of the sum of individual variances. Computing the all-important variance between samples is finally within reach. The only step left is to divide this square root into the difference between the two sample's aggregate means.

Adding any more variables to the mix complicates these calculations further; the deviation of the mean of one variable's sample, essentially, has to be compared to the deviation of every other variable's sample, be that one, two, three, etc. This is best done by first coming up with the mean value for each and using it to find a sample grouping's deviates. These are then squared and added together. Determining the variance "within" groups, the next step, is now simply a matter of computing the mean of the sum of these sums. With one notable additional step, the same calculations are repeated to arrive at the variance of the "between" group data.

To begin with, the mean of the total data set is first determined and then subtracted from the mean of each sample group and the results squared. Since the number of data points observed may differ between groups, however, the squared deviates cannot simply be added together. That is because the fewer the observations, generally speaking, the harder it is to accurately estimate how many are random. Sample sizes among "between" groups may thus not be homogenous, potentially skewing the analysis if not properly accounted for. This is done by multiplying each "between" group's sum of squares by the number of its recorded observations. The variance "between" groups is the sum of these weighted figures.

Separately, these two composite means do not give a precise, one figure rendering of the variance of the "signal" in relation to the variance of the "noise." That requires one last calculation. Here, the mean variance of the "within" and "between" groups must first be divided by its sample's degrees of freedom. Dividing the resulting "between" group's quotient by the "within" group's, at long last, yield the desired proportion otherwise known as the F factor. A figure greater than 1 here suggests the likelihood that the results are random, while a figure less than 1 suggests that the results are not. The lower the F score, then, the greater the likelihood there is a cause-and-effect relationship between variables.

Sometimes, though, data for different variables tends to converge more than diverge, requiring a different type of treatment: analysis of covariance (ANCOVA). A synthesis of linear regression analysis and ANOVA, it gauges not the difference but the likeness between multiple sets of data and answers the all-important question: How can we be certain that two random variables are in fact causally linked? What if they are under the sway of an undetected outside factor, a "covariate"? Well, if influence of this covariate can be statistically eliminated from the data samples, it no longer poses a problem. Whenever a covariate is suspected, then, its known values are plotted, a trend-line computed, and additional values estimated using regression analysis. The resulting correlation coefficients, in turn, are used to predict an alternate set of values for the dependent variable that can, in turn, be compared to the reported values. With these values in hand, an analysis of variance can determine how much or how little the two fluctuate, quantifying the covariate's influence on each random variable. An ANOVA reading of 0 indicates the results are coincidental, a positive reading indicates that they are not. Whatever difference between the "real" and the "covariate-linked" values is the error that must be filtered out. And there in lies ANCOVA's usefulness.

CONCLUSION

All in all, econometrics is an exacting discipline. The statistics employed can be relatively simple like the techniques described above. Or, they can be devilishly complicated, as is the case when a number of variables are examined. (Recognizing this, and the importance of integrating financial accounting examples into an introductory undergraduate business statistics course, Drougas, Harrington, and Miller (2011) describe a project challenging students to review financial statement data for 27 firms in the restaurant industry, generate a multiple regression using software, and interpret the results in the language of business [i.e., which financial items impact a company's stock price]). But no matter how complex the equations, how massive the numbers-crunching and how limited the conclusions that can be drawn, statistics map the uncertainty ever present in the real world in general and in macroeconomics in particular. With statistics, economists can test assumptions, refine or discard models, make forecasts, and bring a scientific rigor to their analyses. Economics would not be nearly as objective or precise a field of study without it.

BIBLIOGRAPHY

Boumans, M. (2001). "Measure for measure: How economists model the world into numbers." *New School for Social Research, 68*, 427–453.

Drougas, A., Harrington, S., & Miller, J. (2011). "Incorporating a practical financial accounting example into an introductory statistics course." *Journal of the Academy of Business Education, 12*, 121–136.

Evans, R. (1999). Chapter 2: "Cherished beliefs and t-statistics." *Macroeconomic forecasting* (pp. 24–49). Oxfordshire: Taylor & Francis Ltd.

Granger, C. (2004). "Time series analysis, cointegration, and applications." *American Economic Review, 94*, 421–425.

Ioannidis, J., Stanley, T., Doucouliagos, H. (2017). "The power of bias in economics research." *The Economic Journal, 127.*

McCloskey, D., & Ziliak, S. (1996). "The standard error of regressions." *Journal of Economic Literature, 34,* 97.

PALSCA S. (2013). "Mathematics in economics. A perspective on necessity and sufficiency." *Theoretical & Applied Economics, 20,* 127–144.

Part Four: 23. "Theoretical assumptions and nonobserved facts." (1985). *Essays in economic theory, theorizing, facts & policies* (pp. 272–282). Piscataway, NJ: Transaction Press.

Soyer, E., & Hogarth, R.M. (2012). "The illusion of predictability: How regression statistics mislead experts." *International Journal of Forecasting, 28,* 695–711.

Wallis, K. (1984). "Comparing time-series and nonlinear model-based forecasts." *Oxford Bulletin of Economics & Statistics, 46,* 383–389.

Vass, C., Rigby, D., Payne, K. (2017). "The role of qualitative research methods in discrete choice experiments." *Medical Decision Making.*

SUGGESTED READING

Jansen, E. (2002). "Statistical issues in macroeconomic modelling." *Scandinavian Journal of Statistics, 29,* 193.

Klein, L. (2006). "Econometric modeling at mixed frequencies." *Journal of Mathematical Sciences, 133,* 1445–1448.

Phillips, P. (1988). "Reflections on econometric methodology." *Economic Record, 64,* 344.

—Francis Duffy, MBA

S

SECURITIES REGULATIONS

ABSTRACT

This article focuses on specific regulations that have been passed in the United States in reference to securities issues. Prior to the Wall Street crash of 1929, there were minimum regulations of securities in the United States at the federal level. Eight specific regulations are discussed, with special emphasis on the Sarbanes-Oxley Act. There will be an exploration of how risk assessment may assist organizations with making sure that regulations are followed. Many organizations are beginning to add risk assessment to their compliance and ethics programs.

Crowd gathering at the Stock Exchange on Wall Street after the 1929 crash. (Courtesy of U.S. Government via Wikimedia Commons)

OVERVIEW

Securities Act of 1933

Prior to the Wall Street crash of 1929, there were minimum regulations of securities in the United States at the federal level. However, as a result of the crash, Congress held hearings to investigate why the situation occurred. After finding abuses, Congress passed the Securities Act of 1933. The purpose of the act was to regulate the interstate sales of securities and make it illegal to sell securities into a state without complying with state laws. The two basic objectives were to:

- require that investors receive significant information concerning securities being offered for public sale.
- prohibit deceit, misrepresentation, and other fraud in the sales of securities.

Securities & Exchange Commission

In addition, the law required organizations to file a registration statement with the Securities and Exchange Commission if they wanted to sell securities publicly. The registration statement was designed to provide information about the organization and made sure that the information was on file as a public record. The information required on the form included the following:

- a description of the issuer's properties and business

Joseph P. Kennedy was the the inaugural Chairman of the Securities & Exchange Commission. (Courtesy of Larry Gordon via Wikimedia Commons)

- a description of the security to be offered for sale
- information about the management of the issuer
- if not registering common stock, information about the securities
- financial statements certified by independent accountants

However, it should be noted that the Securities and Exchange Commission does not provide approval for the statement. Rather, it is responsible for validating the statement if the organization has provided sufficient details, especially information about potential risk factors. Once the statement becomes effective, the organization can begin to sell the stocks. The stocks tend to be sold via investment bankers.

It should also be noted that not all offerings have to be registered with the Securities and Exchange Commission. Some of the exceptions from the registration requirement include the following:

- private offerings to a limited number of persons or institutions
- offerings of limited size

- intrastate offerings
- rule 144 (When you acquire restricted securities or hold control securities, you must find an exemption from the SEC's registration requirements to sell them in a public marketplace. Rule 144 allows public resale of restricted and control securities if a number of conditions are met.)
- securities of municipal, state, and federal governments

Additional Securities Regulations

Other pertinent securities regulations passed in the United States include the following.

The trading floor of the New York Stock Exchange six months after the crash of 1929. (Courtesy of the U.S. Government via Wikimedia Commons)

Regulation Fair Disclosure (Reg FD): A regulation that requires publicly traded companies to disclose information to all investors at the same time. The purpose of this regulation is to create an environment in which all investors have the same information and to reduce the problem of selective disclosure.

The Securities Exchange Act of 1934: An act responsible for regulating the secondary market trading of securities. After the introduction of the act, it only applied to stock exchanges and their listed companies. However, in the late 1930s, the act was amended to include regulation of trades between individuals when no stock exchange was involved. The act also regulates broker dealers without a status for trading securities. A telecommunications infrastructure was developed for those trades that do not require a physical location.

Today, a digital information network is used to connect the brokers. This system is called the National Association of Securities Dealers Automated Quotation System (NASDAQ). The act of 1934 regulates NASDAQ through relations that apply to the association and by requiring that it have an independent organization overseeing it (i.e., self-regulatory organization). The self-regulatory organization for NASDAQ is the National Association of Securities Dealers (NASD). There was an amendment in 1964 that extended the change in the late 1930s to include the regulation of companies trading in the over-the-counter market.

The Public Utility Holding Company Act of 1935: A law passed by Congress that facilitated regulation of electric utilities by limiting their operations to a single state, which made them subject to state regulations and/or forcing divestitures so that each became a single integrated system servicing a limited geographic area. In addition, the act was designed to keep utility holding companies involved in regulated businesses from engaging in unregulated businesses. Therefore, the Securities and Exchange Commission would have to approve a holding company's activities in non-utility business prior to their engaging. This requirement was to ensure that the holding companies kept regulated and unregulated businesses separate.

The Trust Indenture Act of 1939: A law passed in 1939 that prohibits bond issues valued at over $5 million from being offered for sale without a formal written agreement (an indenture), signed by both the bond issuer and the bondholder, that fully discloses the particulars of the bond issue. The act also requires that a trustee be appointed for all bond issues, so that the rights of bondholders are not compromised. The Trust Indenture Act of 1939 was passed for the protection of bond investors. In the event that a bond issuer becomes insolvent, the appointed trustee may be given the right to seize the bond issuer's assets and sell them to recoup the bondholders' investments (Investopedia, n.d.).

The Investment Company Act of 1940: Investment companies were still new in 1940. Given the problems

that happened in the late 1920s and the passage of the initial acts in the early 1930s, Congress felt compelled to pass an act that would provide investors confidence in these new companies as well as protect the public interest from this type of security. As a result of these concerns, the Investment Company Act of 1940 was passed. The act established separate standards for investment companies as well as defined and regulated investment vehicles, including mutual funds. However, certain investments (i.e., hedge funds) were exempted.

The act categorized the investment companies into three different classifications:

- **Face-amount Certificate Company:** An investment company in the business of issuing face-amount certificates of the installment type.

- **Unit Investment Trust:** An investment company, which, organized under a trust indenture, contract of custodianship or agency, or similar instrument, does not have a board of directors, and issues only redeemable securities, each of which represents an undivided interest in a unit of specified securities, but does not include voting trust.

- **Management Company:** Any investment company other than a face-amount certificate company or a unit investment trust. The most well-known type of management company is the mutual fund.

The Investment Advisers Act of 1940: A federal law that was implemented in order to regulate the actions of investment advisors.

The Securities Investor Protection Act of 1970: A federal law created as a special scheme for the liquidation of insolvent securities' brokerage firms and established the Securities Investor Protection Corporation (SIPC) to administer a fund to protect customers of failed brokers. The primary purpose of the act is to reimburse customers for losses due to broker failures and to boost public confidence in securities markets (Joo, 1999).

If a customer has cash and securities missing from their customer accounts, he/she may be eligible for SIPC assistance. However, SIPC's fund cannot be used to pay claims of any failed brokerage firm customer who is also a general partner, officer, or director of the firm; the beneficial owner of 5 percent or more of any class of equity security of the firm (other than certain nonconvertible preferred stocks); a limited partner with a participation of 5 percent or more in the net assets or net profits of the firm; someone with the power to exercise a controlling influence over the management or policies of the firm; and/or a broker, dealer, or bank acting for itself rather than for its own customer or customers (Securities Investor Protection Corporation, n.d.).

Senator Paul Sarbanes (D-MD) and Representative Michael G. Oxley (R-OH-4), the co-sponsors of the Sarbanes–Oxley Act. (Courtesy of U.S. Government via Wikimedia Commons)

The Sarbanes-Oxley Act of 2002: An act introduced to Congress by Senator Paul Sarbanes, Democrat from Maryland, and Representative Michael G. Oxley, Republican from Ohio. Legislation passed in 2002 with the purpose of encouraging employees to become effective corporate monitors and report misconduct and unethical behavior in corporations. This act is discussed in greater detail in the next section.

The Dodd-Frank Wall Street Reform and Consumer Protection Act of 2010: Named for the legislation's sponsors, Senator Christopher Dodd (D-CT) and Representative Barney Frank (D-MA), this 848-page law is "the most ambitious since the Great Depression" (Rao, MacDonald, & Crawford, 2011). It places increased regulations on credit rating agencies, banks, hedge funds, buyout shops, and the derivatives market. Under the act, the government will audit lending programs of the central banks and "rein in" speculative proprietary trading activities of big insured banks. Another big

President Barack Obama meets with Rep. Barney Frank, (D-Mass), Sen. Dick Durbin, (D-Ill), and Sen. Chris Dodd, (D-Conn), in the Green Room of the White House prior to a financial regulatory reform announcement June 17, 2009. (Courtesy of Pete Souza, White House, via Wikimedia Commons)

piece of the law is the creation of an independent Consumer Financial Protection Bureau to monitor mortgage and credit card products. Furthermore, Title I, subtitle A of the Dodd-Frank Act created the Financial Stability Oversight Council (FSOC) to monitor and respond to "systemic risk to the U.S. economy caused by the actions of large complex companies, products, and activities" (Rao, MacDonald, & Crawford, 2011).

APPLICATION

The Sarbanes-Oxley Act of 2002

The Sarbanes-Oxley (SOX) Act was signed into law on July 30, 2002, and was created in response to

Arthur Andersen witnesses, Enron's accounting office, testify at the Subcommittee on Oversight and Investigations of the Committee on Energy and Commerce House of Representatives (107th Congress) hearing on January 24, 2002. Arthur Anderson, one of the world's largest accounting firms, was found guilty of obstruction of justice for destroying documents related to the Enron audit. (Courtesy of the U.S. Government via Wikimedia Commons)

the major scandals in corporations such as Enron, WorldCom, and Tyco. When these scandals occurred, there was a decline of public trust in accounting and reporting practices. Some believed that the SOX Act was "a controversial reaction by Congress to investor and public companies, compounded by excessive compensation to executives" (Bumgardner, 2003). The law covers a wide area of a business and establishes new or revised standards for U.S. public company boards, management teams, and public accounting firms. The act has 11 titles, which address issues such as corporate board responsibilities and criminal penalties. The 11 titles (or sections) are the following:

- Public Company Accounting Oversight Board (PCAOB). The Supreme Court later ruled in 2010 that the establishment of the PCAOB was actually beyond Congress's constitutional authority. The ruling did not declare the entire act unconstitutional; however, the Supreme Court did acknowledge that the act's establishment of the PCAOB as an independent board allows for no accountability or presidential oversight (Lenn, 2013).
- Auditors Independence
- Corporate Responsibility
- Enhanced Financial Disclosures
- Analyst Conflicts of Interest
- Commission Resources and Authority
- Studies and Reports
- Corporate and Criminal Fraud Accountability
- White Collar Crime Penalty Enhancement
- Corporate Tax Return
- Corporate Fraud Accountability

"The law itself amended the regulatory provisions of the Securities Commission Act of 1934" (Britt, 2003, par. 3) by requiring that the Securities and Exchange Commission implement rulings on requirements to comply with the law. Lastly, the law established a new agency, the Public Company Accounting Oversight Board, which is responsible for overseeing, regulating, inspecting, and disciplining accounting firms in their roles as auditors of public companies.

Learning from SOX

Although the SOX Act has had a profound effect on public companies, it was not set up to cover private companies. However, that does not mean that private companies should not take note of the costs and benefits of the SOX implementation. Based on interviews with legal and accounting experts, Anthony (n.d.) was able to develop a list of four key areas that small businesses and private companies should learn about from the Sarbanes-Oxley Act. Some of his important points include the following:

Work with two accountings instead of one. When a large public company works with one firm, it can raise red flags. Small companies should consider having an auditor as well as a separate CPA firm handling areas such as tax filing and consulting services. Private companies are starting to hire smaller firms even though there may be additional expenses.

Have an audit committee. Private companies and small businesses should consider having an internal mechanism that acts as a "checks and balances" system.

Make the independent board truly independent. The external board of advisers should be allowed to voice their opinions versus being cronies of the chief executive officer. They are there to offer objective advice to the senior management team in an effort to keep the organization in compliance with various regulations.

Institute whistleblower protection. The SOX Act has two approaches that encourage employees to become corporate whistleblowers (Moberly, 2006). The first step is a clause that provides protection to whistleblowers from employer retaliation once they have disclosed improper behavior. The second step requires employers to provide employees with guidelines, policies, and procedures to report organizational misconduct within the organization.

VIEWPOINT

Risk Assessment

In the past, the compliance and ethics functions fell in the scope of the organization's legal department. However, with the recent creation of scandals units, such as internal auditing, the organization's initiatives with ethics and compliance have reported directly to the senior management team and the board of directors. As a result of these changes, many organizations are beginning to add risk assessment their compliance and ethics programs.

Phases of Risk Assessment Implementation

Aon created a four-phased process to assist with this task (Kaufman, 2006).

Phase 1 (Risk Identification) includes the following:
- Identify and characterize key risks (i.e., surveys, workshops, interviews, data analysis/documents).
- Categorize risks according to business functionality within the organization (i.e., strategic, operational, financial, human capital, technology, legal, and regulatory).

Phase 2 (Risk Prioritization) includes the following:
- Prioritize/score risks (i.e., frequency, severity, time to impact).
- Develop risk map graphically detailing impacts of risks.
- Establish risk ownership (i.e., may be assigned by function, geography or business unit).
- Group risks into categories of risk magnitude (i.e., low, moderate and high).

Phase 3 (Critical Risk Analysis) includes the following:
- Perform financial modeling of key risks using proprietary loss simulation models.

- Evaluate risk/return (cost/benefit) of competing strategies.
- Consider expected value and distribution of modeled key performance indicators.
- Ensure awareness of correlations of risks.

Phase 4 (Implementation) includes the following:
- Recommend risk mitigation strategies.
- Implement and monitor risk mitigation activity.
- Report results periodically to key stakeholders.
- Review risks and strategies to account for changes over time.

Criticisms of the Risk Assessment Process

With any new system, there have been criticisms of the risk assessment process. According to Kaufman (2004), the most commonly cited arguments are as follows:

Threat of legal discovery. Legal counsel may be concerned that information collected during the risk assessment process must be disclosed if a lawsuit were to arise. There is a concern that this exposure will be perceived as organizational knowledge that a risk was present and the organization failed to act on it.

Fear of retribution. Participants in the process may be afraid to share information if they believe they will be reprimanded.

Lack of senior level support. The senior management team has to support the risk assessment initiative, and it is important that the leaders of this function report directly to their level or the board.

Insufficient resources. Risk assessment programs can be expensive. Organizations will have to be committed to seeing this process succeed. Therefore, short-term profits may be reduced in order to fund the process.

Inability to operationalize the process. Organizations must find a way to maintain real-time risk control, monitoring, and communication.

In many cases, the risk assessment initiative works in conjunction with an organization's enterprise risk management program by acting as the preliminary test to evaluating the organization's strategic, financial, operational, technological, and human capital initiatives. The approach provides "holistic and risk-based views of the organization's legal and social responsibilities" (Kaufman, 2006, p. 8).

CONCLUSION

Prior to the Wall Street crash of 1929, there were minimum regulations of securities in the United States at the federal level. However, as a result of the crash, Congress held hearings to investigate why the situation occurred. After finding abuses, Congress passed the Securities Act of 1933. Other pertinent securities regulations passed in the United States include Regulation Fair Disclosure, the Securities Exchange Act of 1934, the Public Utility Holding Company Act of 1935, the Trust Indenture Act of 1939, the Investment Company Act of 1940, the Investment Advisers Act of 1940, the Securities Investor Protection Act of 1970, the Sarbanes-Oxley Act of 2002, and the Dodd-Frank Wall Street Reform and Consumer Protection Act of 2010.

The Sarbanes-Oxley (SOX) Act was signed into law on July 30, 2002, and was in response to the major scandals in corporations such as Enron, WorldCom, and Tyco. When these scandals occurred, there was a decline of public trust in accounting and reporting practices. Some believe that the SOX Act was "a controversial reaction by Congress to investor and public companies, compounded by excessive compensation to executives" (Bumgardner, 2003). The law covers a wide area of a business and establishes new or revised standards for U.S. public company boards, management teams, and public accounting firms. The act has 11 titles, which address issues such as corporate board responsibilities and criminal penalties.

The Dodd-Frank Wall Street Reform and Consumer Protection Act of 2010 is widely considered the most ambitious and far-reaching renovation of financial regulation in the United States since the 1930s. Together with other regulatory reforms both in the United States and overseas, the act aims to put an end to the "too big to fail problem" and is expected to substantially alter the structure of financial markets (Acharya, Cooley, Richardson, Sylla & Walter, 2011). Acharya et al. do point to the following as remaining wholly or partially unaddressed by the Dodd-Frank Wall Street Reform and Consumer Protection Act, however: pricing of explicit and implicit government guarantees; dealing with inevitable opportunities for the financial sector to engage in regulatory arbitrage; and containing the systemic risk arising from collections of small institutions and markets such as money market funds and repo contracts (2011).

The current trend supports initiatives such as risk assessment and enterprise risk management programs. There have been recent mandates and guidelines that support the popularity of these two initiatives. Kaufman (2006) listed some of the developments as:

- Section 404 of the Sarbanes-Oxley Act of 2002 mandating that organizations file an annual internal control report. One of the requirements is for organizations to affirm that the management team has approved the establishment and maintenance of a risk assessment program in order to be in compliance with regulations.
- The Federal Sentencing Commission made changes to the Federal Sentencing Guidelines by requiring organizations to continuously audit their programs by implementing risk assessment initiatives to reduce the risk of violations of laws.
- In 2004, COSO released the Enterprise Risk Management (ERM) framework, which is a method used to analyze risk.
- The Open Compliance and Ethics Group (OCEG) drafted a framework that provides a holistic approach to implementing, managing, evaluating, and improving compliance and ethics programs.
- Mark Zmieski, the director of Strategic Learning and Research at the Risk Management Association, believes regulatory expectations are the main reason why the ERM approach is becoming popular at many organizations (RMA study, 2007). The study that his organization conducted revealed that respondents believed the following benefits could materialize as a result of an effective ERM system being in place:
- Improved understanding of risk and controls (48 percent of the respondents).
- Ability to set a common risk culture (48 percent of the respondents).
- Opportunity to identify and assess risk in total (45 percent of the respondents).
- Ability to apply consistent policy and standards (45 percent of the respondents).

- Ability to improve strategic decision-making in the next 18 to 24 months (over 50 percent of the respondents).

BIBLIOGRAPHY

Acharya, V.V., Cooley, T., Richardson, M., Sylla, R., & Walter, I. (2011). "The Dodd-Frank Wall Street Reform and Consumer Protection Act: accomplishments and limitations." *Journal of Applied Corporate Finance, 23*, 43–56.

Anthony, J. (2007). "Private companies: 4 lessons from Sarbanes Oxley Act." Retrieved from "http://www.microsoft.com/smallbusiness/resources/finance/legal%5fexpenses/private%5fcompanies%5f4%5flessons%5ffrom%5fsarbanes%5foxley%5fact.mspx"

Britt, P. (2003, July/August). "Professional perspective: Implications of Sarbanes Oxley." Retrieved from "http://www.nareit.com/portfoliomag/03julaug/professional.shtml"

Bumgardner, L. (2003). "Reforming corporate America: How does the Sarbanes Oxley act impact American business?" *Graziadio Business Report, 6.*

Georgiev, G. (2017). "Too big to disclose: Firm size and materiality blindspots in securities regulation." *UCLA*, Rev. 602.

Investopedia (n.d.). "Trust indenture act of 1939." Retrieved November 21, 2007, from xlink:href="http://www.investopedia.com/terms/t/trustindentureactof1933.asp"

Joo, T. (1999, May). "Who watches the watchers? The securities investor protection Act, investor confidence, and the subsidization of failure." *Southern California Law Review, 72.*

Kaufman, C. (2006, February). "A strategy for incorporating risk assessment in the compliance and ethics agenda: Evolution of the risk assessment process as a compliance and ethics tool." *Aon Corporation*. Retrieved from "http://www.aon.com/us/busi/risk%5fmanagement/risk%5fconsulting/ent%5frisk"

Lenn, L.E. (2013). "Sarbanes-Oxley Act 2002 (SOX)-10 years later." *Journal of Legal Issues & Cases In Business, 2*, 1–14.

Rao, H., MacDonald, J., & Crawford, D. (2011). "The Dodd-Frank Wall Street Reform and Consumer Protection Act of 2010." *CPA Journal, 81*, 14–25.

"RMA announces results of enterprise risk management survey." (2007). *Secured Lender, 63*, 14.

Securities Investor Protection Corporation. (n.d.). "How SIPC protects you." Retrieved, "http://www.sipc.org/how/brochure.cfm"

SUGGESTED READING

Fitzsimons, A.P. & Silliman, B.R. (2007). "SEC and PCAOB plan to grant relief to smaller companies." *Bank Accounting & Finance, 20*, 42–46.

Hail, L. & Leuz, C. (2006). "International differences in the cost of equity capital: Do legal institutions and securities regulations matter?" *Journal of Accounting Research, 44*, 485–531.

Johnson, C.L. (2013). "Understanding Dodd-Frank's reach into the financing of Main Street." *Journal of Public Budgeting, Accounting & Financial Management, 25*, 391–410.

Kennedy, D. (2007). "FINRA is at the back door of index annuity regulation." *National Underwriter / Life & Health Financial Services, 111*, 20.

—Marie Gould

SHADOW BANKING SYSTEM

ABSTRACT

"Shadow banking system" refers to a collection of financial institutions and practices that are outside of the traditional, more regulated banking system. Traditional banks are monitored by the government to ensure that they remain financially sound by not taking on too much risk. Institutions such as investment banks, hedge funds, structured investment vehicles, and off balance sheet securitizations all fall outside of traditional financial regulatory regimes, creating a shadow banking system that has grown large enough to rival the traditional banking system.

George Soros appears at the Festival of Economics 2012 in Trento, Italy. Soros is the fund manager of Quantum Group of Funds, a hedge fund. (Courtesy of Niccolò Caranti CC BY-SA 3.0 via Wikimedia Commons)

This exposes the economy to greater levels of risk as was seen in the financial collapse of 2008.

OVERVIEW

Traditional banks are more heavily regulated because they are known as deposit banks—that is, they accept deposits from investors, pay interest to the depositor at a specified rate, and then use the investor's money to make loans and secure other types of investment. Each such loan made by a bank includes an amount of risk because there is a chance that the borrower will not be able to pay the money back to the bank, leaving the bank in the position of having to cover the loan by using its own assets. If a deposit bank were not required to follow certain rules regulating risk, then the bank might taking on excessive risk to earn money. Carrying too much risk backfires, because when too many of the bank's loans fail to be repaid, the bank finds itself in the position of having to cover (pay back) more money than it has available in the form of assets. Banking regulations exist to prevent this type of scenario (United States, 2011; Gennaioli, Shleifer, & Vishny, 2013).

However, banking regulations were developed to control traditional, deposit banks. Most regulations do not apply to institutions that do not fit into the traditional model of deposit banks, so in order to be able to take on greater amounts of risk and earn higher returns, the financial industry has often developed alternative institutions and higher risk types of investment (e.g., credit default swaps), which are not subject to such strict regulation and often do not need to be included on balance sheet reports of an entity's financial health. As these alternative institutions

The former New York City headquarters of Lehman Brothers at Rockefeller Center is now owned by Barclays, a British multinational bank. Lehman Brothers declared bankruptcy in 2008 because of its involvement in the subprime mortgage crisis and is now defunct. (Courtesy of David Shankbone CC-BY-3.0 via Wikimedia Commons)

have grown in number over the years, they have attracted more and more investors, to the point that the amount of money invested in the alternative, or shadow, banking system rivals that of the traditional banks (Longworth & C.D. Howe Institute, 2012).

This has been a major area of concern because many of the investors in the shadow banking system are traditional financial institutions. This means that even traditional financial institutions are able to take on greater risk than many of their depositors might be comfortable with. The shadow banking system played a major role in the financial collapse of 2008. The collapse was caused by a classic case of institutions taking on excessive amounts of risk. When markets began to correct themselves after several years of inflated housing prices and subprime mortgage lending, several major financial institutions found themselves owing far more money than they had the ability to repay (England, 2011).

FURTHER INSIGHTS

Shadow banking institutions had grown so huge and had become so diversified by the first decade of the twentieth century, that the failure of one or two of them threatened to bring down other institutions as well, because so many parts of the shadow banking system had become intertwined with one another. Institutions that took on too much risk in the mortgage markets also invested in hedge funds to try to mitigate their risk, but when multiple investors in the mortgage markets lost their investments, then they all sought to recover on their hedge fund investments, causing those to begin to collapse as well.

Through lack of oversight, the shadow banking system became like a set of dominos, so that when one institution fell it brought down others, which threatened to bring down others, and so on. This is precisely the kind of scenario that banking regulations are set up to prevent, and ultimately the federal government had to step in and provide enough cash to prop up the economy, preventing a complete collapse. After these events, calls for greater regulation of the shadow banking system were renewed and intensified (Haugen & Musser, 2011).

A major complaint about the shadow banking system has long been that it exists primarily because of the close relationships between the leaders of major financial institutions and the government. Critics of this system complain that it operates like a revolving door: Government employees charged with implementing and enforcing financial regulations often spend a few years working for the government, and then resign to enter the private sector, taking very high-paying positions with the very companies that they previously regulated.

These companies—many of whom operate or invest in major players in the shadow banking system—benefit from the former government employees' knowledge and connections, often allowing them to discover new ways of increasing revenue by avoiding regulatory scrutiny (Hirsch, 2012). Furthermore, it is common practice for the heads of government agencies in charge of financial regulation to be drawn from the ranks of banking executives, leading some to observe that the revolving door turns in both directions. The problem with this, according to critics of the system, is that finance executives and government regulators become so intertwined with one another that no one wants to disrupt the ecosystem by creating and enforcing financial regulations that are tough enough to curtail the problematic practices of the shadow banking system. Doing so would harm one's career prospects by interfering with the investment goals of future employers.

For example, an employee at a government agency charged with supervising shadow banking activities is in a position to push for greater oversight of investment banks. However, if this employee knows that in the near future he or she can quit a government job and go work for one of these investment banks, then it is not in his or her interest to inconvenience the investment banks. This type of scenario has led some to suggest that the best way to begin regulating the shadow banking system is by putting in place regulations that would require the passage of a certain amount of time after employees leave government service before they can take a position with private investment firms, and vice versa (Luttrell et al., 2012).

VIEWPOINTS

Economic theorists point out that the activities of the shadow banking system are not problematic in and of themselves, but become so because they are largely unregulated. The financial markets operate on basic principles of supply and demand capitalism, and investment resources that are not required to be asset backed will tend to flow toward investment vehicles that offer the largest potential returns (Annual International Banking Conference, & Claessens, 2015). In the modern context, this explains why investments in the shadow banking system have tended to increase over the years, to the point where they rival investments in traditional deposit banks (Nesvetailova, 2015).

The primary way to combat this trend is by implementing regulations that require activities in the shadow banking system to follow risk allocation requirements similar to those that exist for deposit banks. Doing this, it is thought, will decrease incentives for capital to flow into the shadow banking system, because if shadow banks are no longer permitted to take on inordinate amounts of risk, then they will likewise be unable to earn the rewards that up until now have made the risk so attractive.

Supporters of this approach point out that shadow banks do most of the same types of things as traditional banks, so it is only fair that they should be subjected to the same types of regulations. There is also historical precedent for enacting such reforms. In 1933 the Glass-Steagall Act placed limits on the types of investments that deposit banks could enter into, in the hope of protecting consumers against banks' practice of increasing their own profits by investing depositors' money in risky ventures. Over time, the Glass-Steagall Act was gradually weakened through prolonged lobbying efforts by the financial sector of the economy, until it was repealed in 1999 (Jenkins & Collins, 2012).

Some economists have suggested that the gradual erosion of many of Glass-Steagall's protections was what made possible the financial collapse of 2008, concluding that it therefore makes sense to reinstate such protections as a means of preventing similar disasters in the future. Critics of such regulations, most of them with ties to the financial sector, point out that free markets can only function well when they are truly free, that is, not bound by excessive government regulation, but able to use their own creativity, ingenuity, and financial acumen to maximize profits (Akerlof, 2014). Plantin (2014) argues that regulation of the banking sector drives capital investment to shadow institutions.

The Dodd-Frank Wall Street Reform and Consumer Protection Act was passed into law in 2010 as a response to the economic collapse of 2008. Some of its provisions include greater oversight of derivatives (complex financial instruments that can lead to unforeseeable amounts of risk). The act fell far short of what critics of the financial industry called for, however. A legislative compromise that affords protection to traditional banking consumers and the economy at large, while still offering higher risk investment opportunities for banks and similar institutions, continues to be sought in Congress. Parties on both sides hope that some type of agreement can be reached before the next financial crisis rears its head, although with the speed and interconnectedness of the modern global economy, it is far from certain that this will be possible (Guttmann, 2015).

BIBLIOGRAPHY

Akerlof, G. A. (2014). *What have we learned?: Macroeconomic policy after the crisis.* London, UK: MIT Press.

Allen, F., Qian, Y., Tu, G., Yu, F. (2017). "Entrusted loans: A close look at China's shadow banking system." *SSRN.*

Annual International Banking Conference, & Claessens, S. (2015). *Shadow banking within and across national borders.* Hackensack, NJ: World Scientific.

England, R. S. (2011). *Black box casino: How Wall Street's risky shadow banking crashed global finance.* Santa Barbara, CA: Praeger.

Gennaioli, N., Shleifer, A., & Vishny, R. W. (2013). "A model of shadow banking." *Journal of Finance, 68(4),* 1331–1363.

Guttmann, R. (2015). *Finance-led capitalism: Shadow banking, re-regulation, and the future of global markets.* New York, NY: Palgrave Macmillan

Haugen, D. M., & Musser, S. (2011). *Reforming Wall Street.* Detroit, MI: Greenhaven Press.

Hirsch, P. (2012). *Man vs. markets: Economics explained (plain and simple).* New York, NY: HarperBusiness.

Jenkins, D. A., & Collins, M. I. (2012). *Shadow banking and its role in the financial crisis.* Hauppauge, NY: Nova Science.

Longworth, D., & C.D. Howe Institute. (2012). *Combatting the dangers lurking in the shadows: The macroprudential regulation of shadow banking.* Toronto, Ontario: C.D. Howe Institute.

Luttrell, D., Rosenblum, H., Thies, J., & Federal Reserve Bank of Dallas. (2012). *Understanding the risks inherent in shadow banking: A primer and practical lessons learned.* Dallas, TX: Federal Reserve Bank of Dallas.

Nesvetailova, A. (2015). "A crisis of the overcrowded future: Shadow banking and the political economy of financial innovation." *New Political Economy, 20(3),* 431–453.

Plantin, G. (2015). "Shadow banking and bank capital regulation." *Review of Financial Studies, 28(1),* 146–175.

United States. (2011). *The financial crisis inquiry report: Final report of the National Commission on the Causes of the Financial and Economic Crisis in the United States.* New York, NY: Public Affairs.

SUGGESTED READING

Batchvarov, A. (2013). "Parallel, rather than "shadow," banking system." *Journal of Risk Management in Financial Institutions, 6(4),* 346–351.

Culp, C. L. (2013). "Syndicated leveraged loans during and after the crisis and the role of the shadow banking system." *Journal of Applied Corporate Finance, 25(2),* 63–85.

Kelemen, V. (2014). *Shadow banking and U.S. financial regulatory policy: Overviews.* New York, NY: Novinka.

Prates, D. M., & Farhi, M. (2015). "The shadow banking system and the new phase of the money manager capitalism." *Journal of Post Keynesian Economics, 37(4),* 568–589.

Sunderam, A. (2015). "Money creation and the shadow banking system." *Review of Financial Studies, 28(4),* 939–977.

—*Scott Zimmer, JD*

SPECIAL PROBLEMS IN ECONOMICS

ABSTRACT

There are myriad factors in economics that can influence fiscal health or anemia. While economists are a constantly evolving breed in search of a relevant mechanism that can help explain economic performance, there are elements that, if unaccounted for, can cause serious problems within the study of economics and, ultimately, for policy. This paper examines a few of these problems in the context of prominent domestic and international economic issues.

OVERVIEW

The iconic economist Milton Friedman once offered his thoughts on the causes of the Great Depression of the early twentieth century, pointing the finger at the government's policy responses to the economic slowdowns that led to the market collapse in 1929. Somewhat contrary to the precepts being proffered

People outside a closed bank in New York City after 1929 stock market crash. (Courtesy of Wikipedia)

by his peer John Keynes, who called for government involvement and intervention in times of economic crisis, Friedman contended that the Depression was "produced by government mismanagement rather than by any inherent instability of the private economy" (Friedman, 2002, p. 38).

What were the forms of mismanagement to which Friedman was referring? In an op-ed piece written after his passing, colleagues Edward Nelson and Anna Schwartz asserted that Friedman was not suggesting that the government was ill advised to issue any responsive policy to the steadily declining economy. Rather, they wrote, the institutions that were established to prevent such a collapse (namely the Federal Reserve) offered solutions that were contradictory to long-term fiscal health, such as raising discount loan rates at a time when banks around the nation were closing (Nelson & Schwartz, 2007).

Similarly, a well-intentioned effort to reinvigorate the economy by installing a series of trade barriers under the Smoot-Hawley Tariff Act of 1930, thereby protecting domestic industries, caused far more harm by making international trade cost-prohibitive for foreign investors. U.S. imports and exports suffered terribly as world trade declined nearly 66 percent over a four-year period (U.S. Department of State, 2007).

Although some loyalists to Keynes assume that Friedman meant that government should have stayed out of formulating policy to counter the market instability of the 1920s and 1930s, in truth he was commenting on the apparent missteps of the government, not on the fact that it had intervened at all. The Depression was to many a "perfect storm": a variety of factors, both in the market and on the part of the government, combined to create a painful, dark period in international history. A large collection of unanticipated factors and conditions joined together to cause the greatest market collapse in U.S. history, and with no control over those elements and no effective policy response on the part of the government, the Depression would take root for years.

The fact that the Fed response created more harm than good, as did Smoot-Hawley, illustrates an important point: There are myriad factors in economics that can influence fiscal health or anemia. While economists are a constantly evolving breed, in search of a relevant mechanism that can help explain economic performance, there are elements that, if unaccounted for, can cause serious problems within the study of economics and, ultimately, for policy. This paper will examine a few of these problems in the context of prominent domestic and international economic issues.

Exchanging Currencies

On September 20, 2007, an extraordinary event occurred. For the first time in more than 30 years, the Canadian dollar became equal in value to the U.S. dollar. For decades, it was considered bad fiscal policy for Canadians to take their business to their neighbor to the south, given the great disparity between the two currencies' values. Conversely, during those three decades, the United States thrived on the currency gap. Americans, taking advantage of "fire sale" business deals, traveled north in droves to do

Dominion Bank at the corner of Bleury and St. Catherine Streets in Montreal, QC, about 1915. (Courtesy of Musée McCord Museum via Wikimedia Commons)

business, so much so that *Fortune* published an article titled "Is Canada for Sale?"

When parity was announced, however, a new way of life was born. Canadians began reversing the tide, flowing south to find fire sales of their own. A 1998 Canadian law prohibits banks in that country from merging. In light of this restriction, banks had no choice but to pursue mergers with American financial institutions, moves that would almost always work to the advantage of the U.S. party. With the development of September 2007, however, Toronto-based Dominion Bank announced its acquisition of New Jersey–based Commerce Bankcorp for $8.5 billion—saving $1 billion Canadian, since the deal was first pursued in June of 2007 (Leonard, 2007).

The flip-flop between U.S. and Canadian dollar exchange rates was unanticipated by most, particularly in light of the long-standing inequity between the two. In fact, currency exchange is one of the most difficult areas to model and predict in the field of macroeconomics. Some modeling can be employed to analyze specifically tailored samples of currency relationships in their current states, but such data becomes less reliable when external macroeconomic variables come into the picture and as the perspective moves from the present to the future. Among the variables that can wreak havoc on currency-exchange modeling are industrial shifts, political instabilities, and countless elements that constitute and affect aggregate supply and aggregate demand. One study looks at the propensity for macroeconomic studies to seek simplicity in modeling currency exchange and concludes that overly simplistic modeling may prove inadequate. As an alternative, the authors propose employing mixed models, the foci of which take into account the variety of influences that may impact expectations formation (Uctum, 2007).

The problem that exists with regard to currency exchange is not analysis of the trends and rates at which one currency performs against another. Empirical data can paint a picture of such situations with relative accuracy. It is the forecasting of and long-term expectations for currencies that create inconsistencies and unpredictability in modeling. Linear modeling has been many economists' preferred method of analyzing currency, but the limitations on the degree to which forecasting can be done are indicative of the need for more reliable data-collection resources. One study concludes that other forms of models, such as nonlinear formulae, yield similar results to linear forecasts and, as they rely on forecast data and environmental conditions, may prove more reliable in data collection than their linear counterparts (Boero, 2002).

Market Instability

Arguably, the most difficult challenge facing an economy is not developing industries or maintaining a stable workforce, although these are indeed challenges in and of themselves; it is ensuring that the delicate balancing act between supply and demand, known as equilibrium, continues for the long term. In a free market system, in which the myriad elements that constitute aggregate supply and demand interact, it is critical that extraneous forces do not cause a disproportionate impact on that balance, lest the market be placed at risk.

Of course, there are a plethora of these external influences, each of which can either have an immediate influence on market stability or set in motion a chain of events that will undermine a market's performance in the long term. While identifying these factors is not necessarily difficult, predicting when and how they will impact the market is.

The implications of market instability are obvious. In the 1970s, when developing economies were already in a fragile state, a sudden spike in oil prices sent currencies into a free fall and markets all over the world into turmoil (Bleaney, 2005). Market crises such as the Mexican peso collapse of 1994, the Asian economic crisis of 1997, the continuing struggles of

After the Asian economic crisis of 1997, President of the Republic of Indonesia Muhammad Suharto presented his address of resignation at Merdeka Palace in Jakarta on May 21, 1998. (Courtesy of Office of the Vice President of the Republic of Indonesia via Wikimedia Commons)

the markets of the former Soviet states, and the U.S. housing market woes that sparked the 2008 global recession lend a sense of urgency to the need to predict and assess the depth of issues that can disrupt market stability.

A market's concentration (the number of viable industries within a given system) is vital to its health, but what happens when the industry or industries that make up the economy suffer adversity from extraneous factors? Ideally, a healthy market that loses the strength of one or more of its industries will be able to correct the blow by substituting a healthy industry in the place of underperforming economic sectors. Then again, here too a problem exists: how to predict when and in what capacity substitution should occur in a concentrated market to maintain equilibrium.

A recent study of concentrated markets and the timeliness of substitution in faltering systems revealed that equilibrium can be maintained if industries are able to quickly react and replace faltering firms. Of course, the devil remains in the details; markets are dynamic and extraordinarily complex in nature, after all. As a result, corrective measures to prevent market instability tend to be reactive, not proactive and preventative (Cetorelli, 2007).

Crisis

Each of the examples above alludes to an important point: Many of the problems in the analysis and subsequent management of economic systems are addressed reactively, not proactively. Often, the most impactful issue facing these systems is a sudden shock, not a long-term trend. Shocks come in a wide variety. The sudden shutdown of a major manufacturing facility that employs a high percentage of its staff from the small town in which it is located has an immediate and unanticipated effect on the local and regional economy. If an oil-producing country replaces its U.S.- and European Union–friendly government with an anti-Western regime in a violent coup, it can send oil prices skyward around the globe. A hurricane making its way up the eastern seaboard might force major airports from Miami to Boston to reroute and cancel flights, which in turn would prevent major conferences and conventions from taking place, prompting innumerable hotel room cancellations and putting a major crimp in local economies.

Pile-up at San Juan's Isla Grande Airport in Puerto Rico, a result of Hurricane Maria's winds. Hurricane Maria struck the island in October of 2017. The essential airport is a part of the National Plan of Integrated Airport Systems. It is categorized as a primary commercial service airport. (Courtesy of Andrea Booher, FEMA)

In truth, the natural progression from economic theory to modeling to forecasting and, finally, to economic policy making is a cautious one, and lurking in the shadows outside of this linear process is a specter known as "the crisis." For this reason, economists, accepting of the fact that one cannot anticipate every one of the potential shocks to the system, look at how to react to crises rather than how to prevent them. In some cases, a reaction to elements that could potentially grow into a crisis may mitigate that situation before it becomes unmanageable.

One study of the Chinese economy supports this concept. Since the 1990s, China has steadily become one of the largest and most powerful economies in the world, enjoying most-favored-nation status with another top-tier trading partner (the United States) and dominating mainland Asia in influence. Still, China has proven to be something of an enigma, particularly for those who still see the country as a communist power. The People's Republic of China is a nation that, every 10 to 20 years, seems to halt its progress toward economic liberalization and take a few steps back to enhance and underscore its Maoist roots. Hence, as Western economies have continued along the capitalist avenue, sometimes for hundreds of years, and more recently formed economies such as the former Soviet states have committed themselves to the free market ideal as well, China's slow political transformation and propensity for strictly governing markets continue to frustrate Western trade partners.

The delay in completely opening Chinese markets without heavy trade barriers or restrictions, while a different approach to economic liberalization, is perhaps not a completely negative one. After all, many of the former countries of the Soviet Union immediately embraced the free market concept, only to find themselves handicapped by weak currencies, homogenous industrial bases, and unprepared fiscal infrastructures. China's approach has been more conservative. As the authors of this study conclude:

One of our most important findings is that the impact of capital controls on multiple equilibria has a dual nature. On the one hand, to enhance the opening of the capital account will increase economic development by greatly accelerating capital inflows and improving investment. On the other hand, it increases the probability of crisis occurring in the future (Luo, 2007).

Whether the Chinese policy of impeding the liberalization of its economic endeavors is a reasonable response or merely an overly conservative way of avoiding dramatic regime change is a debate for another forum. Still, that nation employed this action in the face of the near collapse of other liberalizing economies—those in the former Soviet Union—that resulted from adoption of the free market system. The point to be made is that China's trade restrictions are a reaction to international economic turmoil and a policy response designed to avoid a potential crisis.

CONCLUSIONS

While Milton Friedman was known for his no-nonsense analysis of economic policy, economics is a field in which nothing is ever completely set in stone. A contemporary of Friedman, Paul Samuelson, once commented on the fact that although he and Friedman took similar career paths, Friedman was rarely wrong, while Samuelson frequently erred. However, Samuelson's "errors" were in fact groundbreaking, leading to the correct application of hypotheses. His work *Economics: An Introductory Analysis,* first published in 1948, was released in its nineteenth edition in 2010 and reads like a modern history of economic theory, covering the hypotheses that held water, the analytical methodologies that proved fruitful, and the ideas and proposals that failed. "I

Paul A. Samuelson is an American economist. He was awarded The Nobel Prize in Economics, in 1970. (Courtesy of Bender235 CC BY 1.0 via Wikimedia Commons)

know better than anyone else does that you have to try out hypotheses that may not turn out to be true," he once said (Schneider, 2006).

Indeed, economics is not an arena that is static; it is a fluid, dynamic discipline, constantly changing and evolving. Economic analysis is therefore necessarily reactive. As Samuelson demonstrated throughout his illustrious career, errors in theory and modeling will occur throughout the life of the study of an economic system, and it is likely that the models and theories that have been long accepted by the mainstream will eventually come up short in explaining developments in local, national, and international economic systems.

This article has provided several examples of situations in which economic analysis and modeling come up short in the face of certain trends and environments. For example, in currency exchange, which is at the heart of international trade and commerce, fluctuations in rates can have enormous implications

for business and cause monumental shifts in economic relationships. In the case of Canadian banks, the financial institutions north of the U.S. border were previously in a bind. Prohibited by law from merging with one another, they could not merge with American banks either—not as a result of any regulation but simply because the exchange rate meant a probable significant loss on investment. In 2007, however, the weakened U.S. dollar gave strength to the Canadian dollar, and Canadian business and tourism flourished south of the border.

Based on this example, it would seem to be important to seek a way to predict shifts in currency strength. Unfortunately, that ability has eluded economists under current modeling practices. The apparent problem is that the mainstream seems committed to the simplest forms of analysis, which may explain certain trends within a larger environment but does not account for other elements within that system. However, a multifaceted form of study, such as nonlinear modeling, may prove to be a more effective tool to address this ongoing problem in economics.

If currency exchange seems a vexing arena for economic analysis, a far more frustrating problem in terms of study is market stability. Furthermore, while the use of nonlinear, or at least similarly unconventional, methodologies may prove useful in addressing the issue, market equilibrium, which contains countless elements and subparts encompassing the two major elements of a free market (supply and demand), represents an extraordinarily difficult problem in terms of forecasting. Economists' approach to assessing the establishment and maintenance of equilibrium therefore tends to become reactive and responsive. The key to understanding market forces thus rests in studying the activities surrounding the equilibria of other markets as a baseline.

Equilibrium may prove daunting and require a more flexible approach. Crisis situations, however, are as challenging to address as they are to understand. Crises come in many forms, and the breadth of their influence is equally varied. The closure of a manufacturing plant in a rural area sends local unemployment rates skyward, tax receipts southward, and local economies into recession. A hurricane moving up the U.S. eastern seaboard causes every major airport to delay or cancel flights, which in turn causes the cancellation of major conventions and conferences, delivers major losses to local hotels and restaurants (who anticipated an influx of guests and customers), and, of course, sends shockwaves across the country by delaying connecting flights.

The ideal aim of studying such crises is not just to predict them before they happen but also to foresee the breadth of the area they will affect. A careful analysis of the elements that could erupt into a crisis is certainly warranted. In the case of China, that analysis also entails a review of how crises played out in other countries.

In the study of the intricacies and innumerable components of the dynamic and ever-evolving field of economics, a number of problems can arise, primarily with regard to assessing complex, fluid trends and predicting significant events. In many circumstances, it seems that the best response is, as Samuelson suggests, to accept that problems will arise and adapt accordingly.

BIBLIOGRAPHY

Bleaney, M. (2005). "The aftermath of a currency collapse: How different are emerging markets?" *World Economy, 28,* 79–89.

Boero, G. & Morrocu, E. (2002). "The performance of non-linear exchange rate models." *Journal of Forecasting, 21,* 513–542.

Boudebbous, T., & Chichti, J. (2013). "Do financial crises occur in advanced economies at regular intervals?" *International Journal of Economics & Finance, 5,* 46–62.

Cetorelli, N., Hirtle, B., Morgan, D., Peristiani, S. & Santos, J. (2007). "Trends in financial market concentration and their implications for market stability." *Economic Policy Review, 13,* 33–51.

Davis, E. & Schwartz, A. (2007). "Who was Milton Friedman?" *The New York Review of Books, 54.*

De Grauwe, P., & Zhang, Z. (2012). "Monetary integration and exchange rate issues in East Asia." *World Economy, 35,* 397–404.

Friedman, M. (2002). *Capitalism and freedom* (40th anniv. ed.). Chicago, IL: University of Chicago Press.

Leonard, D. & Demos, T. (2007). "The new south of the border." *Fortune, 156,* 19.

Luo, J. & Tang, W. (2007). "Capital openness and financial crises: A financial contagion model with multiple equilibria." *Journal of Economic Policy Reform, 10,* 283–296.

Schneider, M. (2006). "Great minds in economics: Paul Samuelson." *Yale Economic Review Online Edition.* Retrieved from xlink:href="http://www.yaleeconomicreview.com/issues/summer2006/samuelson"

Uctum, R. & Prat, G. (2007). "Switching between expectation processes in the foreign exchange market: A probabilistic approach using survey data." *Review of International Economics, 15,* 700–719.

US Department of State. (2007). "Smoot-Hawley tariff, 1930." Retrieved from xlink:href="http://www.state.gov/r/pa/ho/time/id/17606.htm"

Yutaka, K. (2013). "Effects of exchange rate fluctuations and financial development on international trade: Recent experience." *International Journal of Business Management & Economic Research, 4,* 793–801.

SUGGESTED READING

Anand Tularam, G., & Subramanian, B. (2013). "Modeling of financial crises: A critical analysis of models leading to the global financial crisis." *Global Journal of Business Research, 7,* 101–124.

Cetorelli, N., Hirtle, B., Morgan, D., Peristiani, S. & Santos, J. (2007). "Trends in financial market concentration and their implications for market stability." *Economic Policy Review, 13,* 33–51.

Chung, S. (2006). "The out of sample forecasts of nonlinear long-memory models of the real exchange rate." *International Journal of Finance and Economics, 11,* 355–370.

Samuelson, Robert J. (2007). "Our great recession obsession." *Newsweek, 150,* 66.

—Michael P. Auerbach

STAGES OF ECONOMIC MATURATION

ABSTRACT

Poverty reduction and disease eradication are goals valued by many in the developed and developing countries around the globe. The approaches taken to accomplish those goals remain questionable and daunting as one considers possibilities for modernizing underdeveloped societies. In general, the modernization of developing nations is an endeavor that appears to be loaded with challenges and diversity. Specifically, the extent to which we can unpack modernization perspectives to ensure their relevance to the economic maturation of developing countries remains open for further inquiry. According to the prominent work of W.W. Rostow, all societies fit into one of five stages of economic growth. The linearity of that growth model is certainly one source of its criticism. One way to move beyond those criticisms is to contemplate whether that model is really prescriptive or descriptive in nature and intent. Toward that end, this essay aims to enhance undergraduate student awareness of modernization theory and to explore the applicability of concepts from basic economics and development economics. In addition, it aims to provide those students with valuable insight into the methods for studying, addressing, and resolving the varied needs of developing countries.

OVERVIEW

A variety of perspectives, publications, and college courses relate to the modernization of developing nations whether one refers to them as the global south, the third world, or whatever descriptor one can imagine. In reality, a multitude of approaches exist for thinking about and acting upon the goal of expediting social, political, and economic development within their countries. Whether those engagements occur at the conceptual or practical level, those individuals with an interest in the topic can expect to find references to modernization theory, growth theory, liberal development theory, dependency theory, world systems theory, and so on.

Plenty of material is available to support inquires that may run deep and/or wide. In the few pages ahead, this essay acknowledges some of those perspectives while directing attention to an articulate political and historical economist's perspective on economic growth and modernization. Many consider the five stages of economic growth model, which was the work of W.W. Rostow, a foundation for almost anyone who initiates a study on the industrial progress of a developing country. It is important to note that the work has generated a lot of controversy in the decades since its publication, making it all the more interesting and fascinating. Similar to what an undergraduate student would find in a course on economic development, this essay contains statements at various points highlighting the model's rationale, assumptions, strengths, and weaknesses.

It seems appropriate to suggest at this early point in the essay that the stages model offers hope to developing countries. In short, the model represents an itinerary for a journey that includes a drive along the winding road of economic maturity heading toward a state of mass consumption; as is the case with most journeys, getting there is half the fun. Nonetheless, many scholars and practitioners criticize the model asserting that it is overly optimistic for third world realities and/or it is excessively linear for real maturation processes. Perhaps the greatest value of the growth model resides in its capacity for comparing stages between countries and for generating ideas among scholars and policy makers. In the sections ahead, readers will find a brief background on the intellectual history behind various theories of development, a summary of applicable economic concepts, and an application of those concepts to the topic at hand.

APPLICATIONS

The main purposes of this essay include enhancing an awareness of the intellectual history behind the first modern theorists of development, refining an ability to assess the relevance of historical facts and recent debates, and recognizing various motivations for an economic development agenda. Sometimes those components are hidden and other times obvious. Perhaps the original and subsequent publication titles will spark some initial interest, which ties in very well with the apparent theme of sustaining a wide array of interest.

Rostow & the Stages of Economic Growth

Publication of the seminal article by W.W. Rostow in 1959 held the title "The Stages of Economic Growth." In the following year, that 16-page publication became part of a 179-page book. More importantly, that famous and widely cited book received the subtitle *A Non-Communist Manifesto*. For reasons that become clear later in this essay, there was a real need to distinguish a superior path to modernization from an inferior one. As a matter of background and context, it is also worthwhile to point out that Rostow was a recipient of funding from the Ford Foundation while authoring those publications. In addition, he was an advisor to the U.S. Defense Department during the Kennedy and Johnson administrations and later served as an assistant to President Johnson during the Vietnam conflict.

Perhaps those affiliations made the publications all the more controversial. Now in its third edition, total sales of the book reportedly number about 300,000 copies. Nonetheless, interest in the book has waned since the early 1980s. Some scholars suggest that this lull coincides with the onset of a postmodern era, the end of the Cold War, and/or allegations that the growth stages model is irrelevant to the maturation of countries comprising the third world. Whatever the case may be, the book presents the growth of underdeveloped countries as a direct function of their ability to emulate developed countries in their drive toward economic maturation and as an indirect function of their rates of domestic saving. Certainly, the growth of developed countries corresponds highly with the savings rate given the notable absence of a guide to chart their progressive maturation.

While avoiding the appearance of being ethnocentric, it is important for us to note that economic markets progress at varying degrees through several stages of economic growth. From a basic economic perspective, employments of the factors of production (land, labor, and capital) in varied combinations ultimately generate physical outputs and nonphysical consequences. One may think of the progression as a successive movement through economies that depend on agriculture, manufacturing, services, information, or knowledge at some points during history.

Though at times there is a significant correspondence between each stage and a dominant perspective, it is far more important to understand the historical context to gain a full and comparative meaning.

Modernization Theory & Practice

The extent to which modernization theories are relevant to the economic maturation of developing countries remains unsettled and open for further inquiry. Scholars continue to examine the plausibility of those theories and of Rostow's claim as set forth in *The Stages of Economic Growth: A Non-Communist Manifesto*. In the book, Rostow postulates that economic modernization occurs in five successive stages of varying length. These scholarly pursuits seek a fuller understanding of how changes in political, economic, and social environments during the 1940s and 1950s connect with the evolution of modernization theories.

Classifications of society as traditional, modern, or postmodern are evident in the academic realm and literature. In general terms, modernization theory is oriented toward the study of the economic maturation of underdeveloped, developing, or third world countries. However, the studies are usually conducted through the lens of observers from developed countries. Consequently, it is quite possible for some researchers to overstate the importance of twin pillars, which are the industrial base and the nation-state, to current modernization processes. At issue is whether contemporary growth originates primarily through domestic means and/or whether developed countries exert an inordinate amount of influence on the developing countries.

Many consider modernization as the goal desirable and attainable by all societies. As experience seems acceptable as a major source of learning, it is natural for a been-there, done-that attitude to manifest itself in any model. Being sensitive to a model's set of underlying assumptions and exercising some amount of care are required to avoid allegations of being an ethnocentric, which by definition is the act of judging others based on our own experiences and local customs and norms. The ethnocentric appearance of Rostow's work generates some of the criticisms lodged against the stages model. In sum, the experiences of the developed countries may or may not be directly transferable to developing countries especially when circumstances change with the passage of time.

Capitalism vs. Socialism

History reveals that two overarching ideologies had bearing on the post–world war path to modernity. In terms of political and economic orientations, there was the United States and its liberal form of capitalism at one end and there was the former Soviet Union and its form of socialism at the other end. Furthermore, the divisive effect of the Cold War influenced resource allocations in ways not yet fully understood. Nevertheless, it is evident that the United States moved into the age of mass consumption just because we are more familiar with a capitalistic economic system.

Capitalist and socialist economic systems represent rival solutions to the problem of underdevelopment. It is obvious that both can lead economies beyond agriculture, manufacturing, and into the post-industrial state of development, but any attempt to transition from one to the other takes a lot of time. The former Soviet Union serves as an example in this regard. One reason for a lengthy transition is that the market-based system accommodates household preferences in the production function. In contrast, a socialist economic system accommodates governmental preferences in the production function and households typically receive items in accordance with a market plan. It is clear that a plan- or command-based economy under a socialistic system is less likely to inhibit mass consumption in comparison to a market-based economy with a pluralistic political system.

If rapid progression through the stages of growth toward mass consumption is any indicator, then the superior path is that made possible through liberal capitalism. Many suggest the postmodern era is evident in the emergence of cultural and social analyses that began in the 1980s with the end of the Cold War and a few transitions away from socialism. As further evidence of that shift, many witnessed the formation of goals in the 1990s dealing with global reductions in poverty and disease.

Before we proceed to the next section and its focus on some relevant economic concepts, there are some additional perspectives on development economics and a few names aside from Rostow that are worthy of brief mention. The classical perspective on economic growth is available in the works of Smith, Malthus, Ricardo, and Marx. With the advent of a development economics perspective, soon after the end of World War II, a list of authors might include Keynes, Harrod, Domar, and Lewis. The next section covers some basic economic perspectives and concepts highly relevant to the five stages growth model.

Perspectives & Concepts Relevant to Development Economics

The linearity of the Rostow growth model is a source of criticism. It may be highly irrelevant for those countries that experience false starts and/or experience a temporary movement toward modernity. Cycles of expansion and contraction are certainly a feature common to most economies around the globe. Whether one refers to the developing or the developed countries, the employments of land, labor, and capital occur in varying quantities over time. Nonetheless, some economists point out the inherent bias of Rostow's work because it seems to assume a Western model of modernization and countries with large populations, renewable and/or abundant natural resources, and huge land masses.

Some of the economics literature highlights the differences between economics and development economics. For example, readers will find assertions in the latter category that the totality of capitalism includes both the developing and the developed countries. Furthermore, some scholars suggest that the field of development economics is more complex than basic economics because of its denial of the simplistic focus on free trade, profit motives, and market exchanges. Polanyi (1957), who took into consideration politics and economics, contends that markets are sustainable only to the degree they interact with social and political institutions. He also advances the idea that institutions regulate, stabilize, and legitimize markets and thereby challenge the usual notions of scarcity and of firms operating in price-taking markets. This line of reasoning argues that markets consist of reciprocity, redistribution, and exchange; it is interesting that Rostow's publications are without any reference to Polanyi, though their ideas are similar and only two years separate their works.

Basic economics also tends to ignore the roles of institutions in bringing about changes in societal cultures and customs. Students who read Rostow and/or pursue a study in development economics will likely find a blend of microeconomics and macroeconomics. In terms of the former, they will find references to standard economic concepts such as the production function, the marginal revenue product of labor, the marginal efficiency of capital, comparative advantage, and diminishing returns. Add to that list an introduction and some unusual applications of the term "compound interest." Readers of the *Stages* book will find several references to that term. Furthermore, many authors who cite that book suggest it is a thesis about interest in the financial sense and about the benefits of saving money.

Striking some resemblance to those interpretations, the first reference in the book carries a footnote that seems to define the term in relation to the perpetual compounding nature of a nation's rate of income growth. Subsequent references seem to expand the meaning of the compound interest term relating it in diverse ways to a widespread focus on sustainable economic growth. In terms of the macroeconomic side, the *Stages* book defines economic growth as being an increase in per-capita real income. In contrast, some recent textbooks (Arnold, 2008; Guell, 2008; McConnell & Brue, 2008) define economic growth in terms of annual increases in per-capita constant-dollar gross domestic product. Whatever the preferred definition may be, real economic growth ultimately leads societies to technological maturity. This process is quite complex, requiring examination through the application of multiple perspectives.

A Macroeconomic Foundation

An attempt to integrate modernization theory, development economics, and basic economics can easily become an exercise in futility unless one first explores the facets of each. To prepare readers for that exploration, a short lesson in macroeconomics seems to be appropriate at this juncture. Let us begin by remembering that savings results from an initial sacrifice in consumption. Personal savings translate into business investments. Some of that investment generates new technologies thereby allowing producers to extract larger amounts of output from a given amount of input. Additional outputs engage workers and earn revenues both of which represent increases in income and potential increases in savings and consumption. More importantly, outputs and consumption increase at a faster rate than does population. Drawing from the work of Rostow, an increase in per capita consumption corresponds with technological maturity. In essence,

this macroeconomic approach tells us that current growth leads to technological maturity and it is also a result of "compound interest" or prior growth. By extension, growth is sustainable by applications of economic concepts and other factors outside the realm of basic economics.

At this point, as we move toward the last section of this essay, the reader will find some additional relief as we close this section with economic concepts that are a bit more concise and straightforward. They are relevant to discussions of quality of life and standard of living. In terms of the latter, there are quantifiable measures such as the income distribution, the poverty rate, the life expectancy of a population, and the access to health care, education, and durable goods. Furthermore, in contrast to the standard of living, the quality of life is more subjective because it is more difficult to measure the value of concepts such as leisure, safety, cultural resources, social life, mental health, and environmental quality, and so on. It is important to note that two nations may be comparable in terms of their standards of living, but vastly different in terms of the quality of life of their citizenry. Moreover, the concept of economic well-being is largely undefined and usually controversial. Almost any discussion of it will take on political dimensions.

This essay may begin to read more like a book review for some. At this juncture, readers should recall its main purpose is to convey some concepts central to understanding development economics. That understanding will, in turn, prepare them for pursuing their own survey of the literature on development economics and for the following summary of the five stages of growth. In terms of the pursuits ahead, one needs to consider whether the stages model is descriptive, prescriptive, or explanatory in its nature and intent.

Rostow & the Five Stages of Economic Growth

As a matter of introduction to the five stages, W.W. Rostow argued that there was a "take-off" to economic growth in the U.S. economy in the years 1843–1860. That take-off occurred during the 1840s. It was a period marked by developments in the rail transport and manufacturing sectors occurring at that time in the eastern part of the United States. The next decade witnessed the great railway push into the middle west and a heavy influx of foreign capital to support it. According to Rostow, all societies fit into one of those five categories or stages. As the reader will see, each corresponds with a specific set of economic dimensions and a succession of strategic choices.

First Stage: The Traditional Society

It is a time containing agriculture- and labor-intensive tasks, including hunting, foraging, and fishing. Economic growth is an unfamiliar and unknown concept to members of the traditional society. Their social network consists primarily of what we refer to as extended family. Their acquisitions of basic needs have linkages to divine spirits and intervention. Any expansion of acreage contributes to an increase in agricultural output. However, the actual and potential levels of productivity are indeterminate and likely to be very low. Technology is virtually nonexistent, remaining unavailable and/or without any interest in its application to existing production processes. Trading activities, if any, occur locally and fluctuate according to the dynamics of political, social, and physical elements.

Second Stage: The Preconditions for Take-Off

Societies in this stage exhibit attempts to adopt technology, to handle diminishing returns, and to develop an investment culture. Their interests require changes in attitudes toward education, finance, and commerce. The list of prerequisites for growth includes the following: an initial commitment to education; an acknowledgement of capital mobility; an institution of a system for banking and currency management; and, an emergence of an entrepreneurial class. The entrepreneurs use land, labor, and capital in various combinations, but with limited success due their lack of familiarity with economic principles for optimizing output level. Nonetheless, increases in domestic output occur as manufacturing facilities open and nation-states emerge.

Third Stage: The Take-Off

Steady economic growth gains acceptance as a norm. Individuals gain a better understanding of the causes and consequences of economic growth. With an expansion in business-related concepts, economic processes rather than social traditions drive that growth. These norms and understandings represent the point at which there is a transition from a traditional

Country	Take-off Period
Great Britain	1783-1802
Russia	1890-1914
United States	1843-1860
Germany	1850-1873
Canada	1896-1914
China	1952
India	1952

Tentative take-off dates according to Rostow's Five Stages. (Courtesy of Wikipedia)

or agriculture-based to a modern or industrial-based economy.

New technology and emergent political collaborations act as stimuli. In the process, new industries expand and communities around them develop into urban centers. At this point, there are increases in incomes coupled with a high rate of savings along with a growing interest in entrepreneurialism. With these interests and some calculated risk taking, all their efforts lead to additional discoveries and extractions of natural resources along with subsequent usage by various manufacturing facilities within a process of mass production.

Differentiated industrial processes during this stage include innovations such as the cotton gin, steam engines, and steel production. Rostow draws heavily on railroad history, for example, to demonstrate its multifaceted utility as a product of natural resources, its contribution to the national infrastructure, and its employment in the spatial distribution of industrial materials. Furthermore, he cites the rail transport of steel within countries such as the United States, Great Britain, Germany, and France as a robust example for sustaining economic growth.

Fourth Stage: The Drive to Maturity

This stage generally draws from the contributions of the automobile and the complementary system of roadways to economic maturation. In addition, this stage recognizes the need for diversification as a means of economic stability. This recognition provides some evidence of thoughts about the cyclical natures of an economy and its manufacturing sector. In other words, most members of society now take interest in and readily accept those fluctuations as a natural component of sustainable growth.

Country	Maturity Year
Great Britain	1850
Russia	1950
United States	1900
Germany	1910
Canada	1950

Rostow's tentative drive to maturity dates. (Courtesy of Wikipedia)

Compound interest becomes evident in the individual, social, political, and economic dimensions of the industrial nation-state. Investments, both financial and non-financial in composition, generate outputs that increase at a rate exceeding the population growth rate. In essence, a larger society attributes changes in the composition of a domestic economy to innovation and industrialization. Technology and industry become more complex, shifting away from railway-type steam-driven heavy engineering toward greater industrial diversity that includes the manufacture and employments of machinery, tools, chemicals, and electric-driven equipment.

Enter international trade as factor in the maturity equation. Drawing from the work of Rostow, former imports of the colonization period become domestic manufactures of the modernization era. A positive trade balance emerges with exports exceeding imports. Readers should also take note that Rostow introduces a slight twist on the comparative advantage concept by suggesting that imports occur first, by omitting references to opportunity costs and resultant specialization, and by skipping over the gains from trade. Perhaps he denies applicability of the concept because of its assumption that climate is irrelevant to the production possibilities frontier.

In this stage, society holds a basic understanding of how innovative and entrepreneurial activities build the capacity to produce whatever specialization it so desires. Consequently, a technologically mature society becomes more dependent on its economic choices and its political priorities and less so on technological and institutional necessities. According to Rostow, some additional consequences of maturity include shifts in: the labor force as seen in a reduction in agricultural employments; the leadership composition as a result of a reduction in trade employments; and, the domestic culture as it begins to exhibit some disenchantment with the industrial nature of the nation-state. Society becomes more interested in issues of national security, welfare, and leisure. Lastly, an optimistic economic outlook and real income growth also signify maturity.

Fifth Stage: The Age of High Mass Consumption

This stage seems to suggest that mass production ultimately leads to mass consumption. If so, that process would entail the following simple sequence of events. An initial increase in incomes when the savings rate is stable leads to an increase in savings. Those savings initially displace consumption, and they provide a source of funding to business investments. Those investments generate additional increases in output and incomes. Those incomes increase savings and consumption. Those increases generate additional income. The sequence repeats itself along as there is optimism. Eventually, consumer optimism paves the way for their purchases of durable goods and diverse services.

There are two outcomes reported for this final stage. First, per capita income increases lead society past its need for basic items such as food, clothing, and shelter and toward its want for luxury items. Second, migrations of the labor force head toward urbanized areas and population centers. In essence, the number of employments in urban office settings increase while those in factory settings decrease. Consequently, the urbanization phase generates widespread interest in the arts, cultural events, professional sports, and other forms of mass consumption and entertainment.

CONCLUSION

In conclusion, this essay presented the reader with an overview of five stages of economic growth. It also presents some information with which to distinguish between development economics and basic economics. In closing, the author hopes readers are better equipped to study and address the needs of developing countries, to compare and contrast countries in terms of their economic growth stage, and to recognize and contemplate the value of linear progression models. Perhaps those models are most useful as a tool for description.

BIBLIOGRAPHY

Arnold, R.A. (2008). *Economics*(8th ed.) Mason, OH: Thomson South-Western.

Austin, K.F., & McKinney, L.A. (2012). "Disease, war, hunger, and deprivation: A cross-national investigation of the determinants of life expectancy in less-developed and sub-Saharan African nations." *Sociological Perspectives, 55*(3), 421–447.

Gualerzi, D. (2012). "Development Economics." *International Journal Of Political Economy, 41(3)*, 3–23.

Guell, R. C. (2008). *Issues in economics today*(4th ed.). Boston, MA: McGraw-Hill Irwin.

McConnell, C. R. & Brue, S. L. (2008). *Economics*(17th ed.). Boston, MA: McGraw-Hill Irwin.

Meierrieks, D. (2012). "Rooted in urban poverty? failed modernization and terrorism." *Peace Economics, Peace Science, & Public Policy, 18*(3), 1–9.

Rostow, W.W. (1959). "The stages of economic growth." *The Economic History Review, 12*(1), 1–16.

Rostow, W.W. (1960). *The Stages of Economic Growth: A Non-Communist Manifesto.* New York: Cambridge University Press.

SUGGESTED READING

Chang, J., Chen, B., & Hsu, M. (2006). "Agricultural productivity and economic growth: Role of tax revenues and infrastructures." *Southern Economic Journal, 72*(4), 891–914.

Kapoor, I. (2004). "Hyper-self-reflexive development? Spivak on representing the Third World 'Other'." *Third World Quarterly, 25*(4), 627–647.

Mobarak, A. (2005). "Democracy, volatility, and economic development." *Review of Economics & Statistics, 87*(2), 348–361.

Polyani, K. (1957). *The great transformation: The political and economic origins of our time.* Boston: Beacon Press.

—*Steven R. Hoagland, PhD*

T

TIME VALUE OF MONEY

ABSTRACT

This article will explain the financial concept of the time value of money. The overview provides an introduction to the principles at work when money grows in value over time. These principles include future value of money, present value of money, simple interest, and compound interest. In addition, other concepts that relate to factors that can impede the growth in the value of money over time are explained, including risk, inflation, and accessibility of assets. Basic formulas and tables have been provided to assist in calculating various formulations of time value of money problems. Explanations of common financial dealings in which the time value of money is an important consideration, such as annuities, loan amortization, and tax deferral options, are included to help illustrate the concept of the time value of money in everyday life.

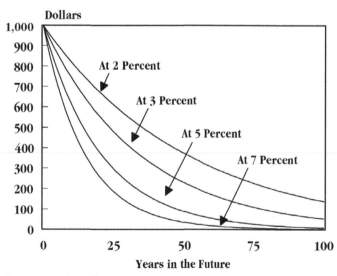

The present value of $1,000, 100 years into the future. Curves represent constant discount rates of 2%, 3%, 5%, and 7%. (Courtesy of Congressional Budget Office via Wikimedia Commons)

The time value of money is a fundamental financial principle. Its basic premise is that money gains value over time. As a result, a dollar saved today will be worth more in the future, and a dollar paid today costs more than a dollar paid later in time. The reason for the increasing value in money over time is that money can be invested to earn interest, and the gain in interest can be significant over time. This is also why a dollar paid today costs more than a dollar paid in the future. Money expended today cannot be invested for the future and thus the loss is essentially twofold—the money is spent on the payment and any earning potential it could have had in an investment vehicle is forgone.

The concept of the time value of money is an important consideration in any long-term, and even short-term, investment or financial obligation. Financial managers and advisers frequently use time value of money formulas to determine the true costs of various investment opportunities. In addition, people consider the time value of money concept—perhaps without even realizing it—in making common financial decisions, such as considering whether to take out a loan or mortgage, sign a lease, deposit money in a savings account or an annuity, or perhaps even to spend the money or pay off bills.

Although calculating the changing value of money over time requires formulas and mathematical computations, the underlying principle that money in hand is more valuable than money down the road is almost self-evident. Most people, if given a choice as to whether they would rather have money today or in the future, would instinctively choose money today. Ready money, or money that is presently accessible, is available to be invested in a range of vehicles that can return the money—plus interest—down the road. The sooner the money is invested, the sooner it can begin earning interest, and the longer the money is invested, the more capacity it has to grow in value. However, money that is not readily available but is to be paid in the future will only then become available for investment upon receipt, and thus it lacks present interest-earning potential.

To understand the economics of the time value of money, it is important to first grasp its underlying concepts of future value of money and present value of money. The future value of money is the value that money will grow to when invested at a given rate for a specified period of time. The present value of money is the amount that an investment earned in the future is worth today. For instance, if a person invests one dollar for one year at a 6 percent annual interest rate, the dollar accumulates six cents in interest while invested and thus is worth $1.06 at the end of the year. Since the time value of money is measured according to the future value and the present value of an investment of money, the future value of the person's dollar is $1.06 at a 6 percent interest rate for a one-year period. The present value of the $1.06 that could be earned at the end of one year is $1.

The following sections provide a more in-depth explanation of these concepts.

BASIC FINANCIAL CONCEPTS
Future Value of Money

The future value of money is the value of a sum of money, invested at a given interest rate for a defined period of time, at a specified date in the future and that is equivalent in value to a specified sum today. The future value of money can be calculated if given the interest rate of the investment, the length of time of the investment, and the amount of the initial deposit. The calculation can determine the future value of a single sum investment that is deposited at the beginning of the duration of the investment. Or, if an investment consists of a series of equally spaced payments, generally known as an annuity, the future value of this investment can also be calculated. When calculating the future value of money, we commonly assume that the future value of an investment will be greater than its present value, and we use mathematical formulas to solve for the exact increase of an investment over time. The rate that money gains in value over time depends on the number of compounding periods that an investment is allowed to grow and the interest rate that the investment is earning. In other words, assume you have $10,000 to

invest today. If you spend it, the money will be gone and thus no interest will be earned on it and the money has no future value. If instead you decide to invest the $10,000, you can increase the future value of your money over time because you will have the $10,000 plus any interest that investment has earned. If you invest the money at 5 percent interest for one year, you would multiply $10,000 by 5 percent to determine annual interest earned of $500. Thus, the future value of your investment is $10,500. This calculation is explained in more detail below.

Calculating Future Value

Investors frequently calculate the future value of their investment options to determine the most profitable way to grow their money. Suppose an investor sets aside $100 to deposit in her money market account at her local bank, which is paying an annual interest rate of 10 percent on money market savings accounts. If she keeps her money in her money market account for one year, at the end of that year she will be able to withdraw both her initial $100 deposit plus the $10 she earned in interest. The following formula illustrates this concept:

Original deposit + Interest on deposit = FV
$100 + (10\%) (\$100) = \$110

Thus, the investor can calculate the future value of her money by plugging in her deposit of $100 plus the 10 percent interest rate that her bank is paying on savings accounts to solve for the future value of her original deposit. When she performs the calculations, she will find that the future value of her $100 after one year is equal to $110 ($100 plus 10). While this calculation is relatively straightforward, another investor may want to calculate how much money he would have if he invested his money in a retirement plan and left it there to earn interest for 20 years. Luckily, there is an easy formula that he could use to determine the future value of his investment:

$FV = P(1 + R)N$
FV = future value
P = principal (initial deposit)
R = annual rate of interest
N = number of years

This equation can be used for any number of years. The investor must simply have the amount of the principal, the annual interest rate of the investment vehicle he is considering, and the number of years the money will be invested. Once an investor has these figures accessible, he can solve for the future value of his investment. For instance, here is how an investor could compare his earning potential of two different investment options by solving for the future value of a $100 deposit at a 10 percent interest rate for one year and again for two years:

1 Year on Deposit

$$FV = P(1 + R)1$$
$$FV = \$100(1 + .10)$$
$$FV = \$100(1.10)$$
$$FV = \$110$$

2 Years on Deposit

$$FV = P(1 + R)2$$
$$FV = \$100(1 + .10)2$$
$$FV = \$100(1.10)(1.10)$$
$$FV = \$121$$

While these calculations illustrate the growth in the value of money over a one- and two-year time period, the same formula can be used to calculate the time value of money for any number of years. For instance, if an investor wanted to figure the amount of her account if she invested $100 at a 10 percent annual interest rate for 10 years, she would need to multiply $100 by 1.10 and then repeat that calculation using the sum of each calculation for a total of 10 times. If she performed this calculation, she would determine that $(1.10)10$ equals 2.594, and multiplying $100 by 2.594, she would discover that the future value of her initial $100 investment at 10 percent annual interest rate for 10 years would be $259.40.

Solving future value of money calculations can become more complicated the longer the money is invested. This is because almost all investments earn interest every year, and this interest is added to the principal at the end of each year, so that the next year interest is earned on both the principal plus all of the interest that has been earned. This financial concept, known as compound interest, is described in more detail below. Because making these calculations grows increasingly complicated the longer the investment, most investors and money managers use future value tables as a shortcut to solve these calculations. These tables have been completed with the calculation of one dollar invested at various annual

interest rates for certain given periods of time. Thus, if an investor knows the annual rate of interest of an investment option and the length of time he plans to invest, he can quickly find the factor he will need to use to multiply by his principal, or initial deposit, to determine the future value of his investment.

The following future value table contains factors that are used in determining various future values. To read the future value table, you simply identify the column that represents the annual interest rate of your investment and the row that represents the duration of your investment. The cell where the column and row meet contains the factor that you will use to multiply by your original investment. For example, suppose you wish to find the future value of an original investment of $1,000 over a five-year period at 10 percent interest. Look up the factor (1.61), and multiply it by the original investment: $1,000(1.61) = $1,610. Thus, the future value of $1,000 invested for five years at a 10 percent annual interest rate is $1,610. You can also calculate how fast your investment will grow over the five years you invest it. To do this, simply deduct 1.00 from the factor and you get the total percentage increase (1.61 − 1.00 = .61, or 61%). In other words, a $1,000 investment that grows to $1,610 in five years represents an increase in value of 61 percent.

You can also use future value tables to determine annual rates of compound interest and the number of years you must invest your principal in order for it to grow by a certain percentage at a known interest rate. For instance, to calculate the annual rate of compound interest that applies to an investment of $1,000, which is expected to grow 61 percent in five years, you would calculate the factor by adding .61 +

Interest Rate												
Periods	1%	2%	3%	4%	5%	6%	7%	8%	9%	10%	11%	12%
1	1.0100	1.0200	1.0300	1.0400	1.0500	1.0600	1.0700	1.0800	1.0900	1.1000	1.1100	1.1200
2	1.0201	1.0404	1.0609	1.0816	1.1025	1.1236	1.1449	1.1664	1.1881	1.2100	1.2321	1.2544
3	1.0303	1.0612	1.0927	1.1249	1.1576	1.1910	1.2250	1.2597	1.2950	1.3310	1.3676	1.4049
4	1.0406	1.0824	1.1255	1.1699	1.2155	1.2625	1.3108	1.3605	1.4116	1.4641	1.5181	1.5735
5	1.0510	1.1041	1.1593	1.2167	1.2763	1.3382	1.4026	1.4693	1.5386	1.6105	1.6851	1.7623
6	1.0615	1.1262	1.1941	1.2653	1.3401	1.4185	1.5007	1.5869	1.6771	1.7716	1.8704	1.9738
7	1.0721	1.1487	1.2299	1.3159	1.4071	1.5036	1.6058	1.7138	1.8280	1.9487	2.0762	2.2107
8	1.0829	1.1717	1.2668	1.3686	1.4775	1.5938	1.7182	1.8509	1.9926	2.1436	2.3045	2.4760
9	1.0937	1.1951	1.3048	1.4233	1.5513	1.6895	1.8385	1.9990	2.1719	2.3579	2.5580	2.7731
10	1.1046	1.2190	1.3439	1.4802	1.6289	1.7908	1.9672	2.1589	2.3674	2.5937	2.8394	3.1058
11	1.1157	1.2434	1.3842	1.5395	1.7103	1.8983	2.1049	2.3316	2.5804	2.8531	3.1518	3.4786
12	1.1268	1.2682	1.4258	1.6010	1.7959	2.0122	2.2522	2.5182	2.8127	3.1384	3.4985	3.8960
13	1.1381	1.2936	1.4685	1.6651	1.8857	2.1329	2.4098	2.7196	3.0658	3.4523	3.8833	4.3635
14	1.1495	1.3195	1.5126	1.7317	1.9799	2.2609	2.5785	2.9372	3.3417	3.7975	4.3104	4.8871
15	1.1610	1.3459	1.5580	1.8009	2.0789	2.3966	2.7590	3.1722	3.6425	4.1772	4.7846	5.4736

1.00 to get 1.61. You would then go to the fifth-year row since you plan to invest for five years, and move along the row until you find 1.61. You would then trace up the column to find the annual interest rate of 10 percent. Thus, you would know that the rate of interest for a $1,000 investment expected to grow 61 percent in five years is 10 percent. Finally, if you want to find out how many years it will take for an investment growing at 10 percent annually to increase 61 percent, you would find the column representing 10 percent and trace down to find the factor of 1.61. You would then follow the row across the table until you reach the Periods column, and you would then find that you must invest your $1,000 at a 10 percent interest rate for five years in order for your investment to increase 61 percent. Thus, the future value formulas and tables provide investors with a relatively quick and easy method to solve for the future value of a range of investment opportunities to decide which options are the most profitable.

Present Value of Money

While the future value of money calculates the value of an investment in the future, the present value of money represents the amount of money that would be required today to equal a desired future sum of money that has been discounted by an appropriate interest rate. The future amount of money could be the result of a long-term investment or the payment of a single sum that will be received or paid at a set date in the future or a series of payments of equal amounts paid or received at equal durations over a period of time. A series of equivalent, equally spaced payments is known as an annuity. Annuities will be discussed in more detail in the sections below. If the principle of the time value of money holds that money today is more valuable than money tomorrow, the inverse of this principle is also true. Money to be received in the future is less valuable than money received today. Thus, the longer an investor must wait to receive her money, the less value she will obtain from the asset.

Like the future value of money, we can use mathematical calculations to determine the present value of money. The reason investors like to solve for the present value of money is so that they can figure out how much money they need to invest today in order to obtain the future value of money that they are seeking down the road. For instance, if a person is planning for his future and he determines how much money he will want to have in his retirement account at age 65, he will want to know how much he will need to invest and save today in order to have that amount available to him when he retires.

One brief example would be as follows: If you received a graduation gift of $5,000 today, the present value of this money would simply be $5,000 because the present value equals the money's spending power, or what your investment is worth today should you decide to spend it. If you are still in school and will not expect to receive your graduation gift for another two years, the present value of the $5,000 upon receipt will no longer be $5,000 because you do not have the money to spend today, in the present. You will not have the opportunity to invest the $5,000 to earn interest on that money until you receive it, and so the $5,000 must be discounted by the appropriate discount rate to determine its present value today.

To calculate the present value of the $5,000 you will receive in the two years, you must first assume that the $5,000 is the future value of the amount of a sum of money you invested today, plus the interest you will have earned on that investment. Depending on the annual rate of interest on your $5,000, we can calculate how much you would have to invest today to earn enough interest over the next two years for you to have the full $5,000 upon your graduation. Since money grows in value over time by earning interest, you would not have to invest $5,000 today to have $5,000 two years from now when you graduate. You would only have to invest the present value today of a sum of money that will grow into $5,000 in two years. The sum of this money will depend on the rate of annual interest that the investment will earn over the two years. Once the annual interest rate of an investment is known, the present value of the investment needed to reach $5,000 can be calculated. In other words, to find the present value of the future $5,000, we need to find out how much we would have to invest today at a specified annual interest rate to receive that $5,000 in the future. The following formulas will show you how to do this.

Calculating Present Value

The present value of a future sum of money is inversely related to the length of time being calculated. In other words, the present value of money decreases as the length of time increases. The reason for this is because the longer money is invested, the more time it has to earn interest. This interest is added to the principal to calculate the future value of money. The more interest a principal deposit can earn, the less the deposit required to grow to a certain amount of money in the future. In other words, the present value of a future return is merely the reverse of a future value calculation.

The equation to calculate present value is:

Due to image rights restrictions, multiple line equation(s) cannot be graphically displayed.

To calculate present value, assume that you wish to find out the present value of $10,000 five years from now, and the annual interest rate of your investment will be 10 percent. To find the future value, use the future value table to determine the interest rate for the period of time in the calculation. In this example, the interest rate is 10 percent per year for a period of five years. Thus, the present value of $1,000 looking five years out can be calculated by multiplying 1.10, which represents a period of one year at 10 percent, by five for the five-year period ($1.10 \times 1.10 \times 1.10 \times 1.10 \times 1.10 = 1.61$). This can also be calculated using the following equation:

$1,000/(1+.10)5 = 620 or $1,000/$620 = 1.61$

Like calculating future value, present values can also be easily computed by using tables that have already calculated various present value factors of a sequence of time periods and discount rates. The cells of the table indicate the factor which, when multiplied by a future value, will yield a given present value. As illustrated by the table below, the present value of money decreases over time and as the discount rate increases.

Learning to calculate the present value of money can be helpful in evaluating the merits of various investment options or business opportunities. The idea behind calculating the present value of money is to discount future returns by a specified level of risk, or a discount rate, plus a specified period of time to evaluate the real-time cost of an investment in today's dollars. Essentially, computing the present value of money helps you to determine the present value, or the cost in today's dollars, of the amount of the net return or cash flow you expect to receive in the future from an investment or a business opportunity. Once you have made this calculation, you can compare your results with the actual real-time costs of an investment or opportunity to determine whether the investment or business opportunity is financially advantageous for you. For instance, if the present value of a project is greater than its actual cost, the project likely will be profitable. If you have multiple projects or investment opportunities, you can compute the present value of each of them and then choose the option with the greatest difference between its present value and cost. Thus, learning to calculate the future value and the present value of investment options is an important part of carefully weighing various investment options so that you make sound financial decisions.

Calculating Interest

The central component of the rising value of money over time is the accrual of interest. Interest is a sum of money that is paid for the use of another's money for a given period of time, usually one year. The lender, or the person whose money is being borrowed, is compensated for allowing her funds to be used for purposes other than her own personal consumption. The original amount lent is known as the principal and the percentage of the principal that is charged for its use over a period of time is the interest rate. The two most common types of interest are simple interest and compound interest.

Simple Interest

Simple interest is interest that is paid or earned solely on the original amount, or principal, that is borrowed or lent. Simple interest is calculated using the following formula:

$X = P \times R \times T$

X = Simple interest: the dollar amount of interest earned or paid only on the principal

P = Principal: the amount of money borrowed or lent

R = Rate: the annual interest rate

T = Time: the number of years the amount is deposited or borrowed

To see this formula at work, suppose that an investor deposited $100 in a simple interest bearing account that paid 10 percent annual interest. For the first year, the calculation to determine the simple interest earned would be: $100 × .10 × .1 = $10 in interest. The next year, the basic calculation would remain the same, with only the initial principal bearing interest. While the interest earned is not added to the initial principal to earn its own interest, it is added to the principal at the end of each period of time. Thus, the growth of the investment is linear, not exponential. Over time, simple interest grows in a stable, predictable pattern as follows:

Year 1: 10% of $100 = $10 + $100 = $110
Year 2: 10% of $100 = $10 + $110 = $120
Year 3: 10% of $100 = $10 + $120 = $130
Year 4: 10% of $100 = $10 + $130 = $140
Year 5: 10% of $100 = $10 + $140 = $150

Compound Interest

Compound interest is interest that is earned on both the principal and on any accrued interest. The use of compound interest is always assumed in time value of money calculations. Interest is compounded at the end of every time period during the life of the investment, which is generally every year. However, interest may be compounded more frequently, and the effect of more frequent compounding is different for lenders and borrowers. Lenders and investors prefer more frequent compounding because compounding produces higher interest earnings in that as interest is added to the principal at the end of each time period, the amount of accrued interest grows with each subsequent time period, and more frequent addition of accrued interest to the principal to gain further interest ultimately yields higher interest returns. Borrowers, on the other hand, prefer simple interest or compound interest with less frequent compounding because this minimizes the amount of accrued interest that they must repay in addition to principal owed.

To calculate compound interest, the interest is calculated not only on the principal, but also on any

interest that accumulates during the specified period of time. The formula for calculating compound interest is as follows:

$X = P(1 + R)N$

X = Compound interest: the dollar amount of interest earned or paid

P = Principal: the amount of money borrowed or lent

R = Rate: the annual interest rate

N = the number of years the amount is deposited or borrowed

For instance, if an investor were to receive 10 percent compound interest on an initial investment of $100, the first year's returns would mirror the earnings of simple interest, or $10. However, the $10 would be added to the $100 principal and thus for the second year, interest would accrue on the sum of the principal plus the first year's interest, or $110. As the interest compounds over the five years of the investment, the growth in the initial principal would look like this:

Year 1: 10% of $100.00 = $10.00 + $100.00 = $110.00
Year 2: 10% of $110.00 = $11.00 + $110.00 = $122.00
Year 3: 10% of $122.00 = $12.20 + $122.00 = $134.20
Year 4: 10% of $134.20 = $13.42 + $134.20 = $147.62
Year 5: 10% of $147.62 = $14.76 + $147.62 = $162.38

Thus, as these illustrations indicate, compound interest grows an initial investment far more quickly than does simple interest. Investments with simple interest grow in a linear fashion while investments with compound interest grow exponentially. Most investment opportunities today, including savings accounts, retirement plans, and securities grow by compound interest. This is part of the reason for the popularity of these investment options, especially for long-term investments. With these investments, the longer they are allowed to accrue compound interest, the more dramatic their growth becomes.

Factors Affecting the Time Value of Money

While the concept of the time value of money holds that money grows in value over time, there are factors that can undermine, or erode, the value that money gains over time. These factors include inflation, risk, and a generalized preference among investors for readily accessible assets. The following sections explain these factors in more detail.

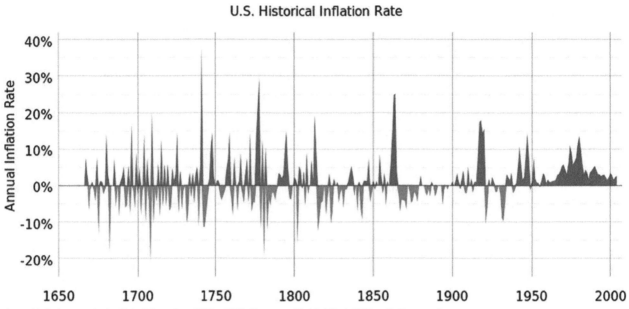

Annual inflation rates in the United States from 1666 to 2004. (Courtesy of Lalala666 via Wikimedia Commons)

Inflation

Inflation refers to a general price increase in the economy. Inflation is defined as a sustained increase in the general level of prices for goods and services. Economists assess the extent of inflation in the economy at specified time periods and then represent its growth as a percentage increase. Most commonly, inflation is measured at one-year intervals and reported as an annual inflation rate.

Inflation affects the time value of money because as inflation rises, the purchasing power of money decreases. This means that as inflation goes up, each dollar buys a smaller percentage of goods and service. Inflation affects the time value of money in that as prices are generally expected to rise in the future, the future value of one dollar will be less one year from now than it is today, and the dollar will buy even less two years from now than it will today. This contradicts the idea that money will become more valuable over time. To illustrate, if general prices for goods and services increase by 4 percent annually, each and every dollar losses 4 percent purchasing power every year. In other words, if inflation rises 4 percent in one year, $1.00 at the beginning of the year depreciates in value to $0.96 by the end of the year. Likewise, if consumers could buy 100 marbles with a dollar at the beginning of the year, they could buy only 96 marbles at the end of the year.

In sum, inflation erodes the value of money by diminishing its value over time. As the rate of inflation rises and the length of an investment increases, the less the investment will be worth in the future. Yet, according to the principle of the time value of money, over time money becomes more valuable because it has an opportunity to earn interest. What happens, then, is that rising inflation undermines the time value of money. The degree to which inflation can diminish the growth in the time value of money depends on the difference between the two interest rates at work. If an investment is growing at a 10 percent annual interest rate and inflation is rising at 3 percent, the money will still gain value over time because the inflation rate is significantly lower than the degree at which the investment is growing. However, if an investment is only growing at a 5 percent annual interest rate and the inflation rate is 4 percent, you can see that inflation will erode most of the purchasing power that the investment will gain over time.

Risk

Another factor that can impede the growth in value of money over time is risk. Risk is the uncertainty about the future growth of an investment, a financial market, or the local, national, or international economy. Risk can potentially minimize the rise in the value of money over time because risk increases with time. Since investors cannot be certain about the future, they may be more hesitant or less likely to invest their money in an opportunity with a higher level of risk, instead preferring to have their money immediately available as cash. However, investors may be willing to forgo their immediate access to cash to invest in an opportunity with a higher degree of risk if the opportunity also has a chance of yielding a higher rate of return. In other words, the assumption of higher levels of risk may be counterbalanced, or compensated, by the potential to earn higher levels of interest. However, the longer investors must forfeit access to their funds, the greater the risk, and thus the lower the likelihood that investors will be open to keeping their money invested and inaccessible. Thus, though the value of money increases over time in the form of interest earned, so level of risk also increases over time.

Every investor, then, must weigh the level of risk against the potential for earning interest when making any investment decision. The higher the level of risk associated with an investment, the greater the financial reward must be to convince an investor to commit to the investment. No financial analyst can precisely predict the future of any investment, financial market, or local, national or international economy. Thus, every investment involves a certain level of risk. Since uncertainty, and therefore risk, increases the further one looks into the future, the value of money decreases going forward into the future because the greater the risk, the greater the possibility that an investment may wind up a loss.

Accessibility of Assets

In addition to inflation and risk, another factor that can erode the growth in value of money over time is the principle that most investors prefer relatively liquid assets. An asset is liquid if it can be converted to cash with relative ease. Investors generally prefer to keep their assets readily accessible; that is, able to be converted into cash within a minimal amount of time and with a minimal amount of effort. Investors would generally decide to liquidate an asset or an investment in instances such as a personal financial need for cash, a decision that an investment is no longer reliable, or because the level of risk associated

with an investment has surpassed the investor's expectation of a profitable return.

While the value of money increases over time, some long-term investments may be less attractive to investors, even though they have the potential to yield higher returns, because the investor would have to give up ready access to a liquid asset for an extended period of time. Most investors would only be willing to make such an investment for the expectation of a very high return. However, there is no guarantee that any particular investment will yield its exact projected return, and so investors must weigh these factors carefully when making any investment decision. In sum, while the increase in the value of money over time is a central tenet of financial theory, inflation, risk, and a preference for easily accessible assets can work to erode the expected returns on an investment and undermine the purchasing power of money in the future.

APPLICATIONS

Time Value of Money at Work in Financial Calculations

Financial planners spend a great deal of time going through calculations to figure out the present value and the future value of money to determine how best to advise clients in managing their assets. Determining the time value of money is an important calculation in several different financial transactions such as purchasing an asset, investing in securities, paying debt, and calculating tax obligations. Tax attorneys, in particular, are often paid to counsel clients on managing their tax payments. Tax attorneys must perform sophisticated tax calculations to determine whether and how much tax obligations can be deferred and how to best structure tax reporting and repayments so that a client complies with the relevant tax regulations while protecting and maximizing their personal and business assets. The following sections illustrate how the time value of money calculation is figured into various financial planning considerations.

Annuities

An annuity refers to a sequence of periodic and equal payments that are made at regular time intervals. Examples are the monthly mortgage payments on a house, pensions or Social Security, and periodic loan payments.

In an ordinary annuity, the investor makes a payment at the end of the relevant time period. In contrast, in an annuity due, contributions are made at the beginning of the time period. Annuities can be calculated to determine not only payments from an investor into an investment, but also payments made from an investment to an investor. For instance, many people contribute to a 401(k) or 403(b) through their place of employment, and this is a form of payment from them into an annuity that will make payments to them upon their retirement. Annuities can be calculated to determine the amount of payment that an investment will pay to an investor over the remainder of his or her life, which is approximated by expectancy of life averages, or the amount of money that an investor will need to deposit in order to accrue a desired investment total. Thus, calculating annuities makes use of the formulas that are frequently used in calculating the future value of money.

Calculating Annuities

Calculating the future value of an annuity requires using the following formula:

$$FVa = P(1 + R)\ 1 + P(1 + R)\ 2 + P(1 + R)\ 3 + \&\&\&.$$
$$+ P(1 + R)\ N\text{-}1$$

This equation can also be expressed as:

$$FVa = P \times \frac{(1 + R)\ N - 1}{R}$$

$$= P \times FVIFAR, N$$

Where FVa = Future value of an annuity

P = Payment

R = Annual rate of interest

N = Number of periods

FVIFAR, N = Annuity factor, or future value interest annuity factor

For instance, an investor may want to calculate the future value of a $1,000 annuity over a period of four years with a 10 percent compound interest rate. To do so, she would use the future value of an annuity formula as follows:

P = $1,000 per year

N = 4 years

R = 10%

Due to image rights restrictions, multiple line equation(s) cannot be graphically displayed.

$$FVa = 1,000 \times 4.641$$
$$= \$4,641.00$$

Loan Amortization

An amortized loan is a loan that requires an equal payment each month that is composed of some interest and some principal. The initial payments made on an amortized loan are mostly interest and the last payments are mostly principal. This is because as the loan begins to be paid off and balance of the loan is gradually lowered, more of each payment goes toward reducing principal while less goes toward paying interest. Thus, at the beginning of an amortized loan, a high percentage of the payment goes toward paying the interest and only the remainder of the payment is applied to reducing the principal. As the interest is paid off, less of the payment needs to go toward the remaining interest, so a greater percentage of the loan payment is allocated to reducing the loan principal.

Loan amortizations are typically represented by an amortization schedule. A loan amortization schedule is a table that shows each payment that is required to pay off an amortized loan. Each row in the table shows the amount of the payment that is needed to pay the accrued interest, the amount that is used to reduce principal, and the balance of the loan remaining at the end of the period. Most mortgages are amortized loans, and thus the homeowner can consult the amortization schedule to track the amount of each payment that is going toward paying the interest and the amount that is actually reducing the amount of the principal.

Ford Motor Company headquarters is located in Dearborn, Michigan. The building is also known as the Glasshouse. It was built in 1956. Ford offers automobile financing to its customers through Ford Motor Credit Company. (Courtesy of Dave Parker CC BY 3.0 via Wikimedia Commons)

Tax Deferral

Deferring the payment of taxes is advantageous to a taxpayer because he can invest the deferred tax and earn income on it until it is paid to the government. However, tax regulations do not permit unlimited, or even extensive, deferrals of tax payments. Thus, while deferring a tax payment can allow the money that would be used to pay the taxes to instead accrue interest, tax payments generally may be postponed for relatively short periods of time and thus the money has a shorter period of time in which to earn interest and gain value. Full compliance with tax requirements is an important part of sound financial management, and because the tax regulations can be more extensive and complicated the more assets an investor has, many investors choose to consult with a tax attorney for advice on their tax deferral options.

CONCLUSION

An investment involves making a present commitment of money with the expectation of a financial gain in the future. The financial gain that most people expect to receive for their investments is known as interest. The time value of money is based on the concept that a dollar today is worth more than a dollar in the future because you can invest the dollar you have today so that it will begin earning interest. The inverse of this is also true—a dollar paid today costs more than a dollar paid in the future. The reason for this is that there are factors that can decrease the value of money over time, such as inflation, risk, and a typical preference for cash or other liquid assets. While inflation can erode the purchasing power of money over time, in general, the longer the period of time between money paid or received today and money paid or received in the future, the greater the increase in the value of the money. This principle, known as the time value of money, is one of the most foundational principles of money management and can be readily seen in common financial transactions such as annuities, amortized loans, and tax deferral considerations.

BIBLIOGRAPHY

Alikar, N., Mousavi, S., Ghazilla, R., Tavana, M., Olugu, E. (2017). "A bi-objective multi-period series-parallel inventory-redundancy allocation problem with time value of money and inflation considerations." *Computers & Industrial Engineering, 104,* 51–67.

Bagamery, B. (1991). "Present and Future Values of Cash Flow Streams: The Wristwatch Method." *The Economic Development Review, 1(2),* 89–92.

Bauman, S. (1965). "The Investment Value of Common Stock Earnings and Dividends." *Financial Analysts Journal, 21(6),* 98–104.

Chen, J. (1998). "An inventory model for deteriorating items with time-proportional demand and shortages under inflation and time discounting." *International Journal of Production Economics, 55(1),* 21–30.

Chiu, H. & Chen, H. (1997). "The effect of time-value of money on discrete time-varying demand lot-sizing models with learning and forgetting considerations." *Engineering Economist, 42(3),* 203–222.

Darwish, M. (2006). "Imperfect production systems with imperfect preventive maintenance, inflation, and time value of money." *Asia-Pacific Journal of Operational Research, 23(1),* 89–105.

Ghosh, D. (2012). "Classroom contents and pedagogy: Time value of money in one lesson." *International Journal of Finance, 24(2),* 7127–7168.

Hariga, M. (1995). "Effects of inflation and time-value of money on an inventory model with time-dependent demand rate and shortages." *European Journal of Operational Research, 81(3),* 512–520.

Hutensky, B. (1999). "Understanding rates of return. In Finance for Shopping Center Nonfinancial Professionals." (pp. 103–137).

O'Leary, J. (2002). "Learn to speak the language of ROI." *Harvard Management Update, 7(10),* 3.

Shankar, S., Anderson, G. A., & Jha, A. (2012). "A few precise and simple methods for understanding changes in cash flow patterns in financial education." *International Journal of Finance, 24(2),* 7169–7185.

Stuebs, M. (2011). "Revealing money's time value." *Journal of Accounting Education, 29(1),* 14–36.

SUGGESTED READING

Eroglu, A. & Ozdemir, G. (2005). "A note on the effect of time-value of money on discrete time-varying demand lot-sizing models with learning and forgetting considerations." *Engineering Economist, 50(1),* 87–90.

Forbes, S. (1991). "A note on teaching the time value of money." *Financial Practice & Education, 1(1),* 91.

Stevens, Sue. (2007). "It's not just money, it's an investment: Help your kids get a good financial start in life." *Morningstar Practical Finance, 3(2),* 1–2.

—Heather Newton

TOPICS IN INTERNATIONAL BUSINESS

ABSTRACT

International business comes in many forms. This paper takes an in-depth look at three such arenas: international development, trade, and multinational corporations. Each of these three forms of international business, while very different in structure, play a significant role in nations' economies, business development and, just as President Wilson envisioned, the establishment and maintenance of close, peaceful relationships.

OVERVIEW

Interstate commerce is by no means a new or even recently introduced concept. For thousands of years, nations have conducted trade with their immediate and regional neighbors. In the fifteenth century, they went much farther, as Europeans traveled across Asia and the Atlantic in search of new trade relationships. In the twentieth century, President Woodrow Wilson used international business as a critical component in his vision of post–World War I peace as one of his historic Fourteen Points: "The removal, so far as possible, of all economic barriers and the establishment

Council of Four at the WWI Paris peace conference on May 27, 1919. From left: Prime Minister David Lloyd George (Great Britain) Premier Vittorio Orlando, Italy, French Premier Georges Clemenceau and President Woodrow Wilson. (Courtesy of Edward N. Jackson (US Army Signal Corps) via Wikimedia Commons)

of an equality of trade conditions among all the nations consenting to the peace and associating themselves for its maintenance" (Halsall, 1997).

Wilson's "point" is one that has reverberated throughout human history. International business is a constant in an ever-changing world. It transcends the politics and sociological disparities that often separate different cultures. This fact is due to the very nature of commerce: Mutual need drives both involved parties into the relationship without consideration of those issues.

International business comes in many forms. This paper takes an in-depth look at three such arenas: international development, trade, and multinational corporations. Each of these three forms of international business, while very different in structure, play a significant role in nations' economies, business development and, just as President Wilson envisioned, the establishment and maintenance of close, peaceful relationships.

International Development Aid

Among the more popular terms applied to nations in varying stages of development (one that is increasingly becoming considered outmoded and derogatory) are the monikers applied to so-called "first world" ("developed"), "second world," and "third world" (or developing) nations. The former of these three is affixed to wealthy and fully industrialized countries, chief among them the United States and the European Union. "Second world" are those countries that have emerged from poverty and have established infrastructures that can foster full industrialization, such as Mexico and the non–European Union countries of Eastern Europe. Developing nations, as logic suggests, are those whose citizens predominantly live in poverty with very few economic or technological resources to help them move "upward" on the international ladder.

The "three worlds" concept is one that, despite its unpopularity among those in academia and government, is reflective of the discernible gulf between wealthier industrialized nations and those that have yet to experience industrialization and the prosperity that comes with it. For a variety of reasons, however, virtually all industrialized nations have in place some sort of program that provides international development aid to less-developed countries. It is to these programs (and the relationships they build) that this paper next turns attention.

Mauritania, A Case Study

In 2005, the government of Mauritania was overthrown in a bloodless coup, with a military junta put in place of what the coup's leaders called a totalitarian regime. Beyond that northwest African country's boundaries, many observers decried the move against a democratically elected government. In the streets of the capital city of Nouakchott, however, people welcomed the move as one toward democracy and away from international isolation. Two years later, the country held its first post-coup democratic and open elections, installing a new president, Sidi Ould Cheikh Abdallahi, as well as a new parliament.

Abdallahi's first order of business was business. Only eight months after his election, Abdallahi declared that the country was dedicated to a free, open market system and that government's role was to guarantee the safety and well-being of its people. Mauritania, he said, would be neighborly and

Sidi Mohamed Ould Cheikh Abdallahi. (Courtesy of Marcello Casal Jr./Abr CC BY 3.0 via Wikimedia Commons)

cooperative with its neighbors. Finally, he said, the nation would be dedicated to building its economic resources so that it could become part of the international business world. His comments, which appeared in a November 2007 edition of *Foreign Affairs*, were in effect an advertisement, inviting countries to join Abdallahi and the new government in rebuilding the new Mauritania. "Mauritania's uniquely strategic position on the northwest African coast and blend of Arab and African culture," he wrote, "sets the stage for mutually beneficial relationships with surrounding nations and particularly European, American, and Asian partners" (*Foreign Affairs*, 2007).

Despite Abdallahi's deposition in 2008, the efforts of Mauritania to attract international development funds and other forms of aid are not unique. Countless developing nations on nearly every continent recognize two important facts about their status: First, they desire to attract potential business, political and security partners from a membership in the international community; and second, they lack

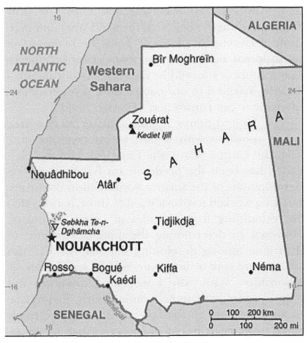

Mauritania is a country located in northwest Africa. (Courtesy of U.S. CIA via Wikimedia Commons)

the infrastructure and/or the economic, social, and political stability necessary to drawing investment.

The Attract & Draw of International Aid

A central theme consistently arises in the discussion of international development aid, one that has been manifest in this author's use of the terms "attract" and "draw." International development, after all, is not a philanthropy. No national government would invest state funds in contributing development aid to a nation that will not use the monies in such a way that there is no sign of improvement, nor a return on that investment.

An examination of the history of the primary source of American international development, the United States Agency for International Development (USAID), presents an illustration of this point. After World War II, efforts to reconstruct a devastated European theater proved successful, lasting until 1951. From that point onward, however, the U.S. international aid system became confused and schizophrenic, with countless congressionally implemented subparts instilled in the place of European reconstruction aid systems. President Eisenhower and his successor, President Kennedy, saw the machinations of that system becoming bogged down in oft-contradictory bureaucracy. They also took notice of the lack of criteria used to determine the recipients of that aid. By 1960, the public's taste for helping war-torn, impoverished, and unstable governments had soured significantly.

Destroyed Warsaw, the capital of Poland, in January 1945 after WW II. (Courtesy of M. Swierczynski via Wikimedia Commons)

President John F. Kennedy was responsible for the United States' Foreign Assistance Program. Here he is meeting with Kwame Nkruman, the first head of an independent Ghana, in March of 1961. (Courtesy of Abbie Rowe, National Park Service, via Wikimedia Commons)

In 1961, however, Kennedy gave new life to the policy of international development. Dismantling the multifarious aid agencies and organizations, he crafted together USAID under his "Foreign Assistance Act." The focus of development programs, he said, would be on developing countries whose stabilization and growth would almost certainly ensure security (particularly at the height of the Cold War) and even trade relationships. A major point he delivered in his proposal was that the economic collapse of developing countries "would be disastrous to our national security, harmful to our comparative prosperity, and offensive to our conscience" (USAID, 2005).

The United States is not alone in its "no free riders" position with regard to international aid. Like the United States, the European Union (EU), which has been the predominant figure in the redevelopment of the former Soviet Union countries, has long worked to provide aid to those nations that are rebuilding from decades of external control. However, in determining the amount of funds to distribute among developing nations, the EU also seeks some sort of intrastate benefit from such relationships. While the European nations do not expect an immediate economic return, its international development funds tend to flow more freely when they are delivered to countries that are strategically and potentially important economic partners (Kostadinova, 2004).

International Development Planning vs. Philanthropic Relief

An important distinction is to be made here between international development funding and disaster or philanthropic relief. The former, to which the above text refers, is a long-term investment designed to build infrastructures, systems, and programs that developing nations can use to restart their own economies, build government institutions, and better address the needs of their citizenry. The latter is usually a short-term contribution, donated in a variety of forms, such as food, supplies, equipment, or even personnel in response to a crisis (as well as money for otherwise stable governments to use to replenish coffers drained by the disaster in question). On many occasions, a nation may be the recipient of both types of aid—USAID operates development programs in the south Asian country of Bangladesh, but after the devastating cyclone that ravaged that impoverished nation's coastline in November 2007, more emergency relief was provided for the people whose lives were uprooted by the storm. Similarly, USAID's decades-long presence in Haiti was expanded after the 2010 earthquake when $773 million was assigned to USAID to facilitate reconstruction efforts (Gootnick, 2013).

Politics & International Aid Development

It was stated earlier in this paper that international business, with its focus on revenue generation and

Cyclone Aila caused extensive damage to India and Bangladesh in November, 2007. Pictured is an area of Bangladesh that was devastated by this storm. (Courtesy of Ferdous CC BY-SA 3.0 via Wikimedia Commons)

development, transcends (or at least eschews) politics. This statement would hold fast were it not for the fact that it is the government (or a counsel thereof, as is the case with the International Monetary Fund) that initiates international development aid programs. Politics presented a problem for USAID's predecessors, for example, not because of a refusal to help. Rather, as the euphemism suggests, there were simply too many cooks in the kitchen. Far too many individual agencies and legislators, following their own political agendas, sent the multitude of development organizations into a myriad of directions and, thus, apparent chaos. USAID may have been the solution to that problem, as it combined the American aid community under one umbrella.

However, another issue arose with similar appearances: With so many needy nations in every corner of the world, and money on limited supply, decisions have to be made. This problem was exacerbated after 9/11, when development funds focused on countries that were either at risk of or attempting to address the presence of terrorist organizations, such as Afghanistan and the countries of the Middle East. Larger, multinational organizations such as the World Bank have fared no better, largely because they are pulled in the directions of each individual country that plays a role in its activities, each of which is focused on its own ideas of local, regional, and international security (Woods, 2005).

International development aid programs may experience a number of problems in terms of policy implementation and conflicts in priorities. Nevertheless, this component of international business remains a critical tool in establishing links not just between so-called industrialized nations and developing countries, but also in terms of potential long-term business partners.

International Trade

Whereas the inequity between the donor and recipient country in international development programs is implicit, trade relationships are more illustrative of a sense of parity among parties. Each participating economy derives some sort of benefit from trade agreements. It comes as no surprise, therefore, that industrialized nations choose to initiate international development programs with developing countries that possess some sort of economic or natural resource (or an intangible form of benefit, such as a willingness to oppose a national enemy) of use to the donor country. After all, if a developing nation succeeds under the aid programs offered by USAID, for example, it is likely to continue its relationship with the United States under the auspices of trade agreements.

The WTO & Trade Partnering

In 1995, the World Trade Organization (WTO) became the chief administrator of the international trade arena. Nearly 100 percent of the world's trade (especially after the accession of China in 2001 and Russia in 2012) falls under the umbrella of the WTO (WTO, 2013). Although that organization is dedicated to the concept of promoting open trade among all interested countries, the fact remains that in recent years, the WTO has been focused largely on the nations of central and Eastern Europe as well as other former Soviet countries as opposed to sub-Saharan African and other distant countries (Madichie, 2007). The rationale is twofold: First, these countries did at one point possess the infrastructure and industrial potential to be contributing trade partners with the rest of the world; and second, these nations are far closer in geography and culture to major European traders.

Of course, such a conclusion does not mean that a sub-Saharan African country has little to offer potential trade partners. Many of the nations in this region have vast diamond mines, oil, and other lucrative resources. However, government instability, poverty, and seemingly endless civil wars have left many of these resources untapped or, at best, risky ventures for trade. Some countries are, however, willing to take the risk if the potential benefit is within sight. For example, China, whose energy needs have skyrocketed in its explosive entry as an economic powerhouse, has been working closely to establish strong commercial relationships with the countries of the former Soviet Union, such as Turkmenistan. Although many former Soviet countries have unstable government institutions, substandard technologies, and poverty levels that rival many sub-Saharan African countries, they were part of the Soviet Union for a reason—they possess vast energy reservoirs, such as oil, coal, and natural gas. China's concern is that if they do not establish close trade relations with such nations before other high-level consumption countries (like the US, Russia, and European Union states) do, they will be

forced to pay a higher rate for the resources they need (Lanteigne, 2007).

The Global Network

Arguably, the most significant attribute of the worldwide economic system over the last century is that it has become a global network. No longer are the isolationist, tariff-laden ways of pre–World War II era economies viable solutions. While many developing economies still apply trade barriers and protectionist measures to ensure the health of their domestic industries, such measures are minute when compared to the potential returns on entering into the myriad of free trade agreements in the post-millennium global economy. With the open, liberal trade mechanisms that are free of convoluted bureaucracies, weighty tariffs, and heavy regulations such accords have to offer, scores of nations have entered into regional and global free trade agreements (FTAs). Among the more prominent is the North American Free Trade Agreement (NAFTA) signed between the United States (one-third of whose economy is dedicated to international trade), Canada, and Mexico. However, there are approximately 300 such agreements around the world, including the Association of South East Asian Nations (ASEAN) and Asia-Pacific Economic Cooperation (APEC), not to mention FTAs in Africa, South America and of course, the European community. In 2013, the WTO implemented the Bali Package, the first such accord approved by all of its members, and one with the focus of lowering trade barriers globally. Free trade encompasses not just the industrialized nations—rather, such agreements create parity among less-developed countries and larger economies alike. Clearly, with a worldwide trend heading in the direction of free trade blocs (Trunick, 2012), international trade remains a fluid, dynamic aspect of international business for any nation, regardless of economic status.

Multinational Commerce

The first two arenas this paper has outlined, while containing private industrial elements, depend on intergovernmental relations (treaties must be signed, agency-to-agency agreements must be forged and contracts must be approved on national, state, and local levels). However, there is a third arena of international commerce that, while affected by

Company painting depicting an official of the East India Company, c. 1760. The pictures made by Indian artists for the British in India are called Company paintings. This one probably depicts William Fullerton of Rosemount, who joined the East India Company's service in 1744 and was second surgeon in Calcutta in 1751. He was present at the siege of Calcutta in 1756 and became mayor of Calcutta in 1757. In 1763 Fullerton became a surgeon to the Patna Agency. He was the only Englishman to survive the massacre of the English during the war with Mir Kasim of Murshidabad. An excellent linguist, he clearly mixed with Indians more than was common and had one or more Indian bibis (mistresses). (Courtesy of Dip Chand (artist) via Wikimedia Commons)

government rules and regulations, centers solely on business relationships.

In the eighteenth century, the East India Company became a pioneer in another form of international business. Enveloping the spice trading corporations of the Dutch and Portuguese, the company dominated an industry that, for two centuries prior, spanned across Asia and traversed two oceans. In essence, that organization, which was much reviled for its monopolistic hold on the business arena, was the world's first multinational corporation (Robins, 2004).

Centuries later, the multinational corporation is still one of the most preferable forms of international business, particularly for industrialized nations. According to the International Labour Organization

(ILO), the vast majority of the most profitable multinational corporations (MNCs) are based in either the United States or Western Europe. By the late 1990s, the 500 largest multinational corporations reported $11.4 trillion in revenues, $404 billion of which were profits. Nearly 36 million people were employees at these companies, which in total possessed assets of over $33 trillion (ILO, 1996).

Controversy

As was the case with the East India Company two centuries ago, multinational corporations have come under fire. This time, however, a major source of that consternation centers on the companies' efforts to minimize expenses while maximizing revenue. Most of these corporations base themselves in locales where the environment is business friendly—real estate is reasonable, labor is inexpensive, and taxes are, of course, at a minimum. The latter of these three is particularly controversial, as many governments are willing to offer disproportionately large tax breaks and similar incentives for setting up shop (Wague, 2013). Again, like the East India Company's case, opponents claim such pro-business breaks do little more than keep wealth among a relative few while exploiting labor and taking away from local economies (*New York Times*, 2007).

Regardless of one's attitudes about the size and wealth of multinational corporations, it cannot be denied that global businesses remain, as has been the case throughout history, a major if not central element of the modern global economy.

CONCLUSIONS

Since the latter half of the twentieth century, countries hoping to provide strength and long-term health to their economies have found these aspects through international business. This paper has provided an illustration of the many different capacities in which such commerce takes place in the new millennium.

For example, some countries still have fledgling economies and continue to struggle with issues of internal stability. Still, if the will exists to join and profit from an increasingly global economy, these countries will likely find receptive audiences in international development programs, especially if they possess potential resources, products, or intangible benefits of interest to donor countries and organizations. Using development aid and grant monies, these developing nations may build the infrastructures and systems necessary to generate intrastate industries and attract foreign investors. Such programs may even give these countries the ability to one day become trading partners on a level playing field with other industrialized nations.

If those resources and linkages do exist on an equitable level, the potential for a trade relationship may be realized. Trade agreements, however, are not without controversy, particularly in light of the assertion that many traders will likely pursue relationships with nearby countries with similar interests and sociopolitical composition. Still, for some countries, those geographical and social similarities may create regional parity and fertile ground for competitive trade agreements. Countries may even link together within free trade agreements, thereby avoiding burdensome tariffs and burdensome government intervention and, once such organizations are forged, attract outside participants to it rather than pursue them.

Beyond government-sanctioned development programs and trade agreements, many businesses will cross borders and even oceans to maximize their economic potential. Multinational businesses have long been the target of those fearful of the imposition of an Orwellian form of corporate governance. After all, the fact that only a handful of businesses can command such astronomical profit margins, possess such large amounts of real estate and assets, and reach virtually any locale on the planet can prove intimidating to the casual observer. Still, the fact remains that this form of international business remains a viable, extensive, and profitable form of commerce, thriving in the modern economic world.

BIBLIOGRAPHY

Bleaney, M. (2005). "The aftermath of a currency collapse: How different are emerging markets?" *World Economy, 28*, 79–89.

Delios, A. (2016). "The death and rebirth (?) of international business research." *Journal of Management Studies, 54*, 3, 391–397.

Fattal Jaef, R. N., & Lopez, J. I. (2014). "Entry, Trade Costs, and International Business Cycles." *Journal of International Economics, 94*, 224–38.

Gootnick, D. (2013). "USAID infrastructure projects have had mixed results and face sustainability challenges." *GAO Reports*, 1–55.

Halsall, P. (1997). Modern Sourcebook: Woodrow Wilson—Speech on the 14 Points Jan 8, 1918. Fordham University.

"Hailing in a new era for democracy and growth." (2007). *Foreign Affairs, 86*, 1.

International Labour Organization, Bureau for Workers' Activities. (1996). Retrieved from "http://www.itcilo.it/actrav/actravenglish/telearn/global/ilo/multinat/multinat.htm#Largest%20corporations"

Kostadinova, P. (2005). "Recipient need or donor interest: Why does the European Union give aid to eastern Europe." *Conference Papers—Midwestern Political Science Association.*

Kulovesi, K. (2014). "International Trade Disputes on Renewable Energy: Testing Ground for the Mutual Supportiveness of WTO Law and Climate Change Law." *Review of European Comparative & International Environmental Law, 23*, 342–53.

Lanteigne, M. (2007). "China's energy security and Eurasian diplomacy: The case of Turkmenistan." *Politics, 27*, 147–155.

Madrichie, N.O. (2007). "Better off out? The costs and benefits of sub-Saharan Africa's membership of the World Trade Organization." *Journal of African Business, 8*, 5–30.

Robins, N. (2004, December 13). "The first multinational." *The New Statesman* Online Edition. Retrieved from "http://www.newstatesman.com/200412130016.htm"

Shapiro, H.S. (2007). "Is the US falling behind on the fast track of international trade?" *World Trade, 20*, 8.

Taxes on the global economy. (2007, July 25). *New York Times, 156*(54016), A18.

Trunick, P. A. (2012). "Building a trading bloc." *World Trade: WT100, 25*, 45–48.

USAID. (2005, January). "About USAID." Retrieved from xlink:href="http://www.usaid.gov/about%5fusaid/usaidhist.html"

Wague, C. (2013). "From tax break to tax haven: Offshore profit shifting and multinational corporations tax avoidance strategy." *International Journal Of Business Strategy, 13*, 115–128.

Woods, N. (2005). "The shifting politics of foreign aid." *International Affairs, 81*, 393–409.

World Trade Organization (WTO). (2014). *Annual report 2014*. Geneva, Switzerland: Author. Retrieved from "http://www.wto.org/english/res%5Fe/booksp%5Fe/anrep%5Fe/anrep14%5Fe.pdf"

SUGGESTED READING

Baltazar, T. & Kvitashvili, E. (2007). "The role of USAID and development assistance in combating terrorism." *Military Review, 87,* 38–40.

McIymont, R. (2007). "Missed opportunities." *Journal of Commerce, 8,* 22–24.

Shapiro, H.S. (2007). "Is the US falling behind on the fast track of international trade?" *World Trade, 20,* 8.

Wilson, M. (2014). "NAFTA's Unfinished Business." *Foreign Affairs, 93,* 128–33.

—*Michael P. Auerbach*

TRADE CREATION AND DIVERSION

ABSTRACT

This article focuses on trade creation and trade diversion. The article provides an overview of trade theory including Jacob Viner's theory of the connection between free trade agreements, customs unions, trade creation, and trade diversion. The relationship between economic integration, trade creation, and trade diversion is explored. The issues and outcomes associated with African regional trade agreements will be addressed.

OVERVIEW

Trade Agreements

Countries actively use trade policy to control national import and export levels and the economy in general. In the twentieth century, free trade agreements emerged as one of the main forms of trade control and cooperation between nations. Under free trade agreements, also referred to as preferential trade agreements (PTAs), goods and services can be exchanged between countries or regions without tariffs, quotas, or other trade restrictions being levied (Holden, 2003). Trade agreements affect trade in two main ways: Trade creation and trade diversion.

- Trade creation refers to the overall increase in trade that results from the displacement of domestic production.
- Trade diversion refers to the diversion of existing trade that results from the displacement of imported goods and services.

Trade Creation vs. Trade Diversion

Economists and policy makers study the effect that the processes of trade creation and trade diversion have on the economy. Trade creation and trade diversion tend to have very different effects on the aggregate economy.

- Trade creation generally produces a net economic gain. Countries enter into free trade agreements, with trade creation a desired result, primarily when the price of a particular imported good or service is lower than the cost of producing the same good or service domestically. The trade relationship allows countries to purchase goods and services at prices less than they would pay domestically for the same goods or services.
- In contrast, trade diversion generally produces a net economic loss. In trade diversion scenarios, countries pay more for imported goods and services than they would under a trade agreement. Domestic purchasers must pay the cost of the imported item and a government tariff.

Reasons for Forming Trade Agreements

According to the U.S. Congressional Budget Office, countries engage in free trade agreements for two main reasons.

- First, foreign trade agreements stimulate and strengthen the economy. Industrialized countries tend to seek out free trade agreements in the interest of promoting and facilitating trade creation. Free trade agreements strengthen national economies and international relationships through trade creation but sacrifice certain domestic business sectors and international relationships through trade diversion. As long as free trade agreements exist between individual countries rather than as an inclusive global pact, trade creation and trade diversion will remain conflicting and competing forces and outcomes. Global free

Canadian economist Jacob Viner. (Courtesy of Wikipedia)

trade, also referred to as multilateral free trade, would end the problem of trade diversion.

- Second, free trade agreements are a form of foreign policy and alliance building. Wealthier nations enter into free trade agreements with developing nations as a means of building international partnerships and aiding developing economies.

The following section provides an overview of trade theory, including Jacob Viner's theory of trade creation and trade diversion. This section serves as a foundation for later discussion of the relationship between economic integration, trade creation, and trade diversion. The issues and outcomes associated with African regional trade agreements are addressed.

Trade Theory
Modern trade theory has its roots in the economic theory of the eighteenth century. Eighteenth-century economists, such as Adam Smith (1723–1790) and David Ricardo (1772–1823), explored how trade between nations affected national economies. Modern trade theory emerged after World War II. Modern

trade theory considers the effect trade barrier removal has on trade flows between countries. Trade theory emerged after World War II as economic theory evolved and grew to address changing global economic relationships. After World War II, economists, world leaders, and governing bodies put trade agreements and economic structures into place, such as the World Bank, United Nations, World Trade Organization, and International Monetary Fund, to prevent the economic depressions and instability that characterized the years following World War I. National agreements promoted and facilitated free trade. Free trade is trade in which goods and services can be exchanged between countries or regions without tariffs, quotas, or other trade restrictions being levied.

Limited Free Trade
Following World War II, the Allied powers, countries in opposition to the Axis powers, promoted a limited form of free trade within a dollar-exchange monetary system. The General Agreement on Tariffs and Trade of 1947 prohibited quantitative restrictions on trade between leading industrialized economies. In the years following World War II, nations have been engaging in trade agreements as a means of increasing economic efficiency, productivity, and growth. Regional trade zones facilitate commercial expansion. Today, trade relationships between nations are also political relationships. Trade relationships, as expressed in customs unions, have become political-economic unions for the world's major trading nations, including the United States, the countries of the European Union (especially those in Western Europe), Japan, China, and South Korea, as well as developing nations.

Modern Trade Theory
Economic theory, after World War II, was deeply engaged with real-world trade concerns and relationships. Modern trade theory began with economist Jacob Viner (1892–1970). Viner's theory of customs unions argues that customs unions have two major effects: trade creating and trade diverting.

- Trade creation refers to the shift of consumption of the importable good from a high-cost domestic producer to a lower-cost external foreign producer.
- Trade diversion refers to a switch from the lowest-cost external producers to a higher-cost producer. Viner's theory argues that trade creation always

improves the country's welfare, but trade diversion dampens the country's welfare (Parai & Yu, 1989).

Trade creation is characterized by a shift in a high-cost domestic product or service to a lower cost imported product or service. Trade diversion is characterized by a shift from low-cost imports from a third-party country to high-cost imports from a member country. Viner believed that all relevant stakeholders in a trade relationship should analyze the economic implications of trade agreements. Trade agreements cause movement between levels of production. This movement can result in a gain or loss of economic efficiency for member nations.

Stakeholders should examine the following variables to judge the economic effect of trade agreements:

- The total volume of trade on which costs have been lowered.
- The total volume of trade on which costs have been raised.
- The degree to which costs have risen on diverted trade.
- The degree to which costs have lowered on created trade, supply curves, and tariffs.

Customs unions and free trade agreements change nations' productive efficiency and consumption habits and levels. Jacob Viner's critics argue that the outcome of customs unions and free trade agreements may reach beyond the fixed outcomes of trade creation and trade diversion (Wexler, 1960).

APPLICATIONS

Trade Creation, Diversion, & Economic Integration
Economic Integration
Trade creation and trade diversion, as outcomes of trade agreements, are part of a larger process of economic integration. Economic integration refers to the integration of commercial and financial activities among countries through the abolishment of nation-based economic institutions and activities. Processes of regional economic integration, such as Europe's, have been shaping the economic relations between countries significantly. At the same time, an increasing integration of all national economies into the global economy has affected these economic relations, too (Krieger-Boden & Soltwedel, 2013).

Economic integration among nations includes the following four stages: free trade agreements (FTA), customs unions (CU), common markets, and economic unions (Holden, 2003). Nations choose different levels of economic integration based on variables such as the strength of their national economy and trade relationships and forecasted trade prospects. Nations may have multiple trade relationships and levels of economic integration with other countries or none at all. Nations that reject or do not pursue the stages of economic integration, as described above, are characterized as autarky.

Autarky, or an autarkic nation, refers to self-sufficient countries that do not participate in international trade. Autarky, which means self-sufficiency in Greek and provides independence from other states, results in both benefits and costs (Anderson & Marcouiller, 2005). The stages of economic integration are rarely fixed or permanent but instead are generally fluid and overlapping. Economic integration, as described below, is an evolving process responsive to the shifting socioeconomic climates. The levels of trade creation and trade diversion decrease as countries move toward greater economic cooperation and economic integration.

Free Trade Agreements
Free trade agreements are agreements that state that goods and services can be exchanged between countries or regions without tariffs, quotas, or other trade restrictions being levied. Examples of free trade agreements include the North American Free Trade Agreement (NAFTA) and the Central European Free Trade Agreement (CEFTA). Free trade agreements may be limited to a business or industry sector or be applied to all levels and types of international trade. Free trade agreements tend to impose two main requirements on member nations:

- First, member nations must agree to follow dispute-resolution procedures.
- Second, member nations must agree to follow rules-of-origin procedures for all third-party products entering the free trade area. Rules of origin, which refer to laws, regulations, and administrative processes that establish a product's country of origin, make up an expensive process for all free trade agreement member nations.

During the 2016 presidential campaign, Donald J. Trump emphasized the importance of renegotiating the United States' trade agreements, including NAFTA. Here he is campaigning in Laconia, Maine, on July 16, 2015. (Courtesy of Michael Vadon CC BY-SA 4.0 via Wikimedia Commons)

East African Community Head of States gather together on April 29, 2009. From left are: Yoweri Museveni of Uganda, Mwai Kibaki of Kenya, Paul Kagame of Rwanda, Jakaya Kikwete of Tanzania and Pierre Nkurunziza of Burundi. (Courtesy of Nukta77 CC BY-SA 2.0 via Wikimedia Commons)

Free trade agreements tend to be applicable to a geographical region and form a free trade area. A free trade area, according to the Organisation for Economic Co-operation and Development, refers to a grouping of countries within which tariffs and non-tariff trade barriers between member nations are generally abolished without instituting common trade policy toward non-members. Free trade agreements result in significant amounts of trade diversion as trade with non-member nations remains an important source of imported goods and services.

Customs Unions
Customs unions, which are free trade areas that also establish a common tariff and other shared trade policies with non-member countries, require trade policy harmony and cooperation between member nations. Customs unions establish a common external tariff (CET) and import quotas on products entering the region from third-party countries but also offer free movement of labor and capital among member nations. Customs unions offer four main benefits to member nations:

- First, customs unions eliminate the need for rules of origin and, as a result, provide member nations with significant administrative cost savings and efficiency gains.
- Second, customs unions establish common trade remedy policies such as anti-dumping and countervail measures.

- Third, customs unions require a level of cooperation that makes trade dispute-resolution procedures between member nations unnecessary.
- Fourth, customs unions work together as a single entity to negotiate multilateral trade initiatives as a single bloc.

The benefits gained from participation in customs unions come at a cost to political and economic independence of member nations. (For example, in 2013 Armenian president Serzh Sargsyan entered his country into a customs union led by Russia—a move that prevents Armenia from being integrated into the European Union.) Member nations exchange their independent trade and foreign policy freedoms for the benefits described above. Trade creation and trade diversion levels in customs unions will vary based on the number of member nations and the remaining trade relationships with non-member nations.

Common Markets
Common markets, as described by the Organisation of Economic Co-operation and Development, are customs unions with provisions to liberalize movement or mobility of people, capital, and other resources and eliminate non-tariff barriers to trade such as the regulatory treatment of product standards. Common markets are a significant step toward economic integration for member nations. Common markets tend to share labor policies as well as fiscal and monetary policies. Common markets, which facilitate increased economic interdependence, tend

The Association of Southeast Asian Nations (ASEAN) is an example of a common market. The flags of ASEAN nations raised in MH Thamrin Avenue, Jakarta, during 18th ASEAN Summit held on May 8, 2011. (Courtesy of Gunawan Kartapranata CC BY-SA 3.0 via Wikimedia Commons)

to produce increased economic efficiency and economic growth for all member nations.

Economic unions, as the final stage of economic integration, are common markets with provisions for the harmonization of certain economic policies such as macroeconomic and regulatory policies. The European Union is one example of a large-scale effective economic union. Economic unions, the last and greatest stage of economic integration among nations, share nearly all economic policies and regulations including monetary policies, fiscal policies, labor policies, development policies, transportation policies, and industrial policies. Economic unions generally share a common currency and a unified monetary policy that controls and coordinates national interest rates and exchange rates. Economic unions require supranational legal and economic institutions to regulate commerce and ensure uniform application of the economic union rules and regulations. Economic unions, with the highest degree of economic integration, tend to promote and facilitate high levels of trade creation.

ISSUES

African Regional Trade Agreements, Trade Creation, & Trade Diversion

Economic integration efforts among nations characterized international relations at the end of the twentieth and beginning of the twenty-first centuries.

Regional economic integration between developing and developed countries is common and believed to lead to economic stability and development. Developing countries and international development organizations, such as the World Bank and the Organisation for Economic Co-operation and Development, promote regional trade agreements as a means of facilitating stability, development, and trade creation. Examples of regional trade agreements include the European Free Trade Agreement (EFTA), Southern African Customs Union (SACU), Gulf Cooperation Council (GCC) Customs Union, Central African Economic and Monetary Community (CEMAC), European Union Taxation and Customs Union, Southern Cone Common Market (MERCOSUR), and West African Economic and Monetary Union (UEMOA).

Regional trade agreements in Africa are characterized by the developing-nation status of most member nations. Regional trade agreements in Africa began appearing in the 1980s. Two treaties, the Lagos Plan of Action (1980) and the Abuja Treaty (1991), created a framework for regional economic integration in central, eastern, northern, southern, and western sub-regions in Africa. A process of trade liberalization and cooperation was developed in the hopes of fostering trade creation, economic development, and, finally, economic integration throughout Africa. Three of the main regional trade agreements in Africa include the Southern African Customs Union, the West African Economic and Monetary Union, and the Central African Economic and Monetary Community. These three regional trade agreements, discussed below, experience different levels of trade creation and trade diversion.

Southern African Customs Union

The Southern African Customs Union (SACU), established in the Customs Union Agreement of 1910, includes the five member states of Botswana, Lesotho, Namibia, South Africa, and Swaziland. The South African Customs Union agreement was revised in 1969 and 1994. The Southern African Customs Union has multiple goals:

- regional integration
- the facilitation of trade between the members of the agreement

Map of Africa showing the member nations of the Southern African Customs Union (SACU). The five member states are: Botswana, Lesotho, Namibia, South Africa and Swaziland.

- improved Trade Negotiations between SACU and third parties
- improved economic development of the member states

The Southern African Customs Union, which provides shared decision-making and a sustainable revenue-sharing arrangement, has been very active in the years following the end of apartheid in 1994. The Southern African Customs Union is challenged by the member nations' varying trade policies and trade policy divergences, and by the perception that South Africa displays an avuncular relationship with its much smaller SACU-member wards because of its greater size, wealth, and overall regional economic dominance (*African Business*, 2013).

As of 2003, The Southern African Customs Union, eager to increase the benefits from economic cooperation, is involved in active trade negotiations with both the European Union and the United States (Kirk & Stern, 2003).

The West African Economic and Monetary Union

The West African Economic and Monetary Union, established in 1994, includes the member nations of Benin, Burkina Faso, the Ivory Coast, Mali, Niger, Senegal, Guinea-Bissau, and Togo. The West African Economic and Monetary Union facilitates trade through the use of a common currency. The West African Economic and Monetary Union has the following goals and objectives:

- "To reinforce the competitiveness of the economic and financial activities of the member states within the framework of an open and competing market and a rationalized and harmonized legal environment."
- "To ensure the convergence of the performances and the economic policies of the member states by the institution of a procedure of multilateral monitoring."
- "To create between member states a common market based on freedom of movement of the people, the goods, the services, the capital and the right of establishment of the people carrying on an independent or paid activity, like on a common external tariff and a marketing policy."
- "To institute a coordination of the national policies by the implementation of common actions, and possibly, of common policies in particular in the following fields: human resources, regional planning, agriculture, energy, industry, mines, transport, infrastructures and telecommunication."
- "To harmonize, to the extent necessary with the correct operation of the common market, the legislations of the member states and particularly the mode of the taxation" (Diop, 2008, p.1)

The Central African Economic and Monetary Community

The Central African Economic and Monetary Community, established in 1994, includes the six member nations of Cameroon, Central African Republic, Chad, Republic of the Congo, Equatorial Guinea, and Gabon. The Central African Economic and Monetary Community has the following goals and objectives:

- Promote the establishment of a Central African Common Market
- Eliminate the obstacles to trade between member nations.

- Coordinate development programs to benefit underprivileged countries and areas.

Economists debate the effects of the African regional trade agreements, described above, on the developing economies of Africa. Regional trade agreements in Africa are intended to foster trade creation but may result in trade diversion. For example, economic community of Central Africa has experienced greater amounts of trade diversion than trade creation. Goods produced outside the regional trade agreements area are priced high due to tariffs and, as a result, pose an economic hardship on the national economy. Regional trade agreements increase the volume of trade without necessarily facilitating trade in areas with high growth potential. Variables that effect trade creation and trade diversion effects of regional trade agreements include the following (Musila, 2005):

- exporting country gross national product (GNP)
- importing country gross national product
- exporting country population
- importing country population
- distance
- regional transportation and communication network
- common language
- willingness of countries to reduce tariffs
- willingness of countries to eliminate non-tariff barriers to trade such as visa requirements, and sociopolitical stability

CONCLUSION

In the final analysis, Jacob Viner's theory of trade creation and trade diversion has had a lasting impact on trade theory and trade policy. Trade creation, which refers to the net increase in trade that results from the displacement of domestic production, and trade diversion, which refers to the diversion of existing trade that results from the displacement of imports, have significantly different effects on national economies. The U.S. Congressional Budget Office promotes more inclusive free trade agreements in an effort to eliminate trade diversion and foster trade creation. Ultimately, the hybrid nature of trade policy, a combination of economic and foreign policy, will likely continue so long as a trade policy is a strategic tool for policy makers.

BIBLIOGRAPHY

Abdel-Latif, A. & Nugent, J. (1994). "Countertrade as trade creation and trade diversion." *Contemporary Economic Policy, 12,* 1–12.

Anderson, J., & Marcouiller, D. (2005). "Anarchy and autarky: Endogenous predation as a barrier to trade." *International Economic Review, 46,* 189–213.

Bendavid, N., & Norman, L. (2013, September 5). "Armenia jilts Europe, ties trade knot with Moscow." *Wall Street Journal - Eastern Edition.* p. A9.

Diop, M. and M. Jubenot. (2008). "New definitions and new indicators for well-being in developing countries: the example of WAEMU." Paper Prepared for the 30th General Conference of The International Association for Research in Income and Wealth. Retrieved from the International Association for Research in Income and Wealth.

Editors, (2013). "The problems of being the rich uncle." *African Business, 394,* 69.

Endoh, M. (1999). "Trade creation and trade diversion in the EEC, the LAFTA and the CMEA: 1960–1994." *Applied Economics, 31,* 207–216.

Esposito, P. (2017). "Trade creation, trade diversion and imbalances in the EMU." *Economic Modelling, 60,* 462–472.

Ethier, W. (1998). "Regionalism in a multilateral world." *Journal of Political Economy, 106,* 1214.

Holden, M. (2003). "Stages of economic integration: From autarky to economic union." Government of Canada Depository Services Program. Retrieved xlink:href="http://dsp-psd.pwgsc.gc.ca/Collection-R/LoPBdP/inbrief/prb0249-e.htm"

Krieger-Boden, C., & Soltwedel, R. (2013). "Identifying European economic integration and globalization: a review of concepts and measures." *Regional Studies, 47,* 1425–1442.

Musila, J. (2005). "The intensity of trade creation and trade diversion in COMESA, ECCAS and ECOWAS: A comparative analysis." *Journal of African Economies, 14,* 117.

Parai, A., & Yu, E. (1989). "Factor mobility and customs unions theory." *Southern Economic Journal, 55,* 842.

"The pros and cons of pursuing free-trade agreements." (2003). Congressional Budget Office. Retrieved from xlink:href="http://www.cbo.gov/ftpdoc.cfm?index=4458&type=0&sequence=0"

Valdes, A. (1995). "Joining an existing regional trade agreement from the perspective of a small open economy." *American Journal of Agricultural Economics, 77,* 1292.

Wexler, I. (1960)." Trade creation and trade diversion: A geometrical note." *Southern Economic Journal, 26,* 316–320.

SUGGESTED READING

Clausing, K. (2001). "Trade creation and trade diversion in the Canada—United States Free Trade Agreement." *Canadian Journal of Economics, 34.*

Hurt, S. R., Lee, D., & Lorenz-Carl, U. (2013). "The argumentative dimension to the EU-Africa EPAs." *International Negotiation, 18,* 67–87.

Koo, W., Kennedy, P., & Skripnitchenko, A. (2006). "Regional preferential trade agreements: Trade creation and diversion effects." *Review of Agricultural Economics, 28,* 408–415.

Nerozzi, S. (2011). "From the Great Depression to Bretton Woods: Jacob Viner and international monetary stabilization (1930-1945)." *European Journal Of The History Of Economic Thought, 18,* 55–84.

Switzer, L., & Redstone, J. (1989). "The impact of a Canada-US bilateral free trade accord on the Canadian minerals industry." *Applied Economics, 21,* 273.

—Simone I. Flynn, PhD

TRADITIONAL MANAGERIAL ECONOMICS

ABSTRACT

Managerial economics pays attention to the firm in ways that other branches of economics never has. No longer seen as the "black-box" buffeted by market forces alone, the firm and how it allocates resources and makes decisions has since become the focal point of quantitative analysis that real-world companies have welcomed. An amalgam of microeconomics, operations research, and management science, the subject's emphasis on the practicalities of running a business day to day using applied mathematics has proven a welcome change of tack for many line managers.

OVERVIEW

Economists build models, think abstractly and, whenever possible, generalize. Business people build customer bases and products lines, think concretely and, whenever possible, quantify. To be sure, traditional economic concepts like supply and demand, profit and utility maximization, "imperfect" information, and marginal analysis sum up the underlying dynamics of markets so neatly that they have become the way business is inherently thought about. But, as a rule, business people are too preoccupied with the hundreds of practical decisions that directly affect their "bottom lines" to ponder economic theory much. And to be fair, there is, without exception, an awful lot to think about: marketing plans, pricing, the size and timing of production runs, quality control, worker productivity, capital budgeting, etc.

The behavior of the firm, along with that of the consumer and a given industry, collectively comprise the subject matter of microeconomics. In relation to business decision-making, its most relevant conceit is "the theory of the firm"; a twentieth-century formulation. In earlier times, classical economists thought exclusively in terms of markets and individual rational actors. When the existence of the "firm" was formally recognized, it was considered a means of eliminating third-party purchases at each stage in the production process; nothing more and nothing less. The elimination of third party purchases occurs only if one entity owns the inputs and outputs required to systematically turn raw materials or component parts into finished goods. By doing so, the firm avoids the costs of researching supplier prices, bargaining, and drawing up legal contracts (collectively referred to as transaction costs), thus improving market efficiency.

Strictly speaking, a firm is a production "function" that maximizes its profits by turning labor and capital (its "inputs") into goods and services (it "outputs") (Williamson, 1996). To succeed at this, a firm must align prices and output levels with market demand and so generates the greatest amount of sales revenue at the least cost. Decision-making at the firm level, essentially, is so largely determined by market forces emanating from beyond its organizational boundaries, the theory insists, that what goes on inside the firm is immaterial. All that really matters is the observable effects of its decisions. For a long time then, economists indifferent to the inner workings of the firm treated it as an impenetrable "black-box" (Loabsy, 1967).

Whether a firm has one, several, or many direct competitors its disposition toward the marketplace is affected. A firm with only one major competitor enjoys a higher price structure and can market a relatively undifferentiated product. By contrast, a firm with a number of competitors enjoys no such luxury and fares better when it markets a more differentiated product. Likewise, a firm can indeed maximize its profits by setting its price exactly at the point where one additional dollar of sales, its marginal revenue, incurs one additional dollar of expense, its marginal cost.

When it comes to the nuts and bolts of *actually* allocating resources in a real-world firm, though, matters turn murkier. For starts, "pure" microeconomic theory, critics contend, is built around a set of unrealistic core assumptions: Firms are not always the rational actors bent on maximizing profits nor do they always enjoy "perfect information." In reality, firms can and do make the "irrational" decision to maximize utility instead of profits; preferring to lower prices to gain market share from competitors. And most decidedly, all firms do not have the same amount or quality of information about current market conditions upon which to base decisions (Hitch & McKean, 1961). Worse still, the markets they compete in are almost always in disequilibrium, subject to external macroeconomic shocks, the sudden introduction of new technologies, the unexpected intervention of government regulators, and the like. Most unrealistically of all, a kind of tunnel vision is necessary to model market behavior; the only way to see a fundamental market principle in action is to zero in on it to the exclusion of any other, effectively reducing a multidimensional dynamic to a one dimensional event.

For business people charged with making specific decisions about very complicated issues, then, microeconomic theories has appreciable limits. It is not that they are wanting too much, but rather, too many variables are at play in the real-world market to see their outline all that clearly. The devil, as the saying goes, is in the details. Economists in this respect deal almost exclusively in observable transaction data (past sales, revenues, and prices, etc.), which by rights must be historical data. Business people, on the other hand, are budgeters and strategic planners: Their concerns revolve around bringing about desirable future outcomes (Calfee & Rubin, 1993). Since the transactions they are most concerned with have not taken place yet, what is more, there is no such data to work with. What data they do have is culled from the numerical minutiae of running a business day to day: entries in accounting ledgers, number of components on order, variable costs of production, inventory of finished goods on hand, etc. Even more to the point, perhaps, the microeconomic models most commonly used do not really lessen the uncertainty surrounding future market conditions enough to be all that helpful. Simply put, they are too static, too simplistic, and too inexact.

By far, the most effective remedy for uncertainty is precision; precision in rendering real-world events, in thinking through problems, and in planning solutions. Fortunately, a means of achieving such precision has gained a considerable following among economists of every stripe in the last thirty years. It is mathematics, and it has given the "dismal science" a powerful new language in which to restate and refine its fundamental tenants in light of the complexity and uncertainty a firm faces in a competitive marketplace every day. A precursor, the graphical representation of key microeconomic phenomena like supply and demand as curves on a plot, has been widely used for a much longer period of time. Merely visual embodiments of the algebraic formula $y = a(x) - b$, these graphs plot the relative values of cost or price per quantity produced or sold. More importantly, because these are linear equations, values for one set of variables can be calculated when the values and rate of change of the other set of variables is known. Older and even more basic, as any accountant will tell you, is the use of addition and subtraction along with multiplication and division to calculate a firm's revenue, costs, and profits. Simple arithmetic in the form of fractions expressed as either percentages or ratios also yield many insightful measures of a company's financial and operational performance.

All of these, of course, were the product of an equation of one sort or another, which raised a very interesting question: What other forms of equations might prove equally as useful in economic analysis? The answer, it turns out, encompasses statistics and probability theory, regression analysis, linear programming, exponentiation, and calculus, and, slightly further afield, decision matrixes, and game theory. Each has proven itself a useful adjunct to more traditional forms of microeconomic analysis. So much so, in fact, they collectively have given rise to the burgeoning new discipline of managerial economics. Be it the employment of statistical techniques in general and regression analysis in particular to test new hypothetical economic models, of maximization and minimization formulae from linear programming to improve the efficiency of production lines, supply ordering and inventory management or of derivatives from calculus to accurately calculate the marginal revenue and marginal cost of a particular product, the marriage of mathematics and microeconomics is proving fruitful indeed.

APPLICATIONS

The management of any firm requires constant attention be paid in equal measure to planning, operations, and control. Mathematics, meanwhile, excels at describing and dealing with subtlety, complexity, and disorder (Cooper, 1961). And, as we have seen, economics concerns itself with the production, distribution, and consumption of goods and services. At the crossroads of management, mathematics, and economics lies management economics, a field of inquiry with a decidedly practical bent. Perhaps too practical for purists who complain, with some

Elon Musk is the founder, CEO and lead designer of SpaceX, co-founder, CEO, and product architect of Telsa, Inc. as well as CEO of Neuralink. Here he tours the commercial rocket processing facility of Space Exploration Technologies, known as SpaceX, along with President Barack Obama at Cape Canaveral Air Force Station, Cape Canaveral, Florida, on April 15, 2010. (Courtesy of Bill Ingalls, NASA, via Wikimedia Commons)

justification, that too many of its tenants and applications are "borrowed" wholesale from operations research and management science to consider the field a bona fide branch of economics. Truth be told, operations research has indeed been the source of mathematical techniques and formulae used in managerial economics. Just as management science has contributed empirically based theories about the organizational behavior instrumental to attempts by managerial economists to systematize and, whenever possible, quantify intra-firm decision-making.

Debating lineages and pedigrees of ideas may well satisfy dogmatists' need for argumentation for its own sake. In the larger context, though, critics ignore the primary reason why economists practice the "dismal" science in the first place: to advance our understanding of how wealth is created to better the human condition. And one constant in our progress toward this understanding is our ability as a species to synthesize new ideas by cross-fertilizing existing ones; if they happen to come from different fields of knowledge, so be it. Philosophic issues aside, drawing from other disciplines in this instance has given economists the tools to open up those "black-boxes" to the light. It is now necessary to give our attention to the imminently more useful matter of what they have found.

Supply & Demand Functions

Managerial economics is all about functions in two senses of the word. A function in mathematics, first and foremost, is an equation or one of its variants such as an inequality or a deduction in symbolic logic. Then, too, of course, a business is often organized by functional area. Regardless, uncertainty about market-driven supply and demand cut right across the entire organization. Accurately projecting the demand curve for a given product not only figures prominently in ramping production up or down but also, critically, in setting prices which, in turn, directly affect the amount of revenue a firm earns. Robust statistical analyses of patterns of past market demand improve the likelihood that forecasts of future demand will have predictive value. Calculating the confidence levels of results, ensuring a data sample is random enough to be indicative of real-world phenomena, applying regression analysis to isolate causes and effects, etc., has also proven very useful in analyzing the consumer research that has proven so instrumental to a firm bringing popular new products and services to market.

Another key determinant to sales, of course, is price for both new and existing products. Here, the venerable demand curve still has much to contribute. How straight the line drawn here determines the kind of function used in calculating consumption levels at different pricing points. A polynomial equation causes the line to be straight, an exponential equation causes it to curve or be more irregularly shaped. The latter's logarithmic function better captures the chaotic character of real-world markets than the former's inherently simpler algebraic one. Crucially, however, both remain approximations of generalized behavior. You see, for all its precision, mathematics is captive of future uncertainty. Mathematics can, however, numerically express the likelihood of a particular outcome using probability theory.

Price directly affects the amount of a good or service supplied to the market place. To calculate the number of units a firm could and probably should market, a firm needs only to determine the price at which consumer demand is the highest. That figure, in turn, can then be plugged into a linear or exponential supply curve equation. The resulting value can then be used to estimate the total cost of production for a firm by plugging it into a cost curve equation. A cost curve equation is much more likely to graphically take the form of a curve than a straight line due to economies of scale. The greater your output, the more able you are to negotiate favorable prices from suppliers that equate to lower costs. Likewise, the greater your output, the more knowledgeable you are regarding the intricacies of the processes involved and thus are better able to improve efficiency.

Profits

The most basic and perhaps the most brutal equation in all business is total revenues minus total costs equals net profit. A firm intent on maximizing profit would be unwise to ignore this tried-and-true microeconomic axiom: Set your price at the point where a product's marginal costs exactly match its marginal revenues. To do this, one must first calculate the two operands: marginal revenue and marginal cost. Both are values that express the rate of change of one variable, price or cost, against another, units either demanded or supplied, a relationship algebra alone

can never capture. Such a calculation can only be performed using the derivative of total revenue or total cost at a given quantity (an application of calculus).

Prices, what is more, do not vary uniformly from one item to the next. Some items are said to be elastic, meaning that the lower the price, the higher the number of items people will buy and conversely; the higher the prices, the fewer items people will buy. Other items, alternatively, are said to be inelastic, meaning that people will buy an item regardless of how much it costs. By this definition, then, basic staples are relatively inelastic; color television sets relatively elastic. The degree to which a product is elastic is determined via algebra by dividing the change in the quantity of demand by the change in its price. If this resulting figure is positive, demand is elastic. If it is negative, demand is inelastic. This very same figure can be plugged into the $y=a(x)$—b formula for a linear demand curve as the value for "a" is to aid in determining demand at different pricing points. Another similar calculation can be done to arrive at the price elasticity of supply.

Productivity

How efficient a firm is can also be readily quantified by dividing a firm's total output by the total number of a firm's workers over a given time frame. The figure yielded is the average product of labor. Marginal analysis, meanwhile, can tell a firm if it needs to hire any additional workers. This is calculated by comparing the changes in total output produced by different numbers of workers. If the derivative of these two values is such that the average wage of one additional worker is greater than the increase in the value of the output he or she contributes, more hiring is unadvisable. It may well be unadvisable at some point for an altogether different reason: diminishing Marginal Returns. Diminishing marginal returns occur in a situation when capital investment is fixed and more workers are hired, and each additional new worker contributes progressively less and less to overall output.

Decision-Making with Uncertainty

Even as brief an overview of the mathematical underpinnings of management economics as this is, it would be negligent to avoid discussion of the progress made in decision theory and game theory. Decision theory allows managers to chart their way through an often elaborate set of options by representing each distinct decision point as a node and each option as a branch extending outward from that node. Its virtue lies in the way very complex problems can be broken down into their constituent parts (the very definition of analysis) and in the way it maps out all the possible consequences of a given decision, outlining those options that are still actionable and those that are not as one goes along in the decision process. In certain cases, decision trees can model the likelihood of actual real-world events. Best-guess probabilities as to the chances a particular node and branch will be followed are assigned, and the overall chances of a given outcome is then ascertained by multiplying the individual probabilities of each successive node leading back to the starting point.

Game theory, meanwhile, tackles the often thorny task of negotiating sales, purchases, cooperative ventures, labor contracts, and the like. Viewing such undertakings as a game with players, strategies and actions, and payoffs gives a firm a clearer understanding of how to best represent its interests. Managers merely need to liken their present situation to a known game scenario. This could be The Prisoner's Dilemma, The Battle of the Sexes, The Deer Hunt, The Lock Out Game, The Chicken Game, or some other exotically named scenario. A game can either be played sequentially or simultaneously and may have well defined or rather vague rules. Its object is always for each player to arrive at a dominant strategy; the course of action that results in the desired outcome. When all the players have decided upon which dominant strategy to follow, the game is said to be in equilibrium.

VIEWPOINTS

The tools and techniques of managerial economics discussed here represent a fraction of those in use today. Though certainly never likely to eliminate the uncertainty inherent in the marketplace, managerial economics nonetheless brings greater accuracy to production planning and pricing, a more agile responsiveness to changing customer needs and wants in product introduction, and a much clearer understanding of the downstream implications of decisions made.

While there is some question as to whether managerial economics is truly economics, the fundamentals

addressed mathematically stem directly from microeconomics and are expressed in terms economists traditionally use.

Managerial economics is most decidedly a work in progress. Today's corporations, for example, are made up of any number of small business units that for all intents and purposes behave like firms in their own right (Egan, 1995). How the corporation per se evaluates its portfolio of products microeconomically given all the cross-selling and bundling going on today is a problem managerial economists have yet to solve. Undoubtedly, there will be other problems in the future, for managerial economics is here to stay.

BIBLIOGRAPHY

Baumol, W. (1961). "What can economic theory contribute to managerial economics?" *American Economic Review, 51,* 142–146.

Calfee, J., & Rubin, P. (1993). "Nontransactional data in managerial economics and marketing." *Managerial & Decision Economics, 14,* 163–173.

Cooper, W. (1961). "The current state of managerial economics." *American Economic Review, 51,* 131–141.

e Silva, C., & Hewings, G. (2012). "Locational and managerial decisions as interdependent choices in the headquarter-manufacturing plant relationship: a theoretical approach." *Annals Of Regional Science, 48,* 703–717.

Egan, T. (1995). "Updating managerial economics." *Business Economics, 30,* 51–56.

Hay, G. (1970). "Production, price and inventory theory." *American Economic Review, 60,* 531–545.

Lenox, M., Rockart, S., & Lewin, A. (2007). "Interdependency, competition, and industry dynamics." *Management Science, 53,* 599–615.

Loasby, B. (1967). "Management economics and the theory of the firm." *Journal of Industrial Economics, 15,* 165–176.

Mintz, O., & Currim, I. S. (2013). "What drives managerial use of marketing and financial metrics and does metric use affect performance of marketing-mix activities?" *Journal of Marketing, 77,* 17–40.

O'Brien, T. J. (2011). "Managerial economics and operating beta." *Managerial & Decision Economics, 32,* 175–191.

Williamson, O. (1996). "Economics and organization: A primer." *California Management Review, 38,* 131–146.

SUGGESTED READING

Hitch, C., & McKean, R. (1961). "What can managerial economics contribute to economic theory?" *American Economic Review, 51,* 147–154.

Liao, S. (1975). "Shareholders-oriented managers versus entity-oriented managers." *Financial Analysts Journal, 31,* 62–71.

Matutinovic, I. (2005). "The microeconomic foundations of business cycles: From institutions to autocatalytic networks." *Journal of Economic Issues, 39,* 867–898.

Shubik, M. (1970). "A curmudgeon's guide to microeconomics." *Journal of Economic Literature, 8,* 405–434.

—*Francis Duffy, MBA*

TRANSFER PRICING

ABSTRACT

Recent growth in international trade and global commerce is increasingly relevant to college students who desire to obtain maximum value from their course work in economics and accounting. Transfer pricing, as a topic spanning those two disciplines, describes a set of strategies through which firms attempt to send a portion of their profits offshore to minimize their income tax liabilities. Because those transactions occur between two firms related through common ownership, transfer pricing historically downplayed the influence of markets in price determination processes. More recently, however, tax regulations and authorities from around the globe are calling for broader perspectives to avoid corporate income tax evasion. Effective involvement in those processes requires a solid understanding of the essential differences and similarities between economics and accounting. The tax laws in many countries define five methods for determining and communicating a firm's transfer price to taxing authorities. Those methods generally involve primary comparisons between two unrelated firms and a secondary comparison of those results to related firms, which is the essence of the so-called arm's length standard. The purpose of this essay is to illuminate standards, methods, and concepts that are relevant to transfer pricing and to demonstrate the importance and value of integrating economics and accounting perspectives. Individuals who gain a better understanding of transfer pricing may find themselves in high demand.

In an era expecting growth in international trade and relations, college students will find additional value from courses in economics and accounting. Professionals at facilitating decision-making and planning, economists, and accountants are becoming integral partners in helping multinational corporations in demonstrating regulatory compliance and developing pricing strategies. Transfer pricing is an interdisciplinary topic that challenges governmental tax authorities, corporate accountants, and market analysts equally. On the one hand, there is a need to describe how the prices of goods and services reflect cost functions, consumer demand, and market conditions. On the other hand, there lies a need to determine prices that maximize profits while using specific methods for minimizing tax burdens.

Transfer pricing, as a topic that traditionally downplays the forces of markets and consumer demand,

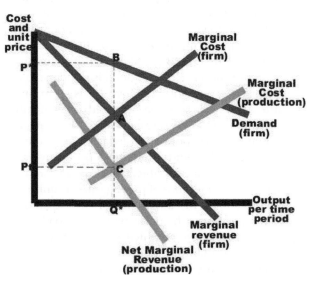

Transfer Pricing with No External Market. (Courtesy of Mydogategodshat CC-BY-SA-3.0 via Wikimedia Commons)

represents a vast opportunity for closing a lingering gap between theory and practice. It also presents a dynamic tension between a group of professionals who seek to minimize corporate income tax burdens and another group whose aim is to prevent tax evasion. In their works related to taxation, accountants are encountering unprecedented challenges to apply sound economic analysis in their tax reduction methodologies and post-tax profit maximization efforts. Transfer pricing practices require interactions between the regulated and regulators. Furthermore, governmental tax authorities around the world are adjusting corporate tax returns and prompting timely explanations. In response, accounting service firms are helping their corporate clients by preparing reports that justify, document, and communicate how they determine prices for transactions between firms (which have relationships through common ownership) that operate in multiple countries.

Involvement in those processes requires a solid understanding of the essential differences and similarities between economics and accounting. Acknowledging the reality that persons learned and trained in one discipline often find it difficult to comprehend other disciplines, this essay tends to emphasize the economics perspective because of its reference in tax regulations that govern the treatment of international transactions. Consequently, several of the largest accounting firms in the world recognize those limitations and are adding economists to their staff. If recent job postings for transfer pricing specialists are any gauge, it appears that the demand for economists is much higher now than it was before the $3.4 billion settlement in September, 2006 between GlaxoSmithKline (GSK) and the Internal Revenue Service. Whether they agree or disagree on this verdict, many professionals are aware of the important and interrelated roles of maintaining data accuracy and assuring assumption reliability. In the pages ahead, the reader will find an exposition of varied aspects with regard to transfer pricing and the apparent need to depart from past inward- or domestic-focused practices.

Firm Profitability & Tax Regulations

In terms of long-standing traditions, a major task of corporate tax departments and accounting staff is to influence firm profitability. Taking a narrow view of that work, accounting is a profession that prepares governmental and financial reports, analyzes costs

Internal Revenue Service building on Constitution Avenue in Washington, D.C. (Courtesy of U.S. Government via Wikimedia Commons)

and revenues, and calculates post-profit tax liabilities. In short, income tax minimization represents a final step toward profit maximization. Therefore, it is reasonable for accountants to invest their time, talent, and energy adding legitimacy to their efforts to minimize the tax burdens of their employers and their clients. Likewise, it is reasonable for government revenue agents to scrutinize that work guarding against potential cases of tax evasion and/or system abuse.

Many tend to view economics in terms of its focus on pre-tax profit maximization conditions. Casting aside any debate regarding views on the inclusion of taxes as an economic cost, economists and some tax authorities expect to observe high levels of profits in industries and markets characterized by new entry, product innovation, and price leadership strategies. Any attempts by corporate tax departments and their accounting staff to understate those profits by transferring them via questionable, inappropriate, and/or undocumented methods of pricing will certainly raise suspicions and garner attention from taxing authorities especially those who understand the broader perspective. As something to which we return later in this essay, it is important for students, practitioners, and clients to focus their attention on a few concepts central to economics including, but not limited to, opportunity costs, economic profits, and market structures.

A cursory review of regulations on transfer pricing makes it apparent that tax accountants, their clients, and other parties stand to benefit from learning more about the price determination processes whether those analyses include or exclude market orientations. Because the regulations contain numerous references to marketplace dimensions, the apparent gap between accounting and economics is quite perplexing given the fact that most students in business programs receive ample exposure to those disciplines early in their studies. Perhaps those studies need to place greater emphasis on transfer pricing mechanisms and on international tax regulations. With some digression at this juncture, that need is real especially in light of the fact that China and other developing nations will become major economic forces in the future.

Transfer Pricing

Returning attention to the central topic here, the field of transfer pricing seems to remain in its infancy although publications on the topic first appeared in academic journals several decades ago. Without tracing the historical roots and development of transfer pricing in this essay, readers can begin to gain a deeper appreciation of this time-honored and current topic by pondering the content and relevance of a clear and concise definition. Using the words from Pearce (1992), transfer pricing is: "The system of setting prices for transactions among subsidiaries of a multinational corporation, where the prices are not subject to market determination. The prices are often deliberately chosen to minimize tax or tariff burdens on the corporation on a world scale, e.g., costs may be overstated in subsidiaries in a country with a high profits tax so that profits can be shifted to a subsidiary in lower tax country" (p. 433).

Readers of this essay will find departure from that fine definition with respect to its dismissal of market influences on transfer price. Furthermore, the applicable regulations call for its inclusion in transfer price determinations and analyses. Moreover, a portion of this essay devotes itself to the division between market and non-market influences.

APPLICATIONS

In the context of international trade and global commerce, tax strategy is largely a function of the geographic locations of the seller and the buyer which

Apple MacBook Pro is a typical laptop. (Courtesy of Ashley Pomeroy CC BY-SA 4.0 via Wikimedia Commons)

also happen to be affiliates by virtue of common ownership. Furthermore, firms that charge their subsidiaries a high (low) price suggests they are booking a higher (lower) taxable income on the sales end of a transaction and a lower (higher) taxable income on the purchase end of a transaction. Those bookings are controlled transactions because one party is under the control of the other party. More precisely, the seller is often the parent firm and the buyer its subsidiary. Moreover, the price of an item in a transaction between two related firms, in contrast to two unrelated firms, may reflect professional creativity more so than market forces.

According to Amram, "transfer pricing is merely an art describing the internal accounting costs assigned to an exchange of goods, services, or intangibles between commonly controlled foreign and domestic entities." Consider the following hypothetical case presented by Amram. Let us say that domestic parent company USCO, which is located in United States, owns foreign subsidiary CaymanCo, which is located in the Cayman Islands. The former entity produces laptop computers at a cost of $50.00 per unit and sells them to the latter entity for $100.00 per unit. CaymanCo incurs an additional $400.00 in costs per computer bringing the total unit cost to $500.00.

CaymanCo distributes those laptops to third parties elsewhere around the globe who pay $1,000.00 for each new laptop. In sum, CaymanCo realizes a taxable income of $500.00 for each computer it sold and USCO realizes $50.00. The hypothetical corporate income tax rate, furthermore, in the United States is 35 percent whereas it is zero in the Cayman Islands. In accordance with Generally Accepted Accounting Principles, USCO and CaymanCo prepare and file consolidated financial statements for a governing agency. In addition, they prepare and file an annual report with their shareholders. On the one hand, the actual post-tax profit on each computer amounts to $482.50. This is the result of subtracting USCO's income tax of $17.50, which is 35 percent of the initial $50.00 transfer pricing profit, from CaymanCo's $500.00 profit per computer. On the other hand, the potential post-tax profit on each computer sold amounts to $500.00 per computer, which would produce $175.00 (35 percent of $500.00) per computer in tax revenue for the United States given the absence of a transfer pricing arrangement.

At issue is whether the shifting of income offshore is legitimate or artificial in nature. In order to ensure legitimacy, the Organisation for Economic Co-operation and Development (OECD) in conjunction with various professionals established a set of methods for determining transfer prices. The specific choice of methods for pricing international transactions will likely affect the allocation of total profit among units within a multinational company. Application of a single method or an inappropriate method without ample justification may give the appearance of being tax evasive whether accidental or otherwise. The challenge is to devise, use, and document the most appropriate methods of transfer pricing thereby proactively avoiding an unfortunate appearance and the associative complexities of reactively untangling an adjustment by a district director at the Internal Revenue Service or another tax authority elsewhere.

Those price determination methods will receive some coverage later in this essay. Meanwhile, this essay directs the attention of readers to a set of economic concepts most applicable to transfer pricing and price determination processes. In doing so, the next section begins without references to market forces and it then concludes with some direct references.

PRICE & PROFIT DETERMINATIONS WITH LIMITED REFERENCE TO MARKETS

Opportunity Cost

Undergraduate business students discover some key differences between accounting profit and normal or economic profit and between accounting costs and economic costs. In general, accountants tend to ignore or downplay the opportunity cost approach advanced in economics. Opportunity cost, by definition, it is the value assigned to the foregone next best alternative. Consider, for example, students cannot attend class and, at the same time, do whatever they would do if absent from class. The opportunity cost of their attendance is the value they receive from the alternative decision, which is the absence. Students will receive compensation, which may take the form of a higher course grade or a grade point average, in return for sacrificing their want to be absent. Likewise, business owners expect incentives to remain in their existing line of business. Consequently, the profits they expect to earn are taken as normal and they are inclusions in the cost of doing business.

Other Key Costs

Shifting gears away from the profit concept for the moment, students in economics courses learn that firms incur a variety of costs with the production of goods and services. Let us consider some key cost definitions and prepare to apply them in a variety of ways. Total cost is the sum of fixed costs and variable costs. Fixed costs are those that exist even without any production. Furthermore, they are constant, as they do not vary with the scale of production. Variable costs are those that vary with production.

Valuable Graphs

The allocation of those costs across larger scales of production results in a variety of cost curve shapes or functions. Graphs depicting these functions show cost on the vertical axis and quantity on the horizontal axis. Readers need to keep in mind that average total cost and average variable cost form important U-shaped curves. Their calculations involve divisions by the production quantity coordinate. The lowest points on those curves are also significant because it is where the marginal cost curve, which is J-shaped, intersects them. Marginal cost is the change in total costs that arise from producing one additional unit.

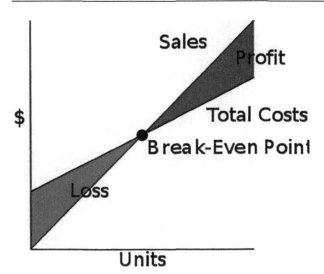

Cost-Volume Profit diagram, showing the Break-Even Point as the point where the Total Costs equals the Sales. (Courtesy of Nils R. Barth via Wikimedia Commons)

Break-even Point

Next, consider one of two key graphical references, which is the break-even point. It occurs where the marginal cost curve intersects the average total cost curve and at the latter's lowest point. The break-even point also marks the location at which those costs are equal and where price needs to be in order for the firm to earn a normal profit. The break-even term is misleading as it seems to indicate an absence of an accounting profit. As mentioned earlier, profits become part of the cost of operations if the owner is remaining consistent with the notion of opportunity cost. Therefore, to remain in business, a firm owner or an entrepreneur will pursue the rate of profit considered normal for the market in which he or she conducts business operations.

Shut-down Point

The second key reference is the shut-down point. It occurs where the marginal cost curve intersects the average variable cost curve and at the latter's lowest point. The shut-down point also marks the location at which those costs are equal and where price needs to be in order for the firm to remain in business as an ongoing economically viable enterprise. For obvious reasons, as the name implies, a transfer price below the shut-down point is likely to grab the attention of tax authorities. It could signify the selling party's attempt to minimize its profit, conversely maximizing

its loss, in transferring an item that is artificially underpriced to the related offshore party. As was the case presented by Amram, the offshore party is then in a position to earn maximum profit by purchasing the item from its parent at an extraordinarily low price and then selling it at the market price.

Price Determination

With this initial reference to market price, we are moving closer to the discussion on how the market influences price determination processes. Though transfer pricing involves a special case in which a firm is selling some of its product to itself or a subsidiary readers should take note of this initial reference to markets. Nevertheless, some product sales occur in the open market regardless of whether transfer pricing is present or absent. In the usual case, a market delineates the acceptable or competitive levels for prices and profits. To realize normal profit, a firm really needs to sell its items or services at a price that equals or exceeds the break-even point. For the sake of simplicity and brevity here, profit maximization under the economic perspective refers to the situation that occurs before the application of income taxes; one could argue that taxes are also a normal part of doing business and are therefore included as costs and by virtue of a net normal profit.

As an early introduction to the next section, readers need to keep in mind that firms produce and sell items and they receive a price for each one sold. Total revenue is the mathematical product of price

"Everyday Low Prices" are widely used in supermarkets. (Courtesy of LateNameGuys CC BY-SA 3.0 via Wikimedia Commons)

times the quantity sold at each price. Marginal revenue is the change in total revenue that arises from selling one additional unit. To reach the normal profit-maximizing output requires a level of production where marginal costs are equal to marginal revenue. Before we depart this section, a discussion of the rules of production is in order. Adherence to these rules allows a firm to continue its operation as a viable entity. First, firms must produce at the profit maximizing output, which is where marginal revenue equals marginal cost. Second, firms need to receive a price that is equal to or greater than average variable cost. Why? Their sales must cover, at the least, average variable costs and contribute something toward average fixed costs. In the context of transfer pricing, this is about as far as an economic analysis can go by excluding specific references to market forces. To recap, most firms face pricing and operating constraints by virtue of their cost functions and profit expectations. As readers are beginning to see, the relationship between market prices and producer costs is critical because it influences whether the production of an item will occur at all and in an efficient and profitable manner. Even with a limited reference to market conditions, business owners expect to earn profits and their firms will incur a variety of costs in their production of goods and services. The next section addresses some market influences that are relevant to transfer pricing, in part, due to necessities for an analysis of markets in accordance with Section 482 of the Internal Revenue Code.

Economic & Market Factors: Possible Relevance to Transfer Pricing Methods & Cases

Tax laws in many of the countries with membership in the OECD define five methods for gauging and auditing a firm's transfer price. The United States is a member, and its tax codes for transfer pricing draw from those of the OECD with the additional stipulation that method choice and supporting documentation need to accompany the tax return at time of its filing. Accordingly, in its absence, district directors at the Internal Revenue Service have explicit authority for adjusting the contents of a corporate tax return and for imposing hefty penalties when they encounter questionable applications of the proscribed transfer pricing methods. The guidelines, as expressed in Section 482 of the U.S. Internal Revenue Code, bring market forces into the regulatory fold. It

Exterior of the Internal Revenue Service office in midtown New York. (Courtesy of Matthew G. Bisanz CC BY-SA 3.0 via Wikimedia Commons)

is clear that government revenue agents expect corporate taxpayers and tax return accountants to use an economic perspective in supporting their transfer pricing methods. This section outlines some additional economic concepts relevant to price determination by directing the reader to a complex array of market characteristics.

Though this essay attempts to simplify the economic perspective, some methods are better and more appropriate for corporate income tax estimation purposes than others. At the least, Section 482 requires tax filers to be in a position to explain the rationale for method selection and to describe the market influences on price determination. Furthermore, that position comes with the abilities to articulate the best model and to define and present it in a clear, concise, and compelling manner. To do otherwise means elevating the likelihood of receiving unwanted and/or unfavorable adjustments to tax returns and experiencing unfortunate determinations by a district director. As part of the process, the guidelines encourage tax filers to conduct economic analyses, to provide accurate documentation, and to offer reliable comparisons.

Using whatever amount of time it takes, analysts need to demonstrate reliability in commercial practices, economic principles, or statistical analyses. The guidelines also make it clear that comparability flows from extensive evaluation processes. In essence, a requirement exists for an evaluation of all factors likely to affect prices or profits in arm's length transactions. Moreover, full compliance requires familiarity with an array of economic concepts.

Demand	Supply
Consumer income	Prices of alternative outputs
Population or number of buyers	Number of sellers
Consumer tastes and preferences	Technology
Prices of related goods	Resource prices
Expected prices	Expected price

Demand Supply Consumer income Prices of alternative outputs Population or number of buyers Number of sellers Consumer tastes and preferences Technology Prices of related goods Resource prices Expected prices Expected price

Competition Type	Structure	Conduct	Performance
Perfect / High	Low concentration	Independent	Allocative efficiency
	Easy entry or exit	Price = MC	Normal profit level
	Standardized products		Low innovation level
Imperfect / Low	High concentration	Maximum profits	Allocative inefficiency
	Entry barriers		Economic profit level
	Differentiated products		High innovation level

Competition Type Structure Conduct Performance Perfect / High Low concentration Independent Allocative efficiency Easy entry or exit Price = MC Normal profit level Standardized products Low innovation level Imperfect / Low High concentration Maximum profits Allocative inefficiency Entry barriers Economic profit level Differentiated products High innovation level

Toward that end, readers of this essay will find brief descriptions of concepts that can help them demonstrate compliance and prepare documentation. From an economics perspective, market price determination involves interactions between demand and supply. More precisely, prices reflect changes in demand and/or supply. Table 1 lists the factors that influence demand and supply.

Those influences exist regardless of the ability of an individual firm or a group of firms to form and implement price determination strategies. A great deal of information will become available from the following overview of the structure, the conduct, and the performance of markets.

Market Structure

Pursuant to the structure-conduct-performance approach to market evaluation, Table 2 lists some key elements for drawing contrasts between a competitive and a noncompetitive market. Key descriptors of market structure include the number of sellers and buyers, the ease at which firms can enter or exit a market, and the level of profit. Imperfect competition produces lower quantities and higher prices than perfect competition. When those prices are higher than the break-even point, firms earn profits greater than the normal level.

Market structure reflects a firm's ability to make the price or to take the price. In microeconomic context, market structures form a continuum portraying the presence or the absence of competition in a market. The opposite ends of that continuum contain perfect competition and imperfect competition. Firms operating in noncompetitive market structures produce less and employ fewer workers than do firms operating in competitive markets. In addition, higher prices result from placement of the profit-maximizing output at a lower level of production in contrast to its placement in competitive markets. It is also important to note that average total costs are higher at lower levels of output and are greater than a competitive market level.

An economic profit occurs when prices are higher than average total cost, which typically invites new firm entry into the market. Economic profits will diminish with entries of new suppliers into the market and the resultant increases in quantity supplied. In turn, an increase in supply will propel prices downward toward the point at which an economic profit evaporates and normal profits resume. Entry into the market may be virtually impossible due to legal constraints such as licenses and patents. Economic profit is sustainable, however, when there are barriers to entry.

The amount of advertising can create differences whether real or perceived in product lines, which by definition is product differentiation. Brand name recognitions and customer loyalties present difficulties for firms contemplating entrance. Economic profit, entry barriers, and product differentiation are likely to result in a concentration of market power among a few firms. As a feature common to noncompetitive market structures, there are at least two techniques applicable to measurements of market power.

Measures of market power include the concentration ratio and the Herfindahl Index (HI). Calculating the concentration ratio for the four largest firms (the CR4) involves dividing the dollar amount of their sales by the total dollar amount of market sales. For example, the CR4 in the soft drink market could be somewhere around a 95, after multiplying the result by 100, meaning that the four largest firms account for 95 percent of product sales within a given market. For a monopolist, the CR1 would be 100 percent, which is the maximum value of a concentration ratio. Calculating the HI involves squaring the market share of each firm in the market and then adding them together; it would be the highest at 100 squared, or 10,000, in the case of a monopolist.

Concentration ratios and the HI as well as levels of profit, price, and output are especially useful in examining industry proposals for merger. A vertical merger occurs when a firm buys one or more of its suppliers; for example, a soft drink manufacturer buys an aluminum can producer. It is important to remember that firms currently engaged in transfer pricing are likely to be the result of an earlier vertical merger. A horizontal merger occurs when a firm buys a competitor; for example, a restaurant owner buys another restaurant. A conglomerate merger occurs when a firm buys a firm in a separate but related industry; for example, a soft drink manufacturer buys a fast-food restaurant.

Market Conduct

Firm conduct within a market economy reflects various strategies. In addition to those centering on price determination, there are firm strategies that involve product line content, research and development activities, and legalistic arrangements. In combination, all these strategies portray their market conduct. The most prevalent behavioral conduct of firms is in the form of their perpetual search for prices. The nature of those search processes may be interactive, collusive, or reactive at any given point in time. Additional objectives may include setting a high price, maximizing a market share, and/or earning a profit. All this involves varying degrees of cooperation including methods that resemble an informal follow-the-leader strategy or those that amount to a formal agreement to fix prices at a specific amount.

Market Performance

Market conduct and market structure jointly determine market performance, which is the last of three dimensions presented in this essay for evaluating economic markets. Evaluation of market performance may include a focus on the statistical association between profit levels and market concentration ratios. Through that examination, analysts should expect to find a strong, positive correlation between the two.

In contrast to imperfect market conditions, analysts may also find that performance in competitive markets exhibits greater amounts of production at lower average cost in concert with higher outputs, employments, and household incomes. Current and future market analysts should take note that it is possible to gather data on these consequences from external sources such as local, state, or federal government agencies and industrial trade associations.

As this section concludes, a number of factors exist that could raise suspicions about tax evasion. For example, features commonly associated with markets in which profits exceed the normal level include the presence of intangible assets such as patents and other intellectual property, barriers to entry, and non-price competition. In essence, the main challenge to the tax departments and staff of multinational corporations is to maximize profit and to minimize taxes by determining transfer prices in accordance with the appropriate methods. The next section provides a brief summary of those methods.

Tax Determination Methods: An Integration of Economic Perspectives & Accounting Practices

The appropriate methods for determining transfer prices generally involve a primary comparison between two unrelated firms and then a secondary comparison of those results with the relationship between two related firms. This is the essence of the arm's length standard usage as a guideline for determining the taxable income of firms with common ownership. Application of the standard is demonstrable under specific conditions. First, there is an expectation of comparing the income generated from the transactions of a firm having a parent (a subsidiary) with those from a firm without a parent firm. The purpose of that comparative analysis is to establish a hypothetical tax liability reference point for transactions similar in content and circumstances similar in nature given the explicit absence of parent-subsidiary relationship. Second, there is an expectation of applying several alternative methods of comparison from which a set of consistent results will emerge. In other words, the purpose is to identify the most appropriate method by minimizing the variance in tax liabilities. That emergent set will contain the best or most reliable method of transfer pricing. A description of the alternative, allowable methods appear in the next section.

On page 20 or so of the 90-page document is the definition of transactions covered by the regulations. With their origins in OECD's initiatives, the transactions governed by Section 482 of the U.S. Internal Revenue Code include sales; assignments; leases; licenses; loans; advances; contributions; transfers of interests in or rights in properties whether tangible, intangible, real, or personal or in money; and whether any of the aforementioned are documented or conducted on the behalf of another taxpayer. In brief, some contend that it covers virtually any interaction that occurs between or among individuals and/or organizations. Other methods involving financial and accounting ratios and concepts are available within the document as well, andreceive cursory treatment here for the sake of brevity. An extraction and synthesis of the basic set of five transfer pricing methods found in Section 482 are as follows:

- The comparable uncontrolled price method reveals a price that is determined by market forces. It attempts to find prices in the transactions of firms controlled by a parent firm and those without a parent firm (uncontrolled) whether the properties in exchange are tangible or intangible. In brief, it compares actual transfer prices.
- The cost plus method employs a mark-up according to normal rate of profit. The base could include actual, standard, variable, and/or marginal costs. It requires decisions regarding treatments of fixed costs and research and development costs. In brief, it compares cost mark-ups in upstream transactions, which are usually those that occur in a parent firm.
- The resale price method reveals a price in cases where there is no additional value added to the tangible product by the reseller. It attempts to draw comparisons on price between controlled and uncontrolled transactions. In brief, it compares mark-ups of price over cost in downstream transactions, which are those that usually occur in a subsidiary.
- The comparable profits method is most applicable when an agreement exists between countries. That agreement governs the applicability of domestic and/or foreign tax rules to various transactions. In special form, an advance pricing agreement establishes future prices as agreed between the taxpayer and the taxing authority, and they diminish the risk of double-taxation. In brief, it compares a variety of financial and accounting ratios.
- The profit split method, the most recent addition to the set, is applicable when services are highly integrated and difficult to separate. An expectation is that the distributions of profit will track closely with an entity's contribution to total revenues. In brief, it is most applicable in the absence of unrelated firms for use as comparables.

Elaborations of these five methods are available from a number of sources including the U.S. Internal Revenue Service and accounting service entities. A few of the big-four accounting firms hold documentation with which to learn about and monitor updates in tax laws of most countries around the globe.

CONCLUSION

In conclusion, the purpose of this essay is to introduce readers and undergraduate students to the topic of transfer pricing and to demonstrate the importance and value of integrating economics and accounting perspectives. As international trade and global commerce continue to bring developing countries into the array, job opportunities for those with a firm understanding of economics will find themselves in high demand.

BIBLIOGRAPHY

Amram, O. (n.d.). "When worlds collide: Transfer pricing tax strategies and securities laws." Retrieved from xlink:href="http://www.kentlaw.edu/perritt/courses/seminar/oren-amram-Tax%20Paper-26apr07-final.htm"

Dogan, Z., Deran, A., & Köksal, A. (2013). "Factors influencing the selection of methods and determination of transfer pricing in multinational companies: A case study of United Kingdom." *International Journal of Economics & Financial Issues* (IJEFI), 3(3), 734-742.

Dürr, O.M., & Gox, R.F. (2013). "Specific investment and negotiated transfer pricing in an international transfer pricing model." *Schmalenbach Business Review* (SBR), 65(1), 27-50.

Pearce, D.W. (Ed.). (1992). *The MIT dictionary of modern economics.* Cambridge, MA: MIT Press.

Internal Revenue Code Section 482. Retrieved xlink:href="http://www.ustransferpricing.com/26CFR%5F1%5F482%5Fcomplete.pdf"

Martini, J., Niemann, R., & Simons, D. (2012). "Transfer pricing or formula apportionment? tax-induced distortions of multinationals' investment and production decisions." *Contemporary Accounting Research,* 29(4), 1060-1086.

SUGGESTED READING

Andreoli, B., & Hryck, D. (2006). "IRS takes aim at service issues in transfer pricing." *Financial Executive,* 22(9), 47-49.

Gold, L. (2007). "International tax: Translation needed: Transfer pricing and FIN 48." *Accounting Today,* 21 (20), 1, 8.

O'Brien, J. (2007). "Transfer pricing." *International Tax Journal,* 33(5), 21-73.

—*Steven R. Hoagland, Ph.D.*

GLOSSARY

Absolute Advantage: Refers to a situation in which a producer recognizes more efficiency in creating a good or service than another producer in the same industry; effectively using the same amount of resources to yield a greater output.

Absolute Liability: A situation where the party responsible for an extremely dangerous situation or operation is completely liable for all resulting harm.

Absorption Costing: The practice of allocating fixed costs evenly across products.

Act of God: A situation usually considered caused by forces beyond human control, such as lightning, floods, earthquakes, etc. Also called force majeure.

Activity-Based Costing: A method of cost accounting that allocates costs based on the activities involved.

Adverse Selection: Market bias towards either the buyer or the seller depending on which party has the best information on the quality of the product.

Agglomeration: The geographic concentration of interrelated industries and economic sectors.

Aggregate Demand: The total demand for goods and services within a nation's economy.

Aggregate Supply: The sum of all goods and services produced in a nation or system.

Agribusiness: A term most frequently used today to describe the upstream and downstream industries that collectively produce, process, and distribute foodstuffs or the equipment and chemicals used towards those ends. It can also refer to a large, vertically-integrated firm engaged in multiple stages of commercial farming.

Agronomics: Once a specialized field of economics concerned with maximizing agricultural output while minimizing soil depletion. Agronomics' current focus is more oriented towards the application of scientific and technical knowledge and less on economic concerns.

Alfred D. Chandler, Jr.: Creator of the Chandlerian Business Theory and business historian.

Algorithm: A procedure or process designed to direct a computer system to execute a specific problem-solving protocol in a finite series of steps.

Allocation of Resources: Apportionment of productive assets among different uses. The issue of resource allocation arises as societies seek to balance limited resources, such as capital, labor and land, against the various and often unlimited wants of their members.

Analysis of Covariance: Determines the likelihood that similar patterns of change in two random variables are the result of some underlying correspondence.

Analysis of Variance: Quantifies the difference in data samples that can be attributed to randomness.

Antitrust Law: The body of law, primarily consisting of federal statutes, designed to promote free competition in trade and commerce by outlawing various practices that restrain the marketplace.

Antitrust Policy: Legislation and analysis that focus on the growth of market power.

APEC: The Asian-Pacific Economic Cooperation is an association of the Pacific Rim economies of Australia; Brunei; Canada; Chile; China; Hong Kong, China; Indonesia; Japan; Malaysia; Mexico; New Zealand; Papua New Guinea; Peru; the Philippines; Republic of Korea; Russia; Singapore; Taiwan (Chinese Taipei); Thailand; the United States; and Vietnam.

ASEAN: The Association of Southeast Asian Nations is a regional free- trade zone encompassing Brunei, Cambodia, Indonesia, Laos, Malaysia, Myanmar (Burma), the Philippines, Singapore, Thailand, and Vietnam.

Assets: Economic resources acquired and owned by an entity.

Asymmetrical Information: The imbalance of information between buyers and sellers in a market.

Autocorrelation: (also called serial correlation): A problem occurring over time in regression analysis when the error terms of the forecasting model are correlated.

Auto-Regression: A multiple regression technique used in forecasting in which future values of the variable are predicted from past values of the variable.

Autoregressive Integrated Moving Average (ARIMA): An integrated tool for understanding and forecasting using time series data. The ARIMA model has both an autoregressive and a moving average component. The ARIMA model is also referred to as the Box-Jenkins model.

Balance Sheet: A balance sheet is a listing of assets and liabilities that acts like a report card showing the overall health of a financial institution.

Bank-Firm Relationships: "The close and continued interaction between a firm and a bank that may provide a lender with sufficient information about, and voice in, the firm's affairs" (Peterson & Rajan, 1995).

Barriers to Entry: Legal, marketing, and scale factors that prevent or inhibit potentially rival competitors from supplying a good or service to a market.

Basel Committee on Banking Supervision: Organization committed to overseeing banking matters the world over.

Bayesian Theory: A statistical theory and method for drawing conclusions about the future occurrence of a given statistical distribution parameter by calculating from prior data on its frequency of occurrence ("Bayesian theory," 2007, p. 757).

Behavioral Economics: "The study of how real people actually make choices, which draws on insights from both psychology and economics" (Lambert, 2006, p. 50).

Berlin Wall: A great barrier that enclosed the entirety of West Berlin, closing off any access to East Germany from West Berlin. Established between 1961 and 1989, the Berlin Wall acted as a representation of the division and separation of East and West Germany following the Cold War.

Binder: A beginning agreement between an underwriter, agent or broker and a binding authority that guarantees the specified coverage until the official policy can be delivered.

Biodiversity: The variety of life forms and the ecosystems in which they live.

Biotechnology: "The use of microorganisms, such as bacteria or yeasts, or biological substances, such as enzymes, to perform specific industrial or manufacturing processes. Applications include the production of certain drugs, synthetic hormones, and bulk foodstuffs as well as the bioconversion of organic waste and the use of genetically altered bacteria in the cleanup of oil spills" (Dictionary.com, 2007).

Bona Fide Player: A player who makes choices and receives payoffs.

Bond: One of a series of notes that are sold to investors.

Branding: Working to associate a feeling or awareness to a product or service through the application and use of a name and logo; aimed at increasing a product or service's visibility.

Break-Even Costing: See Marginal Costing.

Break-Even Point: The point in a graph of cost functions at which average total cost and marginal cost curves intersect.

Bretton Woods agreement: "A 1944 agreement made in Bretton Woods, New Hampshire, which helped to establish a fixed exchange rate in terms of gold for major currencies. The International Monetary Fund was also established at this time" ("Bretton Woods agreement," 2007).

Bretton Woods System: A defunct economic system which specified that free market world currencies would be pegged to the dollar.

Budget Constraint: The consumption options available to someone with a limited income to allocate among various goods.

Business Climate: The combined factors, such as tax structure, public services, government regulations, labor force, and infrastructure, as that affect the profitability and experience of conducting business in a particular country or region of the world.

Business Cycle: A continually recurring variation in total economic activity. Such expansions or contractions of economic activity tend to occur across most sectors of the economy at the same time.

Business Ethics: Field concerned with whether or not (or to what degree) a business's activities are at odds with purely social values.

Business Process: Any of a number of linked activities that transforms an input into the organization into an output that is delivered to the customer. Business processes include management processes, operational processes (e.g., purchasing, manufacturing, marketing), and supporting processes, (accounting, human resources).

Business Process Outsourcing: The transfer of a business process to a foreign third party provider that is guided by a set of performance standards determined by the outsourcing entity.

Business Process Reengineering (BPR): A management approach that strives to improve the effectiveness and efficiency of the various processes within an organization.

Business Regulations: The use of laws or rules by a government regulatory agency to protect consumers and investors as well as provide orderly and predictable business procedures.

Business-to-Business (B2B) Applications: Applications software that supports interaction and transactions between businesses including supply chain systems, order entry and processing, and collaboration on design or fulfillment requirements.

Calculus: The branch of mathematics specializing in the calculation of the precise rate of change (the derivative) and the total amount of that change (the integral).

Cap and Trade: An improvement method used to control pollution by providing economic incentives to producers for reducing their emissions of pollutants.

Capital Budgeting: Method for choosing which long-term projects to invest in by comparing the costs with the rates of return.

Capital Costs: The costs assumed when the decision is made to invest in one project over others; is equal to the possible rate of return on the projects which were not invested in.

Capital Goods: Goods requiring an investment like machinery employed to produce other goods like farm commodities.

Capitalism: Economy which is run and determined through a free market system. An economic system in which the means of production and distribution are owned and controlled mostly by private individuals and businesses for profit, thus what is produced and the quantities of that production are determined by consumer demand and competition.

Capitalization of Earnings: The computation of the investment amount that will yield, at a desired rate of return, an amount equal to the net income of a company.

Capital Mobility: The degree to which investors may infuse or remove their money from a given system.

Capital Movements: Capital movements define the economic status and position of a nation as it relates to other countries. Capital movements are comprised of both the current account as well as the capital account.

Captive Model: The model of outsourcing that involves an overseas business operation that is directly owned by the outsourcing entity and that does not involve a third party.

Carbon Dioxide: A greenhouse gas generated naturally and by human activity such as the combustion of fossil fuels; carbon dioxide is a Greenhouse Gas.

Cash Crop: A crop grown exclusively for sale, not for direct consumption by the producer or the producer's livestock.

Cash Flow: The cash that can be generated by a business, or a particular project, over a period of time.

Casualty: Any losses or liabilities incurred in an accident (except for when covered by fire or marine insurance).

Caveat Emptor: Let the buyer beware. The legal principle that, unless the quality of a product is guaranteed in a warranty, the buyer purchases the product as it is and cannot hold another liable for any defects. Statutes and court decisions concerning product liability and implied warranties have substantially altered this rule.

Central American Free Trade Agreement (AKA DR-CAFTA): (2005) A pact among the United States, Costa Rica, the Dominican Republic, El Salvador, Guatemala, Honduras, and Nicaragua that eliminates tariffs on U.S. goods and contemplates direct foreign investment by the U.S. in each of the signatory countries.

Central Place Theory: Central place theory states that there exists an economic rationale behind the concentration of human settlement that involves a trade-off between two fundamentals: the minimum market size it takes to sell a good or service and the maximum distance consumers are prepared to travel to acquire that good or service. The wider the scope of goods sold in a given area, the higher its population density.

Central Tendency: The clustering of normally distributed data around a sample mean.

Certificate of Origin: Under the provisions of NAFTA, the certificate that a manufacturer or importer is required to obtain from a supplier that verifies the origin of a product.

Ceteris Paribus: A key assumption in economics, which translates from Latin into English meaning "all else held constant."

Chandlerian Business Theory: A business theory developed in the mid-1970s by Alfred D. Chandler, Jr. that says American economic success in the 20th Century was due to the emergence of large firms that dominated important industries and had more efficient internal structures in place than family-owned businesses.

Chandlerian Firms: Large, management-heavy companies with tiered structures which had emerged and dominated business within the United States' most important industries in the early part of the 20th century.

Channel: A route used by a business to market and distribute its products or services (e.g., wholesalers, retailers, mail order, Internet).

Chicago Board of Trade: A major U.S. futures exchange established in 1848. Early on it traded only agricultural commodities such as corn, wheat and oats but it has now grown to include non-storable agricultural commodities and non-agricultural products. In 1859 it was chartered by the state of Illinois to oversee the distribution and price of wheat.

Chief Financial Officer: Executive position responsible for a company's financial planning and recordkeeping.

Claim: A request for payment to cover a loss that falls under the purview of a predetermined insurance policy; estimated or actual amount may be demanded.

Classical Economics: School of economic thought begun during the late 18th century which stresses economic growth and freedom, laissez-faire policy and free competition; supported by the works of Adam Smith, David Ricardo and John Stuart Mill.

Clean Production: The initiatives undertaken by businesses to reduce the environmental impact of production activities.

Climate Exchange: Greenhouse Gas emissions allowance trading system.

Coase Theorem: A theorem that states that externalities are more efficiently remediated privately through bargaining among concerned parties rather than through government regulation or legal action, with the caveat that if property rights are not clearly established at the onset and transaction costs quickly mount, the chances for successful negotiations are practically nil.

Code of Federal Regulations: The Code of Federal Regulations is the organizational system for the rules published in the Federal Register.

Cold War: Specifically refers to the aggression and discord between the United States and Soviet Union following World War II; more generally refers to political and military tension that does not evolve into a war.

Collections: An alternative to letters of credit, collections refer to shipping documents which allow customers to collect payments quickly and easily.

Collective Bargaining: A process in which an employer negotiates working conditions such as wages, hours, and fringe benefits with representatives of their organized employees.

Collective Bargaining Agreement: A contract between a labor union and an employer that outlines working conditions.

Colonialism: National control over a foreign dependent.

Command-and-Control Measures: Government intervention in the marketplace to correct a negative externality via enforceable regulations and quotas.

Command Economy: An economic system where decisions about how to allocate resources are made administratively by a central planning authority.

Committee of Sponsoring Organizations (COSO): A voluntary private sector organization dedicated to improving the quality of financial reporting through business ethics, effective internal controls, and corporate governance.

Commodity Markets: Trade in basic agricultural products like wheat, corn, soybeans sugar, coffee, cattle, and pork bellies.

Common External Tariff (CET)::Common external tariffs are a simple form of economic union that implies shared customs duties, import quotas, preferences, or other barriers imposed by a customs union or common market on imports to any or all countries in the union or market.

Common Law: A legal system derived from the broad and comprehensive principles encompassed within the unwritten laws of England that have been adopted by the United States, although with some exceptions in the State of Louisiana. The principles are created and modified by judicial decision and passed on through custom, traditional usage and precedent.

Common Markets: Customs unions with provisions to liberalize movement or mobility of people, capital and other resources and eliminate non-tariff barriers to trade. Although common markets promote duty-free trade for the member nations, they impose common external tariffs on imports from countries that are not members. Common markets have unified or harmonized social, fiscal, and monetary policies.

Common Tariff: A concept being considered that would create a common tariff on similar products manufactured in the U.S., Canada and Mexico the funds from which would be used to finance the development of infrastructure in central Mexico.

Community Reinvestment Act: The 1977 law which requires depository institutions, such as federally insured banks and thrifts, to help meet the credit needs of the communities in which they operate through with safe and sound business practices and operations.

Comparative Advantage: The economic theory that proposes free trade as an enhancement of the wealth of all trading partners. Comparative advantage encourages nations to trade in what they produce most effectively and import that which they do not.

Compensatory Damages: Payment to someone who has suffered harm, such as for loss of income, expenses incurred, property destroyed or personal injury.

Competition: Rivalry, as between two individuals or entities to secure an advantage over another for customers or a share of the marketplace.

Competitive Advantage: The ability of a business to outperform its competition on a primary performance goal (e.g., profitability).

Competitive Intelligence Systems: Applications and processes designed to help provide managers with insights and understanding of industry trends and business conditions outside of their organization.

Competitiveness: The set of institutions, policies, and factors that determine the level of productivity.

Competitive Strategy: A plan of action by which a business attempts to increase its competitive advantage.

Concentration Ratio: A metric that estimates the concentration of market power among a small number of firms.

Condition: Part of an insurance policy which, in conjunction with the insuring agreements, helps define the rights and responsibilities of both the insurer and the insured in keeping with the policy.

Conglomerate Merger: Occurs when firm ownership expands across different industries and when firms buy their suppliers or competitors.

Congress: The United State government's legislature, granted the power to make laws.

Consumer Confidence Index: Economic indicator which measures the attitudes of consumers regarding the current economic environment.

Consumer Equilibrium: Occurs when the marginal utility per dollar spent for one item equals that for all other items.

Consumer Price Index (CPI): An economic indicator tracked by the U.S. Department of Labor which measures monthly changes in the prices of goods and services purchased by people. The CPI can be a measure of inflation (Gilman, 2006).

Contribution Margin Costing: See Marginal Costing.

Controlled Transactions: Transactions between two or more related firms controlled through common ownership.

Convergence: The tendency of poor economies to grow more rapidly than rich economies.

Core Competency: Specialized expertise a company has in the design and manufacture of products or delivery of services that competitors cannot easily duplicate.

Corporate Social Responsibility (CSR): Corporate Social Responsibility (CSR): Idea that an organization has an obligation to its stakeholders in all of its operations; stakeholders include employees, customers, suppliers, community organizations, subsidiaries and affiliates, joint venture partners, local neighborhoods, investors, and shareholders.

Corporation: A firm that is owned by stockholders and operated by professional managers.

Corruption: The abuse of the agent-client relationship, misuse of public office, legal violations, opposition with public opinion, and acting in ways that hinder the public interest, trust, or duty.

Cost: The amount of money or other asset paid for a purchase, expense or other asset, such as inventory.

Cost-Benefit Analysis: A quantitative assessment of the total value of all of a proposed investment's inputs and outputs, including its opportunity, marginal, and financing costs and its expected, marginal, and future utility.

Cost-Based Valuation: When first proposed in 1883, the cost of raising a child from birth to age 25. Refined periodically from the 1960s onwards, the term now refers to the monetary investment made in a person's maturation and the investment subsequently made in enhancing the quality or productivity of his or her labor.

Cost Benefit: Study that weighs expected expenses versus potential positive returns.

Counter-Trade: Trade in which the exporter agrees to take good or services from the importer or the importer's country as partial or complete payment.

Countervailing Duty: A duty that protects domestic industry from imports that have been produced using government subsidies in the exporting country.

Credit Default Swaps: A credit default swap is an investment vehicle involving an agreement between two parties to take some action in the event that a specified loan is defaulted upon. The seller and buyer of the credit default swap agree in advance that, if the loan defaults, then the seller of the credit default swap will compensate the buyer. Interestingly, there is no requirement for either seller or buyer to be financially obligated by the loan. Credit default swaps were one of the questionable investment strategies used by financial institutions to over leverage themselves in the years leading up to the financial collapse of 2008.

Crop Yield: The amount of a grain produced during a growing season in a standard-sized unit of farm land.

Cross-Border Alliance: International agreements on collaboration between two or more independent companies who exploit a tangible or intangible asset.

Cross-Sectional Analysis: Examines data collected all at one time.

Cross-Sectional Data: Quantifiable observations or measurements on a wide variety of variables during one time period rather than across time periods. (Cf. time series data).

Currency: Money that is circulated and generally accepted for the exchange of goods or services within a given jurisdiction. Domestic governments typically set their own currency and penalize individuals or businesses under its authority that do not accept it. Although currency is technically only legal within a given jurisdiction, some countries informally accept the currency of another country or countries. Resources for two or more countries can also be pooled to make an international currency accepted by all parties to the agreement.

Currency Devaluation: Policy in which a currency's rate of exchange is lowered.

Currency Exchange Rate: The monetary figure at which two or more individual currencies are exchanged.

Current Population Survey: A household survey conducted monthly by the Census Bureau to provide labor force data - including information regarding employment, unemployment, and non-labor force persons - to the Bureau of Labor Statistics.

Customer Relationship Management: The process of identifying prospective customers, acquiring data concerning these prospective and current customers, building relationships with customers, and influencing their perceptions of the organization and its products or services.

Customs: Duties or taxes that are imposed by a country, sovereign state, or common union on imported goods. In some situations, duties or taxes may also be imposed on exported goods.

Customs Unions: An agreement between two or more nation states to impose a common external tariff, remove trade barriers, and reduce or eliminate customs on trade among members of the union. These unions generally place the common external tariff on imports from countries outside the group, but do not allow free movement of capital or labor among the member countries.

Damages: Financial compensation recovered in court by any entity who has incurred loss through the unlawful act of another.

Data: (*sing.* datum) In statistics, data are quantifiable observations or measurements that are used as the basis of scientific research.

Debt: The state of owing something; often refers to the ability to make a purchase today and pay tomorrow.

Decision Making: "The process of choosing between alternative courses of action. Decision making may take place at an individual or organizational level. The process may involve establishing objectives, gathering relevant information, identifying alternatives, setting criteria for the decision, and selecting the best option" ("Decision making," 2007, p. 2285).

Decision Support Systems: Applications software designed to aide managerial decision making in a specific industry or corporate environment.

Decision Theory: A branch of statistical theory concerned with quantifying the process of making choices between alternatives ("Decision theory," 2000, p. 298).

Decomposition: The process of breaking down time series data into the component factors of trends, business cycles, seasonal fluctuations, and irregular or random fluctuations.

Deductive Reasoning: A type of logical reasoning in which it is demonstrated that a conclusion must necessarily follow from a sequence of premises, the first of which is a self-evident truth or agreed-upon data point or condition. Deductive reasoning is the foundation upon which predictions are drawn from general laws or theories.

Demand: The amount of a good or service an individual consumer or group of consumers wants at a given price.

Demand Curve: A graph representing the number of items consumed at each of a number of pricing points.

Demand Schedule: The actual quantities that consumers are willing and able to purchase at various prices.

Department Stores: Larger versions of the five and dime store, offering a large selection and variety of goods at reduced prices and in one location.

Dependent Variable: An event that could be triggered by another event.

Depression: A sustained economic recession.

Deterministic Variables: Variables for which there are specific causes or determiners. These include trends, business cycles, and seasonal fluctuations.

Development Organization: An organization, either public or private, that leads the economic development and regeneration efforts in developing countries or regions of the world.

Developing Country: A country characterized by an underdeveloped industrial base, low per capita income, and widespread poverty.

Developing Region: A region or country characterized by an underdeveloped industrial base, low per capita income, and widespread poverty.

Development Agency: An organization, either public or private, that leads the economic development and regeneration efforts in developing countries or regions of the world.

Differential Theory of Rent: The value of fertile land increased disproportionately as less and less fertile land was brought under cultivation to feed a growing population.

Diffusion: The process in which an innovative idea moves across firms within and across markets.

Diminishing Returns: The notion that additional inputs of capital and labor combinations into the production process eventually reach a point at which the output per unit of input decreases.

Direct Costs: Those costs that can be directly attributable to the production of a specific product.

Direct Foreign Investment: The investment by an outsourcing company into a foreign enterprise equal to or greater than 10%. Direct foreign investment involves a company from one nation that makes some form of investment into a different nation that is not its own. In other words, it is the creation of some enterprise or business venture by a foreign institution or individual. The parent enterprise has authority over the foreign affiliate, which forms the basis of the direct foreign investment relationship that occurs between the two.

Discounted Cash Flow Analysis: Analytical tool which measures valuation; follows the capitalization approach to value.

Disequilibrium: A period in any market when supply and demand are not evenly aligned.

Distribution Theory: National income is divided into rents, wages and profits and any change in one comes at the expense of another.

Distribution of Wealth: The income enjoyed by each of a number different groups or classes in a society.

Division of Labor: Specialization and compartmentalization of the firm's workforce to achieve significant productivity gains.

Dodd-Frank Act of 2010: The full name is the Dodd-Frank Wall Street Reform and Consumer Protection Act. It was passed into law in 2010 as a response to the economic collapse of 2008. Some of its provisions include greater oversight of derivatives (complex financial instruments that can lead to unforeseeable amounts of risk), measures to protect consumers by simplifying financial agreements and creating a new agency to respond to consumer complaints, and implementing some measures to help the country prepare for future financial crises and respond more quickly when they occur.

Doha Round: The current round of negotiations by the WTO aimed at implementing the agreements originally established under GATT which call for the elimination on all tariffs among the participating countries.

Dollarism: A process in which a country formally adopts a foreign currency as it legal tender.

Domain Name: A unique, easily understood identifier for a set of addresses on the Internet.

Dominant Strategy: Economic concept whereby one strategy is beneficial to the individual regardless of the strategies of others within a relationship or system.

Dominant Strategy Equilibrium: The balance point at which two or more dominant strategies converge.

Due Process: A constitutionally determined doctrine requiring that any legal proceeding or legislation protect or respect certain rights of the persons or groups involved in the proceedings or affected by the legislation.

Dumping: The practice of selling goods below their fair market value in an effort to eliminate competition.

Durable Goods: Manufactured goods which are neither consumed nor destroyed during use and which can be used for a period of time.

Duty: 1A tax imposed on an imported good.

E-Business: E-business (i.e., electronic business) is an enterprise that operates electronically rather than through conventional means.

Ecologically Sustainable Development: The business practice of using, conserving, and enhancing the community's resources so that vital ecological processes are maintained for present and future generations.

E-Commerce: Online business transactions such as sales and information exchange. E-commerce is supported by e-business activities and applications.

Econometrics: The statistical analysis of macroeconomic data to predict future conditions and test the accuracy of theoretical models.

Economic Analysis: Study and understanding of trends, phenomena, and information that are economic in nature.

Economic Contraction: The downward phase of the business cycle.

Economic Development: Programs and strategies aimed at promoting growth in a part or whole of an economy.

Economic Disinvestment: The decision of a company not to replenish depleted capital goods in a region.

Economic Expansion: The upward phase of the business cycle.

Economic Exposure: The vulnerability of a firm's earnings to exchange rate fluctuations.

Economic Fundamentals: The ratio of non-gold foreign exchange reserves to imports, the ratio of the current account balance GDP, growth, and inflation.

Economic Growth: The quantitative change or expansion in a country's economy.

Economic Integration: The integration of commercial and financial activities among countries through the abolishment of nation-based economic institutions and activities.

Economic Model: "A simplified, small-scale version of some aspect of the economy expressed in equations, graphs or words" (Baumol & Blinder, p.13).

Economic Policy: Legislation and/or regulation designed to develop or redevelop growth within a certain geographic or industrial area.

Economic Problem: Occurs as a result of unlimited wants and scarce resources; forms basis for studying economics.

Economic Problems: Factors that hinder the functioning and growth of an economy.

Economic Profit: Realized when market price exceeds average total cost; invites rival firm entry into a market in the absence of barriers.

Economics: The study of how people choose to limited use resources which can include land, labor, money, equipment, taxes and investments ("What is economics," n.d.).

Economic System: The distinctive way in which a society parcels out scare resources among its members.

Economic Underdevelopment: A historical process that creates poverty often with lack of access to adequate health care, food, education and housing.

Economic Unions: A type of common market that permits the free movement of capital, labor, goods, and services. Economic unions harmonize or unify their social, fiscal, and monetary policies. When economic unions also have a common currency with a concomitant central bank for all member states, they may be referred to as economic and monetary unions.

Educational-Stock: The amount of formal education a company's employees or a nation's citizens have.

Efficiency: The production of the desired effects or results with minimum waste of time, effort or skill.

Elastic: When percentage change in supply or demand quantity is greater than percentage change in price or income.

Elasticity: The degree to which one variable changes when another related variable is increased or decreased. Both supply and demand can be said to be either elastic or inelastic. When they are elastic, supply and demand are sensitive to changes in costs or price; when they are inelastic, they are not.

Elasticity of Demand: The degree to which a change in price alters a product's sales.

Emerging Market Economy: A system (or collection thereof) that is less than fully developed but contains the qualities that are enticing to international investors.

Emerging Markets: Emerging markets are defined as a foreign financial market that is adapting to the emerging capitalism by initiating its own form of stock market. They are analogous to smaller growth companies, which involve high gains and high risks.

Emissions Controls: Technologies employed to reduce emissions pollution.

Empirical: Based on data obtained in the field, not in theory.

Endogenous Growth Theory: Endogenous growth theory contends that features particular to an area or region above and beyond its natural resources contribute directly to its economic development.

Entrepreneurial Pricing: Viewed as the "Cinderella" approach because the strategy deviates from the traditional pricing approaches and takes innovativeness, assumption of risk and pro-activeness into consideration when setting prices.

Enterprise Resource Planning Systems: Integrated suites of applications software designed control administrative, manufacturing, and logistics functions of an organization.

Enterprise Risk Management: Methods and processes used to manage those risks, possible events or circumstances that can have an influence on business enterprises. By identifying and proactively treating such potential effects, one protects the existence, the resources (human and capital), the products and services, or the customers of the enterprise as well as external effects on society, markets and environments.

Environmental Footprint: The environmental impact associated with an individual's or business's activities, products, and services.

Environmental Management: The process of managing business operations or activities in the best way to minimize the impact, or the potential to impact, on the environment.

Environmental Management Systems: An arrangement of methods and routines that allow for a company to consistently evaluate and control its environmental footprints.

Environmental Regulation: State and federal statutes that are arranged to guard the environment from harm, counteract pollution and over-foresting, protect endangered species, conserve water, create and initiate general plans, and attempt to stop various dangerous practices.

Equation of Exchange: Since total expenditures can be expressed as the product of multiplying the money stock by the velocity and separately by multiplying total output by the average aggregate price, the two calculations are equivalent. Also called the Quantity Equation.

Equilibrium: Balance at which aggregate supply and aggregate demand within an economy meet.

Ethnocentric: The act of judging other yet unfamiliar entities based on values originating from what is familiar.

Eurocurrency: A term for deposits in a bank in one country which are denominated in the currency of another country.

Eurobond: A bond denominated in the currency of a particular nation, but is not sold in that nation.

Exchange Currency: A paper currency that the bearer can have converted into an equivalent amount of gold or silver and thus has intrinsic value. Also called Commodity Money.

Exchange Rate: The price of a domestic currency in terms of foreign currency.

Exchange Rate Regimes: Specific institutional structures designed to produce specific exchange rate outcomes.

Exclusion Game: — Game that provided players two alternatives. One alternative rewarded all of the players equal benefits, whereas, the other alternative only rewarded the active players.

Exogenous Growth Theory: Exogenous growth theory contends that economic growth in a particular area or region is entirely a function of outside market forces.

Exponential Equation: An equation where one or more terms is raised to a certain power. Such a term is multiplied by itself as many times as the value of the number displayed above and to the right of the term.

Export: An item produced in one country and sent to consumers in another country.

Export-Import Bank: A United States government institution designed to encourage exports by providing such financial services as working loan guarantees, export credit insurance; and, when necessary, direct loans.

Export Management Company (EMC): A business venture that manages export sales for other companies.

Export Orientation: The deliberate policy in developing countries of concentrating investments in industries that produce goods in demand in world markets as opposed to demand in domestic markets.

Export Trade Company (EMC) or International Trade Company (ITC): A company that purchases goods in one country for subsequent sale in others.

Exposure: Possibility of loss or hazard.

Expropriation: The action of the state in taking or modifying the property rights of an individual in the exercise of its sovereignty.

Extensive Economic Growth: Growth scenarios in which an increase in the GDP is absorbed by a population increase without any increase in per capita income.

Externalities: Spillovers from products and market transactions that can benefit or harm parties unrelated to or excluded from a transaction or exchange.

Factor Endowments: The total amount of resources available to a country for manufacturing; includes land, labor, capital, and entrepreneurship.

Factors of Production: In classical economics, land, labor, and physical capital are all considered necessary prerequisites for the manufacture of goods or the provision of services. Contemporary economics considers entrepreneurship and human capital to also be full-fledged factors.

Fair Trade Marketing: A philosophy that supports the marketing and sale of products at greater than fair trade prices.

Federal Government: A form of government in which a group of states recognizes the sovereignty and leadership of a central authority while retaining certain powers of government.

Federal Register: The Federal Register is the government's official daily publication which delineates all the current rules, proposed rules, notices from Federal agencies, executive orders, and other presidential documents. Proposed business regulations that become law are added to the Code of Federal Regulations (CFR).

Fiat Currency: A paper currency that's value is assigned to it by the government or central bank and is thus entirely artificial.

Financial Globalization: The linkages created from cross-border financial flows.

Firm: A business owned by stockholders and managed by professional managers.

Fiscal Policy: The expenditures by federal, state, and local governments and the taxes levied to finance these expenditures.

Five and Dime Stores: Small one-stop shops offering a wide variety of goods at lower cost.

Fixed Costs: Those costs, generally overhead costs, which are shared across production units.

Forecasting: In business, forecasting is the science of estimating or predicting future trends. Forecasts are used to support managers in making decisions about many aspects of the business including buying, selling, production, and hiring.

Forex Markets: Markets in which buyers and sellers conduct foreign exchange transactions.

Foreign Demand: The sum of consumer expenditures, investment, goods and services to be met by foreign imports.

Foreign Exchange (FX) Market: This market can be broadly defined as the decentralized network in which currency traders located across the world buy and sell the money of different nations.

Forward: A transaction in which the buyer and seller agree on a price for currency with delivery scheduled for a later date, say, two weeks after the purchase.

Franchises: Branches of a main company or business which are run and owned by individual entrepreneurs in the manner of the authorization granted to someone to sell or distribute a company's goods or services in a certain area.

Free Market: Economic system concept wherein industrial mechanisms operate with little to no government intercession.

Free-Market Economy: An economic system where supply and demand alone decide how resources are allocated.

Free Trade: The exchange of goods and services between countries or sovereign states without high tariffs, non-tariff barriers (e.g., quotas), or other onerous requirements or processes. Free trade does not apply to capital or labor.

Free-Trade Agreement: An agreement that states that goods and services can be bought and sold between countries or sub-national regions without tariffs, quotas, or other restrictions being applied.

Freight Forwarder: A company or individual who assists an exporter-importer in the movement of cargo from one location to another. Freight Forwarders can assist with such things as documentation and the selection of a carrier.

Frictional Unemployment: A type of unemployment temporary in nature where workers are searching for a new job, undergoing training, etc.

Full Costing: See Absorption Costing.

Full Employment: The point in a national economy when every available worker, both skilled and unskilled, earns a steady wage from the most productive work they're capable of. What residual unemployment that does exist is entirely frictional in nature.

Functional Strategies: "Functional strategies take the form of marketing, manufacturing, and logistics strategies" which when implemented in a coordinated manner result in the achievement of the grand strategy (Novack, Dunn & Young, 1993).

Future: The sale and purchase of some item at a specific price today for delivery at some point in the future, even though at that time the actual market of the commodity may have risen or fallen.

Future Value: The value that a payment today will have at a specified date in the future.

Game Theory: The branch of mathematics concerned with deciding upon a strategy that maximizes an individual's gain once the strategies of all other participants is known.

GATT: The General Agreement on Tariffs and Trade; the basic agreements of the WTO. The General Agreement on Tariffs and Trade is the legally binding instrument governing worldwide free trade. GATT is amended and expanded periodically through negotiations among about seventy countries.

General Agreement on Tariffs and Trade ("GATT"): The agreement entered into in 1947 that established international trade policy among the signatory nations in an effort to ensure economic security after WWII.

General Equilibrium: The notion that all economic activity is interrelated and any change in one market has a knock-on effect in every other market.

General Theory of Employment, Interest and Money: The 20th century work by Keynes that pioneered the ideas and techniques of macroeconomic analysis by its study of aggregate demand.

Genetically Modified Organisms (GMOs): Organisms which have been altered through a process of gene structure manipulation; results in desired outcomes or traits.

Global Economy: A model economy characterized by growth of nations, both in populations and in output and consumption per capita, interdependence of nations, and international management efforts.

Globalization: A process of economic and cultural integration around the world caused by changes in technology, commerce, and politics. The increasingly free flow of ideas, people, goods, services, and capital that leads to the integration of economies and societies.

Global Marketing: International efforts undertaken by corporations, mostly in the form of licensing, franchises and joint ventures, to expand their product and service offerings overseas.

Global Outsourcing: The delivery of services and other functions that can be performed by a firm in another country. Outsourcing involves shared management and control; a cooperation between divisions of a company that are located in different countries.

Global Strategy: Methods, approaches, and objectives developed by a business to increase competitive advantage in the market by increasing competitive scope worldwide.

Global Warming: Refers to increasing temperatures of ocean water and air nearest the surface of the earth.

Gold Standard: The practice by which currencies were converted into gold at fixed prices per ounce.

Government Regulations: Statutes established by federal departments or agencies that are enforceable by law.

Grand Strategy: The grand strategy, or master strategy, is a result of an analysis of the environment in which the company operates. The grand strategy "is the mechanism by which the separate entities within the firm develop their strategies and operational plans" and determine their resources requirements (Novack, Dunn & Young, 1993).

Grants-in-Aid: The federal funds appropriated by Congress for distribution to state and local governments to implement and support public policy initiatives.

Green House Gases: Atmospheric gases (natural or produced by humans) that contribute to the Greenhouse Effect.

Green House Effect: The natural process by which the sun's heat is captured in the atmosphere closest to the earth, thus maintaining the temperature of the earth's surface. The gases that capture and retain the heat, (greenhouse gases) include naturally occurring gases as well as manufacturing byproducts such as carbon dioxide, methane, and nitrous oxide.

Gross Domestic Product (GDP): The total market value of all final goods and services produced within the borders of a country during a given period of time. The gross domestic product includes the total consumer, investment, and government spending in addition to the value of exports minus the value of imports.

Growth Cycles: Repeated fluctuations in the growth rate of collective activity in relation to the long-run growth rate trend.

Guiding Principles: An established set of rules published and enforced by prominent property and liability trade associations for addressing complicated losses covered by several insurers, especially regarding the way in which losses should be divided under different circumstances.

Harrod-Domar Growth Model: A theory that emphasizes the primacy of savings as a source of investment funds and the importance of output achieved from a given level of investment.

Heckscher-Ohlin theory: Contends that competitive advantage in international trade can be attributed to differences in the resources countries are endowed with.

Hedge Funds: A hedge fund is a type of financial investment that was originally designed to help investors protect against, or "hedge" against, risk. Hedge funds are essentially large conglomerations of other investments—sometimes large numbers of very diverse investments. The first hedge funds mitigated risk by including instruments that took both long and short positions on the same investment. The long position functions like a bet that the stock price will go up, while the short position functions like a bet that it will fall. Risk is hedged because no matter what the stock price does, the investor receives some financial return. The financial crisis of 2008 was largely related to the widespread failure of subprime mortgages (mortgages made to borrowers unlikely to be able to afford the payments), and there was considerable controversy about the practice of many mortgage lenders authorizing loans and then using hedge fund investments to basically bet against those loans being paid off.

Herfindahl Index: Results when multiplying by 100 the total sum of the market shares held by individual firms in a market; at a maximum of 10,000 in the case of monopolist.

Heuristics: A method for problem solving or decision making that arrives at solutions through exploratory means such as experimentation, trial and error, or evaluation ("Heuristics," 2007, p. 3609).

Hicksian Income: The maximum amount of money that can be spent without taking away from preexisting capital.

High-Performing Organization: Businesses that consistently out-perform their competitors.

Hold Harmless Agreement: Contract provision where a party with potential legal liability for damages payable in the occasion of a future loss is protected by another party to the contract which assumes that liability.

Horizontal Merger: Occurs when firms buy their competitors.

Human Capital: The economic value of a worker's cumulative training and experience, both of which can be broadened and deepened through an additional investment of time and money, further increasing the worker's value.

Human Capital Theory: Firms materially benefit from having a knowledgeable, skilled workforce and should therefore invest in its education and training just as individuals do.

Human Resources: A business support function tasked with finding, screening, hiring and training employees and administering their benefits.

Hyperlinks: Text or symbols on a website that allow the user to automatically link to another page or document. Hyperlinks are usually identified by being different from regular, unlinked text by being in a different color font or underlined.

Hypothesis: An uncertain proposal made to explain certain observations or facts that require further investigation in order to be verified.

Illusion of Validity: "A complete lack of connection between the statistical information and the compelling experience of insight" (Kahneman, 2002).

Imperfect Competition: Exists when large firms rely on discount pricing or smaller production runs to maintain their current revenue levels, undermining the marketplace's efficient allocation of resources.

Imperialism: Practice of furthering a nation's reach by acquiring new territories or exerting political strength over other nations.

Import: An item produced in one country and received by consumers in another country.

Import Substitution: The deliberate policy of erecting high tariffs and other restrictions on imports for the express purpose of stimulating their domestic production.

Income-Based Valuation: A person's human capital is equivalent to The net present value of his/her anticipated lifetime's earnings minus his/ her living expenses originally formulated in 1853.

Income Effect: The influence that a change in income will have on consumption decisions.

Independent Variable: An event that could trigger another event.

Indirect Costs: Those costs that are not directly related to production.

Inductive Reasoning: A type of logical reasoning in which inferences and general principles are drawn from specific observations or cases. Inductive reasoning is a foundation of the scientific method and enables the development of testable hypotheses from particular facts and observations.

Industrial Districts: Business areas containing similar industries with a variety of specialties, similar to today's Silicon Valley in California and Manhattan's Financial, Fashion, and Art districts.

Inelastic: When percentage change in supply or demand quantity is less than percentage change in price or income.

Inferential Statistics: A subset of mathematical statistics used in the analysis and interpretation of data. Inferential statistics are used to make inferences such as drawing conclusions about a population from a sample and in decision making.

Inflation: A sustained rise in prices caused by the amount of cash in circulation being greater than the intrinsic value of goods and services available for purchase.

Information Flow: Refers to the way in which data is collected, processed and reported throughout an organization.

Information System: A system that facilitates the flow of information and data between people or departments.

Information Technology: The use of computers, communications networks, and knowledge in the creation, storage, and dispersal of data and information. Information technology comprises a wide range of items and abilities for use in the creation, storage, and distribution of information.

Information Technology Outsourcing: The transfer of the preparation of some or all of the IT systems to a foreign service provider.

Innovation: The use of a new product, service, or method in business practice immediately subsequent to its discovery.

Insurance: Contractual relationship that exists when one party agrees to reimburse another for loss caused by certain events, activities or contingencies in exchange for payment.

Integrated Supply Chain: A supply chain in which the component organizations are coordinated and integrated into an efficient system with the dual purposes of meeting customer demands and improving the competitiveness of the supply chain as a whole.

Intellectual Property: A product of the intellect that has commercial value, including copyrighted property such as literary or artistic works, and ideational property, such as patents, appellations of origin, business methods, and industrial processes.

Intellectual Property Rights: Refers to right of a creator to prevent another from using a creation and the right to negotiate payment for its use.

Intensive Economic Growth: Growth scenarios in which GDP growth exceeds population growth creating a sustained rise in living standards as measured by real income per capita.

Internal Auditing: An independent and objective opinion to the accounting officer on risk management, control and governance, by measuring and evaluating their effectiveness in achieving the organizations agreed objectives.

Internal Rate of Return: The interest rate on an investment in equipment or a project that would generate income equal to the cash flow from the equipment or project.

International Aid: Grants and appropriations designed to assist a developing nation in building systems necessary for self-subsistence.

International Banking: Banking transactions crossing national boundaries.

International Banking Federation: A consortium of banking associations from Europe, the United States, Australia, and Canada charged with addressing financial service issues on a national and international level.

International Business Operations: Activities and guidelines involved in creating value for an international business's stakeholders.

International Capital Budgeting: When projects are located in host countries other than the home country of the multinational corporation.

International Counter Trade: Agreement in which one country imports goods from a country to which it exports goods.

International Development: Program whereby assistance, grants and projects are offered by an industrialized country or organization thereof to a less-developed nation.

International Financial Markets: A term which sometimes refers to the FX Market, the Eurobond Market, and the Eurocurrency Market considered as a whole.

International Markets: When the target population is in more than one country.

International Monetary Fund (IMF): An institution of over 180 nations who agreed to advocate worldwide financial cooperation as well as the wellness and endurance of the international monetary system. Every nation within the IMF donates by paying quotas, which emulate the nation's role in the global economy and decide what its voting power will be (the United States has a 17% voting stake, for example). The IMF supports worldwide economic growth by granting loans and technical assistance to countries in need. The organization was established in 1944 with the help of 45 nations who wished to avoid the issues and uproar experienced during the Great Depression.

International Political Economy: A social science and historical perspective that analyzes international relations in combination with political economy. It is about the consequences on an international level of the interaction between the state (politics) and the market (economics).

International Strategy: Introducing an international operations component to an organization's strategy in order to capitalize on market need or shortcomings in a foreign market.

International Trade: The exchange of goods and services between countries; creates a world economy in which prices, or supply and demand, affect and are affected by global events.

International Trade Theory: Theory which attempts to explain the phenomenon of international trade patterns and distributions; speaks to the benefits of free trade.

Intranet: Intranets use Internet technologies (browsers, uniform resource locators, routing, and TCP/IP protocols) to serve the internal needs and constituencies of an organization. Thus the key difference between an Intranet and Internet application is the underlying mission of the Intranet portal. The Internet is used to facilitate communications outside the organization and the Intranet is used for internal purposes.

Intuitive Prediction: "A willingness to make extreme predictions about future performance on the basis of a small sample of behavior" (Kahneman, 2002).

Invention: The development of a creative new idea or concept that could lead to a new products or processes in the market.

Irrational: "Not endowed with reason or understanding; lacking usual or normal mental clarity or coherence; not governed by or according to reason" ("Irrational," 2000, p. 618).

Irreversibility: The idea that there is an upper limit to the amount of greenhouse gases the atmosphere can absorb, beyond which catastrophic global warming is inevitable.

Job Openings and Labor Turnover Survey: A U.S. Bureau of Labor Statistics survey that measures labor demand and provides analysis of the U.S. labor market showing how changes in labor supply and demand affect the economy as a whole.

Joint Ventures: A partnership or conglomerate, formed often to share risk or expertise.

Judgment: "The process of forming an opinion or evaluation by discerning and comparing; the capacity for judging" ("Judgment," 2000, p. 632).

Judgment by Adjustment & Anchoring: Adjustment involves estimating using a base number that is then altered to garner the final value. Anchoring refers to the phenomenon that "different starting points will yield different estimates that are biased toward the initial values" (Tversky & Kahneman, 1974, p. 1128).

Judgment by Availability: An assessment of "the frequency of a class or the probability of an event by the ease with which instances or occurrences can be recalled" (Tversky & Kahneman, 1974, p. 1127).

Judgment by Representativeness: A determination of "the probability that object A belongs to class B, or that event A originates from process B, or that the probability that process B will generate event A" (Tversky & Kahneman, 1974, p. 1124).

Judgment under Uncertainty: The assessing of probabilities and the predicting of values (Tversky & Kahneman, 1974, p. 1124). Tversky & Kahneman identified three heuristics that individuals employ in order to predict values in judgments under uncertainty: Judgment by representativeness, judgment by availability, and judgment by adjustment & anchoring (1974, p. 1124, 1127, 1128).

Just-in-Time Manufacturing (JIT): A manufacturing philosophy that strives to eliminate waste and continually improve productivity. The primary characteristics of JIT include having the required inventory only when it is needed for manufacturing and reducing lead times and set up times. Also called "lean manufacturing."

Kaldor-Hicks Compensation Principle: A transfer mechanism intended to maximize overall utility wherein those who gain directly from a change in the economy reimburse those who suffer.

Keynesian Strategy: Policymaking that entails government actively pursuing legislation and/or regulation that promotes economic development via focus on demand-side sectors.

Labor: The sum of all human physical and mental effort that is used to produce goods or services. Although labor includes the application of knowledge to produce goods or services, it does not apply to the knowledge itself.

Labor Agreement: An agreement between an employer and a union that governs working conditions, wages, benefits, and grievances.

Labor Demand: The aggregate need for labor in a given region.

Labor Dispute: A controversy between an employer and his or her employees concerning the terms and conditions of employment, or concerning the association or representation of those who negotiate or seek to negotiate the terms or conditions of employment.

Labor Economists: Economists who study the relationship of labor markets to the economy at large.

Labor Force: All persons classified as employed or unemployed in the civilian, non-institutional population 16 years old and over.

Labor-Management Relations: The broad spectrum of activities concerning the relationship between employers and employees, both union and nonunion.

Labor Relations: Discussions surrounding the issues of work stoppages, strikes, and negotiations for salaries and benefit packages.

Labor Supply: The number of workers available in the local or national work force.

Labor Theory of Value: The wages of workers producing an item constituted its price.

Laissez-Faire: The doctrine that governments should not interfere with the workings of the marketplace.

Land Tenancy: An economic arrangement where sharecroppers cultivate some one else's farm land, compensating the landowner with either a portion of the actual harvest or a percentage of the revenue earned by the sale of a cash crop. For their part, land owners typically provide tools, fertilizer and living stipends to support sharecroppers during the lean months of the growing season.

Latency: The measureable delay or gap in a computer system between the time of data input and desired result going effective.

Lausanne Theory: — A theory that values individual planning as well as connecting individual plans so that they are interrelated.

Law of Demand: Specifies the inverse or negative relationship that exists between an item's demand quantity and its price; quantity and price move in opposite directions.

Law of Diminishing Marginal Utility: Key principle suggesting that total utility or satisfaction increases at decreasing rate as more units are consumed.

Law of Diminishing Returns: Once a certain threshold is reached, the more one variable factor of production like labor is increased, the less additional output it contributes.

Law of Supply: Specifies the direct or positive relationship that exists between an item's demand quantity and its price; quantity and price move in same direction.

Lean Manufacturing: A set of tools and techniques used to eliminate all waste from production processes.

Lease: A written agreement relative to rent of facilities such as buildings and equipment. It obligates the owner (lessor) of the facilities to rent them to the user of the facilities (lessee) over a period of time for a specified rent.

Lessee: One who rents facilities from the owner of the facilities.

Lessor: One who owns facilities that he or she rents to a lessee.

Letter of Credit or Documentary Credit: a letter issued by a bank or other financial institution guaranteeing that a payment made that bank or institution's client will, in fact, be made. If the client can't make the payment, the institution provides the necessary fund and then charges the client. LOCs are used extensively in international trade.

Liability: A legally enforceable obligation, or a debt to pay an assessed amount.

Liberalism: The philosophy of international political economy that emphasizes the role of markets in maximizing aggregate social welfare. Liberalists argue that market surpluses do not exist over time and that attempts to achieve them interfere with efficient production and consumption, stifling welfare.

Liberalization: A process in which an economic system is made open and as free as possible from government intervention or involvement.

Libertarian Paternalism: Programs that provide guidance in a way that allows individuals to make the best choices without limiting them. This is a term invented by Richard Thaler and Cass Sundstein to describe a suggested consumer financial literacy technique by financial institutions (Thaler & Sundstein, 2008).

Limits-to-Growth Model: A model that states that finite supplies of natural resources and energy will eventually make continuously expanding productive capacity and consumption for consumption's sake economically untenable.

Linear Programming: A mathematical technique used to find the maximum and minimum value of a function bounded by constraints.

Linear Regression: A statistical technique used to develop a mathematical model for use in predicting one variable from the knowledge of another variable.

Liquidity: The degree at which a stock can be bought or sold in the market without negatively impacting the stock's value, a measure of the environment of trading and the confidence of investors in the viability of the market.

Loan: A transfer of an asset from a person or entity to another person or entity with the expectation it will be repaid.

Location theory: Location theory states that the longer the distance between buyer and seller, the high the transaction cost of bringing a good or service to market; as such, economic activity tends to cluster in high density areas.

Logistics: In business, logistics is the way companies plan, execute, and control the flow and storage of goods, services, and information in an effective way as to ensure customer satisfaction.

Long Distance Exchanges: Business transactions occurring by boat or post, over time, and usually involving a third-party agent.

Loss: An outgo of expenses or costs without offsetting revenue.

Macroeconomics: The study of aggregate or total behavior in an economy such as within a nation or between countries (Heijman, 2001). It is a subset of the field of economics and looks at behaviors in the national or regional economy. Macroeconomics looks at large scale indicators like the unemployment rate and tries to find relationships between these indicators ("What is macroeconomics," 2009).

Macro-Economy: An economic system that includes supply and demand elements.

Managed Care: A type of health care management where a third-party, a health maintenance organization, for example, acts as an intermediary between a health care provider and a patient for the purpose of controlling access and payment for health care.

Managed Competition: An approach to health care management where independent companies, HMOs, and medical insurance companies, for example, compete for patients in an environment of universal coverage and limited market intervention by the federal government.

Marginal Analysis: The impact one additional unit of input is found to have on output as it applies to revenues, costs and utility.

Marginal Cost: The additional cost of one more unit of output.

Marginal Costing: A method of cost accounting and planning that determines a production unit's

contribution margin and level of production needed to cover fixed costs and a defined profit margin.

Marginal Efficiency of Capital: A measure of the additional output generated from an additional unit of a physical resource such as equipment, machinery, tools, and buildings; taken as an assessment of the productivity of capital.

Marginal Cost: The contribution to total cost from the production of one additional item.

Marginal Resource Cost of Labor: The extra costs associated with hiring one more worker.

Marginal Revenue: The added revenue earned from marketing one more unit of output.

Marginal Physical Product of Labor: The additional output achieved by hiring one more worker.

Marginal Productivity of Capital: The increase in the value of the firm's output when one more unit of capital services is employed.

Marginal Utility: The additional satisfaction an individual receives from the consumption of one additional amount of an item.

Market: A virtual space where consumers and producers interact while exchanging a specific item in accordance with their demand and supply schedules.

Market-Based Instruments: Subsidies, tradable permits, tax breaks, and other incentives to encourage private-sector solutions to negative externalities.

Market Conduct: The behavior of firms in setting prices and pursuing non-price competition.

Market Economy: A market in which the prices of items, products, and services are agreed upon by both sellers and buyers.

Market Equilibrium: The price and quantity associated with the intersection of the demand and supply curve reflecting alignments among consumers and producers on an item's price and quantity.

Market Failure: The result of information being imperfect or unavailable for consumer and producer decisions, of an individual or group holding and bringing a disproportionate amount of influence into a market transaction, or of an imposition of costs or harm on third parties and those outside the exchange or transaction.

Market Opportunity: The future growth capacity of a country as an outsource market and its ability to readily deliver quality products to the market.

Market Performance: Measured in terms of allocation efficiency.

Markets: A social arrangement that allows buyers and sellers to discover information and carry out a voluntary exchange of goods and services.

Market Share: The proportion of total sales of a given type of product or service that are earned by a particular business or organization.

Market Structure: The degree of competition that exists among firms within a market.

Market volatility: The fluctuations in market activity caused by internal and external forces.

Marxism: A major school of thought that views international relations as a struggle between rich and poor classes rather than as a contest between national governments and national states.

Mathematical Statistics: An offshoot of mathematics concerned with the analysis and interpretation of data. Mathematical statistics provides the theoretical underpinnings for various applied statistical disciplines, including business statistics, in which data are analyzed to find answers to quantifiable questions.

Measures of Central Tendency: Descriptive statistics that are used to estimate the midpoint of a distribution. Measures of central tendency include the median (the number in the middle of the distribution), the mode (the number occurring most often in the distribution), and the mean (a mathematically derived measure in which the sum of all data in the distribution divided by the number of data points in the distribution).

Measures of Variability: Descriptive statistics that summarize how widely dispersed the data are over the distribution. The range is this difference between the highest and lowest scores. The standard deviation is a mathematically derived index of the degree to which scores differ from the mean of the distribution.

Medical Economics: A subfield of economics that examines production and markets in health and medicine.

Medical Insurance: Insurance that is purchased to be used in the event of illness, injury, or disease.

Mercantilism: The philosophy of international political economy that emphasizes the role of state power in obtaining advantageous trading arrangements for states. It presumes that states should aggressively seek to maximize exports and to minimize imports.

Mercantilist Theory: Protectionist view which purports that a country should focus on enabling a high number of exports while discouraging imports through tariffs.

Mercosur: Mercosur (Mercado Común del Sur) is the common market of Southern Latin America. It is an intergovernmental agreement aimed at reducing and eliminating trade barriers between Argentina, Brazil, Paraguay, Uruguay, and Venezuela. Those countries that participate to a lesser extent as associates are Bolivia, Chile, Colombia, Ecuador, and Peru.

Merger: Occurs when firm ownership expands combining firms that may be competitors, suppliers, or buyers of an item within a given market or different industries.

MFN: Most Favored Nation-a benefit WTO membership that eliminates discriminatory trade practices by requiring that a trade privilege granted to one nation must also be granted to all WTO members.

Microeconomics: A division within economics for studying behaviors of firms and households as they engage themselves in the exchange of resources and goods.

Ministerial Conference: The highest decision-making body of the WTO which has to meet at least every two years. It brings together all members of the WTO and can make decisions on all matters under any of the multilateral trade agreements.

Mixed Economy: An economic system where certain industries are publicly owned and the government takes an active interest in the efficient, equitable operation of free markets.

Model: A representation of a situation, system, or subsystem. Conceptual models are mental images that describe the situation or system. Mathematical or computer models are mathematical representations of the system or situation being studied.

Modeling: Research method in which trends and subjects are connected for purposes of empirical study.

Monetary Policy: The regulation of the supply of money and interest rates by the central bank (e.g., the Federal Reserve in the United States) of the country or union to control inflation and stabilize currency.

Monetary Stock: Coins, paper currency, traveler's checks and checking account deposits.

Monetary Union: A process in which a group of economies adopt a single currency and a common central bank.

Monetization: Assigning a financial value to the outcomes of inherently intangible processes.

Monopoly: A market where one and only one producer sells a good or service.

Moral Hazard: The effect of having insurance on the behavior of the insured.

Most Favored Nation: Status given to a signatory nation to GATT (and its successor, the WTO), that ensures equal treatment of all signed countries regardless of size, economic status, etc.

Moving Average: A method used in forecasting in which the average value from previous time periods is used to forecast future time periods. The average is updated in each ensuing time period by including the new values not available in the previous average and dropping out the date from the earliest time periods.

Multinational Company: A company that operates in more than one nation; frequently in the form of a parent-subsidiary relationship.

Multinational Corporations (MNC): Companies with holdings in multiple countries.

NAFTA: The North American Free Trade Agreement entered into among the U.S., Canada and Mexico that eliminated trade barriers.

Nash Equilibrium: A balance struck when two or more individuals' strategic decisions meet in such a way that the convergence of those strategies establish a common point.

Nationalization: Seizure of private, foreign-held assets by a host regime.

Nations: Large aggregations of people sharing rules of law and an identity based on common racial, linguistic, historical, or cultural heritage; rarely act unilaterally.

National Technical Commission on Biosecurity (CTNBio): The government agency overseeing the transgenics issue in Brazil.

National Treatment: WTO principle that eliminates discriminatory treatment of foreign goods, services and intellectual property by requiring that the host country treat and protect an imported product as if it were a domestic product.

Natural Monopoly: Usually occurs in industries such as the supply of electric power, natural gas, or communications.

Neoclassical Growth Model: The theory that savings, investment and all other aspects of economic activity operate most efficiently when prices rise and fall in unregulated markets.

Neoclassical Growth Theory: A growth model, also referred to as the exogenous growth model, which focuses on productivity growth.

Net Exports: The difference after subtracting import expenditures from export expenditures; if value is negative, it is a trade deficit; zero is balanced trade; and, positive is a trade surplus.

Net Present Value (NPV) Technique: Method for determining the value of an investment; accounts for the initial costs of the investment along with the present value of the expected cash flows.

New Growth Theory: A growth model, also referred to as the endogenous growth theory, which developed in the 1980s in response to criticism of the neoclassical growth theory.

Non Tariff Barriers: Any impediment to free trade other than tariffs; may include quotas, excessive paperwork requirements and undisclosed trade rules.

Normal Profit: The amount of profit considered enough for an owner to remain in business; occurs when price equals average total cost.

Normative Economics: A branch within economics that suggests what should occur to achieve a goal or objective.

Normative Law: A legal theory based upon queries into what the law should be like. It overlaps with moral and political philosophy, and includes questions of whether individuals should obey the law, on what grounds law-breakers might properly be punished and the proper uses and limits of regulation.

Norms: Rules that dictate behavior.

North American Free Trade Agreement: A trade bloc established by the United States of America, Mexico, and Canada to encourage the free exchange of goods and services between them.

N. S. B. Gras: An economic historian who taught business history at Harvard and was largely responsible for the evolution of the study until his retirement in 1950.

Null Hypothesis: The claim that the data under examination was generated randomly.

Occupation: The set of activities that an employee is paid to complete.

Occurrence: Continued or repeated exposure to conditions that results in unexpected injury during the insurance policy period.

Off Balance Sheet Securitizations (OBSS): Investment banks are subject to financial regulations and reporting requirements to make sure that their investment decisions are sound and do not expose the bank and its investors to unsustainable levels of risk. However, it has long been possible for these investment banks to conduct some of their business in ways that fall outside of the reporting requirements they must follow, so that some transactions do not legally need to be included on the bank's reports. Securitization is simply the financial practice of pooling different forms of debt; off-balance sheet securitization amounts to investment banks finding ways to avoid the inclusion of some of the debt they carry on the bank's balance sheet. This has the effect of making the bank appear to be in a much better financial position than it actually is.

Offshoring: The establishment of third party entities in developing nations for the purpose of performing functions being outsourced by businesses in developed nations.

Oligopoly: A market where a just few producers sell a good or service.

Oliver Williamson: Followed up on Chandler's Business Theory, using Ronald Coase's essay as a starting point. Introduced the theory that subjective-thus imperfect–information allows for exploitation in business transactions (1963-1964).

Operations Management: Those areas of management that are concerned with productivity, quality, and cost in the operations function (i.e., activities necessary to transform inputs such as business transactions and information into outputs such as completed transactions) as well as strategic planning for the organization.

Opportunity Cost: The cost of an alternative that must be forgone in order to pursue a certain action.

Optimum Scale of Enterprise: The size at which a firm most efficiently meets market demand.

Output: The quantity of items or services produced by a firm or group of firms in a market.

Outsourcing: The transfer by a business of ancillary jobs functions to a third party in order to lower costs and improve efficiency and to focus on core responsibilities.

Outsource Model: Model of outsourcing strategy that involves the outsourcing of functions to a third party provider.

Panel Analysis: The simultaneous application of times-series and cross-sectional analysis to a set of data.

Pareto Optimality: The allocation of resources distributed in such a way that no one person is better off or worse off given a change in that allocation.

Perfect Competition: The condition of a market in which several buyers and sellers exist but none of them can influence price, although entry and exit are easy to accomplish.

Penetration Pricing: The lowering of prices so as to increase sales and market share.

Physical Capital Stock: Physical capital stock is one example of an economic aggregate. The stock is needed in order to divide the total output among various other factors that may be involved. It is used also to evaluate the advancement of capital and the productivity of labor.

Policy Cycle: The four major stages of the policy-making process, including agenda setting, policy formulation, implementation, and evaluation.

Policy Regimes: The preparations and understanding involved in facilitating global agreements and the coordination of financial, environmental, and political affairs.

Policy Risk: The potential effects on a business resulting from change in policy or rights.

Polimetrics: Field of political science tool which studies how economic conditions affect voter behavior.

Political Economy: The interactions between political processes and economic variables such as economic policies.

Political Environment: A country's regulatory environment, local attitudes to corporate governance, reaction to international competition, and labor laws.

Political Risk: The threat that social, political or economic factors in a foreign country may affect the feasibility and profitability of an organization's global operations.

Political Risk Insurance (PRI): Insurance that protects businesses engaged in international business from loss associated with political upheaval such as regime or policy change.

Polynomial Equation: An equation where two or more terms are added, subtracted, multiplied and/or divided; commonly used in Algebraic expressions.

Population: The entire group of subjects belonging to a certain category (e.g., all women between the ages of 18 and 27; all dry cleaning businesses; all college students).

Positive Economics: A branch within economics that deals with facts and their accuracy.

Positive Law: The body of laws that have been enacted in a particular community and that are upheld by the courts of that community.

Precautionary Demand for Money: A Keynesian term used to describe income cash held in reserve to meet sudden, unexpected expenditures.

Predatory Pricing: Selling products at low prices so as to negatively affect competitors: Could be in order to get rid of them, weaken them for mergers, discipline them or prevent new competitors from entering the market.

Premium: Payment required for insurance.

Premium Pricing: Pricing that is set high so as to present an air of product exclusiveness.

Present Value: The value today of a future sum of money, either paid or received.

Price: The amount of money that is required to obtain an item.

Price Controls: Restrictions that prevent prices from rising above or falling below a specific amount.

Price Elasticity of Demand: The percent change in quantity demanded in response to a 1 percent change in price.

Price Fixing: The act of conspiring with competitors to establish prices, thus alleviating competition and preserving market share.

Price Inelasticity of Demand: The case when demand for a product remains relatively unchanged at different pricing-points.

Price Skimming: Pricing strategy that involves setting prices high initially and then incrementally lowering the price to entice a wider market; objective is to "skim" the market for profits, layer by layer.

Price Supports: Government subsidies paid to farmers when the market price of a commodity falls below an economically tenable threshold.

Pricing: One of the four elements of the marketing mix; refers to the cost of a product exchange.

Pricing Strategies: Creating a plan for pricing structure so as to reflect consumer wants, product characteristics and competition in a way that generates the most profit.

Prisoner's Dilemma: Analytical game whereby two subjects are left to decide their best strategy without knowing their respective counterpart's plan.

Private Sector: All enterprises that are outside of government control, including micro, small, medium, and large enterprises.

Private Sector Development (PSD): Strategy for promoting economic development by private industries that benefits the poor in developing countries and regions of the world.

Privatization: The transfer of ownership or responsibility from the government (public) sector to the business (private) sector.

Producers: Firms that supply or provide goods or services desired by consumers.

Production Function: An expression of the relationship between outputs and costs.

Production Possibilities Frontier: A model portraying all combinations an entire country can produce while holding constant the state of technology, the amount of resources, and the productivity of workers.

Product: Goods and services that are manufactured and ultimately traded among countries.

Productive Capacity: The total goods and services generated through economic activity.

Productivity: A measure of economic efficiency regarding the effectiveness of economic outputs from economic inputs.

Profit Maximization: The price at which a seller earns the most revenue at the least cost. It occurs when marginal costs exactly equal marginal revenues.

Prospect Theory: "A branch of decision theory which attempts to explain why individuals make decisions that deviate from rational decision making by examining how the expected outcomes of alternative choices are perceived" ("Prospect theory," 2007, p. 6032).

Protectionist: A foreign trade policy that protects national industry with tariffs and other barriers to trade.

Public-Private Partnership (PPP): A collaboration between private and public sectors in which financial and administrative resources are pooled to achieve shared goals and objectives.

Public Choice: The situation in which the public and their elected representatives must decide which values and facts to prioritize and use when solving a public problem.

Public Good: An event, item, or location that is indivisible, jointly consumable, and non-exclusive in nature.

Public-Interest Theory of Regulation: The perspective that government intervention maintains competition, promotes industrial stability, and protects consumers from abuses by firms holding market power.

Public Policy: The basic policies that provide the foundation for public laws.

Public Problems: Undesirable conditions that impinge on a society.

Public Problem-Solving: The approaches and strategies that citizens and their elected representatives undertake to solve or alleviate public problems.

Public Sector: The economic and administrative enterprises of a local, regional, or national government.

Punitive Damages: Damages that are not awarded to compensate the plaintiff, but to reform or deter the defendant and similar persons from pursuing a course of action such as that which damaged the plaintiff.

Purchase: Acquisition of goods or services, either for business use or for resale to customers. A purchase occurs when title to goods is passed or services are rendered.

Purchasing Power: The amount of goods and services that can be bought using a given currency. Because currencies' values frequently change relative to each other, a consumer may be able to purchase more per unit value in one currency than another. Problems arise when imports must be paid for in a strong foreign currency with a weak domestic one because the unfavorable exchange rate makes these imports more expensive.

Psychology: "The science of mind and behavior; the mental or behavioral characteristics of an individual or group; the study of mind and behavior in relation to a particular field of knowledge or activity" ("Psychology," 2000, p. 940).

Quantitative Analysis: An analysis technique used in finance, business and research to assess and understand process behavior with the use of mathematical and statistical modeling. It is a mathematical means of assessing the reality of a current system or process.

Quantity Demanded: The amount of goods or services that consumers desire at given prices.

Quantity Theory: In its most basic formulation, the theory asserts that prices will rise in direct proportion to an increase in the money stock.

Quantity Supplied: The amount of goods or services that suppliers are willing and able to produce at given prices.

Quota: A limit imposed by governmental action on the quantity of an item imported into a country.

Quants: Nickname for computer software designers with mathematical expertise able to perform quantitative analysis on data.

Rate of Substitution: The minimum rate where an agent will be willing to exchange units of one product for units of another.

Rates of Return: Comparison of the money gained or lost on an investment with the amount of money invested.

Rational Choice Theory: "Attempts to explain all conforming and deviant social phenomenon in terms of how self-interested individuals make choices under the influence of their preferences. It treats social exchange as similar to economic exchange — where all parties try to maximize their advantage or gain, and to minimize their disadvantage or loss. It's basic premises are that human beings base their behavior on rational calculations, they act with rationality when making choices, their choices are aimed at optimization of their pleasure or profit" ("Rational choice theory," 2009).

Real vs. Nominal Value of Money: The real purchasing power of a currency versus its face value.

Recession: Period of decline in economic activity.

Redistribution of Income: The transfer of income through government taxation, spending and assistance programs targeted at particular income groups, and programs designed to provide training to workers or to encourage private investments in education or other kinds of human capital. The goal is to transfer money from higher-income groups to lower-income groups.

Regional Development: A strategy for promoting economic growth and development in discrete geographic regions.

Regression Analysis: A family of statistical techniques used to develop a mathematical model for use in predicting one variable from the knowledge of another variable.

Regulation Fair Disclosure: A regulation which required publicly traded companies to disclose material information to all investors at the same time.

Reinsurance: Insurance involving two insurers: the reinsurer and the ceding insurer. The reinsurer agrees to assume part or all of the liability owned by the ceding insurer to reduce the ceding insurer's vulnerability to risk.

Reservation Wage: The lowest possible real wage that makes workers indifferent between consumption and leisure.

Rentier Income: Earnings from assets as opposed to labor.

Rent-Seeking Behavior: The penchant for individuals and firms to secure largely unearned income by obtaining favorable treatment or concessions from government officials.

Resource-Based View of the Theory of the Firm: States that the critical core competencies that give a firm a competitive advantage must be developed internally and remain exclusive to the firm.

Return on Marketing Investment (ROMI): Represents the ratio of money gained or lost on a marketing investment relative to the amount of money invested.

Revenue: The proceeds from the sale of an item; the mathematical product of the quantity of the item sold times the price of the item.

Risk: The quantifiable probability that a financial investment's actual return will be lower than expected. Higher risks mean both a greater probability of loss and a possibility of greater return on investment.

Risk Adjusted Discount Rate: Sum of an investment's risk premium (the risk characteristics of the investment) along with the risk-free rate (generally the return on short-term U.S. Treasury securities).

Risk Assessment: A report that shows assets, vulnerabilities, likelihood of damage, estimates of the costs of recovery, summaries of possible defensive measures and their costs and estimated probable savings from better protection.

Risk Management: A management discipline whose goal is to protect an organization from financial loss.

Return to Scale: A return to scale is the degree to which a change in input results in a proportionately higher, lower, or the same change in output.

Robinson Crusoe Economy: A type of economy focusing on how the economic well being a single person is influenced by a single will.

Ronald Coase: Won the 1991 Nobel Prize in Economics and wrote an influential piece on economic theory that was later used to enhance the Chandlerian Business Theory.

Rowstow's Stages of Growth: The theory that economic growth progresses through five distinct phases: traditional, transitional, take-off, drive to maturity, and high mass consumption.

Rulemaking: The process by which federal departments and agencies establish, change, or revoke a regulation.

Rules of Origination: Provisions established under NAFTA that require the verification by a supplier that a good or service contains products exclusively from the providing country or one of the trading partners.

Rules of Production: Two rules determine the economic viability of a firm: first, a profit-maximizing output level occurs marginal revenue is equal to marginal cost; second, price for output must be equal to or greater than average variable cost.

Sample: A subset of a population. A random sample is a sample that is chosen at random from the larger population with the assumption that such samples tend to reflect the characteristics of the larger population.

Sarbanes-Oxley Act: A law, enacted in 2002, which introduced highly significant legislative changes to financial practice and corporate governance regulations.

Scarcity: Resources including time, money, effort, and so forth are limited and subject to depletion or extinction.

Scarcity of Resources: The perpetual state of man where there is a finite amount of resources available.

Scientific Method: A cornerstone of the social sciences in which a systematic approach is used to understand some aspect of individual or group behavior. The scientific method is based on controlled and systematic data collection, interpretation, and verification in a search for reproducible results. In organizational behavior theory, the goal is to be able to apply these results to real-world applications.

Search Engine: Application software within an Internet browser that is used to scan for a keyword or phrase.

Seasonal Fluctuation: Changes in economic activity that occur in a fairly regular annual pattern. Seasonal fluctuations may be related to seasons of the year, the calendar, or holidays.

Sector Analysis: Methodology in which elements of a macro-economy are separated and studied individually.

Securities and Exchange Commission (SEC): A United States government agency having primary responsibility for enforcing the federal securities laws and regulating the securities industry/stock market.

Securities Regulation: The field of the U.S. law that covers various aspects of transactions and other dealings with securities.

Self Regulatory Organizations: An independent organization that oversees a network of broker-dealer transactions.

Shift-Share Analysis: Shift-share analysis examines the effects on local employment rates attributable to changes in national, industry-mix, and regional factors.

Shut-Down Point: The point in a graph of cost functions at which average variable cost and marginal cost curves intersect.

Signaling Mechanism: The means by which suppliers gauge demand.

Six Sigma (6s): An approach to improving quality. The term "six sigma" is a statistical term referring to the degree to which a product reaches its quality goal. At six sigma, a product is reaching its quality goal 99.9999997 percent of the time, or has only 3.4 defects per million. The six sigma system was originally developed by Motorola.

Small and Medium-Sized Enterprise (SME): The term most often used by development agencies and governments to describe a small business, whether formal or informal.

Social Exchange Economy: A theory that suggests that human behavior is rewards received as a result of what is important to the players.

Social Indicators: A social statistic that has significance for the quality of life in a society.

Social Policy: Policy, enacted through social welfare programs and serving as a social safety net, that regulates and governs human behavior in areas such as general morality and quality of life.

Social Reports: An organized collection of social indicators.

Social Responsibility: Belief that every part of a society, whether a corporation, organization, government or individual, has some obligation to that society. This could refer to the responsibility to act (positive responsibility) or the responsibility to avoid action (negative responsibility).

Social Welfare: The relationship and responsibilities of governments to their members.

Social Welfare Provision: Government program that provides a minimum level of income, service, or other support for disadvantaged groups such as the poor, elderly, disabled, and students.

Social Risk: Pressures put on businesses by environmental or other pressure groups.

Sovereign: The idea that each nation has supreme and ultimate authority over affairs and individuals within its borders and does not have to answer to any higher authority.

Specie: Metallic coins. For much of our recorded economic history, said coins contained a small, fixed amount of silver that had intrinsic worth.

Speculative Demand for Money: A Keynesian term used to describe income put into time-deposit accounts and other financial instruments for the express purpose of earning a profit.

Spot: A transaction in which the buyer and seller agree on a price for currency with delivery scheduled within a very short period, usually two days at most.

Spread: The difference in a stock's value between an actual bid and the asking price at any specific time.

Stabilization Policies: Measures recommend by the IMF and World Bank designed to control and ameliorate financial crises.

Standard Cost Accounting: See Absorption Costing.

Standard Deviation: A measure of the distribution-frequency of data around the sample mean.

Standard of Living: Aggregate of costs and expenses an individual or household must incur in order to live comfortably within an economic system.

Stationarity: The condition of a random process where its statistical properties do not vary with time.

Statistical Modeling: Refers to the process of collection, analysis, interpretation and presentation of data. Statistical modeling assists decision-makers with more informed decisions based on mathematical analysis.

Statistical Significance: The degree to which an observed outcome is unlikely to have occurred due to chance.

Statistical Significance: A basic measure of the extent of randomness active in a normally distributed data sample.

Stochastic: Involving chance or probability. Stochastic variables are random or have an element of chance or probability associated with their occurrence.

Strategic Planning: The process of determining the long-term goals of an organization and developing a plan to use the company's resources – including materials and personnel – in reaching these goals.

Strategy: In business, a strategy is a plan of action to help the organization reach its goals and objectives. A good business strategy is based on the rigorous analysis of empirical data, including market needs and trends, competitor capabilities and offerings, and the organization's resources and abilities.

Strike: An organized cessation or slowdown of work by employees to compel their employer to meet their demands.

Structural Unemployment: Prolonged unemployment caused by underlying shifts in market supply and demand.

Structured Investment Vehicle: Structured investment vehicles are financial institutions that were first used in the late 1980s by Citigroup. Structured investment vehicles earn money by using a credit spread: They acquire capital from an initial pool of investors and then use this capital to make short- and medium-term loans. Income from these activities is then used to acquire long-term securities at higher rates. From the perspective of large financial institutions, the main advantage offered by structured investment vehicles is that they often do not need to be included on the institution's balance sheet, making them similar to off balance sheet securitizations.

Subsidy: A grant made by the government to an enterprise that is judged to be in the public interest.

Subsistence Farming: The near total consumption of crops and livestock directly by the producer to the detriment of any saleable or tradable surplus.

Substitution: The process by which an economic system replaces faltering industries with healthy corporate or business entities.

Substitution Effect: Where two or more factors of production are more or less interchangeable, a price rise in one triggers its replacement by the other. When the price in question is a wage, laborers reduce their leisure time to work longer hours at the higher rate. Employers, conversely, adapt cost-efficient new technologies or outsource parts of the production process.

Supply: The amount of a good or service an individual producer or a group of producers will provide at a given price.

Supply Chain: A network of organizations involved in production, delivery, and sale of a product. The supply chain may include suppliers, manufacturers, storage facilities, transporters, and retailers. Each organization in the network provides a value-added activity to the product or service. The supply chain includes the flow of tangible goods and materials, funds, and information between the organizations in the network.

Supply Chain Management Systems: Applications software which is integrated into a communications network that enables organizations to communicate about and support their purchasing, sales, and shipping needs.

Supply Curve: A graph representing the number of items that will be produced at each of a number of pricing points.

Supply Schedule: The actual quantities that producers are willing and able to purchase at various prices.

Survey Research: A type of research in which data about the opinions, attitudes, or reactions of the members of a sample are gathered using a survey instrument. The phases of survey research are goal setting, planning, implementation, evaluation, and feedback. As opposed to experimental research, survey research does not allow for the manipulation of an independent variable.

Sustainable Competitive Advantage: Exists whenever a firm leverages a core competency to create unique value for customers other firms cannot easily duplicate and so locks in above-average long-term profits.

Sustainable Development: A wide view of human welfare, a future-oriented view regarding the results of the present activities and designed to aid the globe in achieving viable solutions.

Swap: An agreement where-by the buyer will contracts purchase a certain amount of currency at a certain time, but to then sell it back to the seller at another specified price.

Tacit Knowledge: Internally-generated knowledge rarely if ever formally articulated embedded in and used collaboratively by a firm's employees.

Target Costing: A cost accounting method that determines the expected, or target, cost of production based on the planned selling price and profit margin.

Tariffs: Taxes levied on imported goods.

Tariff bindings: Agreements to limit; reduce or eliminate tariffs over a given period of time.

Taxation: The practice of imposing a tax.

Technical Change: A change in the amount of output produced from the same inputs.

Theory of Comparative Advantage: The theory of comparative advantage argues that a country's economic self-interest is best served by developing only export industries in which its physical, human, and productive resources enable it—more so than other countries—to sell goods more cheaply and efficiently in global markets.

Theory of Constraints: A management practice that focuses on maximizing throughput (output) of product by resolving bottlenecks or constraints in the value stream.

Theory of Production: How a firm uses factors of production to earn a profit.

Theory of the Firm: How a firm interacts with a market and what it wants to achieve is at the heart of this microeconomic construct.

Theory of Value: In classical economics, the process whereby prices are set and resources allocated most efficiently.

Threshold Model of Collective Behavior: A theory of public problem-solving that asserts that individuals have tolerance costs and thresholds that must be met before they will take a public stand and declare a condition, issue, or event to be a public problem.

Throughput Accounting: A method of cost accounting, based on the Theory of Constraints, where all costs are considered either Total Variable Costs or Operating Expenses.

Time-Series Analysis: Examines data collected at regular intervals over an extended period.

Time Series Data: Quantifiable observations or measurements gathered on a specific characteristic over a period of time. Time series data are used in business forecasting. To be useful, time series data must be collected at intervals of regular length. (Cf. cross-sectional data)

Time Value of Money: A financial concept describing the effect of interest on money over a set period of time.

Total Revenue: The proceeds from the sale of an item; the mathematical product of quantity of item sold times the price of item.

Total Quality Management (TQM): A management strategy that attempts to continually increase the quality of goods and services as well as customer satisfaction through raising awareness of quality concerns across the organization.

Total Utility: The total amount of satisfaction a consumer gains from the consumption of a good or a service.

Trade: Trade or commerce, in its simplest form, is the agreed transaction of good and services from one willing party to another. Trade is facilitated through a working market. Traditionally, trade involved bartering, but modern times have called for negotiating through a similar medium like money.

Trade Creation: The net increase in trade that results from the displacement of domestic production.

Trade Diversion: The diversion of existing trade that results from the displacement of imports.

Trade Liberalization: The easing of trade regulations and policy so as to allow freer competition in domestic and international markets.

Trade Marking: A unique distinguishing mark, logo, or device used by manufacturers or merchants to create exclusivity for their goods or service.

Traditional Economy: An economic system where custom and cultural reciprocity play a part in the allocation of resources.

Transaction: A record of business; the occurrence of a business event.

Transaction Costs: The expense of researching different suppliers' prices, of successfully bargaining with one, and of drawing up and enforcing a purchase contract.

Transaction Demand for Money: A Keynesian term used to describe income spent as cash on immediate purchases.

Transfer Pricing: The price of the sharing of goods between different parts of the same company; allows for the individual calculation of each division's profit and loss.

Transparency: Refers to full and accurate disclosure of the content and function of a body of rules.

Treaty: A written agreement between nations; can be bilateral, between two parties or multilateral, among three or more.

Trend: The persistent, underlying direction in which something is moving in either the short, intermediate, or long term. Identification of a trend allows one to better plan to meet future needs.

Umbrella Liability: A type of liability insurance providing excess liability coverage for third party losses over and above all types of "underlying" insurance, which includes commercial general liability, automobile liability and employer's liability plus other liability coverage that can be negotiated into the policy.

Unemployment Rate: The number unemployed as a percentage of the total labor force.

Union: An organization that represents employees in negotiations with employers for salary, benefits, hours, and working conditions. Unions mostly represent skilled trades and craftsmen.

Urban Decline: The worsening social and economic problems of urban regions.

Urban Development: Largely government initiated and sponsored enterprises focused on redeveloping derelict urban land and communities.

Uruguay Round: (1986-1994) Trade negotiations that established the WTO from what was the General Agreement on Tariffs and Trade, and called for elimination of duty restrictions and the easing of certain tariffs.

USAID: United States Agency for International Development; chief administrator of American international development programs.

Utility: The satisfaction gained from an activity.

Utility Maximization: A term that specifically refers to a consumer trying to get the most value for the least price. When used in relation to firms, it refers to decision-making criteria based on considerations other than profit.

Utility-Maximizing Behavior: The assumption made by economists that because people are rational, they will pursue a course of action that best satisfies their needs and interests.

Utility Theory: Psychological attempt to ascertain the value, or "utility," of choice.

Utility Theory of Value: As rational actors, individuals make economic decisions based on their wants and needs.

Validity: The degree to which a survey or other data collection instrument measures what it purports to measure. A data collection instrument cannot be valid unless it is reliable. Content validity is a measure of how well assessment instrument items reflect the concepts that the instrument developer is trying to assess. Content validation is often performed by experts. Construct validity is a measure of how well an assessment instrument measures what it is intended to measure as defined by another assessment instrument. Face validity is merely the concept that an assessment instrument appears to measure what it is trying to measure. Cross validity is the validation of an assessment instrument with a new sample to determine if the instrument is valid across situations. Predictive validity refers to how well an assessment instrument predicts future events.

Value Chain: A network of businesses working together to bring a product or service to the market. Value chains typically comprise one or a few primary suppliers supported by many secondary suppliers, each of whom add value to the product or service before it is offered to the customer.

Values: Personally and culturally specific moral judgments.

Variable: An object in a research study that can have more than one value. Independent variables are stimuli that are manipulated in order to determine their effect on the dependent variables (response). Extraneous variables are variables that affect the response but that are not related to the question under investigation in the study.

Variable Costs: Those costs that vary in direct proportion to the level of production.

Variable Factor of Production: One of several basic inputs to production — labor, capital, technology, etc. — that can be changed in the short run.

Variance: The variance is one of several indices of variability that a statistician uses to characterize the distribution among the measures in a given data set.

Velocity of Money: The rate at which the money stock is transacted, i.e. the number of times currency in circulation changes owners over a set period of time.

Wage Rate: The rate per hour paid for a specific job.

Welfare Economics: The branch of economics that examines the effects that free markets have on the well-being of the community at large.

Whistleblowers: An employee, former employee, or member of an organization, especially a business or government agency, who reports misconduct to people or entities that have the power and presumed willingness to take corrective action. Generally, the misconduct is a violation of law, rule, regulation and/or a direct threat to public interest — fraud, health, safety violations, and corruption are just a few examples.

Wholesaling: The selling of goods in large quantities for the purpose of retail sale to consumers.

Wholesalers: Firms that engage in the selling of wholesale goods.

Wire Transfers: Allow for the purchase, sell or transfer of any major world currency.

World Bank: An international economic development assistance organization that was founded in 1944.

World Development Report: Yearly report published by the World Bank which comments on the economic, social and environmental state of the world. The WDR analyzes one detailed factor of development per year; reports in the past have involved subjects like labor, health, poverty, and the role of the state, to name a few.

World Trade Organization (WTO): A multinational organization that attempts to regulate world trade and encourage the free exchange of goods and services.

WTO: World Trade Organization, organization of 150 trading nations committed to liberalizing world trade.

Zero-Sum Games: A game where there are two players and the payoff for all players is zero regardless of the strategy.

INDEX